Collective Redress in Europe — Why and How?

Collective Redress in Europe – Why and How?

Edited by

Eva Lein, Duncan Fairgrieve, Marta Otero Crespo
and Vincent Smith

British Institute of International and Comparative Law

Published and Distributed by
The British Institute of International and Comparative Law
Charles Clore House, 17 Russell Square, London WC1B 5JP

© BIICL 2015

British Library Cataloguing in Publication Data
A Catalogue record of this book is available from the British Library

ISBN 978-1-905221-56-1

All rights reserved. No part of this publication may be reproduced or transmitted in any form or by any means, electronic, mechanical, photocopying, recording or otherwise, or stored in any restricted system of any nature without the written permission of the copyright holder, application for which should be addressed to the distributor. Such written permission must also be obtained before any part of this publication is stored in a retrieval system of any nature.

This publication has been produced with the financial support of the Civil Justice Programme of the European Union. The contents of this publication are the sole responsibility of their authors and can in no way be taken to reflect the views of the European Commission.

Typeset by Cambrian Typesetters
Camberley, Surrey
Printed in Great Britain by Polestar Wheatons Ltd
Cover design by Ian Wileman

Contents

Foreword   ix
A. Stadler

Part I Collective Redress in Europe – Why ?

Section 1 Economic Perspectives

The Economics of the European Commission's Recommendation
on Collective Redress   5
G. Barker and B.P. Freyens

The Economics of Class Actions: Fundamental Issues and
New Trends   31
M. Doriat-Durban, S. Ferey and S. Harnay

Section 2 Behavioural Sciences Perspectives

A Behavioural Perspective on Collective Redress   47
A.L. Sibony

Section 3 Lawyers' Perspectives

To 'Opt-in' or to 'Opt-out' – That is the Question   61
A. Johnson

Collective Redress: A Lawyer's Perspective   67
P. Lomas and M. Raja

Section 4 Judicial Perspectives

Collective Redress from a Judicial Perspective   83
M. Wösthoff

Part II Collective Redress in Europe – How?

Section 1 Models for Collective Redress in Europe – The Commission Recommendation and Beyond

Recent United Kingdom and French Reforms of Class Actions: An Unfinished Journey *R. Mulheron*	97
Class Actions – Some Reflections from a European Perspective *G. Kodek*	117
Rebuilding the Pillars of Collective Litigation in Light of the Commission Recommendation: The Spanish Approach to Collective Redress *M.P. García Rubio and M. Otero Crespo*	133
Recent Collective Redress Developments in Lithuania – Key Issues in Light of the Implementation of the Commission Recommendation *D. Bublienė*	153
The New Belgian Law on Consumer Collective Redress and Compliance with EU Law Requirements *J.T. Nowak*	169
Cross-border Actions for Collective Redress – Some Lessons from Canada *J.P. Brown and B. Kain*	203
The Commission Recommendation on Common Principles for Collective Redress: Some Reflections from Australia *D. Grave and J. Betts*	219
The Commission's Recommendation on Common Principles of Collective Redress and Private International Law Issues *A. Stadler*	235
Forum Shopping and Consumer Collective Redress in Action: The Costa Concordia Case *C. Poncibò*	251
The Israeli Class Action – A Foundation for a European Model? *A. Flavian*	273

Section 2 Specific Areas of Collective Redress in Europe

Collective Redress and Product Liability in the European Union:
The Outcome of a Legal Transplant in Italy   295
C. Poncibò and E. Rajnieri

Collective Redress in Environmental Liability Cases:
The Spanish Approach   327
A. Ruda González

Collective Redress and Competition Law Claims:
Some Specific Issues   337
M. Danov

Where to Next? The European Law Institute's Statement on
Collective Redress and Competition Damages Claims   357
M. Clough

Collective Redress and Health Care Law: The Specific Characteristics
of Group Compensation under Portuguese Law   385
R. Vale e Reis

Section 3 Alternative Dispute Resolution and Collective Redress

Collective Consumer ADR in the European Union   399
M. Tulibacka

Non-Judicial Means of Collective Redress   423
S.I. Strong

The Effect of EU Public Enforcement Proceedings on Collective
ADR   443
V. Smith

Finnish and Swedish Legislation in Light of the ADR Directive –
Boards and Ombudsmen   455
L. Ervo and A. Persson

Section 4 Lessons from Public International Law

Mass Claims Processes under Public International Law   481
S. Giroud and S. Moss

Annex 1: European Commission Recommendation of 11 June 2013 on common principles for injunctive and compensatory collective redress mechanisms in the Member States concerning violations of rights granted under Union Law   505

Annex 2: Directive 2014/104/EU of the European Parliament and of the Council of 26 November 2014 on certain rules governing actions for damages under national law for infringements of the competition law provisions of the Member States and of the European Union   517

Foreword

*Astrid Stadler**

I. THE BACKGROUND TO THIS BOOK

In 2012, the British Institute of International and Comparative Law (BIICL) was awarded a grant by the European Commission to conduct a study on collective redress mechanisms in different EU Member States. The European Network on Collective Redress which was established as a result involves academics, practitioners, policy-makers, litigation funders and consumers, and it has contributed to cross-national comparisons from many perspectives. This book results from the cooperation in this network, particularly from series of seminars and conferences. When the BIICL project started in 2012, some very interesting collective redress reform projects had already been implemented in national law, such as the Dutch Collective Mass Settlement Act (WCAM 2005) or group litigation proceedings in the Nordic countries, but a considerable number of Member States were waiting for a European harmonized instrument on collective redress. Meanwhile, collective redress has become very fashionable in academic literature and has been a highly topical subject for international conferences. Despite the attention the topic received in academia and among lawyers engaged in mass disputes, the story of collective redress in Europe is a "story of missed opportunities and small steps forward."[1]

After many years of intensive debate, the Commission's Recommendation of 2013[2] was anything but path-breaking. Apart from its main deficiency that it is only non-binding soft law[3] it suffers primarily from two shortcomings:

---

* University of Konstanz – Erasmus University Rotterdam.
[1] V Harsági and CH van Rhee in V Harsági and CH van Rhee (eds) *Multi-Party Redress Mechanisms in Europe: Squeaking Mice?* (Intersentia, 2014) XIX.
[2] Recommendation on common principles for injunctive and compensatory collective redress mechanisms in the Member States concerning violations of rights granted under Union Law, (2013/396/EU), OJ L 201/60, 26 July 2013.
[3] The Recommendation is based on art 292 TFEU. The Recommendation does not even include an obligation of the Member States to report on their efforts to comply with the Recommendation. Member States must only provide statistical data on the number of proceedings conducted within a specified period (Recommendation points 38–41).

(1) The idea of private enforcement originally adopted from the US class action system has spread from DG Competition's Green and White Papers[4] on competition law in 2005 and 2008 to consumer law in 2008[5] and finally resulted in the all-embracing horizontal approach taken by the Commission's Recommendation. The intention of creating a gapless system of remedies for all violations of European law which includes individuals, representative entities or public bodies as potential group representatives is too ambitious an approach.[6] This book therefore tries to illuminate collective redress from different angles in order to illustrate the peculiarities of competition cases[7], product liability or environmental pollution cases[8].

(2) By contrast to its wide scope of application, the procedural framework provided by the Recommendation seems too cautious. The Commission tried to steer a middle course between a better access to justice and the advantages of bundling many similar claims into a single court action on the one hand and safeguards against a potential misuse on the other, as have often been described in the context of US class actions. The concern to avoid harm to businesses due to abusive litigation had a strong influence on many parts of the Recommendation and it has therefore also been described as "a mix of a 'wish list' or demands of a lobby".[9]

II. SOME OBSERVATIONS ON THE IMPLEMENTATION OF THE COMMISSION'S RECOMMENDATION

A. Mixed Reception in the Member States

Two years after the Recommendation was published there is definitively no wave of collective redress reform sweeping across the European Union (EU). Some Member States will ignore the Commission's proposals more or less completely, others are at best willing to implement instruments of collective redress with a limited scope of application and as a kind of pilot project. The contributions in Part II of this book describe some of the new models developing in Europe and existing prototypes elsewhere (Australia, Israel). In 2014, France and Belgium after long and controversial debates enacted new representative actions which picked only part of the 'common principles'. The

---

[4] COM (2005) 672 (19 February 2005) and COM (2008) 165 (2 April 2008).
[5] COM (2008) 794 (27 November 2008).
[6] For a similar critical review see M Dawson and E Muir, 'One for All and All for One? The Collective Enforcement of EU Law – Guest Editorial' 41 *Legal Issues of Economic Integration* 3 (2014) 215–224 at 216.
[7] M Clough, 357–384 and M Danov, 337–356.
[8] E Rajnieri and C Poncibò, 295–326 and R Vale e Reis, 385–396.
[9] I Tzankova, 'Case management: the stepchild of mass claim dispute resolution' 19 *Uniform L Rev* (2014) 329–250 at 332.

new French representative action[10] can be brought only by long-standing consumer associations, not by private individuals. Its scope of application is restricted to consumer sales and service contracts, and follow-on damages claims in competition law. Consistent with the Recommendation's default rule in point 21, the French collective instrument is based on an opt-in mechanism. Belgium,[11] by contrast, decided to leave it to the court seized to decide whether an opt-in or opt-out scheme would be more appropriate for the particular proceedings (*système d'option d'inclusion ou d'exclusion*). This rejects the Commission's approach of opt-in proceedings, but it may come under the Recommendation's exception clause in point 21. Like the French counterpart, Belgium group action proceedings can also be instituted only by an 'ideological plaintiff'[12] such as an officially accepted consumer association. The scope of application of the new rules is, however, much broader, as Article XVII.37 of the Belgian *Code de droit economique* refers to the violation of rights provided for in eight books of the Code and another 30 legal provisions and regulations.

The British Ministry of Business, Innovation and Skills (BIS) has also published plans to implement a representative collective action before the Competition Appeal Tribunal (CAT) for follow-on and stand-alone damages actions in competition law.[13] They are critically assessed by Rachael Mulheron in this book.[14] As in Belgium, the mechanism of how to constitute the plaintiff's class can be either opt-in or opt-out, depending on a case-by-case decision of the CAT.[15] The proposal is furthermore in line with the Recommendation regarding a 'preliminary merits test' and an explicit ban of punitive damages and contingency fees, but it absolutely favours conditional fees[16] and after-the-event-insurance thus ignoring the Commission's skepticism of third party funding.

---

[10] Book 4, title II, Chapter III Code de la consommation: 'action de groupe'. The text is available at http://www.assemblee-nationale.fr/14/ta/ta0295.asp. For details see F Ferrand, 'Collective litigation in France: from distrust to cautious admission' in Harsági and van Rhee (above n 1) 127–152 and R Mulheron in this book 97–116.

[11] L'action en réparation collective, Code de droit économique (titre 2, livre XVII, art XVII.35 – XVII.69), for details see the contribution of JT Nowak in this book, 169–202 and S Voet, 'European Collective Redress: A Status of Quaestionis' 4 *Int J of Procedural Law* (2014) 97.

[12] S Voet, 'Een Belgische vertegenwoordigende collectieve rechtsvordering: vier bouwstenen voor een Belgische class action', 18 *RW* (2012-13) 682, at 689; DOC 53 3300/001, 25.

[13] http://www.biicl.org/files/6310_10_12_2012_urn_13_501_front_and_back_covers_22-jan-13_private_actions_in_competition_law_a_consultation_on_options_for_reform_government_~_response_pdf.

[14] See 97–116.

[15] Government response (above n 13) 31 sub 5.15.

[16] For details on conditional fee arrangement (CFA), C Hodges, in C Hodges and A Stadler (eds.) *Resolving Mass Disputes – ADR and Settlement of Mass claims* (Edward Elgar, 2013) 106 et seq, at 121 et seq.

Even the Dutch Ministry of Justice has plans to further improve the collective redress situation in the Netherlands. At present, representative entities have only limited standing to bring court actions and cannot sue for damages on behalf of absent claimants. In July 2014, the Ministry published a consultation on a draft of collective damages actions (Article 1018b-1018j of the Dutch Civil Procedure Code – a new horizontal instrument which will cover all kinds of mass disputes.[17] The new rules set forth a potential preliminary stage of the WCAM proceedings, but they primarily allow the achievement of a compensation scheme with the help of the judge ('damage scheduling').[18] By contrast to the Recommendation, the primary objective of the new proceedings is not a court decision on individual damages, but either an amicable solution achieved by the parties themselves or a court-suggested compensation scheme. Depending on the way litigation develops, absent claimants can join the settlement either by opt-in or opt-out.

Looking at recent developments at the national level therefore gives the impression that even those Member States which are open-minded to reform are designing new instruments more or less independently of the Recommendation's ideas. However unsurprisingly, one can also put it the other way around: as the common principles laid out in the Recommendation are sometimes vague and allow exceptions to a considerable extent (see for example point 21 on the opt-in and opt-out mechanism) there is enough leeway for Member States to argue that their new instruments are coherent with the Recommendation's principles.[19]

B. *Economic Theory of Group Litigation*

One of the positive effects which the intensive debate on collective redress has produced is a closer cooperation of legal academics and economists which still cannot be found in many fields of law. Economic analysis of collective redress has a long tradition in the US,[20] but is only gradually being accepted in Europe. Insight from economic analysis and behavioural science has proven very helpful in understanding the dynamics within a group of individuals, the potential risks involved in principal-agent relations or litigation and settlement strategies in collective proceedings. It also highlights problems inherent to a

---

[17] Consultatieversie Juli 2014, Wijziging van het Burgerlijk Wetboek en het Wetboek van Burgerlijke Rechtsvordering teneinde de afwikkeling van massaschade in een collectieve actie mogelijk te maken (http://www.internetconsultatie.nl/motiedijksma) 7.

[18] Art 1018g Dutch Civil Procedure Code.

[19] Dawson and Muir (above n 6) at 221 describe it as "a blessing rather than a curse" with respect to the level of access to justice in those Member States which already had a extensively developed system of collective redress.

[20] One of the seminal works in this respect is M Olson, *The logic of collective action – public goods and the theory of groups* (Harvard University Press, 1965).

more active role of judges[21] or resulting from the idea that representative entities should be encouraged to become key actors in collective litigation.[22] Therefore the editors of this book also invited authors to describe lessons to be learned from the economic[23] and behavioural science perspective.

Risks identified by economists can often be addressed by lawmakers once they are aware of the problem. The free-rider problem, for example, which appears if (particularly opt-out) group litigation provides a benefit for passive group members without any contribution (then all claimants will probably wait for others to institute group proceedings)[24] can be remedied to some extent by providing rather short periods of limitation for damages claims to put some pressure on the group. With respect to injunctive relief, where the public goods characteristics are evident because everybody benefits from successful litigation, European lawmakers have often tried to avoid free-rider strategies by granting legal standing to representative entities instead of individuals and thus building on public interest litigation and ideological incentives. However, another issue clearly illustrated from the viewpoint of law and economics is that a successful system of collective redress requires sufficient incentives or even some extra benefits for those suing on behalf of a group. Nevertheless, this either remains unheard by lawmakers or is ignored as it may require unpopular political decisions. The German representative action for skimming-off illegally gained profits from businesses violating competition rules[25], for example, failed to work in practice because consumer associations simply have no incentive to take the procedural risk involved in these proceedings. Furthermore the Commission's skepticism to profit-based lead plaintiff organizations[26] or third-party funding of collective litigation and the idea to ban any influence of third-party funders on litigation strategies[27] seems unrealistic. Admittedly it is difficult to find a midway between the US legal culture of 'litigation as a business' with its profit-oriented law firms as key actors in the class action system and the (at least partly)

---

[21] A Biard, *Judges and Mass Litigation, A behavioral law and economic perspective*, doctoral thesis, Erasmus University Rotterdam (forthcoming 2015); M Faure, 'CADR and settlement of claims – a few economic observations' in Hodges and Stadler (above n 16) 38–60.

[22] RJ Van den Bergh and LT Visscher, 'The Preventive Function of Collective Actions for Damages in Consumer Law' *Erasmus Law Review* (2008) 5–30; RJ Van den Berghand and S Keske, 'Rechtsökonomische Aspekte der Sammelklage' in M Casper, A Janssen, P Pohlmann and R Schulze (eds), *Auf dem Weg zu einer europäischen Sammelklage* (Sellier, 2009) 17 et seq., 35–39.

[23] G Barker and BP Freyens, 5–30 in this book and M Doriat-Durban, S Ferey and S Harnay, 31–44 in this book.

[24] For details see A Szalai, 'Beyond opt-in and opt-out: the law and economics of group litigation' in Harsági and van Rhee (above n 1) 75 et seq. at 77.

[25] Sec. 10 Unfair Competition Act; Sec. 33, 34a Antitrust Act.

[26] Recommendation point 4.

[27] Recommendation point 14–16, 32.

European tradition of non-profit associations[28] which can successfully handle injunctions and small consumer claims, but are probably unable to cope with complex investment disputes, securities or cartel cases. Economic analysis will not solve legal problems, but it plays a very important role in identifying these issues and in pointing out potential options for policy makers.

C. Settlement Proceedings on the Rise?

1. Settlements in complex mass disputes

Another observation which can be made is a clear trend towards new settlement mechanisms. Particularly for big cases arising from the global financial crises (like Madoff[29] or Fortis[30]), the securities and product liability cases settled under the Dutch WCAM or mass personal injury cases like the South African silicosis action which recently failed to obtain the High Court's support in arguing for the jurisdiction of English courts,[31] settlement is often the only reasonable option for both parties. However, sometimes it takes at least a court decision on some key issues of the defendant's liability to stimulate his cooperation. Settlement of mass disputes was not a major issue in the Commission's Recommendation,[32] but national policy makers realize the need for non-contentious proceedings and special instruments to support a defendant's or liable party's willingness to get mass claims 'out of the books'. The 2005 Dutch Collective Settlement Act for mass claims (WCAM) was breaking new ground and although its opt-out mechanism and the matter of international jurisdiction cause considerable concern, it has been successfully used in a number of big cases. In July 2013, an important amendment to the WCAM came into force: the act can now be applied to settlements reached if the liable person is declared bankrupt. Another reform of the WCAM followed from the experience that an early

---

[28] A strong position of non-profit organizations has not only been advocated by the Commission's Recommendation, but also in academic writing: eg R Stürner, 'The role of judges and lawyers in collective actions, equality among parties, conflicts of interest' in *Procesos colectivos-class actions* (XXIII Iberoamerican Procedural Law Conference Buenos Aires, 2012) 67 at 86 et seq.; A Stadler, 'Collective redress litigation - a new challenge for courts in Europe' in A Bruns, C Kern, J Münch, A Piekenbrock, A Stadler and D Tsikrikas (eds.), *Festschrift für Rolf Stürner zum 70. Geburtstag* (Mohr Siebeck, 2013) 1801–1816.

[29] http://jurist.org/paperchase/2011/11/madoff-victims-file-class-action-suit-against-jp-morgan.php.

[30] http://www.investmenteurope.net/regions/benelux/second-investor-group-files-claim-against-fortis/.

[31] http://www.leighday.co.uk/News/2013/July-2013/UK-Court-decision-in-gold-miner%E2%80%99s-silicosis-cases. The UK Court of Appeal heard the case on appeal on 25 March 2014.

[32] Recommendation points 25, 26, Recital 13.

involvement of the court – eg by court hearings already during settlement negotiations – may help to achieve better results, to obtain court approval of the settlement contract more easily and to reduce the number of opt-outs.

In England and Wales, the BIS intends to copy the model of special court proceedings for declaring out-of-court settlements legally binding upon the claimants on whose behalf the settlement has been negotiated by representative associations or individual claimants. Furthermore the trend is confirmed by the French and Belgium group proceedings which both emphasize the need for amicable settlements. The French law provides rules for alternative dispute resolution where a consumer association may negotiate a settlement on behalf of consumers.[33] In Belgium, the new rules on group proceedings do not only include a mandatory mediation phase at the beginning of the litigation,[34] but also offer an instrument very similar to the Dutch WCAM: representative entities which have legal standing may institute proceedings with the sole objective of obtaining court approval for an out-of-court settlement.[35] Even in Germany, the 2012 reform of the Capital Market Test Case Act (*Kapitalanleger-Musterverfahrensgesetz*) alleviated the settlement of securities disputes: the plaintiff of the selected test case may negotiate a settlement for all claimants who have already filed actions. When the court approves the settlement contract, an opt-out procedure will take place in order to declare the settlement binding for all claimants.

2. ADR as a substitute for individual or collective consumer claims?

Nevertheless, while judicial avenues are important they are rather costly in some Member States and at least for typical consumer contract disputes the European legislature strongly favors non-judicial mechanisms such as ADR and ODR as a complementary procedure or even as a substitute for individual court proceedings. Although ADR proceedings might be a necessary option for consumers to enforce small claims if access to courts is burdensome, the approach is rather ambiguous: For many years the European legislature has developed complex and elaborated provisions on consumer contracts and now, finally, consumers are expected to resort to ADR institutions which are not bound by the law and will mostly provide equitable solutions. Once again developments in Europe follow those in the US with delay and without taking seriously objections and criticism already raised there: In the US system the trend to ADR and arbitration has long been criticized for its abandonment of the rule of law and its lack of transparency due to

---

[33] Art L. 423-15 und 423-16 Code de la consommation.
[34] Art XVII. 38 Code de droit économique.
[35] Art XVII. 36 Code de droit économique; DOC 53 3300/001, 14.

proceedings behind closed doors and the non-publication of decisions.[36] Whereas in complex mass disputes court-assisted settlements are an often welcome or inevitable solution in extraordinary situations, a far-reaching privatization of the judiciary with consumers being regularly steered towards ADR institutions by direct or indirect pressure (eg imposed by cost sanctions) is not acceptable.

There is not only a risk that the ADR Directive's obligation imposed on the Member States to establish a network of ADR institutions covering all areas of consumer related law will lead ministers of finance or ministers of justice into temptation of reducing necessary investments in the state court system. It is also undeniable that the implementation of the ADR Directive may be a (temporary?) alibi for policy makers to completely rely on the ADR mechanism even as a remedy for mass consumer damage claims and to pretend that no further reform of collective actions is necessary.[37] It is therefore necessary to critically analyze the suitability of ADR mechanisms for collective enforcement of claims.[38] It cannot be ruled out that European and national policy makers have done a disservice to consumers and tort victims who are suffering from small or trivial individual damage only: Despite the fact that ADR proceedings might be almost free of cost, claimants will probably not bother to use them by filling in and submitting standard forms in order to obtain a few Euros – and they will also refrain from costly and time-consuming individual court proceedings. Should this happen, efficient proceedings for skimming-off illegally gained profits (either by representative entities or public bodies) must be considered by policy makers in order to provide at least a deterrence against violations resulting in small and dispersed damages (which cannot be compensated effectively anyhow).

C. Issues to be Tackled in the Future

Some of the major challenges involved in collective actions have more or less been circumnavigated in the Commission's Recommendation: one is the cross-border dimension of mass disputes which is dealt with elsewhere in this book[39] and, another, the need for effective case management. The Recommendation

---

[36] D Luban, 'Settlements and the Erosion of the Public Realm' 83 *Geo L J* (1995) 2619; RC Reuben, M Moffitt, und WD Brazil 'ADR and the Rule of Law' 16 *Dispute Resolution Magazine* (2010) 4 et seq; R Kulms, 'Mediation zwischen effizientem Rechtsschutz und Privatisierung der Justiz' in KJ Hopt and F Steffek (eds), *Mediation, Rechtstatsachen, Rechtsvergleich, Regelungen*, (Mohr Siebeck, 2008) 923 et seq. See also the contributions in J Zekoll, M Bälz and J Amelung (eds), *Formalisation and Flexibilisation in Dispute Resolution* (Leiden, 2014).
[37] H Eidenmüller 2 *ZZP* (2015) (forthcoming); J Zekoll, 'Die Bedeutung der ADR-Richtlinie für die Durchsetzung von Verbraucherrechten' 2 *ZZP* (2015) (forthcoming).
[38] M Tulibacka, 399–422.
[39] A Stadler, 235–250 and C Poncibò, 251–272 .

mentions in various contexts the active role of judges without going into details.[40] From various case studies[41] across different legal systems it has become evident that the introduction of some kind of collective proceedings is not sufficient. Even with a certain degree of aggregation, proceedings that involve a large number of claims require considerable judicial case management skills, furthermore smoothly operating IT systems in courts and law firms and last but not least a procedural framework which allows judges a flexible handling of cases in close cooperation with the parties' lawyers (eg in an early case management conference which identifies relevant issues and fixes a realistic time table).[42] The German KapMuG (Capital Market Test Case Act) illustrates clearly how courts can be "stuck in formalities and inflexible civil procedure"[43]: The *Deutsche Telekom* case which started in 2003 and forced the German legislature to enact the KapMuG ('lex Telekom') is still pending. More than ten years later, in December 2014, the German Federal Supreme Court partially granted the appeal on points of law filed by the test case plaintiff and referred the case back to the court of appeal.[44] At present, it is impossible to predict how long the litigation will last as the proceedings are still in the intermediate test case stage and have not reached the final stage when all the individual claims will have to be decided on the basis of a binding test case decision.[45] A first-hand account is provided by Judge Wösthoff in this book.[46]

Depending on tradition and legal culture, the attitude of judges towards a more active role in managing cases and in handling proceedings for scrutinizing and approving proposed settlements are a real challenge for the judiciary. One academic even frankly takes the position that in his country no

---

[40] Recommendation Recital 21, point 8, 9, 15.

[41] D Hensler, C Hodges and I Tzankova (eds), *Class actions in context: how economics, politics and culture shape collective litigation*, (Edward Elgar, 2014); W van Boom and G Wagner, *Mass Torts in Europe, Cases and Reflections* (Vol 34, European Centre of Tort and Insurance Law Vienna, 2014).

[42] A more detailed analysis is given and similar suggestions are made by Tzankova (above n 9).

[43] Tzankova (above n 9) at 333.

[44] Bundesgerichtshof (BGH) 11 December 2014 (file no. XI ZB 12/12).

[45] For the failure of the KapMuG see also A Halfmeier, 'Litigation without an end: the failure of the German approach to private enforcement of securities law' in Hensler, Hodges and Tzankova (above n 41). A much better example for effective case management is given by the *Buncefield* case in the UK. 2,700 claims based on the explosion of one of the biggest oil storage terminals in the UK were filed by residents, businesses and insurance companies. Within four years, Justice Steel issued a judgment on the liability of Total UK, a 60% owner of the of oil storage terminal, and managed to settle 92 % of the claims subsequently; for details see Tzankova (above n 9). She rightly points out that this case was handled without a formal collective redress mechanism.

[46] See 83–92.

appropriate personal or organizational design for complex litigation exists. Given the fact that even individual litigation was slow and ineffective one could not expect collective litigation devices to be handled more effectively, he concludes.[47] Taking the poor performance of the judiciary as an argument to reject the private enforcement approach altogether (despite the fact that public administration is also inefficient)[48] seems, however, a hardly acceptable capitulation to the 'old structures' in some middle and eastern European Member States.[49]

Mass claim disputes have their own dynamics and party strategies for settlement negotiations differ from normal cases. Courts must be aware that in collective redress proceedings in which absent claimants are represented by a lead plaintiff and do not have the chance of or interest in participating in the negotiation of a settlement, it is necessary to protect them from 'cheap settlements' and principal-agent conflicts. In this context it seems noteworthy that the Amsterdam Court of Appeal which is in charge of the WCAM proceedings until recently accepted all proposed settlements without much hesitation. Only recently, in the DSB case, the court required a number of amendments to be made before it gave its final approval on 4 November 2014.[50] Continental judges can benefit from the experience of their English and US colleagues in aggregate litigation with respect to management skills and the techniques necessary to identify deficiencies and pitfalls in a mass settlement, but it takes a clear specialization of courts with the corresponding rules on jurisdiction and formally embedded training programs for judges.[51] As a supplementary instrument informal manuals on case management following the US example may assist courts in handling complex cases and help to avoid protracted litigation.

III. WHAT NEXT?

The Commission must be prepared to take further action when revisiting the

---

[47] A Uzelac, 'Why no class actions in Europe? A view from the side of dysfunctional justice systems' in Harsági and van Rhee (above 1) 53–69.

[48] *Ibid,* at 68 (Croatia).

[49] For a more positive attitude with respect to group litigation in Poland see R Kulski, 'Polish perspectives and provisions on group proceedings' in Harsági and van Rhee (above n 1) 225 at 227.

[50] Gerechtshof Amsterdam, 4 November 2014, file no. 200.127.525/01, http://uitspraken.rechtspraak.nl/inziendocument?id=ECLI:NL:GHAMS:2014:4560.

[51] The ELI Statement on collective redress 2014, at 15 also emphasizes the need for formal training programs at the European level. The statement is available at the BIICL website: http://www.collectiveredress.org/collective-redress/. The same is strongly advocated by Tzankova (above n 9).

Recommendation in 2017, but it should also consider its room for manœuvre realistically. Indeed the story of collective redress has been one of small steps forward so far. Different legal culture and institutional infrastructure across Member States cannot easily be overcome by providing 'common principles' which are not clearly extracted from existing regimes in the Member States or 'best practices' examples but based on a political compromise. The idea of private enforcement meets limits if one is not prepared to adopt more or less the US class system and its 'law as a business' approach.[52] Some Member States will always be more apt to follow this route than others. A well-balanced mixture of public and private enforcement[53] will probably be the European future and it seems more likely that this balance can be found at the national level than at the European. The Commission should focus on an adequate legal European framework for cross-border issues (jurisdiction and enforcement of judgments and settlements) which will become of increasing importance as some Member States start to compete for the resolution of mass disputes. It should also establish and operate a platform for the exchange of information on similar and parallel proceedings and offer judicial training programs in order to help the judiciaries to learn from each other.

---

[52] Stürner (above n 28) at 86.

[53] This approach has been strongly advocated by F Weber, *The law and economics of enforcing European consumer law – a comparative analysis of package travel and misleading advertising* (Ashgate, 2014); furthermore F Cafaggi and HW Micklitz, *New frontiers of consumer protection – the interplay between private and public enforcement* (Intersentia, 2009).

Part I

Collective Redress in Europe – Why?

1
Economic Perspectives

The Economics of the European Commission's Recommendation on Collective Redress

*George Barker and Benoît Pierre Freyens**

I. INTRODUCTION

The 2013 European Commission (EC) Recommendation on collective redress established a set of common principles for injunctive and compensatory collective redress mechanisms in Member States concerning violations of rights granted under Union Law.[1] The EC's stated objectives for its collective redress policy are to promote an efficient justice system that contributes to European competitive growth, and serves European citizens, and businesses. From an economic perspective this can be understood to require the maximization of European social welfare, including consumer and producer surplus.

This chapter examines the social efficiency of collective redress relative to individual suits. It critically reviews the economic literature on the costs and benefits of the collective redress mechanisms, and explores from an economic perspective the issues or problems which the EC's specifically European model of collective redress seeks to overcome, and which Member States will need to address to promote efficient outcomes, or social welfare in Europe.

---

* George Barker is Visiting Fellow, British Institute of International and Comparative Law; Research Associate, Centre for Law and Economics and Society, University College London; Director, Centre of Law and Economics, The Australian National University. Benoît Pierre Freyens is professor of Economics, Faculty of Business, Government & Law University of Canberra and Research Associate, Centre of Law and Economics, The Australian National University. An Australian Research Council Discovery Project DP0988956 – A Comparative Law and Economics Analysis of Class Actions in Australia, the US and the UK – supports this research.

[1] Commission Recommendation of 11 June 2013 on common principles for injunctive and compensatory collective redress mechanisms in the Member States concerning violations of rights granted under Union Law (2013/396/EU).

II. THE COMMISISON'S RECOMMENDATION ON COLLECTIVE REDRESS

On 11 June 2013 the EC issued a Communication 'Towards a European Horizontal Framework for Collective Redress',[2] which presented their position on some central issues regarding collective redress. This Communication was accompanied by an EC Recommendation on common principles for injunctive and compensatory collective redress mechanisms in the Member States concerning violations of rights granted under Union Law.

The EC recommended that all Member States of the EU have national collective redress systems based on a number of common European principles (The Recommendation).[3] The EC defined collective redress as a procedural mechanism that allows, for reasons of procedural economy and/or efficiency of enforcement, many similar legal claims to be bundled into a single court action. Depending on the type of claim, collective redress can take the form of injunctive relief, where cessation of the unlawful practice is sought, or compensatory relief, aimed at obtaining compensation for damage suffered. This Communication and the EC address both forms of collective redress, without interfering with means of injunctive relief already in place in Member States on the basis of Union law.

The Recommendation identifies the following as areas where the supplementary private enforcement of rights granted under Union law in the form of collective redress is of value: consumer protection, competition, environment protection, protection of personal data, financial services legislation and investor protection. The EC however advocates a horizontal approach, so that the principles set out in the Recommendation should be applied horizontally and equally in these different areas, but also in any other areas where collective claims for injunctions or damages in respect of violations of the rights granted under Union law would be relevant. The Recommendation therefore applies to the field of competition law, an area for which specific rules are included in a proposal for a Directive on certain rules governing actions for competition law damages.[4] While the Recommendation encourages all Member States to follow the principles suggested therein, the proposed Directive leaves it to Member States whether or not to introduce

---

[2] Communication from the Commission to the Council, the European Parliament and the European Economic and Social Committee "Towards a European Horizontal Framework for Collective Redress" COM (2013) 401 Final.

[3] Commission Recommendation of 11 June 2013 (above n 1).

[4] The Recommendation's content therefore applies to the field of competition law, an area for which specific rules – justified by the specificities of competition law – are included in a 'Proposal for a Directive on certain rules governing actions for damages under national law for infringements of the competition law provisions of the Member States and of the European Union' COM (2013) 404.

collective redress actions in the context of the private enforcement of competition law.[5]

The EC thus recommends that all Member States of the EU have national collective redress systems based on a number of common European principles relating both to judicial and out-of-court collective redress that should be common across the Union, while respecting the different legal traditions of the Member States. The EC Recommendation thus seeks to establish a framework to ensure a coherent horizontal approach to collective litigation in the EU context without harmonising national systems.

III. THE COMMISSION'S OBJECTIVES

The EC notes that "a sound legal environment and efficient justice systems can contribute decisively to the European Union's goal of achieving competitive growth". This indicates a fundamental concern with economic efficiency and the effects of the policy on economic growth, which this paper will explore in depth. The EC further states on objectives that "EU Justice Policy aims to develop a genuine area of freedom, security and justice that serves citizens and businesses.[6] This confirms the EC is seeking to maximize the welfare of both European citizens and businesses, or is concerned with what economist call both consumer and producer welfare.

On its more specific concerns, the EC notes that "any measures for judicial redress need to be appropriate and effective and bring balanced solutions supporting European growth, while ensuring effective access to justice. The EC is concerned that any mechanism must not attract abusive litigation or have effects detrimental to respondents regardless of the results of the proceedings." The Commission thus argues that "the European approach to collective redress must thus give proper thought to preventing negative effects and devising adequate safeguards against them" noting that "examples of adverse effects can be seen in particular in 'class actions' as known in the United States." It is clearly helpful then to consider lessons from the US, and other international experience with collective redress.

---

[5] For the Commission, the horizontal Recommendation and the sector-specific Directive are a 'package' that, seen as a whole, reflects a balanced approach deliberately chosen by the Commission. While the adoption procedures differ for both measures under the Treaties, significant changes to this balanced approach would require the Commission to reconsider its proposal.

[6] See the Commission's Communication 'Action Plan Implementing the Stockholm Programme' COM (2010) 171 20.4.2010. See Stockholm Programme – 'An open and secure Europe serving and protecting citizens', adopted by the European Council on 9.12.2009, OJ C 115, 4.5.2010, 1.

IV. INTERNATIONAL CONTEXT AND LESSONS

Measuring the social efficiency of collective redress relative to individual suits is a matter of importance and controversy. It ultimately requires examining the evidence on collective redress in those jurisdictions which have adopted them. Given the US legal system, has long authorized claim aggregation procedures it is useful to consider the results from the major US empirical studies at the outset.[7]

Hensler et al conclude their extensive cost/benefit analysis of class actions in the US in the following terms:

> At the heart of the long controversy over damage class actions is this dilemma: the litigation derives its capacity to do good from the same feature that yields its capacity to do mischief [...] How to respond to the dilemma ... is a deeply political question, implicating fundamental beliefs about the structure of the political system, the nature of society, and the roles of courts and law in society ... at present, there is not a consensus that the mix of good and ill consequences of damage class actions requires public policy makers to do away with this form of litigation entirely.[8]

Hensler's analysis has often been criticized as narrowly based on a qualitative case study approach involving a limited number of cases. By comparison Eisenberg and Miller[9] recently updated and analysed a comprehensive class action data set from the US covering the period 1993–2008 involving nearly 1,000 cases. The 2010 paper updates an earlier study by Eisenberg and Miller[10] for the period 1993–2002, nearly doubling the number of cases in the database, and enabling the examination of class actions over time using a large database. The 2010 study confirms the results from the 2004 study. Fees display the same relationship to class recoveries in both data sets and neither fees nor recoveries materially increased over time.

The Eisenberg and Miller studies have thus revealed a remarkable relationship between attorney fees and class recovery size in the US which has been stable over time: regardless of the methodology for calculating fees ostensibly employed by the courts, the class recovery size was the over-

---

[7] This question has at times been referred to as the 'great big question' of claim aggregation through representative proceedings, see DR Hensler, 'Revisiting the Monster: New Myths and Realities of Class Action and Other Large-Scale Litigation' 11 *Duke Journal of Comparative and International Law* (2000) 179, Ch 15.

[8] *Ibid*, Ch 16, 471–2.

[9] T Eisenberg and GP Miller, 'Attorney Fees and Expenses in Class Action Settlements: 1993-2008' 7 *Journal of Empirical Legal Studies* (2010) 248.

[10] T Eisenberg and GP Miller, 'Attorney Fees in Class Action Settlements: An Empirical Study' 1 *Journal of Empirical Legal Studies* (2004) 27.

whelmingly important determinant of the fee. In particular Eisenberg and Miller find a scale effect – fee percent decreases as client recovery increases – providing empirical support for a key normative justification underlying class actions (ie economies of scale). By aggregating smaller claims into a single larger action, economies of scale in legal services are achieved, which can be passed onto class members in the form of enhanced recoveries. As Eisenberg and Miller note in the context of proposals for US class action reform: 'Reform efforts that might undermine class actions should consider this efficiency'.

The EC clearly aims at distinguishing collective redress in Europe from the US approach. In which case attempts to design national collective redress mechanisms which comply with the EC's recommendations need to be mindful of the results from the Eisenberg and Millar studies, and the cautionary conclusion from Hensler's work.

There are also potential lessons to be learnt from empirical research in other jurisdictions outside the US, although this research currently lags that undertaken in the US. EU Member States that already have forms of collective redress of the kind anticipated by the EC may offer insight, although the apparently short history of this experience may impose limitations. The experience of countries that have a longer history with a collective redress procedure may thus offer more insight. This includes Canada, where Quebec was the first to introduce class action procedures in 1978, with Ontario next in 1992. As of 2008, 9 of the 10 provinces in Canada have enacted comprehensive class actions legislation, while the Federal Court of Canada permits class actions under Part V1 of the Federal Courts Rules. Australia also introduced a class action procedure to its Federal Court in 1995. Ultimately however any empirical analysis of the economic effects of collective redress needs to be grounded in sound economic theory. This is what we turn to next.

In the remainder of the document we will use the terms collective redress and class actions interchangeably. Rather than engaging in a definitional or lexicographical exercise, the focus of our analysis will instead be upon the potential economic effects of the various rules affecting group litigation. Different rules affecting group litigation can have different settings, and this can lead to combinations of different settings. For example contingency fees may be allowed, or not, and if allowed fee percentages may be capped, or not. The group membership rule on the other hand might involve either an 'opt out', or 'opt in' procedure; and damages awards may be penal or compensatory, or based on some other principle. Different settings on different rules imply there are a large number of possible combinations. Rather than try to distinguish the various possible combinations of the different procedural rules, and assign different names to different combinations of rules, we will instead use the generic term class actions interchangeably with collective redress, and focus on the underlying economics or costs and benefits of class actions which may be affected by variation in procedural rules.

V. THE COSTS AND BENEFITS OF COLLECTIVE REDRESS

What are the benefits and costs of class actions? On the benefits side, the main purpose of class actions[11] is to: (i) minimize the private and social cost of repeating a very large number of conciliation meetings and court hearings for claims originating in the same causes – a productive efficiency argument (class actions deliver economies of scale to litigants and to the judiciary), (ii) make it economically viable to provide justice when individual claims are too small- a public good argument (class actions enable supply of justice that would otherwise not take place or could be distorted by free riding)and (iii) minimize the risk of unequal treatment of the victims (or the defendant) – a fairness or consistency argument (decisions taken by the same authority, based on the same evidence and legal defence).

On the costs side, class actions like all collective actions are exposed to free riding and agency issues. If claims are heterogeneous (ie when victims have been inflicted varying degrees of harm) members have different stakes in the action, which makes class actions more complex and difficult to manage than repeated individual suits. Claims heterogeneity leads to class instability through game-theoretical incentives to mimic other members or defect rather than collaborate to the action's success. For instance, in mass torts or product liability cases, which may involve severe accidents where causality and individual harm may be harder to establish, there are powerful incentives for claimants of a certain type (say, low claim) to misreport their type (say, high claim). Prisoner's dilemma-type conflicts amongst members can lead to the collapse of certified, meritorious class action through members' opt-out, a commonly-used strategy when claimants know that the fund (the defendant's balance sheet) is insufficient to settle all claims. It pays then to launch an individual suit and reach a quick settlement for the value of the individual claim prior to the settlement of the class action.

Furthermore, the decisive feature of the class action, relative to other ways of aggregating grievances into a single hearing, is its initiation by an entre-

---

[11] Point (i) is fully spelt out in US Federal Rule 23(a). Points (i) and (iii) correspond roughly to the justification for class actions types (b) (3) and (b) (1) of Federal Rule 23, see JR Macey and GP Miller, 'The Plaintiffs' Attorney's Role in Class Action and Derivative Litigation: Economic Analysis and Recommendations for Reform' 58 *University of Chicago Law Review* (1991) 1, 9.

preneurial attorney and a representative claimant.[12] With class representation comes agency cost. The class counsel may pursue profit maximisation goals quite distinct to the collective interest of the class (which is to maximize net per capita recovery). For instance, if legal fees are paid as a percentage of class recovery, counsel may settle early with the defendant for an insufficient recovery that nonetheless maximizes her net return. This inefficient result arises because the marginal fee gains of pursuing the action are less than the marginal cost of legal time and effort. Conversely, if legal fees are calculated based on input (eg the 'Lodestar' formula used in the US), the counsel has incentives to delay proceedings and settle for a low amount just prior to the hearing (the counsel having by then maximized her fee-to-risk ratio). The legal counsel then acts as independent entrepreneur rather than as loyal agent of the class.[13]

The costs and benefits of class actions are therefore difficult to ascertain. Even when class heterogeneity and representation do not reduce the social efficiency of class actions, other incentive problems may arise. Whenever claim aggregation creates unbalanced stakes between the two parties, one party has incentives to spend excessively large amounts on winning the case, relative to the other party. The defendant, whose stake consists of a potentially large liability brought about by claim aggregation and the cost of legal representation usually faces higher stakes than the class attorney.[14] With asymmetric stakes a defendant has incentives to commit large resources to his defence, which risks depleting the fund that would be used to settle all claims. If the class action is eventually successful fund depletion is detrimental to all parties. A related issue is the presence of cost differentials between class representatives and the defendant. Cost differentials arise from risk aversion and accumulated experience in the conduct of class action lawsuits. With the possible exception of insurance firms, which are repeat (experienced) defendants in class action litigation, it will often be more costly to defendants to litigate because they lack the specialized class actions skills of class representatives.

A final source of inefficiency is class action failure – the non-initiation or non-authorisation of an action when undertaking the action would have been beneficial in net terms. This is again a problem of collective action. Whereas

---

[12] In the US, where the legal system requires class certification (authorisation), the class representative has to demonstrate the typicality and adequacy of her claim *vis-à-vis* other victims, together with the scope and relevance of the grievances.

[13] JC Coffee, 'The Regulation of Entrepreneurial Litigation: Balancing Fairness and Efficiency in the Large Class Action' 54 *University of Chicago Law Review* (1987) 877, 882–3.

[14] We assume throughout this paper that courts operate under the US 'common fund' doctrine rather than the UK 'fee shifting' doctrine, so that each party bears its own representation costs regardless of the litigation's outcome.

market failure (eg unmarketable individual claims, as mentioned above) can arise from the lack of legislated class actions procedures, class action failure may arise from judicial failure to authorize claim aggregation (non-certification) despite substantive merit, or failure by class representatives to initiate the action in the first place. Similarly to companies in which numerous small shareholders have little personal incentive to control or sue the manager given the cost of doing so, class actions with small individual stakes sometimes never see the light of day due to a lack of incentive. The high cost of notifying all parties may deter a potential class representative from initiating the class action. An entrepreneurial attorney may also fail to initiate a class action if economies of scale (lower representation cost as a percentage of class recovery) make class actions less profitable than multiple individual lawsuits.

What emerges from this cursory introduction is that the fundamental trade-off between the social and private motives of using legal procedures is particularly exacerbated in class actions. Class actions tend to minimize social costs but they generate agency and other private costs. Are class action procedures flexible enough? A more tailored approach, eg allowing efficient class repartitioning and deregulating contract design could help realign the interests of class members with their representatives. How this realignment is to proceed is a long-standing research question among economists studying the efficient contracting of legal services. The answer is however largely contextual and depends on the particular type of class action failure examined.

In what follows we review in detail the broad literature on the economic effects of class actions, with a view of isolating the major effects from aggregation and representation and identifying critical trade-offs between class actions and the conduct of multiple individual law suits.

VI. SOCIAL EFFICIENCY IN COLLECTIVE REDRESS

A. Litigation Research

In this section we review some of the most salient economic questions surrounding the resolution of mass litigation through class actions. At this point it is worth specifying commonalities class action economics share with a wider body of law and economics research, as these common elements will play an important role in the models reviewed. There is for instance a long-standing literature analysing efficiency rules for litigation and dispute resolution – whether through settlement or arbitration. Most theoretical contributions to this literature stress the benefits to litigants of developing a bargaining strategy driven by the potential mutual gains from settling the dispute prior to arbitration.

These theories rest on the rationality of the agents involved and builds on the well-known argument that market-based (ie off-court) arrangements leaving rational agents better off will provide powerful incentives for settling disputes early and out of courts, rather than through lengthy arbitration and trial procedures. In these models, settlement agreements depend on the expected trial outcome and on the type and size of the transaction costs involved with court arbitration. Risk aversion and uncertainty expand these transaction costs and provide further motivation to settle early. The number of suits that do proceed to trial are then usually explained by irrational or misinformed behaviour such as undue optimism or incomplete information. In fact some researchers have noted that population-based liability determination creates plaintiff optimism as a result of 'strength in numbers' effects, which are a characteristic feature of mass tort actions.[15]

Much of this 'suit, settlement and trial' literature is of somewhat generic nature, applying to unspecified types of legal disputes. Class action as a dispute resolution mechanism is generally more complex than the average type of litigation because to the traditional components of litigation and settlement (attorney fees, discovery cost, divergent expectations, attitudes to risk and uncertainty) it adds other, more specific economic effects, such as economies of scale, small claim viability and crowding effects. Although we will integrate this additional complexity into a standard model of litigation, these effects per se do not drive our motivation for a specific review of the class action literature. John Coffee aptly isolates the distinctive feature of class action litigation relative to standard litigation models:

> Ultimately, entrepreneurial litigation should be seen less as a process by which the adversaries come to agree on the litigation odds and then settle in order to avoid further transaction costs and more as a variety of Nash equilibrium in which each side assumes the other is committed to an established litigation strategy.[16]

Although these issues set class action apart from standard litigation, the US regulatory framework authorising class actions has been criticized for failing to sufficiently take account of these differences. Macey and Miller for instance claim that 'regulatory shortfalls can be traced ultimately to a single fundamental error: the inappropriate attempt to treat entrepreneurial litigation as if it were essentially the same as standard litigation'.[17]

What regulators may have failed to capture was not lost to economists. Indeed game theoretical considerations stemming from class representation

---

[15] AF Daughety and JF Reinganum, 'Population-Based Liability Determination, Mass Torts, and the Incentives for Suit, Settlement, and Trial' 26 *Journal of Law, Economics and Organization* (2009) 460.
[16] Coffee (above n 13) 895.
[17] Macey and Miller (above n 11) 3.

and class heterogeneity will play an important part in the economic models examined in this paper. In this review, we will therefore proceed in two steps: we will first integrate scaling effects and small claim viability arguments into a basic class action model based on a standard model of litigation settlement, and will then examine how adverse selection and moral hazard affect incentives to settle.

A second piece of literature relevant to the economic study of class actions examines the efficiency of different contracting schemes for legal counsel services. This discussion is somewhat related to the performance pay conundrum analysed in labour economics and hovers around two main methods of contingent fee payment: (i) input-based fee, such as the 'Lodestar' formula used in the US, where attorneys are paid their cost inclusive of reasonable profit and (ii) percentage fees, where attorneys are paid a specific percentage of their clients' recovery. The former usually assumes that attorney cost (time, effort, expenditures, etc.) is verifiable by third parties, whereas the latter will generally be used when this information cannot be verified by courts.[18] These two fee setting methods are of particular importance for the economic analysis of class actions because they affect differently attorneys' incentives to initiate a class action, settle early or go to trial (we review this literature later in the paper).

B. Productive Efficiency

It is often assumed that the fundamental underlying justification for class action procedures is the generation of economies of scale in seeking damage redress through courts. Collectively, plaintiffs typically face a lower average litigation cost. Potentially, scaling effects could also benefit defendants – who may find it less costly to settle one expensive suit rather than many smaller ones, although this point is more controversial. To the defendant, there may be scaling benefits from settling all claims in a single settlement or hearing, rather than through long-term, protracted and repeated individual suits over similar claims.[19] By aggregating his defence cost over a larger number of claimants, the defendant spreads her per-claimant cost of defence, a benefit of

---

[18] On both counts it is the judge rather than the clients who determines the appropriate level of the fees. Judges will decide what represents a 'fair fee' based on a number of parameters, including the size of the recovery settled for (or awarded at trial), the difficulty of the case, the risks faced by the counsel, etc.

[19] Note that this argument is not entirely specific to class actions; a test case that establishes precedent and makes further re-litigation irrelevant would also achieve similar economies of scale (See D Rosenberg, 'Mass Tort Class Actions: What Defendant Have and Plaintiffs Don't' 37 *Harvard Journal on Legislation* (2000) 393). In this paper we will ignore this distinction and assume class actions also act as test cases.

significant importance in large scale class actions.[20] Avoiding the expense of redundancy (repeated) costs enables the defendant to protect her assets.[21] However, class actions also increase claimants' bargaining power relative to that of 'deep pockets' defendants and the scaling benefits to defendants of facing aggregate claims have to be compared to the cost of reduced bargaining power.

Thus, by spreading the fixed cost of undertaking legal action, scaling effects minimize the amount of private resources committed to evaluating a large number of similar claims, improving the productive efficiency of private litigation processes. Class actions also generate social or public economies of scale. By spreading the fixed cost of trying a case over numerous players, society economises on significant judicial and legal resources that would otherwise be wasted in repeated games of litigation and settlement. To courts, class actions may minimize the cost of conducting conciliation and arbitration proceedings (mainly staff time), such as cost of granting motions, evaluating the evidence, determining causality or exercising judgement on any settlement offered. In a very narrow sense, courts can be viewed as defending the interest of the taxpayer by minimising the burden of their own operational costs to society. An efficient court system would be expected to yield more decisions per unit of time and public dollars and class actions would be expected to contribute to such efficiency gains.[22] Besides whom they accrue to, economies of scale also differ in the source of the cost reductions, such as through:

1. Cost-sharing effects: If attorney fees are calculated based on input formulas, spreading the fixed cost of legal counsel work over a larger number of class members reduces average litigation costs relative to individual suits;
2. Recovery effects: If attorney fees are proportional to the amount of the recovery (settlement amount or damage award), there may also be scaling effects in the recovery itself. Judges who award very large recovery also often reduce the percentage of the recovery allocated to attorneys, as they may perceive an imbalance between the percentage fee and the actual work effort of the attorney. Due to cost-sharing and recovery effects, aggregate claims can be worth more than the sum of the separate claims, and;
3. Information externalities: the legal counsel can act as platform transmitting and relaying information amongst the members: the larger the class,

---

[20] *Ibid*.

[21] Avoiding redundancy costs also keeps a larger fund for class action settlement, reducing incentives for class fragmentation through fear of fund insufficiency – a benefit to plaintiffs.

[22] For a contrary but relatively uncommon view, see K Dam, 'Class Actions: Efficiency, Compensation, Deterrence, and Conflict of Interest' 4 *Journal of Legal Studies* (1975) 47.

the higher the chance of a class member contributing information critical to the success of the representative procedure, benefiting all claimants. A related argument is that class actions internalize positive informational externalities. In multiple individual hearings, later plaintiffs benefit from the information disclosed through the discovery process in earlier individual hearings, which may lead to a collective action problem: no-one lodges the first claim. Class actions may correct this market failure by ensuring simultaneous and universal sharing of benefits from the discovery process.[23]

While claim aggregation may decrease the relative cost of litigation, these positive effects may potentially be offset by the costs of managing the class: monitoring incentives for members' opt-outs (eg divergent objectives), facilitating information flows, managing conflicts and disagreements amongst members. Two commonly encountered issues are:

1. Over-inclusion (congestion) effects: when too many victims with different stakes or objectives join the class, or when sheer class size makes coordination difficult, maintaining a common objective with common rules will prove difficult. At some extreme, chaos may ensue if unharmed parties join the class pretending to be victims.
2. Under-inclusion (cost of collective action) effects: upon initiating a class action the onus is on the class representative (or her legal counsel) to inform all affected parties about the procedure. While many harmed parties are easily notified (through standard media channels), others are harder to reach. Thus there is an increasing marginal cost of notifying all potential class members, including the opportunity cost of failing to notify some high-stake claimants.

C. Allocative Efficiency

Counterbalancing the scaling benefits from class actions are the agency and other information costs arising from the representation of the class. Commonly, class actions are initiated by prospective, 'entrepreneurial' lawyers[24] seeking court approval of both the aggregation of the suit (certification) and its representation by the same lawyer. To make this possible, the lawyer needs a class representative, a 'typical' and 'adequate' victim who may be a figurehead or perhaps someone with a somewhat active participation in

---

[23] B Deffains and E Langlais, 'Informational externalities and settlements in mass tort litigations' 32 *European Journal of Law and Economics* (2011) 241–262.

[24] The term entrepreneurial litigation suggest that the attorney behaves as a profit-maximizing entrepreneur rather than as a trusted agent of the plaintiffs.

proceedings. Most other class members will never meet one another, the lawyer, the class representative or the judge administering the case. The judge determines the payment of the lawyer turned attorney as a percentage or an input-based amount taken from the recovery and the class receives the remainder. If the class action fails, neither attorney nor claimants receive anything. One of the most striking features of the class action, relative to individual litigation is that attorney fees are not bargained nor even determined between the class and their legal counsel. Instead, fees are 'centrally' determined ex post by a third party (the judge). We isolate three main issues associated with class formation and representation.

1. 'Additionality'

Class action procedures enable the pursuit of claims that may otherwise not see the light of day – when individual claims are too low relative to the cost of litigation or because of free riding. In that view, class actions provide 'additionality' – they create economic welfare by enabling justice transactions in situations where they would otherwise not materialise. Put differently, class actions deliver a public good by overcoming barriers between human wants and satisfied needs in a relatively cost-effective way.

We note that additionality (small claim viability) is a contested point in the US. It has been argued that in some cases with little merit (small or frivolous claims), aggregating claims blackmails risk-averse defendants into settling 'under pressure' even though the claims carry little chance of success in courts. With limited solvency and strict liability (rather than negligence) standards, the resulting outcome may also be inefficient as defendants may use bankruptcy as a shield against liability, which also reduces their incentives to care. Counterarguments have been provided based on portfolio diversification and risk neutrality amongst large corporations and insurance companies. Whilst we note this controversy, we take the main economic line that additionality, by enabling justice transactions to proceed in the market for small claims, create economic benefits to consumers and producers of these transactions and increase deterrence for plaintiffs – empirical but ageing evidence is provided by.

The additionality argument is less suited to mass tort class actions, where stakes are typically large enough that claimants could just as viably initiate individual suits. Realistically, the 'additionality' argument only applies to a sub-segment of all class actions; that characterized by individually unviable (ie small) claims. John Coffee distinguishes amongst three types of class actions:[25]

---

[25] Coffee (above n 13) 904–5.

- type A where individual claims are 'marketable' in the absence of a class action alternative (economically viable, eg many torts or property damage class actions) and where opt-out is therefore always a credible fallback option.
- type B where individual claims are 'unmarketable' (too low to stand on their own, eg many consumer class actions) in the absence of a class action alternative, and where opt-out is not a credible option for plaintiffs.
- type C where individual claims are a high-variance mix of marketable and/or unmarketable claims, and where conflicts between different subgroups are likely.

Type A and type B class actions will be homogeneous and stable, with scaling and additionality factors driving class membership, but class actions of type C will predictably be unstable. The basic adverse selection (lemon) problem mentioned above ensures that low-stake claimants will be drawn to the class action by sheer want of any other alternative, but as we explain later this may not be the case for high stake claimants.

2. Collective action

Class actions as a collective endeavour may fail due to a free riding problem:[26] potential class representatives with small individual stakes may not register a meritorious class action because they have no incentive to bear the high time (and sometime monetary) cost of notifying all parties. Although each claimant has an interest in the action being initiated, none has incentives to start it. Contingent fees and entrepreneurial attorneys, whereby the action is initiated and managed by a third party, was the obvious solution to the collective action problem, but as discussed above this solution entails agency costs and we will discuss other solutions as well. A related collective action problem is the ever present danger of the class collapsing under the weight of free riding behaviour, progressively returning to multiple individual lawsuits through opt-out attrition, possibly degenerating into inter-plaintiff competition driven by an instinctive fear of fund depletion.[27]

The highly decentralized nature of the US judicial system accentuates these concerns. Attorneys representing geographic clusters of claimants may initiate representative procedures in State courts, which are later consolidated

---

[26] RK Winter, 'Aggregating Litigation' 54 *Law and Contemporary Problems* (1991) 69.

[27] There are potentially optimal risk-sharing remedies to bankruptcy and fund depletion – as a source of class instability. The solution is to balance the awards of present- relative to uncertain future plaintiffs – who bear a larger share of the risk when the fund is depletable, K Ayotte and Y Listokin, 'Optimal Trust Design in Mass Tort Bankruptcy' 7 *American Law and Economics Review* (2005) 403.

through multi-districting. At that stage, a lead counsel would have to emerge from possibly hundreds of attorneys representing the interest of very motley groups of plaintiffs. A host of well-known political economy failures ranging from rent-seeking to unhealthy compromises may then inflate the dead weight cost of further consolidating a spatially fragmented class action. The result is a 'tragedy of the commons' (overexploiting the fund available for recovery) and yet again, the class action may degenerate as losers decide to opt-out.

When a harm, though large in aggregate terms, has been visited in small doses over many victims, organisational cost and free riding should be expected to prevent collective action. In this view, a class action is essentially a public good supplied to its members by a single individual: the class representative who initiates the action. In the absence of an entrepreneurial attorney, the class representative could also be viewed as the individual bearing the whole cost of the legal proceedings, hiring the legal skills and technical expertise required to conduct the action and covering his cost out of the expected recovery. This is not the role traditionally assigned to the class representative in the literature, which sees him as a figurehead with little role in any decision making. In this section, we will temporarily ignore this traditional take on the class representative and assume that, in the absence of an entrepreneurial attorney, some claimant will have to take the initiative to lodge and manage the class action. We will then show that the collective action problems that arise from this situation are sufficiently large to motivate the intervention of a third party.

In the absence of legal counsel, which claimant will step forward as class representative? A prospective class representative facing the choice of initiating or not a class action would rationally leave the task to others given the significant sunk cost (time, stress, liability and pecuniary cost) involved with class notification and subsequent class management. Dewees et al suggest that the free rider problem will be more pronounced still in jurisdictions, which adopt fee shifting rules.[28] If a class action is lost at trial, under fee shifting rules the plaintiff must compensate the defendant for his legal cost. This burden would fall upon the class representative, further reducing any incentives to initiate and lead a class action. In addition, there may also be a liquidity problem: even if a class representative were to step forward out of a sense of moral duty, or following a game of attrition, he may not have the means to contract a lawyer or obtain credit from a lender.

There are various possible avenues to deal with the free rider problem. Since the presence of transaction costs amongst the plaintiffs prevents collective action, the government may license a third party to act on behalf of the

---

[28] DN Dewees, JRS Prichard and MJ Trebilcock, 'An Economic Analysis of Cost and Fee Rules for Class Actions' 10 *Journal of Legal Studies* (1981) 155, 163.

interest of victims. This third party could be the government itself, acting pre-emptively through regulatory responses designed to reduce large-scale harm, such as environmental or health contamination. The third party could also be a profit-motivated private entrepreneur who will incur the transaction costs and take a payment from the class fund contingent on the success of the action. This is of course how most class actions are initiated and we discuss the subsequent agency issues it raises in the next section.

Some have nonetheless argued that there will be situations in which a class representative initiates the class without external intervention.[29] If we consider a heterogeneous class (type C) and examine class formation as a waiting game in which no plaintiff has a stake large enough to motivate taking a leadership role. An equilibrium with class formation will be a rare outcome whereas free riding and market failure will be the most common outcome. Deffains and Langlais show how entrepreneurial class representation solves this type of problem.[30]

3. Agency cost

Class representation by entrepreneurial attorneys[31] may solve the initial problem of collective action, but it is in turn characterized by principal-agent relationships cascading into different basins. Several issues stand out in particular: class representative may pursue different interests when initiating the class action than those of many other class subgroups (ie the representative may not be representative). Attorneys may also pursue different settlement strategies than those maximising the average per capita outcome for the class. In entrepreneurial litigation, attorneys take much fuller control of the case than in standard individual litigation where clients exert much stronger control and influence over the settlement process. As discussed earlier, under a percentage fee payment, attorneys may attempt to minimize effort and maximize their fee by settling early in the proceedings. The resulting settlement is likely to fail to reflect the merit of the case. Finally, attorneys will

---

[29] N Marceau and S Mongrain, 'Damage Averaging and the Formation of Class Action Suits' 23 *International Review of Law and Economics* (2003) 63.

[30] Deffains and Langlais (above n 23).

[31] Technically, the class representative is always a claimant. However, an entrepreneurial attorney taking over the management of a class will usually select and appoint the class representative so that the latter's role is typically subdued. A Klement and Z Neeman, 'Incentive Structures for Class Action Lawyers' 20 *Journal of Law, Economics, and Organization* (2004) 102, and Macey and Miller (above n 11). As suggested before, unless the class representative is one the highest claim plaintiffs, she has little incentive to spend time and effort in the conduct of the class, whereas the attorney has high incentives to do so. And a highest claim plaintiff is typically not a likely class representative because she is a plaintiff with the most incentive to opt out in case of damage averaging (Coffee (above n 13), Macey and Miller (above n 11)).

often have no incentives to show regard for the variance of claims within large heterogeneous classes, thereby creating tensions amongst claimants. These tensions may lead a number of claimants to opt out of the class to seek individual recovery. Along the way, productive efficiency deteriorates although the outcome may be fairer.

These matters are issues of allocative efficiency because they create a wedge between the demand and supply of justice, particularly for large-scale/small-claims actions (large overall liability but small stakes for individual class members). Whilst it is true that judges exert a very high degree of discretion on the whole process (certifying the genuine nature of the class action, examining the adequacy of settlements, etc.), the information asymmetries behind the representation problem also apply to judges who administer judgement based on incomplete information.[32] Some of the agency costs mentioned above could be minimized if plaintiffs exerted a higher degree of monitoring and participation in proceedings. For instance, plaintiffs with a high stake could potentially play this role provided expenditure on monitoring does not exceed some specific magnitude. However, high stake plaintiffs often have higher incentives to conduct individual litigation rather than join a class.

In contrast with standard litigation in which legal fees are agreed *ex ante*, class actions proceed with no explicit prior agreement on the terms of attorney compensation. Largely, this is due to the much higher transaction costs involved. The legal counsel managing the representative procedure is a private agent who usually advances her effort and time and is compensated later, typically on a contingent basis (ie upon winning – settlement or trial). The judge administering the case decides *ex post* (after the recovery is known) what a reasonable amount for legal fees is. Conditional on winning the case, a fee payment drawn from the recovery then compensates the legal counsel for her time, effort and expenses. An amount of economic profit may be part of the fee payment depending on the competitiveness of the market for lawyers (we later discuss why the market for class action lawyers is typically non-competitive). The judge determines the level of this payment by evaluating counsel costs, effort, expertise provided and risk taken against the difficulty of the case. Whether determined through a 'Lodestar' formula or a direct percentage of the recovery.[33]

---

[32] Note that this a specific feature of US class actions. Other countries having legalised class actions do not require a certification process.

[33] In fact, empirical findings suggest that while the two methods of fee setting provide different incentives to the class attorney, either method deliver similar dollar amounts to the legal service. WJ Lynk, 'The Courts and the Market: An Economic Analysis of Contingent Fees in Class-Action Litigation' 19 *Journal of Legal Studies* (1990) 247.

Whereas the class counsel is paid a contingent fee, this is usually not the case for defence attorneys. Contingent fees are typically used for non-corporate clients, as a response to a liquidity problem, as a way to spread the risk and realign the interest of many small clients with their counsel's. These incentives are somewhat redundant in the corporate client segment. Most defendants in class actions are corporations or insurance companies, which do not face significant liquidity problems, whose shareholders have diversified portfolios and whose legal counsel is either 'in-house', or has invested in durable and prestigious long-term professional relationship with the corporation (which they will not put at risk for short-term agency gains).[34] Finally, what should the defendant counsel's fee be contingent on? Whereas plaintiffs can expect the judge to peg attorney fees to the class recovery, the defendant has no such benchmark and defendant attorneys are therefore usually paid hourly fees.

VII. OPTIMAL ATTORNEY CONTRACTING

The problem of collective action suggests that individual plaintiffs will usually wait for other claimants to take action rather than take the costly initiative of lodging and representing a class action. The rationale for free riding is that a more impatient plaintiff will eventually take the lead and deliver a public good to the remaining, more patient claimants. Understandably, few equilibria will support class formation in this context. A more effective alternative is therefore to authorize a third party representative, the entrepreneurial attorney, to initiate and manage the class on behalf of the collective of plaintiffs. This solution resolves the collective action problem since instead of a large number of passive individuals with few incentives to reduce their claim by the cost of class formation; we now have a single individual who runs the class as a profit-making venture.

However, transferring the representation function to an entrepreneur who is not a claimant, has no personal stake in the action and will gather and hold private information about the value of settlement offers raises obvious contracting questions. The third party representative may pursue different objectives than maximising class welfare. It is easy to show that if plaintiffs can perfectly monitor the effort and cost of the attorney, a time-rate contract is the most efficient solution. However, if, as is usually the case, the actions of the attorney cannot be perfectly monitored by her clients, paying the attorney on an hourly basis runs the risk of misalignment between counsel and class interests. For instance, one would expect an hourly-paid attorney to

---

[34] JB Heaton, 'Settlement Pressure' 25 *International Review of Law and Economics* (2005) 264.

advise against settlements (which reduce the length of her work) and in favour of trials (which extend work duration), even though a settlement may offer a higher net expected recovery to the class. This point is pressed further by Polinsky and Rubinfeld who stress that: "Although lawyers have a professional obligation to do what is best for their clients...it seems obvious that a lawyer's financial incentives will affect this decision-making to some, and possibly to a significant, extent".[35]

As noted earlier, using a contingent[36] (outcome-based) rather than input-based method of payment removes attorney preferences for lengthy procedures and for going to trial. It also solves a loss aversion/liquidity problem for many plaintiffs and experimental research suggests this effect is very important in shaping plaintiffs' preferences for contingent fees. Contingent fees have seen remarkable growth over the 1980s and are now the most commonly used method to pay attorneys in class actions. In the US however,[37] contingent contracts introduce a speculative motive to the attorney's actions: since a trial is risky and the attorney is not paid a fee if the outcome is negative, she may now find it in her interest to settle the suit quickly for a suboptimal amount in order to reduce her effort and time cost and guarantee the collection of the fee. Moral hazard thus emerges through the risk that the entrepreneurial attorney settles too early and for too little.

The agency costs of third party representation of poorly informed (or uninformed) claimants under contingent fee contracts have now been extensively studied by economists. This literature offers key insights into the question of efficient representation contracts but it is only seldom developed in a class action context. The main drawback from this omission is that the incentives arising from optimal contract design theory are unlikely to work in a class action context where the contract remains unspecified until a judicial decision is made. Since the class attorney and her clients do not specify the legal fee *ex ante*, the literature on optimal fee design should be viewed as offering potential ways to reform legal fee determination in a class action context, rather than as providing practical advice to plaintiffs with regard to their moral hazard problem.

---

[35] AM Polinsky and DL Rubinfeld, 'Aligning the Interests of Lawyers and Clients' 5 *American Law and Economics Review* (2003) 165.

[36] A contingent fee can be 'pure' if the percentage rate is independent of the size of the recovery, PJ Halpern and SM Turnbull, 'Legal Fees Contracts and Alternative Cost Rules: An Economic Analysis' 3 *International Review of Law and Economics* (1983) 3, or it can be tied to the size of the recovery and a source of economies of scale, as we assume in this paper.

[37] Rosen suggests that the rise of both class action procedures and contingent fees as a method of payment explain much of the income growth in the legal profession over the 1980s, S Rosen, 'The Market for Lawyers' 35 *Journal of Law and Economics* (1992) 215.

A. Class Attorney Contracts

In the only analytical study of this question so far, Klement and Neeman answer in the affirmative but qualify their answer:[38] attorney incentives will respond better to a menu of fee schedules, which they would be free to select from, than to the simple hourly or percentage fee offers. Their analysis starts from two stand-out features of class actions: the ex post determination of legal fees by administering courts and attorney self-selection (the market for class action lawyers is not competitive).

Can judges effectively substitute for clients for the purpose of contract design? Several features of class actions make this task difficult. First, as we have discussed, the collective action problem (i) precludes the use of non-contingent fees and (ii) weakens incentives to monitor attorney actions. Contingent fees have to be adjusted to the probability of success: a low probability requires a higher fee to keep the expected value of the fee to such a level as to ensure attorney participation. The attorney then has incentives to always declare facing low success probability to obtain higher fee adjustments. Overpayment can only be averted by lowering acceptable hours of attorney work for low probability cases, which in turns induces suboptimal attorney effort.

Overpayment vs. sub-optimal effort is the main trade-off. Of course, if the actions of the attorney were observable, Klement and Neeman, along with the literature just reviewed, agree that this problem can be solved through a contingent hourly fee – although they suggest the fee should be decreasing rather than proportional to the number of hours worked. In practice, attorney effort is largely unobservable to all parties so the moral hazard problem remains and is for the court to resolve.

Second, attorney markets in class actions are characterized by self-selection and market power. Whereas in individual suits clients choose their attorney in a competitive market, in class actions an entrepreneur attorney selects a representative client, have him endorsed by a judge, and initiates the lawsuit on behalf of all potential claimants. From that stage onwards, the attorney is no longer subject to competitive forces. Market power in turn is a source of adverse selection: since the attorney self-selects into her role, the court cannot observe her degree of ability. If this problem is compounded by moral hazard, a problem similar to that studied by Rubinfeld and Scotchmer – with a much subdued role for clients – now confronts the judge in charge of the case.[39] Competitive attorney contracting would force candidate class attorneys to elicit information about their ability and their private assessment of the case,

---

[38] Klement and Neeman (above n 31).
[39] DL Rubinfeld and S Scotchmer, 'Contingent Fees for Attorneys: An Economic Analysis' 24 *RAND Journal of Economics* (1993) 343.

reducing the potential rents they would otherwise later extract from their protected position.

What could judges do to reduce strategic behaviour and informational rents, which both reduce plaintiff welfare? The mechanism design literature offers some guidance: a regulator with an additive separable objective function can elicit optimal incentive responses from a monopolist with unknown cost by offering a menu of linear contracts. In the context of class actions, judges could screen attorneys *ex ante* (prior to class certification) by announcing a menu of linear fee schedules consisting of a fixed percentage fee g and a recovery threshold R under which the attorney wins no fees. Incentive compatibility is guaranteed if the menu of fees increases monotonically in q (a hybrid measure of attorney ability and case quality).

Attorneys of different abilities q_1, q_2 exerting the same effort on the same case receive the same payment but with different probabilities. The optimal menu can be implemented both through an hourly fee and a percentage fee arrangement. Under hourly fees, incentive compatibility requires the optimal contract to multiply every additional hour by a decreasing factor of q (to reduce incentives to exceed the optimal amount of hours), whereas under the percentage fee method, the optimal menu should increase linearly in the recovery. Here, the attorney fee should at the margin consist of a percentage fee g (the slope of the linear contract) and a moving threshold $R(g)$ below which the attorney receives no fee (the intercept). A higher percentage fee is coupled to a higher threshold.

B. Class Lemons

Class actions where individual claims are a high-variance mix of marketable and unmarketable claims are usually settled or arbitrated using a damage averaging rule, under which individual recoveries from class actions are simply the average per capita recovery. Hence, low-stake claimants make a net gain compared to the individual merit of their claim, whereas high-stake claimants make a loss. If high-stake claimants are risk averse, they may actually prefer a lower but more certain average payoff than in individual suits (where early individual raids on the defendants' fund may leave an 'empty nest' for many claimants). Otherwise, risk-neutral high-stake claimants will recognize that the net expected recovery from the class action serves the interest of low-stake claimants, and would logically opt-out of the class action, at the expense of productive efficiencies for the class (a reduced scale).

Initially, single high-stake opt-outs will have only minor effects on expected values and so opt-outs go unhindered until the class degenerates. According to this line, the public good argument for using and certifying class action would appear tenuous at best. This argument follows the classic line of the market for lemons argument. The result is a class action market full of lemons (a class largely composed of low-stake claimants and suboptimal class membership). To the extent that these compositional changes are recognized by the judge administering the case, the average recovery will be a low-stake amount and economic distortions are minimized (although productive efficiency remains lowered by the loss of scale and the repeated individual suits of high-stake claimants).[40] There is a further loss of efficiency if judges fail to recognize the exit of high-stake claimants and if low-stake claimants manage to disguise their claims as high-stake, which we will discuss later in this paper.

The decision to opt-in or out is in fact largely determined by the regulatory context, and economists' interest for class action efficiency has exclusively focused on opt-out models. The decision to opt-out is often analysed in a context where victims differ in the extent of their harm and where courts indicate that they will award damages based on the aggregate merit of the case (through damage averaging). It is indeed often the case that victims will have different stakes in the class action; shareholders with different degrees of investment in a failed project, injuries varying with the degree of exposure to a toxic substance, frequent versus irregular consumers of a product sold at an excessive price by a collusive industry, etc.

In some of these examples, the extent of individual damage may be easy to demonstrate (eg by using medical technology or proofs of product purchase). In other cases, measuring individual harm is difficult and costly, and the difficulty may increase in the extent of the injury. For instance, large individual harms, such as developing an incurable disease, can be multifactorial (attributable to other factors than the defendant's action), whereas a smaller individual damage (eg a broken leg, or a small amount of money lost by paying undue fees) can more readily be attributed to the defendant's action.

Establishing causality will be harder in heterogeneous class actions (type 'C' in Coffee's taxonomy), which involve a mix of high and small claims and in which it will generally be very costly to ascertain the extent of individual harm. Therefore, in such cases, courts can significantly reduce the time and costs of establishing causality for differing levels of claims by using damage averaging rules. With damage averaging, courts determine awards on the principle that it is enough to establish causality for the class as a whole so that individual recoveries are identical amounts determined by the aggregate claim and the class size. However, damage averaging makes plaintiffs choices more complex. The law and economics literature often assumes that high

---

[40] That is, unless high-stake claimants have a separate high-stake class action certified later on but such a procedure is risky because (i) by then the fund may have been raided first by the low-stake class action, and (ii) claims variance amongst high-stake claimants is likely to re-iterate the process (with ever increasing risk of a raided fund to the remaining higher-stake claimants).

stake plaintiffs will opt-out rather than be bound by accepting an average recovery, which less than compensates them for the high level of harm incurred. This is essentially what the theory of a market for lemons would predict, but as we shall see later this outcome is by no means certain if we factor in signalling games by heterogeneous plaintiffs.

C. Claim Heterogeneity

The degree of claim heterogeneity also plays a key role in the class formation outcome: if high claims are proportionally larger than small claims, there is a high cost to the defendant of making the wrong payment to a low-claim plaintiff and the defendant requires a large proportion of high-claim plaintiffs in the class to be persuaded that the likelihood of making this mistake is low. Assume for instance that, if all claimants were to join the class, economies of scale are sufficiently high to offset the losses to high claim plaintiffs from damage averaging. Further assume that the proportion λ of high-claim plaintiffs is less than the proportion that would make them indifferent between class and individual action but more than the proportion τ of the stakes' gap in the extended contract zone.

In a two stage signalling game with backward induction, Che suggests that in this case class size will be larger the higher is λ, the lower the stake gap and the larger the scale economies.[41] Otherwise, if λ is less than τ, class size is larger the lower is λ and the larger is the stakes' gap (economies of scale no longer play a role on class size). Thus class formation will be stronger the more homogeneous the class is and will collapse to multiple individual suits if the proportion of high stake claimants is equal to or less than the proportion τ of the stakes' gap in the extended contract zone (only low stake plaintiffs join the class).

Spier recasts claim heterogeneity in terms of bargaining externalities.[42] Here individual plaintiffs with different degrees of commonality in their cases separately sue a defendant whose fund is limited (ie where the defendant would be made insolvent by the aggregate claim should all plaintiffs prevail in court). Her model assumes two plaintiffs and one defendant but is easily extended to a collective of k plaintiffs. Positive bargaining externalities are of the information externalities type: if there are unresolved questions common to the plaintiffs, a decision in the first individual hearing can set a precedent under *stare decisis*, which saves litigation cost to all subsequent claimants. Negative bargaining externalities arise from fund limitation: a settlement

---

[41] Y-K Che, 'Equilibrium Formation of Class Action Suits' 62 *Journal of Public Economics* (1996) 339.
[42] KE Spier, 'Settlement with Multiple Plaintiffs: The Role of Insolvency' 18 *Journal of Law, Economics and Organization* (2002) 295.

between one plaintiff and the defendant decreases the fund available for subsequent bargaining by other plaintiffs.

Spier's main criteria is the degree of correlation between claims: if individual claims are positively correlated, evidence revealed through one plaintiff's settlement benefit other claimants (eg *stare decisis*), whereas if claims are negatively correlated such information reduces the chances of other claimants (eg a criminal case). Spier finds that in case of high correlation, decentralized bargaining fails (due to traditional hurdles – excessive optimism, moral hazard, etc.) whereas collective bargaining increases private and social welfare. In this case, the interests of the defendant and society will coincide and the defendant will attempt to consolidate claims prior to bargaining. If correlation is low, the defendant forces individual settlements that are detrimental to the plaintiffs' welfare.

Here collective bargaining would yield superior outcomes and it is the collective of plaintiffs who will have an incentive in consolidating claims prior to bargaining. Intermediate correlation leads to strategic behaviour with respect to externalities and inefficient individual settlements transferring surplus to the defendant. Thus, mandatory class actions (ruling out opt-outs) for limited-fund litigation improves social welfare. Whilst US Rule 23(b) already provides for mandatory class action in limited-fund cases, Spier notes that the transaction costs associated with proving the commonality of claims and assessing the net value of defendant assets will usually be sufficiently large for defendants to instead file for bankruptcy under Chapter 11, a procedure that would achieve similar claim aggregation results without the transaction costs imposed by Rule 23. Once again, this study questions whether class action procedures provide the main players with the right set of incentives when there other claim consolidation alternatives and when stakes and commonality vary among plaintiffs.

VIII. CONCLUSION

Ultimately, the social efficiency of any legal procedure is determined by its effect on deterrence and the cost-effectiveness with which it is administered when needed. Class action procedures are legislated with those goals in mind: providing deterrence through higher liability when there is commonality of claims, and reducing the per capita cost of obtaining and supplying justice to a large collective of claimants. As we discussed in this article, increased deterrence and economies of scale both materializes through parameters that increase the bargaining power of injured parties and the range of settlements – the contract zone.

We contrasted these social benefits to four main potential sources of social cost: collective action failure, agency costs in representation, settlement pressure and signalling games in heterogeneous classes. Regardless of the extent of their claim, no single plaintiff has incentives to bear the cost of initiating and leading the class. If claims are homogeneous, class failure results from free riding. We saw that the collective action problem can be solved by assigning the rights to initiate and lead a class action to a third party, the class counsel, who bears the cost of managing the action in lieu of the – now figurehead – class representative.

Entrepreneurial attorney representation may resolve the collective action problem but introduces agency costs, which are detrimental to claimants' objectives of seeking adequate redress for their grievances. Incentives for legal entrepreneurship work better through the payment of contingent fees, but more sophisticated contracting arrangements than those currently used are needed to address and prevent moral hazard. If claims are heterogeneous, adverse selection dynamics and court's use of damage averaging rules destabilise the class through likely defection of the most likely class representatives – high stake claimants. We saw that if claimants act strategically, signalling games can nonetheless lead to a variety of class formation equilibria, including polar cases (full inclusion and class failure). The degree of dispersion in claims' size and the weight of each group of claimants were the main factors driving class formation outcomes.

The costs and benefits of class actions litigation remain largely an empirical matter, and not one that will easily be resolved. The lack of comparable and systematically recorded data on class actions characteristics and outcomes makes social efficiency assessments very hard to conduct. The aforementioned comparative exercise the RAND Corporation conducted throughout the 1990s provides of an in-depth analysis of several prominent case studies. The RAND researchers summed up their investigation in inconclusive terms:

> ... plaintiff attorneys seemed sometimes to be driven by financial incentives, sometimes by the desire to right perceived wrongs, and sometimes by both. They sometimes devoted substantial resources to investigating case facts and law, but at other times moved quickly to negotiating settlements. Some of these settlements served class members' interests better than others. Most produced substantial fees for the lawyers themselves. Judges sometimes used their authority to ensure that settlements provided more for class members and the public than for the lawyers, but at other times seemed reluctant to do so.[43]

Generalisation is unsurprisingly difficult: not all attorneys think alike, neither do plaintiffs, nor defendants, nor judges, and the degree of social efficiency

---

[43] Hensler (above n 7) Ch 15, 401.

of class action procedures will remain the 'great big question' of representative proceedings. In this review of the literature, we isolated and analysed the main cost and benefits and emphasized theoretical considerations put forward by economists. We showed in a basic model of class action settlement that although the reality is extremely complex, there is some degree of predictability in class formation equilibria depending on the types of claims, degrees of commonality, damage rules, and ex post rules used to set attorney fees. This exercise derived the fundamental trade-offs between the social and private gains from achieving critical mass and the losses from agency costs and collective action failure. The paper thus explores from an economic perspective the issues or problems which the EC's specifically European model of collective redress seeks to overcome, and what Member States will need to address to implement it, in order to promote efficient outcomes, or social welfare in Europe.

There are several potential ways for research to further expand our understanding of the welfare effects of class actions, by analysing the effects of variation in rules between countries and over time. On the one hand, opt-in class actions have not been the subject of much relevant economic research, perhaps because they are less extensively used than opt-out actions.[44] If potential claimants join the class voluntarily rather than be members by default, the economic theory of clubs seems relevant. Socioeconomic research suggests that decisions taken under active membership differ significantly from those taken under passive membership.[45]

Gains in allocative efficiency may well result from letting potential claimants determine the optimal size and composition of the class they want to be part of, which in turn should lead researchers to study questions of club membership and optimal partitioning. If the economic merits of class actions have proved so difficult to quantify and evaluate, it is due in no small part to the one size fits all nature of the regulatory constraints facing market players. The EC's recommendation thus offers an opportunity to analyse the effects of variation in rules between EU countries, and the effects proposed changes in these rules have over time.

---

[44] DR Hensler, C Hodges and M Tulibacka, *The Globalization of Class Actions* (Annals of the American Academy of Political and Social Science Series, Vol 622, March 2009, Sage 2009).

[45] JD Dana and KE Spier, 'Expertise and Contingent Fees: The Role of Asymmetric Information in Attorney Compensation' 9 *Journal of Law, Economics and Organization* (1993) 349.

The Economics of Class Actions: Fundamental Issues and New Trends

Myriam Doriat-Duban, Samuel Ferey and Sophie Harnay[*]

I. INTRODUCTION

The economics of class actions, representative proceedings, and collective redress is one of the classical fields in law and economics literature. Indeed, issues behind collective litigation illustrate a famous social dilemma: defending private interests of individuals does not equal serving the public interest. It would be efficient for society as a whole if injured victims went to court and recovered their loss because this would internalize all the costs generated by an economic activity. However, it is quite unlikely that such an outcome spontaneously emerges in a purely decentralized economy because the individual costs of litigation are sometimes more important that the expected value of the individual claim. Therefore, a rational agent seeking to maximize his utility will not go to court even if it would have been efficient from the social point of view. As such, the law and the judicial system must play a major role in reducing these costs by properly organizing procedures which help to solve the dilemma.

The dilemma covers a lot of actual or potential litigation, such as consumer law, contract law, mass torts, and antitrust law. In the European context, antitrust is a good illustration. Nowadays, public enforcement is well-organized in European countries by both governments and antitrust authorities, but private enforcement remains weak. This weakness prevents victims from recovering harm caused by anti-competitive practices. The economic literature on this topic now covers a large and growing spectrum of subtopics, including empirical aspects, case studies, and theoretical analysis. In recent years, the law and economics literature has been renewed with new arguments beyond the initial paradox. Arguments include issues such as pressure groups and rent seeking theory, asymmetric information and agency problems, transaction costs theory, strategic behaviour, and behavioural economics.

---

[*] Myriam Doriat-Duban and Samuel Ferey, both of the Faculté de droit, sciences économiques et gestion, University of Lorraine, acknowledge financial support from the French National Agency for Research (JCJC Damage program, ANR-12-JSH1-0001, 2012–2015). Sophie Harnay is also of the Faculté de droit, sciences économiques et gestion, University of Lorraine.

The aim of this chapter is to examine a series of fundamental theoretical issues of collective redress from a law and economics perspective. It illustrates the main reasons for the consensus in economics, which states that collective redress is required to avoid a social dilemma. Part one of this chapter explains why collective redress is required to avoid free-riding problems and to improve efficiency; part two focuses on the role and risks assumed by the key players of class actions, namely lawyers and associations.

II. FREE-RIDING AND ACCESS TO LAW AND JUSTICE: THE CASE FOR CLASS ACTIONS

A. The Individual Decision to Go to Court

According to the economic analysis of law, the individual decision to litigate and to file a suit before a court is determined by an *ex ante* cost-benefit analysis though which a victim compares the expected costs and benefits associated with a suit. The victim then decides to bring the suit before a court when his or her expected gain (the expected damages) exceeds the legal expenses (the compensation of the lawyer, expected duration of litigation, etc), taking the probability of winning and the relative asymmetry of the parties at stake into account. Conversely, when the expected expenses are larger than the expected gain, the victim has no incentive to litigate. Hence, judicial decisions acknowledging individual and collective rights may not be produced when victims do not find it profitable to go to court. Due to the high individual costs associated with the production of a judicial decision, the victim is not induced to bear that cost and prefers not to go to court if there is no expected gain.

Evidently, this situation may entail serious consequences in social terms. Indeed, judicial decisions can be seen as collective goods.[1] On one hand, the consumers of judicial services freely take benefit from past judicial decisions that provide them with free information to resolve their conflict. On the other hand, the stock of judicial decisions grants judges with an input in their production function. Hence, parties in past conflicts contribute to the production of a collective good that benefits parties for the future. However, most of the time, parties are unable to internalize the benefits that their private investment – taking the form of private legal expenses – brings to society. Therefore, the level of judicial decisions that are actually produced may be insufficient. In particular, parties may adopt free-riding behaviour and prefer not to contribute to the production of judicial decisions while using decisions that have been previously produced and financed by other

---

[1] W Landes and RA Posner 'Legal Precedent: A Theoretical and Empirical Analysis' 19 *Journal of Law and Economics* 2 (1976) 249.

agents. An extreme situation occurs when all agents wait for the others to pay for the production of judicial decisions while not contributing themselves.

The consecutive problem with the access to law and justice deriving from that situation thus makes it necessary to search for legal mechanisms that allow the production of a socially-optimal level of judicial decisions. Legal aid is the first device that aids individuals in accessing justice as it reduces the individual cost of contribution to the production of judicial decisions. Mainly due to its costs, its scope remains limited in most countries, and therefore other institutions, including class actions, must be examined.

B. The Reasons for Collective Litigation

In comparison to the dissemination of individual actions and their distinct treatment, class actions display several advantages from a legal and economic standpoint.

First, class actions enhance judicial consistency in rulings, as compared to sequential trials. While sequential trials may lead to different legal decisions in both time and space, owing to the diverging preferences of the judges or to the particular circumstances of the environment, class actions bring a unique and homogeneous solution to the cases that are brought before the court, thereby ensuring the equality of all citizens before the law.[2]

Second, from an economic perspective, class actions foster economic efficiency, as they avoid the duplication of legal costs derived from multiple legal actions which are oriented toward achieving a similar goal. On the one hand, as far as victims are concerned, the grouping of individual actions within a unique claim allows for the realization of economies of scale. As has been mentioned, in situations where the expected gain is low and the cost of litigation is high for an individual, a victim may have no incentive to go to court individually. By contrast, the collection and grouping of several individual claims with a common interest can make litigation profitable, as litigation costs are borne collectively and compared with the sum of the individual expected gains – an implicit argument is that legal costs entail large fixed costs. In that view, class actions thus enlarge the scope of access to justice for citizens. On the other hand, the argument of economies on legal costs is not

---

[2] Two DES Cases recently brought before different French courts provide an example for the inconsistency of legal decisions where no representative proceedings exist. In a first case, the Court of Appeal of Versailles held that each of the two tortfeasors – two pharmaceutical companies – had to pay half of the loss; and one year later, the Court of Nanterre held that the market share liability doctrine could be applied in French law and apportioned the loss to be paid to the victim according to their market shares (97 percent for the first tortfeasor and 3 percent for the second). If these cases had been resolved in a class action suit, such inconsistency and unfairness would not have occurred (S Ferey and F G'Sell, 'Pour une prise en compte des parts de marché dans la détermination de la contribution à la dette de réparation' *Recueil Dalloz* 41 (2013) 2709).

limited to victims, but it also applies to defendants. Indeed, the repetition of several suits based on analogous facts implies a duplication of costs for defendants facing sequential suits. The gathering of claims within a unique claim avoids costs associated with a multiplication of suits.

Third, the advantages of collective actions are not only beneficial for the parties, but also for courts as collective redress reduces administrative and management costs of the judicial system. Indeed, class actions reduce the total number of cases treated by courts and therefore profitably reduce their workload in the general context of court congestion in most countries. This may result in indirect advantages for litigants benefiting from higher-quality judicial services. The total impact of class actions on the efficiency of courts is nevertheless ambiguous. Thus, class actions must be certified by judges through a prior certification process – at least in the US – which adds to the already important workload of judges. Furthermore, precisely because the realization of scale economies makes some judicial actions profitable for victims where they would not be engaged absent a collective procedure, class actions may also contribute to the congestion of courts, as they may encourage excessive litigation in the form of frivolous litigation. The enlargement of the access to justice deriving from the possibility of class actions may thus have a correlation of poorer quality of judicial service actually delivered to citizens. In addition, the advantages of class actions may be lower than expected, since individual agents are able to adopt opportunistic behaviour likely to undermine the efficiency of collective redress procedures.

Fourth, by avoiding a sequence of different individual cases, class actions could be said to improve the quality of justice. Indeed, when trials occur sequentially, a deep pocket defendant could have a rational interest to over-invest in the first trial – exceeding the value of the claim and investing much more than what the victim could pay for his case – either to get a ruling in his favour, or to create a threat to the other plaintiffs. Over-investment strategy decreases the plaintiff's probability of winning and may be used strategically to prevent other victims from bringing their cases before the courts.

C. Collective Litigation and Free-Riding

1. Free-riding in class actions

The conditions of a free-riding problem occur frequently in the context of class actions.[3] Indeed, class members find themselves in a group-like situation in which they have an incentive to free-ride, as the outcome of collective litigation is appropriated collectively whereas the cost of contributing is borne

---

[3] A Cassone and GB Ramello, 'The Simple Economics of Class Action: Private Provision of Club and Public Goods' 32 *European Journal of Law and Economics* (2011) 205.

at the individual level. Hence, the outcome of the joint effort of class members has some features of a non-rival and non-excludable collective good. On the one hand, indeed, the production of a favourable decision by a court benefits all class members, including those who have not contributed, or have contributed less, to the collective effort of the class. However, at the collective level, the deterrence effect associated with class action lawsuits through the avoidance of harmful behavior in the future benefits all members of the class. Class actions may thus be seen as a mechanism of private provision of a collective good.[4] As a consequence, despite their common interest in the collective good, class members may lack the incentive to volunteer and thus refuse to incur the corresponding cost; they may evidently prefer to free-ride on the provision of the good by other class members.

The problem with free-riding becomes pertinent where representative litigation is at stake, as is the case in American proceedings. When one injured individual – the so-called representative plaintiff – initiates a class action suit and bears the cost of litigation privately, he actually supplies a collective good. Then, provided that the court maintains the class action suit through certification, other individuals that have been harmed in a similar way can take benefit from the suit that has been initiated by the representative plaintiff.[5] Thus, as the representative plaintiff expects free-riding behaviours from other agents, they may have no incentive to act as an instigator and initiate the class action, which may result in a non-optimal collective good.

In addition, free-riding behaviour can also originate in conflicts between the members of the class.[6] First, the representative claimant may reflect the preferences of the members of the class only imperfectly. Second, members of the class may have heterogeneous preferences over the different dimensions of the class action. For instance, they may have different views on the distribution of compensation, the settlement versus trial trade-off, and the optimal timing of the class action procedure. Divergences over the level of current and future damages may also occur at the intergenerational level between present and future plaintiffs – future plaintiffs may thus have an interest in low damages being paid in the current period, thereby preserving the perpetrator's solvency for future claims, while present plaintiffs prefer to be compensated

---

[4] M Olson *The Logic of Collective Action* (Harvard University Press, 1965); T Bergstrom, L Blume, and H Varian, 'On the Private Provision of Public Goods' 29 *Journal of Public Economics* 1 (1986) 25; S Vicary, 'Joint Production and the Private Provision of Public Goods' 63 *Journal of Public Economics* 3 (1997) 429.

[5] JC Coffee, 'Class Wars: The dilemma of the Mass Tort Class Action' 95 *Columbia Law Review* 6 (1995) 1343. N Marceau and S Mongrain, 'Damage Averaging and the Formation of Class Action Suits' 23 *International Review of Law and Economics* (2003) 63.

[6] JC Coffee, 'Class Action Accountability: Reconciling Exit, Voice, and Loyalty in Representative Litigation' 100 *Columbia Law Review* 2 (2000) 370.

for their actual loss in the current period. Furthermore, plaintiffs may also be characterized by different levels of risk aversion.

2. *Overcoming free-riding problems*

The development of the free-riding problem in relation to class actions in recent years appears quite surprising. It can be mainly explained by several legal devices that intend to mitigate and overcome the free-riding problem in class actions.

Furthermore, lawyers may also be allowed to initiate a lawsuit on the behalf of a class of individuals without having obtained the prior explicit consent from all potential plaintiffs. Although this can be seen as a source of potential abuse from lawyers leading to over-litigation,[7] this can also be positively interpreted as a way to reduce the cost of group formation for members and to overcome the free-riding problem – such devices can be observed in the US and facilitate the emergence of classes that would not exist otherwise.

The practice of some US lawyers to hire 'professional plaintiffs' to play the role of representative plaintiffs in class actions – usually for monetary compensation – also provides a solution to the free-riding problem, as the representative plaintiff is compensated for the cost of providing a collective good.[8] In the same manner, the possibility of offering additional compensation to class representatives 'for shouldering the extra burden in class action litigation' is also a way to overcome the free-riding problem.[9]

Finally, one can also mention opt-in or opt-out rights in class actions that aim to guarantee class homogeneity and cohesion. Indeed, the opt-in system provides that class members who want to become involved in a class action have to expressly consent to its terms. By contrast, the opt-out class action includes all members of the class, unless they explicitly express their choice to retain their right to sue individually. Although the relative efficiency of opt-in and opt-out rights in increasing class homogeneity may be discussed, both practices can be expected to limit free-riding in class action suits, as they both contribute to aligning the interests of claimants with each other. Some behavioural arguments have been recently stated in favor of the opt-out over opt-in. Indeed, when bounded rationality arguments are considered, individual behaviour may demonstrate a status-quo bias. In a famous example, Thaler and Benardski show the relationship between the status-quo bias and the default rule chosen by the law. They stress the importance of framing

---

[7] J Haymond and J West 'Class Action Extraction' 116 *Public Choice* (2003) 91.

[8] MA Perino, 'Institutional Activism Through Litigation: An Empirical Analysis of Public Pension Fund Participation in Securities Class Actions' (2006). Legal Studies Research paper 0055/2006, St. John's University School of Law, http://www.ssrn.com/abstract=938722.

[9] CM Sharkey, 'Punitive Damages as Societal Damages' 113 *Yale Law Journal* 2 (2003) 347.

the context of a decision and how it enables individuals to act in their best interests. Therefore, the default rule implemented by the law (opt-in or opt-out) may have an effect on the efficiency of the proceedings and opt-out is preferable if the legal system aims at increasing the number of individuals involved in a class action.

III. LAWYERS OR ASSOCIATIONS, THE KEY PLAYERS OF CLASS ACTIONS

Due to problems of coordination, a class action cannot be conducted by all plaintiffs but by a unique agent, such as a lawyer or an association, charged with representing the plaintiffs' interests. From an economic perspective, this results in a transfer of risks concerning the trial from the plaintiffs to the lawyer or the association. The question is to determine whether this transfer of risks is efficient (*A*), and what problems this transfer creates (*B*). Finally, some solutions to the problems triggered by representation are examined (*C*).

A. Class Action and the Best Risk Bearer

The aim of this part of the paper is to determine who the best risk bearer is: a class counsel or an association. This is also important for the determination of a best method for the introduction of class actions in European countries, avoiding the problems observed in the US.

1. The lawyer is the best risk bearer

In a class action, the class counsel can be considered a 'litigation entrepreneur'[10] because he assumes the risk of failure in exchange for a share of the expected returns greater than the incurred costs. This mechanism allocates the risk to the actor best equipped to manage it,[11] mainly for two reasons: specialization and diversification.

The specialization aspect can be justified by the economies of scale (ie, the numbers of plaintiffs) and of scope (ie, the skills of the lawyer). More precisely, economies of scale justify a specialization of the lawyers in a specific case, even if competition may exist among them at the moment of selecting the case, while economies of scope imply that the space of potential legal cases is occupied strategically, each lawyer being specialized in a different legal issue.

---

[10] HB Schaefer 'The Bundling of Similar Interests in Litigation. The Incentives for Class Action and Legal Actions taken by Associations' 9 *European Journal of Law and Economics* 3 (2000) 183.
[11] Cassone and Ramello (above n 3).

The diversification comes from the fact that the class counsel has incentives to create a portfolio of diversified risks, which, taken together, lower the average risk.[12] Thus, the lawyer appears to be the best risk bearer, both due to his expertise in a specific case and his capacity to spread the risk among several cases.

2. Association as an 'alternative' risk bearer

From an economic perspective, there is no fundamental difference in terms of the transfer of risk between a lawyer and an association. Indeed, the association may be the best risk bearer for the same reasons as the class counsel: specialization and diversification. The system of remuneration is similar, as the association is awarded a part of the returns if the case is won.

Nevertheless, a difference exists if we consider the duration of the relationship with the claimants. Indeed, the relationship between the claimants and the lawyer is for a short-term, limited to the litigation. Conversely, the relationship between the claimants and the association is a long-term relationship that may have existed before the lawsuit through membership and that may be extended beyond the trial. This argument may have an impact on the specialization but may play on the pooling of the risks too: the association, financed on a long-term basis by the contributions of its members and public subsidies, can better bear the risk of losing individual lawsuits than a lawyer who runs the risk of personal losses.[13]

One point should be stressed here: in European countries where no class action exists, private actors try to bring forth other proceedings. This trend is quite interesting to observe. For example, Cartel Damages Claims (CDC), a company in Belgium, has tried to sue members of cartels in Germany or Finland on behalf of the victims. For that purpose, CDC used a peculiar procedural tool, which consists of purchasing the claim of the victims. Then CDC bundles all claims purchased and brings them to Court, *de facto* joining them, and asserts that it is entitled to compensation.[14] While German Courts are still reluctant to accept this purchase, Finnish Courts have recently considered such a purchase as admissible.

---

[12] J Backhaus 'The Law Firm as an Investment Bank in Class Actions' 32 *European Journal of Law and Economics* (2011) 225; Cassone and Ramello, *ibid*.

[13] Schaefer (above n 10).

[14] CDC purchased claims from 28 German firms, which could recover damages from the members of a cement cartel. The antitrust damages claimed now amount to approximately €176 million. Each claim has been purchased for 100 euros, and CDC will be awarded an additional 75 percent of the damages recovered if the proceedings succeed (see B Deffains and S Ferey 'Vers une action en responsabilité en droit de la concurrence: à propos de l'affaire du ciment allemand' 131 *Revue d'économie industrielle* (2010) 1).

B. The Problems Related to the Transfer of Risk

Regardless of who the best risk bearer may be, they will only support the risk of a class action if the expected gains exceed the incurred costs. Thus, lawyers or associations have incentives to initiate a class action only if they can appropriate part of the benefits if the case is successful.[15] The solution is a contingency fees reward system.[16]

But this method of transferring the risk may be problematic for two reasons. The first one stems from the very high losses incurred by the defendant, substantially higher than the losses expected in the trial because of the impact of the collective litigation on his reputation. The second problem results from the anonymous relationship between the claimants and the counsel or the association. The consequence is a moral hazard problem, usually observed in this form of agency relationships. The solutions mainly consist in monitoring the agent's behaviour (lawyer or association) or in instituting a compensation scheme that aligns the interests of the lawyer/association with those of the claimants. However, the aforementioned solutions are difficult to apply in a class action suit. The consequence is that 'the class action creates incentives for [a] lawyer to conduct meritless lawsuits and to opt for early settlements that can be disadvantageous for his clients.'[17]

1. The problem of meritless cases

Class actions confront two economic theories. The first is the theory of law enforcement according to which class actions play a positive social role by increasing the potential tortfeasors' incentives to comply with the law (see part I). The second is the theory of capture where class actions might increase meritless and opportunistic litigation and play a negative social role.[18] The problem of capture appears when lawyers/associations attack a firm even if they know that the defendant will not be found liable (meritless case). The

---

[15] This argument is based on doctrine according to which contingency fees are not only the best way to transfer the risk from the plaintiff to the lawyer but also the best way for the plaintiff to monitor the lawyer (see WJ Lynk, 'The Court and the Market: An Economic Analysis of Contingent Fees in Class Action Litigation' 19 *Journal of Legal Studies* 1 (1990) 249; WJ Lynk 'The Courts and the Plaintiff's Bar: Awarding the Attorney's Fee Class Action Litigation' 1 *Journal of Legal Studies* 23 (1994) 185; T Miceli and K Segerson, 'Contingent Fees for Lawyers: The Impact on Litigation and Accident Prevention' 2 *Journal of Legal Studies* 20 (1991) 381).

[16] "The only practicable solution thus appears to be to grant a right to appropriate potential returns in exchange for known costs; this solution is called a contingent fee reward scheme, because it sets benefits discounted by a probability of less than 1 against known costs, and in order to be economically acceptable to the attorney requires the attribution of profits far exceeding the cost in case of success" (Cassone and Ramello (above n 3) 218).

[17] Schaefer (above n 10).

[18] *Ibid*.

strategy of the lawyer/association is to obtain an agreement from the defendant who wants to preserve his reputation[19] by avoiding a large publicity of the lawsuit.[20] The internet site ActionsCivile.com, recently created in France, illustrates such strategies. The website is presented as a simple tool for consumers to join a class action.[21] But actually, the business model of the website is first and foremost to settle cases and to avoid bringing the case before a court. From an economic perspective, the social desirability of class actions depends on the positive social effect in terms of higher deterrence and enforcement of the law compared to the negative social effect.

2. The problem of disadvantageous settlements

Another problem that may emerge concerns the control options class members have with respect to their lawyers. The Anglo-Saxon law and economics literature frequently emphasizes the key role played by lawyers in class actions. It then depicts the relationship between the client and the lawyer as a principal-agent relationship, in which the latter – a legal "expert" – has a higher degree of information than the former. This asymmetric information phenomenon enables the lawyer to possibly adopt opportunistic behaviour resulting in an inappropriate level of effort regarding the actual needs of the client.[22] Within this framework, a class action can be described as a multi-faceted principal-agency relationship in which the principal shares a common interest which is to control the agent effectively. However, each principal has no incentive to bear the cost of control individually, as the benefits are granted to all class members collectively. An insufficient production of control may derive from this free-riding situation. Hence, insufficient monitoring of lawyers may enable them to adopt opportunistic behaviour that is harmful to all class members and society.[23] This can take the form of excessive fees, frivolous class actions, or a wrong timing in the trade-off between litigation and alternative dispute resolution.

---

[19] "The bundling of rights through class actions increases the possibility of opportunistic behavior by lawyers. It enables them to appropriate for themselves and for the members of the groups they represent parts of the reputational assets of the firm along with creating unavoidable litigation costs that are still incurred by the firm even if it wins the suit" (Schaefer (above n 10) 188).

[20] Thus, Ulen explains that "there are circumstances in which the mere act of certifying a class may be enough to convert low-merit claims into such a high risk of catastrophic failure that the defendant will be impelled to settle" (TS Ulen, 'An Introduction to the Law and Economics of Class Action Litigation' 32 *European Journal of Law and Economics* 185 (2011) 196).

[21] See http://www.actioncivile.com.

[22] M Dewatripont and J Tirole, 'Advocates' 107 *Journal of Political Economy* 1 (1999) 1.

[23] Haymond and West (above n 7) 91.

This moral hazard may be observed if the client (principal) does not have all the information about the lawyer's (agent) representation who has the opportunity to act in his/her own interests rather than in the interest of the client. This problem is aggravated in class actions due to the aggregation of the claimants (free-riding, as exposed in part I), but also due to the difficulties in monitoring the representation of the lawyer. A way to create incentives for the lawyer may be to pay a contingency fee. But, according to Schaefer, "if the lawyer works on the basis of contingent fees, he will not maximize the difference between the expected benefits of the lawsuit and his effort, but the difference between his expected fee and his effort" and the consequence is that "the lawyer will invest an effort lower than the one which is optimal for the client." [24]

Thus the class counsel might be induced to conclude a disadvantageous settlement, below the initially expected trial value.[25] More precisely, Ulen explains that the:

> class counsel may have an incentive to arrange a 'sweetheart settlement,' under which counsel agrees with the defendant to settle the claim for a high attorney's fee and a low class recovery. In the same vein (but distinguishably), class counsel may agree to a high fee for itself and something less than complete compensation for the class members.[26]

Two factors can explain this behaviour: the inability of the claimants to monitor the effort of the lawyer,[27] and the difficulty for the judge to verify that the agreement is not disadvantageous for the claimants.[28]

C. *Suggested Solutions*

Several solutions come to mind, among them the substitution of contingency

---

[24] Ulen (above n 20) 194.

[25] "A widely recognized risk is that the class counsel may in effect 'sell out' or enter into a 'collusive' settlement, thus yielding the class members an amount much smaller than the actual value of their claims" (B Hay, 'The theory of fee regulation in class action settlements' 46 *The American University Law Review* (1997) 1429, 1482).

[26] Ulen (above n 20) 193.

[27] "For instance, the lawyer, who is no more controlled by his client due to class action is more inclined to agree to unfavourable settlements as long as payment of his fees is guaranteed" (Schaefer (above n 10) 184).

[28] "The class members are often unable to protect themselves against this danger; and courts, in policing settlements to safeguard the class members' interests, frequently lack the information necessary to detect instances in which the class members are receiving less than their claims are worth" (*ibid*, 1430–31). Ulen (above n 20) exposes the same idea: "The judge, in his or her capacity to review settlements, should identify and prevent abusive outcomes. But judicial review of class settlements is imperfect".

fees with hourly fees; control exercised by the judge; and finally a stricter surveillance of the lawyer's representation by the plaintiffs.

1. Alternatives to the contingency fee system

Regarding the relationship between lawyers and their clients, contingency fees help lower the cost of the class formation. When lawyers are allowed to advance the litigation expenses of their clients – by subsidizing class actions – against the promise that they will receive a percentage of the class recovery in case of a victory, this facilitates the formation of a group of plaintiffs, as the cost for plaintiffs to go to court is reduced *ex ante*.[29] Although such contingency fees are prohibited in France and prohibited or limited in most European countries, their use explains the success and development of class actions in the US.

Contingency fees induce lawyers to bear the risk of the class action but also to act in the best interest of their clients. A proposed solution is, according to Hay,[30] to limit the percentage of contingency fees to preserve the claimant's interest in case of settlement. But more generally, the authors question the nature of the fee: should they use an hourly fee,[31] a contingency fee,[32] or an alternative solution. Thus, for Klement and Neeman,[33] the hourly rate must be decreased to prevent the lawyers from spending too much time on the case only to increase their payment. However, according to Schaefer,[34] there is no optimal fee system because no matter which system is used (contingent or hourly fee), the lawyer is always induced to conduct meritless lawsuits and to conclude disadvantageous settlements.

The negative effects of contingency fees could be also reduced by the introduction of an association. Thus, Schaefer explains that "the lawyer who lost a suit can recover his fees from the association whereas in class actions he either has to bear the risk of litigation himself so that he needs an additional

---

[29] WB Rubenstein, 'Why Enable Litigation? A Positive Externalities Theory of the Small Claims Class Action' (2006) Public Law and Legal Theory Research Paper Series, UCLA School of Law 6/2010, http://www.ssrn.com/abstract=890303.

[30] B Hay, 'Asymmetric rewards: why class actions (may) settle for too little' 48 *Hastings Law Journal* (1997) 479.

[31] For example, in the United States, the 'lodestar method' according to which the court multiplies the hours declared by the class counsel by a reasonable hourly fee, with a possibility for the judge to take into account the particularities of the case (number of parties involved, complexity of the legal issues).

[32] For example, in the United States, the 'percentage of the recovery' method, under which the judge fixes the share of the recovery to award to the attorney.

[33] A Klement and Z Neeman 'Incentive structures for class action lawyers' 20 *The Journal of Law, Economics, & Organization* (2004) 102.

[34] Schaefer (above n 10) 195 and 204.

payment (a risk premium or a contingent fee) or the lost lawsuits have to be financed by the state."[35]

2. *Control of the attorney by the judge*

All the aforementioned problems justify judicial intervention to control the lawyers' action and compensation. This control is exercised *ex ante* by the judge through the class certification procedure. Control by a judge allows a court to filter meritless cases, however it may be inefficient for several reasons: the lack of information available to the judge and the difficulty of distinguishing between honest and opportunistic behaviour, or a problem of forum shopping.[36] The control is carried out *ex post* when the judge approves or disapproves the fee awarded to the class counsel. However, the judge may not possess all the necessary information. The introduction of an association acting on a level between claimants and lawyers may reduce the negative effects of the principal-agency relationship *ex ante* through the pre-conditions of the association's right of action (requirement of a number of members, an effective representation of the interests of the claimants, etc.) and *ex post* through the control exercised by the association over the lawyer, in particular if the association has its own lawyers.

3. *The exercise of control by the litigants*

Another solution to the principal-agency problem depends on the incentives of some claimants to monitor the lawyer. These incentives could consist of selecting the claimants with highest stakes and giving them the responsibility to choose the class counsel based on the assumption that they are most motivated to monitor him.[37]

The control of lawyers exercised by litigants can also be realized through competition between lawyers. As explained before, the economies of scale and scope reduce the competition between lawyers,[38] but a solution could consist, according to Ulen,[39] of auctioning the position of the class counsel. In this system, the court chooses the lowest bid among the lawyers.

Another traditional mechanism of monitoring is based on reputation. But according to Schaefer,

---

[35] *Ibid*, 205.
[36] G Calabresi and KS Schwartz, 'The Costs of Class Actions: Allocation and Collective Redress in the US Experience' 32 *European Journal of Law and Economics* (2011) 169.
[37] Ulen (above n 20) 193.
[38] J Backhaus 'The Law Firm as an Investment Bank in Class Actions' 32 *European Journal of Law and Economics* (2011) 225.
[39] Ulen (above n 20).

the reputation mechanism which often prevents the misconduct of the lawyers can hardly emerge among lawyers who specialize in class action suits. This is because in class action the lawyer does not depend on the recommendation and repeated briefing by his clients. He is able to create the demand for his services himself.[40]

Moreover, especially because of their apathy, the claimants do not use their exit option.

Finally, we can wonder whether the introduction of an association could be an efficient solution to solve principal-agency issues. This question has been asked by Schaefer, who distinguishes several configurations relative to the control exercised by the group on the association and by the association on the lawyer. The ideal situation appears to be where the members of the association can exercise strong control over the association and where the lawyer is strongly controlled by the association. Such ideal situation occurs where there is a small group of highly interested injured individuals who are represented by an association, which can effectively control its lawyers. Conversely, the worst situation is observed where the members hardly exercise any influence on the association, and where the association itself is under the influence of the lawyer.

IV. CONCLUSION

Solving social dilemma is never easy. Class actions and collective redress aim at solving this dilemma. Legal proceedings help provide the most efficient tools to handle this issue. The main conclusion of law and economics doctrine is that collective redress mechanisms are needed to improve efficiency and to ensure that social cost created by some behaviour will be properly internalized. As such, class actions play an important role in creating incentives on those who impose such costs on others. However, law and economics doctrine also focuses on the practical difficulties of such proceedings. Indeed, implementing an efficient system of class actions depends on many issues identified by recent studies. The main risk is that class actions may be captured by interest groups. These statements mitigate the assessment of the ability of actual proceedings to correctly play the role they were created for.

---

[40] Schaefer (above n 10) 204.

2

Behavioural Sciences Perspectives

A Behavioural Perspective on Collective Redress

*Anne-Lise Sibony**

I. INTRODUCTION

Collective redress is a holy grail in Europe. For more than fifteen years, it has been the subject of policy initiatives, solid political fights and a vast legal literature. More recently, a new trend has emerged, both in the literature and in the practice of rule-making. It is often referred to as 'nudging' in reference to one of the best-known pop science books which brought the gist of behavioural sciences to the wider public.[1] Nudging is a misnomer because nudges are only one of the possible uses of behavioural insights in policy making.[2] The real debate is broader and pertains to whether, when and how to use behavioural insights sensibly in policy making.[3] Be that as it may, the use of behavioural insights in rule-making is gathering increasing interest from governments and international organisations at national, European and international level. So far, the reflection on class actions and that on behavioural law-making have not met. Collective redress has not to date received attention from a law and behavioural sciences perspective. This is quite surprising as behavioural findings represent an important contribution to any debate on

---

* Professor of EU Law, University of Liège.

[1] R Thaler and C Sunstein, *Nudge: Improving Decisions about Health, Wealth, and Happiness* (Yale University Press, 2008). Other helpful introductions include D Ariely, *Predictably Irrational: the Hidden Forces that Shape our Decisions* (Harper Collins, 2008); S Levitt and S Dubner, *Freakonomics: A Rogue Economist Explores the Hidden Side of Everything* (William Morrow, 2005); D Kahneman, *Thinking Fast and Slow* (Farrar, Straus and Giroux, 2011); M Bazerman and A Tenbrunsel, *Blind Spots: Why We Fail to Do What's Right and What to Do about It* (Princeton University Press, 2011); J Lehrer, *How We Decide* (Houghton Mifflin Hartcourt, 2010); S Mullainathan and E Shafir, *Scarcity: Why Having Too Little Means So Much* (Times Books, 2013).

[2] R Baldwin, 'From Regulation to Behaviour Change: Giving Nudge the Third Degree', 77 *Modern Law Review*, 6 (2014) 831–857.

[3] For an elaboration, see AL Sibony and A Alemanno introduction to A Alemanno and AL Sibony (eds), *Nudge and the Law: What Can EU Law Learn from Behavioural Sciences?* (Hart, forthcoming 2015).

opt-in versus opt-out, one of the much-discussed topics about collective redress. This short chapter aims to explain why the European debate on class actions would benefit from more research conducted in a behavioural perspective and outline questions for further study.

It may be useful to start by introducing briefly the growing behavioural trend in scholarship and government practice. I will then outline behavioural findings on the status quo bias, the most relevant behavioural insight for a reflection on collective redress and offer a preliminary analysis of how these insights may impact policy making at national and EU level. Finally, I will conclude by identifying questions calling for empirical research.

II. A VERY SHORT HISTORY OF LAW AND BEHAVIOURAL SCIENCES

Economists were the first to be hit by the behavioural wave. Indeed, the seminal work by Kahneman and Tzversky[4] showed empirically that people were not behaving in the way standard economic theory assumed. Not only were ordinary mortals not *homini oeconomici* (even economists knew that), but they did not seem to be even close cousins. From there, a new branch of economics emerged: Behavioural Economics.[5] On the law side, Law and Economics, a dominant paradigm in American scholarship, was hit next. Since economic analysis of law relied on the premises of standard price theory, its premises too needed to be revised in light of behavioural findings. Economic analysis of Law became behavioural, giving rise to a new field – Behavioural Analysis of Law –[6] recently described as 'one of the two most important innovations that is going on in legal scholarship today'.[7] In Europe, behavioural legal scholarship is only emerging.[8] One reason why European legal scholars got less excited about behavioural studies than their American counterparts is because European lawyers had been less excited

---

[4] D Kahneman and A Tversky, 'Prospect Theory: An Analysis of Decision under Risk' 47 *Econometrica*, (1979), 263–292. In *Thinking Fast and Slow* (above n 1), Kahnemann offers an account of this research for the lay reader.

[5] F Heukelom, *Behavioral Economics: A History* (Cambridge University Press, 2014).

[6] This labelling is ironic because it suggests that behavioural insights are brought to the law via economics when in facts these insights come from psychology and economists resisted them for several decades. D Kahneman, foreword to Mullainathan and Shafir (above n 1) at IX. This is why I prefer to refer to "Law and Behavioural Sciences".

[7] T Ulen, 'European and American Perspectives on Behavioral Law and Economics' in K Mathis (ed.), *European Perspectives on Behavioural Law and Economics, Economic Analysis of Law in European Legal Scholarship*, vol. 2 (Springer, 2015), 3–16 at 4. The other most important innovative field, according to Ulen, is empirical analysis of law, a field closely related to behavioural analysis of law.

[8] *Ibid*; Sibony and Alemanno (above n 3).

about economic analysis of law in the first place.[9] The critique of something which was never very important to them (law and economics), strong as it was, could not cause much arousal.

Academic neglect is not always a good predictor of practical significance. Irrespective of what place economic analysis of law occupies in the landscape of legal scholarship, behavioural studies are relevant for law-making, also in Europe. Law generally seeks to regulate behaviour and its effectiveness depends on how people behave in response to rules. Therefore, it is reasonable for regulators and law-makers to inform themselves of behavioural insights that could be relevant to the rules they are contemplating. This realisation took place first in the US,[10] then in the UK[11] and, to a lesser extent, in several other Member States.[12] Behavioural insights also garner attention at EU level with the recent creation of a Foresight and Behavioural Insights Unit.[13] On an

---

[9] K Purnhagen, 'Never the Twain Shall Meet?' in K Mathis (ed.) *Law and Economics in Europe – Foundations and Applications* (Springer, 2014), 3–21. Other reasons are outlined in Ulen (above n 7). They include the less competitive functioning of legal academia in Europe, which accounts for the fact that scholarly innovations are less valued.

[10] Cass Sunstein, one of the authors of *Nudge*, served as a chairman of Office of Information and Regulatory Affairs (OIRA) during the first term of the Obama administration. Behavioural analysis informed in particular the way cost benefit analysis is conducted. See: Executive Order 13563 of January 18, 2011, Improving Regulation and Regulatory Review, Federal Register, Vol. 76, No. 14, 3821. Sunstein shares his government experience in *Simpler: The Future of Government* (Simon & Schuster, 2013).

[11] A Behavioural Insights Team, better known as the 'Nudge Unit' was created in 2010 within the Cabinet Office. In February 2014, it was partly privatised. The Unit still provides services to the UK government but also to private sector entities and foreign governments. http://www.behaviouralinsights.co.uk/.

[12] In Denmark, a bottom-up organisation, called iNudgeU, animated by academics, civic advocates and behavioural professionals, has been increasingly involved in advising government and local authority and has created a Danish Nudge Network (http://inudgeyou.com/). In Germany, the government announced it was hiring psychologists, behavioural economists as well as anthropologists to test new methods of 'efficient government': P Plickert and H Beck, 'Kanzlerin Angela Merkel sucht Verhaltensforscher', *FAZ*, 26.08.2014, http://www.faz.net/aktuell/wirtschaft/wirtschaftspolitik/kanzlerin-angela-merkel-sucht-verhaltensforscher-13118345.html. In France, the government is showing signs of interest as part of the effort to modernise public administration: http://www.modernisation.gouv.fr/les-services-publics-se-simplifient-et-innovent/par-des-services-numeriques-aux-usagers/le-nudge-au-service-de-laction-publique. In the Netherlands, the scientific advisory council (WRR) published a report on 'Policymaking with knowledge of behaviour', available (in Dutch) at: http://www.wrr.nl/publicaties/publicatie/article/met-kennis-van-gedrag-beleid-maken/. The Commission commissioned a survey on use of behavioural insights in policy making at national level. It is underway at the time of writing.

[13] In 2014, the Commission set up a 'Foresight and Behavioural Insights Unit', which is located within the EU Commission Joint Research Centre. The unit's *raison d'être* is to centralize the efforts currently undertaken by some Directorates General of the EU Commission, such as DG Consumer Protection and Health (SANCO), to integrate behavioural insights into EU policymaking.

international level, OECD[14] and the World Bank are raising awareness among governments of developed and less developed countries about how small changes in rules can achieve large changes in behaviour at a minimal cost.[15] While behavioural insights are relevant to law-making in general, more attention has been given to their teachings in some fields of law than in others.[16] In EU Law, consumer law has received the most attention from behavioural scholars,[17] but the focus has been on substantive rules rather

---

[14] P Lunn, *Regulatory Policy and Behavioural Economics* (OECD, 2014); Workshop 'Behavioural Insights and New Approaches to Policy Design', Paris 23 January 2014, http://www.oecd.org/naec/NAEC_Behavioural-Insights-Programme_23-Jan.pdf. OECD is in particular investigating the potential of behavioural policy design Tax and Environmental policy and Antitrust.

[15] World Bank Group, *World Development Report 2015: Mind, Society, and Behavior* (Washington, DC, World Bank, 2015) available at https://openknowledge.worldbank.org/handle/10986/20597.

[16] A Tor, 'The Next Generation of Behavioural Law and Economics' in Mathis (above n 7) 17.

[17] F Rischkowsky and T Döring, 'Consumer Policy in a Market Economy: Considerations from the Perspective of the Economics of Information, the New Institutional Economics as well as Behavioural Economics' 31 *Journal of Consumer Policy* (2008) 285; E Avgoulea, 'The Global Financial Crisis and the Disclosure Paradigm in European Financial Regulation: The Case for Reform' 6 *European Company and Financial Law Review* (2009) 440; G Low, 'The (Ir)Relevance of Harmonization and Legal Diversity to European Contract Law: A Perspective from Psychology' 2 *European Review of Private Law* (2010) 285; M Faure and H Luth, 'Behavioural Economics in Unfair Contract Terms: Cautions and Considerations' 34 *Journal of Consumer Policy* (2011) 337; V Mak and J Braspenning, 'Errare humanum est: Financial Literacy in European Consumer Credit Law' 35 *Journal of Consumer Policy* (2012) 307; HW Micklitz, LA Reisch and K Hagen, 'An Introduction to the Special Issue on "Behavioural Economics, Consumer Policy, and Consumer Law"' 34 *Journal of Consumer Policy* (2011) 271; G Spindler, 'Behavioural Finance and Investor Protection Regulations' 34 *Journal of Consumer Policy* (2011) 315; J Trzaskowski, 'Behavioural Economics, Neuroscience, and the Unfair Commercial Practises Directive' 34 *Journal of Consumer Policy* (2011) 377; WH van Boom, 'Price Intransparency, Consumer Decision Making and European Consumer Law' 34 *Journal of Consumer Policy* (2011) 359; O Bar-Gill and N Helberger, *Forms Matter: Informing consumers effectively*, study commissioned by BEUC (European Consumer organisation), 2013; J Malbon, 'Consumer Strategies for Avoiding Negative Online Purchasing Experiences: A Qualitative Study' 20 *Competition & Consumer Law Journal* (2013) 249; A Tor, 'Some Challenges Facing a Behaviorally-Informed Approach to the Directive on Unfair Commercial Practices', in T Tóth (ed.), *Unfair Commercial Practices: The Long Road to Harmonized Law Enforcement*, (Pázmány Press, 2013) 9-18; O Bar-Gill and O Ben-Shahar, 'Regulatory Techniques in Consumer Protection: A Critique of European Consumer Contract Law' 50 *CMLRev* (2013) 109-126; JA Luzak, 'To Withdraw or Not to Withdraw? Evaluation of the Mandatory Right of Withdrawal in Consumer Distance Selling Contracts Taking Into Account Its Behavioural Effects on Consumers' 37 *Journal of Consumer Policy* (2014) 91; K Purnhagen and E Van Herpen, 'Can Bonus Packs Mislead Consumers? An Empirical Assessment of the ECJ's Mars Judgment and its Potential Impact on EU Marketing Regulation', Wageningen Working Papers Series in Law and Governance 2014/07, http://papers.ssrn.com/sol3/papers.cfm?abstract_id=2503342; A Pape, 'Miscounselling in the German Insurance Market: Utility-Orientated Implications for the

than on procedural issues. More generally, the rules on collective redress have not been confronted with the teachings of behavioural sciences. In this chapter, I do not purport to fill this gap, only to underscore that collective redress deserves attention from a behavioural law perspective.

III. BEHAVIOURAL INSIGHTS AND COLLECTIVE REDRESS: OF THE STATUS QUO BIAS

Among the noteworthy findings of experimental psychology regarding 'deviations' from perfect rationality, one is the inertia bias, also known as status quo bias.[18] Both names refer to our tendency to not call into question the current state of affairs even when we do not have a positive preference for it. This can manifest itself in a variety of situations, for example, as a tendency to keep a pre-ticked box ticked or in the form of procrastination when it comes to changing a mobile phone plan even if it would be beneficial. Kahneman and Tzversky first evidenced the status quo bias.[19] They showed experimentally that subjects have a strong tendency to take the current baseline (or status quo) as a reference point for making decisions – even if it is random and artificially created for the purpose of an experiment. In addition, any change from that baseline tends to be perceived as a loss. This is important because of loss aversion, a separate but related bias. Loss aversion refers to people's tendency to strongly prefer avoiding losses over acquiring gains. It implies, for example, that loosing €100 will cause an amount of unhappiness greater than the amount of happiness generated by a €100 windfall gain. This asymmetric perception of gains and losses is well known from marketers who know it is much better to frame an option as a price reduction (if you return the empty bottle, you get a refund) rather than as a price surcharge (you have to pay for the bottle separately from its content). The two options are equivalent for the seller but buyers interpret a price reduction from a high baseline as a gain while the equivalent price increase from a low baseline is interpreted as a loss. This makes the first option much more appealing.

Meaning of Miscounselling' 37 *Journal of Consumer Policy* (2014) 561; AL Sibony 'Can EU Consumer Law Benefit from Behavioural Insights? An Analysis of the Unfair Practices Directive' *European review of Private Law*, 6, (2014), 901–942; G Hellerinher 'Retail Investors and Disclosures Requirements' in Mathis (above n 7) 193–210.

[18] W Samuelson and R Zeckhauser, 'Status quo bias in decision making', 1 *Journal of Risk and Uncertainty* (1988) 7–59; D Kahneman, J Knetsch and R Thaler, 'Anomalies: The Endowment Effect, Loss Aversion, and Status Quo Bias', 5 *Journal of Economic Perspectives* 1 (1991), 193–206.

[19] Above n 1.

The general lesson about status quo is simple: defaults matter.[20] They matter for retirement plans, which are far more subscribed when subscription is the default than when people have to opt-in.[21] They matter for organ donation, where presuming consent leads to a manifold increase of the proportion of donors in the population.[22] They matter for collective redress too. Though data specific to collective redress is not available, empirical evidence of the status quo bias in various other contexts and cultures is robust enough to suggest that the choice of default is absolutely essential in the design of class actions. If the default is that anyone qualifying to be part of the class for a given action automatically joins (opt-out), there will be far greater enrolment than if the default is that any person concerned by the action has to express her will to enrol (opt-in). From a behavioural standpoint, a legislator who is serious about class actions should make them opt-out.

IV. COLLECTIVE REDRESS IN EUROPE AND THE STATUS QUO BIAS

At present, there are no EU rules on collective redress, only a Recommendation.[23] The informal nature of EU action on class actions can be explained by several factors, including powerful lobbying. From a strictly legal standpoint, the explanation is to do with the absence of a clear competence of the Union. Such a competence could be inferred in the field of competition law where, following the Court judgments in *Courage v Crehan*[24] and *Manfredi*,[25] there is a duty to ensure that those who have suffered a loss as a consequence of anti-competitive behaviour are fully and

---

[20] Sunstein (above n 10), chapter 5.

[21] B Madrian and D Shea, 'The Power Of Suggestion: Inertia In 401(k) Participation And Savings Behavior', *Quarterly Journal of Economics* (2001) 1149–1187 and other references cited by Sunstein (above n 10) 55.

[22] For a survey of empirical studies, see M Palmer, *Opt-out systems of organ donation: International evidence review*, Welsh Government Social Research paper n° 44/2012, http://wales.gov.uk/docs/caecd/research/121203optoutorgandonation.pdf; for a policy discussion, see *The potential impact of an opt out system for organ donation in the UK: An independent report from the Organ Donation Taskforce* (2008), http://www.nhsbt.nhs.uk/to2020/resources/ThepotentialimpactofanoptoutsystemfororgandonationintheUK.pdf; for a critical discussion, see M Quigley and E Stokes, 'Nudging and Evidence-based Policy in Europe: Problems of Normative Legitimacy and Effectiveness,' in Sibony and Alemanno (above n 3).

[23] Commission Recommendation of 11 June 2013 on common principles for injunctive and compensatory collective redress mechanisms in the Member States concerning violations of rights granted under Union Law, OJ L 201 of 26.07.2013, 60–65.

[24] Case C-453/99, *Courage v Crehan*, EU:C:2001:465.

[25] Joined cases C-295/04 to C-298/04, *Manfredi a.o.*, EU:C:2006:461.

adequately compensated.[26] Arguably, effective compensation entails, at least in certain cases, collective redress. However, the EU chose to leave the matter to Member States and abstained from including any provision on collective redress in the recent Directive on actions for damages for infringements of the competition law.[27]

In other areas of EU law, such as consumer protection or environmental law, it is even more difficult than in antitrust to assert EU competence to legislate on collective redress. It is not possible to reason by analogy with antitrust as EU legislation manly consists of directives, which, unlike Article 101 and 102 TFEU, do not have horizontal direct effect and can therefore not be invoked by consumers (however many of them) against companies.[28] In such contexts, collective redress may be necessary for effective enforcement of individual rights granted under UE law, but the competence to adopt measures regarding class action clearly stays with Member States. Where the EU is undoubtedly competent is to adopt measures facilitating mutual recognition of judicial and extrajudicial acts in relation to cross border class actions (in any domain) under Article 81 TFEU.

It is therefore Member States who are in a position to rely on behavioural insights in designing rules on collective redress. By recommending opt-in, the Commission is not helping. From a behavioural perspective, this recommendation is unsound. Both the political choice to recommend opt-in and the principles articulated about the possibility of opt-out beg questions.

As explained above, the message from behavioural sciences is very straightforward: if you want people to do something, make it simple. Therefore, if any government wants to make collective redress available, they should make it simple to use. Opt-out seems to be the easiest way to make things simple and could make a very large difference in the actual use of collective actions, though other factors also affect recourse to the judiciary. It should be stressed that adopting an opt-out principle does not preclude incorporating all sorts of safeguards to avoid the much-dreaded excesses of US-style class actions, notably by prohibiting multiple damages and regulating contingency fees. Instead, the preferred option of the Commission seems to be for Member States to adopt both all sorts of safeguards to avoid abusive collective litigation *and* opt-in.[29]

---

[26] See among many expressions of the official position, J Almunia (then Commissionner for Competition policy), 'Common standards for group claims across the EU', SPEECH/10/554, http://europa.eu/rapid/press-release_SPEECH-10-554_en.htm; Commission, Green Paper – Damages actions for breach of the EC antitrust rules, COM(2005) 672 final at 4; Recital 4 of directive 2014/104/EU cited at fn. 27.

[27] Directive 2014/104/EU on certain rules governing actions for damages under national law for infringements of the competition law provisions of the Member States and of the European Union (OJ L 349 of 5.12.2014, p. 1–19) does not address this aspect, see its Recital (13).

[28] Case 152/84, *Marshall*, EU:C:1986:84.

[29] Above n 23, para 21.

By favouring opt-in, the Commission seems to ignore evidence about the power of the status quo bias. This is surprising as the Commission itself, in another context, showed that it was precisely very aware of the importance of inertia. Indeed, such insights provided the rationale for the prohibition of inertia selling. The Consumer Rights Directive adopted in 2011 prohibits the use of pre-ticked boxes on e-commerce websites.[30] It is no longer possible for a website selling air tickets to tick by default the box "yes, I want an insurance". In other words, a common way for private companies to leverage the status quo bias to their advantage and to the disadvantage of consumers has been outlawed. Apparently, it is not as important in the Commission's view to protect consumers from a procedural rule that certainly works to their detriment though the same mechanism (inertia) is at stake. National legislators are discouraged to provide for inertia enrolment in a class as though this were comparable to inertia selling. In my view, a legislator who realises the power of inertia should use it consistently to foster its policy objectives. Assuming that the policy objective for class actions really is to provide effective remedies in situations where individuals do not have incentives to go to court (rather than keeping appearances of a pro-consumer policy and protecting the interest of businesses), the consistent position for the Commission would be to admit that inertia can work to the detriment of consumers when it is exploited by businesses (which the consumer rights directive does) but also where procedural rules governing class actions follow the opt-in principle. In the first case, the proper role of the law is to regulate businesses when they design choice architecture. In the second case, it is to nudge consumers to make the choices most favourable to them and to effective enforcement of the law. Opt-in should be mandated in the first case (consumers have to actively choose the extra insurance) and banned in the second case (in their own interest and in the interest of justice, litigants should not have to make an active choice).

The way in which the Commission articulates the opt-in principle and the principle of sound administration of justice is very striking. According to paragraph 21 of the Recommendation on collective redress, "any exception to [the opt-in] principle, by law or by court order, should be duly justified by reasons of sound administration of justice". It seems curious that opt-out, which should be the recommended default, needs to be justified on a case-by-case basis. The opposite should be the case both from a behavioural point of view and as a matter of EU law. The right to an effective remedy, protected under Article 47 of the Charter of fundamental rights, must be considered a component of 'sound administration of justice', and in relation to effective-

---

[30] Article 22 of Directive 2011/83/UE on Consumer Rights, OJ 2011, L 304/64. The prohibition, which had to be enacted by Member States before 31 December 2013 is effective since 13 June 2014.

ness of remedies, the more reasonable presumption is that the effectiveness principle commands opt-out rather than opt-in. Nevertheless, it cannot be ruled out that, even in the face of policy-relevant evidence about the magnitude of the inertia bias (see below section V), there will be no political agreement to recommend opt-out. This is why it is important to look beyond the most immediate legal translation of behavioural insight, as a reversal of the principle articulated in the Recommendation.

With the Recommendation as it stands, there are two ways for Member States to rely on behavioural insights in designing collective redress mechanisms and explaining their design choices to the Commission. First, they can seek to justify opt-out on grounds of sound administration of justice by showing that it is the only way to obtain compensation for large-scale damages made up of significant, but low-value, claims. While this seems common sense, the Commission requires Member States to adduce evidence, though there is no formal standard of proof regarding such evidence. It will not be easy for Member States to gather relevant data because that would require gaining insights in how many actions were *not* brought before court because of inadequate collective redress mechanisms. Short of statistics, case studies might suffice.

Alternatively, Member States can choose to follow the Recommendation and adopt an opt-in principle. In this case, there is a second best way to legislate in a behaviourally sound manner. It consists in making opt-in *really simple*,[31] for example by allowing one-click opt-in and making it practically possible for consumer associations and for anyone interested to publicise actions in ways that will produce a good click-through rate, in particular through social media. If consumers can learn about a class action of concern to them via Facebook, follow a link and click to opt-in, there may be a future for opt-in class actions, albeit a biased one in favour of the connected fraction of the population.

Besides the issue of how a class is formed, there is another element in the design of a collective redress mechanism where the status quo bias could be relevant. This element relates to another vexing issue with class actions, namely financing. The idea would be to nudge successful claimants to donate part of the money they have been awarded in the trial or settlement. At first glance, this may seem a strange idea. In many class actions, especially consumer class actions, the sums awarded to each member of the class will be quite small. Would people want to share the small amount of money that is owed to them as a compensation for a wrong they have suffered? My hunch is that they might. The collective dimension of the class action may affect individual perception of what is at stake. Perhaps litigants feel they are part of something bigger, bigger even than the class of which they are a member,

---

[31] On the art of making things simpler, see Sunstein (above n 10).

a mechanism that produces distributive justice. If it is the case, it might be possible to leverage this engagement to make class actions financially sustainable by creating a fund, preferably at EU level, that would receive donations from successful litigants. Here, behavioural insights on the status quo bias could inspire procedural rules. The law could either mandate or let courts decide that members of a class are presented with the choice between two options when informed of the successful outcome of the trial: they could either take the whole sum or donate a fraction of the money to a fund which would finance future collective actions.

To sum up: the status quo bias could be taken into account in relation with two distinct elements of collective action design: class constitution and financing through voluntary contributions. For each of these elements, the suggestions that can be made from a behavioural perspective are clear, but they are only suggestions. Before rule-makers can adopt or reject them, more evidence is needed.

V. NEED FOR EMPIRICAL EVIDENCE

To test the foregoing arguments, four empirical research questions deserve attention. They are offered as starting points for empirical research on collective redress and are by no means exhaustive.

A. How Strong is Inertia in the Context of Class Actions?

Behavioural studies show that the status quo bias exists, that it is strong and robust. This provides a powerful effectiveness argument in favour of opt-out. Yet, resistance to opt-out is great. Therefore, it would be extremely useful to conduct studies to test the existence and magnitude of the inertia bias in the context of collective actions. It would be very difficult to do in real context, because it would be impossible to control the all factors in a real environment that affect decisions to join a collective action. The problem would lend itself to laboratory testing. The experimental design would have to involve lawyers next to psychologists in order to simplify reality (for the purpose of the experiment) in a way that is acceptable, ie in a way that will let the simplified model be informative for the policy debate, notably in the framework of the revision of the Commission Recommendation scheduled for 2017.

B. How Much Does Opt-in/Opt-out Matter?

In real context, opt-in and opt-out matter but many other variables matter as well. It would be extremely interesting to model and test the effect of default in relation to that of other variables, which can impact the choice to join a collective action (such as, for example, the perception of the efficiency of the judiciary, of fairness of trial, of chances of success).

C. How Should One-click Opt-in be Designed?

The design of one-click opt-in should be tested. The difficulty will be in designing a system that allows for sufficiently simple opt-in while being compatible with other procedural principles. In particular experiments could shed light on when it is best, from an effectiveness perspective, to introduce the indispensable checks (eg, to make sure that each click represents one person). For example, results with ID verification before or after the "I join the class" click may lead to very different results.

D. Can Contributory Financing of Class Actions Work?

To test the validity of the proposal outlined above, several elements would deserve empirical scrutiny. First, the motivation of litigants would need to be assessed. Do people want justice more than they want €30 (a realistic sum in the case of a follow-on suit to obtain compensation for a cartel overcharge on consumer goods or services)? Does the willingness to share gains (if indeed there is such a willingness) depend on amounts?

If there is evidence of some willingness to share, the design of the above proposal should be tested. The basic design would be that members of a class which was awarded compensation are presented with the choice between two options: (a) take their money (often a small sum) or (b) donate a fraction of the money they obtained to a fund which would finance future collective actions.

The generous option (b) should be the default, with a possibility to opt-out and choose the selfish option (a). What would need to be tested is what fraction generates the most contribution. Should successful claimants be nudged to donate 5%, 10%, 15%, more? Should they be given a choice on how much they want to contribute to the fund? How should that choice be framed?

It is my hope that these questions will meet with the research interests of empirically minded lawyers working together with experimental psychologists and/ or behavioural economists. Experimental work on collective actions is much needed to move in the direction of more evidence-based policy making on collective redress at national and at EU level.

3

Lawyers' Perspectives

To 'Opt-in' or to 'Opt-out' – That is the Question

Adam Johnson*

This paper gives the personal point of view of an English litigation lawyer on the current state of English law as it concerns the aggregation of related claims. It looks in particular at the issue of whether the current 'opt-in' model should be replaced by an 'opt-out' model.

Leaving litigation (and other) lawyers aside, most members of the public would say that the legal system exists to provide redress to those who have sustained a wrong. The conventional structure is that the victim (now called the claimant in civil cases) initiates a suit against the alleged perpetrator (the defendant), and if the claim is successful redress is usually in the form of an order requiring the payment of money (damages) to the victim.

This conventional structure has a number of obvious characteristics. We might call them benefits. It requires direct engagement between the claimant and the defendant. The defendant knows who is making a claim against him. The precise manner in which the claimant says his rights have been infringed by the defendant must be spelled out. The defendant must respond, and (if that is his position) explain precisely why he says he should be absolved of responsibility vis-à-vis the claimant. If the claimant is awarded damages, in order to compensate him for what he has lost, he must say what he has lost and be able to quantify it. The defendant will be required to pay a sum representing the amount of the claimant's loss, plus the claimant's costs of bringing the action, but no more.

This seems sensible and fair. The party with the most direct interest in the outcome (ie, the claimant) controls the process. The defendant is required to pay, but only to the extent the claimant can show he has actually suffered a loss. From a purely structural stand point, there seems little to take issue with.

Yet this traditional claim structure has some significant limitations. Two points bear emphasis in the present context. First, it can come under considerable stress in the case where there is not only one claimant, but instead multiple claimants – perhaps many hundreds or even thousands of them, each

---

* Partner, Herbert Smith Freehills LLP. The views expressed are the personal views of the author.

of them advancing positions which are potentially different (most usually as regards the calculation of loss). The second point is about costs. Litigation is expensive. If, for an individual claimant, the amount at stake is relatively limited, it may simply not be cost effective to bring the claim at all. So how should a civilised legal system deal with mass claims, including those where the amounts at stake for individual claimants are limited? What structures should apply, and to what extent should the established orthodoxy be modified and perhaps compromised?

It is perhaps best to start with what we should want to avoid. It may be too simplistic to say that what we should want to avoid are the excesses of the US class action system. The US system in fact has much to commend it, and is often maligned by English lawyers who overlook the fact that it springs from a rather different cultural and philosophical tradition. Nonetheless, even an objective observer must express some concerns.

At the heart of it is the concern that the US 'opt-out' system is one in which claims can be advanced on behalf of parties who may be entirely apathetic about the outcome, and who may not even care whether a claim is being advanced or not. This leads to an odd dynamic, in which class action litigation is driven by the lawyers – the 'plaintiffs' bar' – since they are the ones who have most direct (and significant) economic interest in the outcome.

In principle, there is something objectionable about a claim being pursued by lawyers on behalf of absent parties who have evinced no positive interest in pursuing it. The problem may be particularly acute in the US system, given the pressures which arise from such features as the US rules on discovery (including oral depositions), jury trials and awards of penal damages. But even leaving those special features aside, important practical (as well as philosophical) problems are likely to arise with an 'opt-out' system, such as what to do if a compensation fund is established which is not exhausted because too few actual claimants eventually materialise to use it up. Should the excess be returned to the defendant, or should it be sequestrated as a quasi-penalty, and allocated to some relevant charitable cause? Again, in principle, it seems unattractive for a defendant to be required to pay compensation calculated by reference to an overall class, but where some of the class members are indifferent to the outcome and in the event make no claim for compensation at all.

This is the nub of the 'opt-in' or 'opt-out' debate. One must ask the question: what is wrong with the idea that litigation should be pursued only on behalf of parties who have actually evinced an intention to support it by opting in? Such a structure necessarily excludes potential claimants who fail to opt-in, but is that in principle unfair?

That rather depends on the reasons why potential claimants might not opt-in. One might be that they are unaware of the on-going litigation, and therefore do not know that making a claim is even an alternative open to them. That is a real concern, but the answer surely is to require those managing the litigation to advertise appropriately. In the modern world, with the possibility of extensive and immediate communication not only by traditional methods but also by the internet and via social media, the risk of affected parties not being notified is presumably one which can effectively be managed. If the potential defendant is in possession of information which will enable potential claimants to be identified, there is no reason why he should not be ordered to produce it.

Logically, one must try to flush out potential claimants either before liability is established against the defendant, or afterwards – when it is necessary to divide up the available compensation package among those who have an interest in receiving it. There will be imperfections in any communication process, but it seems better to conduct the exercise before the litigation is very far advanced, rather than after it has effectively been concluded, if it is to be conducted at all.

Cost is no doubt another major factor influencing the decision whether to opt-in or not, but one of the features of the English litigation landscape over the last 10 years or so has been the growth of the litigation funding market, and there is good reason to think that that will only continue. Meritorious claims should be of interest to funders. There are no doubt problems of scale, and perhaps something of a chicken-and-egg situation: funders are only likely to want to fund if the scale of the litigation warrants the investment, and that will not be so unless a sufficient number opt-in. But the answer again should be to give them the opportunity of doing so, and to see what they say, rather than to assume that they all want to be claimants whether they have said so or not.

None of this is to undermine the importance of having a reliable and robust mechanism for the aggregation of claims. One can see the obvious need for such a feature in any developed system of law. Modern experience with issues such as the bank-charges litigation makes that clear. The 2008 financial crisis has spawned other mass claims across a range of areas, including the large-scale litigation currently being pursued on behalf of many thousands of investors in the RBS Rights Issue of April 2008. And those examples are drawn only from the area of financial services. There are many others.

It is a matter of regret and perhaps surprise that English procedural law did not have a serviceable system for the aggregation of claims until 2000, with the introduction by Lord Woolf as part of his reforms of the Group Litigation Order or "GLO". But now that English law has the 'opt-in' GLO, one is entitled to ask what is wrong with it, and why in philosophical and practical terms a move to an 'opt-out' structure is justified. The 'opt-in' structure provides a procedural vehicle enabling those who are sufficiently motivated to make a complaint to bring their claims together under a group structure, provided the claims are sufficiently closely connected. That seems a proportionate response and does not appear unfair. An 'opt-out' structure, however, enables an action to be advanced on behalf of class members who may not even know or care that claims are being pursued on their behalf. That is a strange result, and one which it is suggested is difficult to justify, either in policy or case management terms.

The GLO mechanism is still relatively new, as a case management device. A practice is developing as to how large scale claims should be controlled by the Court. Control will usually involve directions being given for the advertisement of the GLO, with a view to encouraging all interested parties to identify themselves so their claims can be added to the group register. In the RBS Rights Issue litigation mentioned above, case management by the Court has been under the supervision of a designated Judge, sitting together with the Chief Master of the Chancery Division. Although the position of many of the claimants is different (the overall group comprises not only institutional but also retail investors), common issues have been identified and are being case managed together.

It is an important feature of the GLO framework in Civil Procedure Rules Part 19 that although it provides an overall structure for the management of claims, it is relatively skeletal. Much is left to the management discretion of the Judge dealing with the individual case. That is eminently sensible. There can be no one size fits all answer in the context of large scale litigation. The flexibility of the GLO mechanism enables bespoke case management responses to be devised, designed to fit the complexities of any particular situation. Such responses might include the resolution of a preliminary issue or issues of law; the identification of test cases; or perhaps the segregation of claimants into different groups. As experience with the GLO structure develops, practice will no doubt become more established, but one hopes the inherent flexibility of the system will remain.

It is also significant that the GLO is a generic structure – that is to say, it applies in principle across the board, in any type of case. This is in contrast to certain of the proposals for development of an 'opt-out' class action model in England and Wales, which contemplate the introduction of a number of different structures on a sector-specific basis (such as the current Consumer Rights Bill, which proposes an 'opt-out' structure but only in relation to competition law claims; and such as the ill-fated provisions in the Financial Services Bill 2010, which were intended to introduce an 'opt-out' scheme for "financial services claims", but which in the event were withdrawn before the Bill came into effect). It is suggested that a sector-based approach is inherently less attractive than a generic system. Immediately problems of definition and delineation are likely to arise. One can see claimants (or perhaps their lawyers) seeking to take advantage of any subtle differences between arguably available sector-specific structures, and the potential for extensive litigation about whether a particular type of claim falls within a particular structure or not. This may be good for the lawyers, but it is not good for clients as the ultimate consumers of legal services and is best avoided.

The over-arching point is that the GLO system is still being tested and is still bedding-in. One feels that its potential is yet to be fully realised. Given other changes which are occurring in the English litigation arena, in particular in the area of costs and funding, there is a strong argument for allowing what is still a relatively new case management mechanism to evolve, before supplanting it with a new, and very different, mechanism designed to address the same objectives.

Ultimately when looking at the 'opt-in'/'opt-out' issue, one is addressing a question of policy. Does English procedural law, at this stage in its development, have the need for an 'opt-out' structure? For the reasons given above, the view of the present author is that such a need has not been sufficiently established. In any event, at present the Court system has other priorities. The effective removal of legal aid in civil cases which has occurred in recent years has given rise to a number of very pressing practical problems. Many individuals and small businesses who have sustained losses and who would wish to take action to vindicate their rights find themselves unable to do so or, perhaps even worse, find themselves caught trying to navigate the intricacies of our legal system without the benefit of representation. This has given rise to the phenomenon of the litigant in person, or 'self-represented litigant'. It is suggested that attention is better focused on allocating resources to the needs of such individuals and companies, who have engaged with the legal process (or who have been forced to engage with it), rather than accommodating the interests of absent litigants under an 'opt-out' system, who may not even be aware that they are parties to a case or who in any case may simply not want to be involved.

There is a temptation to think that every wrong requires redress, but that is not necessarily so. Sometimes, for some people, other priorities intervene. Sometimes, some people would rather put their grievances and irritations behind them and move on. That is a matter of personal choice. If people do put their hands up and complain, then by all means give them the procedural mechanism which will enable them to advance a claim efficiently. But if they do not, then it is difficult to see why the law should intervene in order to allow others to do it for them.

A Lawyer's Perspective

*Mira Raja and Paul Lomas**

I. INTRODUCTION

Collective redress mechanisms are steadily, if slowly, spreading across Europe. Even where reforms have not yet resulted in legislative changes, this topic stirs debate at national level across Member States. Claimants, and claimant lawyers, are seeking to exploit the opportunities that the procedures currently offer.

Recent national legislative developments include the adoption of laws in a number of jurisdictions (such as Belgium and France) and well advanced draft legislation in the UK that may be adopted in 2015. At a Community level, on 11 June 2013, the European Commission published a series of common non-binding principles in relation to collective redress mechanisms in the form of a Recommendation and is proposing further sector-specific legislation (in the anti-trust area).[1] But what are we really trying to achieve with collective redress in Europe? Why, and how, should Europe's legal systems provide for mechanisms to enable individuals/small numbers of parties to obtain compensation?

There is widespread political acceptance in Europe that there is a need to shift the balance, to a degree, in favour of claimants (particularly mass claimants) largely to improve 'access to justice'. This typically addresses the situation where many have suffered losses that, at an individual level, might not justify litigation but collectively amount to material compensation by the defendant company to a sizeable section of society. More and more countries are considering that, without some form of collective redress, harm (financial or physical) is going uncompensated. Where these mechanisms are well established, eg the USA and Australia, they tend to be widely used. The data shows that there is a materially higher degree of compensation for loss by claimants, whether by litigation or settlement. This evidence seems to demonstrate both a need and a mechanism.

---

* Freshfields Bruckhaus Deringer.
[1] European Commission Recommendation of 11 June 2013 on common principles for injunctive and compensatory collective redress mechanisms in the Member States concerning violations of rights granted under Union Law (2013/396/EU). For further information, see http://www.collectiveredress.org/collective-redress/eu-cross-border.

However, the 'full-on' generic class action mechanism, seen particularly in the USA, supported by legal system drivers that make it such a potent threat to defendants, does not exist in Europe. Indeed, there is a very high degree of sensitivity in Europe as to the adverse effects in Europe of adopting a system that has too many of the adverse features of the US litigation market. The US system is often criticised for acting for the benefit of the plaintiff bar law firms rather than claimants and as encouraging claims without, or with little, merit – so-called blackmail suits – pressurising defendants to settle to avoid unpredictable litigation before a jury.

As things currently stand, therefore, there are significant differences in the evolving collective redress regimes across Member States in Europe as compared with the US system. Whilst countries have adopted, or are adopting, different elements, all are wary of the full US cocktail of generic class action procedures, penal or triple or jury-awarded (rather than compensation-based) damages claims, jury trials on liability, very high levels of results-based compensation for plaintiff bar law firms including contingency fees and limited 'loser pays' costs arrangements.

Critically, the US approach uses 'opt-out' processes. These enable the claimant's lawyers to define the class of claimants and to act on behalf of all of them. Members of the class may not be aware of the litigation but, under court control, they are nevertheless parties to it and bound by the result. To avoid this result, class members need pro-actively to 'opt-out' of the class, which is a rare occurrence. This gives the claimant law firms immense commercial leverage. European jurisdictions have traditionally been very cautious about litigation that is conducted by lawyers rather than clients and there are real difficulties in many countries with the recognition or enforceability of a judgment (eg the waivers and releases against further claims) in respect of a case that the claimant did not even know he or she was fighting.

The range of options seen in Europe include such measures as:

1. broad 'opt-out' class actions such as in Portugal[2] but with a very different litigation climate and incentives;
2. the new regime in Belgium,[3] which provides for an optional opt-in/opt-out mechanism, again in a very different litigation climate;
3. the recent legislation in France[4] which is only available to consumers,

---

[2] Created by virtue of the Law 83/1995, of 31 August 1995. For further information, see http://www.collectiveredress.org/collective-redress/reports/portugal/overview.

[3] The law of 28 March 2014 introduced a new section in the Belgian Economic Law Code entitled 'actions for collective redress', also known as 'class actions.' For further information, see http://www.freshfields.com/en/knowledge/class_actions_belgium_september/?LangId=2057.

[4] Introduced by virtue of the *Loi Hamon* of 17 March 2014. For further information, see http://www.freshfields.com/uploadedFiles/SiteWide/Knowledge/Briefing%20Class%20Action_VGB%282%29.PDF.

represented by a consumer association and the Italian class action[5] which allows collective claims to be brought in respect of claims for breach of contract, unfair or anticompetitive commercial practice, and product or service liability, neither of which includes opt-out mechanisms;

4. sector-specific opt-out mechanisms (such as is likely to be introduced in the UK towards the end of 2015 through the Consumer Rights Bill but only in relation to competition law claims);
5. sector-specific opt-in systems (such as the Capital Market Model Claims Act (*Kapitalanleger – Musterverfahrensgesetz* (KapMuG) in Germany;[6] and
6. class actions settlement (to be contrasted with litigation) mechanisms such as in the Netherlands via the 2005 Act on Collective Settlement of Mass Damages (*Wet collectieve afwikkeling massaschade*, WCAM)[7], in Germany (where there is a sector-specific opt-out settlement system in the KapMuG) and in the UK (where there are proposals for opt-out collective settlements for breaches of competition law).

This chapter comments on some of the key drivers behind collective redress reforms across Europe, touches upon the US experience and examines what a model European collective redress mechanism might look like, taking into account the need for various safeguards and some fundamental principles of European jurisprudence.

II. KEY DRIVERS BEHIND COLLECTIVE REDRESS REFORMS ACROSS EUROPE

The European Commission has said that citizens and businesses are often reluctant to initiate private lawsuits against unlawful practices, in particular if the individual loss is small in comparison to the costs (and risks) of litigation. As a result, illegal practices have caused significant aggregate loss to European citizens and businesses which remain uncompensated.

The Commission is also well aware of the differences in approach and procedures at Member State level and is concerned that the diversity of national systems and their different levels of effectiveness, in particular a lack of a consistent approach to collective redress at EU level, undermines the effectiveness of the rights of citizens and businesses (in particular those granted by EU law) and gives rise to uneven enforcement of those rights.

---

[5] For further information, see http://www.collectiveredress.org/collective-redress/reports/italy/overview.

[6] For further information, see http://www.collectiveredress.org/collective-redress/reports/germany/overview.

[7] For further information, see http://www.collectiveredress.org/collective-redress/reports/the netherlands/overview.

This is contrary to basic principles of EU law. The principles in the Recommendation therefore aim to help citizens and companies enforce the rights granted to them under EU law, with the aim of ensuring a coherent horizontal approach to collective redress across the range of areas where rights are granted under EU law, albeit without harmonising Member States' systems. Member States have, therefore, been requested by the EC to put into place appropriate measures on collective redress within 2 years. The Commission will then assess whether further measures are required.

The Recommendation relates purely to collective redress. However, there have been other developments relating to enhancing consumer rights at a European level. For example, the Commission hopes that the new Antitrust Damages Directive[8] will encourage and facilitate the bringing of antitrust damages claims, particularly compensation claims by business and consumers who have suffered loss as a result of cartel conduct. In addition, the ADR Directive[9] aims to give European consumers greater access to informal redress for their purchases of goods or services.

For understandable reasons, in Europe, some reforms in relation to collective redress at a national level have been introduced as part of the political reaction to high profile cases leading to subject-specific laws to deal with the 'problem'. For example in Germany, the *Deutsche Telekom* securities case led to the introduction of the KapMuG which provides for redress in relation to breaches of capital markets laws and the WCAM in the Netherlands was originally created for collective redress after a particularly difficult case of physical injury arising from pharmaceutical products.

However, whether it is due to a specific problem, or the wider recent global financial crisis and loss of confidence in corporate behaviour, or a desire generally to empower individuals/small businesses, or the loss of State funding for litigation or the reducing role of the Church or Trade Unions in supporting individuals against powerful defendants, there is clearly a current renewed Europe-wide political will to strengthen consumer rights/rights for small parties. In the current economic climate, any measures which are designed to empower the 'little man' will be politically popular, and a desire to claim compensation for losses suffered is likely to appeal to consumers more when times are hard.

A. A Specific Example

In the UK, a much discussed, if slightly dated, example of the issues was the *Which?/JJB Sports* replica football shirts litigation. This case has been cited by

---

[8] http://ec.europa.eu/competition/antitrust/actionsdamages/damages_directive_final_en.pdf.
[9] Directive 2013/11 of 21 May 2013 on alternative dispute resolution for consumer disputes. http://eur-lex.europa.eu/LexUriServ/LexUriServ.do?uri=OJ:L:2013:165:0063:0079:EN:PDF.

many as highlighting a need for a different mechanism for collective redress for consumers (at least in the competition context). An action was commenced in March 2007 against JJB Sports for follow-on litigation for compensatory damages alleging that the price of replica football shirts had been fixed contrary to competition law. The action was brought using section 47B Competition Act 1998 (as amended by the Enterprise Act 2002), which provided a specific opt-in approach for an action brought by Which?, a consumer rights organisation (designated with the power to act, under these provisions), on behalf of consumers. Most of the fundamental issues in the case such as breach of the relevant competition law provisions had already been determined.

However, instead of the thousands of consumer claims some had predicted, only a few hundred consumers eventually joined the action. A settlement agreement was reached under which JJB Sports agreed to pay compensation of £20 to consumers who had purchased one of the affected football shirts (for up to £39.99). Which? subsequently said the number of consumers opting in was very low considering the degree of publicity, the amount of resources spent and the external legal costs, and has doubted that it would bring such an action in the future given the costs to it of proceeding with the claim and the limited benefit to consumers. It has said: "Had the collective redress system been based on 'opt-out' and '*cy-près*', the case would have made a greater financial impact thereby ensuring that affected consumers were properly compensated, either directly or indirectly, and tangentially this would have had the effect of acting as a stronger deterrent to companies from engaging in activities that cause consumer detriment."[10]

However, did this case 'fail' because of the limitations inherent in an opt-in system that prevented justice, or are consumers just not interested in pursuing such claims? And if they are not, what is the purpose of improving the processes in a compensation led system? The deterrence of bad behaviour and related punishment are for the public enforcers and not to be left in the random hands of private litigants. Depending on the view taken as to which of these was the real reason for the low participation rate, collective redress mechanisms in the UK either should, perhaps, be expanded to encompass opt-out actions, or restricted to higher value claims.

This case was settled in January 2008 in a different economic climate; perhaps more consumers would have been interested in claiming compensation had the action been brought a few years later, when attitudes might have been different. That aside, on its face, there seems to be some force in the argument that the case showed that consumers were not interested in obtaining compensation when the compensation value was relatively small. Does it

---

[10] http://www.which.co.uk/documents/pdf/collective-redress-case-study-which-briefing-258401.pdf.

follow that there is no genuine consumer need for, or interest in, compensation for widely-spread but relatively low-value losses? Some would argue that there is no social utility in compensation-based claims being run in such circumstances when claimants have suffered no material loss, and that behavioural issues are rightly resolved by regulators imposing fines in the public interest.

Whatever the analysis, the prevailing view across many Member States is clearly that there should be an effective (and in many cases enhanced) mechanism for such consumer claims, leading to the growing number of collective redress mechanisms emerging across Europe. The question remains, however, as to what a collective action should look like, and how that redress should be administered (by regulators or the courts). Member States have not all taken a consistent view on these topics.

III. A CAUTIONARY TALE FROM THE US

Unlike in the US, in Europe damages are primarily compensation based and not intended to be penal, tend to be much lower level and are awarded by judges and not juries. In many countries, lawyers cannot participate to the same degree in the fruits of success (thus changing the economic incentives of bringing such mass actions) although there are limited models of contingency fees (for example 'damages-based agreements' are permitted in the UK and Germany allows some contingency fee arrangements). Perhaps most importantly, there are only a limited number (as yet) of opt-out mechanisms. Are the fears of importing the US system and the abuses within it, simply by way of introducing a European 'class' action, justified?

In Europe, there is dramatically less power in the drivers behind the full blown US model of class actions. There is also a clear political wish to avoid its excesses (such as the blackmail suits which force companies to settle even those claims lacking in merit, to avoid becoming embroiled in a full-blown merits trial class action lawsuit). Is it possible, therefore, by incorporating safeguards into any new system, learning from the US experience, to develop a collective redress mechanism which meets the needs of consumers, but at the same time, respects the legitimate interests of businesses?

Policymakers will need to give a lot of thought to the necessary safeguards, and to grapple with difficult decisions, to avoid any unintended consequences and to exclude abuse of a system that is certain to be tested by those wanting to exploit it (in either direction). However, as a matter of theory, it does seem that if a few fundamental guiding principles are kept in mind, any new mechanism could strike a fair balance. Such fundamental principles, which are entrenched in many European legal systems, would include:

1. the idea that damages are compensatory and judge-determined;
2. the loser pays rule;
3. tight control of the definition of a class, the nature of the representative claimant and the behaviour of those representing him (including whether it is better to bring an action by collective redress methods and the claim is meritorious) by a properly qualified court; and
4. close attention to the incentives operating on claimant law firms to ensure that they do not incentivise actions that it is not in the interests of society to have brought.

IV. A MODEL EUROPEAN COLLECTIVE REDRESS MECHANISM

In order to meet the objectives of enabling access to justice, any such approach must incentivise claimants to bring small claims (arguably something which the current UK mechanisms do not do, as shown by the Which? case mentioned earlier). Yet, in order to maintain the balance referred to above, the approach must also discourage excessive or frivolous claims to prevent an unfair burden on business. Further, it must create a regime which will, to an extent, hold businesses accountable for the damage caused by illegal behaviour but not punish businesses for such behaviour, which is a responsibility for national regulators rather than the courts.

It is, in part, a political, and a social, question as to how the balance is struck between the legal rights of consumers, or businesses, on the claimant side and those of business and State entities on the defendant side. However, unintended consequences which may be exploited must (and should) be a real fear for European policymakers. Much of the litigation environment in the US has been created by the plaintiff bar. Such law firms have, as their business model, the exploitation of the litigation rules for 'class' or 'collective' actions to the maximum extent possible. There is an emerging plaintiff bar in Europe adopting, so far as they can, similar models, as adapted for local conditions. One important lesson from the US experience is that at least some members of the plaintiff bar will seek to exploit all available collective redress mechanisms to go beyond the policy purposes unless strong features are built in to prevent/discourage them from doing so.

Some relevant aspects are discussed below. Some issues obviously leave room for abuse on their face (such as an opt-out mechanism) and need to be carefully considered, or controlled if adopted. However, arguably others, which have been fairly widely promoted and which do not in themselves leave obvious scope for abuse by the plaintiff bar, upon further analysis could potentially have unattractive consequences (such as using a regulator to administer redress).

A. Opt-in or Opt-out?

It is often argued that an opt-out system risks importing many of the abuses of the US system. It shifts the balance of power in favour of those who control the litigation strategically (often plaintiff bar law firms) and away from defendants and can lead to irrational outcomes. It may also lead to litigation being pursued in the name of people who do not necessarily want to litigate, take no part in the litigation and exercise no control over what is being done in their name.

The Recommendation states that rules on collective redress should be based on the opt-in model. In this world, affected parties remain free to litigate individually and the decision is only binding upon the parties that opted-in. The issue becomes one of how best to facilitate and finance the action making it easy and cost effective to build the group of claimants and to run the resulting case.

Although some Member States have introduced or are introducing opt-out models, it is suggested that if this is the prevailing policy, such models need to be used with great care and precision, focussed on very specific issues, under tight control from the courts so that an opt-out approach in a given case has to be clearly (a) workable; and (b) superior to other approaches. There would also need to be very tight control on the incentives and identity of the representative claimant or those representing them (for example, that an opt-out claim can only be brought by a recognised consumer group acting in the public interest and not for individual profit).

B. A Generic or Sectoral Basis?

Europe seems to be experimenting with the sectoral route in individual Member States, with collective redress mechanisms applying to one or more specific industrial sectors or types of claim. Examples include the UK, via the Consumer Rights Bill, which proposes a regime which is limited to competition claims and Germany where only specified forms of securities claims can be brought collectively.

The obvious problem with the sectoral approach is that disputes and claims frequently cross fields and definition and demarcation can give rise to secondary litigation. If different procedural rules and mechanisms apply in different industrial sectors or different fields of law, what happens to claims that do not fit easily into such definitions? It seems a valid concern that claims would be defined (perhaps artificially) to take advantage of the added momentum and negotiating power of a collective action system. Why should one group of claimants benefit because of a particular feature of its case which means that it qualifies, but another be excluded, essentially for reasons outside of its control?

A related question is therefore whether as a matter of theory, it is necessary for different sectors to benefit from different mechanisms, or could they all be governed by one over-arching set of rules? It may be that some sector-specific rules are inevitable to meet the needs of different areas of redress, but what does seem appropriate is to move progressively and proportionately. Dramatic changes may be particularly vulnerable to unforeseen consequences.

C. Incorporating Safeguards into the Mechanism

The importance of building-in safeguards into any new mechanism has been mentioned above. These should include the following.

1. The court as gatekeeper to protect against frivolous claims being brought – the importance of judicial control by properly qualified and trained judges who are in a position to prevent abuse of collective action techniques cannot be underestimated. The tests applied need to include not only whether there is a genuine class that can be defined and has a sufficiently congruent interest, but also, critically, that the adoption of a given form of class action really is in the interests of justice and the claimants, given the other remedies available to them and the merits of the claim.
2. Standing – it seems critical that there is some form of control on the party that leads any proceedings seeking collective redress. It seems fairly obvious that the more weight and effectiveness that there is behind any collective redress procedure, the greater the degree of control required. As a matter of logic and justice, it seems only right that the control of a collective action is in the hands of those who have suffered the loss themselves, and not in the hands of a party pursuing personal profit. This is particularly critical in those jurisdictions that permit financial incentives for lawyers based on their success in obtaining damages.
3. The loser pays rule – certainly as a matter of English law, and in some other European legal systems (eg Germany, Italy and Spain), this is common. It has been seen as a very important control on spurious litigation that claimants take some element of risk as to a successful defendant's costs to act as an effective economic disincentive both on claimants and their funders as regards claims that should never be brought. Such a regime also makes it more likely that reasonable and fair settlements will be reached. There seems no logical reason why this should not be applicable to any form of collective redress, which, at its core, should only be a procedural mechanism for allowing multiple claims to be brought. This need not be a bar to claimants bringing reasonable actions because insurance has been available in appropriate cases (although this practice needs to operate in such a way as not to undermine the rationality that the loser

pays principle brings) and the circumstances and the level of the award of adverse costs are (and should be) subject to judicial control to ensure fairness.

D. *The Role of Non-Party Funding*

The role of funding in any regime is more controversial and more complex.

Should contingency fees, or the increasingly frequent third party funding, be permitted for collective redress? Contingency fees have been one of the driving factors in the US litigation experience: giving lawyers the possibility to receive a very material percentage of the financial recovery for their own benefit is a shot in the financial arm to plaintiff litigation. It significantly improves the incentives for the plaintiff bar and, therefore, on the margin materially increases the risk of spurious and unmeritorious cases being brought because of the size of the pay-off for the law firm that is, in reality, running the action. The Commission shares these concerns, commenting that certain methods of attorney compensation, such as contingency fees, may create an incentive to unnecessary litigation. The Recommendation states that contingency fees are in principle prohibited for collective actions but leaves the door open in that, if a Member State nevertheless wants to allow for the application of contingency fees, it may do so provided there is appropriate national regulation to prevent abuse.

However, it must also be recognised that many meritorious claims could not be brought without some form of external funding, as the claimants themselves do not have the necessary resources to provide the working capital for a case or to take the risk of having to pay the legal fees (far less the other side's costs) if the case is unsuccessful. If the main driver behind the introduction of collective redress mechanisms is to enable access to justice, it then seems that some form of funding, be that via government schemes, third parties or lawyers, must be permitted to enable these claims to be brought in practice.

There is an active and evolving third party funding market in some parts of Europe whereby financial institutions, usually specialist funds, are prepared to advance the legal fees based on a share of damages. Although this raises many of the same issues as contingency fees, such a third party funder is usually more remote from the litigation, performing some kind of objective review of the merits of the case and is exposed to risk, such as adverse costs (particularly in the UK), which provides (or should in theory provide) a degree of rationality in relation to the cases that receive funding. Rather than prohibiting external funding outright, perhaps a better way is to ensure that there are proper controls which do not change the dynamics of the litigation to such an extent to tempt spurious claims to be brought but, rather, enable legitimate claims to be pursued.

E. The Calculation of Damages

The appropriate basis for calculating damages is another area which has provoked controversy. The rationale behind the introduction of a collective redress system is compensation and justice for consumers/small parties who would not otherwise be able to bring their claims. Were such claims to be brought on an individual basis, damages would clearly be compensatory under the current principles adopted in EU Member States and, indeed, under EU law. It should, therefore, follow that the basis for, and quantum of, damages ought not to change merely because of the introduction of a new procedural mechanism which allows for multiple claims to be grouped together. This principle seems fundamental to protecting the values of a European legal system. It is an important part of the distinction from the US system which is more open to a punitive, rather than simply compensatory, element.

However, collective actions raise particular issues as to whether there should be some formulaic calculation of damages without the need for each individual to prove his or her personal loss. In true collective redress involving large numbers of claimants with small individual claims, individual proof of loss would not be economic. Indeed, the simple calculation of loss, making assumptions as to circumstances, is one of the societal benefits of collective redress. However, to provide compensation on such a formulaic basis, without taking account of individual specific circumstances does, at least on a jurisprudential basis, undermine the philosophical position that each claimant seeking compensation should prove his or her loss. It is likely that Member States will take a pragmatic approach to such issues in the interests of seeing an effective redress system in place, with the debate as to the right to redress happening as part of the definition of sub-classes of claimants whose compensation formula will be adjusted to reflect the position of that sub-class; this would be a more specific and circumstances-sensitive approach, without actually resorting to individual calculations.

A further issue arises in the context of discussions as to the distribution of any unclaimed sums in an opt-out regime. In keeping with the principle of claimants proving individual loss and only being compensated for their actual damage, it can be strongly argued that any sums not claimed by a claimant should be returned to the defendant: if the purpose is compensation, and claimants do not want to be compensated, or are not prepared to make the effort to collect sums to which they are entitled, why should the funds not be returned to the defendant? Is this not the logical consequence of any system that is based on compensation and not punishment?

Moreover, in circumstances where a penalty has been imposed by the regulator, which is frequently the case, it seems unfair that there should be a further, or alternative, penalty imposed by the failure to repay to a defendant damages that are not needed to provide compensation. It seems a fair working assumption that governments will have given (or should give) regulators the power to fine for behaviour which is regarded as wrong, looking at it from the perspective of public policy. This is not something which should be passed to the judiciary.

However, a common fall-back position of those arguing for collective redress is that an approach equivalent to the doctrine of *cy-près* should apply so that unclaimed funds should be paid by the defendant to benefit generally the community affected by the issue being litigated (such as a charity operating in the relevant area). Not only is it questionable how this meets the objectives of compensation (because the benefits of such application of funds would be shared on different precepts from those governing compensation) or indeed, the efficient use of capital, but it is also not clear why those who did receive their compensation through a claim in the litigation (which presumably reflected their loss and the merits of their claim) should be further be benefitted by the receipt of indirect benefits through the application of *cy-près*.

F. The Role of the Courts and Regulators

The issue as to the division of roles between the courts and regulators arises in the debate about whether a regulator should determine compensation/redress levels. It is quite frequently suggested that one way to address the lack of a procedural collective action at national level is to award powers to the regulators to award compensation where there has been collective loss, removing the need for collective redress litigation procedures. Indeed, a previous UK government indicated a preference for enhanced powers for regulators to award compensation between private parties and the elements of the necessary legislation are in place. It is strongly suggested that this is confusing the role of the courts and regulators in a number of very troubling respects.

Regulators do not generally have the necessary resources and skills to award compensation. This is not their primary role; they do not have the right processes, powers or people.

Moreover, in most European jurisdictions, civil rights are determined by adversarial proceedings before a neutral arbitrator (and the European Convention on Human Rights has given rise to detailed case law on this issue). There are legitimate concerns about inherent conflicts of roles and overlaps of interests. Regulators are pursuing policy objectives for the market or activity that they regulate. For that purpose, in the public interest, they have enforcement powers and sanction powers. Their powers of investigation may well go well beyond what would be available to a private litigant. Because they have a policy agenda (and the powers to back it up, which they exercise, in effect, of their own volition), it is difficult to see how they can ever be a neutral decision maker for private rights of compensation between a claimant who believes he has suffered loss and a defendant (who is regulated) who will have to pay compensation. The regulator will not be able to keep the two roles separate and it is fundamentally undesirable that there should be a trade-off between public sanction for misbehaviour and private compensation. This trade-off is already actively seen in the settlement of regulatory claims, but that is, at least, consensual. If a regulated entity offers to pay compensation to those affected by an infringing activity as part of settling regulatory proceedings, that is a matter for that entity. However, that is a very different matter from giving the regulator both the power to impose public sanctions and to determine private redress.

The better solution must be that claims are adjudicated in the courts, before a truly independent tribunal, in an independent manner, free from the wider interests of regulators and any regulatory (ie political) agenda, and which can be challenged in the appellate courts, whilst regulators impose fines and other behavioural remedies in the public (not private) interest.

V. CONCLUDING THOUGHTS

It seems fairly unlikely that there will be just one model for collective actions across all of Europe, given the various existing mechanisms, and the approach taken in the ongoing reforms, across Member States. These various developments give rise to complex cross-border implications; the possibilities that exist for forum shopping, the effect of decisions in one jurisdiction on rights in another and the conflict of laws issues are only starting to be considered.

A practical example of this is the attraction of the WCAM in the Netherlands, which has been used to settle claims with non-Dutch European claimants who have only a marginal connection to the Netherlands (for example the *Converium* case in circumstances where the alleged misconduct did not occur within the Netherlands, and the investor class included few investors resident in the Netherlands.) Another is the UK competition law opt-out proposal which only applies to UK members of the class.

Over time, and as collective actions are used more widely across Europe, these differences will need to be addressed and resolved. It also needs to be worked out how any developments at a European level will sit with existing national regimes. To that end, the framework proposed by the Commission in its Recommendation which contains common principles is helpful and to be respected by Member State regimes in developing their own mechanisms.

When developing policy and reforms in this area, it is important for policymakers to remember the fundamental principles that are the foundations of European legal systems. Clearly it is right to be cautious given the experience in other jurisdictions; but there is no reason to fear the rise of the European collective action in and of itself.

4

Judicial Perspectives

Collective Redress from a Judicial Perspective

Meinrad Wösthoff[*,1]

I. INTRODUCTION

Few topics in recent years have stimulated more excitement in European legal circles than the necessity of creating collective redress mechanisms in order to facilitate judicial practice with mass actions. On the one hand, consumer protection organisations and, in the area of capital markets, investor associations canvass for creating such mechanisms with the idea that this is the only method of effective redress. On the other hand, business associations warn against adopting an American style class action because they fear mischievous and abusive litigation. There are strong arguments in favour of both viewpoints, and to further complicate the question, different legal traditions within the European Union (EU) have led Member States to adopt conflicting positions. Some Member States have already adopted instruments for collective redress whereas in other States a more individual approach to such claims is the norm. It is against this background that the Commission Recommendation of 11 June 2013[2] should be seen. The Commission suggests non-binding principles for collective litigation albeit without explaining the details of such a mechanism. The Commission's expectations are unambiguous. Its intention is to ensure a coherent common concept for collective redress within the EU without harmonising the legal orders of the Member States. It is up to the Member States to offer national collective redress mechanisms in order to support claimants both with access to justice and enforcement of judgments, particularly in areas such as consumer protection, competition, environmental protection and financial services.[3]

---

[*] The author is Director of the Amtsgericht (Lower Regional Court) Hanau and between 2003 and 2010 was the Presiding Judge of the 7th Commercial Court of the Landgericht (Regional Court) Frankfurt am Main where he presided over the *Telekom* case.

[1] This work was translated from German to English by Laurence Grafton, LLB and Dipl-Jur Johannes Ungerer – both are Research Assistants at the Institute for Private International and Comparative Law, University of Bonn.

[2] Commission Recommendation of 11 June 2013 (2013/396/EU).

[3] Cf Press Release of the European Commission of 11 June 2013 (IP/13/524).

The aim is therefore already defined within the EU. It is: yes to collective redress, but no to uniform regulation. The effective protection of individual rights and their enforcement is to be achieved by creating collective redress mechanisms, though it will be up to each Member State to define the rules so long as those rules are coherent. The European Parliament suggested in its Resolution "Towards a coherent European approach to collective redress" of 2 February 2012[4] that the legal traditions and legal systems of each Member State should be reasonably considered. The reason that both the European Parliament and the Commission are pushing ahead with the creation of a collective redress instrument is summarised in Recital 2 of the Commission Recommendation of 11 June 2013. It is definitely true, as the Commission points out, that in today's world events can take place where a large number of people will be harmed and incur loss as a result of one and the same illegal action. In these cases of 'mass harm situations' the courts have thus far been somewhat powerless and unable to help individual victims within an appropriate timeframe and for a reasonable cost.

II. THE *TELEKOM* CASE BEFORE THE LANDGERICHT (REGIONAL COURT) FRANKFURT AM MAIN

Since 2001 a total of 2,700 actions have been brought before the Landgericht Frankfurt am Main against Deutsche Telekom AG, the former state telecoms monopoly that was turned into a joint stock company. The author of this paper dealt with these actions between 2003 and 2010. About 17,000 claimants seek the return of money invested in shares during the initial public offering (IPO) of Deutsche Telekom AG.[5] They argue that the prospectuses issued by Deutsche Telekom AG prior to its IPO were inaccurate, and consequently the claimants have a right to repayment of their investment by virtue of §44 *Börsengesetz* (Stock Exchange Act). Not all 17,000 claimants gave the same reasons as to why they thought that the prospectuses were inaccurate. Rather, the claimants have pointed to different mistakes and omissions for the inaccuracy. Additionally, the claimants bought the shares at different times and in different denominations. The statements submitted by the claimants, who are represented by more than 800 lawyers, and statements submitted in reply by the defendant's lawyers fill the shelves of two large storage rooms in the Landgericht Frankfurt am Main. This example already shows how challenging it can be for courts to deal with mass actions.

---

[4] EU 2011/2089(INI).
[5] See Court Order of the *Landgericht Frankfurt am Main* from 11 July 2006, file reference number 3/7 OH 1/06 KapMuG.

Contrary to actions brought for injunction, for instance, against an act that is in breach of competition law, actions for damages are not about the behaviour of the defendant or defendants but are also about subjective factors relating to the individual claimant. For the author it is less about the question whether collective redress makes sense – this is something that one can answer in the affirmative depending on the design of the instruments of collective redress – rather the question is about how it works in practice. On this very point the underlying legal framework of each Member State is pivotal.

III. OVERVIEW OF THE GERMAN LEGAL TRADITION

In the area of civil law, the German legal tradition focuses on individual claims. A person or legal entity that claims damages has to assert that claim against the person who is considered by the claimant to be obliged to pay the compensation sought. The *Zivilprozessordnung*[6] allows for few exceptions, but Article 60 ZPO states that a plurality of persons can act as joint litigants in a single action if similar claims or obligations form the subject matter in dispute and such claims are based on an essentially similar factual and legal cause.[7] This, however, is not a mass claim or a form of collective redress as such action requires differentiation between the legal relations of each individual claimant with the defendant or defendants. In such an action, attention needs to be paid to individual submissions made by each claimant. To take a decision in a joint litigation case, the court has to consider each legal relationship separately, ie determine whether each claimant is individually entitled to the claim. There is no requirement that the outcome of a joint litigation case be the same for each individual claimant. Instead, it is possible that some claimants succeed, while the claims of others are dismissed. This already demonstrates problems that could potentially be triggered by collective redress instruments, especially in cases of damages claims. In these cases not only is it necessary to determine whether the defendant's behaviour was indeed unlawful but also whether it caused harm to the individual claimant. This is especially challenging for the court where a large number of claimants act collectively. In these cases both the defendant's behaviour and the extent to which the individual claimant has been affected by this behaviour have to be considered carefully in order to assess whether the individual claimant is entitled to his or her claim. Hence, according to the traditional understanding of German law, only questions of general importance can be answered in a collective action, ie the questions which concern all parties alike. The individual

---

[6] ZPO, German Code of Civil Procedure.
[7] See Münchener Kommentar zur Zivilprozessordnung – ZPO, vol. 1: arts 1-354 (4th ed., Beck, Munich 2013) art 60.

conditions that a claimant must prove he has satisfied in order for the claim to succeed cannot be dealt with by collective litigation.

IV. DEALING WITH MASS ACTIONS

Mass actions, whatever their origin, in which hundreds or thousands of claimants seek damages, must be divided into two parts. The first part deals with the general questions, which are those relevant to all litigants. Collective redress mechanisms would be very suitable for this exercise. For instance, there is the opportunity to ascertain questions of fact through collective inquiry and to take common decisions on questions of law. The second part deals with the questions relating to the individual claimants. More general and thus collective mechanisms for mass damages cases can be envisaged only in cases where the damage suffered by each claimant is ascertained and enforcement does not depend on further individual conditions (eg as to whether the claim became time-barred), and where the claimant's standing is not in doubt. In such cases, collective redress could well be possible for those who submit that they have suffered loss because of the conduct of a single defendant. This category includes actions brought by a plurality of persons suffering minor losses resulting from the unlawful behaviour of the defendant, and where the individual victims' claims would simply be economically unreasonable because they have incurred only a marginal loss.

V. POSSIBLE INSTRUMENTS FOR COLLECTIVE REDRESS

In cases of the type discussed above, an instrument of collective redress can be a 'skimming off action' (*Abschöpfungsklage*),[8] which is an action that ensures that the person causing the damage has to compensate for the whole loss incurred by his behaviour; however the compensation is not to be distributed among the victims but used for other purposes such as to finance consumer protection organisations. It could also be possible for certain institutions to be granted standing to claim damages and distribute the compensation awarded by the court among the victims. One can see that the question as to the suitability of collective redress mechanisms mostly depends on the type of infringement that has caused loss to a large number of people. It is more difficult to use collective redress mechanisms where the loss suffered by each claimant is particularly unique, ie where the right to compensation depends on the claimants meeting subjective conditions.

---

[8] Cf http://www.collectiveredress.org/collective-redress/reports/germany/overview.

VI. A NEW WAY IN GERMAN PROCEDURAL LAW –
THE *KAPITALANLEGER-MUSTERVERFAHRENSGESETZ* (CAPITAL MARKET
INVESTORS' MODEL PROCEDURE ACT)

The difficulties outlined have been made abundantly clear to the German legislator by the *Telekom* case, as briefly illustrated above. At the time when the cases were filed, all claims had to be treated and decided individually according to the civil procedure rules that were in force. For each and every claim, evidence had to be taken of relevant but disputed facts submitted by the parties. It was not possible to transfer the outcome of each inquiry to parallel cases, even if those cases were based on the same facts and contained the same witness statements, as the procedural principle of 'evidence to be taken directly' (*Unmittelbarkeit der Beweisaufnahme*) states that only evidence that has been heard in that very case is admissible. The German legislator realised the difficulties involved and the exorbitant amount of time wasted, resulting in the adoption of the *Kapitalanleger-Musterverfahrensgesetz* (Capital Market Investors' Model Procedure Act)[9] on 1 November 2005, which was subsequently amended on 19 October 2012.[10] The Act mainly introduces a 'model' or 'test case procedure'. Litigation of such nature requires a large number of claims that concern damages for incorrect, misleading or omitted capital market information or the wrongful use of capital market information. So far, the Act only applies to some areas of law, where mass loss has occurred and a claim can be brought before the court. It has been considered, and already suggested, that this Act be applied not only to the actions of capital market investors but also in other cases, for instance for the purposes of consumer protection.

VII. THE MECHANISMS OF THE *KAPITALANLEGER-MUSTERVERFAHRENSGESETZ*

What are the advantages of this Act when dealing with mass actions? The Act allows the court that deals with hundreds or thousands of damages claims, which are based on identical facts, to issue an order to refer all these matters to the competent *Oberlandesgericht* (Higher Regional Court). That court has to decide on the factual or legal issues, where ten or more claimants request this order. This decision is binding on all other claims based on the same facts – for instance an incorrect prospectus or ad hoc announcement. Therefore, only one hearing of evidence is needed for all the facts in question. The *Oberlandesgericht* will decide common legal questions uniformly too. The results of this form of

---

[9] For the legislative history see F Reuschle, 'Ein neuer Weg zur Bündelung und Durchsetzung gleichgerichteter Ansprüche – Zum Entwurf eines Kapitalanleger-Musterverfahrensgesetzes (KapMuG)' *WM (Zeitschrift für Wirtschafts- und Bankrecht)* 2004, 2334 et seq.

[10] BGBl. (German Federal Law Gazette) I 2012, 2182.

'model procedure' litigation are binding on all claimants and defendants who can be said to relate to the litigation, even if they have not requested the order themselves. After the 'model/test case procedure' litigation before the *Oberlandesgericht* has come to an end, the original court that issued the order will then continue to deal with all the individual claims – taking into account the findings of the *Oberlandesgericht*. Only where individual disputes require further discussion will it be up to the (original) court to decide on these issues. The collective approach set out in the *Kapitalanleger-Musterverfahrensgesetz*, relates to some of the factual and legal questions, but is not concerned with all the details of the cases. With 'model procedure' litigation the German legislator created a legal instrument that combines both a collective and an individual approach, when it comes to how to deal in court with a single claim that is part of a capital market mass case. Furthermore, the judicial role can be eased by virtue of the Act's provision on 'collective settlements'. The Act offers the possibility of reaching a settlement which will bind most or even all litigants involved in the 'model procedure' litigation. This collective approach can have a positive benefit on the judicial process of mass actions too. Lastly, the collective approach is further strengthened by the 2012 amendment of the Act. While being party to the outcome of the 'model procedure' litigation requires filing an initial action (cf §22 Abs. 1 and §9 Abs. 1 *Kapitalanleger-Musterverfahrensgesetz*), §10 Abs. 2 of the Act as amended still allows those who do not join the 'model procedure' litigation for cost reasons to register their claim. The act of registering the claim has the sole effect of preventing the claim from being rejected later because of a lapse of time.[11] The advantage for those who register their claim, but do not file it as an action, is that they can wait for the outcome of the 'model procedure' litigation without the risk that their claim will be rejected as time-barred. Upon the outcome, they can decide whether or not to file an action, most likely the latter where the 'model procedure' litigation has not been successful for the investors.[12] This last approach has collective implications too, insofar as many can benefit from collectively undertaken 'model procedure' litigation at no risk of having their claims rejected due to lapse of time. However, it should not be forgotten that § 10 Abs. 3 of the Act calls for certain conditions to be met. The Act states, among other things, that when registering the claim the reasons and amount

---

[11] Art. 10 (2) KapMuG: Innerhalb einer Frist von sechs Monaten ab der Bekanntmachung nach Absatz 1 kann ein Anspruch schriftlich gegenüber dem Oberlandesgericht zum Musterverfahren angemeldet werden. Die Anmeldung ist nicht zulässig, wenn wegen desselben Anspruchs bereits Klage erhoben wurde. Der Anmelder muss sich durch einen Rechtsanwalt vertreten lassen. Über Form und Frist der Anmeldung sowie über ihre Wirkung ist in der Bekanntmachung nach Absatz 1 zu belehren.

[12] Cf F Wardenbach, 'KapMuG 2012 versus KapMuG 2005: Die wichtigsten Änderungen aus Sicht der Praxis', *GWR (Gesellschafts- und Wirtschaftsrecht)* 2013, 35 et seq.

shall be stated. The case law on this requirement implies that a claim based on an incorrect prospectus cannot be rejected later because of lapse of time, if and only where the specific incorrect prospectus information was mentioned when the claim was registered.[13]

VIII. SUGGESTIONS FOR DEALING WITH MASS ACTIONS

Several aspects are now clear to the author of this paper, who, for seven years, has been the presiding judge in the chamber of the Landgericht Frankfurt am Main dealing with the *Telekom* case. These aspects will now, in this last section of the paper, be addressed from a judicial perspective. It is trivial – but important to mention – that this perspective is that of a German judge expressed in the context of German procedural law. The author is very well aware of the fact that the issues he regards as being important may not be, or may perhaps only partly be, relevant issues in other Member States of the EU that have a different legal tradition.

A. Fundamental Basis

Global relations and the increasingly complicated structure of economic systems leads today, more than ever, to a situation where the actions of single persons or companies can cause damage that has varied repercussions for a large number of people. A legal system that, against this background, only provides for and permits legal disputes between single claimants (victims) and defendants (those who have caused the damage) makes it difficult or even impossible for the court, where actions have been filed in droves, to reach a decision in cases that are based on similar grounds, for instance when incorrect capital market information is given. Litigation of this type comes with the danger that it is no longer justiciable. In any case, there is an obvious risk that such actions cannot be decided by the court in reasonable time according to European standards that have been put in place in order to ensure the right of access to justice.

B. Different Approaches in Different Situations

Mass loss can occur in many different areas and result in mass actions. An example in the area of capital markets is the *Telekom* case, which has been

---

[13] Ruling of the *Oberlandesgericht* (Higher Regional Court) Frankfurt am Main from 16 May 2012, file reference number 23 Kap 1/06, GWR 2012, 301; for an opposing view see A Halfmeier, 'Zur Neufassung des KapMuG und zur Verjährungshemmung bei Prospekthaftungsansprüchen' *DB (Der Betrieb)* 2012, 2145 et seq.

illustrated above. Similarly, in the service sector, mass loss can occur as a result of the incorrect drafting of a telecommunications contract – it is imaginable that thousands of contracting parties of a telecommunication company end up slightly overpaying on their monthly fee because of wrongful contractual terms. Furthermore, a mass action can come about as a result of the fact that a company manufactured a product that contains a defective part, and consequently thousands of consumers suffer loss. While, on the one hand, a mass action can also depend on subjective conditions relating to the claimant, it can, on the other, be quite conceivable that in a different mass action only objective conditions will be taken into account. According to the guideline criteria set out in the Commission Recommendation of 11 June 2013, these different starting points have to be considered when creating instruments of collective redress for the Member States of the EU. The more complicated the litigation process is due to the consideration of subjective conditions relating to every single claimant – which happens where a legal system is designed for two-party disputes (*Parteienprozess*) between an individual claimant (victim) and an individual defendant (tortfeasor) – the more complex and time consuming litigation will be.

In essence, the considerations above suggest that the national legislators have to provide mechanisms to aid the courts in dealing with mass actions. This is the only way that citizens can be granted their right of access to justice. This right includes the ability to realise a claim within a reasonable time frame, as is required by case law, including that of the European Court of Justice.[14] Hence, in its Recommendation of 11 June 2013 the Commission explicitly points out that mechanisms for collective redress, either those already introduced or those to be introduced, should be "fair, equitable, timely and not prohibitively expensive."[15] From the author's experience it is clear, at least as far as the German legal system is concerned, that these criteria, and thereby effective redress, can only be achieved by derogation from the stringent requirements of the *Parteienprozess* characterising today's law of civil procedure. This raises the question of whether litigation mechanisms are conceivable without abandoning the relevant fundamental requirements of the rule of law – which require hearing the claimant and the defendant equally – in order to deal with all the factual and legal questions raised in mass actions potentially brought by thousands of litigants. It is therefore necessary to create mechanisms that reduce the mass of factual and legal questions, ie the parties' submissions, to what is essential. Although the Commission Recommendation

---

[14] Eg Court Order of the European Court of Justice from 16 July 2009, file reference number C-385/07 P; Court Order of the European Court of Justice from 8 December 2011, file reference number C-389/10 P.

[15] Commission Recommendation of 11 June 2013 (2013/396/EU), section I para 2.

excludes "intrusive pre-trial discovery procedures"[16], one can still imagine litigation mechanisms allowing the gathering of information prior to trial and the assessment of its relevance to the case. It is inconceivable that a small group of judges – or even a single judge – have to arrive in a 'timely' fashion at a satisfactory conclusion in a mass action where hundreds of lawyers submit thousands of documents forming hundreds of thousands of pages in total, and where submissions are made by lawyers in many different ways.

C. The Necessity of Uniform Rule of Law Standards

The litigation mechanisms, which, in part, are still to be created, can and will certainly have to be adapted to the legal culture of individual Member States. There is no need for an EU wide uniform approach. The Commission Recommendation of 11 June 2013 stresses this repeatedly. The crucial point is that existing collective redress instruments, and those which are still to be created, comply with uniform EU rule of law standards focusing on the interests of the claimants as a group. Additionally, the procedural rights of mass claim defendants, who are likely to be big companies, need to be respected. This is the only way that mass actions in which ultimately thousands of claimants are to be granted their individual claims could become justiciable. If the court dealt with mass loss by considering all individual questions submitted by thousands of claimants, the duration of proceedings would threaten the right to justice and discourage investors and consumers from bringing claims. The objective of the European Commission to not only ensure effective legal redress for investors or consumers through injunctive or compensatory collective redress, but also to "stop illegal practices" would thus not be met.[17] It will be necessary to find a way of appropriately dealing with mass actions *cum granum salis*, without losing sight of rule of law principles.

D. Other Approaches than Actions Brought by Individuals

Finally, in the case of small and micro damages one should think about actions filed by associations and 'skimming off actions'. In cases where a large number of people suffered from small or even micro loss, society at large still has an interest in sanctioning the behaviour that has caused mass harm. Within the German legal framework, such cases are now dealt with by Article 10 of the *Gesetz gegen den unlauteren Wettbewerb* (Unfair Competition Act). The provision states that in cases where a company profits from an unfair

---

[16] *Ibid.*, Recital 15.
[17] *Ibid.*, section I para 1.

commercial practice at the expense of a large number of consumers, those who have standing to bring a claim (eg consumer protection organisations) can sue to skim off these economic profits. If they succeed, skimmed off profits go to the German Treasury. This and the fact that the claimants often face difficulties in proving the loss does not encourage collective litigation. Consequently, only a few cases of this type have been brought so far. It is up to the legislator to increase the attractiveness of such collective action and encourage litigation, which certainly interests and benefits the economy as a whole.

IX. CONCLUSION

In conclusion, if collective redress is to be efficient and outcomes are to be reached within a reasonable time, then this mechanism cannot be achieved without some sacrifice to procedural rights granted in the traditional *Parteienprozess*. Balancing in particular the efficiency of collective redress mechanisms against subjective procedural rights (of both claimants and defendant), and the oft-pleaded principle of a right to a fair trial, will be the basis for the creation of further collective redress mechanisms in the Member States.

Part II

Collective Redress in Europe – How?

1

Models for Collective Redress in Europe – The Commission Recommendation and Beyond

Recent United Kingdom and French Reforms of Class Actions: An Unfinished Journey

Rachael Mulheron[*]

I. INTRODUCTION

When the civil procedure of a jurisdiction does not enable its substantive law to be applied and adjudicated in the judicial forum, then that legal system has, in some measure, fallen into disrepute. With that conundrum in mind, and with varying degrees of conservatism, the French Parliament and the legislature of the United Kingdom, have recently taken steps to address this conundrum, by promulgating proposals concerning the introduction of a form of class, or collective, action that will, if implemented, modify their landscapes of civil litigation considerably.

As a backdrop to this reform, on 11 June 2013, the European Commission published a series of common, non-binding principles for collective actions, via its Recommendation on Common Principles for Injunctive and Compensatory Collective Redress Mechanisms in the Member States concerning violations of rights granted under Union Law.[1] The Recommendation "aims to ensure a coherent horizontal approach to collective redress in the European Union without harmonising Member States'

---

[*] Professor, Department of Law, Queen Mary University of London. The author is a member of the Civil Justice Council of England and Wales (CJC), was a former member of the CJC/MOJ Working Party on Contingency Fees, was a former member of the CJC/MOJ Working Party on Third Party Funding, and is a current member of the Competition Appeal Tribunal (CAT) Class Actions Working Party responsible for drafting rules of court for the foreshadowed class action. However, the views expressed in this article are written in a personal academic capacity, and should not be taken to necessarily represent the views of any entity with which the author is associated or of which the author is a member. The author wishes to gratefully acknowledge and thank Marie-Lise Grare, Co-eLearning Projects Co-ordinator, Universite Catholique de Lille, France, for her assistance in translating the French legislation referred to herein (however, any errors remain solely the author's responsibility).

[1] European Commission, 2013/396/EU, of 11 of June 2013, available at http://www.rwi.uzh.ch/lehreforschung/alphabetisch/domej/archiv/hs13/ccphs13/ccpunterlagen/05-1-CommissionRecommendation.pdf.

systems",[2] and envisages that collective redress will enable the private enforcement of rights as a supplement to the 'core task of public enforcement'.[3] The Commission proposed that national redress mechanisms would be valuable in areas of personal data protection, financial services, consumer protection, competition, environment protection and investor protection,[4] and noted that the common principles will, when implemented, enhance access to justice and deter unlawful behaviour, whilst also "ensuring appropriate procedural safeguards to avoid abusive litigation."[5] That theme of balance and moderation has been translated to the newly-proposed regimes in France and the UK too – albeit in differential respects.

Part II of this chapter briefly outlines the background to each of the French and UK proposals. Part III undertakes a tabular comparative examination of some key aspects of the regimes' designs, together with a comparison as to what the EC Recommendation itself proposed for each aspect. That these proposals are very different in their design and scope reflects, primarily, the divisive policy conundrums which occur in this area of law reform. It is an instance of political will and law reform meeting 'head-on', in disputes of which political decision-making will inevitably prevail. However, the 'gate-keeper' role of certification is one class design feature upon which all three reform proponents have agreed, albeit that the stipulated certification criteria vary widely. A comparative tabulation of certification under the French and UK regimes is undertaken in Part IV, and Part V concludes the chapter.

II. A BACKGROUND SUMMARY

Whilst their designs may differ greatly, one of the common features of the French and UK regimes is the length of time which each has taken to promulgate. Reform – especially in such a contentious area as collective actions reform – does not occur overnight, and both jurisdictions have shown a distinctly measured and cautious approach.

A. The French Group Action

French class actions reform has been lengthy in consideration, and stultified

---

[2] To quote the summary of the Recommendation by the Commission at http://ec.europa.eu/consumers/redress_cons/collective_redress_en.htm#comrec.
[3] See EC Recommendation, Recital 6.
[4] *Ibid*, Recital 7.
[5] *Ibid*, point 1.

in implementation. Over the years, political intentions were stated,[6] and Bills put forward,[7] but no tangible progress occurred. The new French collective actions regime ('the French Group Action') is contained in Chapter III of the French Consumer Code, which was promulgated by the French Parliament on 12 February 2014,[8] several months after it was submitted.[9]

Entitled, 'Group Action', the regime is sectoral, not generic.[10] It relates only to breaches by a defendant of its legal or contractual obligations pertaining to 'the sale of goods or provision of services',[11] or 'injuries result[ing] from anti-competitive conduct' (the latter as a follow-on action, where the unlawful conduct has been formerly adjudicated on by the national or European competition authorities).[12] Although it has been envisaged, politically, that the possibility of group action would be extended to the health sector,[13] that has not yet occurred. It is an opt-in regime (ie, requiring the express consent or mandate of a group member, for his or her claim to be included within the group of consumers who are entitled to claim compensation).[14] The law itself was the subject of an appeal to the Constitutional

---

[6] Eg a statement by President Chirac on 4 January 2005 that, "I am asking the Government to amend the current legislation so as to enable consumer groups and their associations to bring collective actions against unfair practices going on in certain markets"; and a statement by President Sarkozy on 20 April 2007 that, '[a]s for class actions, I am favourable to them in general', and as cited in P Karlsgodt (ed), *World Class Actions: A Guide to Group and Representative Actions Around the Globe* (OUP, 2012) 160.

[7] The several Bills are described at *ibid*, 162–164, commencing with two Bills presented in 2006: Reform Proposal No 322 to the French Senate dated 25 April 2006, and Reform Proposal No 3055 to the French National Assembly dated 26 April 2006. Subsequent Bills followed, including, but not limited to: Reform Proposals No 2677 to the French National Assembly dated 24 June 2010; Reform Proposal No 657 to the French Senate dated 9 July 2010. Also, see Hogan Lovells, 'France: Introduction of Class Actions Expected in Early 2014' (Nov 2013) 1.

[8] Inserted in Book IV of the Consumer Code, 14th Parliament (Session of 13 Feb 2014), http://www.assemblee-nationale.fr/14/ta/ta0295.asp. This is the version accessed and cited for the purposes of this chapter.

[9] The Bill was submitted to the French Council of Ministers on 2 May 2013; was adopted by the French National Assembly on 3 July 2013; and then modified by the French Senate on 13 September 2013.

[10] Generic regimes are those which can deal with a range of legal disputes, provided that the procedural requirements for commencing the action are met.

[11] *Ibid*, art 423-1.

[12] *Ibid*, art 423-17. The action must be brought within five years of that decision: art 423-18.

[13] Per the Minister for Social Affairs and Health, Marisol Touraine, when presenting the National Health Strategy on 23 September 2013 ('we will improve collective rights by making way for class actions in the health sector. The prospect of class actions "à la française" will constitute a decisive evolution', as cited in Hogan Lovells, 'Class Actions in the Health Sector: One More Step Forward?' (9 Oct 2013); and supplemented by Benoit Hamon, the Minister for Social and Cooperative Economy and Consumer Affairs, as cited in: Hogan Lovells, 'France: Introduction of Class Actions Expected in Early 2014' (Nov 2013) 2.

[14] French Group Action, art 423-5.

Court on the basis that it was contrary to the French Constitution,[15] and the law could not come into effect until the Court had adjudicated. At the time, commentators suggested that, even if amended in some respects, the law would indeed be promulgated.[16] That optimism proved well-founded, in that the French Constitutional Court approved the constitutionality of the new law on 13 March 2014. It is known as the 'Hamon Law'.[17]

While the newly-proposed French Group Action is not particularly expansive, it does herald a significant reform for the benefit of consumers. However, it contains at least three important restrictions (apart from its sectoral nature). First, it can only be brought by a representative entity,[18] being a nationally-approved consumer association,[19] of which there are fewer than 20 at the time of writing.[20] In that regard, the opt-in and representative nature of the action replicates those which have been previously introduced, in respect of investor[21] and environmental[22] actions. Secondly, as the regime can only relate to compensation for 'pecuniary damage resulting from damage suffered by consumers',[23] certain types of claims which may otherwise arise from breach of legal or contractual obligations cannot be brought. For example, claims for bodily injury arising from alleged medical negligence, product liability and environmental harm will be excluded from its ambit.[24] Thirdly, given that the regime only entitles consumers to give their express mandate for inclusion in the group action, corporate entities that are, say, victims of alleged anti-competitive practices, are excluded.

---

[15] Eg the adversarial principle is breached; the defendants' rights are violated; and the principle of equality of arms is violated, see Hogan Lovells, 'Class Actions Introduced in French Law' (February 2014) 2.

[16] http://www.mwe.com/France-Finally-Embraces-Class-Actions-02-27-2014/.

[17] The 'Loi Hamon', No 2014-344, of 17 March 2014. The law is named after Benoît Hamon, the deputy-Minister for the Social and Mutually-Supportive Economy and Consumer Affairs. For further commentary about the law, at the time of its enactment, see, eg Allen and Overy, 'New Legislation Introducing Group Actions in France' (March 2014) 1.

[18] French Group Action, art 423-1.

[19] These are approved under art 411-1, by the Ministry of Economy and Finance.

[20] Presently, there are 16 such associations eligible to act as representative entity: per McDermott, Will & Emery, 'France Finally Embraces Class Actions', *National L Rev* (28 February 2014); and Clifford Chance, 'Introduction of Class Actions in France' (February 2014, *Briefing Note*) 1.

[21] Per art 452-2 of the Monetary and Financial Code, and discussed in, eg D de Nayves and B Javaux, 'France Chapter', in I Dodds-Smith and A Brown (eds), *Class and Group Actions 2014* (6th ed, ICLG, 2014) [1.1], [1.8].

[22] Per art 142-3 of the Environment Code, cited *ibid*.

[23] French Group Action, art 423-1.

[24] A particular exclusion noted in topical commentary, eg Hogan Lovells, 'France: Introduction of Class Actions Expected in Early 2014' (November 2013) 1.

In that respect, the French Group Action rather resembles the opt-in regime which was implemented in England in 2003, in respect of follow-on actions for anti-competitive conduct,[25] which could only be instituted by the sole 'specified body' approved under that regime, the English Consumers' Association. That follow-on regime has been extensively-criticised for its lack of utility, both for small-and-medium businesses, and more widely.[26] At least the French Group Action has the marked advantage of permitting any one of several consumer organisations to initiate such actions.

The French Group Action contains a two-stage process.[27] The first may conveniently be described as the 'proof-of-liability' stage. The court must decide on individual consumer cases of alleged grievance, which the consumer association (as representative entity) has the task of presenting, and where those individuals have been placed in 'a similar or identical situation'. The court will need to identify the common legal and factual issues arising in those individual cases.[28] The court then defines the consumer group for whom the defendant's liability is engaged, and fixes the criteria which determine the group members' admission to the group.[29] With no minimum number of individual cases prescribed in the French law, it has been suggested that the class may comprise only two consumers.[30] At this first stage, the court will also determine either what level of damage would compensate each consumer (or each category of consumer), or what determinants are needed by which to assess those damages.[31] If the defendant's liability is proven, then in the same decision, the court will order the measures by which consumers will be notified of their rights as potential group members[32] (which measures are to be at the defendant's expense),[33] and it will set a date for consumers to join the group in order to obtain compensation for the damage which they have suffered (which must be a date between 2–6 months after the notice period expires).[34]

---

[25] Contained in s 47B of the Competition Act 1998.

[26] See, for a more detailed discussion of the s 47B regime, eg Mulheron, *Reform of Collective Redress: A Perspective of Need* (Report for the Civil Justice Council, February 2008), Section 8.

[27] Some commentators, however, have described it as a four-stage process, eg Latham and Watkins, 'Introduction of Class Actions in France: A Growing Threat to Professionals?' (25 March 2014) 2–3.

[28] Foreshadowed in, eg de Nayves and Javaux (above n 21) [3.3].

[29] French Group Action, art 423-3.

[30] de Nayves and Javaux (above n 21) [1.5]; Hogan Lovells, 'Class Actions Introduced in French Law' (February 2014) 1.

[31] Eg it has been hypothesised that a court may stipulate, by its judgment, 'the different types of injury and, for each type, the fixed sum to be paid by the [defendant] to the victims': *ibid*, [5.5].

[32] French Group Action, art 423-4.

[33] *Ibid*, art 423-4.

[34] *Ibid*, art 423-5.

The second stage may conveniently be described as the 'implementation' stage. This is where the consumers who fall within the already-defined group come forward to claim under the 'opt-in' procedure, and where the defendant trader must compensate each consumer for the damage suffered within the terms and conditions set by the court at the first stage.[35] Those damages may be paid directly by the defendant to the group members, or via the representative entity.[36] In the latter scenario, the group members, in coming forward, mandate that the consumer association receives compensation on the group's behalf. The compensation payment is to be paid into a deposit account,[37] which cannot be debited except for payment of sums to those injured parties.[38] Any difficulties raised during the implementation of the judgment will be ruled upon at this stage, by the same judge who ruled on liability.[39]

There is also a so-called 'simplified procedure' which applies 'where the identity and the number of injured consumers are known, and when those consumers have been harmed in the same amount, in respect of the same service, and by reference to the same period or duration'.[40] In that scenario, the court may order that the defendant compensate those consumers directly and individually, under specified terms. However, it is also an opt-in system, in that the court must provide information to the consumers affected by the defendant's breach, and thereafter the consumer must agree to be paid by the defendant (ie, take a positive step to agree to be bound), within the terms set in the court's decision.[41] As noted elsewhere, '[t]his simplified procedure is therefore not an opt-out procedure, but a specific and unique opt-in procedure'.[42] It is probably best-suited to the repayment of uniform overcharge-of-fees scenarios[43] (eg, the type of dispute which England witnessed in respect of allegedly-improper bank fees charged to several bank customers, some years ago).[44]

---

[35] *Ibid*, art 423-11.
[36] *Ibid*, art 423-5.
[37] At the Caisse des Depots et Consignations.
[38] French Group Action, art 423-6.
[39] *Ibid*, art 423-12.
[40] *Ibid*, art 423-10.
[41] *Ibid*, art 423-10.
[42] McDermott, Will & Emery, 'France Finally Embraces a Class Action', *National L Rev* (28 February 2014) 2.
[43] Hogan Lovells, 'France: Introduction of Class Actions Expected in Early 2014' (November 2013) 2.
[44] As outlined, eg in R Mulheron, 'Disgruntled Customers and Bank Charges: Class Actions (Reform) Activity' in S Grundmann and Y Atamer (eds), *Financial Services, Financial Crisis and General European Contract Law* (Wolters Kluwer, 2011), ch 11, 279; and R Mulheron, *Reform of Collective Redress in England and Wales: A Perspective of Need* (Research Paper for the CJC) (February 2008), Section 17.

B. The UK Proposal

Meanwhile, the UK legislature has recently debated the introduction of a collective proceedings regime for competition law grievances. Here, again it is a sectoral, and not a generic, regime.

The relevant proposal is contained in Schedule 8 of the Consumer Rights Bill 2013–14, and is entitled, 'Private Actions in Competition Law'[45] ('the UK Competition Class Action'). The reform proposal followed from the Government's 2012 consultation on private actions in competition law.[46] The Bill had its First Reading in the House of Commons on 23 January 2014.[47] The relevant Rules of Court have been drafted.[48] At the time of writing, the Bill has passed through both Houses of Commons and Lords, and although the relevant provisions in Schedule 8 were not the subject of disagreement between those Houses during debate, other provisions of the Consumer Rights Bill will require further debate before the Bill, as a whole, can be passed into law.

Unlike the French law, the UK regime will adopt an opt-in or opt-out approach for the formation of the class, depending upon judicial choice.[49] The claims will be heard exclusively by the Competition Appeal Tribunal (CAT). The regime is proposed to cover civil proceedings brought in any part of the United Kingdom.[50]

In fact, the current reform proposal in Schedule 8 of the Consumer Rights Bill, regarding a class action for competition law infringements, is the second time in four years that a sectoral class action has been considered by the UK Parliament. The previous attempt – which concerned a collective action for 'financial services claims'[51] – was a casualty of the legislative 'wash-up' which followed the calling of the General Election in 2010.[52]

---

[45] The relevant provisions will be inserted in the Competition Act 1998 and the Enterprise Act 2002.

[46] The reform was promulgated by the Department of Business, Innovation and Skills (BIS), via the consultation, *Private Actions in Competition Law: A Consultation on Options for Reform* (April 2012). The *Government Response* on this important consultation was published on 29 January 2013.

[47] See, for history and progress of the Bill, the discussion on the relevant Parliamentary website: http://services.parliament.uk/bills/2013-14/consumerrights.html.

[48] Prepared pursuant to s 15B(1) of the Enterprise Act 2002, as inserted by Sch 8 of the Consumer Rights Bill 2013–14, and are available at http://www.catribunal.org.uk/247-8406/Draft-Tribunal-Rules-on-Collective-Actions.html. The draft rules will be subject to a formal consultation in the near future.

[49] Sch 8, s 47B(7)(c).

[50] Sch 8, s 47A(2).

[51] Contained in cll 18–25 of the Financial Services Bill 2010 (Bill 51 09–10) ('FSB'). The rest of the Bill progressed through wash-up, and achieved Royal Assent on 8 April 2010: Financial Services Act 2010, c 28.

[52] See, further R Mulheron, 'Recent Milestones in Class Actions Reform in England: A Critique and a Proposal' (2011) 127 *Law Quarterly Rev* 288.

A relevant time-line of collective redress-related reform in England and Wales is shown below, for convenience:

– **Dec 2008** Civil Justice Council, *Improving Access to Justice Through Collective Actions: Developing a More Efficient and Effective Procedure for Collective Actions: Final Report* (A Series of Recommendations to the Lord Chancellor) and draft legislation, based upon a series of 'evidence of need' factors (sourced from the author's legal and empirical study undertaken for the CJC, *Reform of Collective Redress: A Perspective of Need*, February 2008).

– **Jul 2009** MOJ, *The Government's Response to the Civil Justice Council's Report: "Improving Access to Justice through Collective Actions"* – no generic regime, but sectoral permissible where need demonstrated.

– **Jul 2009** HM Treasury, *Reforming Financial Markets* – recommended a new collective redress regime.

– **19 Nov 2009** Presentation of Financial Services Bill 2009 to Parliament, with cll 18–25 containing the provisions regarding 'collective proceedings' for 'financial services claims' (with a CJC/MOJ Working Party formed to draft a new CPR Pt 19.IV to underpin the proposed regime).

– **Apr 2010** Relevant parts of FSB, containing the collective proceedings, were 'washed up', when the General Election was called.

– **Apr 2012** BIS, *Private Actions in Competition Law: A Consultation on Options for Reform*.

– **29 Jan 2013** *Actions in Competition Law: A Consultation on Options for Reform: Govt Response*.

– **1 Apr 2013** The Damages-based Agreements Regulations 2013 came into force, the DBA Regs 2010 were repealed, and the definition of a 'damages-based agreement' in s 58AA of the CLSA 1990 was amended. Contingency fees will be expressly prohibited for opt-out collective proceedings under the UK Competition Class Action (per Sch 8, s 47C(8)).

– **11 Jun 2013** The EC published a series of common, non-binding principles for collective actions, via its *Recommendation on Common Principles for Injunctive and Compensatory Collective Redress Mechanisms in the Member States Concerning Violations of Rights Granted under Union Law*.

– 23 Jan 2014   Consumer Rights Bill, Sch 8, *'Private Actions in Competition Law'*, introduced into Parliament (House of Commons).
– 10 Mar 2014   *Draft Tribunal Rules* published on the CAT website, prepared for collective proceedings and collective settlements in the CAT and to underpin the Sch 8 regime once enacted, and subject to forthcoming public consultation.
– as at 13 Jan 2015   The Consumer Rights Bill is at the 'ping pong' stage, having passed through both Houses of Parliament.

Indeed, prior to that financial services reform proposal in 2010, the English reform landscape had been almost as stultified as the French experience. There had been a number of proposals for collective redress reform, dating back to 1995, but all had recommended an opt-in model.[53] The path of opt-out reform really started its course in the UK with the publication of the CJC's seminal report of December 2008, and the momentum of that reform has continued throughout the intervening period, albeit with some 'rocky' moments brought about by timing issues and a divergent political will across different sectors at times.

Of course, the opt-out approach which is possible under the UK Competition Class Action renders it quite disparate from the French Group Action. Also, under the proposed UK regime, the action may be instituted by either a directly-affected class member, or by an ideological claimant.[54] In that regard too, it differs from the French Group Action significantly.

Where an opt-out regime is authorised by the CAT, then aggregate damages are permitted;[55] and in the case of a judgment, any unclaimed damages are to be paid to the Access to Justice Foundation.[56] By contrast, where an opt-out collective proceedings is settled on the basis that its terms are 'just and reasonable'[57] (with a certification order having previously been

---

[53] *Viz* Law Society Civil Litigation Committee, *Group Actions Made Easier* (1995), which proposed an opt-in rule of 14 parts; Lord Chancellor's Dept (LCD), *Proposed New Procedures for Multi-Party Situations: Consultation Paper* (1997); and the subsequent *Draft Rules and Practice Direction* (1999); LCD, *Representative Claims: Proposed New Procedures: Consultation Paper* (2001), and *Consultation Response* (2002), all discussed further in R Mulheron, *The Class Action in Common Law Legal Systems: A Comparative Perspective* (Hart Publishing, Oxford, 2004) 94–97.

[54] Sch 8, s 47B(8), as amended by the Public Bills Committee (Commons), dated 6 March 2014.

[55] Sch 8, s 47C(2).

[56] Sch 8, s 47C(5), referring to the fund established by s 194(8) of the Legal Services Act 2007 (and described in R Mulheron, *Costs and Funding of Collective Actions: Realities and Possibilities* (Research Paper for the European Consumers' Organisation, BEUC), Section 23), and subject to s 47C(6).

[57] Sch 8, s 49A(5).

made[58]), then the unclaimed damages sum can be paid to any destination which forms part of the judicially-approved settlement (including *cy-près* distributions, reversion to the defendant, or other destination). This differential treatment of the unclaimed sum, as between a judgment and settlement, was a deliberate Government decision.[59] The Government also provided some guidance that, in any judicially-approved settlement, certification would not require satisfaction of the superiority or merits tests, given that the settlement was consensual.[60] There is also a rather extraordinary provision in the Bill, whereby a collective settlement may be judicially approved but where a collective proceedings certification order has not previously been made (ie, because no representative claimant has instituted an action at all).[61]

III. A COMPARISON OF KEY DESIGN ISSUES

As the author has detailed elsewhere,[62] the design framework of a collective action potentially entails the consideration of at least 60 separate issues, whether statutorily or judicially. It is a complex and divisive issue. The three recent reform proposals being considered herein can conveniently be contrasted, on several points relating to class actions design, as Table 1 demonstrates:

TABLE 1 Class action design features: a comparative perspective

The design feature	EC Recommendation	French Group Action	UK Competition Class Action
standing to sue:	a representative entity, an *ad hoc* certified entity, or a public authority	an approved national consumer representative entity	an *ad hoc* representative entity or a directly-affected class member (Sch 8, s 47B(8))
type of dispute covered by the regime:	generic – any 'mass harm situation', where two persons	Wide, but sectoral – applies to 'consumer grievances' re sale	sectoral only – re anti-competitive conduct, and covering

---

[58] Sch 8, s 49A(1).
[59] *Private Actions in Competition Law: Government Response* (2012) [5.64]–[5.65], [5.70].
[60] *Ibid*, [6.22]. This relaxation for settlement-only classes is typical of North American jurisdictions too, as discussed, eg in Mulheron (above n 53) 390–95.
[61] Sch 8, s 49B.
[62] R Mulheron, 'Building Blocks and Design Points for an Opt-Out Class Action' [2008] *J of Personal Injury Law* 308, 317–323. This drew upon the author's more detailed study undertaken in Mulheron (above n 53) Parts II and III.

TABLE 1 continued

The design feature	EC Recommendation	French Group Action	UK Competition Class Action
	(legal or corporate) have allegedly suffered damage	of goods or provision of services; or from anti-competitive conduct (Article 423-1)	any action which is stand-alone (re an *alleged* infringement) or a follow-on (re a *proven* infringement), either under the Competition Act 1998 or Article 101(1) or 102 of the EU Treaty
type of class member:	natural or corporate persons	individual consumers (natural persons only)	natural or corporate persons
opt-in or opt-out:	opt-in – with opt-out only 'exceptional'	opt-in only	opt-in or opt-out, depending upon judicial discretion
type of damage recoverable:	compensatory damages (unrestricted)	pecuniary damages only (Article 423-1)[63] (i.e., no damages for personal, physical or psychiatric injury permitted)	compensatory damages (unrestricted)
is certification required?	yes – 'for verification at the earliest possible stage of litigation' (Article 8)	yes – under the first stage of the regime (Article 423-3)	yes – necessary for the CAT to make a collective proceedings order
aggregate assessment:	none specified	none specified	yes – damages can be awarded 'without undertaking an assessment of the amount of damages recoverable in respect of the claim of each represented person' (s 47C(2))
res judicata effect:	none specified	yes – for any group member whose injury was remedied (whether by judgment,	yes – 'binding on all represented persons, except as otherwise specified', in respect of

---

[63] Those damages may be paid directly by the defendant, or through the consumer's association, or via a legal professional who represents the association for the purposes of obtaining such compensation: arts 423-5–423-9.

TABLE 1 *continued*

The design feature	EC Recommendation	French Group Action	UK Competition Class Action
		simplified procedure, or settlement) (Article 423–21)	judgment or settlement (Sch 8, s 47B(12) and s 49A(9))
exemplary damages:	no – would 'lead to overcompensation in favour of the claimant party' (Article 31)	not specified – but punitive damages are permitted in very limited circumstances in French law[64]	No – expressly prohibited for collective proceedings (Sch 8, s 47C(1))
third party funding:	permitted, but tightly controlled; and a stay of proceedings ordered in certain eventualities	not specified	not referred to, and hence, not prohibited (unlike lawyers' contingency fees, below)
lawyers' contingency fees:	yes, but only where 'appropriate national regulation of those fees in collective redress cases' occurs (Article 30)	not specified	percentage contingency fees (damages-based agreements) expressly prohibited, for opt-out collective proceedings (Sch 8, s 47C(8))
notice of funding arrangements to the court:	yes, 'at the outset of the proceedings' (Article 14)	not specified	not specified
relevant costs rules:	costs-shifting (ie, the 'loser-pays principle'), subject to national laws (Article 13)	costs-shifting[65] (the judge may order that the defendant make payment to the representative entity for its expenses) (Article 423–8)	costs-shifting (CAT r 26(1))

---

[64] D Fairgrieve, 'The Human Rights Act 1998, Damages and Tort Law' [2001] *Public Law* 695, 704–5 ('Non-compensatory damages are *prima facie* contrary to the underlying principles of *responsabilité administrative*. But principle and practice diverge. The lower courts' "sovereign power of assessment" in awarding damages provides a veil behind which, as in French civil law, a punitive element for egregious fault may be included': citations omitted); D de Nayves and B Javaux, 'France Chapter', in I Dodds-Smith and A Brown (eds), *Class and Group Actions 2014* (6th edn, ICLG, 2014) [5.3], http://www.iclg.co.uk/practice-areas/class-and-group-actions/class-&-group-actions-2014#jurisdictions.

[65] Per art 696 of the French Civil Procedure Code (costs 'shall be borne by the losing party'), subject to judicial discretion to order otherwise, noted *ibid*, [6.1].

TABLE 1 continued

The design feature	EC Recommendation	French Group Action	UK Competition Class Action
settlement:	permitted and 'encouraged' – but the 'legality of the binding outcome of a collective settlement should be verified by the courts' (Articles 25 and 27)	permitted – the consumer association may enter a mediation as representative claimant (Article 423-15), but the outcome must be judicially approved (Article 423-16)	permitted – both where a collective proceedings order has, and has not, been made (CAT rr 22–23, and 24–25, respectively)
national registry of class actions:	yes, to be established by each Member State, 'through electronic means' (Articles 35–36)	not specified	not specified
cross-border cases:	yes – representative entity can represent 'natural or legal persons from several Member States', but only where that entity is designated by their Member State as being able to seize the jurisdiction (Article 17)	not specified	for any class member not domiciled in the UK at the specified date, that party must opt-in to opt-out collective proceedings, in order to be included in that collective proceeding (Sch 8, s 47B(11)(b))
the relevant court:	not specified	any civil court (*tribunaux de grande instance*)	only the CAT
suspension of limitation periods for individual actions:	yes – 'from the moment the parties agree to attempt to resolve the dispute by [ADR]' (Article 27)	yes – suspended when the consumer association brings the action, and starts running again from a point at least six months after any appeal expires (Article 423-20)	yes – different limitation periods apply, depending upon whether the claim arose prior to, or after, the new regime taking effect

IV. CERTIFICATION: THE DEVIL IN THE DETAIL

Neither the French nor the UK legislators, nor the Commission itself, endorsed the notion (as practised elsewhere)[66] that a class action should

---

[66] Eg under Pt IVA of Australia's federal class action, per ss 33C and 33N(1).

proceed until a defendant challenged its suitability in representative form and sought to bring the action to a halt. Indeed, quite the reverse: certification is mandatory.

In this author's view, this strategic design factor was entirely correct. Indeed, there were three separate advantages to certification which were outlined by the Civil Justice Council,[67] in forming its recommendation for generic opt-out reform for England and Wales.

First, it would ensure that the court could 'assess and decide on the most appropriate mechanism through which a claim should progress', when a number of various procedural tools are available in the jurisdiction. In that way, it would 'act as a diligent gatekeeper at the outset of the action'. The UK Government has also noted, more recently, that certification is vital 'to prevent unsuitable cases taking up time in the courts',[68] given that judicial efficiency should be enhanced, and not damaged, by the introduction of a new procedural regime.

Secondly, in a wider context, certification would ensure that any extra-judicial, out-of-court regimes would also be considered, for the dispute, in order to ensure that the use of court resources was the most appropriate for its resolution.

Thirdly, certification would best facilitate 'effective access to justice for both claimants and defendants alike. … Absent an express certification process, the risk will arise, as was the experience in Australia, that a *de facto* certification process will develop through defendants issuing a large number of interim applications challenging the legitimacy of any individual claim proceeding on a collective basis. The possibility of such large scale procedural skirmishing must be avoided in any reformed process.'[69]

The 2013 Recommendation states no conditions for certification, other than that the case should not be 'manifestly unfounded'.[70] The certification matrix for the French Group Action remains quite light-handed at this juncture, and as remarked elsewhere,[71] the conditions to institute a group action will require clarification. The certification criteria for the UK Competition Class Action, on the other hand, are very detailed – arguably more extensive than those which exist in the longstanding opt-out regimes elsewhere in the common law world.[72] This is a particular instance in which the law-makers

---

[67] *Improving Access to Justice through Collective Actions* (2008), 151, and Recommendation point 4.//
[68] BIS, *Private Actions in Competition Law* (2012) [A.3]; and *Government Response* (2013) [5.35]–[5.37].//
[69] CJC, *Improving Access to Justice through Collective Actions* (2008) 152–153; and Mulheron (above n 53) 23–29.//
[70] Recommendation, point 8.//
[71] Hogan Lovells, 'Class Actions Introduced in French Law' (February 2014) 2.//
[72] For a detailed comparative legal analysis and case authorities re relevant certification criteria, see Mulheron (above n 53) Pt II, chh 5–8.

responsible for the UK regime have been willing and able to learn from the jurisprudence which has emanated in other common law class actions jurisdictions.

Table 2 sets out the comparative certification criteria proposed by the French and UK law-makers (except for those relating to the representative claimant, which are dealt with further below).[73]

TABLE 2 Comparative certification criteria

Certification criterion	French Group Action	UK Competition Class Action
commonality	group members must have been placed 'in a similar or identical situation', regarding a failure of a defendant of a professional or legal obligation (Article 423–1)	class members must have claims that 'raise common issues' (CAT r 7(1)(b)), where 'common issues' means 'the same, similar or related issues of fact or law' (CAT r 1(2)(j), Sch 8 s 47B(6))
superiority to other means of resolving the dispute	N/A	it must be 'an appropriate means for the fair and efficient resolution of the common issues' (CAT r 7(2)(a)) CAT must take into account 'the availability of ADR and any other means of resolving the dispute' (CAT r 7(2)(g))
minimum numerosity	not specified, except for 'individual cases', hence presumably at least two cases are required (Article 423–3)	none specified – but there must be 'an identifiable class of persons' (CAT r 7(1)(a)); plus CAT is required to consider 'the size of the class' (CAT r 7(2)(d))
preliminary merits	N/A	the representative claimant 'believes that the claims … have a real prospect of success' (CAT r 3(2)(h)) when deciding between opt-in and opt-out, CAT shall consider 'the strength of the claims' (CAT r 7(3)(a))
cost–benefit criterion	N/A	CAT will take into account 'the costs and the benefits of continuing the collective proceedings' (CAT r 7(2)(b)

---

[73] See Table 3.

TABLE 2 *continued*

Certification criterion	French Group Action	UK Competition Class Action
an adequate class definition	the court must define the group of consumers to whom the defendant is liable, and the criteria for group membership (Article 423-3)	CAT must be satisfied that the claims sought to be included in the collective proceedings 'are brought on behalf of an identifiable class of persons' (CAT r 7(1)(a))
need	N/A	CAT must take into account 'whether any separate proceedings making claims of the same or a similar nature have already been commenced by members of the class' (CAT r 7(2)(c))
general suitability	N/A	class members' claims must be 'suitable to be brought in collective proceedings' (Sch 8 s 47B(6)) CAT must consider 'whether it is possible to determine for any person whether he is or is not a member of the class' (CAT r 7(2)(e)) CAT must take into account 'whether the claims are suitable for an aggregate award of damages' (CAT r 7(2)(f)) when deciding between opt-in and opt-out, the CAT must consider 'the estimated amount of damages that individual class members may recover' (CAT r 7(3)(b))

The importance of certification cannot be overstated. For example, the Canadian regime has followed the lead of the US litigation, in which the certification hearing has become the 'chief battleground' of class actions disputes, with one court remarking that an 'unintended consequence' of the class actions statutes was to transform certification "from preliminary step to battleground; in some senses, the certification proceeding is the trial",[74] whilst another has noted that, "[a]s a practical matter, the effect of a denial of certification will often terminate the proceeding."[75] It is predictable that a similar pattern will follow, under the French and UK regimes.

---

[74] *Consumers' Assn of Canada v Coca-Cola Bottling Co* [2006] BCSC 863, [35], citing: *Gariepy v Shell Oil Co* (2002), 23 CPC (5th) 393, [5].

[75] *Stewart v General Motors of Canada Ltd* (Ont SCJ, 8 June 2007) [3].

In addition to the certification criteria described above, both regimes provide detail as to which party may commence the respective collective actions. From a design point of view, there are three options for the conferral of standing: to permit only a directly-affected class member to initiate the action on behalf of the class members; to permit the so-called 'ideological claimant' (ie, one who does not have a direct cause of action against the defendant/s itself, but which can adequately represent the class members) to commence proceedings on behalf of the class; or to permit both to have standing to sue under the regime. At its broadest, an ideological claimant can be one of three types: (i) an entity which fits the requirements of an 'adequate representative' for the case at hand (the '*ad hoc* ideological claimant'); (ii) a body which is specified under a legislative instrument as being an appropriate body to bring such a claim (the 'designated ideological claimant'); or (iii) a recognised public authority (such as a national competition authority).

The UK regime permits the widest possible standing to sue, in that a representative claimant can be either a representative entity or a class member.[76] On the other hand, the EC Recommendation and the French Group Action do not endorse the notion of directly-affected class members commencing collective actions, but favour the ideological claimant as having the exclusive capacity to sue.

Interestingly, while all three types of ideological claimant are provided for in the EC Recommendation which proposes the horizontal implementation of collective redress regimes in Member States,[77] neither the French nor the UK regimes goes nearly so far. The French Group Action opts only for the designated ideological claimant (specifying[78] that it must be an approved consumer representative entity). The UK Competition Class Action, on the other hand, prefers the *ad hoc* representative (which, presumably, could be either an entity or an individual),[79] whereby the CAT must assess whether to authorise that entity or person to act as a representative for the action.[80]

Table 3 sets out the criteria which apply to the representative claimant at certification, under the French and UK regimes. Given that the latter endorses an *ad hoc* ideological claimant, it necessarily follows that far more criteria must be stipulated under that regime.

---

[76] Sch 8, s 47B(8)).
[77] See the definition of 'representative action' in art 3(d), and the further provision in arts 6 and 7.
[78] Per art. 423-1.
[79] Section 47B(8).
[80] Per the proposed provision in the Enterprise Act 2002, s 15B(2)(c).

TABLE 3 Comparative certification criteria for the representative claimant

The criterion	French Group Action	UK Competition Class Action
adequacy of the representative:	not relevant – given that a national consumer association must have been pre-approved under Article 411-1, thereby pre-determining adequacy	it is 'just and reasonable for that person to act as a class representative' (CAT r 6(1)(b), Sch 8 s 47B(8)(b)) – and it would 'fairly and adequately act in the interests of the class members' (CAT r 6(2)(a))
financial adequacy of the representative:	not specified	the representative 'will be able to pay the defendant's recoverable costs if ordered to do so' (CAT r 6(2)(d)); and will be able to satisfy any cross-undertaking in damages, required by the CAT, where an interim injunction is sought (CAT r 6(2)(e)); and must also give an 'estimate of and/or details of arrangements as to costs, fees and disbursements' which the CAT orders that the representative must provide (CAT r 6(3)(d))
an absence of conflicts of interest:	not specified	the representative 'does not have, in relation to the common issues for the class members, a material interest that is in conflict with the interests of class members' (CAT r 6(2)(b))
veracity:	not specified	the contents of the collective proceedings claim form 'shall be verified by a statement of truth signed and dated by the proposed class representative or … his legal representative' (CAT r 3(3))
pre-existence:	the entity must be pre-designated under Article 411–1	CAT will consider whether the representative is 'a pre-existing body, and the nature and functions of that body' (CAT r 6(3)(b))
a plan:	not specified	the representative must have 'a plan for the collective proceedings', including a method for notifying the class members of their progress, and 'a procedure for governance and consultation which takes into account the size and nature of the class' (CAT r 6(3)(c))

V. CONCLUSION

The prospective changes in class actions law are being keenly observed by consumer associations in both France[81] and in England.[82] A time of fundamental change in civil litigation, and an evolution in the way in which group grievances are addressed, lie ahead.

The way in which the opt-in model operates in France will undoubtedly be closely observed by reformers in other European Member States, given the EC's preference for such a model. The UK legislature has justifiably departed from that preference, for legal, historical and cultural reasons, and its operation will provide much debate for EC policy-makers as to whether the EC's strongly-stated preference was, indeed, justified. It is intended that Member States will implement the principles in the Recommendation, via national collective redress systems, by 26 July 2015,[83] and that the Commission will assess the implementation of its Recommendation, 'on the basis of practical experience', by 26 July 2017.[84]

However, policy-makers and legislatures can only achieve so much. It will be the task of both litigants and courts to render the French and UK reforms workable and fair. The divergent paths which each jurisdiction has chosen to take, in order to implement significant legal change, will make for a rich and fascinating landscape.

---

[81] Eg 'UFC, one of the most important consumer associations that has been approved by the government to introduce group actions, has already declared that several group actions are ready to be filed and that it is simply waiting for the promulgation of the law to introduce them': McDermott, Will & Emery, 'France Finally Embraces a Class Action', *National L Rev* (28 February 2014) 2.

[82] The Association was a respondent to the Government's consultation on *Private Actions in Competition Law* (2012) (above n 59).

[83] EC Recommendation, point 38.

[84] *Ibid*, point 41. The Member States are to communicate 'reliable annual statistics' to the Commission by 26 July 2016.

Class Actions – Some Reflections from a European Perspective

*Georg E. Kodek**

I. INTRODUCTION

The Recommendation on Collective Redress recently issued by the European Commission (EC) has given new impetus to the discussion on collective redress.[1] While clearly intended to encourage Member States to introduce some form of collective redress, this document ironically reflects in large measure the traditional concerns raised against collective redress which have been voiced in the discussion on collective redress in continental Europe for the past 10 years. Thus, the Recommendation tells us in some detail what a future group proceeding is not going to look like. For example, there are to be no contingency fees;[2] the Recommendation states that lawyers' remuneration shall not create an incentive to litigation 'that is unnecessary from the point of view of the interest of the parties.'[3] Furthermore, there are to be no punitive damages,[4] and it is prohibited to base remuneration to the fund

---

* Judge on the Austrian Supreme Court and Professor of Civil and Commercial Law at WU, the Vienna University of Economics and Business.
[1] See European Commission Recommendation of 11 June 2013 on common principles for injunctive and compensatory collective redress mechanisms in the Member States concerning violations of rights granted under Union Law (2013/396/EU). See also Statement of the European Law Institute on Collective Redress and Competition Damages Claims (2014); A Bruns, 'Einheitlicher kollektiver Rechtsschutz in Europa', 125 *Zeitschrift für Zivilprozess* (2012) 399 with further references; H Willems, in C Brömmelmeyer (ed.), *Die EU-Sammelklage, – Status und Perspektiven* (Frankfurter Institut für das Recht der Europäischen Union, 2013) 17; WH van Boom and G Wagner (eds.), *Mass Torts in Europe: Cases and Reflections* (de Gruyter, 2014); DR Hensler, C Hodges and IN Tzankova (eds.), *Class Actions in Context* (Edward Elgar Publishers, 2014). See also C Hodges, *The Reform of Class and Representative Actions in European Legal Systems* (Hart Publishing, 2008) 70–76; A Stadler, 'Group Actions as a Remedy to Enforce Consumer Interests', in F Cafaggi and HW Micklitz (eds.), *New Frontiers of Consumer Protection – Interplay between Private and Public Enforcement* (Intersentia, 2009) 305, at 325–27.
[2] Para 30 of the Recommendation.
[3] *Ibid*, para 29.
[4] *Ibid*, para 31.

provider on the amount of the settlement reached or the compensation awarded.[5]

The author of this chapter was a member of a working group which devised a new group litigation proceeding in Austria in 2007.[6] The scope of this chapter, however, is not limited to, nor indeed focused on, Austria. Nor does it attempt to provide a comprehensive analysis of the extensive discussion on collective proceedings throughout Europe.[7] Rather, its aim is more limited. It will briefly discuss the main concerns of the introduction of such a scheme in Europe. While many of these concerns are not specifically directed against class actions as such, but rather against the US legal system as a whole, some concerns affect the ongoing opt-in versus opt-out debate. These concerns are addressed in more detail, with special emphasis on possible limits the European Convention on Human Rights (ECHR) may impose on a collective proceedings mechanism. A final section will seek to explore a possible middle ground between the opt-in and opt out-models.

II. THE IMPORTANCE OF THE LEGAL FRAMEWORK

It has long been recognized that when facing new challenges, the development of the law may greatly benefit from an examination of other legal systems.[8] Yet, the solutions found in these systems often are embedded in an

---

[5] *Ibid*, para 32.

[6] This draft (which was to become the Austrian Civil Procedure Reform Act of 2007) was never enacted. While the government announced its intention to introduce a group proceeding mechanism, the proposal was met with severe resistance from the chamber of commerce. This, together with meager support of the initiative on part of the government parties, ultimately prevented the introduction of the procedure. For a discussion of the draft see G Kodek, *Die Gruppenklage nach der ZVN 2007* (Recht der Wirtschaft 2007) 722. For the discussion preceding the formation of the working group see G Kodek, Gesetzliche Möglichkeiten zur Regelung von Massenverfahren, in BMSG (ed.), *Massenverfahren – Reformbedarf für die ZPO, Wilhelminenberg Gespräche* VI (2005) 311; G Kodek, *Möglichkeiten zur gesetzlichen Regelung von Massenverfahren im Zivilprozess* (Ecolex 2005) 751; G Kodek, Massenverfahren – Reformbedarf für die ZPO, *AnwBl* (2006) 72; G Kodek, 'Collective Redress in Austria', in R Hensler, C Hodges and M Tulibacka, 'The Globalization of Class Actions' 622 *Annals of the American Academy of Political and Social Sciences* (2009) 86; G Kodek, Massenverfahren und Verfahrensmassen: Einige Gedanken zur aktuellen Diskussion, 132 *Zak* (2012) 66.

[7] The British Institute of International and Comparative Law website on Collective Redress (funded by the Civil Justice Programme of the European Union) includes overviews of the relevant national systems, with regular updates on reforms: www.collectiveredress.org.

[8] On the importance of a comparative approach in this context see TD Rowe, 'Debates over Group Litigation in Comparative Perspective: What Can We Learn From Each Other?' 11 *Duke J Comp & Int'l L* (2001) 157.

entirely different (factual and legal) framework.[9] Therefore, when comparing mechanisms of different foreign systems with our own, the differences between the systems always have to be taken into account. Due to these differences, foreign solutions may serve as inspiration, but often cannot be simply copied on a one-to-one basis. One example illustrating this difficulty is the common law doctrine of *stare decisis*. Because of this principle of binding precedents, a judgment in a test or pilot proceeding will, at least from a theoretical point of view, be far more important than in continental Europe where prior court decisions, while clearly often followed in practice, are not technically binding.

Another example are different concepts of *res judicata* in this context. If *res judicata* extends to preliminary questions, such as under the concept of issue preclusion, and is not necessarily limited to the parties of the case (non-mutual estoppel), this seems to open ways to deal with mass damages or similar problems in a way totally unthinkable in many continental European countries. Also, the American class action cannot be discussed adequately without a discussion of contingency fees which provide an incentive for lawyers to take up proceedings of this kind.

Nonetheless, an examination of the US system of class actions is valuable in many respects. Such an examination shows that, because of the different legal framework, many problems likely to be encountered in Europe do not arise in the US. These differences militate against a transfer of the US class action model to Europe. Two examples illustrate this point: First, American procedural law facilitates class action proceedings because the availability of contingency fees is a powerful incentive for lawyers to organize and fund such proceedings. A legal system which – for good cause – does not want to allow contingency fees will have to introduce other solutions for the funding of such type of proceedings.

Another aspect is the summary determination of the amount of damages in class action proceedings. Here, of course, one has to take into account that most proceedings are disposed of by way of settlement, not by way of judgment. Often the problem of individual compensation is shifted into a post-settlement proceeding. This solution, however, seems problematic in light of Article 6 of the ECHR if the settlement is to include persons who did not actively consent to the settlement. Also, it has to be pointed out that in the US, due to the often quite generous awards, the 'cake' is big enough to leave room for negotiations about the distribution. If in a group proceeding only the aggregate amount of actual losses suffered by the members of the group

---

[9] Valuable insights on the importance of the legal framework and the possibility of a class action outside the US are offered in PH Lindblom, 'Group Actions: A Study of the Anglo-American Class Action Suit from a Swedish Perspective' 3 *Group Actions and Consumer Protection* (1992) 15–6.

is awarded, the question of distribution becomes more critical if certain members of the group want to avoid remaining undercompensated and, thus, in spite of the group litigation being successful, have to bear a part of their loss themselves. Therefore, the fair and efficient determination of quantum (of damages) presents a particular challenge in devising rules for a group proceeding.

III. SOME ARGUMENTS AGAINST CLASS ACTIONS

The US type class action is often viewed with skepticism in Europe.[10] However, often this criticism does not distinguish between general reservations against the US legal system and specific problems of class actions. Examples include the (in the eyes of critics) sometimes far-reaching exercise of international jurisdiction by US courts, the excesses of discovery proceedings, grossly inflated verdicts and the availability of punitive damages. Also, contingency fees are abhorred by many European observers. Yet all these points of criticism do not address specific defects of class action proceedings, even if the high awards expected, be it compensatory or punitive damages, clearly make the US an attractive forum for plaintiffs.[11] Due to the American rule on costs, a class action is an ideal device to exercise pressure on a defendant in order to bring about a favourable settlement.[12]

---

[10] C Hodges, 'Multi-Party Actions: A European Approach' 11 *Duke J Comp & Int'l L* (2000) 321: 'Europe neither needs nor wants US-style class action litigation'. See also M Taruffo, 'Some Remarks on Group Litigation in Comparative Perspective' 11 *Duke J Comp & Int'l L* (2001) 405: 'The European rejection of class actions – essentially based on ignorance – has usually been justified by the necessity of preventing such a monster from penetrating the quiet European legal gardens.' Another question is the recognition of US class action judgments on the basis of current law. Here, some authors argue that the test should be whether the rights of the absent members of the class were adequately represented (see B Hess, 'Die Anerkennung eines Class Action Settlement in Deutschland' 55 *Juristen Zeitung* (2000) 373; F Stein and J Martin, *Kommentar zur Zivilprozeßordnung* (21st ed. Mohr Siebeck, 1993) § 328 para. 141. This, however, is highly controversial. Some authors take the view that such judgments could not be recognized in Germany at all (R Mann, 'Die Anerkennungsfähigkeit von US-amerikanischen "Class-action"-Urteilen', *Neue Juristische Wochenschrift* (1994) 1187).

[11] This aspect is graphically illustrated by Lord Denning, Master of the Rolls, in *Smith Kline & French Laboratories Ltd v Bloch*, 2 All ER 72 (1983): "As a moth is drawn to the light, so is a litigant drawn to the United States."

[12] See eg LA Bebchuk, 'Suing Solely to Extract a Settlement Offer', 17 *JLStud* (1988) 437; JM Landers, 'Of Legalized Blackmail and Legalized Theft: Consumer Class Actions and the Substance-Procedure Dilemma', 47 *S Cal L Rev* (1974) 842. See also HB Schäfer, 'Anreizwirkungen bei der Class Action und der Verbandsklage', in J Basedow, KJ Hopt, H Kötz and D Baetge, *Die Bündelung gleichgerichteter Interessen im Prozeß* (Tübingen, 1999) 67 (68, 71: *Beutetheorie* = theory of prey).

These points of criticism, however, do not support a rejection of group actions altogether, since such a procedure would be part of a totally different substantive and procedural framework in Europe. If one leaves the above-mentioned points of criticism aside, the main argument against an introduction of group proceedings is the opt-out system which subjects all members of the class, regardless of whether they took part in the proceeding, to the outcome of the proceeding. By allocating the procedural burden of opting-out to the members of the class, this system was criticized as a 'forced community' (*Zwangsgemeinschaft*) of the members of the class. This is problematic not only from the point of view of the right to be heard, as it may also pose problems in light of the rule of law in some countries. In an international context, these objections are aggravated if foreign class members without any relation to the US are subjected to the jurisdiction of US courts.

On a different level, the concept of opt-out class actions may also be criticized because it violates the principle of party autonomy (*Dispositionsgrundsatz*),[13] the procedural law maxim that it is the prerogative of the parties to decide whether or not to pursue a claim. It is by no means clear why persons should be subjected to the outcome of a proceeding and have their subjective rights determined in that proceeding, even though they do not pursue these rights by themselves.

IV. THE OPT-IN VERSUS OPT-OUT DEBATE – AN OVERVIEW

Most of the issues discussed above in some form or another involve the question of whether the group proceeding is of the opt-in or opt-out type. The principal arguments in favour of opt-in type proceedings are well-known. It is argued by proponents of such a scheme that opt-in type proceedings increase the efficiency of proceedings. Perhaps more importantly, an opt-in type system ensures that cases of similar facts and law are decided alike. It also minimizes concerns as to the jurisdiction of the court since the members of the group join the proceeding on their own volition, thereby clearly accepting the court's jurisdiction. Clearly, a stronger degree of 'aggregation' or 'bundling' facilitates settlements of mass claims.[14] Finally, the strong aggregation brought about by

---

[13] See also R Stürner, 'Verfahrensgrundsätze des Zivilprozesses und Verfassung', in Festschrift für Baur (Tübingen, 1981), 647–666 ff; A Stadler, 'Verhandlungen' 62 *Deutscher Juristentag* (1998) Vol II/1 I 48.

[14] T Arons and WH van Boom, 'Beyond Tulips and Cheese: Exporting Mass Securities Claim Settlements from the Netherlands', 21 *European Business Law Review* (2010) 85; XE Kramer, 'Enforcing Mass Settlements in the European Judicial Area: EU Policy and the Strange Case of Dutch Collective Settlements' in C Hodges and A Stadler (eds.), *Resolving Mass Disputes* (Edward Elgar, 2013) 63.

opt-out type proceedings can also contribute to solve problems under substantive law, in particular very small value mass claims.

In spite of these advantages, opt-out type proceedings are heavily criticized in many countries. Thus, it is argued that the members of the group should be able to decide by themselves whether they want to bring a claim and in what way they want to pursue it. This probably, in large measure, can be explained by the 'individualistic' tradition of many European legal systems (and, particularly, lawyers), with small firms or even sole practitioners being the rule in many countries until fairly recently. Also, the costs of the proceeding would be easier to handle in an opt-in type proceeding.

In addition, in an opt-out system, definition of the 'group' is critical since it defines the number of persons bound by the proceeding even against their will. On the other hand, even in an opt-in type proceeding, certain problems concerning the definition of the group still remain because, for determining whether or not a plaintiff can bring an individual lawsuit in spite of a pending group proceeding, the court would have to determine whether or not the plaintiff falls within the definition of the group.

While an opt-out system can contribute to solve the problems of very small claims or 'atomized losses,' opponents of such a scheme would argue that this is a problem of substantive law and, accordingly, should be solved by substantive law, eg, by requiring a business to pay profits gained by some unlawful method to a certain compensation fund.

While the Commission Recommendation clearly favours the opt-in system as the default option, it also recognises that too rigid an approach to the structuring of collective redress may not be in the interests of justice. One possible way for Member States to implement the Recommendation would be to permit their courts to adopt the form of collective redress procedure best suited to the particular circumstances of the case at hand, as under the new Belgian legislation.[15] Under this model, the choice between opt-in and opt-out should be made by national courts taking into account the specific features of each case, including such matters as the characteristics of the claimants (big business, SMEs, trade associations, NGOs such as consumer associations, large numbers of individual consumers, or public bodies); the nature of the claim; and the overall context of the proceedings.[16]

---

[15] See also E Falla, *Powers of the judge in collective redress proceedings*, Université Libre de Bruxelles, 2 February 2012; European Parliament, Directorate General for Internal Policies, Overview of existing collective redress schemes in EU Member States, July 2011, IP/A/IMCO/NT/2011-17; BEUC, Country survey of collective redress mechanisms (updated in December 2011); Les actions de groupe. Les documents de travail du Sénat Belge, Mai 2010; Strooischade: Een verkennend (rechtsvergelijkend) onderzoek naar de mogelijkheden tot optreden tegen strooischade, Juli 2009.

[16] ELI Statement at 44 et seq.

V. SOME PRACTICAL ASPECTS

Where there is a default option, people tend not to actively choose a different option even when they could ('inertia bias'). This is why default options constitute such a powerful 'nudge.'[17]

While experience gained in the US clearly shows that only very few class members actually opt out of a class litigation, the same need not be true in Europe. If class members in the US are reluctant to opt out of a proceeding, this can be explained not only by their inertia bias, a lack of care or a lack of initiative, but also by the enormous amount of legal fees an individual lawsuit would accumulate. If a class action is pending, an individual member of the class will often face difficulty in finding a lawyer ready to take up the case on the basis of a contingency fee because this fee could only be calculated on the basis of the amount in controversy in the individual lawsuit. In Europe, the cost of litigation tends to be lower in many countries; also, in many countries legal expenses insurance is widely available. Thus, experience from Austria gained in our biggest civil proceedings ever, the WEB proceedings, shows that many plaintiffs decided to proceed individually rather than by way of a group action. An opt-out is not only unsatisfactory from a procedural point of view, but also in light of the harmony of decisions to be brought about by the group proceeding. If a group proceeding affords an adequate level of protection (which has to be guaranteed both in an opt-in and an opt-out system), there seems to be no need to provide for a possibility to opt out. It should be noted that occasionally it has been suggested in the US to exclude the possibility to opt out altogether.[18] Both from a point of view of procedural economy and with a view towards deciding all relevant questions of law and fact alike, opt-out type proceedings seem to be preferable because they prevent a large number of individual lawsuits in which questions already disposed of in the group proceeding have to be re-litigated. A system with an opt-out possibility without restrictions could not effectively cope with the practical and procedural economic difficulties mass litigation brings about. The following sections will attempt to explore to what extent an opt-out proceeding would be compatible with principles of European law.

VI. JURISDICTIONAL CONCERNS

An opt-out type system may pose problems in cross-border proceed-

---

[17] ELI Statement 43, citing C Sunstein and R. Thaler, *Nudge*, (Yale University Press, 2008) at 1 and 105 et seq.
[18] Note, 'Developments in the Law – Class Actions' 89 *Harv L Rev* (1976) 1318, 1488.

ings.[19] The reason for this is that an opt-out system would subject members of the group to the jurisdiction of the court, even if they have no connection whatsoever with the country where the proceeding is pending. While the Brussels I Regulation only addresses jurisdiction from the perspective of the defendant, this is due to the fact that it only has traditional two party-proceedings in mind. In such a proceeding the plaintiff chooses the forum; thus the Regulation only has to protect the interests of the defendant by imposing limits to the plaintiff's freedom of choice. This is different, however, in a proceeding where a member of the group would be bound by the outcome of a proceeding in another country even if he has no connection to this country. In such a case, the criteria set forth in the Regulation as to where a defendant can be sued may also provide guidance as to where a member of a group can be 'hauled into court' in a foreign country.

It is no coincidence that the only opt-in type class action ever certified in the US concerned a cross-border case, namely the ski train accident in Kaprun, Austria. In what certainly was one of Austria's most terrible accidents, 155 passengers were killed when a ski train caught fire in a tunnel. This accident led to extensive litigation both in Austria and abroad, many of the passengers being foreign tourists. Some survivors of American passengers brought suit in the US. While these actions originally proceeded as individual lawsuits, the court later certified it as a class-action. Contrary to regular American practice, this class was to include non-Americans only if they actively opted in.[20] This opt-in type class action, however, was short-lived, being overturned quickly by the Second Circuit Court of Appeals.[21]

The recent reform of the Brussels I Regulation unfortunately failed to address this problem.[22] Therefore, at least for the foreseeable future, collective redress will be limited to purely domestic proceedings (or proceedings where the inclusion of foreign class members is justified by some other recognized ground for the exercise of jurisdiction) unless foreign members of the group actively opt in or submit to the court's jurisdiction in some other form.

While Articles 29 and 30 of the Brussels I Regulation address the problem of parallel proceedings and irreconcilable judgments by giving preference to the court where proceedings were first initiated, Article 29 requires not only 'the same cause of action' in all proceedings, but also the participation of 'the

---

[19] A Nuyts and N E Hatzimihail (eds.), *Cross-Border Class Actions: The European Way* (Sellier European Law Publishers, 2014).

[20] In *re ski train fire in Kaprun*, Austria, 229 November 11, 2000, 220 FRD 195, 211 (SDNY 2003). This author was a legal expert in this proceeding.

[21] *Kern v. Siemens Corp.* (2d Cir.2004) 393 F.3d 120 [cert. denied, 544 U.S. 1034, 125 S.Ct. 2272, 161 L.Ed.2d 1061 (2005)].

[22] For an interesting discussion of the *Kern v Siemens* type problem, see R Mulheron, 'In defence of the requirement for foreign class members to opt in to an English class action', in D Fairgrieve and E Lein, *Extraterritoriality and Collective Redress* (OUP, 2012) 258.

same parties' and, therefore, will not apply to parallel proceedings initiated by (different) representative entities.[23] Article 28, however, confers broad discretion on the courts to stay proceedings (Article 28(1)) or even to decline jurisdiction with regard to the possibility of consolidating the proceedings in the court first seized (Article 28(2)). Consolidation depends, however, on the procedural law applicable in the Member State where the first action has been filed. In order to avoid irreconcilable judgments, the European Law Institute (ELI) Statement on Collective Redress and Competition Damages Claims recommends that Member States should consider the implementation of national rules generously permitting the consolidation of 'related actions' within the meaning of Article 28(2) of the Brussels I Regulation.[24]

The ELI therefore recommends that the European legislature initiates a broad discussion on private international law issues relating to collective redress in order to come up with a solution when the Commission revisits the situation in its review four years after the Recommendation's implementation.[25]

VII. 'FORCED COMMUNITY' OR LEGITIMATE 'BUNDLING': THE INFLUENCE OF THE ECHR

A. Introduction

One point of criticism against an opt-out type class action often voiced in Europe is that such a system forces all members of the class into a proceeding, regardless of whether they actually want to participate. This, it is often argued, constitutes a violation of Article 6 ECHR. This argument has to be taken seriously as in Europe a group proceeding has to be compatible with the requirements of Article 6 ECHR and Article 47 of the Charter of Fundamental Rights of the European Union.[26]

The case law of the European Court of Human Rights certainly recognises that a proceeding with a particularly large number of parties can take longer than a simpler proceeding. Indeed, the difficulty of the case is one of the criteria which have to be taken into account when assessing the duration of the proceeding for purposes of Article 6 ECHR.[27] Yet, a State, in order to fulfil its obligations under Article 6 ECHR to provide access to justice, has

---

[23] ELI Statement at 38.
[24] *Ibid*.
[25] ELI Statement 36. See also A Stadler, 'Conflicts of Laws in Multinational Collective Actions – a Judicial Nightmare?' and D Fairgrieve, 'The Impact of the Brussels I Enforcement and Recognition Rules on Collective Actions', both in Fairgrieve and Lein (above n 22) 191.
[26] See B Hess, 'EMRK, Grundrechte-Charta und europäisches Zivilverfahrensrecht' in HP Mansel (ed.) *Festschrift für Erik Jayme* (Sellier, 2004) I 339.
[27] See C Grabenwarter, *European Convention on Human Rights* (CH Beck, 2014).

to devise procedures which make it possible to dispose of a case even in difficult and complex proceedings.[28] Since a group proceeding inevitably brings about a limitation of the procedural rights of individual parties, the following section will discuss whether such a limitation is compatible with the requirements under Article 6 ECHR.

B. The Possibility of Limiting Individual Procedural Rights

Any attempt to introduce some form of group proceeding inevitably has to limit the procedural rights of individual group members; otherwise the proceeding would quickly become unmanageable. A proceeding with hundreds or even thousands of plaintiffs with different lawyers, different and sometimes maybe outright contradictory allegations and motions would be impossible to handle. Thus, the question arises whether such a limitation is in line with the guarantees under Article 6 ECHR.

In this context, two decisions of the European Court of Human Rights offer valuable insights. The first decision, *Lithgow v United Kingdom*,[29] concerned the nationalization of large parts of the British shipbuilding industry according to the Aircraft and Shipbuilding Industries Act 1977. Section 41(1) of the 1977 Act provided that a Stockholder's Representative was to be appointed in respect of each acquired company 'to represent the interests of holders of securities of that company in connection with the determination of the base value of those securities.' He was to be appointed by the holders of the securities at a meeting held within a prescribed time-limit, or, if the shareholders failed to appoint a representative in time, by the Secretary of State; he could be removed by resolution passed at a meeting of the security holders (Schedule 6). His remuneration and expenses were to be met by the Secretary of State.

The *raison d'être* for the institution of Stockholders' Representative was that it was considered essential, in order to prevent negotiations and arbitration being rendered unworkable by a multiplicity of individual claims, that they be conducted, on behalf of the former owners, exclusively by a nominee representing their collective interests. As a result, although the individual shareholders had voting rights at stockholders' meetings, they had no direct standing in compensation negotiations.

According to the Government, stockholders would have had a remedy in domestic courts against a Representative for failure to comply either with his obligations under the 1977 Act or with his common law obligations as agent. They further maintained that he could not refuse to institute arbitration

---

[28] *Ibid*.
[29] ECHR, 24 June 1986, *Lithgow and others v United Kingdom*, E 24.6.1986, application nr 9006/80.

proceedings if so directed by the stockholders or, probably, a majority of them and that, as a matter of pure practice, he would not agree the quantum of compensation in negotiations without their consent.

The Court found no violation of the applicant's rights under Article 6 ECHR: 'Notwithstanding this bar on individual access, the Court does not consider that in the particular circumstances the very essence of Sir William Lithgow's right to court was impaired.'[30] The Court pointed out that the 1977 Act established a 'collective system for the settlement of disputes concerning compensation,' in that the parties to proceedings before the Arbitral Tribunal would be the Secretary of State for Industry on the one hand and the Stockholders' Representative on the other.[31] The latter was appointed by and represented the interests of all the holders of securities of the company concerned and thus the interests of each individual shareholder were safeguarded, albeit indirectly. This, the Court continued, was borne out by the fact that the Act made a provision for meetings of shareholders at which they could give instructions or express their views to the Representative. Furthermore, in addition to the power of removal conferred by Schedule 6 to the 1977 Act, remedies were available to an individual who alleged that the Representative had failed or was failing to comply with his duties under the Act or with his common law obligations as an agent. [32]

Moreover, the Court agreed with the Commission's view that this limitation on a direct right of access for every individual shareholder to the Arbitral Tribunal pursued a legitimate aim, namely the desire to avoid, in the context of a large-scale nationalization measure, a multiplicity of claims and proceedings brought by individual shareholders. Neither does it appear, having regard to the powers and duties of the Stockholders' Representative and to the Government's margin of appreciation, that there was not a reasonable relationship of proportionality between the means employed and this aim.

This view was affirmed more recently in another decision concerning Germany.[33] In *Wendenburg et al v Germany*, the European Court of Human Rights had to deal with applications of several German lawyers who contested the abolition of the single court admission system (*Singularzulassung*) by a judgment of the German Constitutional Court. According to section 25 of the German Attorneys Act (*Bundesrechtsanwaltsordnung* – BRAO), a lawyer admitted before a Court of Appeal was not entitled to appear before lower courts in civil cases, and vice versa. This provision was overturned by a judgment of the Constitutional Court on 13 December

---

[30] *Ibid*, para 196.
[31] *Idem*.
[32] *Ibid*, para 28.t
[33] ECHR, 6 February 2003, *Wendenburg v Deutschland*, application no. 71630/01.

2000. The applicants, lawyers previously admitted to the Court of Appeal, saw this as a violation of their property rights under Article 1 of the First Protocol. In addition, they alleged a violation of Article 6 ECHR, because the change in the law was affected by a decision of the German Constitutional Court against which no appeal was available.

The European Court of Human Rights dismissed the application as obviously ill-founded. While the proceeding before the German Constitutional Court had concerned civil rights in the sense of Article 6 ECHR of the applicants, the fact that the applicants could not appear in the proceeding did not violate Article 6 ECHR. The Court referred to its decision in *Lithgow* and pointed out that in proceedings involving a decision for a collective number of individuals, it is not always required or even possible that every individual concerned is heard before the court. The Court stressed that 'the legislative change resulting from the Federal Constitutional Court's decision affected the position of numerous lawyers.'[34] The Court went on that, 'given the practical implications, the Federal Constitutional Court had sufficiently fulfilled the requirements of Article 6 of the Convention by hearing associations defending the professional interests of lawyers on all matters including the transitional arrangements.'[35]

These decisions clearly show that a group action without a possibility to opt out may well comply with Article 6 ECHR.

C. *Equality of Arms*

The limitation on individual procedural rights, however, is not the only aspect where a group proceeding may pose concerns under Article 6 ECHR. From this provision, the European Court of Human Rights has derived the so-called principle of equality of arms.[36] In certain cases, availability of a group proceeding could even be mandated under this principle. A possible example would be a case where a defendant faces a large number of similar claims from a large number of people. This may be problematic particularly where injunctive relief is sought. This problem might become relevant if injunctive relief is available not only to certain associations, but also to individuals. Without a group proceeding being available, a defendant would be exposed to a multitude of identical claims. Even if he succeeded in one proceeding, another member of the group could bring another lawsuit and,

---

[34] *Idem*.
[35] *Idem*.
[36] See, inter alia, ECHR, 6 February 2001 in *Beer v Austria*. For a discussion, see G Kodek, 'Zur Zweiseitigkeit des Rekursverfahrens. Überlegungen aus Anlass der Entscheidung Beer gegen Österreich', *Österreichische Juristenzeitung* (2004) 534.

thus, had a second chance while a defeat of the defendant in at least one proceeding and in practice would have effects vis-a-vis all members of the group because the defendant would be required to comply with the injunction.

Another aspect of group litigation where the principle of equality of arms could become relevant is the scope of *res judicata*. Some authors suggest a system of *res judicata* graded according to the outcome of the case (*secundum eventum litis*).[37] Under this system, in case group litigation fails, individual group members could still bring individual lawsuits.

Evidently, such a system is highly problematic. While a defeat in the group litigation would be final for the defendant, and, thus, all members of the group would benefit from this outcome, a success of the defendant in the proceeding would not protect him from future proceedings brought by individual group members.

This also seems objectionable in light of general principles of equality. In addition, such a system provides no viable solution for mass claims because in case of a large number of claims brought after dismissal of a group action, the system is faced with the very same problems that a group action proceeding seeks to avoid.

A final point concerns standing for an application to initiate a group proceeding. While so far the focus has been on the side of the claimants, the principle of equality of arms arguably requires that the defendant should also have standing since he also has an interest in getting a single consistent decision on a multitude of claims.

VIII. PARTY AUTONOMY AND THE INTENSITY OF THE 'AGGREGATION EFFECT'

The strongest argument against an 'American style' opt-in type proceeding is that the members of the group are not only bound by the outcome, but that individual claims of individual members of the group are determined without any initiative on part of the respective members. This is incompatible with the principle of party autonomy (*Dispositionsgrundsatz*). In most countries, the creditor always has to take the initiative when he wants to pursue a claim.

---

[37] Such a system seems to be in place in Brazil (A Gidi, 'Class Actions in Brazil – A Model for Civil Law Countries' 51 *American Journal of Comparative Law* 313 [370, 388]). A similar model was proposed by ECLG, The need for group action for consumer redress, ECLG/033/05, 10. Such a model would be remarkably different from the US system. While according to *Cooper v Federal Reserve Bank of Richmond*, 467 US 867 (1984), a discrimination case, individual class members could still bring suit if a class-wide discrimination could not be shown, under US law at least the determination in the class action proceeding that there was no class-wide discrimination is binding on all members of the group (Gidi, *ibid*. at 391).

Thus, in ordinary civil litigation, the creditor has to file a complaint. Also in an insolvency proceeding, which due to its character as mass proceeding bears some resemblance to collective litigation, generally has to lodge his claim by himself and, thus, has to take the initiative in order to benefit from the proceeding. Exceptions to this general rule mainly comprise creditors whom the law wants to specifically protect such as, eg, the owners of insurance policies in the insolvency of an insurance company. Also, the European Insolvency Regulation seems to presuppose that the creditors have to lodge their claims in order to be able to take part in the proceedings. While an administrator can lodge claims in a particular proceeding, this applies only to creditors who have actively taken part in at least one proceeding.

This conflict with established principles of civil procedure can be avoided by a system in which all members of the group (regardless of whether or not they actively take part in the proceeding) are bound by the determination of preliminary questions, such as liability of defendant or other common questions of law or fact. These issues common to all claims could be placed 'outside the brackets' so to speak, and would be determined in a collective proceeding while the determination of an individual claim would require an initiative on part of the respective member of the group.

Regardless of whether the group proceeding is an opt-in or opt-out proceeding, in the interest of concentration and procedural economy the initiation of such a proceeding should constitute a bar against individual litigation.[38] Otherwise the group proceeding cannot fulfil its designed task to reduce the workload of the courts.[39] As has been shown above, Article 6 ECHR does not require the availability of a possibility to opt out. Nor does Article 6 ECHR require that a person, in order to be bound by the decision rendered in a proceeding, actually take part in it. Rather, for the purpose of Article 6 ECHR, the opportunity to take part is sufficient.

While the 'aggregation effect' suggested here in some respects is even stronger than the one in class actions in the US,[40] this is mitigated by the fact that the decision of preliminary questions is binding on all members of the group, but the decision on an individual claim would always require an initiative by that individual member of the group. In light of the danger of the

---

[38] See A Stadler, 'Verhandlungen' 62 *Deutscher Juristentag* (1998) Vol II/1 I 52. The approach by Gidi (above n 37) [400] ('Traditional civil-law rules of *lis pendens* must be sacrificed in the interest of absent class members. The best solution would be a flexible mechanism to merge the actions, to choose the class action with the broadest scope, to allow the plaintiff in one class action to intervene in the other and make a new claim if necessary, or a combination of these devices.') hardly offers a workable alternative.

[39] See F Reuschle, *WM* (2004), 2334 (2338).

[40] The same conclusion was reached by B Hess, *WM* (2004), 2329, with regard to the German *Kapitalanleger-Musterverfahrensgesetz* (*KapMuG*).

claim becoming time-barred if the group member remained passive, such a bar to individual litigation together with the possibility to take part in the group proceeding, could very well serve as an incentive to take part.

Under such a system, one has to clarify what court should decide on the stay of individual proceedings. Under general principles, this would be the court where the individual proceeding was pending. Alternatively, this power could, and probably should, be given to the court before which the group litigation is pending, because this court is in the best position to determine whether a certain proceeding can be expected to also clarify aspects of an individual proceeding.

IX. ATOMIZED LOSSES

Proponents of opt-out type class actions argue that this system also solves the problem of 'atomized losses' – losses so small that the victims do not think pursuing them worthwhile. By combining all members of the group in a single proceeding, the amount in controversy is high enough to serve as an incentive to lawyers to organize such a proceeding. Yet, by this the underlying problem is obscured rather than solved. In essence, the distribution of the proceeds of such a proceeding is a question of substantive law. The low amount of the individual losses and the difficulties in finding the actual victims lead to a collective form of compensation generally resulting in damages being paid to institutions rather than individuals.[41] Only occasionally courts and lawyers seem to be more imaginative. Thus, in one case, a taxi company which had charged excessive fares agreed to reduce the fares and, thereby, to pay back the customers the amount it had overcharged.[42] However, in this case individual claims are not satisfied anymore;[43] rather on a supra-individual level, the taxi company is deprived of its unlawfully gained profits. Then, a more direct (and indeed, simpler) approach would be the introduction of a system

---

[41] That damages are often awarded to institutions rather than individuals as is the legal issue behind Finkelstein's controversial book on the 'Holocaust Industry'. This, however, is not a peculiar feature of holocaust-related proceedings. A discussion of Finkelstein's controversial views is beyond the scope of this paper.

[42] *Daar v. Yellow Cab Co.* 67 Cal. 2d 695 (1967). This so-called '*fluid recovery*' is criticized from an economic point of view by HB Schäfer in Basedow, Hopt, Kötz and Baetge (above n 12) 91, especially n 58; see also JA Jolowicz, *On Civil Procedure* (CUP, 2000) 113 at n 25.

[43] This is sometimes clearly seen by American authors. Such small claims class actions are, eg, criticized by SM Hill, 'Small Claimant Class Actions: Deterrence and Due Process Examined' 19 *Am J of Trial Advoc* (1995) 147; M Handler, 'The Shift from Substantive to Procedural Innovations in Antitrust Suit – The Twenty-Third Annual Antitrust Review', 71 *Colum L Rev* 1 (1971); JM Landers, 'Of Legalized Blackmail and Legalized Theft: Consumer Class Actions and the Substance-Procedure Dilemma', 47 *S Cal L Rev* 842 (1974).

of disgorgement of illegal profits which is enforced by public authorities rather than achieving a similar effect in the guise of a private law group action.[44]

X. CONCLUSION

Our short discussion has shown that the concerns voiced against the introduction of group proceedings in large measure are directed against the US legal system as such, not against class actions specifically. An examination of the case law of the European Court of Human Rights shows that a group proceeding can comply with the requirements of the ECHR. Jurisdictional concerns are more difficult to overcome since for cross-border cases the revised Brussels I Regulation does not provide special rules for collective proceedings. Thus, for the foreseeable future, group proceedings in Europe will probably be limited to domestic cases or cases where the court can base its jurisdiction as to foreign members of the group on some other valid ground. In a cross-border context, an opt-in type system has some advantages in that by opting in, the respective member of the group clearly submits to the jurisdiction of the court. Possible concerns in light of the principle of party autonomy (because members of the group could receive an award (or be subjected to a ssettlement regardless of whether they took some form of initiative) could be addressed by a system in which only the common questions of law and fact are put 'outside the brackets' and determined in a collective proceeding, whereas an individual claim is only judged upon if the respective member of the group takes some form of initiative. This shows that it may well be worth examining alternatives to the traditional opt-in or opt-out models. The concept of collective litigation is broad and flexible enough to encompass an enormous variety of proceedings. Some of these should be acceptable also in light of traditional European procedural maxims.

---

[44] Such a system is in force in Germany under section 10 of the Unfair Competition Act and sections 34a, 33 of the Antitrust Act. This system, however, is rightly criticized as being too cumbersome.

Rebuilding the Pillars of Collective Litigation in Light of the Commission Recommendation: The Spanish Approach to Collective Redress

María Paz García Rubio
Marta Otero Crespo[*]

I. GENERAL REMARKS

Over the last few decades, procedural mechanisms aiming to group together similar claims arising from a single or closely related wrongful act into a single proceeding – ie, collective redress mechanisms – have become a widely discussed legal phenomenon across Europe, in both the European Union and its Member States.[1] In fact, the occurrence of a number of mass disasters has highlighted the need to establish adequate mechanisms in order to enforce the rights of EU citizens, both effectively and efficiently. In this regard, there have been significant developments in the collective redress field within the EU itself particularly in two different areas, Consumer and Competition Law. Looking back, it is evident that until late 2010, both DG SANCO and DG COMP were working in parallel producing a series of uncoordinated works. With the aim of avoiding duplicity, they were joined by DG JUSTICE, in order to develop the so-called 'horizontal approach' to collective redress.

---

[*] Dr María Paz García Rubio is a Professor of Civil Law (University of Santiago de Compostela). Dr Marta Otero Crespo is a Senior Lecturer of Civil Law (University of Santiago de Compostela) and BIICL Consultant in Collective Redress. This contribution is substantially based on M Otero Crespo, 'The Collective Redress Phenomenon in the European Context: the Spanish Case', *Procedural Science at the Crossroads of Three Generations* (provisional title), forthcoming, Nomos Verlagsgesellschaft, Baden-Baden, Germany.

[1] See B Hess, 'Collective Redress and the Jurisdictional Model of the Brussels I Regulation', in A Nuyts and NE Hatzimihail (eds) *Cross-border class actions. The European Way,* (Sellier, 2014) 59. Collective redress is a broad term ('umbrella term') that includes group litigation, model case proceedings, actions brought by ombudsmen or representative entities, collective settlements, skimming-off actions and injunctions.

Leaving aside the Consultation on collective redress[2] or the European Parliament Resolution 'Towards a Coherent Approach to Collective Redress',[3] the European Commission's initiative on collective redress of 11 June 2013 constitutes the greatest step towards the establishment of effective and common collective redress mechanisms within the EU. The European Commission's initiative is made up of the European Commission Recommendation on common principles for injunctive and compensatory collective redress mechanisms in the Member States concerning violations of rights granted under Union Law[4] along with its corresponding Communication.[5] Following its previous work in the field, the Commission Recommendation declared that its purposes are to facilitate access to justice in mass harm situations, to ensure adequate procedural safeguards against abusive litigation, to stop illegal practices and enable injured parties to obtain compensation through collective redress when a right granted under EU Law has been violated. The Recommendation declares that all Member States should have collective redress mechanisms at a national level not only for injunctive purposes, but also for compensatory relief. Furthermore, the respect of the basic principles that are set out in the Recommendation is defined as mandatory,[6] which should also be common across the EU. Member States should then ensure that the collective redress procedures are fair, equitable, timely and not prohibitively expensive.

---

[2] 'Towards a coherent approach to collective redress.' (2011) This public consultation aimed at identifying common legal principles on collective redress and to examine how such principles could fit into the EU legal system, as well as the jurisdictions of the Member States. Further, the consultation analysed the areas in which different forms of collective redress could help to better enforce EU legislation or protect the rights of EU citizens and businesses.

[3] European Parliament resolution of 2 February 2012 'Towards a Coherent Approach to Collective Redress.'

[4] (2013/396/EU), OJ 26.7.2013. http://eur-lex.europa.eu/legal-content/EN/TXT/?qid=1398263020823&uri=OJ:JOL_2013_201_R_NS0013.

[5] Communication from the Commission to the European Parliament, the Council, the European Economic and Social Committee and the Committee of the Regions 'Towards a European Horizontal Framework for Collective Redress', COM (2013) 401 final, available at http://ec.europa.eu/consumers/archive/redress_cons/docs/com_2013_401_en.pdf.

[6] However some exceptions are allowed with respect to theoretically 'mandatory rules'. Nevertheless, it should be highlighted that this is a mere Recommendation instead of a binding Directive or Regulation. It has been argued that the current political situation would not allow a Directive or Regulation, which would impose an obligation on the Member States to implement new instruments for the collective enforcement of mass claims. See A Stadler, 'The Commission's Recommendation on common principles of collective redress and private international law issues', 4NiPR 2013, 483 again, A Stadler, in this volume, 235–249; ELI Statement on Collective Redress and Competition Damages Claims, available at: http://www.europeanlawinstitute.eu/fileadmin/user_upload/p_eli/Projects/S-5-2014_Statement_on_Collective_Redress_and_Competition_Damages_Claims.pdf, 12–14.

Currently, the Recommendation advocates the establishment of collective redress mechanisms ensuring injunctive and compensatory relief when rights granted under Union Law are violated. From a substantive point of view, the expression 'violation of rights granted under Union Law' covers all the situations where a breach of rules established at the EU level has caused or is likely to cause prejudice. Explicit reference is made to areas such as consumer protection, competition, environment protection, protection of personal data, financial services regulation and investor protection.[7] This unifying approach to collective redress mechanisms, ie the so-called 'horizontal approach', does not match current Spanish legislation, where there is no general collective redress device. On the contrary, disperse rules allowing for forms of collective litigation are actually stipulated in the Code of Civil Procedure (*Ley de enjuiciamiento civil*, LEC) and within certain specific areas such as consumer law, product liability, competition law, equality law, labour law, environment protection, etc.[8]

Departing from the chaotic and fragmented Spanish regulation and using consumer protection in collective redress cases as a model case, this chapter will examine the Spanish provisions allowing for collective litigation, as well as their potential compliance or non-compliance with the principles proposed in the European Commission Recommendation of 11 June 2013.

II. THE CURRENT SPANISH APPROACH TO COLLECTIVE REDRESS AND ITS COMPLIANCE WITH THE PRINCIPLES ESTABLISHED IN THE EC RECOMMENDATION

A. The Current Spanish Regulation on Collective Litigation: a Response to Late XXth Century Needs

Upon examining the current Spanish procedural regulation, it is evident that the existing provisions were not designed to be applied to collective litigation. This inadequacy has a historical explanation. First of all, when the new LEC was passed in 2000,[9] as a general rule, the Spanish legislator opted to avoid incorporating the so-called 'special proceedings' (*procesos especiales*).[10] Consequently, a special regulation on collective litigation was not promulgated. Secondly, and closely related to the first reasoning, the minds of the drafters of the new LEC were on traditional forms of litigation, ie one

---

[7] Nevertheless, those areas may not be interpreted as a closed list as Point (7) allows for its application 'in any other areas where collective claims for injunctions or damages in respect of violations of the rights granted under Union law would be relevant.'

[8] Consumer law and/or product liability are the most relevant in practice. We refer to both areas at the same time, as it is very difficult to clearly distinguish between consumer protection and product liability cases. Typically, the categories overlap.

[9] The LEC 2000 came into force on 8 January 2001.

[10] See Title XIX of the Preamble of the LEC 2000.

claimant versus one defendant, with only a few exceptions. This reductionist approach may explain why they were not aware of the potential needs arising from mass litigation. They consequently only inserted a single specific article in the LEC (Article 11) dealing with collective claims in consumer law scenarios,[11] and some other scattered provisions which explicit or implicitly deal with mass harm situations.[12] Article 11 of the LEC was a late and ill-conceived reaction to the mass harm situations related to product liability/consumer law cases and natural disasters, which occurred within national boundaries in the late 80's[13] and early 90's.[14]

Prior to 2000, as a legislative consequence of mass harm situations, provisions of many consumer law rules began to recognize the right of consumer and users' associations to file collective action claims before the Courts.[15] However, those actions were devised to ask for purely injunctive relief. At the time, consumer and users' associations were frequently denied legal standing to commence class actions requesting compensation for damages suffered by a group of people.[16]

---

[11] For a brief historical evolution on the regulation of collective litigation from 1985 until now, see M Otero Crespo 'The Collective Redress Phenomenon in the European Context: the Spanish Case', Procedural Science at the Crossroads of Three Generations (provisional title), forthcoming, Nomos Verlagsgesellschaft, Baden-Baden, Germany.. Prior to 1985 the General Act on Consumer Protection of 1984 included art 20 which states that consumer and users' associations shall file claims for the defence of their members, the association itself and the general interests of consumers and users. This wording has become typical in Spanish consumer law procedural provisions influencing subsequent regulations on the matter.

[12] See art 6.1.7 and 8 LEC, arts 7.7, 11, 13.1, 15, 43, 52.1, 76.2.1,78.4, 221, 222.3, 249, 250, 256.1. and 6, 519 LEC and finally, art 711. 2 and 728.3 LEC.

[13] See the 'Colza' case (decision of the Tribunal Supremo (Criminal division) 5661/1997, 26 September), one of the most important product liability cases in Spain. The Supreme Court granted compensation for the injuries caused by the consumption of rapeseed oil. The product caused more than 1,000 deaths and left more than 25,000 people seriously injured, many of whom were permanently disabled.

[14] In 1982, the Tous dam in Valencia crumbled causing personal injuries and material damage to 28,000 people. For further details on the 'Tous dam' case, see decision of the Tribunal Supremo (Administrative chamber), 323/1999, 25 January, and the decision of the Tribunal Supremo (Administrative chamber) 8084/1997, 20 October. The Courts granted reparation to those claimants affected by the disaster.

[15] Amongst the areas where consumer and users' associations were entitled to start collective proceedings, we can refer to unlawful advertising (art 25.1 of the Act 34/1988, of 11 November), unfair competition (art 19.2.a) of the Act 3/1991, of 10 January), oppressive clauses (art 16.3 of the Act 7/1988, of 13 April), or in art 20.1 of the Act for the General Defence of Consumers and Users of 1984. For further details, M Requejo Isidro and M Otero Crespo, 'Collective redress in Spain: recognition and enforcement of class actions judgments and class settlements', in D Fairgrieve and E Lein (eds) *Extraterritoriality and collective redress* (Oxford University Press, 2012) 310–311.

[16] This is the reason why one of the most important decisions on collective redress in Spain must be considered as exceptional. The Spanish Consumers' and User's Organization (OCU)

The legal panorama changed in 2000. The enactment of the new LEC coincided with the insertion of a specific litigation procedure before a Court concerning consumer law issues – a representative action – in Article 11 LEC. This provision has since been amended on several occasions, broadening both its scope of application[17] and the 'subjects' which may be granted legal standing.[18] According to its current wording, "notwithstanding the individual standing of those injured"[19] signifies that legally constituted consumer and users' associations, authorized public entities and even the Public Prosecution Service may file a claim asking for injunctive and/or compensatory collective redress. This amplification may be closely related to a sociological issue: the traditional Spanish reluctance towards collective litigation seems to be in the process of being overturned. The economic crisis started in 2008, along with the occurrence of a number of mass harm situations, such as the air traffic controllers strike in 2010 or scandals related to the sale of complex financial products to small investors or consumers have undoubtedly influenced the way in which people injured by the same legal infringement seek relief. With this behavioural change, consumer and users' associations, as well as some law firms are playing a crucial role in overcoming hesitancy towards collective litigation. Collective proceedings are frequently being publicized through the media (websites,[20] newspapers, radio, etc) so that individual consumers have the opportunity to join *demandas colectivas* which are initiated by both the associations and the law firms.[21] This new form of propaganda may

---

joined proceedings as a civil party representing a high number of affected consumers; the Supreme Court awarded compensation also to victims *'even though they were not directly represented in the trial'* (emphasis added).

[17] An art 11 *bis* LEC was inserted in 2007, granting standing to Trade Unions and other legally constituted associations whose primary goal is the defence of equal treatment for men and women, but with the peculiarity that in these cases they are only permitted to represent their own members. Subsequently, public bodies competent in the matter were permitted to preside over cases, but exclusively when the aggrieved parties are unidentified. Individuals are also entitled to bring proceedings in order to defend their own rights. An individual also has standing in defence of collective and diffuse interests. However, when claiming these supra-individual interests, each individual is not a named claimant also representing someone else: he/she is only defending his/her own singular right(s) before the courts.

[18] In 2002 and more recently in March 2014. On both occasions the *leit motiv* was the need to adapt the Spanish provisions to the requirements imposed by EU Directives.

[19] Literally, art 11 LEC seems to recognize the compatibility between the exercise of individual actions and collective actions.

[20] A good example is the *Asociación de usuarios de bancos, cajas y seguros de España* (ADICAE) website, where an individual consumer can gain free access to information on collective claims (http://colectivos.adicae.net/. Further, art 15 LEC establishes some publicity requirements, which influence the admissibility of a collective action initiated by a consumer or users association.

[21] On the other hand, as the Communication from the Commission to the European Parliament, the Council, the EESC and the Committee of Regions has already pointed out, it

increase some avoidable risks, such as abusive litigation or the generalization of contingency fees.

Considering the aforementioned legislative and social background, it can be observed that the approval of the EC Recommendation in 2013 has offered national legislators in the EU a new rulebook to look at when developing rules on collective litigation. In this sense, the question the paper shall assess is whether the EC non-mandatory instrument will constitute the pillar of new, or at least improved, Spanish legislation on collective proceedings.

B. Spanish Legislation and its Compliance with the Proposed EC Recommendation Principles: Remarkable Issues that Need to be Addressed

Departing from the mandatory principles set out in the EC Recommendation and comparing them to the Spanish provisions on the matter, some procedural and substantive issues may need to be revisited by the Spanish legislator by 26 July 2015, the deadline given by the Recommendation for Member States to put appropriate measures in place,[22] and notably by 2017, when the Recommendation is due to be reviewed.[23] As we have already mentioned, the purpose of this chapter will focus only on consumer law scenarios, as it is the area that has historically been developed by the Spanish legislator, and has proven to be the most fruitful when collective redress devices are applied.[24]

1. Legal Standing

It must be noted that the EC Recommendation is based on representative actions. In fact, Chapter III on principles common to injunctive and compensatory collective redress begins by examining standing for bringing a representative action. The EC, as a matter of policy, favours granting standing to associations who initiate collective or representative actions, as opposed to a single representative claimant acting on behalf of others. Representative entities are required to meet certain requirements in order to guarantee the viabil-

---

cannot be overlooked that advertising the opportunity to file a collective action may negatively affect the reputation of the potential defendant, which could have adverse effects on its economic standing. See Communication from the Commission to the European Parliament, the Council, the European Economic and Social Committee and the Committee of the Regions 'Towards a European Horizontal Framework for Collective Redress', COM (2013) 401 final, 12.

[22] See point 38 of the Recommendation.
[23] See point 41 of the Recommendation.
[24] The open question is whether Spanish consumer law provisions may be applicable to non-consumer law scenarios.

ity of the claim.[25] Furthermore the Recommendation encourages Member States to empower public authorities to bring representative actions.[26]

Granting standing to representative entities is consistent with the Spanish legal system. In this regard, the aforementioned Article 11 of the LEC states that "notwithstanding the individual standing of those injured", consumer and users associations shall be empowered to defend the rights and interests of their members and of the association itself, as well as the general interests of consumers and users. When those damaged by an event are a group of consumers or users whose components are perfectly determined or may be easily determined, the standing to apply for the protection of these collective interests corresponds to the associations of consumers and users, to the entities legally constituted whose purpose is the defence or protection of these, and the groups affected (Article 11.2 of the LEC).[27] In cases of diffuse interests,[28] ie the identification of the injured parties is not easy to determine, only associations that are considered representative may start proceedings (Article 11.3 of the LEC). The criteria for representation is not defined by the LEC, but is defined by the Consumer Law Act 2007. Article 24 of the Consumer Law Act 2007 completes the regulation on standing in cases of collective and diffuse interests, stating that for the purposes of Article 11.3 of the LEC, associations that are members of the Consumers and Users' Council are considered to hold the legal status of representative consumers and users associations.[29] In order to become a member of the Council, it is necessary to comply with certain prerequisites, and there have been renowned cases in which consumer associations have lost their status.[30]

---

[25] See points 4–7, and particularly point 6, where it is stated that only entities that have been designated in advance or entities that have been certified on an *ad hoc* basis by Member States' national authorities or courts for a particular representative action should be allowed to initiate representative collective actions.

[26] See also the regulation on follow-on actions, which are also available under the application of the EC Recommendation.

[27] See the Decision of the Provincial Court of Madrid (*Sección* 14), 13 October 2014, on the '*thalidomide babies*' case. The Court granted standing to a group of victims acting as an association.

[28] See below the difference between collective and diffuse interests according to the Spanish legislation. The distinction between both types of interests has been taken from Italian sources. See G Alpa, *La tutela degli interessi diffusi nel diritto comparato: con particolare riguardo alla protezione dell'ambiente e dei consumatori*(Giuffrè, Milano, 1976); U Ruffolo, *Interessi collettivi o diffusi e tutela del consumatore*(Giuffrè, Milano, 1985).

[29] See also art 37 c) of the General Act on Consumer Protection 2007. This provision recognizes that legally constituted and registered consumer and users' associations have the right to represent and defend the rights of their associates, the association itself and the general collective and diffuse interests of the consumers and users.

[30] Listed members of the Consumers and Users Council may be found here: http://consumo-inc.gob.es/asociaciones/home.htm?id=131. AUSBANC (*Asociación de Usuarios de Servicios Bancarios*) has been excluded from the Register on two occasions, first in 2005, and more recently in 2014.

Furthermore, legally authorized entities (Article 6.1.8 LEC) are permitted to request injunctive relief in order to protect both collective and diffuse interests of consumers and users. This standing was incorporated to comply with EU Consumer Law Directives.[31] Most recently, paragraph 5 of Article 11 LEC, added in March 2014 by Act 3/2014, grants standing to the Public Prosecution Service (*Ministerio Fiscal*) to file "any type of claim for the defence of the interests of consumers and users". Prior to this amendment, the Public Prosecution Service was only entitled to file actions looking for injunctive relief. From our perspective, the amendment appears to broaden the scope of standing for the Public Prosecution Service. First of all, it may recognize the public interest nature or relevance of mass harm situations.[32] Second, the amendment to some extent publicizes private wrongs.[33] The Preamble of Act 3/2014 does not explain the aforementioned procedural change so the question is whether the Public Prosecution Service will adopt a new attitude towards compensatory collective redress or not.

Concerning the adoption of a new attitude, it is important to note certain difficulties the Public Prosecution Service may face. The lack of material and personal resources available for the Administration of Justice system, as well as the inherent complications arising from collective litigation (identification of the injured parties, publicity of claims, quantification of damages, etc), may limit the powers of the Public Prosecution Service in the exercise of injunctions and/or mere declaratory relief, at least in the immediate future.

2. Remedies: Injunctive and Compensatory Relief

The EC Recommendation advocates injunctive and compensatory relief and these goals are expressly referred to in the instrument title, thus both compensatory and injunctive relief may be achieved under the Spanish system. Nevertheless, the Spanish system was historically reluctant to legally implement the recognition of damages as an essential part of collective relief.

Before the LEC 2000, the majority of claims were designed for cessation or prohibition purposes (declaratory and injunctive relief), which is consis-

---

[31] See Act 39/2002, of 28 October 2002, on the transposition of Consumer Law Directives into the Spanish system. This paragraph was amended in March 2014. Regarding injunctive collective redress, the interplay between the Recommendation and the Injunctions Directive is an interesting issue, seeing as the pre-requisites to apply for legal standing under the Directive are fewer than those established by the Recommendation (point raised by the ELI Statement on Collective Redress, at 23-24).

[32] Cf art 51 of the Spanish Constitution.

[33] See Otero Crespo (above n 11); F Cordón Moreno, 'Reformas procesales introducidas por la Ley 3/2014 de 27 de marzo. En especial, la legitimación del Ministerio Fiscal para el ejercicio de las acciones en defensa de los consumidores', 9 *Revista CESCO de Derecho de Consumo*, 2014, 1–9.

tent with civil law norms which provide that damages should not be awarded to non-parties. However, in 2000, legislation made compensatory relief available for consumer affairs. This compensatory role of collective actions filed by groups or consumer associations has been already acknowledged by case law. Significant decisions of the Spanish Supreme Court (Civil Chamber) confirm that representative entities have standing to file claims seeking injunctive relief, and may also seek the award of both patrimonial and non-patrimonial damages.[34]

The traditional connection between collective redress and injunctive relief is still formally present in the General Act on Consumer Protection 2007. Until March 2014, Title V, Chapter I of the General Act on Consumer Protection 2007 only expressly regulated *Acciones de cesación* (injunctions). The March 2014 reform revised the wording of Article 53 of the General Act on Consumer Protection 2007, which now includes not only the exercise of actions looking for injunctive relief, but also compensatory actions, amongst others.[35] Surprisingly, injunctions are still regarded as the principal action to be exercised (Article 53 paragraphs 3 and 4) whereas actions looking for compensatory relief, unjustified enrichment claims, etc, are devised as secondary *petitum*.

With regard to injunctive relief, a judgment upholding an action for cessation in defence of collective interests and of the diffuse interests of consumers and users may impose a fine ranging from 60,000 to 600,000 euros per day for delay in the enforcement of the court decision within the time limit set forth therein. The fine for the delay is to be paid to the Public Treasury (Article 711 LEC).[36]

---

[34] In one of the leading cases of the Supreme Court (Civil Chamber) 473/2010, 15 July, a motorway collapsed and people were stuck for around 17 hours due to winter snowfall. The Court granted patrimonial and non-patrimonial damages to the drivers and users affected following their finding that the motorway operating company was not diligent in establishing adequate measures to avoid such damaging circumstances. The action was filed by the consumer association AUSBANC. More recently, the Supreme Court decision (Civil Chamber), 241/2013, 9 May, where the Supreme Court considered the so-called floor-clauses in mortgages contracts to be null and void. The claim was filed by AUSBANC in the defence of the interest of consumers and users against banks and savings banks. The Court held that those clauses were oppressive but did not impose any compensatory damages for the amounts already paid by consumers. See also the Supreme Court decision of 8 of September 2014, 464/2014.

[35] Please note that this provision does not have a retroactive effect, so it is only applicable to consumer contracts entered into after 13 June 2014 (*Disposición Transitoria Única de la Ley 3/2014, de 27 de marzo de 2014*).

[36] As was mentioned above, the Member States should establish appropriate sanctions against the losing defendant with a view to ensuring effective compliance with the injunctive order – including the payments of a fixed amount per day of delay. See EC Recommendation 'Efficient enforcement of injunctive orders', point 20.

Given the new wording of Article 53 of the General Act on Consumer Protection Act 2007 and the new paragraph 5 of Article 11 LEC, compensatory relief is also available to the Public Prosecution Service when bringing an action before a court. However, as has already been mentioned, it remains unclear whether the Public Prosecution Service will change its practice and file any compensatory actions. Prior to the March 2014 amendment, the standing of the Public Prosecution Service to file a compensatory action was denied by the Provincial Court of La Coruña in its writ (*Auto*) 18/2013, 15 February.[37] If the Public Prosecution Service follows its current practice, individuals may have the opportunity to go to court asking for their own personal damages, individually or collegially, by constituting a group or via consumer and users' associations.[38] Evidently, this option does not seem to comply with either the literal application of the LEC provisions, or a proper collective redress mechanism, as the judicial economy and efficiency of the Courts may be questioned. Furthermore, the pleas of *res judicata* and *lis pendens* and even the stay of proceedings may need to be reinterpreted in light of the new legislation, which will be discussed below.

In addition to the General Act on Consumer Protection 2007, claimants may bring a compensatory claim founded on Article 12.2 of the General Contractual Conditions 1998 Act and Articles 32 and 33 of the Competition Law Act. However these claims are limited to cases where consumers are involved. In other areas, compensatory relief for collective losses is not recognized under Spanish Law. Other than the aforementioned limitation, each victim is entitled both to claim damages individually, and to join other claimants through a joint action with several co-plaintiffs.

In terms of the compensatory scheme, like many other European jurisdictions, punitive damages are not available at the moment. In this regard, the Spanish legislation does not conflict with the European Commission Recommendation.

3. Opt-in versus Opt-out. The Res Judicata *Effect*

While the EC Recommendation advocates the creation of a claimant party through its opt-in principle[39] as the default option, the EU accepts exceptions

---

[37] In the case, the Public Prosecution Service filed a joint injunction and a compensatory action. The Provincial Court affirmed the First Instance ruling (*Juzgado de Primera Instancia* núm. 11, *Auto* of 18 September 2012), stating that the Public Prosecution Service did not have legal standing to ask for the individuals' compensation.

[38] This occurred in the preference share cases in Galicia. See, ia, Decision of the Provincial Court of La Coruña 49/2014, 26 February.

[39] Note that the constitution of the claimant party by opt-in principle is curiously included under the chapter V, the section on specific principles relating to compensatory collective redress.

under its opt-out principle.[40] Spanish regulation therefore does not offer a clear answer to this fundamental issue. This signifies that the final implication of the Commission Recommendation is subject to diverging interpretations, as the academia and the judiciary have differing views on the matter.

In reality, the LEC does not contain any specific rule on the issue. Nevertheless, following the LEC provisions potentially applicable to group litigation, when an individual plaintiff, an association, or legal entity or group has brought proceedings, the remaining aggrieved parties can join the claim, thus assuming the personal defence of their interests in court (Article 15 LEC).[41]

However, several concerns may be raised. What if the aggrieved party does not take part in the proceedings? Is the victim bound by the final judgment of the process, even if the judgment is unfavourable to the aggrieved parties who took part in the proceedings? Is the victim then allowed to file a new action or may the new action be neutralized by the *res judicata* or *lis pendens* replies?[42] The positive answer to the application of the *lis pendens* or *res judicata* replies seems to be a sound option. However, Spanish Courts do not seem to follow this precedent and recently, in August 2014, two requests for preliminary rulings were sent to the ECJ.[43] In both cases, the referring Court (*Juzgado de lo Mercantil nº 9 de Barcelona*) questioned the compatibility of Article 43 LEC (stay of proceedings) with the Directive 93/13 on Unfair Terms in Consumer Contracts in application to cases where an individual action is brought after the exercise of a collective claim. By applying Article 43 LEC, the individual action filed in the second place must be stayed and

---

[40] Following the EC Recommendation, 'any exception to this principle, by law or by court order, should be duly justified by reasons of *sound administration of justice*' (emphasis added). The question is to determine the meaning of 'sound administration of justice', which should be clarified on a case-by-case basis. Further, the EC seems to ignore on-going collective redress national reforms, which have been introduced or are in the process of being introduced. The recently passed Belgian legislation is a good example as it is a combination of opt-in and opt-out (for further details, visit http://www.collectiveredress.org/collective-redress/reports/belgium/overview). The European Law Institute Draft Statement on Collective Redress and Competition Damages Claims (2014) has also highlighted the convenience of revising this restrictive approach towards the opt- out option (for further details, visit http://www.europeanlawinstitute.eu/fileadmin/user_upload/p_eli/General_Assembly/2014/Draft_Statement_on_Collective_Redress_Competition_Damages_Claims.pdf).

[41] The Public Prosecution Service shall be a party to these proceedings when social interest justifies this. The court which knows of these proceedings shall notify the Public Prosecution Service of their commencement in order to evaluate its appearance.

[42] M Otero Crespo, 'Ignorancia de la ley, error y tutela jurisdiccional de los derechos de los consumidores: el puzle de las "acciones colectivas" en la LEC', Coloquio Derecho civil- Filosofía del Derecho, Zaragoza, 2014, draft version available at https://sites.google.com/site/coloquio26septiembre/comunicaciones-1/otero-marta.

[43] OJ 3.11.2014. Available at http://eur-lex.europa.eu/legal-content/EN/TXT/PDF/?uri=OJ:C:2014:388:FULL&from=ES.

treated as a preliminary issue pending final judgment in collective proceedings. The consumer is bound by the decision adopted in those proceedings without having the opportunity to put forward the appropriate pleas or adduce evidence with full equality of arms. So the questions sent to the ECJ are (1) whether the Spanish legal system provides an effective means or mechanism pursuant to Article 7 (1) of Directive 93/13, (2) to what extent does a stay of proceedings preclude an individual consumer from pleading in court in a case where the unfair terms in the contract individually concluded with him are void, thereby infringing Article 7(1) of the Directive, and (3) whether the fact that a consumer is unable to dissociate himself from collective proceedings constitutes an infringement of Article 7(3) of Directive 93/13.

The ECJ has also been requested to examine whether the effect of a stay of proceedings provided for in Article 43 of the LEC is compatible with Directive 93/13 on the grounds that the rights of consumers are fully safeguarded by a collective action, because the Spanish legal system provides for other equally effective procedural mechanisms for the protection of consumers' rights and by the principle of legal certainty. Both requests for a preliminary ruling will hopefully shed light on the intricate Spanish procedural regulation.

To illuminate the opt-in versus opt-out debate, Spanish civil procedure rules currently in effect must be examined. It is clear that pursuant to Article 15 of the LEC, that when associations, legal entities or groups bring proceedings, aggrieved parties will be summoned to the hearing, and are to be given the opportunity to join the ongoing proceedings.[44] The Court Clerk (*Secretario Judicial*) makes a general announcement by publishing the admission of the claim through corresponding media that covers the geographical location where the damage has occurred. Additionally, the LEC places different criteria on bringing claims based on whether the injured parties are known or easy to identify (collective interests) or whether they are an indeterminate number of persons or a number which is difficult to ascertain (diffuse interests).

If the aggrieved parties are determined or may be easily determined, the LEC establishes an additional informative burden upon the plaintiff, as he must communicate his intention to file the claim to the other aggrieved persons already known prior to such general announcement. After the obligation is fulfilled, the consumer or user may join the proceedings at any time. However, the victim will only be allowed undertaking those procedural steps that have not yet precluded. The LEC does not specify the type of notification required, nor the content to be communicated.[45]

---

[44] See Requejo Isidro and Otero Crespo (above n 15) 314–315.

[45] The communication could be a personal notice with acknowledge of receipt or any similar method, which guarantees the receipt of the notice by the injured consumer or user. Cf, see the Decision of the Provincial Court of Madrid (*Sección* 14) of 13 October 2014.

In cases where the damage is caused to an indeterminate number of persons or a number which is difficult to ascertain, the call made by the Court Clerk can suspend the proceedings for a time of up to two months. The Court Clerk will decide the timing of each case depending on the circumstances, the complexity of the event, and the difficulties in finding those injured.[46]

After the suspension, the proceedings can resume with the intervention of all the consumers who have obeyed the call. The individual appearance of consumers or users is not subsequently allowed, notwithstanding the fact that the consumers may assert their rights or interests in accordance with the provisions of Articles 221 and 519 of the LEC.[47] According to Article 221 LEC, as it pertains to claims for a money award or personal services, the judgment upholding the claim must individually specify the consumers or users that will benefit. When individual identification is impossible, the judgment must determine the conditions to be met in order to be eligible for payment. If specific consumers who are to benefit from the judgment cannot be identified, the enforcement court will issue an order on whether the requirements established in the judgment are satisfied by the individuals who claim damages (Article 519 LEC).[48] Upon examining both provisions (Articles 221 and 519 LEC), it can be deduced that the procedural rights of 'absent members of the class' are fully guaranteed.

Evidently, some scholars have asserted that the Spanish system advocates for an opt-out *sui generis* regime under these circumstances.[49] Nevertheless, the question remains theoretically unclear, as it leads to conflicting solutions. On one hand, fundamental procedural rights are at stake (right of access to

---

[46] If the Spanish system is interpreted as an opt-out regime, this could perhaps constitute the period which the aggrieved parties have to declare whether or not they will join the proceedings in order to bind themselves to the final result of the process.

[47] Furthermore, art 256.1.6 LEC provides for a preliminary investigation with the aim of identifying the aggrieved parties when they may be easily singled out (collective interest). This provision states that "By an application by whomever intends to initiate legal action for the defence of the collective interests of consumers and users with a view to specifying the members of the group of aggrieved parties when, not having been determined, it can easily be determined. To this end, the court shall take the appropriate measures to verify the members of the group, in accordance with the circumstances of the case and the details provided by the applicant, including a request to the defendant to cooperate in the said determination". This preliminary measure may be contrary to the fundamental right to the protection of personal data, as it has been declared by the Constitutional Court Judgment 96/2012 of 7 May. See Otero Crespo (above n 11).

[48] The Public Prosecution Service also has standing to seek enforcement on behalf of the consumers and users affected.

[49] F Gascón Inchausti, *Tutela judicial de los consumidores y transacciones colectivas* (Ed. Civitas, Madrid, 2010) 26, asserts that the Spanish system is based on an opt-out model. However, its current legal design is far from being complete.

justice, due process, etc).[50] On the other hand, it has been argued that 'the need to harmonise the right to protection of the aggrieved party, and that of the professional against which the claim is brought',[51] and yet it is further argued that effective procedural economy is achieved under the opt-out regimes rather than under the opt-in schemes.[52] Our view on this debate is that taking into account the fundamental procedural rights granted by Article 24 of the Spanish Constitution, together with Article 6 ECHR and Article 47 (1) of the Charter of Fundamental Rights, it cannot be stated that a non-party to a process is absolutely bound by its final outcome, irrespective of the interpretation provided to those LEC articles. A solution supporting this view might be contrary to fundamental procedural rights.[53]

However, in practice, the functioning of the Spanish judicial system supports this opt-in approach when it concerns consumers' pleas for compensation. The famous 'preference shares' cases may serve as an example. In brief, over a series of years, small investors bought billions in preferred savings banks shares, completely unaware of the complexity of those financial products.[54] Following the financial crisis, thousands of non-professional investors suffered a significant financial loss. In order to compensate the investors for their losses, a specific consumer arbitration option was made available to those who had suffered economic damage.[55] Nevertheless, those who rejected the individual consumer arbitration or those who were not eligible for that mechanism followed the judicial path. As a result, thousands of individual claims flooded the Spanish courts, mainly in the autonomous regions of Galicia and Madrid. The social impact of the 'preference share' cases

---

[50] See art 24 of the Spanish Constitution. This article proclaims the right to action in court, along with judicial guarantees. Literally, '1. All persons have the right to obtain effective protection from the judges and the courts in the exercise of their rights and legitimate interests, and in no case may there be a lack of defence. 2. Likewise, all have the right to the ordinary judge predetermined by law; to defence and assistance by a lawyer; to be informed of the charges brought against them; to a public trial without undue delays and with full guarantees; to the use of evidence appropriate to their defence; not to make self-incriminating statements; not to plead themselves guilty; and to be presumed innocent. (...)'.

[51] P Grande Seara, 'Capacidad y legitimación en los procesos para la tutela de los derechos de consumidores y usuarios', in *Resolución de conflictos en materia de consumo: proceso y arbitraje* (Ed. Tecnos, 2010), 67.

[52] A Planchadell Gargallo, *Las 'acciones colectivas' en el ordenamiento jurídico español* (Ed Tirant lo Blanch, Valencia, 2014) 44, considers that opt-in mechanisms are more respectful to Spanish constitutional rights, but are less effective from the procedural economy viewpoint, as opt-in systems do not generally avoid the existence of multiple claims, where multiple claims should ideally be accumulated in the first proceeding.

[53] Otero Crespo (above n 42).

[54] In fact, many of the buyers were told that their investments were as safe as a savings deposit.

[55] This arbitration mechanism operates on an individual basis. Through consumer arbitration tribunals, banks have settled with thousands of clients, thus avoiding Court proceedings.

appeared to be an occasion to test the existing collective procedure. However, reality shows us that other than injunctive relief (an example being the injunction against NGC Banco, which was filed prior to the March 2014 amendment by the Public Prosecutor Service)[56] compensation can only be awarded through the exercise of individual claims before first instance courts and through either collective or group claims. However, only a few investors have opted for collective or group claims.[57] Reality shows us that current procedural mechanisms are not capable of effectively resolving a large number of individual claims for compensation of damage. This is disappointing considering that almost every single small investor has requested or must request individually the reimbursement of the losses suffered after acquiring preference shares fraudulently sold by former saving banks, with approximately 71,000 savings bank customers implicated in the financial losses.

4. Funding Mechanisms and Legal Costs

Funding and costs issues are closely related to effective access to justice, notably when cases concern consumer law issues, as the costs of civil litigation are usually high.[58] However, the existence of funding mechanisms aimed at facilitating access to justice for consumers, cannot be a source of abusive litigation. In this regard, the Commission Recommendation contemplates both funding and costs principles.

Regarding funding (points 14 ff), bearing in mind that representative actions would constitute the majority of actions, the Recommendation states that the claimant party (representative entity) should be required to declare to the court at the outset of the proceedings the origin of the funds that will be used to finance the legal action. Third party funding is also expressly taken

---

[56] Commenting on this *Auto* of the *Audiencia Provincial de A Coruña*, Sección 3ª, of 15 February 2013, F Cordón Moreno, 'El Ministerio Fiscal y las acciones para la protección de los derechos de los consumidores y usuarios', *CESCO*, https://www.uclm.es/centro/cesco/pdf/notasJurisprudencia/jurisprudencia/nj25.pdf, 1–2.

[57] Thousands of lawsuits have been filed against the Galician former saving bank (more than 4,000 cases – see the Annual Report 2014 of the Galician Public Prosecutor Service/ *Fiscalía de la Comunidad Autónoma de Galicia. Memoria 2014*, 253. This Report is available at https://www.fiscal.es/memorias/memoria2014/FISCALIA_SITE/recursos/fiscalias/superiores/galicia.pdf). To avoid the high risk of collapse of the first instance courts, the Spanish Justice Administration has set up two specific courts in La Coruña and Vigo which are competent to hear these claims. These Courts have been authorized to accumulate all the individual lawsuits, and they are to be dissolved by the end of 2014. Nevertheless, the large number of cases may extend the duration of their existence.

[58] Those costs include court fees, remuneration of legal representatives, costs of expert analysis, etc. Over the last few years, issues pertaining to court costs have been a source of conflict in Spain, especially since the new Act 10/2012 of 20 November on Judicial Fees.

into account. Concerning the latter, the court should halt the proceedings if a conflict of interests arises where the third party has insufficient resources to meet its financial commitments to the claimant party initiating the collective redress procedure or to meet any costs should the procedure fail. However, the Recommendation only contemplates private financing. This restriction has been explained by the Communication as an issue directly connected to the private nature of the dispute between two parties: "the Commission does not find it necessary to recommend direct support from public funds, since if the court finds that damage has been sustained, the party suffering that damage will obtain compensation from the losing party, including their legal costs."[59] Regardless of its express recognition in the Recommendation, Spanish litigation ignores the third-party funding institution in itself, although nowadays this is neither regulated nor used in practice. In our view, third party funding may be allowed if safeguards are kept to guarantee the sound administration of justice, the transparency of the proceedings and the lack of conflict of interests.

Another issue connected to funding is legal aid, notably the significant barrier for access to justice due to the application of the new fee system of Spanish Courts. Spanish Consumer organizations may obtain legal aid (Article 37 General Act on Consumer Protection 2007) to defend consumer interests (both collective and diffuse interests). In addition Act 1/1996 on Free Legal Assistance [60] provides the right to apply for free justice benefits for associations that represent the public interest or foundations registered in the corresponding administrative register (Article 2 c) who cannot afford litigation costs.

Concerning the costs debate, the Commission Recommendation adopts an ambiguous approach. The 'loser pays principle' seems to be the preferred rule under the Recommendation principles. In this regard, Member States are required to ensure that the lawyers' remuneration and the method by which it is calculated do not incentivize litigation. As a general rule, national legislators in EU Member States should not permit contingency fees which risk creating such an incentive. Specifically, these fees may be allowed when there is national regulation for collective redress which takes into account the right to full compensation of the members of the claimant party already in effect.

Regarding costs, the Spanish system follows the abovementioned principles. Similar to the EC Recommendation, Spain's general principle is the 'loser pays' rule. However, contingency fees/*quota litis* agreements are also available and valid in Spain (which includes lost cases) after the decision of

---

[59] See Communication from the Commission to the Parliament, the Council, the EESC and the Committee of the Regions, 15.
[60] Act 1/1996, of 10 January (*Ley de Justicia Gratuita*).

the Supreme Court of 4 November 2008.[61] No express regulation, as required by the Recommendation, is available in Spain at the moment. However, no abuses of the system have been reported so far.

5. ADR Mechanisms

Collective Alternative Dispute Resolution and settlements are taken into account by the Recommendation as a means of settling disputes concerning compensation either consensually or out-of-court, both at the pre-trial stage and during civil trial (see points 25–28 of the Recommendation). Through observation, it appears as though the European Commission tries to incentivize collective conflict resolution through non-litigation channels, however this is limited to the cases where the parties effectively consent to non-judicial mechanisms. If the parties involved agree to submit the dispute to these alternative channels, the ADR procedure may suspend any limitation period applicable to the claims. If an agreement is reached, the courts should verify the legality of the binding outcome. Therefore, in order to avoid abuse, the judicial authority should revise and approve the agreement.

From the Spanish perspective, collective settlement procedures or collective ADR mechanisms appear irrelevant in practice.[62] Following an ADR model, on March 2013, the Spanish Ombudsman (*Defensor del Pueblo*) suggested setting up a special arbitration system (*arbitraje universal*) designed to compensate investors for their losses in the abovementioned preference shares cases. Although it might have been a good starting point to test collective arbitration as well as claims brought before the courts, most of those cases have been settled through individual arbitration or individual lawsuits.

In contrast, it should be noted that the use of arbitration mechanisms is expressly regulated when dealing with collective claims that concern a certain or determinable number of consumers. Collective consumer arbitration is available under Act 231/2008 regulating the Consumer Arbitration System (Articles 56–62).[63] The goal of collective consumer arbitration is to resolve a series conflicts that are based on the same factual presumptions that have injured the collective interests of consumers and users, and that have affected a determined or determinable number of such persons by using a single

---

[61] On contingency fees/ *quota litis* agreements, see also the Decisions of the Supreme Court 357/2004, 13 May, 446/2008, 29 May and 314/2013, 27 May. Formally, art 44.3 of the *Estatuto General de la Abogacía*, has not been repealed. However, its wording does not comply with subsequent Acts dealing with lawyers' remuneration. Consequently, Supreme Court decisions have supported the legality of contingency fee arrangements under Spanish law.

[62] On collective settlements and their potential regime under Spanish law, Gascón Inchausti (above n 48) especially 147 ff.

[63] Royal Decree 231/2008 of 15 February.

consumer.[64] It should be noted that the decision to proceed collectively is not made by the parties themselves. The President of the relevant Consumer Arbitration Board, either acting on his own initiative or responding to a request from a local consumer association, makes the initial determination as to whether and to what extent a collective arbitration may be appropriate. Then, the respondents (who are either businesses or professionals) must agree to collective arbitration within 15 days of being notified. Respondents may then propose a settlement at the time that they indicate their agreement to collective proceedings, although a settlement offer is not required. If the respondent agrees to collective arbitration, then the Consumer Arbitration Board provides notice to potential claimants in the relevant territory through publication in the territory's Official Journal. Additional means of publicity may be used as well. According to Article 59 of Act 231/2008, the notice must indicate that consumers can protect their individual rights and interests through the collective proceeding; where the consumers and users may access the terms of any proposed settlement; and the consequences of a failure to join the action in a timely manner. The notice period runs for 2 months beginning from the date of publication in the Official Journal. Once the notice period has run, the President of the relevant Consumer Arbitration Board appoints the arbitral tribunal. It is important to highlight that the agreement by the respondent to pursue collective arbitration automatically suspends any individual arbitrations that may be underway. Arbitral submissions presented outside the notice period will only be accepted when the presentation is before the date anticipated for the hearing. The admission of those petitions will not have a retrospective effect on the submissions, as the consumer or user will only be able to intervene in all steps following the date of admission.[65]

III. CONCLUSION

At the end of 2014, the need to reform current Spanish legislation on collective proceedings in order to implement or clarify the principles set out in the Commission Recommendation did not seem to be on the agenda of either

---

[64] As this paper has assessed above, the articles of Act 231/2008 suggest that the precise identity of the members of the collective may be determined after the initiation of the arbitration. See European Parliament Resolution of 2 February 2012.

[65] For further details, see SI Strong, 'Collective consumer arbitration in Spain: a Civil Law Response to US- Style Class Arbitration', 5 *Journal of International Arbitration* 30 (2013), 495–510.

the Spanish legislative or executive powers.[66] However, restructuring of the legislation is required, as existing Spanish provisions do not conform entirely with the Recommendation and some of its proposed tools are not available at the moment. Realistically, the 2015 deadline may not be met by the Spanish legislator, so the question is whether the restructure of legislation will be complete by 2017, when the European Commission will review the implementation of the Recommendation.

Taking into account the current chaotic and incoherent regulation and its negative impact on the functioning of the judicial system – highlighted by certain recent cases mentioned above – the Spanish legislator must clarify how the claimant party is constituted. We have selected to analyse this fundamental matter due to its close correlation to many other collective litigation issues, such as standing to sue, *res judicata*, *lis pendens*, etc. All pressing issues pertaining to collective litigation depend on Spain's opt-in versus opt-out approaches. It has been said that opt-out mechanisms work well in consumer law scenarios involving small claims. However, these type of mechanisms may not comply with our Constitutional requirements, nor will they comply with Article 6 of the ECHR, nor Article 47 (1) of the Charter of Fundamental Rights.

---

[66] Nevertheless, given major cases involving economic damage to thousands of citizens ie the preference share cases, criticism of the inadequacy of the existing collective redress mechanisms has been raised by relevant authorities as the Spanish Ombudsman or the Public Prosecutor Service in Galicia – see Annual Report 2014 of the Galician Public Prosecutor Service (in Spanish); https://www.fiscal.es/memorias/memoria2014/FISCALIA_SITE/recursos/fiscalias/superiores/galicia.pdf.

Recent Collective Redress Developments in Lithuania – Key Issues in Light of the Implementation of the Commission Recommendation

Danguolė Bublienė [*]

I. INTRODUCTION

In June 2013, after long and thorough deliberations concerning a European vision and approach towards collective redress, the European Commission adopted a Recommendation on common principles for injunctive and compensatory collective redress mechanisms in the Member States concerning violations of rights granted under Union Law (the Recommendation).[1] The goal of the Recommendation is not to harmonise the national systems of the Member States of the European Union,[2] but rather to create a unified approach towards collective redress across the EU by establishing common, non-binding principles. The principles set out in the Recommendation should be implemented by the Member States by 26 July 2015 at the latest.

In March 2014, after almost two years of discussions,[3] the Parliament of the Republic of Lithuania adopted amendments to the Civil Procedure Code of the Republic of Lithuania (CPC),[4] introducing in essence a new instrument into civil procedure law – the group action. Although the group action was already introduced in Lithuania in 2003 with the adoption of a new Civil

---

[*] Associate Professor, Private Law Department, Faculty of Law, Vilnius University.
[1] Recommendation of 11 June 2013 on common principles for injunctive and compensatory collective redress mechanisms in the Member States concerning violations of rights granted under Union Law, OJ L 201, 26.7.2013.
[2] European Commission Press release 'Commission recommends Member States to have collective redress mechanisms in place to ensure effective access to justice,' 11 June 2013, available at http://europa.eu/rapid/press-release_IP-13-524_en.htm.
[3] The proposal to the Lithuanian Parliament was provided in June 2012 by the Government of the Republic of Lithuania.
[4] Law of the Republic of Lithuania Amending arts 49, 80, 182 of the Civil Procedure Code of the Republic of Lithuania and Supplementing the Civil Procedure Code of the Republic of Lithuania by Article 261/1 and XXIV/1 division.

Procedure Code, it was surrounded by uncertainty due to ambiguous wording, and has not yet been used in practice.

The 2003 mechanism was replaced by new collective redress legislation, which came into force on 1 January 2015. Given that it is difficult to predict how the new mechanism will function in practice, rather than assess its potential application, this Chapter will instead provide an overview of the differences between the 2014 and 2003 mechanisms, examining the key features of the new model and assessing its compliance with the principles of collective redress provided by the Recommendation. Evaluating the implementation of the Recommendation in the Lithuanian legal system is of particular importance: it is unclear whether the Recommendation was taken into account in the process of the adoption of the Amendments to the CPC as neither the wording of these Amendments, nor their *travaux praparatoires* provide reference to it.

II. THE HISTORY OF GROUP ACTIONS IN THE LITHUANIAN LEGAL SYSTEM

As mentioned, the group action was first introduced in Lithuania in 2003. The then new Civil Procedure Code established two types of collective redress mechanisms: (i) representative actions (Paragraphs 1–5 of Article 49); and (ii) group actions (Paragraph 6 of Article 49). The representative action was applied mainly in the area of injunctive collective redress,[5] eg to protect consumer interests in cases where the State Consumer Protection Authority initiated a claim against businesses regarding amendments of unfair terms in consumer standard contracts. As to the group action mechanism, it was mainly designed for cases of compensatory collective redress, but it was never implemented in practice due to ambiguous and incomplete legislation.

Firstly, the group action was only regulated in one sentence of Article 49 CPC: '6. Group claims may be submitted to protect a public interest.' The CPC did not elaborate detailed regulation to define the model of a group claim nor the grounds for formulating such claims, the definition of a group or its legal consequences. The primary intent of the Lithuanian legislator was to create the general legal background allowing for a group action mechanism to be developed and elaborated upon through case law. However, the single sentence on group actions gave insufficient impetus for the courts to develop the mechanism in practice. Contrary to the purpose of the regulation and due to its laconic character, the Lithuanian courts refused to hear group

---

[5] The term injunctive redress is understood to encompass claims concerning the cessation of illegal behaviour and/or claims concerning recognition and/or modification of legal relationships.

actions brought before them. The Court of Appeal of Lithuania limited the application of the collective group action mechanism by acknowledging the lack of regulation and by declaring it impossible to bring such an action.[6]

Secondly, the group action instrument was based on the objective of protecting a public interest. Although the scope of 'public interest' had been often interpreted by the courts and was therefore a known concept, Article 49 provided no guidance on the scope of a group action or its restrictions. The concept of 'public interest' suffered from uncertainties and vagueness of its own and its interpretation by the Constitutional Court of the Republic of Lithuania has become an obstacle in applying the collective redress mechanism.[8]

Despite the fact that the group action mechanism was specifically designed to deal with mass harm situations, it did not help to resolve compensatory claims. This situation led to attempts by Parliament to resolve the issue by initiating the Draft on the Protection of Public Interests and amendments to the CPC in 2007,[9] which aimed at clarifying *locus standi* and at elaborating

---

[6] Decision of the Court of Appeal of Lithuania, 2 June 2009, in civil case No 2-492/2009. In this case, the Court of Appeal of Lithuania concluded that that there were no objective and real grounds for the implementation of the group action, declaring that the right stipulated in Part 6 of art 49 CPC could not be realized because the mechanism of group action is not regulated by law. In particular, the use of a group action mechanism was deemed impossible because the laws do not specify who may have standing in a group claim, what the particular content and conditions of such claim are, and which rules are to be followed for the submission and assessment of the claim. Evidently, the law does not provide any rules regulating the consequences of such action or its *res judicata* effect.

[7] In the ruling of the Constitutional Court of the Republic of Lithuania of 21 September 2006, the court declared that: "It also needs to be noted that not any legitimate interest of a person or a group of persons is to be considered as a public interest, but only such interest, which reflects and expresses the fundamental values which are entrenched in, as well as protected and defended by the Constitution; these are inter alia openness and harmony of society, the rights and freedoms of the person, the supremacy of law, etc. It is such interest of society or part thereof, which the State, while implementing its functions, is obliged to ensure and satisfy, inter alia through courts that decide cases at law within their jurisdiction. Thus, every time when the question arises whether a certain interest is to be considered as a public one, it must be possible to reason that without satisfying a certain interest of a person or a group of persons, certain values entrenched in, as well as protected and defended by the Constitution, would be violated. While in situations where the decision on whether a certain interest has to be considered as public and is defended and protected as a public interest, must be taken by the court, which considers a case, it is necessary to reason it in the corresponding act of the court. Otherwise, a grounded doubt would arise that what is protected and defended by the court as a public interest, actually is not a public but a private interest of a certain person." The official English version of this ruling is available at http://www.lrkt.lt/dokumentai/2006/r060921.htm.

[8] Ruling of the Supreme Court of the Republic of Lithuania, 30 July 2009, in civil case No 3k-3-333/2009.

[9] The Draft Law on Protection of Public Interests and the Draft Law Amending and Supplementing arts 5, 27, 49, 83, 274, 275, 296 of the Civil Procedure Code and Supplementing arts 96/1 of the Civil Procedure Code.

rules on a group action mechanism. The Government did not approve the drafts, arguing that they lacked legal clarity and a systematic approach.[10] The drafts were never adopted.

In 2008, the Ministry of Justice initiated research on the situation concerning group actions. Three years later – in 2011 – the Lithuanian Government adopted a Concept Paper on Group Actions,[11] describing the essence of the reform of the group action system and its implementation. The improved group action mechanism was designed with the intent of consumer protection, aiming to ensure the right balance between the interests of consumers and businesses. However, the Concept Paper itself did not propose to limit the group action mechanism to merely the protection of consumer interests. It was designed as a measure to protect individual rights and interests in different areas of society, transforming the philosophy of the group action mechanism from public to private. This reform was based on the explanation that the interests of the group may not always coincide with the public interest, as they were interpreted by the aforementioned jurisprudence of the Constitutional Court. This was also transposed into the amendments to the CPC. In 2011, the Ministry of Justice charged a working group with the enactment of the Concept Paper. The draft of the amendments to the CPC was accepted by the Government in 2011, and was adopted by Parliament after two years of thorough consideration.

Therefore, as a result of legislative initiatives and reforms, two different mechanisms coexist in Lithuania: one linked to the protection of the public interest and a new mechanism for group action proceedings. It should be possible for a victim to pursue both injunctive and compensatory collective redress. However, the realisation of compensatory collective redress through the collective redress provision in Article 49 CPC remains a matter for discussion.

III. THE KEY FEATURES OF THE LITHUANIAN GROUP ACTION

A. General Characteristics of the Group Action

The main aim of the group action instrument is twofold: (i) to protect the interests of the weaker party, notably in the areas of consumer protection, unfair commercial practice, employment, competition and environmental matters[12] and (ii) to create an effective procedural mechanism, which allows for reduced costs of litigation, for both the parties and the State.

---

[10] Resolution No 1243 of the Government of the Republic of Lithuania of 21 November 2007.

[11] Resolution No 855 of the Government of the Republic of Lithuania of 13 July 2011 on the adoption of the concept of group action.

[12] *Travaux preparatoires* of the Draft on the Amendments to the CPC, 2; available at http://www.lrv.lt/Posed_medz/2012/120627/04.pdf.

The formation of the group depends on two factors: numerosity and commonality. The CPC establishes the minimum threshold for the formation of the group – the minimum number of members should be 20 plaintiffs. If the number falls below the mandatory threshold, it is at the discretion of the court to decide whether to pursue the claim. The commonality factor requires the members of the group to share common questions of law or fact, including protection of rights and interests.

The commonality factor renders the collective group action mechanism similar to a joinder of claims, where a plaintiff shares the same legal and factual grounds of a case with other plaintiffs. However, the group action is to be distinguished from a joinder of claims, as specific rules are established to regulate it. The main procedural difference is that in the case of a joinder of claims, each plaintiff acts in his own name. Each plaintiff is able to conduct his case independently and could be summoned to a court hearing. The plaintiffs may also agree to have the case conducted by one of them. However, the agreement of all participants (co-plaintiffs or co-defendants) is in general mandatory to conclude a settlement, or waive or accept a claim, except where it does not exceed the requirements indicated in the claim. The situation is different with the group action mechanism: the group members, with a few exceptions provided in the CPC, do not have any right to manage their case independently, or to appear before the court to represent themselves in person at a hearing or in other procedural actions. The representative of the group represents their interests. There is no requirement for the group to issue a formal power of attorney to the group representative. This ensures a more effective and expedient procedure.

Furthermore, the adequate or proper representation principle is applied in the case of a group action. The arguments proving the legitimacy of the representative should be indicated in the statement of the group claim. Accordingly, the court, while considering the issue of admissibility of the case, should consider the legitimacy of the group representative, by evaluating the fairness of the representative, their reputation, whether the representative is competent to take on the role, their experience and behaviour in similar cases, and whether a conflict of interest exists between the group representative and the group members. The principle of proper representation requires the court to suggest a change of representative if it finds that the latter does not act properly on behalf of the group.

The new regulation on group actions does not clearly stipulate how many individuals could be appointed as representatives of the group. On the one hand, the law uses the singular form to describe the legal status and role of the group representative. On the other hand, the law does not indicate any prohibitions or restrictions on having more than one representative to a group. However, if an excessive number of representatives were appointed to the group action procedure, the court may decide not to accept the case as a group action and instead consider individual procedures more effective.

It should be added that a representative action cannot be brought under the rules for group actions.[13] However, an association or trade union is entitled to be a group representative, (i) if the claims provided in the form of a group action arose from the legal relationship directly related to its objectives provided in its articles of association, and (2) if no less than ten group plaintiffs are members of the association or trade union. In this case, not all group members might be members of the association or trade union. However, the association or trade union should represent the interests of all group action plaintiffs alike. Unlike in representative actions, the victims in a mass harm situation are also a party to the group action proceedings.

A rule on mandatory group representation by a lawyer was introduced in the group action mechanism. This rule is considered an important safeguard for individual rights and interests, as it ensures that the claim form will be drafted in a professional way, that professional representation is guaranteed and that the possibility of abuse is reduced.[14]

B. Requirement for an Out-of-Court Settlement

The group action is subject to mandatory out-of-court negotiations, and the court will only accept a group action if the parties have failed to resolve their dispute peacefully by prior mutual agreement. The requirement for an out-of-court settlement can be met in two ways: (i) through the submission of a written petition to the defendant. The written petition should state the group's intention to submit the claim in court, describe the group, the claim, and indicate that the group will proceed with court proceedings if no settlement is reached; or (ii) through out-of-court negotiations following a procedure regulated by law. However, it has to be noted that the provisions regulating the out-of-court settlement procedure need to be reviewed before being useful in practice, as they do not contain any special rules regarding group actions. For example, an out-of-court procedure is provided for by law in consumer disputes. However, the relevant rules do not indicate any possibility of a group action procedure. Undoubtedly, taking into account that out-of-court procedures in consumer matters are under the jurisdiction of the state institutions, which are responsible for market surveillance, it would be useful to coordinate

---

[13] The representative action as described in the Recommendation cannot be brought under Lithuanian rules on group actions.

[14] Resolution No 855 of the Government of the Republic of Lithuania of 13 July 2011. On the adoption of the Concept on the group action, para 19.2 of the Concept; *Travaux preparatoires* of the Draft Amendments to the CPC, 4; available at http://www.lrv.lt/Posed_medz/2012/120627/04.pdf.

the processes and to establish effective consumer protection mechanisms. It should also be noted that the law does not establish any rule providing that the courts should verify the outcome of out-of-court negotiations.

C. Opt-in Model

The Lithuanian legislator has decided to adopt a group action mechanism based on an opt-in model. The opt-in model signifies that the group of claimants is constituted on the basis of consent of all those claiming to have been injured or harmed. The justification for the model was based on the fact that only a few European countries have started implementing an opt-out system in their national law. Furthermore, Lithuania does not have experience with group action lawsuits, and there are still doubts whether the opt-out system is contrary to the provisions of the European Convention on Human Rights and Fundamental Freedoms.[15]

The opt-in principle is evident in several articles of the CPC. First, the CPC clearly states that an individual shall express in written form their consent to participate in a group action, and must submit it to the court (point 1 of Part 2 Article 441/3). Accordingly, the individual joining the group must submit a statement form to the group representative.[16] The written statements of the group plaintiffs, together with the list of participants in the group action, shall be submitted to the court. Secondly, the group representative should publish an announcement with information about the group action, as well as information for the individuals who wish to join the group. It should be noted that the law does not indicate any criteria or methods of publicising a group action. Thirdly, new plaintiffs may be added to the group. When accepting the claim, the court will establish a deadline for joining the group action. After amendments to the claim are made, the court shall finally decide whether all plaintiffs may be included in the group, and confirm the final composition of the group (Article 441/7 and 441/8 of the CPC). A person is free to decide whether to join or withdraw from the group, and this right cannot be restricted. After the final confirmation of the group's composition, new plaintiffs may only be added if there are serious grounds to do so, and only upon approval by the defendant and the group representative.[17] The

---

[15] Resolution No 855 of the Government of the Republic of Lithuania of 13 July 2011. On the adoption of the Concept on the group action, para 14 of the Concept; *Travaux preparatoires* of the Draft Amendments to the CPC, 4; available at http://www.lrv.lt/Posed_medz/2012/120627/04.pdf.

[16] Order No 1R-378 of the Minister of Justice of the Republic of Lithuania of 22 December 2014.

[17] This does not apply where an individual claim has been submitted before the final confirmation of the group. In that case the claimant shall withdraw the claim on the basis of art 139 CPC and become a member of the group.

application in such a situation is made to the court and not to the group representative. In case the number of plaintiffs in the group falls below the minimum requirement, it is at the discretion of the court to decide whether the action should go forward, taking into account the effectiveness, suitableness, and expedience of the process (Article 441/11 of the CPC).

D. Loser Pays Principle and Financing of the Group Action

Similar to many other Member States, the loser pays principle is the prevailing practice in Lithuanian civil procedure. The regulation of the group action mechanism does not overrule this principle. Moreover, this principle was maintained as the main safeguard against abusive litigation for group action lawsuits.[18] The CPC establishes special rules for the split of litigation costs between the group members. The dominating principle is equality; litigation expenses incurred by the party in whose favour the judgment was made shall be awarded by the court to the other party (and if this is the claimant side, should be attributed to the group action plaintiffs in equal parts). It would seem that the rule is quite simple and clear. However, an exception to that rule could potentially be applied in the following cases: (i) in case of individual claims in group action cases, the litigation expenses incurred after an interim decision are ascribed to the individuals who submitted individual claims; (ii) in case a member of the group does not wish to proceed with their claim, they shall cover the expenses incurred before leaving the group (which might lead to complications in determining exactly which expenses were incurred before the opt-out).

The CPC neither regulates litigation financing nor contingency or success fees. It only provides that expenses that are reasonable and necessary for the group representative shall be ascribed to the litigation expenses. The expenses pertaining to legal assistance are included in the litigation expenses, in accordance with the general rules of the CPC. The representative of the group supervises the allocation of the litigation expenses between the group plaintiffs. However, there are no indications or restrictions in the CPC as to financing from third parties.

The financing of group actions was not taken into account and regulated when the group action mechanism was introduced into the Lithuanian legal system. A success fee was enacted in 2004 through the adoption of a new Law on the Bar.[19] This law establishes that in civil cases a party is allowed to agree that the lawyer's fee would depend on the outcome of the case, unless such agreement on a success fee would contradict the rules governing good

---

[18] See the *travaux preparatoires* of the Draft Amendments to the CPC, 8; available at http://www.lrv.lt/Posed_medz/2012/120627/04.pdf.

[19] Law No IX-2066 of 18 March 2004.

practice of lawyers.[20] This rule was not changed or amended with the enactment of the group action. Despite the fact that the rule is permissive in nature, it is quite vague. Moreover, the Code of Professional Conduct for the Advocates of Lithuania does not address success fee matters, nor does it explain exceptions to the rule. It does not create boundaries for the application of the rule, but rather only provides general principles of conduct for lawyers. It will therefore depend on judicial interpretation where the success fee would not be acceptable with respect to group action scenarios.

E. The Main Procedural Peculiarities of the Group Action Mechanism

The main procedural peculiarities of the group action under Lithuanian law are related to (i) the rules concerning admissibility, (ii) the role of the court, (iii) the requirement to publish information, (iiii) rules on the allocation of the litigation expenses (discussed above) and (iv) rules relating to changes of the group and the realization of the group's procedural rights and obligations. Lastly, the time limits set in group action proceedings need to be taken into account.

As to the rules on admissibility a fairly broad discretion is assigned to the court to decide whether the claim can be admitted as a group action. The admissibility is examined in the process of acceptance of the group action claim, and, to a certain extent, in a later phase of the proceedings. While examining whether the court should accept the claim, the court shall evaluate whether the claim satisfies the requirements of the group action legislation (ie numerosity and commonality – correlation between the group action claims and the individual claims). Furthermore, the court takes all circumstances into account in order to ensure that the group action mechanism is more expedient, effective, and the most efficient way to solve the claim compared with individual claims. Finally, as was discussed above, the court decides on the legitimacy of the group representative.

The court will be quite active during the group action proceedings. It is entitled to decide *ex officio* whether there is a necessity for the group members to participate in the court hearing, or to dismiss the group lawyer or group representative if the court believes that they act improperly.

The publicity requirement is directed at both the group representative and the court. The group representative is obliged to publish an announcement inviting potential plaintiffs to join the group action. The court has to publish, on a specific website, information about any developments (after the group action's acceptance), eg whether the group disapproves of or has been ordered to replace its representative, or any other developments.

---

[20] See art 50, Law No IX-2066 of 18 March 2004.

The statement of the claim shall indicate the list of plaintiffs. However, at the time of acceptance, the list of plaintiffs is not final and may be amended during proceedings. New plaintiffs might join the group during a period of time indicated by the court (between 60 to 90 days, extendable for an additional 30 days). After the consolidation of the plaintiff list, the court shall once again examine whether the action meets the requirements established by law and adopt a final list of group members. From then on, only plaintiffs justifying that they were unable to join the group action earlier for important reasons can join if both the group action representative and the defendant give their consent. This contrasts with the situation of plaintiffs joining the action at the beginning, where consent of the defendant is not required.

The CPC establishes further procedural peculiarities for group actions. These concern the right to change the grounds of the claim, to withdraw or waive the claim or the right to settle the case. A withdrawal requires consent of more than half of the group members. The essence of these rules is related to the right to opt-out from the group action. In case group members do not exercise their right to opt-out, they are bound by any withdrawal, waiver or settlement.

F. The Particularities of the Group Action in Appeal and Cassation

There are special rules for group actions in appeal and cassation. These firstly relate to mandatory representation by the group representative and the lawyer and secondly, to the right of group members to waive their rights and obligations in appeal or Supreme Court proceedings. If half the members of the group waive their right to an appeal, the latter will not be possible. However, an appeal or cassation judgment, if rendered, is imposed on the members, even if they waived their right to an appeal. Thirdly, the law establishes rules on how the group representative may be replaced during an appeal. Fourthly, there is a provision concerning the right to submit an individual appeal or a cassation appeal in case the group does not file an appeal. The statute of limitation for an individual, both for an appeal to the second instance or a cassation appeal, is 30 days.

IV. IMPLEMENTATION OF THE COMMISSION RECOMMENDATION IN THE LITHUANIAN LEGAL SYSTEM – AN EVALUATION

A. Impact of the Recommendation on the Interpretation of National Law

The Commission Recommendation[21] is a non-binding legal instrument of

---

[21] Above (note 1).

the *acquis communautaire*. Its objective is not to achieve a level of harmonisation of the Member States' legal provisions that regulate collective redress, but rather to establish a common policy and legal framework for collective redress in the EU. However, taking into account points 38–41, it is evident that the Recommendation could lead to a harmonisation of collective redress systems. It is therefore worth considering what influence the Recommendation could have on national law in the area of collective redress. Taking into account the practice of the Court of Justice (CJEU), the legal status of the Recommendation and its effect on national law remains unclear and there is uncertainty as to how the Recommendation is going to be implemented.

The CJEU has had several opportunities to interpret the legal status of EU Recommendations, but instead of clarifying their status, the CJEU case law has rather created more obscurity concerning the influence of a Recommendation on national law. This is reflected in the *Alassini* case:[22]

> In that connection, it should be borne in mind that the Court has consistently held that, even if Recommendations are not intended to produce binding effects and are not capable of creating rights that individuals can rely on before a national court, they are not without any legal effect. The national courts are bound to take Recommendations into consideration in order to decide disputes brought before them, in particular where such Recommendations cast light on the interpretation of national measures adopted in order to implement them or where they are designed to supplement binding provisions of EU law.[23]

The view of the CJEU could be summarized as follows: (i) Recommendations do not create legal rights on which individuals can rely before national courts. Therefore, in contrast to EU directives, individuals cannot claim damages from the State for the non–implementation of Recommendations; (ii) the national courts have to take into account Recommendations when interpreting the national rules that implement Recommendations or where they are designed to supplement binding provisions of EU law. The latter rule developed by the CJEU renders Recommendations rather unclear, especially since the CJEU recognized that 'Recommendations are generally adopted by the institutions of the Community when they do not have the power under the Treaty to adopt binding measures or when they consider that it is not appropriate to adopt

---

[22] Judgment of the CJEU, of 18 March 2010, in joined Cases C-317/08, C-318/08, C-319/08 and C-320/08 *Rosalba Alassini ao v Telecom Italia SpA* [2010] ECR I-02213.

[23] See also Case C-322/88 *Grimaldi* [1989] ECR 4407, paras 7, 16 and 18, and Case C-207/01 *Altair Chimica* [2003] ECR I-8875, para 41.

more mandatory rules.'[24] It is not clear whether it is mandatory to take Recommendations into account in interpreting national rules, given their non-binding character. Taking the example of collective redress in Lithuanian law, the situation is particularly unclear as the CPC Amendments were not designed to transpose and implement principles established in the Recommendation, or at least there is no clear indication of such intention. Furthermore, it is not clear whether the court should interpret national law in light of a Recommendation if national law contradicts it. Should the court then interpret national law *contra legem*? The practical effect of the CJEU's interpretation in the aforementioned cases is unclear due to the fact that the Court, upon examining the effects of Recommendations, has not stated to what extent the national court should take into account the provisions of a Recommendation, what possible effect such interpretation could have on the rights of individuals and what influence it could have on the obligations of Member States.

Besides the CJEU's interpretation concerning the legal effect of Recommendations, the Commission Recommendation on collective redress itself creates uncertainty concerning its legal effect and consequences due to its section VII. Firstly, the Recommendation indicates the date of its implementation. Furthermore, the Recommendation requires the Member States to collect statistical data and provide the information to the Commission. It should be noted that similar rules have not existed in other instruments such as the ADR Recommendation.[25] Finally, the Recommendation on collective redress requires that the Commission evaluates the Recommendation's impact and effect on access to justice after four years and assesses whether there is a necessity for further regulatory measures in the EU (point 44 of the Recommendation). It is evident that such rules are not in line with a non-binding nature.

B. The Lithuanian Group Action Model in Light of the Commission Recommendation on Collective Redress

Regardless of how the CJEU will interpret the Recommendation in the future, it is clear that the Recommendation is the legal instrument which reflects to some extent the political and legal consensus of the EU in the area of collective redress. This is further evident in the fact that the rules were

---

[24] *Grimaldi* (above n 22), para 13.
[25] Commission Recommendation of 30 March 1998 on the principles applicable to the bodies responsible for out-of-court settlement of consumer disputes (OJ L 115, 17.4.1998, 31–34) and Commission Recommendation of 4 April 2001 on the principles for out-of-court bodies involved in the consensual resolution of consumer disputes (OJ L 109, 19.4.2001, 0056–0061).

considered in depth and many stakeholders, including the EU institutions, participated in the elaboration process. Therefore, the established principles demonstrate an important common concept at the EU level, taking into account the European legal traditions, culture and social environment. The Recommendation is designed to both guarantee the protection of individual rights and interests indicated in EU law, and to facilitate access to justice. Therefore, it is worth evaluating how this concept is translated into the Lithuanian group action model.

The Recommendation provides two types of principles: common principles of collective redress and specific principles concerning injunctive and compensatory collective redress. Generally, the principles contained in the Recommendation could be summarized as principles establishing two types of rules which are different by nature: (i) safeguards against abusive litigation (limited standing for representative actions, admissibility check, loser pays principle, opt-in rule with the exception to apply an opt-out system, conditions for funding and legal fees, and the prohibition of punitive damages); (ii) measures promoting collective redress (fair, speedy and not prohibitively expensive procedures, adequate information, cross-border collective redress, effectiveness of injunctive collective redress, consensual dispute resolution, and registration of collective redress actions).[26]

The Lithuanian group action model corresponds in essence to the concept of European collective redress, as it reflects the main safeguards established in the Recommendation.

1. Convergences

First, the Lithuanian group action model is based on the opt-in system, the main procedural safeguard and guarantee for the parties to group actions. Despite the fact that the Recommendation admits the opt-out system as an exception, the Lithuanian legislator has established stricter regulation and does not provide for the application of an opt-out model. As is pointed out in the Recitals of the Recommendation, the opt-out model is alien to the legal traditions of most Member States. The same is true for punitive damages, which cannot be awarded to a plaintiff under the Lithuanian Civil Code. The same is also true for both intrusive pre-trial discovery and jury trials.[27] According to the Recommendation, the opt-in system is closely

---

[26] Communication from the Commission of the to the European Parliament, the Council, The European Economic and Social Committee and the Committee of the Regions 'Towards a European Horizontal Framework for Collective redress', COM 2013) 401/2; European Commission Press release 'Commission recommends Member States to have collective redress mechanisms in place to ensure effective access to justice', 11 June 2013, available at http://europa.eu/rapid/press-release_IP-13-524_en.htm.

[27] Recommendation, Recital (15).

related to the right to freely join the group or leave the group. Although the CPC only grants the right of joining the group without restrictions during a time period indicated by the court (except if there are important reasons for the non-respect of the time period), these rules can be considered in compliance with the Recommendation (point 23).

Further, whereas the Recommendation aims at limiting representative actions by establishing strict eligibility criteria, the representative action in Lithuanian law does not reflect the spirit of the Recommendation. Representative actions are possible for the protection of public interests. Therefore, the eligibility criterion becomes important for these particular cases. However, Lithuanian law does not limit the power of representative entities along the criteria established in the Recommendation.

Furthermore, the rules on admissibility enacted in Lithuanian law ensure that the admissibility check occurs at the first stage of the proceedings. The rules are quite conservative and cautious, and refer to the priority of individual litigation over group action litigation. This is clearly evidenced by the numerosity criteria. It shall be noted that the numerosity criteria does not coincide with the description of the term 'collective redress' provided in the Recommendation. According to the latter, both injunctive and compensatory collective redress mechanisms should be allowed where two or more plaintiffs are entitled to bring an action collectively. In contrast, the Lithuanian group action model is based on the threshold of 20 or more plaintiffs. Moreover, even reaching the threshold does not guarantee that the case will be examined according to the group action rules. As stated above, Lithuanian law requires the court to evaluate all circumstances, ensuring that the group action mechanism is a more expedient, effective and appropriate way to resolve group claims compared to individual claims. It is doubtful whether a court would consider the group action mechanism a more expedient, effective and appropriate way to solve the claim if there are only two claimants.

In addition, similar to the Recommendation, Lithuanian law provides for an active role of the court in group action proceedings. The court must manage the collective group action proceedings effectively in order to help protect the rights of the group members.

Lastly, as mentioned above, the loser pays principle prevails in both the Lithuanian CPC and in the Recommendation.

2. Divergences
At same time the lack of implementation of some concepts of the Recommendation in the Lithuanian legal system should be noted.

Firstly, Lithuanian law lacks rules pertaining to litigation funds. The Lithuanian rules do not oblige the group representative (or the group members) to disclose the origin of the funds financing the group action. Furthermore, the court is neither entitled to stay the proceedings under

Lithuanian law when faced with situations stipulated in point 15 of the Recommendation which allows for such a stay, nor is there a rule in Lithuanian law pertaining to third party funding. Although Lithuania does not customarily practice third party litigation funding, this does not mean that no demand for third party financing will arise in the future. Moreover, Lithuanian law allows success fees and does not provide any particular restrictions on such fees in cases of group actions. It is unclear whether ethical principles will be appropriate safeguards. Therefore, in this regard, the Lithuanian law should be revised.

Secondly, the new rules in the CPC have not clarified the relationship between public and private enforcement. As indicated in the Recommendation, collective redress mechanisms should supplement public enforcement (Recommendation, Recitals (7) and (22), points 33, 34). The *ratio legis* of the principle is twofold: first, the collective redress mechanism should be consistent with public enforcement; second, in follow-on[28] actions ie actions following a final decision of a public authority finding that there has been a violation of Union law, the public interest and the need to avoid abuse can be presumed to have been already taken into account by the public authority. In Lithuanian law, there is no ground for a stay of a group action if proceedings of a public authority are launched after the commencement of the former. According to the CPC, it is mandatory to stay proceedings when a case cannot be heard because another related case is pending in either a civil, criminal or administrative procedure. However, this is only applicable in the event where both cases are pending before courts. It is doubtful whether a court will order a stay in the cases encompassed by the Recommendation. However, these scenarios would be an ideal basis to realize the CJEU's approach that the national court should take the Recommendation into account when applying national law implementing it. The CJEU's view, if put into practice, would prevent national law from contradicting the Recommendation and the latter would influence the application of national rules.

In addition, in order to correctly comply with the Recommendation as to the consistency of the collective redress mechanism with public enforcement, administrative processes in Lithuanian law which are designed to protect individual rights consecrated in EU law should be reviewed, and the Lithuanian collective redress provisions should establish clear rules regarding those mechanisms, whilst ensuring the mechanism's effectiveness.

Thirdly, the Recommendation instituted the provision of effective access to information, thus attempting to ensure a balance between freedom of expression and the right to access information on the one hand and the

---

[28] The description of follow-on action is established in point 3 e) of the Recommendation.

protection of the reputation of the defendant on the other. As mentioned above, the CPC Amendments indicate two types of requirements for publicity of a group claim: through the announcement of the group representative and through a specially designated website. The law does not indicate any criteria or method for the announcement by the group representative. Taking into account points 10 to 12 of the Recommendation, it should be examined whether the general regulation of mass media in Lithuania would help ensure the right balance or whether some specific rules should be enacted to ensure such balance.

Fourthly, the Recommendation obliges the Member States to establish a national registry of collective actions. At present, no registry is available in Lithuania.

V. CONCLUSION

Even though no reference was made to the Recommendation when the group action mechanism was enacted in Lithuanian law, the Lithuanian group action model corresponds in essence to the concept of 'European' collective redress, as it reflects the main safeguards established in the Recommendation. The adoption of detailed rules on group actions clearly reflects new trends and movements within the jurisdictions of EU Member States' laws in the area of collective redress. It is further evident that there is a clear intention to develop an additional mechanism for the protection of the rights and interests of individuals, by improving access to justice and avoiding an abusive litigation culture while conserving the legal culture of each Member State. Even though the Lithuanian group action model contains procedural safeguards, the Recommendation has not fully been implemented into the Lithuanian legal system and Lithuanian law should be better aligned with it.

Areas to be addressed are: third party funding, for which a higher demand may arise in the future; potential restrictions for success fees in the context of group actions; improved coordination of public and private enforcement which requires a review of administrative processes designed to protect individual rights based on EU law; clear criteria regarding the provision of information by the group representative; and the creation of a registry for collective actions.

The New Belgian Law on Consumer Collective Redress and Compliance with EU Law Requirements

Janek Tomasz Nowak[1]

I. INTRODUCTION

The Belgian Law on collective redress for consumers[2] entered into force on 1 September 2014 and marks a new phase in the development of Belgian procedural law, which has traditionally preferred individual claims.[3] The aim of this chapter is to place the new law in the existing procedural landscape and to provide an assessment of its most salient points in the light of EU law. To that end, Part I will assess the history of collective redress in Belgium before the adoption of the law of 28 March 2014. It appears that despite the preference for an individual treatment of claims, certain instruments of collective redress were already available. Part II gives an overview of the main features of the 2014 Law, which will provide the reader with an insight into the functioning of the procedure. Part III will add a European perspective and assess to what extent the law corresponds to the demands of EU law, in particular the 2013 European Commission (EC) Recommendation on collective redress.[4]

II. COLLECTIVE REDRESS IN BELGIUM BEFORE THE ADOPTION OF THE LAW OF 28 MARCH 2014

A. *Principle: No Collective Redress Unless Specifically Allowed by the Law*

Article 17 of the Belgian Civil Procedure Code (CPC) states that proceedings

---

[1] Junior Researcher, Institute for European Law, KU Leuven and Visiting Lecturer, MCI Management Center Innsbruck. The author wishes to thank Eva Lein, Marta Otero Crespo, Sven Sobrie and Jogchum Vrielink for their valuable comments. All errors remain my own.
[2] Law of 28 March 2014 concerning an action for collective redress, *Belgian State Gazette* 2014, 35201.
[3] L Frankignoul, 'L'action en réparation collective ou un mécanisme procédural permettant de prendre le droit au sérieux', *Revue Générale de Droit Civil Belge* (2012) 207.
[4] Commission Recommendation of 11 June 2013 on common principles for injunctive and compensatory collective redress mechanisms in the Member States concerning violations of rights granted under Union Law, OJ 2013, L201/60.

will be declared inadmissible if an applicant does not have an interest in the outcome of the proceedings or no capacity (power) to bring a claim. The interest should be personal and direct, meaning that the proceedings should provide a benefit for the applicant himself and that his legal situation will be changed if the case is decided in his favour. Furthermore, the interest should be vested and present, meaning that hypothetical future interests cannot be protected. The only exception to this principle that the law permits is an action brought to protect a 'severely threatened' right.[5] The capacity to bring proceedings refers to the connection between the applicant and the right he seeks to protect.[6] When the applicant is also the beneficiary of the right he seeks to protect, the notion of capacity adds very little – if nothing – to the notion of interest.[7] If however, the applicant is not the beneficiary of this right, the notion of capacity will play an important role in evaluating whether the person bringing the proceedings is entitled to do so.[8]

Given the fact that a collective redress mechanism generally entails the possibility for a representative to bring an action on behalf of a possibly indeterminate number of applicants, a number of potential difficulties may arise in light of these conditions. The notion of 'interest' appears key in this respect since a representative in principle does not protect any personal or direct interest. Most actions defending collective interests therefore failed before the courts due to lack of personal and direct interest. 'Capacity' only comes into play when a representative has been given the power by law to defend a certain collective interest. The judge will then assess whether a sufficient connection exists between the interest such a representative seeks to protect and the specific interest at stake.

1. Interest

The definition of the notion 'interest' is controversial. A former prosecutor-general of the Belgian Supreme Court once stated that 'interest' is likely to be one of the least clear notions of the Belgian Civil Procedure Code.[9] It is clear, however, from the case law of the Supreme Court, that bringing an action defending a collective interest is, in principle, only possible when explicitly

---

[5] Art 18(2) CPC.

[6] ME Storme, 'Procesrechtelijke knelpunten bij de geldendmaking van rechten uit aansprakelijkheid voor de burgerlijke rechter, in het bijzonder belang, hoedanigheid en rechtsopvolging', in *Recht halen uit aansprakelijkheid* (Mys & Breesch, 1993), 198; H Boularbah, 'La double dimension de la qualité, condition de l'action et condition de la demande en justice', *Revue Générale de Droit Civil* (1997) No A.1. 'Capacity' should be understood as having the power/competence to bring proceedings and not as 'being capable of' bringing proceedings.

[7] Boularbah (above n 6).

[8] *Ibid*.

[9] J Krings, Opinion in Cass. 19 November 1982, *Arr Cass*, 1982–83, 374.

provided for by the law. Or, to put it differently, collective actions are prohibited unless allowed by the law. The Supreme Court has made its view on collective interest litigation explicit in the *Eikendael* case. The case concerned an action brought by an environmental protection association against a decision of a local planning authority to change the designation of the Eikendael domain, an area of high ecological value, in order to allow the owner to build apartments there. The association brought proceedings before the Conseil d'Etat in order to have the decision annulled.[10] While the annulment proceedings were pending before the Conseil d'Etat, an action was brought before the civil courts in order to have the planning decision suspended. A recourse to the civil courts system was necessary because, at that time, the Council of State had no power to suspend an act at issue pending the outcome of the annulment proceedings. The planning decision was suspended at first instance,[11] a decision confirmed on appeal.[12] The Supreme Court, however, reversed the decision of the Court of Appeal, holding that:

> [U]nless the law provides otherwise, an action brought by a natural or legal person is not admissible when the applicant does not have a personal and direct interest in the outcome of the case, meaning an own interest; the general interest cannot be considered to be an own interest for that purpose. [13]

The Court then went on to consider that "the own interest of a legal person only concerns that what affects their existence or their material and moral rights, in particular their assets or reputation" and that "the sole fact that a legal or a natural person pursues a goal, be it or not a statutory goal, does not have as a consequence that an own interest is established, for everyone can potentially pursue any goal."[14]

The *Eikendael* doctrine proved to be a limit to collective actions before the courts of the judiciary for decades. Only recently, in a 2013 judgment concerning an action for damages brought by an environmental association, has the Supreme Court departed from its *Eikendael* doctrine. In reference to the Aarhus Convention it held that:

---

[10] Conseil d'Etat 11 September 1981, *Arr RvSt* 1981, 1283.
[11] President of the Antwerp Court of First Instance 20 October 1980, *Rechtskundig Weekblad* 1980–81, 2553.
[12] Antwerp Court of Appeal 12 March 1981, unpublished.
[13] Belgian Supreme Court 19 November 1982, *Pasinomie* 1983, I, 338 (Translation by the author).
[14] *Ibid*.

Belgium has imposed upon itself the obligation to secure access to justice for environmental protection associations seeking to challenge the action or inaction of private parties or state authorities in breach of environmental law, in so far as they comply with the conditions that national law requires. [15]

The court further held that "those criteria cannot be interpreted in such a way as to render access to justice for such associations impossible" but should be interpreted "in compliance with the objectives of Article 9.3 of the Aarhus Convention."[16]

It is not clear yet whether this jurisprudence will have any effect outside the area of environmental law. Given the fact that the Supreme Court based its reasoning solely on the Aarhus Convention, it seems very unlikely that the *Eikendael* doctrine will be relaxed in relation to collective interest actions brought in other areas of the law.

2. *Capacity*

The notion of capacity plays a particular role in the admissibility of proceedings brought by interest groups before the Belgian Conseil d'Etat and the Belgian Constitutional Court. Contrary to the Supreme Court, they quite easily accept proceedings brought by interest groups, especially the Constitutional Court. The notion of capacity is being used to determine whether a sufficient connection exists between the interest group's founding statute and activities on the one hand and the collective interest it seeks to protect on the other.[17] Given the fact that the debate on collective redress mechanisms in the EU mainly centres around the possibility to seek damages for violations of consumer and competition law, we will not delve further into how the notion of capacity is being analysed for the purposes of judicial review.[18]

The question of capacity in regards to interest groups before the ordinary courts has not generated much case law since actions were often defeated on the ground that associations could not bring an action to defend a collective interest. Also, in cases where associations sought to defend their own mater-

---

[15] Belgian Supreme Court 11 June 2013, No P.12.1389.N/1, 4 (Translation by the author).
[16] *Ibid*.
[17] Boularbah (above n 6) No I.A.2.c.
[18] See further, J Wouters, G De Baere and JT Nowak, 'Iets over de invloed van het internationaal en Europees recht op het administratief recht' in D D'Hooghe, K Deketelaere and AM Draye, *Liber Amicorum Marc Boes* (Die Keure, 2011), 619–634 (Conseil d'Etat) and JT Nowak, 'Wettigheidstoetsing van handelingen van de instellingen van de Europese Unie: complementaire rechtsbescherming in een meerlagige rechtsorde', *Tijdschrift voor Bestuurswetenschappen en Publiekrecht* (2013) 195-2011 (Constitutional Court).

ial or moral rights, the question of capacity was not at stake since the association was defending its own interest.

An exception in this regard is the case of environmental protection associations. A 1993 Act seeking to mitigate the consequences of the Supreme Court's *Eikendael* doctrine conferred upon environmental protection associations a right to apply for cessation orders to stop actual or imminent violations of environmental law without the need to demonstrate a personal and direct interest within the meaning of Article 17 CPC.[19] Environmental protection associations nevertheless had to demonstrate that they had the capacity to bring proceedings, meaning the existence of a sufficient link between their statutory goals and the collective interest they sought to protect in a specific case.

It appears that the courts interpreted the notion of capacity very rigidly, often not finding a – territorial – link between the collective interest an environmental protection association sought to defend in a concrete case and its statutory goals and/or activities.[20] Hence, the right of these associations to act in protection of the environment was, despite the law, rather limited. It therefore does not come as a surprise that a number of Belgian environmental protection associations have filed complaints with the Aarhus Convention Compliance Committee.[21] Legislative activity in this regard has so far not yet resulted in any modification of the law.[22] That is why the 2013 judgment of the Supreme Court is all the more important, as it recognised that the conditions under which environmental protection associations could bring proceedings should not be interpreted to such an extent that it would make it impossible for them to bring a claim.[23] More successful claims for interim relief can thus be expected in the future.

B. Germs of Collective Redress in Belgian Procedural Law

The previous section demonstrated the Supreme Court's restrictive approach towards actions brought by associations in defence of a collective interest. Actions brought outside the traditional remit of an association were basically unthinkable. A claim by a lose group of persons to defend a collective interest or by a representative of an undetermined group of persons by way of a

---

[19] Law of 12 January 1993 concerning a right of action with a view to protect the environment, *Belgian State Gazette* 1993, 3769.
[20] J Joos, 'De Wet vorderingsrecht leefmilieu: overzicht van rechtspraak', *Tijdschrift voor procesrecht en bewijsrecht* (2003) 145-146.
[21] See, for example, ACCC/2005/11 concerning compliance by Belgium with its obligations under the Convention, http://www.unece.org/env/pp/pubcom.html.
[22] Belgian Senate 1 April 2007, Proposal to amend the Law of 12 January 1993 concerning a right of action for the protection of the environment, No 3-2442/1.
[23] Belgian Supreme Court 11 June 2013, No P.12.1389.N/1.

collective action would thus fail with absolute certainty. Nevertheless, a number of procedural mechanisms in Belgian procedural law allow parties with similar claims to bring proceedings together. Secondly, the Belgian legislator has adopted various laws providing for specific forms of collective redress.

1. Procedural Techniques to Bring Claims Collectively

A number of procedural techniques allow for a plurality of claimants to bring or to be involved in proceedings against the same defendant. These encompass well known techniques in the field of procedural law that do not amount to a proper collective redress mechanisms but nevertheless allow for a participation of multiple claimants instead of the classical two-party proceedings.

A first possibility is the cumulation of claims (*jonction directe* or *cumul d'actions*).[24] Article 701 CPC states that various claims between two or more parties can be brought together when they are sufficiently connected. This presupposes that the claims are connected to such an extent that it is preferable to hear them together in order to avoid conflicting outcomes.[25] A prime condition is that the claims of the various applicants have the same cause of action, meaning that their claims are based on the same set of (legal) facts and (legal) acts.[26] A notable example is the case of *NV P Belgium*, in which 117 independent opticians brought a case against a competitor for a violation of Belgian competition law.[27] It should be pointed out, however, that the technique of cumulative claims does not amount to a proper collective redress mechanism. It essentially enables a bundling of claims in a single application for the sake of proper administration of justice.[28] The admissibility of each claim will be assessed separately and claims will be rejected on an individual basis. In the case at hand the applicants each individually received a EUR 1000 damages award, which does not correspond with the idea of a collective redress mechanism through which damages are awarded to a group as a whole.

It should be pointed out that a cumulation of claims is nothing other than a joinder of claims on the initiative of the claimants. Claims that are sufficiently connected can thus also be cumulated at the initiative of the court.[29]

---

[24] G de Leval and F Georges, *Droit Judiciaire – Institutions judiciaires et éléments de compétence* (Larcier, 2014), 423–424.

[25] Art 30 CPC.

[26] S Voet, *Een Belgische vertegenwoordigende collectieve rechtsvordering* (Intersentia, 2012), 23, with reference to P Thion, 'Kwalificatie van oorzaak en voorwerp van de vordering. Mysteries uit het procesrecht', *Nieuw Juridisch Weekblad* (2003) 727–737, nr. 4–19.

[27] Antwerp Court of Appeal 11 October 2007, *Revue Générale de Droit Civil Belge* (2009) 139–141.

[28] de Leval and Georges (above n 24) 423.

[29] Art 856(2) CPC.

A second technique is the so-called litigation mandate (*mandat ad agendum*), by which a representative is given a mandate to bring proceedings by multiple claimants with similar claims.[30] The principle *nul ne plaide par procureur* has been departed from in Belgian procedural law and proceedings can be brought via a third party who has no interest in the outcome of the case. While the holder of the litigation mandate resembles to a certain extent the representative in a collective redress claim, the technique of a litigation mandate only amounts to a bundling of separate claims for the purposes of proper administration of justice. Each individual claimant is exercising its right to go to court individually through the holder of the mandate. It requires the claimant to take the initiative, which he is unlikely to do if the damage or other benefit pursued is relatively small. This is, however, exactly what a collective redress mechanism seeks to overcome.

The intervention (*demande en intervention*) is a third technique which facilitates the possibility of having multiple claimants opposing a single defendant.[31] Article 15 CPC allows a third party to become part of the proceedings either to protect its own interest or the interest of a party to the proceedings, or to obtain a judgment against one of the other parties. Again, the individual nature of this mechanism distinguishes it from collective redress.

All three techniques thus entail some elements that correspond to collective actions, respectively: (1) a plurality of claimants bringing a single case (multiple claimants bringing a cumulative claim versus a claim brought on behalf of a group of which the actual members are not necessarily yet identified), (2) the possibility of having proceedings brought by a representative (holder of a litigation mandate versus a group representative) and (3) the possibility to become part of the proceedings after they have been started (intervention versus opt-in). However, they cannot be equated to collective redress mechanisms. First, the claim is not brought to protect or vindicate the rights of a collective but to protect a bundle of individual claims. The focus on individuality clearly distinguishes these mechanisms from collective redress. Second, the possibility in the CPC to allow multiple claimants to take part in a single set of proceedings is not motivated by the protection of a collective interest nor the facilitation of private enforcement of a government policy. The sole objective appears to be procedural economy. Collective redress mechanisms however, while contributing to procedural economy, have been devised primarily to enhance legal protection or to facilitate the enforcement of government policies.

---

[30] Boularbah (above n 6) No I.A.3.a).
[31] de Leval and Georges (above n 24) 409–414.

2. Collective Redress Provided For by the Law

In addition, a number of mechanisms facilitating collective proceedings already existed in the Belgian legal order before the Law of 28 March 2014. They were developed outside the confines of the CPC and provide for collective redress in specific areas of law. It is very likely that similar mechanisms exist in other Member States since they were partly based on EU law.[32] However, while various mechanisms are indeed the result of the implementation of Belgium's obligations under EU law,[33] a number of them already existed in Belgium before an obligation to provide them was imposed by EU law. The most important ones will be briefly addressed in the following section.[34]

(a) Collective Redress and Consumer Protection

Collective redress in the context of consumer protection has taken on the form of cessation orders. This corresponds to the approach taken by the EU which, until the EC's Recommendation on collective redress, mainly focused on prevention or limitation of consumer rights infringements (see, eg, the Injunctions Directive[35]).

By 1971, the power had already been given to consumer rights associations to seek injunctive relief against acts constituting a violation of the Unfair Commercial Practices and Consumer Protection Act (UCPA). This Act, however, did not provide for an express derogation from Articles 17 and 18 of the CPC, described above, which led the Supreme Court to conclude that the conditions set out there still applied and that an interest other than a mere collective interest needed to be proven.[36] In 1991, an express derogation to the CPC was inserted in the UCPA, which eliminated the main limitation for consumer rights associations to bring a claim for injunctive relief.[37] The associations' right to bring such claims is now consolidated in Article 7, 4° of Book XVII of the Economic Law Code,[38] which allows consumer protection associations that have legal personality and are either a member of

---

[32] Eg Directive 98/27/EC of the European Parliament and of the Council of 19 May 1998 on injunctions for the protection of consumers' interests, OJ 1998, L166/51.

[33] Voet (above n 26) 44.

[34] For a comprehensive overview, see K Wagner, 'Collectieve acties in het Belgisch recht', *RDJP* (2001) 150–182.

[35] Directive 98/27/EC of the European Parliament and of the Council of 19 May 1998 on injunctions for the protection of consumers' interests, OJ 1998, L166/51.

[36] M Storme and E Terryn, 'The Globalization of Class Actions: Belgian Report on Class actions' in *The Globalization of Class Actions* (Oxford, 2007) 8.

[37] See now Art XVII.7, second para. Economic Law Code.

[38] Loi du 26 décembre 2013 portant insertion du livre XVII "Procédures juridictionnelles particulières" dans le Code de droit économique, et portant insertion d'une définition et d'un régime de sanctions propres au livre XVII dans ce même Code, *Belgian State Gazette* (2014) 6923.

the Council for Consumption (*Conseil de la consommation*) or have been recognised by the competent minister to file for a cessation order.

(b) Collective Redress and Anti-Discrimination Law
The Law of 30 July 1981 on the punishment of certain acts inspired by racism or xenophobia (Anti-Racism Law)[39] was adopted to combat growing racial tensions in Belgian society. Ten years later it appeared necessary to found a permanent structure securing the application of the Anti-Racism Law, resulting in the Interfederal Centre for Equal Opportunities (ICEO)[40] being founded in 1995. One of its tasks is to support victims of racist acts with advice, and to assist in mediation or court proceedings. Shortly afterwards the Centre was also given the competence to act of its own right against violations of the Anti-Racism Law.

Since the implementation of Directive 2000/43/EC on equal treatment between persons irrespective of racial or ethnic origin,[41] the ICEO's power to act in judicial proceedings can be found in Article 32 of the Anti-Racism Law. It provides that the ICEO can act in court to denounce any violation of the Anti-Racism Law. It can act both in criminal and civil proceedings and can take any form of action it sees fit. It can do so of its own right, without a mandate of the victims. Note that this goes further than Directive 2000/43/EC, which obliges the Member State to ensure that entities having a legitimate interest in ensuring the application of the provisions of the Directive, may engage in any judicial or administrative proceedings but only on behalf or in support of the victims and with their approval.[42]

Belgium has given the ICEO the larger power to act on the basis of a collective interest without the need for a (potential) individual claim to be available. In addition, the actions that the ICEO can undertake are not limited to injunctions but also cover damages claims. In case the ICEO is acting in support of or together with a victim of discrimination, courts will generally only award damages to the victim.[43] However, when the ICEO acts alone and damages are being awarded, it is allowed to keep and use them for its own activities.[44] This is different from the collective redress paradigm

---

[39] *Belgian State Gazette* 1981, 9928.
[40] See http://www.diversitybelgium.be/.
[41] Directive 2000/43/EC of the Council of 29 June 2000 implementing the principle of equal treatment between persons irrespective of racial or ethnic origin, OJ 2000, L180/22.
[42] Art 7(2) Directive 2000/43/EC.
[43] See, for example, Criminal Court Veurne 12 November 2002, to be consulted on www.diversiteit.be.
[44] Not every judge, however, is convinced that the Centre should be able to claim damages: see, for example, Criminal Court Luik 21 december 1998, *JLMB* 1999, 78. See further J Vrielink, *Van haat gesproken? Een rechtsantropologisch onderzoek naar de bestrijding van rasgerelateerde uitingsdelicten in België* (Maklu, 2010), No 453–454.

adhered to by the EC, and also differs from the Belgian Law of 28 March 2014, according to which the representative bringing a collective action should not benefit from the claim.[45]

(c) Collective Redress and Environmental Protection
In order to mitigate the effects of the restrictive doctrine of the Supreme Court concerning the ability of environmental protection associations to bring claims with a view to protect the environment, in 1993 the Belgian legislator adopted a Law conferring a right of action concerning the protection of the environment.[46] It allowed non-profit environmental protection associations meeting certain conditions to file for a court order stopping or preventing an infringement of environmental protection rules.

The 1993 Law did not prove to be an enormous success for two reasons. First, it included the condition that an association had to exist three years before proceedings are brought. This largely excluded associations set up in relation with a particular event, eg a group of persons seeking to challenge the permit for the expansion of a neighbouring industrial plant, which could not be expected to have existed three years before. Second, as already mentioned above, the condition that such association had to prove its capacity to bring a claim was interpreted restrictively by the courts, only giving rise to a handful of claims in its first ten years of application.[47]

That being said, the Law was a success for other parties, namely individual citizens or groups of individual citizens. While individual citizens were not listed amongst the parties that could claim interim relief on the basis of the 1993 Law, municipal councils were. Article 194 of a 2005 Flemish Decree concerning the organization of local government[48] allowed inhabitants of a municipality to start legal proceedings on behalf of their municipality in order to protect municipal interests if their municipality failed to do so. From 2005 onwards, citizens started to resort to their power under Article 194 of the Decree to file for cessation orders on behalf of their municipality on the basis of the 1993 Law.[49] This is an interesting evolution from a collective action perspective, as it allowed a group of citi-

---

[45] See Recommendation, No 29–30 and Report on the introduction of a collective redress mechanism, Chamber of Representatives 17 February 2014, No 3300/004, 17–18 and 25.

[46] Law of 12 January 1993 concerning a right of action with a view to protect the environment, *Belgian State Gazette* (1993) 3769.

[47] See also Joos (above n 20) 145–146.

[48] Gemeentedecreet, *Belgian State Gazette* (2005) 38153.

[49] S Sobrie, 'Art. 194 (nieuw) Gemeentedecreet: het optreden namens de gemeente (heimelijk) aan banden gelegd', *Rechtskundig Weekblad* (2012–13) 1323.

zens to bring an action on an *ad hoc* basis, outside the confines of an environmental protection association, in order to protect a collective interest. Article 194 of the Decree was not limited to environmental protection cases; all sorts of cessation orders could be applied for. Municipal councils, however, were not very pleased with the extensive use of Article 194 of the Decree as in various situations, proceedings brought by their inhabitants were actually against the interest of the municipal council. The possibility to bring collective claims was therefore largely abolished in 2012, however, not with respect to environment claims. Article 194 of the Decree still allows citizens to act on behalf of their municipality in case inaction of their municipality either causes damage to the environment or seriously threatens to damage the environment. It is expected that the situation will not change much, if at all, with respect to the application of Article 194 of the Decree and the 1993 Law.[50]

C. Absence of a General Collective Redress Mechanism

It appears from the previous sections that the idea of collective redress was certainly not alien to the Belgian legal order. The CPC contains a number of procedural techniques which show elements of collective redress. Furthermore, a number of specific collective redress mechanisms did exist outside the confines of the CPC. They were, however, fragmentized and not part of a general approach towards collective redress. Also, apart from cases in which the ICEO was competent to act, collective redress mainly took the form of cessation orders sought by certain associations or authorized bodies. A general collective redress mechanism to obtain compensation for damage caused to a large group of victims was lacking.[51]

III. AN OVERVIEW OF THE LAW OF 28 MARCH 2014

On 17 January 2014, the Belgian government introduced its proposal for a collective redress mechanism, which eventually formed the basis of the Law of 28 March 2014.[52]

The Law of 28 March 2014 allows for a limited group of representatives to bring an action on behalf of an undetermined group of consumers in the

---

[50] *Ibid*, 1323–1324.
[51] Voet (above n 26) 36–47.
[52] Project of law on the introduction of a collective redress mechanism, Chamber of Representatives 17 January 2014, No 3300/001 and 3301/001 ('Project of Law'). For an overview of previous attempts, see Frankignoul (above n 2) 197–198.

Brussels courts in order to claim damages caused by violations of an exhaustive list of legislative provisions. The procedure consists of four phases – admissibility, settlement, merits and execution – and its main objective is to facilitate a negotiated settlement between the group representative and the defendant,[53] which would bind all claimants involved.

The law has not been inserted into the CPC but is part of a separate chapter in the Economic Law Code. It illustrates the special nature of the collective redress mechanism as an exception to the general rule laid down in Articles 17 and 18 CPC.[54] The Law of 28 March 2014 therefore also contains an explicit derogation clause.[55] The Civil Procedure Code nevertheless remains applicable to all issues not dealt with in the Law of 28 March, such as certain time-limits or rules on evidence.

A. The Admissibility Phase

An application for collective redress should be brought before the court of first instance or the commercial court of Brussels.[56] The application should contain a number of mandatory elements allowing the judge to evaluate the admissibility of the application. They pertain to the specific admissibility requirements to bring an action for collective redress, the description of the collective damage, the choice between an opt-in or an opt-out system, and a detailed description of the group of potential consumers on behalf of which the representative brings the claim.[57]

1. Special Admissibility Criteria

Article XVII.36 contains a list of three special admissibility criteria for a collective redress application.

First, the collective redress mechanism can only be used to obtain compensation for damages sustained on account of a breach by an undertaking of its contractual obligations, of a number of EU regulations, or of a number of Belgian laws or their implementing acts. The EU regulations and the Belgian laws are exhaustively listed in Article XVII.37 ELC.[58] The list contains 31 instruments and covers most relevant Belgian legislation in the area of consumer protection, including competition law, as well as a

---

[53] Report on the introduction of a collective redress mechanism, 26.
[54] *Ibid*, 27.
[55] Art XVII.36 ELC.
[56] Art XVII.35 ELC.
[57] Art XVII.42 §1 ELC.
[58] Art XVII.36 1° ELC.

number of EU regulations pertaining to passenger rights when travelling by air,[59] on water,[60] or on land.[61]

Second, an application for collective redress can only be made by an applicant who complies with the necessary legal requirements. The law makes provision for two categories of group representatives, namely a consumer protection association with legal personality who is either a member of the Council of Consumption or recognized by the competent minister;[62] or an association with legal personality recognized by the competent minister, whose statutory goals have a direct link with the collective damage sustained by the group, and who is not pursuing an economic aim in a sustainable manner.[63] A third possible group representative is the Consumer Ombudsman, who can only act as a representative of a group of consumers in the course of settlement negotiations.[64]

Further, the judge has to assess whether the applicant is an appropriate representative in relation to the claim.[65] This allows the judge to evaluate the relationship between the representative and the (potential) group members as well as his capability to manage the collective action. In case a more suitable representative exists, the judge can reject the application. This role of the judge provides an important control as a representative acts independently from the consumers affected by the collective redress proceedings.[66] The

---

[59] Council Regulation (EC) No 2027/97 of 9 October 1997 on air carrier liability in the event of accidents, OJ 1997, L285/1; Regulation (EC) No 261/2004 of the European Parliament and of the Council of 11 February 2004 establishing common rules on compensation and assistance to passengers in the event of denied boarding and of cancellation or long delay of flights, and repealing Regulation (EEC) No 295/91, OJ 2004, L46/1; Regulation (EC) No 2111/2005 of the European Parliament and of the Council of 14 December 2005 on the establishment of a Community list of air carriers subject to an operating ban within the Community and on informing air transport passengers of the identity of the operating air carrier, and repealing Article 9 of Directive 2004/36/EC, OJ 2004, L344/15; Regulation (EC) No 1107/2006 of the European Parliament and of the Council of 5 July 2006 concerning the rights of disabled persons and persons with reduced mobility when travelling by air, OJ 2006, L204/1.

[60] Regulation (EU) No 1177/2010 of the European Parliament and of the Council of 24 November 2010 concerning the rights of passengers when travelling by sea and inland waterway and amending Regulation (EC) No 2006/2004, OJ 2010, L344/1.

[61] Regulation (EC) No 1371/2007 of the European Parliament and of the Council of 23 October 2007 on rail passengers' rights and obligations, OJ 2007, L315/14; Regulation (EU) No 181/2011 of the European Parliament and of the Council of 16 February 2011 concerning the rights of passengers in bus and coach transport and amending Regulation (EC) No 2006/2004, OJ 2011, 55/1.

[62] Art XVII.39 1° ELC.
[63] Art XVII.39 2° ELC.
[64] Art XVII.39 3° ELC.
[65] Art XVII.36 2° ELC.
[66] S Voet and B Allemeersch, 'De rechtsvordering tot collectief herstel: een Belgische *class action* voor consumenten', *Rechtskundig Weekblad* (2014–15) 649.

power also allows a judge to select the most appropriate representative if multiple representatives bring an action for collective redress in relation to the same cause at the same time.[67] The 'first come first served' principle does not apply.[68]

A group representative has to remain an appropriate representative throughout the whole of the proceedings.[69] He will lose his status if at some point during the proceedings he no longer complies with the conditions set out in the law.[70] In case the judge cannot find a suitable replacement, he will order the closure of the collective redress proceedings.[71]

Third, the group representative will have to prove that an application for collective redress will be more effective than separate actions brought by individual consumers.[72] This reflects the idea that an action for collective redress is still the exception and that an individual action is preferred by Belgian procedural law. The judge has to assess whether this requirement has been met. The law does not lay down any criteria but inspiration can be drawn from the preparatory documents, which refer *inter alia* to the complexity and the efficiency of the application for collective redress, the potential size of the group, and the impact of the proceedings on the individual consumer.[73]

2. The Method of Selecting Group Members

Upon the application for collective redress the group representative has to indicate how the group of consumers affected by the action should be composed.[74] The law leaves him the choice between an opt-in model and an opt-out model.[75] The final decision lies, however, with the judge, who will select the model in his admissibility decision.[76] In two instances, the law has prescribed the mandatory use of the opt-in model, namely in case of persons who do not have their habitual residence in Belgium,[77] or in case the collective action seeks to redress moral or bodily harm.[78]

---

[67] S Voet, 'Samen sterk: Belgische consumenten class action is een feit' (105) *Droit de la Consommation – Consumentenrecht* (2014) 10.

[68] F Danis, E Falla, and F Lefèvre, 'Introduction aux principes de la Loi relative à l'action en réparation collective et premiers commentaires critiques', *Revue de Droit Commercial Belge* (2014) 573.

[69] Art XVII.40 first para ELC.
[70] Art XVII.40 second para ELC.
[71] Art XVII.40 third para ELC.
[72] Art XVII.36 3° ELC.
[73] Project of Law, 8-9.
[74] Art XVII.42 §1 ELC.
[75] Art XVII.38 §1 1° ELC.
[76] Art XVII.43 §2 3° ELC.
[77] Art XVII.38 §1 2° ELC.
[78] Art XVII.43 §2 3° ELC.

In his decision on the admissibility of the application for collective redress, the judge will lay down a time limit for consumers to exercise their right to opt-in or to opt-out of the action. This time limit may not be shorter than thirty days and not be longer than three months.[79] In order to make sure that all affected consumers are informed of the decision to proceed with a collective action, it will be published in the Belgian State Gazette and on the website of the Federal Public Service of Economy, SMEs, the Self-Employed, and Energy.[80] The judge is allowed to order supplementary publication measures if those prescribed by the law do not suffice.[81]

The proper dissemination of information is important as the decision to opt-in or to opt-out is irrevocable.[82] An exception is, however, provided in case of the opt-out system. A member of the group will not be bound by a final court decision or a settlement if he can prove to a reasonable extent that he could not have been aware of the admissibility decision.[83]

3. The Admissibility Decision

The judge has two months to assess the admissibility of the collective redress application. Various authors have suggested that this time limit is far too short to be complied with, especially in highly complex cases.[84] The failure to meet the two-month time limit will, however, not be penalized in any way. It should therefore be considered a term of order that indicates the preferred pace of the proceedings.[85]

The admissibility decision will contain a description of the collective damage, the cause of the collective damage, the applicable method to select group members, a precise description of the group of affected persons, the identification of the group representative, the identification of the defendant, time limits for exercising the right to opt-in or to opt-out, a time limit allowing for the parties to negotiate a settlement, and ancillary measures of publication of the admissibility decision.[86]

B. The Settlement Phase

The law provides for a mandatory settlement procedure between the group

---

[79] Art XVII.43 §2 7° ELC.
[80] Art XVII.43 §3 ELC.
[81] Art XVII.43 §2 9° ELC.
[82] Art XVII.38 §1 third subpara ELC.
[83] Arts XVII.49 §4 and XVII.54 §5 ELC.
[84] Voet and Allemeersch (above n 66) 653 (calling the time limit 'unrealistic'); Danis, Falla and Lefèvre (above n 66) 570 (calling the time limit 'surrealistic').
[85] Voet and Allemeersch (above n 66) 653.
[86] Art XVII.43 §2 ELC.

representative and the defendant.[87] The judge will determine in his admissibility decision a time limit by which a settlement should be reached. The period cannot be shorter than three months and not be longer than six months and starts to run upon the expiration of the period by which affected persons had to exercise their right of option.[88] Upon a joint request of the parties, a judge may extend the period once, for a maximum six months.[89]

In case no settlement has been reached within that period, the judge will proceed with the collective redress proceedings. The same applies when the judge refuses to homologate a settlement agreement or when the settlement agreement does not satisfy all legal requirements to be homologated and parties have failed to complete the agreement within a prescribed time limit.[90]

When parties have reached a settlement agreement they can submit it to the judge in order to have it homologated. The agreement shall contain a number of mandatory entries;[91] persistent failure to include them can eventually lead to the discontinuation of the proceedings.[92] Mandatory are: a reference to the admissibility decision, a detailed description of the collective damage, a description of the group and a detailed assessment of the affected consumers, the identification of the group representative, the identification of the defendant, the modalities and the substance of the redress, the time limit within which members of a group formed by an opt-out selection system should make themselves known to the registry, the amount the defendant has to pay to the group representative in order to cover his costs, the responsibility for the costs of supplementary publication measures, the guarantees the defendant has to give, a procedure to revise the agreement if more damage would occur after the agreement has been concluded, supplementary publication measures, the text of the agreement, the date of the agreement and the signatures of the parties.[93]

The judge will homologate the agreement upon verification of whether the agreement contains all mandatory entries.[94] He will, however, refuse to do so when: it appears that the agreed redress is manifestly unreasonable for the group or a subcategory of the group, the time limit by which members of a group selected on the basis of an opt-out system have to make themselves known is manifestly unreasonable, the supplementary publication require-

---

[87] Art XVII.45 §1 first subpara ELC.
[88] Art XVII.43 §2 8° ELC.
[89] Art XVII.45 §1 second subpara ELC.
[90] Art XVII.52 ELC.
[91] Art XVII.45 §3 ELC.
[92] Art XVII.52 ELC.
[93] Art XVII.45 §3 ELC.
[94] Art XVII.49 §1 ELC.

ments of the agreement are manifestly unreasonable, or the remuneration paid to the group representative surpasses his real costs.[95]

The decision by which the judge homologates the agreement has the same force as a judgment.[96] In his decision the judge will appoint an administrator who will deal with the distribution of the damages amongst the members of the group.[97] The decision will be published in the Belgian State Gazette and on the website of the Federal Public Service of Economy, SMEs, the Self-Employed, and Energy.[98] Neither the conclusion of a settlement agreement nor the homologation of it implies an admission of guilt or civil responsibility on the part of the defendant.[99] Individuals who have not taken part in the settlement procedure thus cannot invoke the agreement to establish the liability of the defendant in a separate individual action for (non) contractual liability.

It should be pointed out that the law also facilitates the homologation of a collective settlement agreement reached outside the scope of collective redress proceedings. A group representative and a defendant may submit a settlement agreement to the judge in order to have it homologated.[100] The requirements such an agreement has to comply with are the same as if the agreement was reached in the context of collective redress proceedings.[101] An important point to take into account is that the settlement agreement reached outside the context of court proceedings is also a form of collective redress. Therefore, a judge who is being requested to homologate a settlement agreement will also have to verify whether the admissibility criteria for bringing collective redress proceedings have been complied with.[102] Thus, in case the group representative who initiated the out-of-court settlement is not allowed to do so under the Law of 28 March 2004, or the rules regarding the selection of group members have not been respected, or recourse to a collective settlement appears not to be the most efficient way of dealing with the damage, or when the agreement relates to the violation of EU or Belgian law to which the Law of 28 March does not apply, the judge will refuse to homologate the settlement agreement.[103]

---

[95] Art XVII.49 §2 ELC.
[96] Art XVII.49 §4 ELC.
[97] Art XVII.49 §3 ELC.
[98] Art XVII.50 ELC.
[99] Arts XVII.46 and XVII.51 ELC.
[100] Art XVII.42 §2 first para ELC.
[101] Art XVII.42 §2 second and third para ELC.
[102] Art XVII.44 §1 ELC.
[103] Art XVII.44 §2 ELC.

C. Proceedings on the Merits

In case no settlement has been reached or no settlement agreement was homologated, the proceedings continue on the merits.[104] The parties are requested to appear in court within one month and the judge will lay down a timeframe for the remainder of the case.[105] If the judge decides that the application for collective redress is successful the judgment has to contain the following elements: a reference to the admissibility decision, a detailed description of the collective damage, a description of the group and its subcategories, a list or a precise estimate of the affected consumers, the identification of the group representative and the defendant, supplementary measures of publication, the modalities and the amount of the redress, a time limit by which members of a group selected on the basis of an opt-out system have to make themselves known, guarantees the defendant should provide, and a revision procedure in case damage arises after the decision.[106] Further to this, the judge appoints a claims administrator.[107]

It should be pointed out that during the proceedings and until the court has rendered its judgment parties can at any time submit a settlement agreement to the judge, who will then proceed to the homologation process as described in the previous section.[108]

D. The Execution Phase

The execution of a homologated settlement agreement or a final judgment is entrusted to a claims administrator. The claims administrator is chosen from a list established by the general meeting of the competent court.[109] Only lawyers, ministerial civil servants and holders of a judicial mandate in the exercise of their profession or office can be put on the list.[110] The claims administrator is under a duty to guarantee the correct execution of the homologated settlement agreement or the final judgment.[111] The case remains however pending before the judge until the agreement or the judgment has been executed in full.[112]

An important task of the claims administrator is to establish the definite list of members of the group that can receive compensation. Within a

---

[104] Art XVII.52 first para ELC.
[105] Art XVII.52 second para ELC.
[106] Art XVII.54 §1 ELC.
[107] Art XVII.54 §2 ELC.
[108] Art XVII.56 ELC.
[109] Art XVII.57 §1 first para ELC.
[110] Art XVII.57 §1 second para ELC.
[111] Art XVII.57 §2 ELC.
[112] Art XVII.60 ELC.

reasonable time, he will put together a provisional list of group members wishing to obtain compensation and who have made themselves explicitly known.[113] The claims administrator will make a mention on the list when he is of the opinion that members of the group who made themselves known do not correspond to the group description or do not comply with the modalities for execution.[114] The provisional list will be serviced on the judge, the group representative and the defendant.[115] Within thirty days, the group representative or the defendant can object to the inscription or the exclusion of a group member on the list.[116] Both the claim administrator and the relevant group member will be informed by the registry within fourteen days in case he or she has been excluded from the group.[117] Within another fourteen days the parties, the claims administrator and the concerned group member can give their views on the exclusion to the registry.[118] In a subsequent hearing, the judge will then establish the definite list.[119] Group members excluded from the definite list can, however, not bring an appeal against the decision to exclude them as they are not a party to the proceedings. It appears also from the preparatory documents that they should not be allowed to bring third-party proceedings since they cannot considered to be third parties to the case.[120] Unless the parties to the proceedings, ie, the group representative and the defendant, want to appeal the decision of the judge on that ground, the excluded group member remains without a remedy. The only solution would be to start proceedings on an individual basis.[121]

The claims administrator will then proceed with the process of execution.[122] If the defendant was ordered to compensate the group members in kind, the claims administrator will supervise the execution of this process.[123] In case the defendant was ordered to compensate the group members by equivalent, the defendant will transfer the sums agreed in the homologated agreement or the judgment to the claims administrator, who will divide them amongst the group members.[124]

---

[113] Art XVII.58 §1 first para ELC.
[114] Art XVII.58 §1 second para ELC.
[115] Art XVII.58 §2 ELC.
[116] Art XVII.58 §3 first para ELC.
[117] Art XVII.58 §3 second para ELC.
[118] Art XVII.58 §3 third para ELC.
[119] Art XVII.58 §4 and §5 ELC.
[120] Project of Law, 69–70.
[121] Voet and Allemeersch (above n 66) 658.
[122] Art XVII.59 §1 ELC.
[123] Art XVII.59 §2 ELC.
[124] *Ibid.*

The claims administrator will file an end report to the judge upon the complete execution of the homologated agreement or the judgment.[125] The report will contain all information necessary to allow the judge to take a decision regarding the closure of the proceedings as well as a detailed assessment of the costs and the remuneration of the claims administrator.[126] The report will also make mention of any sums not distributed amongst the members of the group.[127] This is likely to happen when an opt-out system has been used to select the group members since the number of claimants cannot be assessed with great precision beforehand.[128] Comparative research has shown that the amount of unclaimed damages may be very high in cases where group members are either discouraged by the formalities of the execution process or there may be a lack of clear publicity.[129]

The decision on the end report is taken by the judge. The approval of the report marks the end of the execution procedure under supervision of the claims administrator.[130] In case of sums not distributed, the judge will decide on how these are to be used.[131] The judge has wide discretionary power in this regard, but the preparatory documents make a number of suggestions. He may for example choose to reverse the sums to the defendant or he may order the defendant to use the sums to offer to its customers a reduction on their bills for a certain period of time.[132] The latter methods are not considered to be punitive damages by the legislator as their aim is to compensate actual damage, even when not all damage has been claimed.[133] It is, however, unclear who will supervise this form of execution as the task of the claims administrator ends with the approval of his final report.

E. *The Effect of a Collective Redress Procedure on Other Proceedings or Procedural Incidents*

A last chapter of the new Law regulates a number of issues on the relationship between a collective redress procedure and other claims/proceedings.

First, the impact of a collective redress procedure on the statute of limitations applicable to individual claims is being considered. The prescription period of the individual claim of a group member who chooses to opt out of the collective procedure will be suspended between the publication of the

---

[125] Art XVII.61 §1 first para ELC.
[126] Art XVII.61 §1 second para ELC.
[127] *Ibid*.
[128] E Falla, *The Role of the Court in Collective Redress Litigation* (Larcier, 2014) 242.
[129] Danis, Falla, and Lefèvre (above n 68) 581.
[130] Art XVII.61 §2 first para ELC.
[131] *Ibid*.
[132] Project of Law, 42.
[133] *Ibid*. See also Report on the introduction of a collective redress mechanism, 30–31.

admissibility decision in the Belgian State Gazette and the moment in which the group member communicates his choice to opt out to the registrar.[134] Furthermore, in case the judge decides to close the collective procedure due to the lack of a suitable representative, the prescription period of the individual claim of a group member will be suspended between the publication date of the admissibility decision and the day on which the judge closed the collective procedure.[135] Lastly, the prescription period of a group member who has been excluded from the definite list established by the claims administrator will be suspended between the said publication date and the communication by the registrar of the final decision to the group member that he or she is excluded.[136]

Secondly, the collective redress procedure remains independent from criminal proceedings. The general principle that civil proceedings should be suspended pending the outcome of connected criminal proceedings does not apply in the case of a collective redress procedure.[137] The independence from criminal proceedings is further reinforced by the exclusion of consumers that have obtained the status of a civil party in criminal proceedings.[138]

Thirdly, the law allows for settlement negotiations between the defendant and an individual group member relating to the same cause of action. Upon reaching an agreement, the group member will lose his status as group member in the collective procedure.[139]

Fourthly, upon the decision declaring the collective redress procedure admissible, all proceedings pending between an individual group member and the defendant having the same object and cause will become without object while all new proceedings started by an individual group member against the defendant having the same object and cause will be inadmissible.[140]

Further to this, a number of derogations from the CPC have been included in regard of certain procedural incidents. Thus, the group representative is not allowed to alter the subject-matter of the proceedings once the claim has been brought.[141] The group representative is also not allowed to discontinue proceedings without approval of the judge,[142] and he can never waive the right to action as this belongs to the holders of the right, namely the individual consumers.[143] In case of discontinuance of proceedings, the

---

[134] Art XVII.63 §1 ELC.
[135] Art XVII.63 §2 ELC.
[136] Art XVII.63 §3 ELC.
[137] Art XVII.67 first para ELC.
[138] Art XVII.67 second para ELC.
[139] Art XVII.68 ELC.
[140] Art XVII.69 ELC.
[141] Art XVII.64 ELC.
[142] Art XVII.65 first para ELC.
[143] Art XVII.65 third para ELC.

prescription period of the individual claims of the group members is suspended from the day on which the application was brought.[144] Lastly, an application for collective redress and an individual application cannot be joined based on the fact that both cases are sufficiently connected.[145] The exclusion of these procedural techniques in the course of collective redress proceedings is motivated by the objective to protect the position of the individual consumer as well as to guarantee the smooth functioning of the collective redress proceedings.[146]

IV. THE BELGIAN LAW ON CONSUMER COLLECTIVE REDRESS IN LIGHT OF THE COMMISSION RECOMMENDATION ON COLLECTIVE REDRESS AND OTHER REQUIREMENTS OF EU LAW: A FIRST ASSESSMENT

A. The EU Legal Framework

The EC has made the effective enforcement of consumer rights a policy priority. To that extent a number of initiatives have been taken, facilitating both in-court and out-of-court solutions. The underlying idea is to create a framework for consumer redress in the EU that encourages consumers to buy goods or seek services abroad more frequently. The Belgian law on consumer redress should be seen in the light of this evolution and should ideally fit in an EU-wide horizontal framework for consumer rights enforcement.[147]

The EC launched the idea of a collective redress mechanism as part of its Consumer Policy Strategy for 2007–2013.[148] After years of consultations and negotiations, it appeared impossible to find a consensus on the introduction of a mandatory EU collective redress mechanism. In order to motivate the Member States to take action, the EC published a Recommendation in 2013,[149] accompanied by a Communication[150] laying down its view on

---

[144] Art XVII.65 second para ELC.
[145] Art XVII.66 ELC.
[146] Project of Law, 43.
[147] In line with a European Parliament Resolution of 2 February 2012 the Commission advocates in its Recommendation a horizontal approach by which each Member State would introduce its own mechanism in line with a common set of principles as opposed to a vertical approach by which the EU legislator would lay down a framework for the whole of the EU.
[148] Communication from the Commission to the Council, the European Parliament and the European Economic and Social Committee, *EU Consumer Policy Strategy 2007–2013: Empowering consumers, enhancing their welfare, effectively protecting them*, COM(2007) 99 final, 11.
[149] Commission Recommendation of 11 June 2013 on common principles for injunctive and compensatory collective redress mechanisms in the Member States concerning violations of rights granted under Union Law, OJ 2013, L201/60.
[150] Communication from the Commission to the European Parliament, the Council, the European Economic and Social Committee and the Committee of the Regions, 'Towards a European Horizontal Framework for Collective Redress', COM(2013) 401 final.

how collective redress should evolve in the EU. The Recommendation set out a number of criteria to which collective redress mechanisms in the Member States should ideally adhere. While a recommendation is not binding upon the Member States,[151] the language is nevertheless relatively strong and the EC encourages the Member States to take the criteria into account when adopting new collective redress mechanisms or amending existing ones. The EC will assess the state of collective redress in the Member States by 26 July 2017 and will propose further measures if necessary.[152]

Collective redress is also relevant with regard to the private enforcement of competition law. Private enforcement of competition law is an important part of the EC's competition and consumer rights policy.[153] The recently adopted directive on private damages actions refers explicitly to the improvement of 'the conditions for consumers to exercise the rights that they derive from the internal market.'[154] Collective redress mechanisms surely contribute to this aim, and while the directive itself does require Member States to adopt collective redress mechanisms for the enforcement of EU competition rules,[155] the Recommendation explicitly lists competition law amongst the areas where the supplementary private enforcement of EU law rights in the form of collective redress is of value.[156]

Redress in cases of mass harm situations should not always be obtained by court proceedings. The EC has put great emphasis on the use of alternative dispute mechanisms. This has culminated in a number of legislative acts, of which the regulation on consumer online dispute resolution[157] and the directive on alternative dispute resolution for consumer disputes[158] are the most recent examples. Also the Recommendation stresses the importance of alternative dispute resolution procedures, which should be available alongside or as part of judicial collective redress.[159]

---

[151] Article 288 TFEU. The Recommendation contains nevertheless an obligation to implement the principles set out therein into national law (see No 38). It is, however, unclear how this can be enforced since, in accordance with the Treaties, a recommendation is not binding.

[152] Recommendation, No 41.

[153] Green Paper – Damages actions for breach of the EC antitrust rules, COM(2005) 672 final, 3.

[154] Directive 2014/104/EU of the European Parliament and of the Council of 26 November 2014 on certain rules governing actions for damages under national law for infringements of the competition law provisions of the Member States and of the European Union, OJ 2014, L349/1, 9th Recital.

[155] Directive 2014/104/EU, 13th Recital.

[156] Recommendation, 7th Recital.

[157] Regulation (EU) No 524/2013 of the European Parliament and of the Council of 21 May 2013 on online dispute resolution for consumer disputes and amending Regulation (EC) No 2006/2004 and Directive 2009/22/EC, OJ 2013, L165/1.

[158] Directive 2013/11/EU of the European Parliament and of the Council of 21 May 2013 on alternative dispute resolution for consumer disputes and amending Regulation (EC) No 2006/2004 and Directive 2009/22/EC, OJ 2013, L165/63.

[159] Recommendation, 16th Recital and No 15 to 29.

Lastly, the case law of the Court of Justice of the EU (CJEU) regarding national procedural autonomy should be taken into account.[160] The CJEU's judgments have already impacted on national procedural rules, not least in the area of consumer protection law, and will also be relevant for collective action mechanisms. Member State legislators adopting new procedural rules that will also facilitate the application of EU law, such as a collective redress mechanism for the enforcement of consumer protection law, should thus not overlook the case law of the CJEU in this regard.

B. Thematic Assessment of the Law of 28 March 2014 in Light of the EU Legal Framework

1. Opt-in or Opt-out and Other Issues Related to the Composition of the Group

The Recommendation on collective redress stipulates that the claimant group should be selected on the basis of the opt-in principle. The use of the opt-out system should be the exception and should be duly justified by reasons of sound administration of justice.[161] It appears from the Communication that businesses were heavily opposed to an opt-out model on account that it would be more susceptible to abuse.[162] The EC also showed a strong preference for an opt-in model. It argued that a clearly defined group would allow for greater respect for the rights of the defence in court proceedings and would be in line with the principle of party autonomy.[163] Furthermore, the collective redress proceedings would be more effective as the value of the dispute as well as the admissibility and the merits of the claim could be assessed more easily.[164] A major argument against the opt-out system for the EC was that it seemed incompatible with the aim of collective redress, namely the obtainment of compensation, since the damages obtained would not be distributed to unidentified persons.[165] A number of consumer protection associations argued against an exclusive reliance on an opt-in system as it would not guarantee effective redress in all situations; the option to choose an opt-out model should always be available as an alternative.[166] Indeed, it has been argued that in cases of diffuse damages, which often occur in the context of consumer protection legislation, an opt-in model does not work. Consumers are not always aware that they are affected or do not act because

---

[160] For an overview, see K Lenaerts, I Maselis and K Gutman (JT Nowak (ed.)), *EU Procedural Law* (Oxford University Press, 2014), Ch. 4).
[161] Recommendation, No 21.
[162] Communication, 11.
[163] Communication, 12.
[164] *Ibid*.
[165] *Ibid*.
[166] Communication, 11.

of 'rational indifference' and the fact that possible benefits are outweighed by the effort that has to be undertaken in order to become part of the group.[167] This line of argument was also adopted by the Belgian legislator.[168] In an explicit reference to the Recommendation, the Belgian legislator stated that the nature of consumer protection legislation warranted the opt-out principle and its inclusion in Belgian law was thus duly motivated.[169] Further, reference was made to the positive consequences of an opt-out system for businesses, namely that a decision would have *res judicata* effect vis-à-vis all members of the group.[170] Lastly, provided that necessary guarantees are included in national legislation, such as sufficient publication measures, the principle of 'opt-out' was considered compatible with Article 6 ECHR.[171]

By allowing a choice between an opt-in and an opt-out system the Belgian legislator seemed to have departed from the EC's choice for an opt-in system. The departure is, however, less radical than would first appear. The choice for either model under Belgian law has to be duly motivated both by the group representative and the judge. This can be reconciled with the Recommendation, which exceptionally allows an opt-out model if duly justified. Furthermore, preference is given to the opt-in model in a number of situations, such as the case of bodily harm and for persons not habitually resident in Belgium. Especially in the latter case the choice for the opt-in model coincides with the EC's concerns regarding the right of the defence. Persons habitually resident in Belgium are presumed to be able to make an informed choice regarding their right to opt-out as the necessary safeguards in the form of publication requirements have been provided for by the law. Since the effectiveness of national publication requirements in guaranteeing an informed choice is less sure for persons habitually resident outside Belgium, the opt-in model has been made mandatory for them. This guarantees the right to an effective remedy in line with the EC's concerns as the person concerned will not be bound by a decision in regard of which he or she was not able to make an informed choice on whether to opt-out or not.[172]

Another issue pertains to the possibility for a group member to leave the group before final judgment is given, which was also included in the Recommendation.[173] The Belgian Law of 28 March 2014 does not allow members of the group to leave once the deadline to exercise their right of option has expired. This is motivated by a desire to have a clear picture of the

---

[167] Voet and Allemeersch (above n 66) 650.
[168] Project of Law, 29.
[169] *Ibid*, 30.
[170] *Ibid*, 29.
[171] *Ibid*, 30.
[172] *Ibid*, 24.
[173] Recommendation, No 22.

group at a very early stage of the proceedings, which would enhance the efficiency of the procedure, in particular with respect to settlements. It would also avoid consumers exercising their right of option depending on the outcome of the procedure.[174] While this does not correspond to the Recommendation, it is worth referring back to the EC's argumentation in favour of an opt-in system: according to the EC, the represented group should be clearly defined at the onset to allow the court to conduct the proceedings consistent with the rights of all parties.[175] Although this was not the Belgian legislator's main concern,[176] the exclusion of the possibility of leaving the group would certainly contribute to that goal. The Belgian *Conseil d'Etat* recognized that the rule was motivated by a concern to safeguard the functioning of the procedure. It questioned, however, whether this was in line with the objective of securing the most appropriate form of legal protection for every individual consumer.[177] That being said, the Law contains mechanisms for leaving the group at a later stage of the proceedings, either because an individual settlement has been reached,[178] or in case of an opt-out system, when a group member can demonstrate to a reasonable extent that he was unable to have knowledge of the admissibility decision within the timeframe in which he could exercise his right to opt out.[179]

2. Funding of Collective Actions

The funding of collective redress is a major issue. One has the immediate preference to regulate it strictly in order to avoid practices commonly associated with class actions in the US, such as staggering contingency fees and politically motivated third-party funding. The Recommendation does not exclude third-party funding but provides for a strict framework that guarantees maximum transparency and allows the judge to intervene whenever necessary.[180]

This contrasts starkly with the Law of 28 March 2014, which contains very little on the financing of collective redress proceedings and no rules at all on third-party funding. This was also explicitly recognized by the government in its proposal,[181] but no further consideration was given to the issue of third-party funding. This is all the more surprising in light of the rules on the distribution of costs of collective redress proceedings.

---

[174] Project of Law, 23.
[175] Communication, 12.
[176] See, however, Project of Law, 18.
[177] Project of Law, 73.
[178] Art XVII. 68 ELC.
[179] Arts XVII.49 §4 and XVII.54 §5 ELC.
[180] Recommendation, No 14–16.
[181] Project of Law, 10.

The principle is that the group representative bears the financial risk for the introduction of a collective redress procedure.[182] He can claim expenses and legal fees back from the defendant if the action has been successful.[183] However, if the case is lost, the group representative has to reimburse the costs of the defendant, including lawyers' fees.[184] The group representative is not allowed to seek reimbursement from the group members.

A main objection to the system is that group representatives will be hesitant to bring certain claims.[185] The government counters this argument with its choice to grant standing only to selected organizations, assuming that these will be guided by the collective interest they represent rather than by the financial risks of collective redress.[186] Costs can also be moderated by the judge in accordance with the CPC. The government further stresses the positive effect that the group representative will assess the claim carefully before bringing collective redress proceedings, which should prevent frivolous cases from being brought.[187]

That being said, respected collective interest associations also need means to operate. Furthermore, the reimbursement of costs and lawyers' fees if collective redress proceedings are decided in favour of the group will not entirely compensate the group representative, given that internal costs, such as personnel, are not part of the calculation.[188] Financial considerations may thus well become important at some point in deciding to pursue certain cases.[189]

This is where the option of third-party funding comes in. It cannot be excluded that some of the selected associations that can bring an action for collective redress may seek money elsewhere. It should be pointed out that the possibility of third-party funders seeking to fund collective redress proceedings in return for part of the damages is largely excluded by the Law of 28 March. Damages will be distributed by the claims administrator directly to the group members. However, nothing prevents a third-party funder from addressing individual group members directly. This could eventually lead to situations in which a third-party funder actively searches for potential group members and promises them to convince a group representative to bring collective proceedings in return for a small fee. Furthermore,

---

[182] Report on the introduction of a collective redress mechanism, 17–18 and 25.
[183] Project of Law, 12. This accords to Recommendation, No 13.
[184] Article 1017, first para. CPC. See also Report on the introduction of a collective redress mechanism, 25.
[185] Voet (above n 67) 22.
[186] Project of Law, 11.
[187] *Ibid*, 12.
[188] Art 1018 CPC. See also Danis, Falla and Lefèvre (above n 68) 574.
[189] See also H Jacquemin, 'Les pratiques du marché et la protection du consommateur dans le Code de droit économique', *Journal des Tribunaux* (2014) 734.

third party funders with non-financial motives may generously fund collective action proceedings against their competitors. These cases are also targeted by the Recommendation.[190]

Some mechanisms of the 2014 Law may nevertheless provide protection against abuse of third-party funding. If it appears that a group representative's conduct is influenced by a third-party funder, a judge may deem the group representative unsuitable and either reject the action or replace him.[191] Another option available to the judge is to decide that collective redress is not an effective method of redress when proceedings are being brought for ulterior motives.[192] Also, the competent minister may revoke the status of group representative conferred upon an association.[193] However, these options have not been included in the Law to tackle potential abuse of third-party funding. Their effectiveness depends largely on a judge's willingness to use them to that end.

The Law is thus clearly not meeting the requirements of the Recommendation in this regard and the argument is unconvincing that the careful pre-selection of a limited circle of potential group representatives allows for protection against abuse.

3. The Obligation to Attempt a Settlement

The Recommendation requires Member States to encourage parties to settle their disputes.[194] It does not specify whether an attempt to settle should be a mandatory step in the proceedings. From the Communication it appears, however, that the EC considers recourse to consensual dispute resolution as voluntary as an obligation could lead to "unnecessary costs and delays" and potentially undermine "the fundamental right of access to justice."[195] It should be pointed out that also according to the judgment of the CJEU in *Alassini* an attempt to settle as a mandatory condition for the admissibility of a claim may impact on the principle of effective judicial protection.[196]

The Law of 28 March 2014 introduces a mandatory settlement phase between the admissibility and the merits phase. Thus, the mandatory attempt to consensual dispute resolution is not a condition for the admissibility of the collective redress proceedings. In that regard it cannot be compared to the CJEU's judgment in *Alassini*.[197] Nevertheless, it is an integral part of the

---

[190] Recommendation, No 16.
[191] Art XVII.36.2° ELC.
[192] Art XVII.36.3° ELC.
[193] Art XVII.39 ELC *a contrario*.
[194] Recommendation, No 21.
[195] Communication, 14.
[196] ECJ, Joined Cases C-317/08 to C-320/08 *Alassini*, EU:C:2010:146, para 62.
[197] *Ibid*.

collective redress proceedings and can thus give rise to "unnecessary costs and delays."

In his admissibility decision, the judge fixes the time period for a negotiated settlement between the parties. It should not be shorter than three months and not exceed six months. Upon request of the parties the period can be extended once for another six months. This means that a collective redress procedure can potentially be delayed for one year. This depends, however, entirely upon the parties. In case the attempt at a negotiated settlement proves unsuccessful, the group representative should notify the judge without delay.[198] This signals the end of the settlement phase and within one month of that notification the judge will convene the parties in order to decide on the organization of the merits phase.[199] The notification to the judge of the lack of agreement between the parties can be done before the expiration of the time periods fixed in the admissibility decision.[200] It is thus possible for the parties to terminate the mandatory settlement phase immediately and to proceed to the merits phase.

While the settlement phase appears to be a mandatory step in the proceedings, it thus depends completely on the parties whether they actually make use of it. In case they have no intention to settle, they can proceed to the merits phase without delay. The month between the end of the settlement phase and the start of the merits phase cannot reasonably be considered a major obstacle to the effectiveness of the proceedings. Furthermore, it may also have been provided for without a mandatory settlement phase by way of time allotted for case management purposes. The mandatory settlement phase appears thus to be an invitation by the judge to the parties to come to a settlement, an invitation which they can accept or reject, rather than a mandatory attempt at settlement. This accords almost completely with the 2008 Mediation Directive,[201] to which the EC refers in its Recommendation.[202] It provides that mediation should be 'a voluntary process in the sense that the parties are themselves in charge of the process and may organise it as they wish and terminate it at any time'.[203]

4. Limitation to Consumers and Consumer Law

The Recommendation mentions consumer protection law, competition law,

---

[198] Art XVII.48 ELC.
[199] Art XVII.53 ELC.
[200] Art XVII.48 ELC.
[201] Directive 2008/52/EC of the European Parliament and of the Council of 21 May 2008 on certain aspects of mediation in civil and commercial matters, OJ 2008, L136/3.
[202] Recommendation, No 25.
[203] Directive 2008/52/EC, 13th Recital.

data protection law, environmental law, the law of financial services and the protection of shareholders as areas of law in which a collective redress mechanism would be particularly useful.[204] The Recommendation does not, however, limit the scope of the Recommendation to those areas of law as the EC clearly envisaged a general collective redress mechanism.

In contrast, the Law of 28 March 2014 limits the scope of application of the collective redress mechanism both *ratione materiae* and *ratione personae*. A first limitation concerns the area of law to which the collective redress mechanism is applicable. The legislator has not chosen to refer in the abstract to an area but has included a list of 31 instruments to which the collective redress mechanism applies. All these instruments are connected with the area of consumer protection law in a broader sense, including classic consumer rights but also passengers' rights and competition law. The technique of referring to a list has been criticized as the Law will need to be changed every time a new instrument is to be included in the list.[205] Furthermore, it is not clear what will happen if a listed piece of legislation is repealed and replaced by a new law or regulation that has the same object.

A second limitation concerns the persons who can benefit from collective redress following a violation of the listed instruments. A clear choice has been made to make collective redress available to consumers only. This is in line with the objectives pursued by the Law but it can be questioned whether the mechanism should not also be available for small and medium enterprises, which often find themselves in a position similar to that of consumers in case of diffuse damage caused by another undertaking.[206]

All specific criticism boils down to the same point, namely that the legislator has limited the collective redress mechanism to a specific area of law.[207] However, it was a deliberate choice to introduce the concept of collective redress first in a limited area of law to gain experience and consumer protection law proved to be a suitable 'test case' in this regard.[208] This also explains the use of a list instead of referring to an area of law in the abstract: proceedings will not be held back by defining the scope of application of the law and the focus will lie on the procedure itself.[209] The government will evaluate the functioning of the 2014 Law within three years of its entry into force. On the basis of that analysis the government may take the initiative to expand the scope of application to other areas of law.[210] The 2014 Law may

---

[204] Recommendation, No 7.
[205] Report on the introduction of a collective redress mechanism, 13.
[206] *Ibid*, 11.
[207] Some have argued this may amount to discrimination in relation to access to justice. See Voet (above n 67) 8.
[208] Report on the introduction of a collective redress mechanism, 40.
[209] *Ibid*, 17.
[210] *Ibid*.

thus well be the first step towards a general collective redress mechanism in Belgium.

5. Exclusive Competence of the Courts of Brussels and the Right to Appeal

For collective redress actions, the Law confers an exclusive competence upon the Brussels courts.[211] The choice is motivated by a desire to create specialized judges and to secure the development of a consistent body of case law.[212] Furthermore, it was deemed appropriate to make the courts of the capital competent given that the damage for which compensation is being sought will possibly affect many persons across various judicial 'arrondissements'.[213] This choice has received approval in legal literature.[214]

Problems could, however, arise in the context of appeal proceedings. If an appeal is brought under Belgian procedural law against a first instance decision, the whole case becomes pending before the appeal court.[215] The same would apply in collective redress proceedings since a derogation from that principle has not been provided for. Consequently, an appeal against the admissibility decision will transfer collective redress proceedings as a whole to the Brussels Court of Appeal, which will then take over the rest of the procedure. A first consequence is that the merits of the case will only be considered once, namely on appeal. This is not necessarily a problem, as a right to appeal as such does not exist. A second, more problematic issue is that the Brussels Court of Appeal is already swamped (further to being an ordinary appeal court it is also the review court for decisions taken by certain regulatory authorities) and that once a collective procedure is transferred to the Court of Appeal it is very likely that it will be a very long time before proceedings can be concluded.[216] This appears to be incompatible with the Recommendation, which prescribes that collective redress procedures should be timely.[217]

As to centralised proceedings and their length, the CJEU was confronted with this problem in the *Agrokonsulting* case.[218] The case concerned the question whether a rule providing for the centralization of a certain type of litigation in the administrative courts of the Bulgarian capital did amount to a breach of the principle of effectiveness and the right to effective judicial

---

[211] Art 633*ter* CPC.
[212] Project of Law, 12.
[213] *Ibid*, 16.
[214] Voet and Allemeersch (above n 66) 652–653.
[215] Art 1068(1) CPC.
[216] Voet (above n 67) 14.
[217] Recommendation, No 2.
[218] ECJ, Case C-93/12 *Agrokonsulting*, EU:C:2013:432.

protection. An element that the Court took into account in its analysis was the length of proceedings. It held eventually that the Bulgarian rule was compatible with EU law provided that the "jurisdiction rule does not cause individuals procedural problems in terms, inter alia, of the duration of the proceedings, such as to render the exercise of the rights derived from European Union law excessively difficult."[219] The judgment seems to suggest that centralization of certain types of litigation becomes problematic if cases cannot be decided in a timely manner. Depending on how the Belgian situation develops, the involvement of the Brussels Court of Appeal could impact on the timely conclusion of collective redress proceedings and thus contradict the principles established by the CJEU.

6. The Application of EU Competition Law

Articles 101 and 102 of the TFEU appear to have not been included in the list of instruments to which the Belgian collective redress mechanism applies. Article XVII.37 merely refers to rules of 'Belgian' competition law. This should, however, not be an obstacle to use the collective redress mechanism for violations of EU competition law. The Belgian competition rules on cartels and abuse of dominant position are straightforward copies of their EU counterparts.[220] A violation of EU competition rules that also affects consumers on the Belgian market will thus very likely be covered by the collective redress mechanism. Furthermore, Article 4 of the Damages Directive provides that, in accordance with the principle of equivalence:

> National rules and procedures relating to actions for damages resulting from infringements of Article 101 or 102 TFEU shall not be less favourable to the alleged injured parties than those governing similar actions for damages resulting from infringements of national law.[221]

Consequently, the collective redress mechanism should also be available for damages claims based on a violation of Articles 101 and 102 TFEU.

V. CONCLUSION

The idea of collective redress existed within the Belgian legal order in various

---

[219] *Ibid*, para 61.
[220] See Arts IV.1 and IV.2 ELC.
[221] Directive 2014/104/EU of the European Parliament and of the Council of 26 November 2014 on certain rules governing actions for damages under national law for infringements of the competition law provisions of the Member States and of the European Union, OJ 2014, L349/1.

ways before the entry into force of the Law of 28 March 2014. Collective actions mainly took the form of claims of associations seeking to protect a collective interest. With the Law of 28 March 2014 Belgium introduced, for the first time, a proper collective redress mechanism. It did so with hesitation, evidenced by the mechanism's limited scope of application. The Belgian legislator nevertheless vowed to undertake a review of the 2014 Law within three years of its application, making a general collective redress mechanism a viable prospect for the future.

The 2014 Law does not only document an internal evolution towards a class action style mechanism, but is also part of a development taking place at EU level. The EC made collective redress an important part of its consumer rights policy. The Belgian legislation should therefore also be seen as part of an EU-wide horizontal enforcement network, in particular with respect to, but not limited to consumer protection law. It is in that context that this chapter assessed the 2014 Law in light of EU law requirements. It appears that the 2014 Law departs on a number of points from EU law requirements. However, in its practical application, the Law may be a perfect fit in the EU-wide enforcement network. A final assessment will only be possible within a few years, when the procedure is up-and-running. A first step has nevertheless been taken.

Cross-Border Actions for Collective Redress – Some Lessons from Canada

John P Brown and Brandon Kain[*]

I. INTRODUCTION

After a lengthy, contentious, controversial and tortuous process, the European Commission published its policy paper on collective redress in June 2013.[1] The paper contains proposals for addressing the violation of rights granted under EU law including a non-binding Recommendation on common principles for injunctive and compensatory collective redress mechanisms in Member States. The Recommendation does not require Member States to implement collective redress regimes or otherwise reform their existing legal systems. As is the case with many political compromises, the Recommendation satisfies almost no one.

Perhaps the most disappointing aspect of the Recommendation (other than its non-binding nature) is the adoption of an opt-in rather than an opt-out model for collective redress regimes. Although an opt-out model is not expressly excluded, it is decidedly meant to be the exception.

Much has been written on the advantages of an opt-out model compared to an opt-in model, and why an opt-in model is not a viable form of collective redress[2] (a view shared by the present authors). There is no intention

---

[*] John P. Brown, Partner, McCarthy Tétrault LLP, Toronto, Canada and Brandon Kain, Partner, McCarthy Tétrault LLP, Toronto, Canada.

[1] Commission Recommendation of 11 June 2013 on common principles for injunctive and compensatory collective redress mechanisms in the Member States concerning violation of rights granted under the Union Law (2013/396/EU), OJ (L 201/60, 26.7.2013).

[2] See for example, R Mulheron, 'A Missed Gem of an Opportunity for the Representative Rule' *European Business Law Review* (2012) 49–60; R Mulheron, 'Recent Milestones in Class Actions Reform in England: A Critique and a Proposal' 127 *Law Quarterly Rev* (2011) 288–315; R Mulheron, 'Opting In, Opting Out, and Closing the Class: Some Dilemmas for England's Class Actions Law-Makers' 50 *Canadian Business LJ* (2011) 376–408; R Mulheron, 'The Case for an Opt-out Class Action for European Member States: A Legal and Empirical Analysis' 15 *Columbia Journal of European Law* (2009) 409–453; R Mulheron, 'Reform of Collective Redress in England and Wales: A Perspective of Need (Report submitted to the Civil Justice Council of England and Wales, February 2008); R Mulheron, 'Competition Law Cases under the Opt-out Regimes of Australia, Canada and Portugal' (Report submitted to the

here to travel down that rabbit hole in this chapter. Instead, the focus will be on how the European Commission's preference for an opt-in model will affect related issues, including (a) jurisdiction and the enforceability of collective redress judgments in other countries, (b) the need for similar collective redress regimes in the Member States, and (c) the need for cooperation and coordination between courts in Member States in cross-border proceedings.

Canada is a federal system, but constitutionally class action legislation falls not only within the purview of the federal government, but also within each province and territory in Canada.[3] As a result, Canadian courts struggle with a number of challenges arising from the filing of multi-jurisdictional, national and/or parallel class actions in more than one province. Canada's experience in this area could therefore be quite relevant to the EU and so this experience will be discussed with a view to offering insights into the challenges Member States will likely face when they begin implementing opt-in collective redress regimes.

II. JURISDICTION AND ENFORCEABILITY

Canadian class action regimes are based on the opt-out model.[4] As a result, in a Canadian action the court certifies a defined class of people and/or entities who are then presumptively bound by a judgment in the action unless they take active steps to opt-out of the proceedings. This legislated provision is uncontroversial when applied to representative plaintiffs, because they attorn to the jurisdiction of the Canadian court by commencing the action. It is equally uncontroversial when applied to 'absent' foreign claimants from other provinces or territories in Canada (ie those who meet the class definition but who fail to opt-out), because they are subject to the court's jurisdiction by virtue of the 'real and substantial connection' to the court that exists from sharing common issues with the attorning representative plaintiff, a

---

Department for Business, Enterprise and Regulatory Reform, October 2008); R Mulheron, 'Improving Access to Justice Through Collective Actions: Developing a More Efficient and Effective Procedure for Collective Actions': Final Report'(A Series of Recommendations to the Lord Chancellor, November 2008), 488 pp (co-author of Report); R Mulheron, 'In Defence of the Requirement for Foreign Class Members to Opt-in to an English Class Action' in D Fairgrieve and E Lein, *Extraterritoriality and Collective Redress* (OUP, 2012), ch 14, 245–266.

[3] Every Canadian province other than Prince Edward Island has enacted class proceedings legislation. Additionally, class proceedings legislation exists at the federal level in the form of Part 5.1 of the *Federal Courts Rules*, S.O.R./98–106, though its use has been limited by the jurisdictional constraints of the Federal Court.

[4] As discussed below, there are three Canadian jurisdictions that follow an opt-in approach for non-residents: British Columbia, Newfoundland and New Brunswick. However, they still require residents to opt-out.

principle that is bolstered by the jurisdictional reciprocity shown by each court within Canada.[5]

However, different considerations apply to absent foreign claimants who are not present in Canada and have never taken positive steps to consent to its jurisdiction.

Pursuant to generally accepted principles of private international law, jurisdiction cannot be asserted over a party for the purposes of a judgment that is intended to be enforceable outside of the state issuing the judgment unless the party was present in the state when the proceedings were commenced, or submitted or consented to the jurisdiction of the state.[6] Moreover, a fundamental principle adhered to in civil law jurisdictions in Europe is that one can only become a claimant in a court proceeding by expressly asking to bring or join a claim. Pursuant to this principle, parties have the right to participate fully in proceedings brought on their behalf and to know the nature and extent of the claims. They also have the exclusive right either to compromise their claims or to have their entitlement to relief determined individually.

Prior to 1990 Canadian courts applied these generally accepted principles of private international law in deciding whether to assert jurisdiction over foreign parties. This changed in 1990 when the Supreme Court of Canada adopted a new jurisdictional test, the 'real and substantial connection' test, which it later extended to international litigation in 2003.[7] This test is a radical departure from the generally accepted principles of private international law adhered to by other countries for asserting jurisdiction for the purposes of a judgment that is intended to be enforceable internationally.

Notwithstanding the radical nature of the real and substantial connection test, within Canada the intended preclusive effect of a class action judgment from one province is regularly recognized by courts in other provinces, even with respect to absent foreign claimants. This is attributable to the fact that the Supreme Court of Canada requires a province to enforce the judgments of another province that assumed jurisdiction over the parties based on the 'real and substantial connection' test, regardless of whether the traditional presence or consent tests are met.[8] As well, all Canadian provinces and territories have either a formal opt-out class proceedings statute or a common law opt- out class proceedings process.[9] Given these features of the Canadian

---

[5] *Meeking v Cash Store Inc*, 2013 MBCA 81, leave to appeal granted and appeal adjourned *sine die* [2013] SCCA No. 443. See also *Club Resorts Ltd v Van Breda* [2012] 1 SCR 572.

[6] *Dicey, Morris and Collins on the Conflict of Laws*, 15th ed. (Sweet & Maxwell, 2012), Rule 43.

[7] *Beals v Saldanha* [2003] 3 SCR 416.

[8] *Morguard Investments Ltd v De Savoye* [1990] 3 SCR 1077.

[9] *Class Proceedings Act*, SA 2003, c. C-16.5, ss. 17 and 17.1; *The Class Actions Act*, SS 2001, c. C-12.01, s. 18; *Class Proceedings Act*, CCSM c. 130, s. 16; *Code of Civil Procedure*, CQLR c. C-25, arts. 1007 and 1027; *Class Proceedings Act*, SNS 2007, c. 28, s. 19; *Class Proceedings Act*,

legal landscape, a court in one province may reasonably expect that another court in another Canadian province will recognize its assumption of jurisdiction over absent foreign claimants and so enforce a corresponding judgment.

The same cannot be said for foreign countries.[10] In contrast to Canadian courts,[11] the courts of foreign countries do not accept the real and substantial connection test as a proper jurisdictional basis for enforcing a judgment issued by a Canadian court. Rather, foreign courts will only enforce a judgment from another country where the other country asserted jurisdiction over the parties based on the traditional grounds of presence or consent. A foreign judgment pronounced on other jurisdictional grounds is considered a nullity and will not be enforced.[12]

As a consequence, when a Canadian court certifies a class that includes absent foreign claimants, it purports to assert jurisdiction over potential plaintiffs on a basis that will not be recognized by the countries in which they reside. This means that a Canadian class action judgment will not have preclusive effect and the issues that are the subject of that judgment may be relitigated by absent foreign claimants in their home countries.

This result is firmly supported by courts and commentators worldwide. Professor Briggs summarizes a widely accepted view outside of Canada that the real and substantial connection test is a radical departure from the law in other countries:

> *As a matter of English law, such a development [ie adopting a 'real and substantial connection' test] would require legislation. And it is important to understand how radical the Canadian departure is.* For the English common law enquires into whether the party to be bound to the judgment has acted in such a way as to have assumed a personal obligation to obey the judgment: his submission to the jurisdiction of the court is the commonest example, but his presence within the jurisdiction also places him in the way of obedience. The Canadian development, however, does not focus on whether the party to be bound has assumed an obligation, but on whether the Canadian court should impose one for reasons of its own.

RSBC 1996, c. 50, s. 16; *Class Proceedings Act*, RSNB 2011, c. 125, s. 18; *Class Actions Act*, SNL 2001, c. C-18.1, s. 17 and *Western Canadian Shopping Centres Inc v Dutton* [2001] 2 SCR 534, ¶49. See also: *Federal Courts Rules*, SOR/98–106, Rule 334.21.

[10] *Teck Cominco Metals Ltd v Lloyd's Underwriters* [2009] 1 SCR 321, ¶30 ("A distinction should be made between situations that involve a uniform and shared approach to the exercise of jurisdiction (e.g. interprovincial conflicts) and those, such as the present, that do not"). See also *Beals v Saldanha* [2003] 3 SCR 416, ¶26–28 and 30 (noting that the real and substantial connection test "may give rise to different considerations internationally").

[11] *Beals v Saldanha* [2003] 3 SCR 416.

[12] TJ Monestier, 'Foreign Judgments at Common Law: Rethinking the Enforcement Rules' 28 *Dalhousie LJ* (2005) 163 at 164–165, 168–171 and 183.

There is nothing wrong with such a development, but far from being a modernisation of the details, it represents a fundamental reorientation of the law on foreign judgments. *It is not clear that the Supreme Court fully appreciated what it was doing.*[13]

Other commentators have expressed similar views that their countries will not recognize and enforce Canadian judgments if the only basis for the Canadian court's jurisdiction over foreign parties is the existence of a real and substantial connection.[14]

Further, a series of judicial decisions from outside Canada have expressly rejected the real and substantial connection test as a basis for recognizing and enforcing foreign judgments. In 2012, the Supreme Court of Ireland held in *Flightlease* that "the Canadian approach would represent a radical change in the common law" which "appears not to have been followed in any other common law jurisdiction", and stated:

> ... The learned trial judge set out clearly his reasons for holding that the Canadian jurisprudence should not be adopted. These are as follows:-
>
> 1. *The court was not referred to judgments of any other common law jurisdiction which suggested that common law courts generally have followed the Canadian lead.* That remains the position.

---

[13] A Briggs, *The Conflict of Laws*, 2nd ed. (Oxford University Press, 2008) at 138–139, emphasis added.

[14] J Fawcett and JM Carruthers, *Cheshire, North & Fawcett's Private International Law*, 14th ed. (Oxford University Press, 2008) at 527 and 530–531 ("The Supreme Court of Canada in *Morguard Investments Ltd v De Savoye* has adopted a radically different approach towards the recognition and enforcement of foreign judgments at common law in inter-provincial cases"); A Briggs, *Agreements on Jurisdiction and Choice of Law* (Oxford University Press, 2008) at 347–348 ("English common law does not and cannot accept the existence of a strong connection between the adjudicating court and the cause of action as a distinct basis for the recognition of a judgment... The developments taking place in Canada, for example, are alien to the structure of the English common law. ... [T]he Canadian approach to the recognition of foreign judgments is not just an updating of the traditional common law, but a revolutionary change in its basic structure"); R Fentiman, *International Commercial Litigation* (Oxford University Press, 2010) at 697-698; Lord Collins of Mapesbury, ed., *Dicey, Morris and Collins on the Conflict of Laws*, 15th ed. (Sweet & Maxwell, 2012), Vol. 1, at 708 ("There is no authority in England which suggests that this is the appropriate test for the recognition and enforcement of foreign judgments in personam"); R. Mulheron, 'The Recognition, and *Res Judicata* Effect, of a United States Class Actions Judgment in England: A Rebuttal of *Vivendi*' 75 MLR (2012) 180 at 208–209; JJ Chan, 'Problems in the Recognition and Enforcement of U.S. Class Action Judgments in Singapore' 25 *SAcLJ* (2013) 51 at 72–74 ("[T]he Singapore courts would and should be extremely cautious before following the directions marked out by *Morguard* and *Beals*"); D Kenny, '*Re Flightlease*: The "Real and Substantial Connection" Test for Recognition and Enforcement of Foreign Judgments Failure to Take Flight in Ireland' 63 *ICLQ* (2014) 197 at 198 ("[I]t has been a lonely revolution for Canada. As of yet, no other common law jurisdiction has decided to follow Canada's lead and reshape the common law rules").

> 2. There has been some academic commentary which cautions against adopting the Canadian approach and *it would not be correct to describe the area under consideration as one where there has been a broad acceptance in the common law world of a new direction.* ...
>
> 4. ... *[A] radical change in common law* has the potential to have a retrospective effect which would not in the ordinary way arise in the event of a statutory amendment. Such a change can work an injustice.
> 5. The courts in this jurisdiction cannot engage in *an alteration of the common law which would amount to legislation* as opposed to allowing for the orderly evolution of common law principles.
> 6. *There is no consensus in the common law world as to the need for the change identified by the Supreme Court of Canada.*
>
> *I concur with each of the foregoing propositions.* In relation to *Indyka v Indyka*, both in the United Kingdom and insofar as that has been followed in other common law jurisdictions, it has not been extended to proceedings other than matrimonial proceedings.
>
> ... *The change contended for by Swissair is of such significance that it would in my opinion exceed the judicial function* to re-state the common law in such a way. Such a change should be by legislation. ...[15]

The United Kingdom Supreme Court (formerly the House of Lords) later reached the same conclusion in *Rubin*:

> Consequently, if *the judgments in issue* on the appeals are regarded as judgments *in personam* within the Dicey rule, then they *will only be enforced in England at common law if the judgment debtors were present... in the foreign country when the proceedings were commenced, or if they submitted to its jurisdiction.* ...
>
> The principles in the Dicey rule have never received the express approval of the House of Lords or the UK Supreme Court... But there can be no doubt that the references by the House of Lords in the context of foreign judgments to the foreign court of "competent jurisdiction" are implicit references to the common law rule...
>
> The Rubin respondents question whether the rules remain sound in the modern world. *It is true that the common law rule was rejected in Canada*, at first in the context of the inter-provincial recognition of judgments. *The Supreme Court of Canada held that* the English rules developed in the 19th century for the recognition and enforcement of judgments of foreign countries could not be transposed to the enforcement of judgments from

---

[15] *In re Flightlease (Ireland) Ltd* [2012] IESC 12, emphasis added.

sister provinces in a single country with a common market and a single citizenship. Instead *a judgment given against a person outside the jurisdiction should be recognised and enforced if the subject matter of the action had a real and substantial connection with the province in which the judgment was given*: Morguard Investments Ltd v De Savoye [1990] 3 SCR 1077, para 45. This approach was applied, by a majority, to foreign country judgments in *Beals v Saldanha* [2003] 3 SCR 416...

There is no support in England for such an approach except in the field of family law. ... *It has never been adopted outside the family law sphere in the context of foreign judgments.*

The Supreme Court of Ireland in *In re Flightlease (Ireland) Ltd* [2012] IESC 12... *also held that the Dicey rule should not be rejected in favour of a real and substantial connection test.* ...[16]

Finally, the Rule 43 in *Dicey Morris & Collins* that was uniformly endorsed and applied by the courts in the cases cited above was revised in the most recent edition to clarify that the rule applies to all parties, including absent foreign claimants, and not just to defendants. Adrian Briggs explained the significance of this in a recent affidavit filed in a Canadian proceeding:

The second point is to note the change in wording in the relevant Rule in *Dicey Morris & Collins*. In the 14th edition, Rule 36 (as it then was) dealt with whether a foreign judgment was liable to be recognised by asking whether the 'judgment debtor' had been present within the jurisdiction of the foreign court, or had submitted to it, *et cetera*. It seemed to me, in my capacity as member of the editorial team with primary responsibility for this Chapter, that this wording had the potential to mislead. *For where a claimant's claim had simply been dismissed by a foreign court, the judgment would be recognised as res judicata as against the claimant, even though it seemed unnatural to refer to him as a 'judgment debtor'. The intended sense of the Rule was that if a foreign judgment purported to tie the hands of a party to the foreign proceedings, that person was bound by the foreign judgment if he had submitted to or had been present within the jurisdiction of the foreign court.* If he were referred to, not as the 'judgment debtor', but as 'the person against whom the judgment was given', it might be easier to see that the proper question was whether that person had submitted to or had been present within the jurisdiction of the foreign court. It can be seen from the

---

[16] *Rubin v Eurofinance CA* [2013] 1 AC 236 (UKSC), para 9 and 108–111, emphasis added. See also *Islamic Republic of Iran Shipping Lines v Phiniqia International Shipping LLC* [2014] HKCFI 1280, para 29–31 and 33–35 (accepting that "[I]n the absence of exceptional justification, the Hong Kong court should and would not see fit to even start considering the application of the Canadian approach in place of the well-established approach").

judgment in *Rubin* that Lord Collins, the General Editor of *Dicey Morris & Collins*, regarded this as a clarification of the existing rule which did not alter its material effect: see *Rubin* at paragraphs 7 to 10.[17]

In other words, the revised Rule 43 in *Dicey Morris & Collins* precludes the recognition and enforcement of foreign judgments against claimants who do not meet the traditional jurisdiction tests of presence, consent or submission, ie, absent foreign claimants in the parlance of this paper. Where an action by an absent foreign clamant is unsuccessful, Rule 43 would permit that claimant to relitigate the action against the defendant abroad. Applied to a Canadian class action involving absent foreign claimants, this deprives defendants of any certainty that those claimants will not relitigate the class action abroad should the defendant be successful in dismissing the Canadian proceeding.

A further obstacle to the enforcement of a Canadian opt-out class action judgment is that very few other countries have opt-out collective redress or class action regimes. Consequently, a Canadian class action judgment is burdened with an additional objectionable element – the fact that parties are presumptively bound by a judgment even though they have not expressly asked to bring or join the claim in question.

In the EU, at least as between Member States, the provisions of the Brussels I Regulation address and resolve most of the jurisdiction and enforceability issues Canada initially struggled with but has largely resolved within its own borders. Like the rules that govern the Canadian federation, Brussels I contains rules that govern the jurisdiction of courts and the recognition and enforcement of judgments in civil and commercial matters in Member States. The Regulations specify which Member State has jurisdiction, and why. The Regulations also require Member States to recognize judgments from other Member States without special procedures applying.

The fact that the EU is urging all Member States to adopt opt-in collective redress regimes rather than opt-out regimes will also eliminate many jurisdiction and enforceability issues as between Member States.

However, just as Canada's laws fail to provide a means of overcoming the serious obstacles to enforcing its class action judgments outside of Canada, Brussels I offers little assistance to Member States in respect of these issues in relation to non-Member States, and in particular in relation to non-European non-Member States such as Canada, Australia and the United States. Moreover, the EU preference for opt-in regimes conflicts with the long-standing opt-out class action systems in federalist countries such as Canada,

---

[17] Supplemental Affidavit of Adrian Briggs sworn 2 January 2014, in *Airia Brands Inc et al v Air Canada et al* Ontario Superior Court of Justice, Court File No. 50389CP, para 6.

Australia and the United States. It will also conflict with the imminently expected opt-out collective redress regime proposed for the UK.

That being said, opt-in regimes have some advantages in respect of matters relating to jurisdiction and enforceability. An opt-in regime eliminates virtually all jurisdiction issues relating to both domestic and foreign claimants. In either instance, anyone who wishes to participate in the action must expressly opt-in to the proceeding, a process that satisfies generally accepted principles of private international law for asserting jurisdiction over a party for the purposes of securing a judgment that can be enforced internationally.

This is the main reason the Civil Justice Council of England and Wales has proposed an opt-in regime in the UK for foreign or non-resident claimants. (Notably the Council has proposed an opt-out regime for domestic or 'resident' claimants because they are subject to the UK courts and corresponding legislation by virtue of their presence in the country.) The opt-in proposal for foreign claimants was designed to address concerns over the enforceability of UK class action judgments abroad:

> Class members who are not domiciled in England and Wales will only be able to join an opt-out action if they give notice to the class representatives that they want to opt into it. This reflects similar provisions in the Financial Services Bill relating to persons not domiciled in the UK. *It is intended to avoid any arguments in relation to national sovereignty which might arise if the provisions purported to assert jurisdiction to decide cases for foreign domiciliaries who have taken no active part in the proceedings.*[18]

Accordingly, the Civil Justice Review Council was concerned that if an English court certified an opt-out class that included non-resident claimants, other jurisdictions would neither recognize nor enforce any judgments issued by that English court against the foreign claimants.

This proposed legislative initiative in the UK mirrors legislative provisions that already exist in the Canadian provinces of British Columbia, Newfoundland and New Brunswick which have implemented opt-out regimes for resident or domestic claimants and an opt-in approach for non-resident or foreign claimants.[19] This opt-in feature of the legislation avoids the jurisdictional issues created when a court applies the real and substantial connection test to absent foreign claimants, instead of requiring their presence or consent.[20] As the British Columbia Court of Appeal explained in *Harrington*:

---

[18] Civil Justice Council, 'Response to European Commission Public Consultation: Towards a Coherent European Approach to Collective Redress' (SEC (2011) 173 Final), 56.

[19] *Class Proceedings Act*, RSBC 1996, c. 50, s. 16; *Class Proceedings Act*, RSNB 2011, c. 125, s. 18; *Class Actions Act*, SNL 2001, c. C-18.1, s. 17.

[20] *Harrington v Dow Corning Corp* (1997), 29 BCLR (3d) 88 (S.C.), para 9 and 13 (QL)

> The authorities and literature to which we were referred do not address the application of s. 16(2) [of the B.C. *CPA*]. However, it is expressed in the same terms as those recommended in 1996 by the Uniform Law Conference of Canada in its *Uniform Class Proceedings Act*, s. 16(2). The latter has been the subject of some comment insofar as the Legislatures have chosen *opting in over opting out. Opting in is seen as having the advantage of "indicating that the non-resident accepts the jurisdiction of the court such that they would be precluded by the doctrine of res judicata from later suing or benefitting from a suit brought in another jurisdiction."*...By opting-in the non-resident class members are accepting that their claims are essentially the same as those of the resident class members.[21]

Member States will face difficult questions relating to the enforceability of collective redress and/or class action judgments from non-Member States, not only based on issues of jurisdiction but also arising from the opt-in versus opt-out dichotomy. The manner in which a Member State decides to resolve these questions will affect the enforceability of its judgments by the courts of non-Member States, and the enforceability of judgments from non-Member States in its own courts.

III. THE NEED FOR SIMILAR COLLECTIVE REDRESS REGIMES

In Canada, nine of ten provinces have formal class action opt-out legislation. Eight of these provinces are common law provinces with class action statutes that are similar or identical in most material respects. The other province, Quebec, is a civil law jurisdiction that has class action legislation which is similar in import and effect to the common law legislation. Moreover, the objectives and goals of all the class action regimes are the same – access to justice, judicial economy and behaviour modification. This similarity of class action regimes across Canada facilitates the enforcement of a class action judgment from one province in another province.

As Member States begin considering whether to implement collective redress statutes it would be helpful to have a common checklist or guide to refer to, not only to assess what provisions might be required in order to develop an effective regime, but also to strive, to the extent possible, to implement similar collective redress regimes in each Member State. This approach will be beneficial on a number of levels.

("The non-resident opt-in procedure avoids potential difficulties in exercising jurisdiction over class members outside the province who have not taken any initiative to attorn to the jurisdiction of the BC court").

[21] *Harrington v Dow Corning Corp* (2000), 193 DLR (4th) 67 (BCCA), para 74, 85 and 99, leave to appeal refused [2001] SCCA No. 21, emphasis added.

First, Member States will be familiar with the provisions and goals of each other's collective redress regimes. This will make it easier to decide whether to recognize and enforce collective redress judgments from other Member States.

Second, similar collective redress regimes would result in complementary judicial decisions concerning similar issues that arise in the various collective redress regimes that can become a valuable resource for all Member States.

Third, if collective regimes are similar, forum shopping should not become an issue. The rights available to claimants will be the same or similar in every Member State.

A useful checklist of provisions that should be considered for a collective redress statute can be found in the International Bar Association's 'Guidelines for Recognising and Enforcing Foreign Judgments for Collective Redress' (Guidelines). In October 2006, the Consumer Litigation Committee of the International Bar Association created the IBA Task Force on International Procedures and Protocols for Collective Redress (Task Force) to study the potential problems associated with judgments rendered in multi-jurisdictional actions for collective redress. The objective of the Task Force was to draft guidelines that could be applied to address the recognition and enforcement of a collective redress judgment in a jurisdiction other than the jurisdiction in which the judgment was granted. The work of the Task Force culminated in the Guidelines which were formally adopted on 16 October 2008 by the Legal Practice Division of the International Bar Association.[22] The purpose of the Guidelines is set out in the introductory paragraphs:

> 7. ... the Guidelines are intended to describe minimum internationally accepted standards for the procedural and substantive rights to be afforded by a court issuing a collective redress judgment to the persons it purports to bind. These standards can be used as a point of reference by a second court wishing to consider whether to treat those persons as bound by the judgment of the first court.
>
> 8. These Guidelines can assist the second court, for example, to determine when, and in what circumstances, it would be fair, just and reasonable for a foreign judgment for collective redress to have preclusive effect in the jurisdiction in which absent claimants reside, where, otherwise, the absent claimants might seek to re-litigate the issues which were the subject of the collective redress judgment.

---

[22] The *Guidelines* are available on the IBA website at: www.ibanet.org/Search/Default.aspx?q=guidelines%20collective%20redress.

9. The Guidelines may also serve as a useful checklist for courts to maximise the likelihood that their judgments will be recognised elsewher

Countries that are considering adopting collective redress legislation or that are in the process of preparing such legislation may find the Guidelines a useful benchmark of international standards that can be taken into account if foreign recognition of their judgments is among the objectives to be achieved.

IV. THE NEED FOR COOPERATION AND COORDINATION BETWEEN COURTS

A major problem between provinces in Canada, and between Canada and the US is multiple, overlapping class actions. Class actions seeking the same or similar relief against the same defendants are often commenced in different provinces in Canada, or in Canada and the US at the same time. Sometimes the various courts become aware of these competing actions and sometimes they do not. When they do become aware of these competing actions sometimes they are willing and able to coordinate the actions to avoid duplication, and sometimes they are unwilling or unable to do so. This creates unfairness and prejudice for all the parties involved. Three measures have been proposed in Canada to try to address these problems.[23]

The first measure was a proposal for a national registry of all class actions, much like the national registry of collective redress actions proposed in the EU policy paper. The national registry in Canada was proposed in 2005 by the Uniform Law Conference of Canada (ULCC). The mandate of the ULCC is to harmonize the laws of the provinces and territories of Canada, and where appropriate the federal laws as well. The recommendation of the ULCC relating to multi-jurisdictional class actions within Canada was as follows:

> An on-line Canadian Class Proceedings Registry of all class action filings in each Canadian jurisdiction should be created and maintained for use by the public, counsel and courts. All current or proposed class proceedings legislation in all Canadian jurisdictions should require that all class action filings be directed to this registry. In addition or alternatively, courts in each jurisdiction should issue practice directions setting out the details of such filings.[24]

---

[23] *Report of the Uniform Law Conference of Canada's Committee on the National Class and Related Interjurisdictional Issues: Background, Analysis, and Recommendations* (March 2005), 2–3.
[24] *Idem.*

Unfortunately, this recommendation has not been implemented to date by any legislature. The Canadian Bar Association (CBA) is a professional, voluntary organization that represents over 37,000 lawyers, judges, notaries, law teachers, and law students in Canada. Following the recommendation of the ULCC, the CBA established the National Class Action Database. The Database was intended to provide lawyers and the public with easy access to court documents relating to class action lawsuits that were currently underway anywhere in Canada. However, the Database is a voluntary initiative which lawyers only infrequently update and so it does not contain a comprehensive listing of all class action lawsuits in Canada. The result is that it is not a very useful resource for lawyers or judges. Member States should strive to create viable, uniform accessible registries with current information in order to monitor and supervise competing collective redress actions.

The second proposal by the ULCC was legislation that obligated courts to take into consideration existing, competing class actions when deciding whether to certify a class action in its own jurisdiction:

> All current or proposed class proceedings legislation in all Canadian jurisdictions should:
> (a) expressly permit the court to certify, on an opt-out basis, a class that includes class members residing or located outside the jurisdiction;
> (b) require that a plaintiff seeking to certify a class proceeding give notice of such an application to plaintiffs in any class proceeding in Canada with the same or similar subject matter;
> (c) permit plaintiffs from other jurisdictions served with such notice to make submissions at or before the certification application, including submissions that their action is the preferable procedure for all or part of the overlapping class;
> (d) require the court, in certifying any class proceeding, to consider whether there are one or more class proceedings relating to the same or similar subject matter that have been commenced in one or more other Canadian jurisdictions and to consider whether such class proceedings may be a preferable procedure for the resolution of the claims of all or some of the class members;
> (e) require the court, in assessing whether related class actions in other jurisdictions may be a preferable procedure for the resolution of the claims of all or some of the class members, to consider all relevant factors including:
>> (i) the nature and the scope of the causes of actions advanced, including any variation in the cause of actions available in the various jurisdictions;
>> (ii) the theories offered by counsel in support of the claims;

(iii) the state of preparation of the various class actions;
(iv) the number and extent of involvement of the proposed representative plaintiffs;
(v) the order in which the class actions were commenced;
(vi) the resources and experience of counsel;
(vii) the location of class members, defendants and witnesses;
(viii) the location of any act underlying the cause of action;

(f) permit the court the court to make any order it deems just, including:

(i) certifying a national or multijurisdictional opt-out class proceeding, if (1) all statutory criteria for certification have been met, and (2) the court determines that it is the appropriate venue for a national or multijurisdictional class proceeding;
(ii) refusing to certify an action on the basis that it should proceed in another jurisdiction as a national or multijurisdictional class proceeding;
(iii) refusing to certify that portion of the proposed class that includes class members who may be included within a pending or proposed class proceedings in another jurisdiction;
(iv) requiring that a subclass with separate counsel be certified within the certified class proceeding. [25]

This second measure has not been adopted in any Canadian jurisdictions, which has resulted in duplicate class actions in different provinces and unseemly 'carriage motions' between competing law firms.[26]

Member States should implement measures similar to the measures proposed by the ULCC to avoid these same problems.

The third measure was the creation and adoption of protocols that would allow judges from the different provincial courts in Canada to communicate with each other in certain circumstances in order to coordinate competing class actions in different provinces.

---

[25] *Idem.*

[26] *Tiboni v Merck Frosst Canada Ltd* 2008 CanLII 11372 (ON SC); *Tiboni v Merck Frosst Canada Ltd* 2008 CanLII 37911 (ON SC); *Tiboni v Merck Frosst Canada Ltd* 2009 CanLII 381 (ON SC); *Tiboni v Merck Frosst Canada Ltd* 2009 CanLII 10678 (ON SC); *Setterington et al v Merck Frosst Canada Ltd et al* [2006] OJ No. 376 (SCJ); *Mignacca v Merck Frosst Canada Ltd* 2008 CanLII 61238 (ON SC); *Mignacca v Merck Frosst Canada Ltd* 2009 CanLII 10059 (ON SCDC); *Mignacca v Merck Frosst Canada Ltd* 2009 ONCA 393 (CanLII); *Mignacca v Merck Frosst Canada Ltd* 2009 CanLII 68180 (ON SC); *Wuttunee v Merck Frosst Canada Ltd* 2008 SKQB 78 (CanLII); *Wuttunee v Merck Frosst Canada Ltd* 2008 SKQB 229 (CanLII); *Wuttunee v Merck Frosst Canada Ltd* 2008 SKCA 79 (CanLII); *Wuttunee v Merck Frosst Canada Ltd* 2008 SKCA 80 (CanLII); *Merck Frosst Canada Ltd v Wuttunee*, 2008 SKCA 125; *Merck Frosst Canada Ltd v Wuttunee*, 2009 SKCA 43 (CanLII).

The CBA developed a protocol for cross border judicial cooperation and communication that has as its purpose facilitating the case management of multi-jurisdictional class action proceedings and the enforcement of any resulting judgments in each participating jurisdiction.[27] The CBA, in conjunction with the American Bar Association (ABA), also developed a similar protocol that can be used between Canadian provincial courts and courts in the US.[28]

These protocols have found favour with judges in both Canada and the US and have been applied on an *ad hoc* basis on numerous occasions with considerable success. Although the current scope for communication and coordination under these protocols is limited, the protocols represent an important step in the right direction and hopefully will lead to protocols that are more comprehensive in the future.

Member States should give serious consideration to developing similar protocols to prevent undesirable forum shopping and to address other inevitable problems that will be created by overlapping multi-jurisdiction collective redress actions between Member States and between Member States and non-Member States.

The IBA Multi-Jurisdictional Collective Redress Working Group (Working Group) was created to provide a forum for the discussion, and potentially the formulation of policy, with respect to the conduct of collective redress proceedings which are multi-jurisdictional in nature from the perspective of the practitioner, the judiciary and the legislators. The Working Group facilitates the exchange of ideas across a variety of stakeholder interests and jurisdictions. It aims to achieve a number of objectives with respect to the conduct of multi-jurisdictional proceedings for collective redress. These objectives include fostering awareness and dialogue with respect to the differing regimes governing collective redress remedies and addressing the possibility of judicial cooperation in simultaneous collective redress proceedings arising in different jurisdictions internationally. The Working Group is currently working on developing protocols, similar to the Canadian and US protocols for broader international applications.

---

[27] The CBA protocol can be found at: http://www.cba.org/cba/resolutions/pdf/11-03-A.pdf, http://www.cba.org/cba/resolutions/pdf/11-03-A-Annex01.pdf, http://www.cba.org/cba/resolutions/pdf/11-03-A-Annex02.pdf, and http://www.cba.org/cba/resolutions/pdf/11-03-A-Annex03.pdf.

[28] This protocol can be found at: https://www.cba.org/cba/resolutions/pdf/11-03-A-bckd.pdf.

V. CONCLUSION

Canadian lawyers, judges and lawmakers have been dealing with cross-border class actions for over twenty years. In the process they have identified many of the key problems that such actions can create and they continue to struggle, mostly on an *ad hoc* basis, to find solutions for the issues of jurisdiction and enforceability as they arise. Some viable solutions have been identified which are largely dependent on the existence of similar class action or collective redress regimes between countries. These solutions also require cooperation and coordination between courts in the different countries in order to address competing and/or overlapping class actions.

Canada has had to reframe its approach to its own class actions after the fact because its lawmakers did not anticipate these problems when the original legislation was drafted. In contrast, Member States have the benefit of the Canadian experience to draw on before they create their own legislation. Ideally they will strive to implement legislation that addresses these matters from the outset.

The Commission Recommendation on Common Principles for Collective Redress: Some Reflections from Australia

Damian Grave and Jason Betts*

I. INTRODUCTION

In June 2013 the European Commission released its Recommendation 'on common principles for injunctive and compensatory collective redress mechanisms in the Member States concerning violations of rights granted under Union Law' (the Recommendation).[1] The Recommendation followed wide consultation and detailed consideration. The term 'collective redress' is defined in the Recommendation as referring to either injunctive collective redress where 'cessation of the unlawful practice is sought', or compensatory collective redress 'aimed at obtaining compensation for damage suffered'. In either situation collective redress refers to a procedural mechanism to allow many similar claims to be aggregated into a single proceeding for a 'mass harm situation'. A 'mass harm situation' is defined to mean a situation where two or more persons claim to have suffered harm causing damage resulting from the same illegal activity of one or more persons.[2]

This Recommendation was accompanied by a Communication from the EC to the European Parliament, the Council, the European Economic and Social Committee and the Committee of the Regions entitled 'Towards a European Horizontal Framework for Collective Redress' (the Communication).[3]

As the Communication made clear, the result of the wide consultation was that most stakeholders agree that establishing common principles for collective redress across Europe is desirable. The Communication said:

---

* Partners, Herbert Smith Freehills.
[1] Commission Recommendation of 11 June 2013 on common principles for injunctive and compensatory collective redress mechanisms in the Member States concerning violations of rights granted under Union Law (2013/396/EU).
[2] See the Recommendation at para 3(b).
[3] COM (2013), 11 June 2013.

219

More specifically, many stakeholders agree with the following basic parameters of a collective redress system in terms of effectiveness and safe guards: any collective redress mechanism should first and foremost be capable of effectively resolving a large number of individual claims that raise the same or common issues and relate to a single alleged infringement of rights granted under EU law. It should be capable of delivering legally certain and fair outcomes within a reasonable time frame, while respecting the rights of all parties involved. At the same time, it should incorporate safeguards against abusive litigation and avoid any economic incentives to bring speculative claims. In examining the concrete building blocks needed to ensure effectiveness and safeguards, the public consultations confirm that collective redress mechanisms vary significantly amongst Member States. These mechanisms differ from each other as regards the type of available collective action and its main features, such as admissibility, legal standing, the use of an opt in or an opt out system, the role of the Judge in collective proceedings and requirements on informing potential claimants about a collective action. Furthermore, each collective redress mechanism operates in the broader context of general civil and procedural rules, rules regulating the legal profession and other relevant rules, which also differ amongst Member States. Given this diversity, stakeholders naturally have very different views as to whether any specific national system of collective redress – or its features – may be particularly instructive when formulating EU-wide standards on effectiveness and safeguards.[4]

In formulating its Recommendation it was common ground that any European approach should: be capable of effectively resolving a large number of individual claims for compensation of damage, thereby promoting procedural economy; be capable of delivering legally certain and fair outcomes within a reasonable timeframe, while respecting the rights of all parties involved; provide for robust safeguards against abusive litigation and avoid any economic incentives to bring speculative claims.[5]

It was thought to be important that the advantages of collective redress procedures in terms of access to justice and stronger enforcement be achieved and the disadvantages be mitigated and, in particular, the risk of abusive litigation. As set out below, the balancing of these considerations was also an important factor leading to the introduction of the class action procedures in Australia.

---

[4] See the Communication at 6–7.
[5] See the Communication at 9–10.

A. The Recommendation

The aim of the Recommendation is to facilitate access to justice in relation to violations of rights under Union Law and to recommend that all Member States should have collective redress systems at a national level.[6] The Recommendation puts forward a set of principles relating to collective redress that should be common across Europe while respecting the different legal systems of the Member States.[7] The principles assist to prevent abuse through the introduction of appropriate safeguards.[8] The Recommendation identifies principles common to injunctive and compensatory collective redress being: standing to bring a representative action; admissibility; information on a collective redress action; reimbursement of legal costs of the winning party; funding and cross-border cases.

The Recommendation then identifies specific principles relating to injunctive collective redress being 'expedient procedures for claims for injunctive orders' and 'efficient enforcement of injunctive orders'. The specific principles relating to compensatory collective redress are identified as being: constitution of the claimant party by opt-in principle; collective alternative dispute resolution and settlements; legal representation and lawyers' fees; prohibition of punitive damages; funding of compensatory collective redress and collective follow-on actions.

The Member States should implement the principles set out in the Recommendation in their national collective redress systems by July 2015.[9] The Member States should also collect reliable annual statistics on the number of out of court and judicial collective redress procedures and information about the parties, the subject matter and outcome of the cases.[10] This information is to be communicated to the Commission each year and for the first time by July 2016.[11] The Commission should assess the implementation of the Recommendation by July 2017.[12]

B. Australian Class Action Procedures

The term 'class action' is not precisely defined under Australian law. At its widest it has been referred to as "a generic term for a procedure where by the claims of many individuals against the same defendant can be brought or

---

[6] See Recommendation at para 10.
[7] See Recommendation at para 13.
[8] See Recommendation at para 13.
[9] See Recommendation at para 38.
[10] See Recommendation at para 39.
[11] See Recommendation at para 40.
[12] See Recommendation at para 41.

conducted by a representative".[13] A class action has been distinguished from the traditional representative proceeding which has its origins in the Court of Chancery. In 1988 the Australian Law Reform Commission (ALRC) recommended the introduction into Australian law of a new grouping procedure of related claims. This recommendation was embodied in the ALRC's report grouped proceedings in the federal court. The ALRC said:

> Allowing proceedings to be brought on behalf of a group or class of persons can ensure that persons who have a cause of action arising from multiple wrong doing are not prevented or discouraged from having that claim determined by a court as a result of lack of resources, costs barriers or ignorance of legal rights. In addition, the grouping of many claims into one proceeding may be a more efficient way of determining the issues which are common to those claims than separate proceedings would be.[14]

The issues with which the ALRC was concerned in its Report included: reducing the cost of court proceedings to the individual; enhancing access by the individual to legal remedies; promoting efficiency in the use of court resources; ensuring consistency in the determination of common issues and making the law more enforceable and effective.[15]

The ALRC recommended that a new procedure be introduced by legislation which advanced the objectives of access to the courts and judicial economy, while providing safeguards against possible abuse.[16] The introduction of the latter is important and is consistent with the approach set out in the Recommendation.

The ALRC outlined the advantages of the proposed new grouping procedure, which may be broadly summarised as reducing the costs of litigation where necessary and worthwhile, whilst not encouraging abuse or the pursuit of the trivial:

1. where a number of people suffer loss, injury or damage as a result of a multiple wrong, a class action or other effective grouping procedure could help to reduce cost for each member of the group as well as promote efficiency in the administration of justice;
2. where the claims are 'individually recoverable', the primary policy goals of such procedures are to enable the most efficient use to be made of resources and to ensure consistency in decision making;

---

[13] Australian Law Reform Commission (ALRC), Grouped Proceedings in the Federal Court, Report No 46 (1988) at [2].
[14] See the Report at [2].
[15] See the Report at [13].
[16] See the Report at [2].

3. where claims are 'individually non-recoverable' (that is, where the cost of legal proceedings is high in relation to the amount claimed), the grouping of claims may reduce the cost of litigation to the individual and thereby enhance access to a legal remedy.[17]

The ALRC also recognised that where claims are so small that even assuming the availability of efficient, economic and fair grouping procedures, the cost of recovery will exceed the total benefits of litigating, then it was not appropriate to extend the new procedures to this kind of case. This particular observation has re-emerged in the context of the debate over third party funding of class action proceedings, including the question of whether third party funders stir up claims for which the costs of recovery are greater than the benefits to group members of litigating, but which may nevertheless generate significant returns to the third party funder.

Part IVA of the Federal Court of Australia Act 1976 (Cth) was introduced by the Commonwealth Parliament of Australia with effect from 5 March 1992. Substantially similar legislation now also exists in both Victoria and New South Wales. Part 4A of the Supreme Court Act 1986 (Vic) was introduced by the Victorian Parliament with effect from 1 January 2000 and Part 10 of the Civil Procedure Act 2005 (NSW) was introduced by the New South Wales Parliament with effect from 4 March 2011.

II. COMMON PRINCIPLES

Set out below are some thoughts and comments on four of the common principles from the Recommendation in light of the experience in Australia to date.

A. Opt in/Opt out

The Recommendation makes clear that the claimant party should be formed on the basis of express consent of the natural or legal persons claiming to have been harmed.[18] This is referred to in the Recommendation as the 'opt in' principle. Any exception to this principle, by law or by court order, should be justified by reasons of sound administration of justice.[19]

In contrast the position in Australia is that there exists an opt-out class action procedure.

---

[17] See the Report at [61]
[18] See Recommendation at para 21.
[19] See Recommendation at para 21.

Under Australian law it is commonly the case that the term 'opt in' is used to describe the means of determining the members of the group where the persons represented must consent in writing before they commence a proceeding (or with leave thereafter) in order to receive the benefit of any judgment. The term 'opt out' on the other hand is used to describe the means of determining the members of the group where the proceeding can be commenced without the consent of the persons represented but where those persons are able to elect not to continue as group members and to pursue their own individual proceeding.

In the context of Europe, the Communication said:

> The 'opt-out' system gives rise to more fundamental questions as to the freedom of potential claimants to decide whether they want to litigate. The right to an effective remedy cannot be interpreted in a way that prevents people from making (informed) decisions on whether they wish to claim damages or not. In addition, an 'opt-out' system may not be consistent with the central aim of collective redress, which is to obtain compensation for harm suffered, since such persons are not identified, and so the award will not be distributed to them.[20]

Similar issues were considered in Australia prior to the introduction of the opt-out class action procedure and particular weight was given to the importance of the opt-out class action procedure in facilitating access to justice. It would be helpful for the issue as to whether Europe should adopt an 'opt-in' or an 'opt-out' collective redress procedure to be considered and reviewed more broadly at the next opportunity.

In considering these issues the ALRC said that the grouping of claims serves a number of purposes. First, it ensures a single decision on issues in which all members of a group have the same interest – that is, consent to becoming a group member is not of significance where the interest of group members are the same. Secondly, it reduces costs and increases efficiency by enabling a single determination of issues which are common to members of a group – that is, consent to becoming a group member gives choice to those who have a real option to pursue rights individually. Thirdly, it enhances access to legal remedies by overcoming cost barriers or lack of knowledge – that is, consent to becoming a group member may defeat this purpose and leave persons with no means of obtaining redress.[21]

The ALRC concluded:

---

[20] See the Communication at 12.
[21] See the Report at [108].

A fair balance will be struck between the interests of group members and respondents if proceedings can be commenced without the consent of group members as long as notice is given to group members and they have an opportunity to withdraw from the proceedings or litigate individually. The respondent's ultimate liability should not, generally speaking, extend beyond those group members who can be identified and prove their claims.

Recommendation: Subject to the provision of appropriate protection, it should be possible to commence a group member's proceeding without first obtaining the consent of that group member. Provision should be made to ensure that group members are notified of the proceedings and that a group member can discontinue his or her proceeding or continue it independently. The rights of persons should not be prejudiced by the commencement of proceedings without consent.[22]

The ALRC also concluded that any mechanism for opting out of representative proceedings needed to be simple and involve little cost. It was important that, as far as possible, the rights of any group member to commence or continue separate proceedings on the same cause of action were preserved.[23]

While indicating a preference for an opt-out procedure, the ALRC accepted that an unfettered right on the part of group members to opt out could pose practical problems for the representative party. The ALRC stated:

If the right of group members to opt out was completely unfettered, there could be problems for the principal applicant and the respondent in dealing with the case as it approached a hearing. Settlement negotiations could be hampered if it was not known how many people were able to exclude themselves. The benefits of economy and of obtaining a uniform decision for all affected might be lost if people could withdraw at any stage. If there was a limited fund from which any settlement or judgment money could be obtained, the proceedings of group members opting out to pursue their claim individually may have to be stayed. To help avoid these problems it would be appropriate to empower the Court to fix a date after which leave would be required to opt out. A group member could discontinue without leave up to the date specified by the Court.[24]

The issue as to whether Australia should adopt a class action model providing for an 'opt-in' or an 'opt-out' procedure was the subject of considerable

---

[22] Footnotes omitted. See the Report at [126]–[127].
[23] See the Report at [181].
[24] See the Report at [183].

debate following the ALRC's recommendation and prior to the enactment of Pt IVA of the Federal Court of Australia Act (Cth).

When the Federal Court of Australia Amendment Bill 1991 (Cth) was debated in the House of Representatives, the Attorney General said that:

> The area of concern to business appears to be whether persons having relevant claims against the respondent should be included in the group covered by the proceedings unless they choose to opt out or whether all such persons should have to take a positive step to be included, that is, to opt out.
>
> The Government believes that an opt out procedure is preferable on grounds both of equity and efficiency. It ensures that people, particularly those who are poor or less educated, can obtain redress where they may be unable to take the positive step of having themselves included in the proceedings. It also achieves the goals of obtaining a common, binding decision while leaving a person who wishes to do so free to leave the group to pursue his or her claim separately.[25]

There is a specific requirement in the legislation to give notice to group members informing them of the commencement of the proceeding and of their right to opt out. The principle purpose of the notice is to inform group members of the right to opt out, when that right must be exercised, and the consequences of exercising or not exercising that right, so that group members are able to make an informed decision concerning their position. It is important that the notice contains sufficient information to enable group members to exercise their rights in relation to the proceeding and that the content of any notice be clear and easy to understand.

A recent study on opt-out rates in representative proceedings found that the average opt-out rate was just under 14% for proceedings under Pt IVA of the Federal Court of Australia Act (across a sample of 153 cases) and just under 21% for proceedings under Pt 4A of the Supreme Court Act 1986 (Vic) (across a sample of 14 cases). This, the study notes, is much higher than was anticipated when the introduction of Pt IVA of the Federal Court of Australia Act was being debated in Parliament, and certainly higher than the experience in the United States, where a median opt-out rate of less than 1% is common.[26]

---

[25] Australia, House of Representatives, *Debates* (14 November 1991) 3175. See also the same observations of Senator Tate when the Bill was introduced into the Senate on 12 September 1991: Australia, Senate, *Debates* (12 September 1991) 1448.

[26] V Morabito, An Empirical Study of Australia's Class Action Regimes – Second Report: Litigation Funders, Competing Class Actions, Opt Out Rates, Victorian Class Actions and Class

B. Funding

The Recommendation sets out a number of common principles on funding and, in particular, third party funding of proceedings. These common principles are clearly intended to minimise the risk of abusive litigation. The claimant party should be required to declare to the court at the outset of the proceedings the origin of the fund that it is going to use to support the legal action.[27] The court should be allowed to stay the proceedings if in the case of resources provided by a third party: there is a conflict of interest between the third party and the claimant party and its members; the third party has insufficient resources in order to meet his financial commitments to the claimant party initiating the collective redress procedure or the claimant party has insufficient resources to meet any adverse cost order should the collective redress procedure fail.[28]

The Member States should ensure that a third party funder does not seek to influence procedural decisions of the claimant party, including on settlements or to provide financing for a collective action against a person who is a competitor of the third party funder or against a person on whom the third party funder is dependant.[29]

The Member States should ensure that in addition to these common principles, in the case of third party funding for compensatory collective redress actions, it is prohibited to base remuneration charged by the funder on the amount of the settlement reached or the compensation awarded unless the funding arrangement is regulated by a public authority to ensure the interest of the parties.[30]

In Australia there have been very similar concerns to those identified above and the courts have been active in this area. The topic of litigation funding has been controversial and has also attracted considerable public attention. Writing extra-judicially in 2010 McDougall J said:

> Few topics in recent years have excited as much controversy as litigation funding and, in particular, the rise of entrepreneurial litigation funding. Advocates of litigation funding argue that it is the means of enhancing access to justice, of enforcing market protections and allowing consumers to hold recalcitrant corporations accountable for their misconduct and the harm they inflict, which would not otherwise be redressed. For critics, entrepreneurial litigation is an example of heinous commodification – an

---

Representatives (Department of Business Law and Taxation, Monash University, September 2010) 29–31.

[27] See the Recommendation at para 14.
[28] See the Recommendation at para 15.
[29] See the Recommendation at para 16.
[30] See the Recommendation at para 32.

anathema that corrupts the Court process and the prosecution of claims (footnotes omitted).[31]

As McDougall J's comments demonstrate, third party funding, depending on one's perspective, is advocated on the basis that it provides access to justice and criticised on the basis that it promotes unnecessary litigation. Particularly following the High Court of Australia decision in *Campbell's Cash and Carry Pty Ltd v Fostif Pty Ltd*[32] the debate about the legitimacy of third party funding has focused on two competing aims of the civil justice system. On the one hand, there is a public benefit arising from the provision of funds to potential claimants who might otherwise be unable to proceed against a large defendant because the cost of prosecuting the claim is prohibitive compared to its size. On the other hand, there is a danger associated with permitting a third party with no direct interest in the issue in dispute to prosecute the claims of persons who are not themselves prepared or able to prosecute them.

The subject of litigation funding also received attention in the recent report of the Australian Productivity Commission entitled 'Access to Justice Arrangements' (the Productivity Commission report) where the Commission noted that litigation funding provides clear access to justice benefits for plaintiffs but that direct regulation of litigation funders is appropriate in order to mitigate the following risks: that agreements may be struck unfairly (for example, with excessive commissions) because consumers have limited capacity and experience compared to funders; that funders may exercise too much control over proceedings, and may place pressure on the court system; potential conflicts of interest between funders, lawyers and plaintiffs and a potential lack of financial supervision and therefore no measures to encourage a funder to hold adequate capital relative to its financial obligations.[33]

The Federal Court of Australia and the Supreme Court of Victoria have released practice notes that require for class action proceedings that the funding agreements be disclosed prior to the initial case management conference.[34]

In relation to the first three risks identified above, the Productivity Commission was of the view that 'courts are both active and well equipped to monitor litigation funders and are capable of introducing the necessary rules themselves'.[35] In relation to the fourth risk identified above, namely the

---

[31] R McDougall, Keynote Address to the New South Wales Young Lawyers Civil Litigation Seminar, 13 March 2010 at 16.
[32] (2006) 229 CLR 386.
[33] Productivity Commission, Access to Justice Arrangements, Report No 72 (2014) at 629 – 630.
[34] See Federal Court of Australia Practice Note CM 17: Representative Proceedings Commenced under Part IVA of the Federal Court of Australia Act and Supreme Court of Victoria Practice Note No 9 of 2010: Conduct of Group Proceedings.
[35] See the Productivity Commission Report (above n 33) at 631.

lack of financial supervision the Commission considered that even though licensing and capital requirements could create some barriers to entry for funders in the market it considered that those barriers were justified and remained of the view that there should be a licensing regime to verify the capital adequacy of litigation funders in addition to court oversights.[36] The Commission noted that it would only be practical for capital adequacy conditions to require management of the financial risk and not its elimination. The Productivity Commission said that 'careful consideration of the exact balance between consumer protection and regulatory burdens would be an important consideration for the consultation process undertaken to develop a licence'.[37]

The Productivity Commission recommended that the Australian Government should establish a licence for third party litigation funding companies designed to ensure they hold adequate capital relative to their financial obligations and properly inform clients of relevant obligations and systems for managing risks and conflicts of interest. It also recommended that regulation of the ethical conduct of litigation funders should remain a function of the courts, and the licence should require litigation funders to be members of the Financial Ombudsman Scheme. Finally, where there are any remaining concerns relating to categories of funded actions, such as securities class actions, these should be addressed directly, through amendments to underlying laws, rather than through any further restrictions on litigation funding.

C. Collective Settlements

The Recommendation makes clear that the legality of the binding outcome of a collective settlement should be verified by the courts taking into consideration the appropriate protection of interests and rights of all parties involved.[38]

In Australia, there is also a requirement for court approval before a settlement or compromise of a class action proceeding can take legal effect. In approving any settlement or compromise of a class action, Australian courts assess whether it is a fair and reasonable compromise of the claims made on behalf of group members, and not just in the interests of the parties.

The court can have regard to a broad range of factors and evidence of these factors will need to be placed before the court.[39] Generally the court, in considering an application to approve a settlement or compromise of a class action proceeding, will take into account at least the following factors:

---

[36] See the Productivity Commission Report (above n 33) at 632.
[37] Ibid.
[38] See the Recommendation at para 28.
[39] See *Williams v FAI Home Security Pty Ltd* (2000) 180 ALR 459 at 465.

1. the complexity and likely duration of litigation;
2. the reaction of the group to the settlement;
3. the stage of the proceedings;
4. the risks of establishing liability;
5. the risks of establishing loss or damage;
6. the risks of maintaining a representative proceeding;
7. ability of the respondent to withstand a greater judgment;
8. the range of reasonableness of the settlement in light of the best recovery;
9. the range of reasonableness of the settlement in light of all the attendant risks of litigation and
10. the terms of any advice received from counsel and/or any independent expert in relation to the issues which arise in the proceeding.[40]

Even though settlements are subject to judicial oversight some commentators have suggested reforms to ensure that class action settlements are subject to even greater scrutiny. In particular it has been suggested that there should be court appointed cost experts to assess legal fees, an independent guardian to represent group members interests, less use of suppression orders in relation to the details of the settlement and ensuring settlement approvals are set out in publicly available judgements.[41]

D. Admissibility

The Recommendation provides that Member States should provide for verification at the earliest possible stage of litigation the cases in which conditions for collective actions are not met, and manifestly unfounded cases are not continued.[42] It is stated that the courts should carry out the necessary examination of their own motion.[43]

It is not clear in this context what 'verification' means. The 'verification' of cases in which the conditions for collective actions are not met appears to provide for the formal certification of the class or group at an early stage of the proceedings, and to cases which require summary judgment at an early stage of the proceeding (the reference to 'manifestly unfounded cases'). The Commission therefore seems to be referring, in addition to a consideration of the formal requirements of the group or class action, to a form of summary

---

[40] See Practice Note CM 17 – Representative Proceedings Commenced under Part IVA of the Federal Court of Australia Act 1976 at para 11.2 and Supreme Court of Victoria, Practice Note No 9 of 2010 – Conduct of Group Proceedings at para 11.2.

[41] See M Legg 'Class Action Settlements in Australia – The Need for Greater Scrutiny' 38 *Melbourne University Law Review* 2 (2014) 1.

[42] See the Recommendation at para 8.

[43] See the Recommendation at para 9.

examination of the merits of the claim. In relation to the latter, the Recommendation does not make clear the criteria to be applied by the courts in considering these issues.

In Australia there is no formal requirement for class certification. There are, however, a number of 'threshold requirements' for the commencement of a class action proceeding. These requirements are set out in Section 33C of the Federal Court of Australia Act. There are three threshold requirements for the commencement of a class action proceeding:

1. There must be:
   a) a claim by seven or more persons; and
   b) the claims must be against the same person;
2. The claims must arise out of the same, similar or related circumstances;
3. There must be a substantial common issue of law or fact.

There are also other considerations relevant to a class action proceeding. These include whether the class action proceeding is an efficient mechanism for the resolution of the claims of group members (Section 33N), whether the proceeding satisfies a cost-benefit analysis (Section 33M) and whether there are fewer than seven group members in the class action proceeding (Section 33L). Satisfying these considerations is not a precondition to the commencement of a proceeding. Rather they are matters relevant to the continued conduct of a class action proceeding.

In recent years Australian courts have not referred heavily to United States jurisprudence surrounding the prerequisites for certification under Rule 23 of the Federal Rules of Civil Procedure (US) for guidance as to the proper interpretation of the threshold requirement under Section 33C of Part IVA of the Federal Court of Australia Act. That is a product both of the statutory differences between the provisions of Part IVA and Rule 23 of the Federal Rules of Civil Procedure (US), and the increasing body of Australian jurisprudence available to provide guidance on such issues.

Some debate existed as to where there should be a formal certification mechanism introduced into Part IVA of the Federal Court of Australia Act requiring an initial showing of compliance with the threshold requirements before the court permits the class action proceeding to proceed through the interlocutory processes.[44] The ALRC recommended against the employment of a certification device in 1988, having considered the experience in the United States and Quebec concluding:

---

[44] See, for example, V Morabito, 'Group litigation in Australia – Desperately Seeking Effective Class Action Regimes (National Report for Australia prepared for the Globalisation of Class Action Conference, Oxford University, 12–14 December 2007) 27.

The preliminary matter of the form of the proceedings has often been more complex and taken more time than the hearing of the substantive issues. Because the court's discretion is involved, appeals are frequent, leading to delays and further expense. These expenses are wasteful and would discourage use of the procedure. There is no need to go to the expense of a special hearing to determine that the requirements have been complied with as long as the respondent has a right to challenge the validity of the procedure at any time.[45]

Australian courts have power to similarly dismiss proceedings in specified circumstances. In general terms this power is exercised if the proceedings are frivolous or vexatious, no reasonable cause of action is disclosed or the proceedings are an abuse of process.

E. Registry of Collective Redress

The Recommendation provides for the Member States to establish a national registry of collective redress actions.[46] The national registry should be available to any interested persons through electronic means and should provide access to comprehensive and objective information on the available methods of obtaining compensation.[47]

This is a very important part of the Recommendation ensuring that this sort of information is both gathered and made available. It will be essential that this occur and in the context of the various supervision and reporting obligations on Member States set out in the Recommendation.[48] It will also be important in the context of the assessment which needs to be made by the EC as to the implementation of the Recommendation by July 2017.[49]

The importance of obtaining accurate and up to date empirical information on specific aspects of the collective redress procedure cannot be underestimated. In Australia, while parties were initially slow to adopt the class action procedure under the Federal Court of Australia Act, such proceedings have become a prominent feature of the Australian litigation landscape, and a popular focus of academic and media attention. It has been suggested that Australia is the jurisdiction outside of North America where a corporation will most likely find itself defending a class action. This proposition had been advanced for many years, however, without any empirical foundation. The

---

[45] See the Report at [146].
[46] See the Recommendation at para 35.
[47] See the Recommendation at para 36.
[48] See the Recommendation at paras 39 and 40.
[49] See the Recommendation at 41.

growth in class action proceedings in Australia has in fact been more modest than many commentators have suggested.

It was not until relatively recently that there existed any empirical analysis of the Australian class action regimes. In 2009 and 2010, two reports were released by Professor Morabito comprising an empirical study of the legislative regimes embodied in Part IVA of the Federal Court of Australia Act and Part 4A of the Supreme Court Act 1986.[50] Professor Morabito's Third Report was released in November 2014.[51] Together these three reports comprise a comprehensive empirical study of the Australian class action regimes.

---

[50] The reports are V Morabito, 'An Empirical Study of Australia's Class Action Regimes – First Report: Class Action Facts and Figures' (Department of Business Law and Taxation, Monash University, December 2009) and V Morabito, 'An Empirical Study of Australia's Class Action Regimes – Second Report: Litigation Funders, Competing Class Actions, Opt-out Rates, Victorian Class Actions and Class Representatives' (Department of Business Law and Taxation, Monash University, September 2010).

[51] V Morabito, 'An Empirical Study of Australia's Class Action Regimes – Third Report: Class Action Facts and Figures – Five Years Later' (Department of Business Law and Taxation, Monash University, November 2014).

The Commission's Recommendation on Common Principles of Collective Redress and Private International Law Issues

*Astrid Stadler**

I. INTRODUCTION

For its new policy on collective redress the European Commission has chosen the form of a mere 'Recommendation' instead of a binding Directive or Regulation with respect to the violation of (consumer) rights granted under EU law. The Recommendation provides some basic principles on collective redress instruments which should be taken into account by the Member States when implementing injunctive or compensatory collective redress mechanisms. There is, however, no obligation for the Member States to implement such procedural tools. Despite the attempt at establishing common principles, the European legislature thus seems to accept a heterogeneous landscape of collective redress in Europe and has missed the opportunity to provide rules on international jurisdiction, recognition and the applicable law particularly designed for cross-border mass litigation. As a consequence forum shopping becomes even more important for plaintiffs in mass damage cases.

II. THE RECOMMENDATION AND ITS BACKGROUND – WHY ONLY A RECOMMENDATION?

In June 2013 the European Commission finally published its long-awaited policy on collective redress. The documents include separate proposals and recommendations for EU competition law and for the violation of (consumer) rights granted under EU law: a Communication to the European

---

* Professor Dr Astrid Stadler, University of Konstanz (Germany) and Erasmus School of Law (Rotterdam). This paper first appeared as A Stadler 'The Commission's Recommendation on Common Principles of Collective Redress and Private International Law Issues' 4 *NIPR* (2013) 483. Reproduced with kind permission of Nederlands Internationaal Privaatrecht (NIPR).

Parliament and the Council entitled 'Towards a European Horizontal Framework for Collective Redress',[1] and a proposal for a recommendation 'on common principles for injunctive and compensatory collective redress mechanisms in the Member States concerning violations of rights granted under Union Law'[2] (the 'Recommendation'). For the competition law sector, the Commission proposed a directive 'on certain rules governing actions for damages under national law for infringements of the competition law provisions of the Member States and of the European Union',[3] and published an impact assessment[4] and some ideas on the calculation of damages in competition cases.[5]

The documents are the final result of a long and very controversial debate on a reform of the European system for enforcing consumer rights and the rights of tort victims in mass harm situations. Although the result is disappointing for those who had hoped for a binding European framework of collective redress instruments, it had been clear for some time that the current political situation would not allow a directive or regulation which would impose any obligation on the Member States to implement new instruments for the collective enforcement of damages claims. Therefore it did not come as a surprise that the Commission's documents were rather cautious. Neither the proposed directive on competition law nor the recommendation on common principles for injunctive and compensatory collective redress for other violations of EU law will oblige the Member States to engage in fundamental reforms of their existing systems.[6]

A brief review of the debate at the European level reveals the controversial positions taken in the Member States and within the Commission. With respect to competition law, Directorate-General (DG) Competition, based on the Ashurst study (published in 2004),[7] from the outset clearly favoured stronger instruments of private enforcement in line with the example of US

---

[1] COM(2013) 401/2.

[2] COM(2013) 354/3); the final document has now been published: Commission Recommendation of 11 June 2013, 2013/396/EU, *OJ* 2013, L 201/60.

[3] COM(2013) 404 final. The Directive is supposed to be adopted during the December meeting of the Council.

[4] Commission Staff Working Document, Impact Assessment Report, 'Damages actions for breach of the EU antitrust rules', SWD(2013) 203 final.

[5] COM(2013) 3440.

[6] For more detailed reviews of the Commission's documents see C Hodges, 'Collective Redress: A Breakthrough or a Damp Squib?', 37 *Journal of Consumer Policy* (2014) 67–89; A Stadler, 'Die Vorschläge der Europäischen Kommission zum kollektiven Rechtsschutz in Europa – Der Abschied von einem kohärenten europäischen Lösungsansatz?', *European Union Private Law Review (GPR)* 2013, 281.

[7] D Waelbroeck, D Slater and G Even-Shoshan, 'Study on the Condition of Claims for Damages in Case of Infringement of EC Competition Rules' (Ashurst) 31 August 2004.

class actions. This initiative, which resulted in a Green Paper in 2005,[8] a White Paper in 2008,[9] and an internal proposal for a regulation (which never appeared in public), prompted a wave of strong resistance from the business sector all over Europe, particularly in Germany and France. DG Competition's stance indeed supported, rather uncritically, the idea that private enforcement would be a more efficient instrument than public enforcement in antitrust cases, although it could not produce empirical data or sufficient research on the relationship between public and private enforcement in Europe. Therefore the argument that the idea of class action that had been developed in the completely different US system should not simply be copied in Europe certainly carried some weight.[10] Unfortunately the Commission thus missed the opportunity to start the idea of a European type of group action which would harmonize better with European traditions and would avoid the negative implications of class actions (such as a claim culture and the blackmailing of defendant companies by unmeritorious but expensive mass claims).

Directorate-General for Health and Consumers (DG Sanco) was, for various reasons, more cautious when it published a Green Paper on collective redress for consumers in 2008,[11] but this could not suppress the strong opposition, particularly against opt-out group actions. Thus, before the re-election of Manuel Barroso in 2009, some Member States took the opportunity to wrest from him the concession that opt-out group or class actions would not be implemented in Europe.[12] As a result, in February 2011 the Barroso II Commission launched a public consultation to obtain 'a more coherent approach to collective redress',[13] which was intended to bring together the different positions in the Member States and to establish a common basis. The response to the public consultation was overwhelming with respect to the number of statements filed, but again the positions taken varied considerably.[14] Finally, as a reaction to the consultation the European

---

[8] COM(2005) 672.

[9] White Paper on damages actions for breach of the EC antitrust rules, COM(2008) 165.

[10] In Germany, in particular, the opposition was and still is quite strong, cf A Bruns, 'Einheitlicher kollektiver Rechtsschutz in Europa', *Zeitschrift für Zivilprozess* (2012), 399 and further references; H Willems, in C Brömmelmeyer (ed.), *Die EU-Sammelklage – Status und Perspektiven* (Nomos 2013) 17.

[11] Green Paper on consumer collective redress, COM(2008) 794.

[12] 'Barroso verheddert sich im Sammelklage-Dickicht', *Frankfurter Allgemeine Zeitung*, 20 October 2009; 'Kroes scheitert mit Kollektivklage', *Frankfurter Allgemeine Zeitung*, 26 October 2009; *Financial Times*, 3 October 2009.

[13] Public Consultation: Towards a coherent European approach to collective redress, SEC(2011) 173.

[14] See the study by B Hess and T Pfeiffer, 'Evaluation of Contributions to the Public Consultation and Hearing: "Towards a Coherent European Approach to Collective Redress"', Study JUST/2010/JCIV/CT/0027/A4' (2011), http://ec.europa.eu/competition/consultations/2011_collective_redress/study_heidelberg_summary_en.pdf.

Parliament published a resolution in 2012,[15] and warned the Commission to take into consideration the potential for collective redress instruments to be misused, and to provide sufficient safeguards. The resolution also stressed the need for effective instruments for alternative dispute resolution (ADR), but correctly pointed out that ADR or ODR (online dispute resolution) mechanisms cannot provide sufficient protection for consumer rights unless there is some pressure on the business sector to adopt these mechanisms and to make them in fact available to consumers. It has become clear that there needs to be both (consumer) ADR instruments and – as a last resort – procedural tools for the enforcement of mass claims in cases where defendants refuse to cooperate in settling cases.[16] Nevertheless, it was also clear at that point of the debate that the development of European instruments of collective redress faces a dilemma that is difficult to deal with: how can efficient tools for enforcing even small and minor damages claims be provided, while the implementation of wrong incentives which may lead to a misuse of these tools is avoided? The Commission's Recommendation is an attempt to balance these diverging interests. It is a compromise based on the realistic estimation that, for political reasons, nothing else would be possible within the remaining time that the Barroso II Commission is in office.

III. THE FRAMEWORK PROVIDED BY THE RECOMMENDATION

With the exception of competition law, the Commission recommends the implementation of a horizontal collective redress mechanism for injunctive and compensatory relief. The basic principles of these instruments laid out in the Recommendation attempt to respect national traditions such as the prominent role of representative entities or public authorities like ombudsmen in enforcing consumer rights in the Member States. The principles comprise a series of safeguards to make sure that there are no wrong incentives to bring unmeritorious claims. This includes an opt-in mechanism only,[17] the maintenance of the 'loser pays' rule,[18] and a prohibition on punitive damages[19] and contingency fees.[20] Paragraphs 8, 14, and 15 of the Recommendation require an initial verification of the case by the court, and

---

[15] Resolution of the European Parliament (2 February 2012) 2011/2089(INI). For a detailed discussion of the position of the European Parliament see Hodges (above n 6).
[16] See Recommendation paras 25–28: Collective alternative dispute resolution and settlements.
[17] Recommendation paras 21–24.
[18] Recommendation para 13.
[19] Recommendation para 31.
[20] Recommendation paras 29–30.

impose restrictions on the influence of third party funders on the litigation.[21] Legal standing to bring collective actions should only be given to designated representative entities that satisfy clearly defined conditions of eligibility.[22] The principles, however, also include many exceptions which will allow Member States to retain existing instruments and even, for example, opt-out group actions.[23] The Recommendation emphasizes the need to protect defendants against a US claim culture,[24] but it fails to provide the necessary safeguards for an adequate representation of group members or 'absent plaintiffs'. Although it stresses the key role which should be given to the courts in protecting the rights and interests of the parties, there is – contrary to international standards for group or class action litigation[25] – no requirement, for example, for court approval of settlements.[26] The most important gap is, however, the failure to provide clear rules for cross-border cases.

IV. PRIVATE INTERNATIONAL LAW ISSUES IN CROSS-BORDER MASS TORTS

A. Competition among (some) Member States for the 'big cases'?

Although it is difficult to predict the future, the consequences of the Commission's current collective redress policy seem obvious. In recent years we have already been able to observe that, owing to the failure of the European legislature to provide binding instruments or at least a framework for collective redress, Member States have taken very different approaches to reform. While some of them, like Germany, were not very ambitious and faced considerable political resistance to the implementation of new instruments,[27] others realized the opportunity to modernize their systems and to

---

[21] For a critical review of these aspects see Stadler (above n 6) 287–289.
[22] Recommendation paras 4–7.
[23] Recommendation para 21 first requires that the claimant party should be formed on the basis of the express consent of the person. Then, however, it states: 'Any exception to this principle, by law or by court order, should be duly justified by reasons of sound administration of justice.'
[24] Recommendation Recitals 13, 15, and 20.
[25] For a comparative overview of mass settlements and their court approval see the contributions in C Hodges and A Stadler (eds.), *Resolving Mass Disputes – ADR and Settlement of Mass Claims*, (Edward Elgar, 2013).
[26] This is mentioned in the Recommendation only with respect to ADR (para 28) and it is not entirely clear whether a verification by the courts is also intended for settlements negotiated during court proceedings.
[27] In Germany, there is, apart from instruments for injunctive relief and for skimming-off illegally gained profits from those violating antitrust laws and the rules on fair competition (Sec. 33, 34a Antitrust Act; Sec. 10 Unfair Competition Act), only the Capital Market Model Case Act. This came into force in 2005 and provides for test case proceedings for damages claims by investors. In 2012 a moderate reform of that Act came into force which adopted to some extent

make their jurisdictions attractive for the 'big cases'. Group action proceedings have been available for some time in Bulgaria,[28] Italy,[29] the Nordic countries,[30] Poland,[31] Portugal,[32] Spain,[33] and maybe soon France,[34] but the number of cases filed under the new provisions is surprisingly small – for various reasons. By contrast, the Dutch Collective Settlement Act (WCAM)[35] enacted in 2005[36] has been extremely successful, perhaps not so much with respect to the number of cases (six settlements have been approved by the Amsterdam Court of Appeal since 2005,[37] and a seventh case – the *DSB* case – is pending), but definitely in terms of the number of claimants and the amounts of money involved. Although the WCAM was designed in the first place for domestic cases, it has turned out to be a very effective and popular instrument for settling big international cases with a large number of tort victims and liable parties willing to buy global peace.

---

the (Dutch) idea of opt-out proceedings for a settlement; for more details, see A Stadler, 'Developments in Collective Redress: What's New in the "New German KapMuG"', *European Business Law Review* (2013) 733.

[28] Bulgarian Civil Procedure Code Chapter 33, Arts. 379 to 388: www.iclg.co.uk/practice-areas/class-and-group-actions/class-&-group-actions-2013/bulgaria.

[29] Art. 140-bis *Codice del consumo*, enacted 1 January 2010 and reformed by the law of 24 March 2012, see K Linhart and E. Finazzi Agrò, 'Kollektiver Rechtsschutz in Italien: die italienische "azione di classe"', *RIW* (2013) 443; www.iclg.co.uk/practice-areas/class-and-group-actions/class-&-group-actions-2014/Italy.

[30] Sweden: Group Proceedings Act SFS 2002:599; Denmark: Law no. 181, 28 February 2007 (§§ 254a-254k Danish Civil Procedure Code); Norway: Dispute Act, Chapter 35 (enacted 2008); Finland: Class Action Act 444/2007 of 13 April 2007.

[31] Law of 17 December 2009 (*Diziennik Ustaw* No. 7 Pos. 44; in force since 19 July 2010).

[32] Law no. 83/95 and no. 24/96.

[33] Art. 11 Spanish Civil Procedure Code.

[34] The French *Assemblée Nationale* accepted the principle of consumer class actions in the summer of 2013 on a first reading. The final decisions are to be made at the beginning of 2014, see www.iclg.co.uk/practice-areas/class-and-group-actions/class-&-group-actions-2014/france.

[35] *Wet Collectieve Afhandeling Massaschade*, abbreviated as WCAM.

[36] For details see X Kramer, 'Enforcing Mass Settlements in the European Judicial Area: EU Policy' and 'The Strange Case of Dutch Collective Settlements (WCAM)', in Hodges and Stadler (above n 25) Ch. 3; W van Boom, 'Collective Settlements of Mass Claims in the Netherlands', in M Casper et al. (eds.), *Auf dem Weg zu einer europäischen Sammelklage?* (Sellier 2009) 171; T Arons and W van Boom, 'Beyond Tulips and Cheese: Exporting Mass Securities Claim Settlements from the Netherlands', *European Business Law Review* 2010, 857; A Mom, *Kollektiver Rechtsschutz in den Niederlanden*, (Mohr Siebeck 2011).

[37] Cf Court of Appeal Amsterdam 1 June 2006, LJN: AX 6440 (*DES*); 25 January 2007, LJN: AZ 7033, *NIPR* 2007, 208 (*Dexia*); 29 April 2009, LJN: BI 2717 (*Vie d'Or*); 29 May 2009, LJN: BI 5744, *NIPR* 2010, 71 (*Shell*); 15 July 2009, LJN: BJ 2691, *NIPR* 2010, 458 (*Vedior*); 12 November 2010, LJN: BO3908, *NIPR* 2011, 85 and 17 January 2012, LJN: BV1026 (*Converium*). For more details cf. Kramer (above n 36) 74 et seq; I Tzankova and D Hensler, 'Collective Settlements in the Netherlands: Some Empirical Observations', in Hodges and Stadler (above n 25) 91 et seq.

The most important WCAM cases settled the claims of thousands of shareholders from all over the world (except the United States) who had previously been excluded from US class actions and therefore sought relief in Europe.[38] In the aftermath of two US Supreme Court decisions restricting access to US courts for securities cases[39] and cases under the US Alien Tort Statute,[40] the WCAM has become even more important for claimants.

In January 2013, the British Government announced that it will also implement out of court settlement proceedings, following the example of the Dutch WCAM – probably sometime in late 2014 or 2015.[41] This is a reaction to the increasing demand even from the business sector for settlement proceedings that provide court assistance but do not require contentious court proceedings in the first place. This is not the place to go into the details of these proceedings, but the way the debate in Europe is obviously moving reveals that there will be strong competition among at least some of the Member States to attract the big cases to their court systems and, what is probably much more important, to their law firms.

Without a uniform instrument of collective redress, forum shopping becomes extremely important for plaintiffs in mass litigation. It is not only the traditional issues of the conflict of laws rules and substantive tort law that have to be taken into consideration. First of all, plaintiffs may look for an answer to the question of which jurisdiction will offer effective instruments for contentious litigation or for court proceedings declaring out of court settlements to be binding upon all the victims of a mass tort. If such a forum is available, the next question will be whether the court will be in a position to apply a uniform set of tort rules to all individual claims or, if not, whether the formation of sub-groups or sub-classes would be possible under the forum's procedural rules.[42] Both options are important for an efficient handling of complex cross-border cases if no settlement of the whole can be achieved.

---

[38] Particularly the *Shell* and *Converium* cases (above n 37).

[39] *Morrison v. First National Bank of Australia*, US Supreme Court, 129 S. Ct. 2762 (June 2010).

[40] *Kiobel v. Royal Dutch Petroleum*, 569 US – (2013) = 133 S. Ct. 1659 (2013). For a detailed review of the decision and its consequences see M Stürner, 'Die territorialen Grenzen der Human Rights Litigation in den USA', *Juristenzeitung* (2014) 13 et seq.

[41] Department for Business Innovation & Skills, 'Private Actions in Competition Law: A Consultation on Options for Reform – Government Response', January 2013, www.biicl.org/files/6310_10_12_2012_urn_13_501_front_and_back_covers_22-jan-13_private_actions_in_competition_law_a_consultation_on_options_for_reform_government_~_response_pdf.pdf. Also see the information on the Consumer Rights Bill 2013–14 to 2014–15, http://services.parliament.uk/bills/2014-15/consumerrights.html.

[42] See also A Stadler, 'Conflicts of Laws in Multinational Collective Actions – A Judicial Nightmare?', in D Fairgrieve and E Lein (eds.), *Extraterritoriality and Collective Redress* (OUP, 2012) Ch. 11, 191.

B. The European jurisdictional regime and the Rome Regulations

The current European system of international jurisdiction and choice of law rules is far from being able to provide satisfactory answers to the questions mentioned above. Neither the Brussels I Regulation[43] nor the Rome II[44] (or Rome I[45]) Regulation has been designed for mass harm situations.[46] On the contrary, the choice of law rules provided by the Rome II Regulation, in particular, take a clearly individualistic approach and try to protect the expectations of a tort victim that the rules of the place where the damage occurred (which will often be the place of the tort victim's domicile)[47] apply or, in product liability cases, that the law of the country where the product was bought and marketed applies.[48]

1. Brussels I Regulation

The Brussels I Regulation, with its well-established jurisdictional regime in Articles 2–24 [now Articles 4-26 of the Brussels I Recast Regulation (EU) 1215/2012], does not provide special rules for mass litigation. Article 6 no. 1 [now 8 no. 1] of the Regulation allows a claimant to sue several defendants in the Member State where only one of them is domiciled if the claims are closely connected and if there is a risk of irreconcilable judgments resulting from separate proceedings. But there is no corresponding provision for the situation where several plaintiffs intend to file an action against the same defendant in respect of a single event or a single cause mass tort like a mass accident or a series of incidents as in a product liability case. The present system of Brussels I requires that a court hearing mass claims in single proceedings has jurisdiction over all the claims of the absent claimants. This results from the binding effect of a judgment or court approval of a settlement upon all the claimants. In tort cases, only the courts of the place where the defendant is domiciled (Article 2 Brussels I Regulation [now Article 4 Brussels I Recast Regulation]) or the courts of the place where the harmful

---

[43] Regulation (EC) No. 44/2001 of the Council of 22 December 2000 on jurisdiction and the recognition and enforcement of judgments in civil and commercial matters, OJ 2001, L 12/1. [The Brussels I Regulation has been revised and is now in force as Regulation (EU) No 1215/2012 of the European Parliament and of the Council of 12 December 2012 on jurisdiction and the recognition and enforcement of judgments in civil and commercial matters (recast), OJ 2012 L 351/1].

[44] Regulation (EC) No. 864/2007 of the European Parliament and of the Council of 11 July 2007 on the law applicable to non-contractual obligations (Rome II), OJ 2007, L 199/40.

[45] Regulation (EC) No. 593/2008 of the European Parliament and of the Council of 17 June 2008 on the law applicable to contractual obligations (Rome I), OJ 2008, L 177/6.

[46] Stadler (above n 42) Ch. 11.11–11.34.

[47] Art 4 Rome II Regulation.

[48] Art 5 Rome II Regulation.

event occurred (Article 5 no. 3 Brussels I Regulation [now Article 7 no. 2 Brussels I Recast Regulation]) have such jurisdiction. The latter refers either to the place where the liable party committed the tortious act (which will often be the same as her place of domicile, as defined for legal persons and companies in Article 60 [now Article 63] of the Regulation) or the place where all the tort victims suffered the injury. Only in the few cases of real mass accidents like a train or plane crash will Article 5 no. 3 [now 7 no. 2] lead to the courts of the place of the accident having jurisdiction for all tort victims. In product or pharmaceutical liability cases, as well as securities cases, the place of injury or damage is not the same for all persons affected by the tort. As a consequence, plaintiffs can file an action on behalf of all tort victims only in the country where the liable party is domiciled. Given the current situation of a very heterogeneous landscape of collective redress, it is more or less a matter of coincidence whether group or class action proceedings are available there.

There have been some proposals to supplement the Brussels I Regulation with respect to these mass harm situations, and to implement a special rule for mass litigation. One could choose, for example, the place where the majority of victims are domiciled, as an additional option for the plaintiffs.[49] Such a rule would particularly fill a gap if the liable party is domiciled outside the European Union. Others generally prefer the place where the defendant is domiciled,[50] leaving it to the national rules of the Member States to determine whether liable parties from outside the European Union can be sued in their courts.

Another quite controversial debate was provoked by the Dutch Collective Settlement Act. With an increasing number of international cases being settled in the Netherlands under the WCAM, the question of jurisdiction came to the fore and turned out to be highly controversial.[51] The WCAM proceedings, which start with a joint application by the parties negotiating the out-of-court settlement, lead to a reversal of the roles of the parties in the

---

[49] A Stadler, 'Cross-border Mass Litigation – A Particular Challenge for European Law', in J Steele and W van Boom (eds.), *Mass Justice – Challenge for Representation and Distribution*, (Edward Elgar, 2011) 73, at 81.

[50] T Arons, *Cross-border Enforcement of Listed Companies' Duties to Inform*, (Kluwer 2012) 322, 325; similarly B Hess, 'A Coherent Approach to European Collective Redress', in Fairgrieve and Lein (above n 42) Ch. 6.29.

[51] For a general discussion of the private international law aspects of the WCAM: Kramer (above n 36); Tzankova and Hensler (above n 37); H van Lith, *The Dutch Collective Settlement Act and Private International Law*, (Maklu 2011); A Halfmeier, 'Recognition of a WCAM Settlement in Germany', *NIPR* 2012, 176; L Perreau Saussine, 'Quelle place pour les class actions dans le règlement Bruxelles I?', *Semaine Juridique* 2011, 911; A Stadler, 'Internationale Zuständigkeit niederländischer Gerichte für "mass settlements"', in *Grenzüberschreitendes Recht – Crossing Frontiers: Festschrift für Kay Hailbronner* (CF Müller 2013) 883.

proceedings. The potentially liable party, who would be the defendant in a traditional action for damages, becomes an 'applicant' together with the representative entity acting on behalf of the aggrieved persons. This latter group of persons – the so-called 'interested parties' – is on the 'defendant' side of the WCAM proceedings. If the Amsterdam court finally approves the settlement, the interested parties who had the chance of opting-out during the proceedings will be legally bound by the settlement. Although the settlement might be the best solution for them from an *economic* perspective, they are *legally* precluded from individual litigation and cannot sue the liable party for a greater amount of compensation. This preclusive effect may not be welcomed by all of them, and as the interested parties become subject to these court proceedings without their explicit consent their situation is at least similar to that of a defendant.[52] They may thus need the protection provided by jurisdictional rules.

However, in terms of jurisdiction the WCAM proceedings do not fit into the categories of the Brussels I Regulation. The Amsterdam Court of Appeal has indeed taken the position that the 'interested parties' are to be deemed to be 'defendants', and the court has offered two different options under the Brussels I Regulation for establishing Dutch jurisdiction over foreign tort victims who are not domiciled in the Netherlands. One option is Article 6 no. 1 [now 8 no. 1], based on the idea that it suffices that only one of the 'interested parties' is domiciled in the Netherlands.[53] As it is the core objective of the whole settlement proceedings to give a binding settlement for all aggrieved persons, the close connection requirement of Article 6 no. 1 [now 8 no. 1] seems to be met. Nevertheless, this has the surprising effect (although it is inherent in Article 6 no. 1) [now 8 no. 1] that it does not take a close link to the Netherlands to establish jurisdiction. The *Converium* case provides a good example: the liable parties were all Swiss companies, and only 3% of the shareholders entitled to compensation were domiciled in the Netherlands. Therefore, the Court of Appeal in Amsterdam preferred to rely on Article 5 no. 1 of the Brussels I Regulation [now Article 7 no. 1 of the Brussels I Recast Regulation], and argued that the settlement is a contract to be fulfilled in the Netherlands,[54] thus ignoring the fact that there is only a

---

[52] For a detailed discussion of 'the person to be sued' under Art. 2 Brussels I Regulation, see Van Lith (above n 51) 42 et seq.

[53] Court of Appeal Amsterdam 29 May 2009, LJN: BI 5744, *NIPR* 2010, 71, *NJ* 2009, 506 (*Shell*); Van Lith (above n 51) 45–47; for a critical review of this position see R Polak, 'Approval of International Class Action Settlements in the Netherlands', 2009, 11, www.iclg.co.uk; J Stuyck, 'Class Actions in Europe', 20 *European Business Law Review* 2009, 483 et seq., 502; see also Arons (above n 50) 316.

[54] Court of Appeal Amsterdam 12 November 2010, LJN: BO3908, *NIPR* 2011, 85 (*Converium*), para. 2.8; Van Lith (above n 51) 37 et seq.

contract between the parties negotiating the settlement and that the contract does not become binding on the 'absent or interested parties' unless the court approves the settlement.

There is a continuing debate on these jurisdictional issues both within and outside the Netherlands. Some authors strongly suggest that under the present rules it is necessary to leave aside the settlement contract and look to the underlying tort or contract obligations instead.[55] Then the WCAM proceedings could be treated like regular actions for the recovery of damages and the liable party would be the 'defendant'. This solution, however, would considerably narrow the scope of application of the WCAM proceedings to cases in which the liable party is domiciled in the Netherlands or the 'harmful event' occurred there.[56] The global attraction of these proceedings would be lost, although there seems to be a demand for such comprehensive settlements. Another solution for establishing jurisdiction in the Netherlands is to include a choice of forum clause in the Dutch settlement.[57] However, again, it seems highly debatable whether 'interested parties' can be bound by a choice of forum clause negotiated by a representative entity to whom they have never explicitly given a power of attorney to act on their behalf.

In sum, neither of the solutions proposed by the Amsterdam court is satisfactory under the Brussels I Regulation system.[58] The more attractive these settlement proceedings become, the more important are clear rules on international jurisdiction. Beyond the issue of jurisdiction, it is still an open question whether all Member States will accept the preclusive effect of such settlements.[59] In particular, those states that reject the opt-out mechanism may object to recognition and enforcement based on the public policy argument of Article 34 of the Brussels I Regulation [see now Article 45 Brussels I Recast Regulation].[60] So far there has been no ECJ case law dealing with these issues, and the parties negotiating WCAM settlements are probably anxious to avoid bringing disputes before the courts. As soon as other Member States start to offer similar proceedings these questions will gain in importance and will require answers.

---

[55] Van Lith (above n 51) 71.

[56] Van Lith (above n 51) 74; she suggests specific jurisdictional rules for collective litigation and collective settlements.

[57] Van Lith (above n 51) 54–56; in the *Refcom* case the ECJ applied rather strict standards for extending choice of forum clauses to third parties (ECJ 7 February 2013, C-543/10, *NIPR* 2013, 154).

[58] Hess (above n 50) Ch. 6.21, fn. 26.

[59] D Fairgrieve, 'The Impact of the Brussels I Enforcement and Recognition Rules on Collective Redress', in Fairgrieve and Lein (above n 42) Ch. 10, at 171.

[60] See Hess (above n 50) Ch. 6.22–29; Halfmeier (above n 51) with numerous arguments as to why the public policy objection cannot be raised in Germany.

Although the European legislature has enacted a fundamental reform of the Brussels I Regulation [in force since January 2015],[61] mass litigation was not taken into consideration and none of the issues mentioned above will be solved by the new provisions. The reason is obvious: at that time there was still a chance (or at least there was thought to be a chance) a harmonization of collective redress, and the answers could have been given in the relevant legislation on collective redress. With only a mere recommendation on collective redress, which we have now received, the whole complex question remains open. The Commission might also have feared the controversial private international law issues to prevent a smooth adoption of the recast of the Brussels I Regulation. This is all the more annoying as the Recommendation will not be able to stop the competition among Member States. Those Member States which have far-reaching reforms on their agenda will continue with these reforms, and even if they are willing to accept the framework established by the Recommendation the many exceptions included in its principles will allow a broad range of approaches. It is only a matter of explaining why exceptions are necessary – and there are always explanations for everything!

2. *The applicable law*

The Commission's failure to tackle the private international law issues may also influence the effective handling of cross-border cases. As mentioned above, only in rare cases will the Rome I Regulation allow the application of a single set of tort rules to the claims of numerous tort victims. In product liability cases in particular, the well-balanced approach taken by Article 5 of the Rome II Regulation protects the individual expectations of purchasers and producers but does not take into consideration the effective handling of mass harm situations. Again there have been proposals for special choice of law rules for mass litigation. These proposals include, among others, the application of the law of the defendant's domicile or principal place of business,[62] or the law of the country where the majority of victims are domiciled.[63] This is a sensitive issue, because altering the private international law rules only for the purpose of an effective handling of proceedings may be interpreted as putting the cart before the horse.[64] Is it really a good solution

---

[61] Regulation (EU) No. 1215/2012 of the European Parliament and of the Council of 12 December 2012 on jurisdiction and the recognition and enforcement of judgments in civil and commercial matters (recast), *OJ* 2012, L 351/1.

[62] Green Paper on consumer collective redress, para. 59 (law of the trader as one option) (above n 11).

[63] *Idem*.

[64] Stadler (above n 42) Ch. 11.48-11.50; for the US see L Silberman, 'The Role of Choice of Law in National Class Actions', *University of Pennsylvania Law Review* 2001, 2022.

to change the applicable law for procedural reasons? Must tort victims accept another (sometimes less favourable) tort law simply because they are not the only tort victim but are part of a large group? The answers must be weighed carefully and should be given by the legislature. But how? The Member States are clearly not in a position to provide binding rules, either in respect of international jurisdiction or in respect of the applicable law. They can improve the situation for their courts by allowing the formation of subgroups and sub-classes in collective redress proceedings. Judges will then be in a position to group the class of tort victims according to the applicable tort law – a well-established way to handle multi-district class actions in the US, for example. In any case, the European legislature missed the opportunity to fill a gap in exactly the area in which it has its key competence and right of existence. Whereas we can probably live with different national approaches regarding the particular instruments of collective redress, cross-border issues can be solved only at the European level. As a Recommendation is clearly not the place for dealing with these problems, supplementary provisions in the Brussels I Regulation and the Rome Regulations were necessary.

3. *Towards a better coordination of parallel mass litigation?*

If – for political reasons – the European legislature was not able to provide clear rules on jurisdiction and the applicable law, one could at least expect some regulations on the coordination of mass damage proceedings in different Member States. In the absence of uniform rules on the legal standing of representative entities, there is a high probability that cross-border mass accidents or mass torts will be picked up by various representative associations in different countries. As a consequence, and depending on jurisdiction, there may be parallel proceedings against the same defendant in several courts and on behalf of different groups of tort victims.[65] The provisions in the Brussels I Regulation on related actions (Articles 27 et seq. Brussels I Regulation [Articles 29 et seq. Recast Regulation]) will not be able to prevent this. Articles 27 and 28 [now 29 and 30] address the problem of parallel proceedings and irreconcilable judgments by giving preference to the court where proceedings have been initiated first. However, Article 27 [now 29] requires not only 'the same cause of action' in all proceedings, but also the participation of 'the same parties' in the proceedings. If different representative entities are acting as lead plaintiffs, Article 27 [now 29] does not apply, and one can only have recourse to Article 28 [now 30]. A consolidation of the

---

[65] R Money-Kyrle and C Hodge, 'European Collective Action: Towards Coherence?', *MJ* (2012), 477 at 485; JN Stefanelli, 'Parallel Litigation and Cross-border Collective Actions under the Brussels I Framework: Lessons from Abroad', in Fairgrieve and Lein (above n 42) Ch. 9, 143; Hess (above n 50) Ch. 6.16, 6.17.

proceedings as mentioned in Article 28(2) [now 30(2)] will often not be permitted by national rules, and one might also dispute whether actions are 'related' if they have different objectives, such as the recovery of damages on the one side or a skimming-off of illegally gained profits on the other (as permitted under German competition and antitrust laws, for example). In any case, the application of Article 28 of the Brussels I Regulation [Article 30 of the Recast Regulation] is not mandatory but gives the courts the discretion to react.

The approach taken in the Commission's Recommendation is a half-hearted one. Paragraph 35 simply asks Member States to establish a national registry of collective redress actions, and the Commission promises to assist in ensuring the coherence of the information gathered and the interoperability of the registers. That is not enough. If the Member States follow the Commission's Recommendation and implement it only for opt-in group or class action proceedings, it is pivotal that information about pending actions is distributed in the best possible way across national borders. Furthermore, the plaintiffs need a platform for the exchange of information in order to cooperate better or even to consolidate their efforts to obtain damages. The Commission could have borrowed inspiration from one of its own documents released almost at the same time:[66] in its proposal for a reform of the European insolvency regulation the Commission envisages national registers with access via the European e-Justice portal. Thus it will not be necessary to search separate national registers. It will also take common criteria in the structure of the national registers in order to search them effectively. An even better solution could be a register operated at the European level implemented by a European legislation supplementing the Recommendation.

V. CONCLUSION

With its Recommendation on collective redress, the Commission has backed down after strong opposition in some Member States to even a moderate reform of private enforcement tools. The non-binding character of the framework and the principles included in the Recommendation is not very likely to change the present situation of collective redress. Whereas some Member States will respect the Recommendation, others will stick to their resistance against collective actions, particularly those for the recovery of damages. Despite the many safeguards against misuse included in the Recommendation, the business sector in some Member States might be tempted to rejoice that a uniform binding instrument has been averted. However, as some Member

---

[66] COM(2012) 744 final, 8.

States are ambitious to strengthen their country as a location for mass litigation or mass settlements, the competition for 'big cases' will continue and will barely be affected by the Recommendation. Articles 6 no. 1 and 5 no. 3 allow, to some extent, companies from abroad to be held liable for torts in Member States other than the Member State of their domicile. Nevertheless, the jurisdictional regime of the Brussels I Regulation is still not sufficiently flexible for the effective enforcement of mass claims.

Therefore, the main failure of the European legislature is not its inability to agree on binding harmonized instruments of collective redress. Consumers, potential litigants, lawyers and courts could at least have expected a clear framework of private international rules. Although, or even because, the issues of international jurisdiction and enforcement involve controversial arguments and require a balancing of different national interests, it is up to the European Union to take the lead and to use its core competence for regulating cross-border issues. With respect to mass torts, these issues have now fallen between the cracks – the European legislature neither tackled them in the context of the recent reform of the Brussels I Regulation nor as a minimum approach for its collective redress policy. According to the Recommendation, the Commission will allow Member States a period of two years to implement the new instruments. The Commission will only revisit the situation four years from now. It is not very likely that the chances for the harmonization of collective redress tools will be much better in four years' time. On the contrary, a successful implementation of far-reaching instruments (for example, based on an opt-out mechanism) in some Member States will not increase their willingness to give them up in order to support a uniform approach in Europe. Thus the European legislature must realize that collective redress is still on the table at the European level. It is necessary to initiate a broad discussion on the private international law issues now, in order to come up with a solution as soon as possible.

Forum Shopping and Consumer Collective Redress in Action: The Costa Concordia Case

Cristina Poncibò[*]

I. INTRODUCTION

On 13 January 2012, the Costa Concordia cruise ship capsized and sank after striking an underwater obstruction off the Isola del Giglio, Tuscany. The captain (Francesco Schettino) is currently under house arrest, facing criminal charges for manslaughter and abandoning ship, because there is now clear evidence that he left the cruise liner before all passengers had been evacuated. The Italian Prosecutor has described captain Schettino's behaviour as 'reckless and inexcusable' in performing a very risky manoeuvre sailing too close to the coast.[1]

The passengers (4,252 people of different nationalities)[2] had bought their tickets either over the internet or through travel agents. Thus, as consumers, they had entered package holiday contracts, ruled by the EU Directive on package travel, package holidays and package tours,[3] having as the object a cruise and related services with the Italian cruise line company, Costa Crociere SpA, which is owned by Carnival in Miami.

Following the accident, one third of the passengers of different nationalities have agreed to the offer arising from a joint conciliation scheme (see Section V), while the others rejected the offer with the aim of pursuing full damage recovery. Among the passengers who rejected the offer, a group filed individual claims in their home jurisdictions and another group joined

---

[*] Lecturer, Department of Law, University of Turin, Italy.
[1] The captain says that it was common practice for the Costa Concordia cruise ship to deviate from its original route and to sail dangerously close to Giglio Island. The so-called 'showboating' was part of Costa's promotional policy.
[2] By nationality, the passengers included 989 Italians, 569 Germans, 462 French, 177 Spanish, 126–129 Americans, 127 Croats, and 108 Russians, 25 Brits, 74 Austrians and 69 Swiss. The remaining 520 passengers were of about thirty different nationalities.
[3] Council Directive (EC) 90/314 on package travel, package holidays and package tours [1990] OJ L158.

the criminal proceedings in Italy against the captain and the members of the crew.[4] Finally, some groups of passengers, including non-US citizens, filed State class actions in the US.

The Costa Concordia disaster raises some fundamental issues about forum shopping and collective redress in cases involving consumer contracts.

II. FORUM SHOPPING

A. *Trans-Atlantic Consumer Litigation*

Advised by their lawyers, some groups of Costa Concordia passengers decided to sue the parent company of the Italian cruise line in the US, ie they filed State class actions in Florida. Despite the parties agreeing on the Italian jurisdiction as indicated in the tickets, they asserted that they were entitled to bring their lawsuits in the US. This was because the umbrella company, Carnival, and the marketing subsidiary from which their travel agent purchased their tickets, were headquartered in Florida. Curiously, the Italian consumer association Codacons, that represented many Italian passengers, rejected any settlement with the Italian company and launched a campaign to inform Italian and non-Italian passengers to join US class actions. Surprisingly, the association has not filed any action according to the Article 140-bis of the Italian Consumer Code providing for the *azione di classe*, the new Italian collective redress mechanism. It seems clear however that actions have been brought in the US seeking larger compensation and the award of punitive damages.

Traditionally, the US has a forum shopping system with two features that encourage plaintiffs to file claims in US courts, even when those claims involve foreign parties or foreign activity. This is a permissive approach to personal jurisdiction, giving plaintiffs broad court access, and a strong tendency of judges to apply plaintiff-favoring domestic law.[5] In addition, from a plaintiff's perspective, litigating before a US court brings some advantages, which are not provided under European jurisdictions. The contingency fee system makes the courts more readily accessible to a group of consumers with limited financial resources. Such a system is extremely important in financing the litigation in consumer cases. The opt-out system in class actions eliminates the financial risks in bringing claims and favors the litigation of disputes, like consumer small claims, which the consumer

---

[4] R Carleo, 'Caos Costa e Class Action Italiana: Le ragioni di un mancato avvio' 1 *Rivista di diritto della navigazione* (2013) 35–69.

[5] C A Whytock, 'The Evolving Forum Shopping System' 96 *Cornell LRev* (2011) 481–534.

would not have been brought to court because of the limited amount of individual loss suffered. Moreover, plaintiffs may benefit from liberal discovery rules that either do not exist in European civil law countries, or are much more limited, like disclosure rules in England. In addition, the prospects of a jury awarding high compensatory damages, and even punitive damages, can convince potential plaintiffs, including Costa Concordia's passengers and their lawyers, that US courts are more favorable than those in the EU. All these elements appear to be relevant in explaining the attempts to start litigating the Costa Concordia case before the courts of Florida. In this case, one particular element has been fundamental in driving the litigation: the organization of US attorneys. They are able to organize groups of consumers internationally (ie outside the US) and have in fact been building relationships with local attorneys and a consumer association in Italy to attract more clients to bring claims to the US and increase pressure on defendants.

In reality, the forum shopping system has evolved and no longer encourages plaintiffs to pursue transnational claims in US courts to the extent it supposedly once did. The Costa Concordia affair is an example of this more restrictive approach of US courts.[6]

In 2013, judges in Florida dismissed the first *class action* in *Warrick v. Carnival Corp*.[7] The US District Court for the Southern District of Florida was the first court to decide the issue in relation to the Costa Concordia accident. It held that Massachusetts' residents-plaintiffs had to litigate their claims against the Carnival/Costa defendants in Italy. In analysing the forum non-conveniens issue,[8] the court found that the private and public interest factors heavily favoured trial in Italy. With respect to the private-interest factors, the court stated that the evidence is located 'predominantly in Italy, held by Italians, likely written in Italian, all of which is difficult and costly, and slow to produce here'. The court viewed the public-interest factors as similarly favouring dismissal due to the heavily congested dockets in the Southern District of Florida. In addition, the judges noted the much stronger interest that Italy has in the resolution of the accident

---

[6] D Fairgrieve and E Lein (eds), *Extraterritoriality and Collective Redress* (Oxford University Press, 2012), Part IV: Extraterritoriality and US Law.

[7] *Warrick v Carnival Corp*, No. 12-61389 (SD Fla, February 4, 2013). See also *Scimone v Carnival Corp*, No. 12-26072-CA02. In this case, the court dismissed the claims of the 35 foreign plaintiffs, but not of the 17 US plaintiffs. See also *Abeid-Saba v Carnival Corp*, No. 12-26076-CA02. In this case, the court dismissed the claims of all 57 plaintiffs, including 5 US residents.

[8] The forum non-conveniens doctrine allows a US Court to dismiss a case over which it has jurisdiction if there is a foreign alternative forum which may hear the case. It enables a US Court to decline to hear a case too remotely connected to it, even if no other court is simultaneously seized.

claims, and the fact that Italy is 'more at home' with the law that will likely govern the action. Finally, the court noted that the presence of two US corporations as defendants did not 'materially change the calculation', because the company that implemented the policies and procedures is Costa Crociere SpA, an Italian entity.

This more restrictive approach of US courts implies that European judges will have to manage a growing number of cross-border collective redress cases.

B. European Forum Shopping

The Green Paper on Collective Redress[9] covers other known regulatory instruments with their legal basis in Article 81 TFEU when dealing with issues relating to jurisdiction and choice of law in consumer collective redress cases.

These are Regulation (EC) 44/2001 on jurisdiction ('Brussels 1 Regulation', now Regulation (EU) 1215/2012)[10] and Regulation (EC) 864/2007 ('Rome II Regulation') on the law applicable to non-contractual obligations, to which Regulation (EC) 593/2008 ('Rome I Regulation')[11] is added with respect to contractual obligations. However, the Green Paper points out that these tools, as well as Regulation (EC) 861/2007 establishing a European procedure for small claims,[12] are not tailored to mass litigation. Thus, they are not equipped to deal with consumer collective redress cases. Most cases before European courts concern the sale of, or services relating to, luxury goods,[13] installment sales,[14] package holiday

---

[9] Commission's Green Paper on Consumer Collective Redress, Brussels, 27.11.2008, COM (2008) 794 final. See also the Recommendation on common principles for injunctive and compensatory collective redress mechanisms in the Member States concerning violations of rights granted under Union Law, [2013] OJ L 201, 60–65, at 17.

[10] Council Regulation (EC) 44/2001 on jurisdiction and the recognition and enforcement of judgments in civil and commercial matters [2001] OJ L 012, 1-23. On 12 December 2012, the European Parliament and the Council adopted Regulation (EC) 1215/2012 ('Recast Regulation') which replaces Regulation (EC) 44/2001 ('Brussels I Regulation) on jurisdiction and the recognition and enforcement of judgments in civil and commercial matters and which has applied since 10 January 2015, [2012] OJ L 351, 1–32.

[11] Regulation (EC) 593/2008 on the law applicable to contractual obligations (Rome I) [2008] OJ L 177, 6–16; Regulation (EC) 864/2007 on the law applicable to non-contractual obligations (Rome II) [2007] OJ L 199, 40–49.

[12] Regulation (EC) 861/2007 establishing a European Small Claims Procedure [2007] OJ L 199, 31.7.2007, 1–22.

[13] *Rayner v Davies* [2002] EWCA Civ 1880 (survey to buy a yacht).

[14] Joint Cases C-240/98, 241/98, 242/98, 243/98 and 244/98 *Oceano Grupo Editorial SA v Quintero* [2000] ECR I-4941 (purchase of an encyclopedia by instalments).

contracts,[15] timeshare agreements,[16] and some ordinary sales[17] and services.[18]

These private international law instruments therefore do not address or resolve the difficulties and inefficiencies that consumers have in order to get damages following the behavior of companies that qualify as mass torts.

The Brussels I Recast Regulation regulates, inter alia, the jurisdiction over persons domiciled in the EU.[19] In particular, this provision, conceived for individual actions, expressly contemplates the involvement of more parties, although from the defendants' perspective. Article 8 of the Recast Regulation provides that, in the case of multiple defendants, the plaintiff may bring an action in the court of the forum of any of them.[20] However, the said article does not regulate the reverse case of the plurality of plaintiffs.

The Brussels I (Recast) Regulation allows the consumer to rely on the courts of the Member States where the defendant is domiciled and provides an alternative forum at the place where the consumer is domiciled.[21] Article 18 of the Recast Regulation is based on the presumption that consumers are generally weaker and need protection both regarding jurisdiction and the applicable law. In terms of jurisdiction, a consumer is always entitled to sue or to be sued in the court of his domicile and the effect of a jurisdiction clause is generally restricted. In terms of choice of law, a consumer will not be

---

[15] *Thomas Cook Tour Operations v Hotel Kaya* [2009] EWHC 720 (QB); *Barton v Golden Sun Holidays* [2007] ILPr 57; *Watson v First Choice Holidays v Flights* [2001] 2 Lloyd's Rep 339.

[16] *Lynch v Halifax Building Society and Royal Bank of Scotland* [1995] CCLR 42.

[17] Landgericht Feldkirch (2R18/08Z) (Austrian buyer purchased a sewing machine on eBay from a German seller by using a pseudonym, stated a delivery address in Germany and payment was made from a German bank account), see S Calabresi-Scholz 'LG Klagenfurt (AT) 12 February 2008 – Brussels I Regulation Articles 5(2), 22(5) – International jurisdiction – Matters relating to maintenance' 1 *European Legal Forum* (2008) 57.

[18] BGH (III ZR 71/08) (a German sued a Greek lawyer regarding services provided in Greece; the lawyer was listed on the websites of the German Embassy in Athens and legal expenses insurers), see S Calabresi-Scholz 'BGH (DE) 17 September 2008 – Brussels I Regulation Article 15(1)(c) – International Jurisdiction – Matters relating to a contract concluded by a consumer' 5 *ELF* (2008) 256; see also OGH 4 Nd 514/97 (language course contract); OGH 9 Nd 509/01 (master education contract).

[19] Italian law No. 218/1995 provides for additional criteria such as residence in Italy, the presence in Italy of a representative authorized to sue and be sued, and other criteria, also referring to the Brussels Convention of 1968 (art 3), then abrogated by Regulation (EC) 44/2001.

[20] Art 8 (1) Regulation (EU) 1215/2012 'allows a person domiciled in a Member State to be sued, where he is one of a number of defendants, in the courts for the place where any one of them is domiciled, provided the claims are so closely connected that it is expedient to hear and determine them together to avoid the risk of irreconcilable judgments resulting from separate proceedings'.

[21] Art 18 (1) Regulation (EU) 1215/2012: 'A consumer may bring proceedings against the other party to a contract either in the courts of the Member State in which that party is domiciled or, regardless of the domicile of the other party, in the courts for the place where the consumer is domiciled'.

deprived of the standard of protection provided by the mandatory rules of the law of the consumer's habitual residence, which is the default law applicable in absence of choice (see Section III). It is a common presumption that a consumer is at a disadvantage in litigation versus a company and therefore requires legal protection. Requiring consumers to sue abroad might lead to procedural difficulties and disadvantages which could deprive them of their right of access to justice. However, it is certainly wrong to presume that the protective jurisdiction rules remove all procedural obstacles to cross-border access to justice. Suing at home is more convenient to consumers, but it may still be undesirable considering the small value of the claim. If a consumer does not decide to sue, however, the rules on jurisdiction and choice of law lose all significance.

Thus, the provisions of the said Regulation may facilitate the practice of forum shopping among European jurisdictions especially in consumer cases. This is evident in the Costa Concordia situation. Taking the case examined here as an example: each passenger could have sued the company in the place of the company's domicile, but also in his place of domicile. Accordingly, passengers' domiciles could have justified actions before the courts of some EU Member States, just to limit the discourse to European jurisdictions. This may result in the proliferation of parallel proceedings against the same defendant in several European courts and on behalf of different groups of consumers. In addition, the rules may lead to conflicting judgments in European jurisdictions. European Consumer Law is closely harmonized within the Member States, but divergences remain in the relevant domestic case law.[22]

To overcome such risk, the Commission suggested in its Green Paper that protective jurisdiction should not be used in representative actions. The suggestion is probably right, as protective jurisdiction enables an individual consumer to always sue or be sued in his domicile. Consequently, this benefit is not compatible with the nature of cross-border collective redress, where consumers may come from different Member States. The Green Paper states at point 58: "In cross-border cases the Regulation on jurisdiction would be applicable to any action including an action brought to court by a public authority, if it is exercising private rights (eg an ombudsman suing for consumers). Representative actions would have to be brought to the trader's court, or the court of the place of performance of the contract (Article 5 (1))".

Indeed, collective redress changes the presumed inequality of litigation power between consumers and professionals. Where a large number of consumers bring actions together, or an association or a public authority represents consumers, against one business defendant, the collective strength

---

[22] JM Smits, 'Full Harmonization of Consumer Law? A Critique of the Draft Directive on Consumer Rights' 18 *ERPL* (2010) 5–14.

of the claimants largely increases the litigation power of the traditional weaker party. This is sufficient reason to abandon the protective jurisdiction in collective redress.

To conclude this section, our point here is that the Brussels I Regime allows consumers to select the jurisdiction in case of litigation. This can lead to a number of actions before the courts of European Member States in the countries of domicile of the consumers involved, and, as in the present case, in the courts of non-European countries. The provisions examined here apply to the Costa Concordia case in the sense that the passengers could have sued the cruise company before the courts of the place where they were domiciled, or before the Italian courts (the Italian cruise liner has its statutory seat in Genoa). By following the Green Paper's suggestion to leave aside the consumer forum in collective redress cases, jurisdiction could be determined by referring to the court of the professional,[23] or the place of performance of the contract.

In addition, specific problems may also arise with respect to the role played by consumer organizations in collective redress in EU Member States and the requirement of homogeneity of consumer rights. This latter point is a common pre-requisite of admissibility for the majority of the collective redress mechanisms adopted in EU Member States.

1. Consumer Contracts

The abovementioned rules contain a discipline for the benefit of the consumer, but they introduce an exception to the normal policy of granting jurisdiction to the courts of the Member State of domicile of the defendant. Due to their exceptional character, their scope is necessarily limited in line with the interpretation of the CJEU.

In interpreting Article 13 of the Brussels Convention,[24] the CJEU had consistently held that the term 'contract' is to be understood as an act that gives rise to reciprocal and interdependent obligations between the two parties.[25] The *Gabriel* case concerned a company that was sending personalized letters to consumers containing a misleading promise to award a prize accompanied by a catalogue of products or a good order. In such cases, the Court stated that jurisdiction should follow the provisions for consumer contracts according to Article 13 of the said Convention. In *Engler*, the CJEU noted that a seller's (misleading) promise to award a prize and the consumer's acceptance of the

---

[23] Art 63 Regulation (EU)1215/2012 para 1: "For the purposes of this Regulation, a company or other legal person or association of natural or legal persons is domiciled at the place where it has its: (a) statutory seat, or (b) central administration, or (c) principal place of business".

[24] Convention of 27 September 1968 on jurisdiction and the enforcement of judgments in civil and commercial matters.

[25] Case C-96/00 *Gabriel* [2002] ECR I-6367, para 39.

prize could create a 'contract between a trader and a consumer' within the meaning of Article 13.[26]

Article 17 of Regulation (EU) 1215/2012 certainly expanded the content of the previous Article 13 of the Brussels Convention.[27] The scope of its application is not limited to consumer contracts in the strict sense (ie contracts concerning the provision of a service or tangible movable property).[28] Package travel contracts are included within such a definition.

When called upon to interpret Article 15 of Regulation (EC) 44/2001, the CJEU, in *Ilsinger*[29] has again shown greater flexibility in interpreting the concept of 'contract' in a case very similar to *Engler*. While stressing the need for the effective conclusion of a contract, in line with the interpretation of Article 13 of the Brussels Convention, the CJEU preliminarily found that the scope of the said provision is no longer limited to those situations where the parties have assumed reciprocal obligations.

Without this limit, there is a contract even when one of the parties, the consumer, is limited to manifesting his acceptance (of a prize) without taking on other legal obligations towards the other party, ie the professional. The latter, however, 'must have clearly expressed their willingness to be bound by that commitment in case of acceptance by the other party, declaring unconditionally willing to pay the premium in question to consumers who have requested it'.[30] In its interpretation of Regulation (EC) 44/2011, the CJEU has thus favoured the extension of consumer protection.

Besides those consumer contracts where the protective rules have been tested in litigation, there are also borderline contracts which generate controversy as to whether they are included in the scope of protection. The European legislator wishes to protect the weaker party, but sometimes it is not clear who the weaker party is. This is especially true in investment contracts[31] and profession-related contracts.[32]

---

[26] Case C-27/02 *Engler v. Janus Versand GmbH* [2005] ECR I-481.

[27] It confirms the extension of the application of its rules to additional consumer contracts, ie contracts for the sale of goods on installment credit terms; or contracts for a loan repayable by installments, or for any other form of credit, made to finance the sale of goods. The extension aims to align the procedural rules with the substantive provisions of EU directives in the area of consumer protection.

[28] J Hill, *Cross-border Consumer Contracts* (OUP, 2009).

[29] Case C-180/06 *Renate Ilsinger v Martin Dreschers* [2009] ECR I-3961.

[30] *Ibid*, 51.

[31] *Ghandour v Arab Bank (Switzerland)* [2008] ILPr 35 (Athens Court of Appeal held that a borrower, who borrowed very substantial funds from a bank relying upon her own expertise and judgment to invest, was not a consumer); *Standard Bank of London v Apostolakis* [2003] ILPr 29; see also Oberlandesgericht Koblenz, 08.03.2000 – 2 U 1788/99, ILPr 14; Case C-318/93 *Brenner v Dean Witter Reynolds* [1994] ECR I-4275.

[32] Case C-464/01, *Guber v BayWA AG* [2005] ECR I-439. Cf *Prostar management v Twaddle* [2003] SLT (Sh Ct) 11 (management agreement providing services to a professional footballer).

2. Consumer Associations

The application of the Regulation (EU) 1215/2012 also involves identifying the notion of 'consumer' and 'consumer association'.

The CJEU has pointed out that the Brussels I Regime applies when the applicant is a person who buys goods or services for non-business purposes. He shall enjoy the protection afforded by the Brussels I Regime, because 'he is personally involved as a plaintiff or as a defendant'.[33]

Second, a consumer must conclude the contract, for a purpose, which can be regarded as being outside his trade or profession. The consumer status must therefore be assessed by reference to the role that person plays within a given contract with respect to the nature and purpose of the latter.[34] On this point, the CJEU also made clear in the *Gruber* case that a contract made by an individual to purchase goods or services for personal purposes couldn't be classified as a contract concluded by a consumer, unless professional use is so limited as to have a negligible role in the overall context of the operation.[35] Moreover, it is necessary that the counterparty acted professionally at the time of the conclusion of the contract with the effect of excluding contracts between two consumers from the scope of the protective provisions as in this case no party is weaker than the other.

The question that arises primarily with respect to the wording of Article 18 of Regulation (EU) 1215/2012 ('a consumer') concerns the legal standing of associations and committees of consumers in collective redress cases.

It should also be noted that, with regard to the actions for injunctions, the recitals of the Directive 2009/22/EC,[36] as well as the previous Directive 98/27/EC,[37] state that 'with regard to the jurisdiction, the proposed action does not preclude the application of the rules of private international law and Conventions in force between the Member States…'. The CJEU has also ruled on the application of the criteria laid down by the Brussels Convention for injunctive relief. In the *Henkel* case, the Court assessed whether a consumer association could be qualified as a consumer within the meaning of Article 16, but it denied this possibility.[38] It has to be noted in this context that actions between a public authority and a person governed by private law fall outside the scope of the Brussels regime only in so far as

---

[33] Case C-96/00 *Gabriel* [2002] ECR I-6367, para. 39.
[34] Case C-269/95 *Benincasa* [1997] ECR I-3788, 3800.
[35] Case C-464/01 *Johann Gruber v BayWa AG* [2005] ECR I-439.
[36] Council Directive 2009/22/EC of June 23 April 2009 on injunctions for the protection of consumers' interests [2009] OJ L 110/30.
[37] Council Directive 98/27/EC of 19 May 1998 on injunctions for the protection of consumers' interests, [1998] OJ 166, 51–55.
[38] Case C-167/00 *Verein für Konsumenteninformation v Karl Heinz Henkel* [2002] ECR I-8111.

the authority is acting in the exercise of public powers. In the case cited, the action was based on the provisions regulating injunctive relief, a procedure where only consumer associations and/or public authorities (and not the single consumer) have standing. In this case, in fact, the associations are acting in their own name as a public authority and their right to obtain an injunction to prevent the use of unfair terms in contracts constitutes a public law power. An organization of that kind takes on the task, in the public interest, of ensuring the protection of the entire group of consumers. For this reason, it has the statutory right to bring an action to obtain an injunction preventing unlawful by-traders, independent of any private law relationship arising out of a contract between a professional and a private individual.

In collective redress cases, the associations (and committees) do not promote action in the collective interests of the consumers, but they act for individual consumers, who have subscribed to an action. They would intervene in the name (and not only on behalf) of victims previously identified or identifiable in any case. For example, Article 140-bis of the Italian Consumer Code, in referring to the homogeneous individual rights of consumers and users, legitimizes each member of the group, also by giving mandate to associations or committees. In doing so, it emphasizes the representation of consumer rights. Proceedings brought by a representative body of consumers based on Article 140-bis of the Consumer Code are therefore not entirely comparable to those already examined by the CJEU in *Henkel*.[39]

III. CHOICE OF LAW

Once jurisdiction has been established, the competent court has to identify the law applicable to the dispute. In this context, it is also appropriate to make some mention of the issues related to the law applicable to contractual obligations under the Rome I Regulation[40] and the existing links with Regulation (EU) 1215/ 2012 in collective redress cases.

With regard to obligations of a contractual nature, the general rule is that the law chosen by the parties governs the contract (Article 3). In the absence of that choice, the applicable law is that of the country with which the contract is most closely connected (Article 4).

---

[39] Recommendation on common principles for injunctive and compensatory collective redress mechanisms in the Member States concerning violations of rights granted under Union Law, [2013] OJ L 201, 60–65, at 17.

[40] Council Regulation (EC) 593/2008 of 17 June 2008 on the law applicable to contractual obligations (Rome I), OJ L 177, 6–16.

The Rome I Regulation also provides for special categories of consumer contracts. For this type of contract, Article 6 determines as the applicable law the law of the country of habitual residence of the consumer and that a choice of the applicable law is limited. Further, Article 6(2) Rome I Regulation ostensibly protects consumers by discouraging party agreement on a pre-dispute basis on the law governing a consumer contract. Thus, European private international law contrasts with the absence of private international law restrictions on choice of forum and choice of law in the US, even in consumer contracts.[41]

The prerequisite for the application of the 'discipline of favour' is, again, that the contract is 'a contract concluded by a consumer' within the meaning of Article 6. Similarly to Article 18 of Regulation (EU) 1215/2012, Article 6 of the Rome I Regulation states that the contract is to be concluded by a natural person for a purpose, which can be regarded as being outside his trade, business and professional activity. Thus, it extends to all consumer contracts provided that the professional: pursues his commercial or professional activities in the country where the consumer has his habitual residence; or by any means, directs such activities to that country or to several countries including that country.

In cross-border collective redress cases, the rights of consumers that are homogeneous according to domestic laws may not be so homogeneous, in particular in light of Article 6.[42] Because of this provision, in mass cases involving consumers from different Member States, the court would have to apply the different national laws of residence of the various consumers. If a collective redress regime were open to consumers habitually resident in different Member States, Article 6 Rome I Regulation would directly lead to the result that a separate law should govern each individual claim. The current Rome I Regulation does not provide consumers with viable options to waive the application of the protective applicable law, which surely poses problems, yet to be resolved, for the proper functioning of cross-border collective redress. In the *Costa Concordia* case, the applicable substantive laws would not have significantly diverged in EU Member States because of the high level of harmonization of EU Consumer Law, and in particular the rules on package travel. Nevertheless, divergences may arise in the application of domestic laws by national judges, leading to conflicting judgments.

A solution advanced in the Green Paper on Collective Redress would be to introduce an amendment to the rules, imposing the law of the profes-

---

[41] R A Brand, 'The Rome I Regulation Rules on Party Autonomy for Choice of Law: A U.S. Perspective' University of Pittsburgh Legal Studies Research Paper Series (2011) No. 2011–29. http://dx.doi.org/10.2139/ssrn.1973162.

[42] Communication 'Towards a European Horizontal Framework for Collective Redress' COM (2013) 401 final, at 3.7.

sional's habitual residence in consumer collective redress cases. Other options are the application of the law of the most affected market, or of the Member State where the representative entity is established.[43]

IV. FORUM AVOIDING

In the Costa Concordia scenario, European private international law rules seem to confirm the jurisdiction of the Italian courts. Thus, a question arises here: is the Italian judicial system for collective redress able to manage the claims of the thousands of victims of the Costa Concordia disaster?

The Costa Concordia case confirms the scant appeal of the Italian jurisdiction. However, how can attempts to avoid this jurisdiction be explained? The litigation environment matters, as well as issues pertaining to substantive law, which, in this case, is quite favourable for victims. In addition, the *azione di classe* has some shortcomings preventing this mechanism from reaching its full potential. This Section points out the fundamental issues behind the choice of a particular forum.

A. Substantive Law

The legal issues at stake are numerous and complex: the liability regime applicable to the claims which will be filed by passengers and third parties, the possibility for ship-owners to invoke limitation of liability (and the regime applying to such limitation), and the consequences of criminal charges against the captain.

It is rather difficult to identify the liability regime applicable to the actions brought by the passengers of Costa Concordia for health damages, and by the relatives of the deceased passengers. Various opinions have been expressed.

First, it can be argued that the claims brought by the passengers are subject to the International Convention on Travel Contracts (CCV)[44] and the EU Package Holiday Directive (90/314/EC),[45] since the casualties occurred during a cruise included in a package offered by the company.

The cruise line company in fact submitted a package to the passengers incorporating Costa's general terms and conditions. The CCV is referred to as a 'residual' regulation in case there is no mandatory domestic or international law applicable to the claim. Nevertheless, the application of the CCV

---

[43] Green Paper on Consumer Collective Redress (above n 9) 59.
[44] International Convention on Travel Contracts (CCV), Brussels, 23 April 1970.
[45] Council Directive 90/314/EEC of 13 June 1990 on package travel, package holidays and package tours, OJ L 158, 23.06.1990, 59–64.

and the EU and Italian legislation on package travel contracts is justified although the accident occurred during the sea transit. This was part of a cruise offering a wide range of activities exposing passengers to risks which are only faintly related to carriage by sea. It is important to underline that the CCV provides some limitation to the amount of damages that could be paid to passengers according to the circumstances of the case.[46]

Second, several commentators have considered the matter to be governed by the provisions of the Athens Convention, which established a comprehensive integrated system governing the liability of cruise ship operators for personal injuries and property damage sustained by its passengers. It also contains standards for establishing liability and permissible defenses as well as its own statute of limitations and venue provisions. In particular, the Athens Convention[47] allows the carrier to limit its liability for personal injury or death of passengers.[48]

Finally, it is also possible to allege that Italian law – namely, the Navigation Code – should apply,[49] since the accident occurred on a ship operating under the Italian flag and within Italian territorial waters, and the package tour was agreed with an Italian company. In this case, there would be no limitation of liability for death or injuries, because the Navigation Code does not expressly contain a limit to the amount of damages that can be awarded in favour of a passenger or his relatives in case of death or injury. Interestingly, however, liability for loss of baggage is very limited.

The position reached by Italian Courts over the last two decades as regards compensation for death or serious injuries is in favour of a progressive increase of the amount of compensatory damages, and the sums awarded often exceed the limits applicable under the CCV, or the Athens Protocol.[50]

---

[46] If the claims were to be brought under the CCV, limitation of liability under art 13 would apply, namely 50,000 Germinal golden francs for cases of personal injury, equal today to around €600,000, whilst limitation for loss or damage to baggage would be slightly less than €24,000.

[47] Athens Convention relating to the Carriage of Passengers and their Luggage by Sea 1974 (Athens, 13 December 1974). The adoption of the Athens Convention was primarily motivated by a series of uninsured ferry disasters, but the Convention has had so far limited success and only a few States have ratified it.

[48] According to the 2002 Protocol and/or EU Regulation n. 392/2009, a carrier's liability for death is capped at 400.000 Special Drawing Rights, equal to around €470,000, ie considerably less than the equivalent limitation under the CCV.

[49] Italian Navigation Code, entered into force on 21 April 1942.

[50] Finally, it is worth mentioning that clauses excluding or limiting liability are considered potentially unfair by Italian law, and are subject to specific and strict conditions of validity. Pursuant to art 1341 Codice Civile similar clauses must be referred to in an ad hoc clause at the bottom of the contract or in the general terms and conditions, and must be specifically approved and accepted; moreover, several clauses of this kind are void if contained in contracts with consumers.

In addition, pursuant to Article 7 of the Italian Navigation Code, the law of the ship's flag regulates limitation of liability. The ship was operating under the Italian flag, the owners (Costa Crociere SpA) are an Italian company, the accident took place in Italian territorial waters, and there is little doubt therefore that Italian law would regulate limitation of liability. The system (set out by Article 275 of the Navigation Code) is peculiar, and there are quite a few significant differences between Italian law and the Conventions.

First, limitation under Italian law is afforded only to the operator (*armature*) whilst the Conventions extend the limitation to other parties involved (eg the manager, charterer and Master).

Secondly, the Italian Navigation Code provides for an 'all inclusive' system, since it extends the limitation to all acts or events occurring during the voyage (including for instance salvage awards, or removal of wreck charges, and liability claims for injured and dead passengers), whilst the Conventions exclude several liabilities from limitation. A major difference exists in respect of the calculation of the limitation fund. Under Italian law, the fund depends on the value of the ship, not on the tonnage. In order to limit liability, the operator of the ship must establish a limitation fund by way of actual payment of a sum to the court.[51] Finally, under Italian law, limitation is excluded in case of fraud or gross negligence of the operator. The recklessness of the captain does, in principle, not prevent the cruise line company from benefiting from limitation, but under Italian law owners are barred from seeking limitation in cases of 'gross negligence' which implies a far less severe degree of negligence.

In light of the above, it seems that Italian law, by permitting compensation beyond the limitation set out by the CCV, is favourable to passengers. So why did their lawyers attempt to pursue claims that are evidently connected with Italy in the US?

This was probably because US courts are more likely to award victims a huge amount of damages, including extra-compensatory damages. Italian private law on the other hand pursues the goal of deterrence through extra-compensatory damages but only to a limited extent and under specific circumstances.[52] For example, in the leading case *Parrott v Fimez SpA*,[53] the Italian courts expressed the view that private lawsuits brought by injured people must only aim at obtaining compensation for loss. Allowing separate

---

[51] The amount is equal to two-fifths of the sound value of the ship (plus the ship's earnings at the end of the voyage); but if the value of the ship at the time when the limitation is applied for is lower than one fifth of the sound value, the limitation fund corresponds to one fifth.

[52] F Quarta, 'Foreign punitive damages decisions and class actions in Italy', in Fairgrieve and Lein (above n 6) 276.

[53] L Ostoni, 'Translation: Italian rejections of punitive damages in a US judgment', 24 *JL&Com* 24.

awards intended to punish the defendant is against public policy. The Court of Appeal of Venice rendered a judgment confirmed by the Supreme Court, refusing the recognition and enforcement of a judgment of the District Court of Jefferson County, Alabama, in a tort case. In this case, an Italian manufacturer had been ordered to pay $1,000,000 punitive damages, having allegedly caused the death of the plaintiff's son in a road accident, due to a defect in the design of the buckle of the crash helmet he was wearing. The US court did not specify the apportionment of compensatory and punitive damages against the Italian defendants, and the Court of Appeal of Venice concluded that the award was punitive in nature, and therefore contrary to domestic public policy.

The Supreme Court confirmed the ruling, and stressed that the Italian system of civil liability is strictly compensatory, not punitive. Hence, any foreign judgment including punitive damages against Costa Crociere SpA would incur serious problems during enforcement, and fight an uphill battle for the exequatur.

B. *The Procedural Gap*

Turning to the procedural aspects, the cost of civil litigation in Italy may represent another relevant factor in opting for the Italian jurisdiction: Italian lawyers are not expensive in comparison with those in other European countries. This is because Italian court fees as well as lawyers' fees in civil proceedings are determined according to a statutory framework. Until recently, any other agreement between plaintiff and counsel, in particular any contingency fee or conditional fee arrangement, was plainly illegal.

Moreover, Italian civil procedure does not allow for pre-trial discovery. This is because there is no strict separation of pre-trial and trial phase in Italy, yet much of the preparatory stage of civil litigation is potentially in the hands of the parties. The rules on discovery are generally similar to those of other European civil justice systems.

So why did some passengers and their lawyers, including some Italian citizens, try to escape the Italian jurisdiction with respect to a claim that is deeply connected to Italy?

The fundamental answer comes from the 'procedural gap' of the Italian civil justice system: 'Justice delayed is justice denied' has a meaning in Italian as well as in other languages. Statistics for the Italian civil judiciary, while constantly improving, remain quite unsatisfactory compared to our neighbours.[54] A study by the OECD finds that the average length of a civil suit

---

[54] E Silvestri, 'Goals of Civil Justice When Nothing Works: The Case of Italy', in A Uzelac (ed), *Goals of Civil Justice and Civil Procedure in Contemporary Judicial Systems Ius Gentium: Comparative Perspectives on Law and Justice* (Springer, 2014) Vol. 34, 79–103.

through all its stages is eight years, far higher than elsewhere.[55] Indeed, when a judge of the Court of Appeal of Turin, one of the biggest cities in the country, became president of the main civil court 12 years ago, he found that the oldest case had started about 43 years earlier.[56] By 2009, the Court of Appeal of Turin had cut the average length of a civil case from seven years to three. How has this goal been achieved? This became possible by improving some basic management techniques; one was to impose a 'First in, first out' principle to cases instead of the 'Last in, first out'. Following this example, the government is considering plans to halve Italy's backlog of cases and ensure that all trial stages are completed within twelve months. The government has undertaken measures to give judges more support for ancillary tasks. It is also encouraging the digitization of proceedings and out-of-court settlements.

B. *Why the Azione di Classe has not Changed the Picture*

Another question arises at this point: has the introduction of the *azione di classe* improved the picture? For some Italian legal scholars, the answer was quite simple before 2010. Before that date, Italy did not allow collective damages actions and the lack of a collective instrument explained the limited attractiveness of Italian Courts with respect to mass litigation. Italy finally adopted collective redress mechanisms from 1 January 2010, by introducing a new Article 140-bis of the Consumer Code (*Codice del Consumo*).[57] The introduction of this action raised many hopes that the level of protection of citizen's rights, or more precisely, consumer rights would increase.

Four years later it is questionable whether these hopes have come true. The reality seems to conflict with the high expectations associated with the introduction of the Italian collective redress mechanism for damages. Indeed, it is very interesting to note that the practice of forum shopping in mass torts to avoid the jurisdiction of Italian courts has continued in spite of the presence of the *azione di classe* in the Italian legal system. The Costa Concordia disaster occurred in 2012, well after the introduction of the *azione di classe*. However, none of the passengers and victims of the cruise have considered bringing such action.

---

[55] OECD, *What makes civil justice effective?* (OECD, 2013).

[56] The judge of the Turin Court of Appeal is now responsible for the project at the Department of Justice of the Italian government.

[57] Law No. 244/2007 originally introduced the old 140-bis, while law No. 99/2009 introduced the new 140-bis. Publications discussing the old 140-bis are still available, of course, and could confuse readers less experienced with the Italian system.

1. Subjective Limitations

Indeed, the new action is inserted in the Consumer Code as a means to protect the consumer. Consequently, only a consumer may file the new action. Under the Consumer Code, the term 'consumer' refers to any natural person who, in commercial activities covered by this Title, is acting for purposes which are outside their trade, business, craft or profession.

Under the new law, consumers (ie natural persons) with homogenous interests, have the right to file the *azione di classe* against a private corporation in three different cases.

It is important to underline that the plaintiff may give a mandate to a consumer association or committee to sue on his behalf. The law does not require the plaintiff to be a member of the consumer association to which he gives such mandate, and does not set forth provisions about the remuneration of the consumer association.

Because of their role, consumer associations and committees are indicated as the 'representative plaintiffs' of the damaged consumers. Indeed, they are the de facto engine behind the *azione di classe*, while the individual consumer, who is an actual plaintiff, plays no role in the civil proceedings.

This choice of limiting the action to 'consumers' in itself implies a restriction. In the case of the Costa Concordia, however, such action would seem to be applicable in view of the fact that passengers were benefitting from a package travel regime. Of course, this excludes the protection of those who worked on the Costa Concordia ship.

2. Objective Limitations

There are also objective limitations. According to Article 140-bis, paras 2 a, b and c, the action enforces:

a) contractual rights of a number of consumers and users who find themselves in a homogeneous situation in relation to the same company (…);
b) homogeneous end-consumers' rights concerning a given product in relation to its manufacturer, even in the absence of a direct contractual relationship;
c) homogeneous rights to payment of damages due to these consumers and users and deriving from unfair commercial practices or anti-competitive behavior.

Thus, it is clear that cases governed by Article 140-bis would be primarily related to actions based on consumer contracts, damages resulting from a defective product, and actions for damages caused to the same consumers and users' by anti-competitive behaviour. For example, according to the letter of the law, behaviour (such as that which Captain Schettino is accused of) causing environmental damage is excluded. In addition, Italian scholars are still discussing whether Article 140-bis may also apply in a case of violation of certain rules protecting the financial markets, such as market manipulation or false information, where these do not qualify as unfair commercial practices.

The situation of the cruise passengers could fall under Article 140-bis, paragraph 2 (a), because they all purchased the tickets for the cruise and, after the disaster, they find themselves in a 'homogeneous situation'. The Court has to verify the presence of such a requirement by issuing an admissibility order.[58] Another problem – a fundamental one that will be quantified later – is the damage caused to the individual passenger. This is damage to the person, ranging from the death of a passenger to the mere stress of the rescue, or damage other than to the person, for example damage to personal property. With respect to the quantification of the various damages, the court may issue a judgment on the final amounts due to those who have joined the action, or it shall establish a homogeneous calculation criterion for the payment of these sums. It also grants the parties a period of not more than 90 days to agree on the liquidation of the damages.[59]

3. Cross-border Cases

The Italian Parliament has not considered the cross-border dimension of collective redress, the law is silent in this respect. In terms of competence, the *azione di classe* adopts the criterion of the residence of the defendant. Article 140-bis para. 4 of the Consumer Code only mentions judicial competence when the claim is submitted to the court located in the capital of the Region in which the company is based.[60]

---

[58] In the admissibility order, the court sets out the terms and the most appropriate forms of notices to the public, so that those belonging to the class can join promptly. Public notification is a condition for the claim. By the same order, the court determines the characteristics of the individual rights involved in the action, specifying the criteria according to which the individuals seeking to join are included in the class or must be regarded as excluded from the *azione di classe*.

[59] The minutes of the agreement, signed by the parties and the judge, is immediately enforceable. If the parties have not reached such agreement within 90 days, the judge, upon the request of at least one of the parties, liquidates the damages due to each member of the class. The judgment becomes enforceable 180 days from publication.

[60] The court of Turin has jurisdiction over Valle d'Aosta, the Court of Venice over Trentino-Alto Adige and Friuli-Venezia Giulia, the Court of Rome over Marche, Umbria, Abruzzo and Molise, and the Court of Naples over Basilicata and Calabria.

It emerges that the main question consists in reconciling the application of Regulation (EU) 1215/2012 with the requirement to concentrate the efforts of the group on a small number of judges previously identified (the court located in the capital of the Region in which the company is based). The application of the criteria provided for by Article 18 of the Brussels I Recast Regulation makes it possible to embed the action in an Italian court, but these criteria do not necessarily coincide with those on which Article 140-bis is based. It should be noted, however, that once jurisdiction has been identified under the Brussels I Regime, national procedural rules complement and support the criteria laid down in the Regulation. This is particularly so in cases where the internal rules enhance the concentration of cases in one forum. Thus, the competent court may be located at the place of performance of the contract, or the place of the damaging event, provided of course that such place is the same for all consumers involved in the proceedings.

V. THE JOINT CONCILIATION

Finally, it is important to underline that a large number of passengers have received compensation by adhering to an ad hoc joint conciliation scheme. This solution results from the exercise of 'Italian creativity' in law to overcome gaps of the ordinary justice system.

Consumer associations have played – and still play – an important role in advancing consumer rights in Italy. The *Ministero delle Attività Produttive* set up a Consumer Council (National Council of Consumers and Users, *Consiglio nazionale dei consumatori e degli utenti*) in July 1998. Article 136 of the Italian Consumer Code expressly mentions it and states its functions.[61] The Consumer Council invites representatives from national consumer associations to take part in meetings with representatives of the government and of the industry. There are about eighteen important consumers associations within the county. Among other requirements, the organizations should be founded by a public or certified private deed, they shall be democratically structured, pursue the sole aim of protecting consumers and users, and shall not be profit making. In addition, a list of members shall be kept and updated annually, with an indication of the fees paid directly to the association for statutory purposes. They also have to demonstrate that they are representative in terms of numbers of members and present throughout the country.

The Consumer Council is responsible, among other tasks, for encouraging initiatives designed to improve consumers and users' access to justice in order to settle disputes.

---

[61] Decree Law 281 of 30 July 1998 – now Consumer Code, Legislative Decree 206/2005.

Based on the above-mentioned legal framework, sixteen of the consumer associations taking part in the Consumer Council promoted a committee of Costa Concordia victims on 12 January 2012. Its aim was to advance the rights of the injured passengers and obtain rapid and satisfactory compensation. Consumer associations contacted the victims of the disaster to obtain their consent to approach the cruise line company with a view to enter out-of-court settlement negotiations between Costa and the passengers. Such out-of-court agreement (protocol) between consumer representatives and the company contains the criteria for compensating the passengers. Indeed, there is no control over the content of the agreement by the courts, nor by the government. The government only supervises private parties during the process of negotiations. The Italian term to denote a form of conciliation is '*conciliazione paritetica*'. The EU Parliament Resolution on alternative dispute resoltion expressly mentions the Italian system, acknowledging that it deserves attention among the various out-of-court settlement procedures. The EU Resolution on alternative dispute resolution in civil matters states that the Italian joint conciliation procedure is a possible best practice model. It is based on "(…) a protocol agreed and signed by the company and the consumer associations, requiring the company to agree in advance to ADR in order to resolve any disputes which arise in the area covered by the protocol".[62]

Thus, the joint conciliation model consists of a voluntary ADR method based on negotiation. It had already been widely applied in sectors such as telephony (where it was tried out initially in 1991 in a pilot project financed by the EC), and postal services (2002).

Joint conciliation may be initiated only after the parties (consumers' associations and businesses) have signed agreements and implementing rules which govern the conduct of the procedure.

With respect to the *Costa Concordia* case, the agreement provides for a compensation package offered to physically uninjured passengers. As to the families of the dead and missing, or hospitalized passengers, separate proposals were to be offered based on their individual circumstances and left to direct negotiations.[63]

The agreement was reached with virtually all the Italian consumer associations and defense organizations, save for one (Codacons), which was preparing class action claims in the US on behalf of passengers and victims. The compensation comprises a payment of €11,000 per person to compensate for all damages (including loss of baggage and property, psychological

---

[62] European Parliament Resolution of 25 October 2011 on alternative dispute resolution in civil, commercial and family matters (2011/2117(INI)), 11.

[63] A group of 32 passengers died and 64 passengers were injured from a total of 4,252 passengers.

distress and loss of enjoyment of the cruise) to be paid within seven days from the acceptance of each passenger. In addition, the agreement provides for the reimbursement of a range of other costs and losses, including reimbursement for the value of the cruise, all air and bus travel costs included in the cruise package, all travel expenses to return home, all medical expenses arising from the event, and all expenses incurred on board during the cruise. Notwithstanding the fact that the joint conciliation has some advantages, it is quite clear that the non-physical damages suffered by the passengers have not been fully compensated in this case, and the gravity of the stress and pain of being involved in a disaster have not been subject to full compensation.

Costa also promised return of all property stored in cabin safes, as far as recoverable, and to grant passengers access to a program for 'psychological assistance'. The offer to uninjured passengers was available for some months only. The uninjured passengers (and consumer associations) agreed not to bring legal actions, including the *azione di classe*, against the company. Because of the joint conciliation about 60% of Italian and non-Italian passengers received compensation based on these terms.[64]

VI. CONCLUSIONS

This case is a starting point from which to observe the practice of forum shopping among European jurisdictions in consumer contract cases.[65]

European private international law provides that a consumer can sue the professional in the courts of the place of his domicile. Taking the Costa Concordia case as an example: each passenger could have sued the company in the city or town of his domicile. Accordingly, passengers' domiciles could have justified actions before the courts of a number of European jurisdictions. Nevertheless, as the Costa Concordia case shows, this benefit for the consumer is not compatible with the nature of cross-border collective redress. Existing rules and lack of any form of coordination risk promoting the proliferation of parallel proceedings in the EU and conflicting judgments. Our analysis confirms that some sort of European coordination is absolutely necessary and urgent to avoid these risks and their negative consequences,

---

[64] In France, the process has been more complex: the cruise line company had set a deadline of 14 February 2012 (only one month after the event) for the acceptance of the offer, but FENVAC (the French national federation of the victims of catastrophes), which represented a large number of passengers, contested this deadline as too close and unreasonable. FENVAC sought an order from the Court of Nanterre to extend the deadline for the acceptance of the offer; the application was upheld and the Court of Appeal of Versailles following Costa's appeal confirmed the order.

[65] S Tang Zheng, 'Private International Law in Consumer Contracts: A European Perspective' 6 *JPIL* (2010) 225–248.

such as different treatment of European consumers involved in the same disaster depending on the place where they are domiciled.

Moreover, while Italian substantive law is relatively favorable to Costa Concordia's passengers (although it does not provide for punitive damages), the Italian civil justice system suffers from serious procedural shortcomings, so that consumers, including Italian consumers, turned to other jurisdictions despite the fact that the case was obviously connected with Italy. In addition, the introduction of the *azione di classe* has not changed the Italian litigation landscape.[66] Eventually, the compensation of a large number of passengers, who were only physically uninjured, was managed by an ad hoc out-of-court settlement scheme (joint conciliation), with the aim of overcoming the downsides of the judicial system. In so doing, the Italian experience shows the potential of out-of-court settlement mechanisms for cross-border consumer collective redress.

---

[66] Costa Cruises, which operated the Concordia, initially offered survivors a 30% discount off future cruises, but consumer associations dismissed the first proposal as 'insulting'.

The Israeli Class Action – A Foundation for a European Model?

Ariel Flavian*

I. INTRODUCTION

A system of collective redress has clear advantages for European consumers, outweighing the problems that may arise from its implementation. The European Union has praised such procedures time and time again, but in 2013, only a very modest recommendation was issued by the European Commission.

Experience from other jurisdictions, such as Israel, shows that the procedure which the Commission outlined in its recent recommendation will not achieve its goals and will leave consumers with no workable redress mechanism. The basic principle of an efficient system of enforcement is that it makes unlawful behaviour inexpedient. The aim is to reach the optimal level of deterrence which will prevent the unlawful business from retaining its illicit gains. Necessary features of a proper redress system should include provisions for the inclusion of all consumers in a class unless they opt out, otherwise the number of plaintiffs would be too small and wrongdoers would not be deprived of their unlawful gains. In addition, financial incentives are necessary for an efficient private action mechanism. The Israeli model illustrates that the combination of an opt-out mechanism with financial incentives may lead to a flood of class actions. It is for this reason that financial incentives should be balanced by safeguards which come into effect at the earliest possible moment, even before an action is submitted to a court. Safeguards play an important role in preventing both frivolous actions and a flood of actions. In Israel, the new legislation brought with it many class actions. The sheer number of class actions has created new challenges for Israeli courts and the legal instrument which was introduced in Israel requires re-thinking.

This article advocates the importance of a coherent European collective redress mechanism. The evolution of the procedure in Europe and the recent

---

* Dr Ariel Flavian is an external lecturer at Haifa University and Partner at Herzog, Fox and Neeman (Israel). He would like to thank Dr Duncan Fairgrieve and Dr Christine Riefa for their useful comments. The contents remain the sole responsibility of the author.

Commission Recommendation are reviewed. A survey of the new Israeli class action model shows how the opt-out machinery and associated financial incentives promote private enforcement, yet require some changes to prevent the flood problem. In light of these developments, the question to be asked is how the Commission Recommendation can be changed to best serve the interest of consumers in the EU.

II. COLLECTIVE REDRESS IS AN IMPORTANT TOOL TO PROMOTE EFFICIENT TRADE

Consumer enforcement suffers from rational apathy, as private consumers find it too costly to become embroiled in legal proceedings. Individual victims often choose to take no action, or to take a free ride on the efforts of the few consumers who decide to resort to the law. The combined effect of rational apathy and free-riding leads to sub-optimal enforcement in consumer cases.[1]

The difficulty with many such cases is that the personal damages are scattered and there is no financial motive to bring individual actions for each small loss.[2] The expected award to the claimant pursuing such an action to judgment is lower than the expected litigation costs, and they have therefore been characterized as 'Negative Expected Value' suits.[3] Class actions are used to turn such suits into 'Positive Expected Value' suits by using economies of scale. By combining many claims based on similar questions of facts or law against the same defendant, an action can become economically valuable for the plaintiffs and for the lawyers, provided that a share of the action income is paid to them, or they are otherwise remunerated.[4]

---

[1] R Van den Bergh and L Visscher 'The Preventive Function of Collective Actions for Damages in Consumer Law' 1 *Erasmus Law Review* 2 (2008) 5.

[2] G Howells 'Cy-près for consumers: Ensuring class action reforms deal with "scattered damages"' in J Steel and W van Boom (eds) *Mass Justice* (Edward Elgar, 2011) 58–72.

[3] LA Bebchuk and A Klement, 'Negative-Expected-Value Suits' in C Sanchirico (ed), *Procedural Law and Economics* (Edward Elgar 2011); Harvard Law and Economics Discussion Paper No. 656, http://papers.ssrn.com/sol3/papers.cfm?abstract_id=1534703. See also A Conter and HB Newberg, *Newberg on Class Actions* (4th ed. West Group, 2002) S 2, §5:7; see also WF Schwartz and AL Wickelgren, 'Advantage Defendant: Why Sinking Litigation Costs Makes Negative Expected Value Defenses, but not Negative Expected Value Suits Credible' (2007), http://www.law.virginia.edu/pdf/olin/0708/wickelgren.pdf; see also JC Coffee, 'The Regulation of Entrepreneurial Litigation: Balancing Fairness and Efficiency in the Large Class Action' 54 *U Chi L Rev* (1987) 877, 904–906.

[4] OM Fiss, 'The Political Theory of the Class Action' 53 *Washington & Lee LRev* 1 (1996) 21.

Collective redress is also used to promote adherence to substantive legal norms.[5] Private enforcement is welcomed in areas where public enforcement is not sufficient. In these areas, private enforcement has a role in promoting the general good of the society. But privately led enforcement is generally less costly to society because it does not rely on public funds. It is also regarded as more efficient because private enforcers have a personal interest in the results of the action.[6] Individuals acting out of personal gain may further common interests shared by represented class members. The idea behind such proceedings is to achieve an optimal sanction so as to deter wrongdoing. Therefore, damages imposed are not always limited to those required to remedy losses suffered by group members; they may also be imposed as a means of disgorgement of ill-gotten gains, and to deter further violations.[7]

Collective redress enables consumers to combat abuse by companies, particularly those which are large and powerful. It helps balance the actors in consumer markets and enables court disputes to be brought in cases involving small amounts of personal damage, both by individuals and by large-scale consumers. It is also an important tool in advancing fair trade and public interest.

III. EUROPE'S NEED FOR A WORKABLE SCHEME OF COLLECTIVE REDRESS

With 500 million citizens in twenty-seven Member States, the EU is one of the largest markets in the world, generating an estimated 30% of nominal gross world product.[8] The problem faced by such a large and geographically widespread market is how to ensure that consumers have confidence when purchasing goods from other countries within the EU in order to maximize the advantages of the internal market. One of the clear requirements of a secure market is consumer assurance that if things go wrong, they have access to effective redress mechanisms.[9] Consumer disputes require tailored, cheap,

---

[5] S Goldstein, 'Class Actions in Israel' 13 *Int Cong Comp Law* 45 (1990) 65; See also Leave to Appeal Request No. 4556/94 (Israeli Supreme Court), *Tezet v. Zilbershatz* [26 May 2006] Piskey Din Mem Tet (5) 774.

[6] See for example GS Becker and GJ Stigler, 'Law Enforcement, Malfeasance, and Compensation of Enforcers' 3 *J Legal Stud* 1 (1974) 13.

[7] See, for example, The Securities Exchange Act 1934, s 78u-2(e) and 78u-3(e) from the US; See also S Kalb and MA Bohn, 'An Examination of the SEC's Application of Disgorgement in FCPA Resolutions', http://www.corporatecomplianceinsights.com/2010/ disgorgement-fcpa-how-applied-calculated/.

[8] http://en.wikipedia.org/wiki/Outline_of_the_European_Union.

[9] European Commission, Communication from the Commission on 'widening consumer access to alternative dispute resolution' Brussels 4 April 2001,http://ec.europa.eu/consumers/redress/out_of_court/adr/acce_just11_en.pdf.

and efficient mechanisms that do not create delays or generate costs disproportionate to the sums at stake.[10] The Single European Market confers many rights to individuals, but these are worthless if there is no effective means to enforce them.[11]

Studies have shown that European consumers feel that their rights as consumers are often left undefended when things go wrong. In its Green Paper on Consumer Collective Redress of November 2008, the EU concluded that the main barriers preventing consumers from enforcing their rights are the high cost of litigation and the complexity of procedures. According to the survey, one in five European consumers would not go to court for a sum of less than €1000. Half of those surveyed said that they would not go to court for a claim of less than €200.[12] Both the lack of faith in current systems and the lack of confidence could be addressed by introducing an EU-wide system of collective redress. Yet the evolution of collective redress in Europe has taken too long and made little progress.

IV. THE EVOLUTION OF COLLECTIVE REDRESS IN EUROPE

Following a decision of the European Parliament, the EC issued a recommendation that requires its members adopt a legal framework for collective redress within their national jurisdictions.[13] This followed a long debate in EU institutions and in Member States regarding the shape of the legal instrument to be adopted. EC officials have repeatedly stressed the importance of collective action for the confidence of consumer trade.[14] As early as 1997, the

---

[10] OECD, Recommendation on Consumer Dispute Resolution and Redress, available at http://www.oecd.org/dataoecd/43/50/38960101.pdf, 6.

[11] Commission Staff Working Document – Public Consultation, 'Towards a Coherent European Approach to Collective Redress' (SEC (2011)173) s 1, 1.

[12] European Commission, 'Green Paper on Consumer Collective Redress, COM(2008)794 final, 4, s 9, available at http://ec.europa.eu/consumers/redress_cons/ greenpaper_en.pdf.

[13] European Parliament, Resolution of 2 Feb 2012 'Towards a Coherent European Approach to Collective Redress', http://www.europarl.europa.eu/sides/getDoc.do?pubRef=-//EP//TEXT+TA+P7-TA-2012-0021+0+DOC+XML+V0//EN, Commission Recommendation of 11 June 2013 on common principles for injunctive and compensatory collective redress mechanisms in the Member States concerning violations of rights granted under Union Law (2013/396/EU), http://eur-lex.europa.eu/legal-content/EN/TXT/PDF/?uri=CELEX:32013 H 0396&from=EN.

[14] The first collective measure was Commission Regulation (EC) 1768/95 (implementing rules on the agricultural exemption for the purposes of safeguarding agricultural production). But later in 1998, the Commission introduced Directive 98/27/EC empowering consumer organisations to apply to courts in fellow Member States for an injunction against any infringement of consumer credit, consumer guarantees or the terms of package holidays, if it is perpetrated in that organisation's home state by an entity based in another Member State.

former Consumer Commissioner, Magdalena Kuneva, stated that one of the EC's plans for 2007–13 was to introduce a European system of collective redress for consumers.[15] This policy statement was followed by a public consultation paper and a green paper.[16] In February 2011, the Commission issued a Public Consultation Working Document noting the need for a coherent European approach to collective redress and soliciting comments on how to structure such a mechanism.[17] The Commissioner for Health and Consumer Policy, John Dalli, following Kuneva's statement, underlined the necessity of collective redress systems for consumers.[18]

There was, however, a continuing struggle over whether intervention at EU level was justified, and there were objections to interference in the way Member States approach the problem of consumer redress. The Commission claimed that the US-style class action is based on a 'toxic cocktail' of punitive damages, contingency fees, the opt-out system, and pre-trial discovery procedures, and said that such a model should not be introduced in Europe.[19] Leading commentators, meanwhile, claimed that judicial collective redress encourages frivolous, fraudulent, or abusive claims, and that it wastes the resources of defendants and courts, with deleterious effects on the economy, and could potentially lead the legal system into disrepute.[20] Alternative

---

[15] European Commission, Communication from the Commission to the Council, the European Parliament and the European Economic and Social Committee 'EU Consumer Policy strategy 2007–2013, Empowering consumers, enhancing their welfare, effectively protecting them' COM (2007) 99 final, http://ec.europa.eu/consumers/archive/overview/cons_policy/doc/EN_99.pdf.

[16] Respectively, http://ec.europa.eu/consumers/redress_cons/docs/consultation_paper2009.pdf, and European Commission, 'Green Paper on Consumer Collective Redress', COM(2008)794 final, http://ec.europa.eu/consumers/redress_cons/greenpaper_en.pdf.

[17] European Commission, Commission Staff Working Document – Public Consultation, 'Towards a Coherent European Approach to Collective Redress', SEC (2011) 173 final (4 Feb, 2011), http://ec.europa.eu/dgs/health_consumer/dgs_consultations/ca/docs/cr_onsultation_paper_en.pdf. The European Parliament stated in its recent report that the Commission has still not put forward convincing evidence that, pursuant to the principle of subsidiarity, action is needed at EU level to ensure that victims of unlawful behaviour are compensated for damages. See European Parliament Committee on Legal Affairs, 'Draft Report on Towards a Coherent European Approach to Collective Redress', 15 July 2011 (2011/20899INI), para D (3) 4.

[18] Commissioner John Dalli, 'Commissioner Dalli delivers a speech on Group Action: A necessity for consumers', http://ec.europa.eu/commission_2010-2014/dalli/docs/20101115_group_action.pdf.

[19] European Commission/DG SANCO, Green Paper on Consumer Collective Redress – Questions and Answers MEMO/08/741. See question No 9 at http://europa.eu/rapid/press ReleasesAction.do?reference=MEMO/08/741&format=HTML&aged=0&language=EN.

[20] See for example C Hodges, 'Response to Consultation: Towards a Coherent European Approach to Collective Redress' (28 April 2010), http://ec.europa.eu/competition/consultations/2011_collective_redress/university_of_oxford_en.pdf; and C Hodges: 'New Modes of Redress for Consumers: ADR and Regulation' (May 2012), http://papers.ssrn.com/sol3/papers.cfm?abstract_id=2126485.

mechanisms were offered, based on public regulatory powers to require or to enforce restitution and ADR,[21] yet judicial collective redress was largely favoured and has been developed by some Member States.[22] It is this background which explains why in June 2013 the Commission chose to publish a Recommendation,[23] rather than using a directly effective instrument binding all Member States.[24]

V. CORE PROVISIONS OF THE COMMISSION'S RECOMMENDATION

The purpose of the Recommendation, as stated in its first provision, is to facilitate access to justice for damages and injunctions against violations of EU law, in a way that is in accordance with the legal traditions of all Member States. The procedure envisaged is based on the activity of representative non-profit entities supervised by Member States.[25] In addition, Member States may empower public authorities to bring representative actions.[26] The preferred mechanism requires members of the affected class to opt into the action. Any exception to this principle should be duly justified by reasons of sound administration of justice.[27]

---

[21] See for example C Hodges, 'Collective Redress in Europe: The New Model' *Civil Justice Quarterly* (2010) 383-384.

[22] See for example the new Belgian law on collective redress adopted in March 2014. Explanatory remarks at http://www.collectiveredress.org/collective-redress/reports/belgium/_generalcollectiveredress. The UK draft Consumer Rights Bill (published June 2013) allows limited opt-out collective actions and an opt-out collective settlements in competition law. See also for the developments leading to the Commission Recommendation and the recent developments in the Dutch, German, France and Belgium jurisdictions S Voet: "European Collective Redress: A status Quaestionis", http://papers.ssrn.com/sol3/papers.cfm? abstract_id=2318809.

[23] See the Recommendation (above n 14).

[24] The European Law Institute mentioned in a recent statement that in the light of the current political situation, it is not realistic to anticipate a binding measure which will require Member States to implement new collective enforcement measures relating to damages. See European Law Institute, 'Statement of the European Law Institute on Collective Redress and Competition Damages Claims' (2014), http://www.europeanlawinstitute.eu/fileadmin/user_upload/p_eli/Projects/S-5-2014_Statement_on_Collective_Redress_and_Competition_Damages_Claims.pdf, 12. See also A Stadler 'The Commission's Recommendation on common principles of collective redress and private international law issues', http://www.nipr-online.eu/upload/documents/20140113T103840-NIPR%202013-4_Stadler.pdf. Prof. Stadler argues that the Commission Recommendation is an attempt to balance diverging interests: "It is a compromise based on the realistic estimation that, for political reasons, nothing else would be possible within the remaining time that the Barroso II Commission is in office", see 484.

[25] Para 3.

[26] Para 3 s 7.

[27] Para 3 ss 21–23.

The Commission Recommendation provides for dissemination of information on collective actions and free-of-charge national registries.[28] As for safeguards, it favours the loser-pays principle, a certification procedure, supervision of settlements, and a prohibition of punitive damages.[29] In addition, it provides that public enforcement should take precedence over private recourse, with the courts permitted to issue orders to stay private collective redress proceedings until public enforcement is exhausted.[30]

With regards to funding, the Recommendation provides that contingency fees should be supervised to limit any incentive to abusive litigation,[31] and that funding by third parties should be regulated by Member States and prohibited where it seems to be provided for an ulterior motive, or where it may unduly harm the procedure.[32] But all these are only guidelines for Member States to implement by July 2015, with the progress and influence of collective redress to be subject to further consideration in July 2017.[33]

VI. LESSONS FROM ISRAEL

Experience from jurisdictions outside the EU suggests that the vague procedure offered by the Commission's Recommendation will not work. The Israeli model in particular sheds light on the probable outcome of a privately-funded opt-out mechanism. It is a good comparison because the Israeli model is based on legal principles rooted in English law,[34] and is therefore not foreign to the European legal culture. The model developed in Israel may be much more acceptable in the eyes of European legislators than the US model, as it has not adopted all the class action features to which Europe objects, such as punitive damages, pre-trial discovery, and settlements which benefit only the class lawyers.

The provisions at the core of the ongoing EU class action debate have already been considered in Israel. The outcome was Israel's adoption of an up-to-date opt-out model, although in specialist cases (such as claims for large individual damages including mass tort actions) claims can be made on an opt-in basis. Of the many class actions submitted to the Israeli courts after 2006, not one has been based on the existing opt-in Israeli model.[35]

---

[28] Para 3 ss 10–12, 35–37 respectively.
[29] Para 3 ss 13, 8, 28 and 31 respectively.
[30] Para 3 ss 33–34.
[31] Para 3 ss 29–30.
[32] Para 3 ss 14–16 and 32.
[33] Para 3 ss 38–41.
[34] Rule 29 of Israel's Civil Law Procedure Regulations 5744-1984 was based on the English R.S.C. Ord. 15 r 12 (1), but abolished in 2006 with the introduction of the Israeli Class Action Law 5766–2006 (CAL).
[35] See Class Action Law 5766–2006, s 12, 'Class action by way of adherence', which has never been applied since its introduction.

Furthermore, the influence of organisational representation on the evolution of the Israeli case law has so far been very limited.[36] The Israeli experience, therefore, may supply some useful considerations as the final European model is shaped.

The number of collective redress cases in Europe is very low, with only few actions brought each year, whereas in Israel (with less than 1% of the population of Europe) there are many. Applications for class actions certified by the Israeli courts are often followed by judgments or settlements which accord benefits to Israeli consumers. However, some detrimental effects of the procedures should not be disregarded.

Class actions were developed in Israel gradually and very cautiously in order to avoid the legal hazards which had come to light in the US.[37] The first attempt was to use existing provisions of the Israeli rules of procedure which allowed joinder of interested parties.[38] This failed, because the Israeli court found that the provision was not detailed enough to cater for such a major legal phenomenon.[39] A second attempt was based on a sectoral approach, which promoted the inclusion of class action sections in specific legislation.[40] This also failed, because many legal actions were not based upon a certain act. For example, consumer cases not directly covered by the consumer protection law might be brought under provisions such as defec-

---

[36] With the very welcome exception of an organization set up by lawyers which has so far succeeded in influencing case law relating to unfair competition: see Court of Appeal (Tel Aviv) 2483-09-12 Hatzlacha V. Cohen Development.

[37] S Deutch, 'Consumer Class Actions: Are They a Solution for Enforcing Consumer Rights? The Israeli Model' 27 *Journal of Consumer Policy* 2 (2004) 179.

[38] It was thought that Rule 29 (based on the English concept of representative proceedings), in conjunction with Rule 19 of Israel's Civil Law Procedure Regulations 5744-1984 (permitting joinder of multiple claims when a common question of law or fact might arise) could enable claimants to bring American-style class actions for damages. See S Goldstein, 'Collective Representative Action: What and for What' 9 *Mishpatim* (1978) 416.

[39] Case no. 3126/00 (Israeli Supreme Court) *The State of Israel v. Eshet Project Management*, Tak El. Nun Zain (3) 220, (2003).

[40] These enactments were introduced gradually between 1988 and 2005 into specific areas of law, where there was the potential minimal harm for a large number of people, who were unlikely to sue unless they were given an incentive to do so. The existing legislation was amended to enable class actions for violations of the law, such as the Amendment to the 1981 Consumer Protection Law; Amendment to the 1968 Securities Act 5748-1988; The Prevention of Environmental Hazards (Civil Suits) Law 5752-1992; Amendment to the 1988 Business Restrictions Law 5752-1992; Amendment to the 1981 Banking (Consumer Services) Law 5756-1996; Male and Female Workers Equal Pay Law, 5756-1996; Amendment to the 1981 Oversight over Financial Services (Insurance) Law 5756-1996; The Companies Law 5759-1999; The Equal Rights of People with Disabilities Law 5758-1998; Supervision of Financial Services (Pension Funds) Law 5765-2005; Prevention of Environmental Hazards Act (Civil Actions) 5752-1992, s 5 and s 6; The Interest Law 5717-1957 (limits permitted interest rates); Amendment to the 1981 Banking (Consumer Services) Law 5756-1996.

tive products, tort, or contract law. As a result, the class action provision in the specific enactments could not assist consumers in recovering their losses.

The current legal position was reached in 2006, when Israel's Class Action Law (CAL) was introduced. The collective machinery in Israel is now embodied in a binding and detailed act which contains 45 sections (by comparison, US Federal Rule of Civil Procedure 23 contains only 8 sections),[41] each of which was considered in great detail by the legislature. Unlike the Commission Recommendation and the rules of civil procedure in England and Wales, which have influenced the Israeli system in the past, class actions in Israel are now enshrined in primary legislation, rather than in secondary legislation of civil procedure. The advantage of primary legislation is that it prevails over secondary legislation, allowing the Israeli enactment to defeat any pre-existing contradictory rules of procedure and to prevent misuse or interpretations different from the legislation.

VII. PROVISIONS AT THE HEART OF THE NEW ISRAELI MODEL

Four major goals are specified in Section 1 of Israel's Class Action Law 5766-2006:[42] (1) to promote access to justice in general, with particular regard to segments of the population not expected to bring individual actions; (2) to enforce the relevant law in the areas subject to such actions and to deter infringements of this law; (3) to impose appropriate remedies to benefit injured parties; and (4) to assist in the fair and effective management of claims.[43]

In essence, the effectiveness of the Israeli system rests on four main pillars in the CAL: Firstly an opt-out provision, which enables large classes to group together. Secondly, the wide range of possible representatives from both the private and public sectors, including organisations which have operated continuously for at least a year in the relevant area, provided that their work is undertaken for non-political motives. The class action law allows stand-alone actions to be brought by all representatives without any filtering machinery before they reach court, subject to an in-court certification procedure. Thirdly, financial incentives, contingency fees, and possible funding by

---

[41] United States Federal Rules of Civil Procedure, rules 23(a)–(h), http://www.law.cornell.edu/rules/_frcp/rule_23.

[42] Published in Hebrew on Israel's Department of Trade and Industry website, http://www.tamas.gov.il/NR/exeres/C2B5FF40-FE01-4D04-A5DC-155A9511D9A5.htm. For a translation see http://weblaw.haifa.ac.il/en/JudgesAcademy/workshop3/Documents/R/5/Class_Action_Law%20in%20Israel%202006.pdf.

[43] In a report on class actions, the Ontario Law Reform Commission in Canada (1982) [Vol 1 Ch 2] described the goals of class actions as improved access to justice, judicial economy, and modification of behaviour.

a special 'class action fund,' with no court fees levied on the submission of class actions. Fourthly, the CAL has a very wide scope which allows class actions to be brought in many areas of law, including consumer law (even against banks and insurance companies), financial markets, environmental law, and employment law. Even actions against the state or state bodies for repayment of unlawful levies are permitted, subject to extensive defences and limitations.

The remarkable openness of the Israeli system derives from the courts' wide notice powers to publish announcements and deliver updates from any critical point of a collective action to the general public, to relevant interested organisations, to state bodies, and to class members (any of whom may raise objections or join the procedure).[44] A further source of transparency in the Israeli model is a free online registry established by the CAL to track and publish developments in each collective action.[45] The registry contains all the relevant information about class actions commenced after March 2007, including the date the action was submitted, the court where it is managed, the essence of the action, the representing plaintiff, the defendant, the description of the represented class, the certification decision, proposed compromise agreements, applications for voluntary dismissal, and any notices to group members. In addition, decisions in cases are published on the registry. The documents in the registry may be viewed in pdf-format, enabling class members and the general public to follow all the developments and issues in every filed case.

VIII. THE EFFECT OF THE NEW ISRAELI MODEL

This new model has revolutionized Israeli consumer law, improving access to justice in cases which otherwise would not been submitted to the courts. Banks have been ordered to repay unlawful charges,[46] insurance companies have been forced to refund consumers who had paid excessive charges for insurance premiums,[47] and even the sizes of crisp packets and other food products have been enlarged.[48] In these and many other respects, Israeli

---

[44] Notices are governed by s 25 of the Class Action Law 5766–2006. For the right of interested bodies to participate in hearings see s 15.

[45] Class Action Law 5766–2006, s 28.

[46] For example, Case no. 1805-09 (District Court of Tel Aviv) *Bashan v. Bank Hapoalim* (2009), concerning overcharging for the production of documents.

[47] For example, Case no. 1251/07 (District Court of Tel Aviv) *Keidar v. Dikla* (2007), concerning unlawful payments for insurance to which the insured were eligible by law. Payments were made to the insured.

[48] In Case no. 1953/06 (District Court of Tel Aviv) *Amar Ashaer v. Osem* (2006), the packets of crisps known as Bisli were ordered to be enlarged after the defendants were found to have misled people by making the packets smaller without changing the weight shown or the price.

consumers are better placed thanks to the use of class actions following the introduction of the CAL. For the first time too, the courts have awarded damages in favour of the general public, using the US doctrine of fluid damages.[49]

However, the procedure set down in the Israeli legislation has increased access to justice so substantially that it has brought a flood of actions. The comparison between the number of claims in Israel and the number of claims in EU Member States shows that the Israeli system is highly efficient – arguably too efficient – as so many actions for damages are brought before the courts. Israel's class action registry shows that between March 2007 and the end of November 2014, some 4795 collective actions were brought. Some 1200 new actions were brought to the courts in 2013, with just as many in 2014.[50] Typically, these involve very high sums because of the large classes represented (none being based on the opt-in machinery). The registry reveals that since implementation of the CAL, most actions have related to consumer issues (approximately 78%), whereas prior to the CAL they comprised only 40% of class action applications.[51] They are divided as follows:[52]

- 78% are consumer related (food industry 14.4%; telecommunications and internet providers 12.8%; banks 9.7%; insurance 8.8%). These consumer actions also involve actions in the transportation sector and other areas relating to the purchase of goods or services;
- 15.3% relate to taxation;
- 5.7 % relate to labour issues;
- Less than 1% relate to competition or environmental issues.

A survey by the Israeli financial newspaper *Globes* showed that in 2010, the average claim was for NIS 564m (approximately GBP 100m) and the average claim in the first six months of 2011 was NIS 131m (GBP 22m).[53] The highest value claims were against telecommunications and internet companies, where the average claim in 2010 was for NIS 283m (GBP 65m) and the figure for the first six months of 2011 was NIS 100m (GBP 16 million). The average claim against a local authority in 2010 was NIS 22m (GBP 3.5m) and the figure for the first six months of 2011 was NIS 26m (GBP 4.5 m).

---

[49] Appeal No. 10085/08 (Supreme Court) *Tnuva v. Rabi* (2011).
[50] Class Actions Registry at http://elyon1.court.gov.il/heb/tovanot_y/list.htm.
[51] Deutch (above n 37).
[52] According to an examination made by the author of 580 actions registered in the Israeli Registry of Class Actions based on class actions submitted before 2010.
[53] 'Sharp Increase in Class Action Suits Submitted, particularly against Communications Companies' *Globes* (6 July 2011) at http://www.globes.co.il/news/article.aspx?did=1000661350?.

The strong impact of such court procedures may have an adverse effect on Israel's market economy. Companies have to concentrate more on legal defence than previously rather than on production, and considerable resources are being spent on defence against legal actions, which are in many cases unsubstantiated and end in a voluntary dismissal or compromises with little benefit to consumers.[54]

The proliferation of cases is unhindered, because no court fee is required to file an action and there is no barrier to bring a stand-alone class action under the Israeli law. In addition, when an application fails to go through the certification stage, the court expenses imposed on the plaintiffs are usually low. Despite a well-developed scheme of judicial safeguards, the huge number of actions being submitted will necessitate some revision of the procedures, yet no voices in Israel are calling for the abolition of the Class Action Law. Its benefits are generally acknowledged as outweighing its drawbacks.

IX. THE OPERATION OF SAFEGUARDS IN ISRAEL

The Israeli legislature was well aware of the problematic side of class actions and the risk of abuse. There was no doubt that frivolous suits can have an adverse effect on the market.[55] Unmeritorious claims can force defendants to compromise and settle a case solely to save the costs of defence in such an action. When collective proceedings are led by private individuals, there can also be major problems of agency involving either with the representative plaintiff or with the attorney representing the class.[56]

The Israeli regime provides a range of safeguards to deal with these hazards. To begin with, a certification process is imposed to filter out unmeritorious claims after their submission to the courts.[57] The courts must exam-

---

[54] R Adini, 'This is also a Way to End Up: On Voluntary Dismissals in Class Actions' forthcoming, Hapraklit Volume Nun Bet, at http://www.hapraklit.co.il/_Uploads/__dbsAttachedFiles/Adini_Article.pdf.

[55] R Van den Bergh and L Visscher, 'The Preventive Function of Collective Actions for Damages in Consumer Law' 1 *Erasmus Law Review* 2 (2008) 5, http://papers.ssrn.com/sol3/_papers.cfm?abstract_id=1101377. AI Vogelsang, N Ramphal, SJ Carrol and NM Pace, 'Economic analysis of consumer class actions in regulated industries', 32 *Journal of Regulatory Economics* 1 (2007) 87–104.

[56] EA Posner, 'Agency Models in Law and Economics' (2000), University of Chicago Law School, John M. Olin Law and Economics Working Paper No. 92, available at http://www.law.uchicago.edu/node/1294. J-J Laffont and D Martimort, *The Theory of Incentives: The Principal-Agent Model* (Princeton University Press, 2001). MD Whinston, JR Green and A Mas-Colell, *Microeconomic Theory* (OUP, 1995). A Klement, 'Who Should Guard the Guardians? A New Approach for Monitoring Class Action Lawyers', http://www.faculty.idc.ac.il/klement/EngArt/TROL.pdf.

[57] Class Action Law 5766–2006, s 8.

ine whether the representatives can properly represent the interests of the class, and some preconditions must be met. These preconditions include showing that the claim is prima facie based on its merits, the good faith of the representatives and the capability is properly ensured to represent the class (both the representative plaintiff and class lawyer may be examined). In addition, there must be sufficient common questions of law or fact to allow a collective procedure. The judge has a specific power to order replacement of representatives (ie, class lawyer or representative plaintiff) when it is found that a representative did not act in the interests of the class members, but the claim nevertheless appears meritorious.[58] The judge may also order the division of the class into subclasses if conflicts of interest exist between class members.[59]

Compromises and voluntary dismissal of the action are regarded as carrying the risk of abuse,[60] so judges are instructed not to allow arrangements between the parties unless they benefit the class members who are not normally present at trial. By acting in bad faith or for their own benefit at the expense of class members, representatives can cause actions to be terminated. The law therefore imposes strict supervision of compromises and voluntary dismissals. This includes routine use of expert evidence to examine the economic benefits to the class members of the suggested settlement.[61] The court may conclude that an expert opinion is unnecessary only for 'special reasons,' for example, where the compromise requires legal evaluation of the strength of the arguments of the parties,[62] or where the compromise is led by the court.[63] In addition, the parties and the lawyers on both sides are required to confirm by sworn affidavit that there are no additional agreements which remain undisclosed to the public.[64] Any compromise is also sent to relevant bodies, the Attorney General, and class members, enabling any of these to object to the compromise and allowing class members to opt out of the suggested settlement if they wish.

Lawyer's fees are supervised under Israeli law. The class lawyer or the plaintiff representative should not accept any payment additional to that set by the court.[65] The law also establishes criteria for representative remuneration, to ensure that payment corresponds to the benefit class members or the

---

[58] CAL, s 8 (c)(2).
[59] CAL, s 10 (c).
[60] CAL, ss 18–19 and 16 respectively.
[61] CAL, s 19 (b). This provision is intended to combat 'sweetheart settlements' and the problems of evaluation of coupons and other undertakings which were heavily criticized in the US).
[62] CAL, s 19 (b).
[63] E.g. Appeal 8479/02 (Israeli Supreme Court) *Sabo v. the Israeli airport authority*.
[64] CAL, s 18 (b) relating to compromise agreements and s 16 (b) in relation to voluntary dismissal.
[65] CAL, s 22.

general public.[66] The principle of 'the loser pays' – under which the losing party pays the costs of the winning party – may be overturned in class actions, so that if an action has benefited the members or to the general public despite finally being dismissed, the winning party may have to pay the costs of the unsuccessful applicant.[67]

All other financial transactions between the representatives and the defendants are supervised. This includes the distribution of funds to the class members or to other beneficiaries named by the court, and in order to prevent the misallocation of funds, the judge has the power to appoint trustees to supervise the collection of damages.[68]

Nonetheless, all these safeguards do not appear to be sufficient to stem the tide of claims now flooding the Israeli courts. How, then, can the Israeli model be fine-tuned before it is recommended to Europe?

X. PROPOSED CHANGES TO THE ISRAELI SYSTEM

The principal change which I would recommend to the Israeli system is the introduction of a mechanism to filter the flood of stand-alone claims. The aim would be to filter out unmeritorious actions at the outset to prevent them from reaching court. One suitable filter might be the prioritizing of out-of-court settlements by establishing a compulsory collective ADR mechanism. A second change might be to introduce a compulsory stage prior to court in which a claim is submitted to an appropriate public body capable of investigating a possible breach of the law (where such a body exists), and then to allow disputes to be submitted to court only after a public regulatory finding has authorized further action.[69] Public enforcement seems to be preferred by leading scholars,[70] though it should be born in mind that public enforcers are short of funds and their record as collectors of damages for consumers has not been good. Public enforcers are likely to be objective and to look at the general good of all players in the market, whereas private enforcers may prioritize their own interests over the class members' inter-

---

[66] CAL, s 22 sets the criteria to the representative plaintiff and s 23 sets the criteria for the payments to the class lawyer.
[67] CAL, s 22 (c).
[68] CAL, s 20.
[69] ADR and public enforcement were both envisaged by the recent commission: see part 3 s 26, 33–34.
[70] Hodges (above n 21), arguing that if ADR proceedings do not bring the parties to a consensual solution, a regulatory public body should intervene. Court procedure would act as a stick if parties (especially the defendants) knew that failure to settle would result in a class action against them.

ests.[71] This is why in 2007 Britain's Office of Fair Trading took the view that public and private enforcement are complementary: the first is best suited to dealing with wrongful activities and practices, while the second helps to deter improper practice by businesses because of the magnitude of the possible damages.[72] This means that follow-on actions should be given preference over stand-alone actions. There may be some ways to award priority to public enforcement, for example, by releasing them from the certification procedure, or to require plaintiffs in stand-alone actions to provide surety to cover the defendant's expenses. In addition, as far as stand-alone actions are concerned, lawyers' fees should be subject to tighter supervision and should be based directly on the sums distributed to the class members.[73] The Israeli model should also be made friendlier to organisational enforcement, with an assumption that supervised and licensed organisations are trustworthy representatives in class actions.[74]

XI. CHANGES FOR THE EU BASED ON THE ISRAELI MODEL

The evidence from Israel shows that an opt-in mechanism does not work. None of the actions in Israel since 2007 have used this machinery. This is in-line with evidence from the US showing that before opt-out machinery was introduced in 1966, class actions were never brought at all.[75]

A very thorough British study led by Rachael Mulheron showed that the rates of participation are very low in opt-in collective redress cases, whereas opt-out class actions are run on behalf of large groups.[76] The creation of a large group of plaintiffs makes an action more viable and creates an incentive for lawyers.

---

[71] WPJ Wils, 'The Relationship between Public Antitrust Enforcement and Private Actions for Damages' 2 *World Competition* 1 (2009) 3–26.

[72] OFT, 'Private actions in competition law: effective redress for consumers and business', Discussion paper OFT916, (April 2007) at http://www.oft.gov.uk/shared_oft/reports/comp_policy/oft916.pdf.

[73] In March 2014 some members of the Israeli Knesset proposed a change to the law, ia adopting such a provision.

[74] This should be done by abolishing the restriction in CAL, s 4 (a) 3 on organizational class actions where private action is possible.

[75] EF Sherman, 'American Class Actions: Significant Features and Developing Alternatives in Foreign Legal Systems', (2003) 215 *FRD* 130–3; also *Amchem Products, Inc et al v Windsor et al* 521 US 591, 592 (1997), in which it was said that "Rule 23(b)(3) was the most adventuresome innovation of the 1966 Amendments, permitting judgments for money that would bind all class members save those who opt out."

[76] R Mulheron, 'Reform of Collective Redress in England and Wales: A Perspective of Need' (Civil Justice Council, 2008), http://www.judiciary.gov.uk/wp-content/uploads/JCO/Documents/CJC/Publications/Other+papers/reform-of-collective-redress.pdf. Opt-in, see 154–56. Opt-out, see 147–153.

Collective redress has a deterrent effect and can prevent improper behaviour by making wrongdoers pay in full for the damage and costs inflicted on others.[77] Some commentators claim that the main purpose of class actions is to use private litigation, not primarily for compensatory purposes, but as a procedural device to assure adherence to substantive legal norms.[78] This means that in order to achieve optimal deterrence, the number of class members should be sufficient to force wrongdoers to give up their unlawful profits. In opt-in cases, however, some illicit gain may remain in the hands of the wrongdoer.[79]

There are calls in Europe to adopt a compromise provision granting judicial discretion to decide whether a case will be heard on an opt-out basis.[80] The problem is that such a mixed model creates uncertainty. If the representatives are to spend their time and resources on the case, they want to know from the outset that the case involves large classes of represented persons, so as to take the advantage of economies of scale. Another disadvantage of giving judges this discretion to decide whether to use an opt-in or an opt-out model is that it might unnecessarily burden judges and could invite additional litigation challenging the judge's decision.

XII. FINANCIAL INCENTIVES AS A LEGITIMATE WAY TO FINANCE PRIVATE ACTIONS

In the Israeli model, collective actions are most often led by private individuals who may be liable to pay the court fees and other party expenses at the end of the case. Some incentives should therefore be introduced in order to persuade such representatives to take the risk. The representative plaintiff usually cannot pay the lawyers' fees, because his personal claim is very small. Despite reservations about the structure of lawyers' fees, the Israeli legislature therefore took the view that since the lawyer has an entrepreneurial role in bringing a collective action, some remuneration should be offered. This is one of the provisions which make the Israeli model able to rely on efficient private enforcement. Contingency fees are, however, foreign to the litigation

---

[77] Klement (above n 56).

[78] S Goldstein, 'Class Actions in Israel' 13 *Int Cong Comp Law* 45 (1990) 65. See also Leave to Appeal Request No. 4556/94 (Israeli Supreme Court), *Tezet v. Zilbershatz*, [26 May 2006], Piskey Din Mem Tet (5) 774.

[79] European Commission 'Commission Staff Working Paper Accompanying the White Paper on Damages actions for breach of the EC antitrust rules' (COM(2008) 165 final, SEC(2008) 404), http://eur-lex.europa.eu/LexUriServ/LexUriServ.do?uri=CELEX:52008SC0404:EN:NOT. See s 58.

[80] See the recent ELI statement cited in n 24 particularly on the Belgian model (42–46).

culture of some European jurisdictions. There is a fear in Europe that lawyers will profit at the expense of the class members. The Commission Recommendation provides that the methods of calculating legal fees should not create any incentive to litigate (s 29). It also provides that contingency fees, which risk creating an incentive for abusive litigation, be regulated by the Member States, taking into account the right of group members to full compensation (s 30). The Commission does not preclude contingency fees so long as they are regulated in a manner that is not harmful to the class members and will not lead to unnecessary litigation.

Another means of finance, preferred by the Commission, is supervised third-party funding.[81] Some jurisdictions which object to contingency fees have already adopted a system of third-party funding. In the Netherlands, for example, members of the bar are not permitted to charge contingency fees, so entrepreneurs fill the gap in financing the expenses of managing the action.[82] The difference between funding by contingency fees and funding by a third party is not crucial, since third-party funders, as participants in the procedure, obtain a share of any gain from the litigation, though their influence on the procedure is less than that of the lawyers running cases in court. The advantage of contingency fees is that lawyers are bound by the rules of ethics and supervised by the law commission in each Member State, and therefore pose less of a risk than private, unsupervised third-party funders.

Finance may also be available from a class action fund such as that set up under Section 27 of the Israeli CAL. This is governed by an independent body, although at present its financial capacity is very restricted. There are suggestions that by diverting all *cy-près* distributions from successful actions into this fund, it could be built to assist future actions.

Scholars who have investigated the use of contingency fees have found that they give rise to significantly greater numbers of frivolous or fraudulent claims.[83] On the other hand, CJC research has concluded that contingency fees improve the quality of claims brought to justice.[84] There is no doubt that

---

[81] See part 3 ss 14–16 .

[82] I Tzankova, 'Class Actions, Group Litigation and Other Forms of Collective Litigation: Dutch Report', http://globalclassactions.stanford.edu/sites/default/files/documents/Netherlands_National_Report.pdf.

[83] E Helland and AT Tabarrok, 'Contingency Fees, Settlement Delay and Low-Quality Litigation: Empirical Evidence from Two Datasets' 19 *The Journal of Law Economics and Organization* 2 (2003) 517–542, http://ssrn.com/abstract=405500 http://papers.ssrn.com/sol3papers.cfm?abstract_id=405500; KM Clermont and JD Currivan 'Improving on the Contingency Fee' 63 *Cornell Law Review* (1978) 529; J Dana and K Spier, 'Expertise and Contingent Fees: The Role of Asymmetric Information in Attorney Compensation' 9 *J Law Econ Org* (1993) 349; H M Kritzer, *Risks, Regulations and Rewards: Contingency Fee Legal Practice in the United States* (Stanford University Press, 2004).

[84] RL Moorhead, 'Improving Access to Justice, Contingency Fees: A Study of Their Operation in the United States' (Nov 17, 2008), http://ssrn.com/abstracts=1302843.

without contingency fees, there is no incentive for lawyers to perform an entrepreneurial role. Contingency fees are particularly appropriate to collective redress cases because the individual representative cannot pay the legal fees and other expenses necessary for a case against large companies, which are usually the defendants in these actions. It is reasonable that lawyers should be compensated for the risk that they may not be paid at all if the action fails, and the risk that lawyers who have to finance an action have no coverage of their expenses.

Any future EU framework for collective redress with private enforcement needs to include a measure compelling member states to allow financial incentives and funding, either by a collective redress fund or by supervised funders.

XIII. WHY THE EU SHOULD PROGRESS TO A BINDING PROCEDURE

Should the imposition of collective redress by the EU be governed by a binding instrument or should it draw only broad principles and leave the implementation to individual Member States? The latter approach might make the introduction of a new model more acceptable to Member States, but will lead to incoherency amongst Member States. The introduction of a unified and binding European collective action model is not at all simple. Basic features of the procedure vary between Member States, with some such as Portugal using an opt-out mechanism, while others such as France strongly object.

On the other hand, detailed legislation benefits from certainty and coherence. A non-binding European provision will not result in a single coherent procedure model, because each Member State will interpret the principles so as not to clash with its national laws. As a result, consumers may feel more confident about purchasing goods from some Member States than from others, and some countries' procedures will serve consumers better than others do. In order to provide coherence, the EU should insist upon introducing a binding procedure that includes a unified registry, an opt-out mechanism and incentives for lawyers and representatives. The procedure should take the form of a clear and effective regulation on collective redress adopted by all Member States. This must be clear and directly applicable to individuals in all Member States in order to avoid the risk of inconsistent implementation.

XIV. CONCLUSION

For the sake of safe trade between Member States in the enormous market of the EU, consumers must have the power and confidence to enforce their consumer rights. The problem with enforcement of consumer rights is often that the personal return for each consumer is very low and only the aggregation of personal rights makes legal action economically viable. The progress in Europe towards the introduction of a collective redress mechanism has been very slow so far, but the Commission Recommendation of June 2013 is certainly a step forward. The Israeli class action system has rendered consumer law in Israel amongst the world leaders, and dramatically improved consumer rights. The only evident problem with the model is that it has promoted too many legal proceedings which are expensive and wasteful. However, the model can be improved if Israel moves towards a better-balanced system by adopting pre-trial filtering mechanisms. Israel's experience certainly suggests that the introduction of a binding and balanced collective action system in the EU would dramatically improve the enforcement of consumer rights.

2

Specific Areas of Collective Redress in Europe

Collective Redress and Product Liability in the European Union: The Outcome of a Legal Transplant in Italy

Cristina Poncibò and Eleonora Rajneri*

I. INTRODUCTION

This chapter discusses whether introducing a mechanism for collective redress may significantly contribute to enhancing the level of consumer protection in product liability litigation in the European Union. It starts by considering the Italian experience following the introduction of the *azione di classe* and shows the very limited impact of the new action on product liability litigation. In fact, the legal transplant of a judicial collective redress mechanism took place in a legal system where the driving forces behind collective redress (ie, consumer associations, entrepreneurial lawyers and judicial case management) are absent and where the legal profession fears opening the Pandora's box known as the class action. In order to be successful, such a transplant should be 'contextualized' within the legal system: collective redress never travels alone. In the EU, collective redress represents a more sophisticated procedural tool with respect to the joinder of parties. However, because of the conservative approach, collective redress is not producing a cultural revolution in advancing product liability mass litigation so far.

II. COLLECTIVE REDRESS AND PRODUCT LIABILITY LITIGATION IN ITALY

A. General Information

Under Italian Law, Article 2043 of the Italian Civil Code (ICC) states the general principle of *neminem laedere* coexists with the strict liability system

---

* Lecturer, Centre for Comparative and Transnational Law, University of Turin; Research Fellow at the IUSE. Cristina Poncibò is the author of paragraphs I, II, III, IV, V and VI; Professor, University of Eastern Piedmont; Research Fellow at the IUSE. Eleonora Rajneri is the author of paragraph VII.

governed by Legislative Decree No. 224/1998,[1] which first implemented the Product Liability Directive.[2]

The Consumer Code consolidates the laws concerning consumer law (eg, consumers' rights, contracts, unfair commercial practices, sale guarantees and litigation) in order to ensure a high level of protection for consumers and users in accordance with the principles of EU legislation.[3] With respect to product liability, the Consumer Code provides a strict product liability regime.[4] It defines 'product,' 'defective product,' 'manufacturer,' 'supplier,' and the scope of manufacturers' and suppliers' liability. The injured party must prove the damage, the defect in the product, and the related causation, but not the manufacturer's liability. Article 117 of the Consumer Code provides that a product is defective when it does not provide the safety that one can reasonably expect, considering all circumstances.[5] Among the circumstances are the way in which the product was distributed; its packaging, evident features, instructions and warnings supplied, the product's reasonably expected use and life cycle and the period during which the product was distributed. Furthermore, a product is not defective simply because the manufacturer markets a safer one later. A product is defective if it does not offer the safety normally offered by other products in the same category. Twenty-six years after Parliament passed Legislative Decree No. 224/1998, the case law is still quite limited.[6] In commenting on the very limited application of the law, one author expressly uses the word 'failure.'[7] Does Italy represent a paradise for product safety? This is highly improbable, even though the scope of Legislative Decree No. 224/1998 was to enhance

---

[1] E Rajneri, 'Interaction Between the European Directive on Product Liability and the Former Liability Regime in Italy' in D Fairgrieve (ed), *Product Liability Law in Comparative Perspective* (Cambridge University Press, 2005), 67–82.

[2] Council Directive (EC) 85/374 on the approximation of the laws, regulations and administrative provisions of the Member States concerning liability for defective products, [1995] OJ L 210 as amended [1995] OJ L 141 ('Product Liability Directive').

[3] Legislative Decree No. 206/2005 (Consumer Code). It has consolidated the provisions of Legislative Decree No. 224/1998.

[4] The Italian Supreme Court confirmed (judgment no. 13432/2010) the double-track protection system, based on both the EU product liability regime and domestic rules on tortious liabilities. In a case concerning damage caused by a defective car, the Supreme Court ruled that product liability claims could be grounded in the tort rules based on fault or negligence set out in art 2043 of the ICC, in addition to the strict-liability regime under the Product Liability Directive.

[5] Rajneri (above note 1).

[6] L Frata, 'L'azione di classe e la responsabilità da prodotto difettoso: quali scenari futuri' 17 *Danno e responsabilità* (2012) 48. In the first ten years after the introduction of the discipline (1988), the Courts decided five cases.

[7] G Ponzanelli, 'Armonizzazione del diritto v. protezione del consumatore: il caso della responsabilità del produttore', 3 *Danno e responsabilità* (2002) 728.

the level of consumer protection against defective products. The many reasons for this failure include the limitations of the recoverable damage, the difficulty in satisfying the burden of proof before the courts and the lack of a collective redress mechanism for damages.[8] In fact, before the introduction of the *azione di classe*, forms of collective action already existed in Italy concerning consumer rights and labour law, but were limited to injunctive relief (Article 139 of the Consumer Code). Existing (but ineffective) mechanisms rely on the impulse of consumer associations, which have no standing in actions to recover damages and can only obtain cease and desist orders to protect consumer interests.[9]

B. The Italian Way: Product Liability Litigation before a Criminal Court

Over the last two decades or so, damaged parties have advanced a significant number of cases of mass torts for product liability through criminal proceedings (*costituzione di parte civile nel processo penale*, see Section III, B).

The Italian Constitution (Article 112 Constitution) and the Italian Code of Criminal Procedure (Article 50 CPC) oblige public prosecutors to bring a criminal action against the defendants in cases of homicide or serious personal injury, as well as for most other criminal offences. In accordance with the provisions of Article 582 of the Italian Criminal Code, injured parties only prosecute minor personal injuries following a complaint. These criminal charges are subject to compulsory prosecution under Italian law.

Italian criminal courts are empowered to decide whether victims are entitled to compensation under Article 185 of the Italian Criminal Code. The article provides that: "Every crime requires restoration according to civil law. Every crime which has caused patrimonial or non-patrimonial damage obliges the perpetrators and the persons who, according to the civil law, are responsible for his or her actions to pay compensation."

In practice, all those harmed by a crime can claim compensation and restitution by appearing as *parte civile* before a criminal court, in accordance with Article 74 of the Italian Code of Criminal Procedure. The *parte civile* is an institution, which features in all codes influenced by the French Code of Criminal Procedure.[10]

---

[8] The EU Commission has openly defined the expression 'Collective redress' in its Communication 'Towards a European Horizontal Framework for Collective Redress', COM(2013) 401 final.

[9] EU Commission, Evaluation of the effectiveness and efficiency of collective redress mechanisms in the European Union (2008), Country report Italy prepared for Civil Consulting and Oxford Economics by HW Micklitz and C Poncibò, 18 August 2008, http://ec.europa.eu/consumers/archive/redress_cons/it-country-report-final.pdf.

[10] N Coggiola and M Graziadei 'The Italian 'Eternit Trial': Litigating Massive Asbestos Damage in a Criminal Court', in WH Van Boom and G Wagner (eds), *Mass Torts in Europe: Cases and Reflections, Tort and Insurance Law* (De Gruyter, 2014), vol. 34, 29.

Readers who are not familiar with the role played by the *parte civile* in criminal proceedings should therefore turn to general works on comparative criminal and civil procedure in order to be better acquainted with it. Under the Italian Code of Criminal Procedure, those who have suffered damage as a consequence of a crime, may decide to be a party to the criminal court proceedings as *parte civile*, to claim compensation, possibly on an interim basis, or restitution in kind from the defendant (and/or the parties who are jointly liable with the defendant). As an alternative, they may decide not to play any role in the criminal proceedings, but rely on the findings and records of the criminal court. In this case, the judgment shall be *res judicata* in respect to subsequent civil proceedings to recover damages. Furthermore, any claimant who does not pursue either course may start parallel and independent civil proceedings (see Articles 75, 651, 652 Code of Criminal Procedure). In the latter case, criminal and civil court proceedings and their outcomes shall be completely independent from one another, and may eventually lead to different and conflicting outcomes.

The *parte civile* has the autonomous power to bring evidence to the criminal court and to assist the prosecutor in proving whether the defendant is guilty. It can therefore, for example, inspect documents and cross-examine witnesses at the trial, and present its own conclusions to the court. Quite often, the reason for the claimant being present at the criminal proceedings as *parte civile* – rather than initiating parallel civil proceedings – is to take advantage of the fact that the court provides and pays for the often needed, but expensive, scientific and medical expert opinions. In addition, the *parte civile* can also appoint experts. Furthermore, if a claimant appears before the court in the capacity of *parte civile*, the evidence heard by the court is formed with the material contribution of the *parte civile* who has the power, for example, to cross-examine witnesses. This may be important to reach a single decision on the issue of criminal and civil liability. As mentioned above, the claimant may also forego the right to present his case to the court as *parte civile*, and decide to bring a separate civil action for damages before a civil court. In this case, however, the burden of proof concerning the facts of the case is entirely on him.

Having considered the above, the absence of any collective redress mechanism becomes less important in damage claims for economic loss lodged in criminal proceedings. This explains why the Milan criminal proceedings have amassed a considerable backlog of civil claims.[11] This also happened in the Italian '*Eternit* trial,'[12] the largest criminal case ever prosecuted in Europe for asbestos-related deaths, injuries, and damages. Eternit was not the only

---

[11] This also happened with respect to Italian financial scandals, such as the Parmalat litigation.
[12] Coggiola and Graziadei (above n 10).

company in Italy which, by working with asbestos, involved its managers in committing criminal offences related to the violation of rules on safety at work.

From our perspective, we assert that the new collective redress mechanism, the *azione di classe* examined below, would not have changed the outcome; the *azione di classe* limited to consumer protection would not have covered the *Eternit* mass litigation.

C. Will the Introduction of the 'Azione di Classe' Change the Litigation Landscape of Product Liability?

The *azione di classe* may be particularly relevant in the field of product liability law. In this case, the liability regime has a strong deterrence function because it aims to induce firms to increase investment to ensure the safety of their products.

Debates about the enactment of a means of collective redress in the Italian legal system have been going on for years. At the end of 2007, Article 140-bis of the Consumer Code was introduced in the original text of the Consumer Code, but its application was postponed several times. In July 2009, the original version of Article 140-bis was replaced in its entirety with the current article, introducing the new collective redress mechanisms beginning on 1 January 2010.[13] Subsequently, Article 6 of Law Decree no. 1 dated 24 January 2012, ratified by Law no. 27 dated 24 March 2012, added a further set of amendments. The recent changes, effective as of 25 March 2012, lowered one of the admissibility thresholds. The lowered threshold provided that the *azione di classe* were inadmissible if class members' rights were not 'identical,' whereas these rights now need to be homogeneous, which evidently widens the spectrum to allow claimants who have similar, but not identical, claims.

1. Scope of the action: product liability cases

The *azione di classe* protects consumers. This means that only a consumer may file a new action. Under the Consumer Code, 'consumer' means any natural person who, in commercial practices covered by this title, is acting for purposes which are outside their trade, business, craft or profession.

Under the new law, each consumer who is a member of the proposed group has the right to file an action. The law considers only physical persons as consumers. The plaintiff may give a mandate to a consumer association or

---

[13] Law No. 244/2007, commonly known as 'Finanziaria 2008'. Publications discussing the old art 140-bis are still available of course, and they could generate confusion for readers less experienced with the Italian system.

to a committee to sue on his behalf. The law does not require the plaintiff to be a member of the association to which he gives a mandate, and does not set forth provisions about their remuneration. Due to their role, they are the 'representative plaintiffs' of the damaged consumers. In fact, they are the de facto engine behind the *azione di classe*, while the individual consumer, who is an actual plaintiff, plays no role in the civil proceeding. Defendants can only sue Italian and foreign companies. More precisely, the law uses the word *impresa* to describe defendants. The word *impresa* seems to include the English concept of 'company,' but there is even dispute over what the word's exact equivalent is in Italian.

Product liability appears among the types of claims that consumers can advance. Article 140-bis, paragraph 2, letter b) of the Italian Consumer Code specifies that the action aims to protect consumer rights concerning defects of products or services, regardless of any contractual relationship between the plaintiffs and the manufacturer. The Tribunal of Milan has interpreted this provision in the *Voden Medical* case discussed below.

2. Procedural aspects

The *azione di classe* is inadmissible in one or more of the following cases: if the claim is manifestly unfounded; if there is a conflict of interest; if the rights infringed upon are not homogenous and/or if the lead plaintiff is unable to represent in an adequate way the interests of the class.

In addition to satisfying the specific requirements for class actions, a proposed class action also needs to satisfy the general requirements for any consumer action: the lead plaintiff must be a consumer and must have 'an interest' in the suit.

If a proceeding on the same issue is pending in front of a government authority or an administrative judge, the court may suspend the admissibility phase until the administrative proceeding is complete. The admissibility phase ends with a court decision. If the decision finds the class admissible, it determines the requirements that each member must fulfil to be part of the class.

The procedure involves two main stages, the first being an admissibility stage, while the second stage concerns liability and damages. Publicity and opt-in take place between the first and the second stages. The courts can consider expert reports at both the phase of admissibility and the liability and damages phase. [14]

---

[14] In case more than one action is filed on the same grounds, the Court may order to consolidate them. If the Court admits an action, any subsequent action on the same matter is dismissed (though each plaintiff can still propose individual actions). Only if the class action is inadmissible may a new individual action be filed in the same matter.

Subsequently, the proceeding moves on to the phase in which liability and, potentially, damages are determined. If the court finds the defendant liable, the court's decision specifies either a damage amount or a uniformly applicable criterion in order to calculate the damage for each individual claim.

The *azione di classe* provides for an opt-in model. Members must affirmatively opt in to the class if they want the decision on damages (or the settlement) to apply to them. If a court decision finds the action admissible, the decision also orders publicity of the admissibility finding and establishes a deadline for consumers to join. This deadline for opting in can be no later than 120 days after the deadline for public dissemination. The judgment is binding for the consumers who joined the action (ie, opted-in). If consumers do not join the action, they retain the option to undertake their own individual lawsuit.

II. EXPLAINING A LEGAL TRANSPLANT

The legal transplant of a judicial collective redress mechanism into Italian civil procedure rules has occurred for at least three main reasons.[15] They are the prestige of US class actions, the reaction of the public opinion to some dramatic failures of existing laws, and political pressure at European and national levels. The Italian experience provides an interesting example for examining the impact related to the introduction of collective redress in Civil Law countries.

A. Dramatic Failures and the Prestige of the US Class Action

The *Parmalat* scandal is "one of largest and most brazen corporate financial frauds in history."[16] Indeed, the scandal affected a country that heavily relies on public enforcement and dislikes the concept of private vindication of the public interest. Yet, the Italian capital markets watchdog Consob only started its investigations in late 2002/early 2003, after the market had signaled that something was wrong at Parmalat. The market already knew something that Consob did not. However, the Italian public learned from the media shortly after Parmalat's collapse that class-action lawyers in the US were launching civil actions at a speed unthinkable for Italy, and that those actions could involve unsuspecting Italian investors. Whenever it has been possible, both Parmalat's Extraordinary Commissioner (who acts on behalf of the company and its creditors) and investors have brought civil actions in the US, escaping

---

[15] A Watson, *Legal Transplants* (University of Georgia Press, 1993).
[16] *Securities and Exchange Commission v Parmalat Finanziaria SpA*, Case No. 03 CV 10266 (PKC) (SDNY), Accounting and Auditing Enforcement Release No. 1936/December 30, 2003.

the jurisdiction of Italian courts. This pattern is not simply a type of forum shopping based on the search for the most convenient substantive rules, it is motivated by the array of weapons that US civil procedures offer plaintiffs in complex cases regarding collective interests.[17]

In any case, this news gave impetus to discussion, albeit ill-conceived, concerning the introduction of class-action mechanisms in Italy, conducted in the mass media and at a political level as a side issue of the main topic concerning new regulation in response to the *Parmalat* cases and other scandals (eg, Argentinian bonds, insurance cartel).[18]

It became possible to file an *azione di classe* before the Italian Courts in 2010. However, lawsuits brought through an *azione di classe* can only cover conduct by defendants subsequent to 15 August 2009. The date Article 140-bis of the Consumer Code came into force is relevant in this respect because it prevents the use of *azione di classe* in the very cases that motivated Italian lawmakers to turn their attention to collective redress. Investors who were crushed by the financial scandals mentioned above (and the infamous Tango bonds) will never be able to aggregate their claims into a single action, as these events took place long before the fateful date of 15 August 2009.

B. Social and Political Pressure

In fact, consumer associations and the public at large have exercised strong political pressure. The words 'class action' remind most people of John Grisham novels and Hollywood movies, where the 'common citizen' manages to prevail over large corporations. Erin Brockovich may be the most famous representative of a class action, so famous, in fact, that Julia Roberts played her in a movie. Given its popularity, the class action, deprived of its negative aspects, has become a widespread electoral promise. Unfortunately lawyers were not able to influence public opinion or politicians, in order to establish a more realistic, technical discussion of the possibility of introducing the *azione di classe*.

C. European Influence over Domestic Consumer Law

The EU has taken an interest in the development of collective actions in the field of consumer law for quite some time.[19] European activism in consumer protection, as an instrument for market integration, has resulted in a number

---

[17] G Ferrarini and P Giudici, 'Financial Scandals and the Role of Private Enforcement: The Parmalat Case' (2005) ECGI Law Working Paper No. 40/2005.

[18] Other scandals involved securities and antitrust cases. On the latter see P Giudici, 'Private Antitrust Law Enforcement in Italy' 1 *Comp L Rev* (2004) 61.

[19] European Commission, Memorandum on Consumer Redress, COM (1984) 692.

of directives. Among those, the most interesting for our purposes is certainly Directive 98/27 on injunctions for the protection of consumer interests, which allows so-called 'qualified entities' in the Member States to apply for injunctive relief in the interest of consumers.[20] Article 139 of the Italian Consumer Code implemented the abovementioned directive.

In fact, the European Commission has been conferring on collective redress schemes since 2005, and the system it is now recommending arose from a series of green and white papers, as well as public consultation. The European Parliament supported this in its Resolution. In its Recommendation, the Commission called for the implementation of its collective redress principles by 26 July 2015 at the latest. Although the Recommendation is not legally binding, the Commission notes that it will evaluate the status of collective redress laws in the Member States after four years.

Undoubtedly, European intervention raised awareness about consumer rights and the role of remedies guaranteeing effective protection of consumer rights in the Member States, and in Italy in particular.

III. THE OUTCOME OF A LEGAL TRANSPLANT

A. Product Liability Cases

The Italian expression *azione di classe* represents an improbable translation of the US class action. An explosion of media coverage, loud proclamations and filings purportedly claiming billions of Euros in damages have occurred due to the new law. A number of scientific contributions are currently trying to analyze the new procedural mechanism.[21]

However, one may question whether the *azione di classe* has cleared the way for product liability mass torts in Italy. Unfortunately, this does not seem to be the case. To date, consumers have only filed thirty actions before the Courts nationwide. One of the cases examined in this paper is about product liability.[22] Of the applications presented so far, nine passed the admissibility test, the court rejected sixteen applications because they did not pass the

---

[20] C Poncibò, 'Consumer Collective Redress in the European Union: The Italian Case", in G Howells, A Nordhausen, D Parry and C Twigg-Flesner (eds) *The Yearbook of Consumer Law* (Ashgate, 2008), 198–231.

[21] N Calcagno, 'Italian Class Action: The Beginning' (15 March 2011), http://ssrn.com/abstract=1875424; R Comolli, M De Santis and F Lo Passo, 'Italian Class Actions Eight Months In: The Driving Forces' (16 September 2010), http://globalclassactions.stanford.edu; R Nashi, 'Note: Italy's Class Action Experiment' 43 *Cornell Int'l LJ* (2013)147.

[22] E Rajneri and C Poncibò, Italian Report, Focus on Collective Redress (2014), http://www.collectiveredress.org/collective-redress/reports/italy/overview.

admissibility test, and twenty actions are currently pending. Between 2010 and 2014, only three cases ended with a judgment.[23]

1. The 'Voden Medical' Case

The lead plaintiff bought a flu test distributed by Voden Medical Instruments Company. The product's instructions claimed it could reveal the presence of any type of flu with almost no margin of error. Relying on this information, the plaintiff purchased the test, but after reading a press release published on the Voden website, he discovered that the test could lead to false negatives. Consequently, he gave mandate to a nationwide consumer association to file an *azione di classe* against Voden and to seek reimbursement and damages compensation.[24] At first, the consumer claimed that this was a product liability case, but the Tribunal of Milan rejected the action because the claim addressed the distributor (Voden Medical Instruments) and not the manufacturer. Article 140-bis Paragraph 2, letter b) of the Consumer Code specifies that the action applies to protect the rights in respect of defects of products or services, regardless of any contractual relationship between the plaintiffs and the manufacturer. According to the interpretation of the Court, the consumer has to file the *azione di classe* against the manufacturer concerning the characteristics of the product marketed. In the present case, it was clear that Voden Medical Instruments was only the distributor of the product and, thus its activities were limited to advertising and marketing of the test. The lead plaintiff in an amended complaint specified that the misleading content of the paper represented unfair commercial practice. The Tribunal of Milan decided to admit the amended complaint presented by the plaintiff in order to have a better understanding of the grounds of the case. Accordingly, the court admitted the action based on the amended complaint and ordered Codacons to publish the decision in three of the biggest Italian newspapers. The defendant appealed the decision, claiming lack of homogeneity between the interests of the plaintiff and those of the members of the class.

Nonetheless, the Court of Appeal of Milan held that the interests at issue were homogenous because they required the same solution to the same questions of fact and law. In particular, the consumers had concluded the same contract with the defendant, by purchasing the test. In addition, the same misconduct had injured the consumers, since the information contained in the illustrative paper of the product had misled them. As far as the other admissibility elements are concerned, the appellate body concluded that since

---

[23] The Osservatorio Antitrust of the University of Trento is publishing the data, see http://www.osservatorioantitrust.eu/it/azioni-di-classe-incardinate-nei-tribunali-italiani.

[24] Tribunal of Milan, VIII Section, no. 98/2010 of 13 March 2012, *Codacons v Voden Medical Instruments*.

Codacons was one of the biggest associations, it possessed adequate economic and organizational means to represent the class. The judge also did not find any conflict of interest between the association and the consumers.

The Tribunal of Milan, with the first merits decision in the history of the application of *azione di classe*, overruled the ordinances taken at the admissibility stage and held the lawsuit groundless and inadmissible.[25] The lead plaintiff failed to prove his consumer status and to show that the information it contained influenced the decision to purchase the test. Consequently, the court rejected the claim and told the lead plaintiff to pay the legal expenses. In addition, the Tribunal of Milan ordered the plaintiff to pay a compensatory damage to the defendant for what it deemed a temerarious lawsuit.[26] It is also surprising that the plaintiff was ordered to pay the legal expenses of the proceedings.

2. Codacons v British American Tobacco

Codacons v British American Tobacco is the first and only case of tobacco mass litigation in Italy.[27] A nationwide consumer association, in its own name and as the representative of several consumers, claimed that the nicotine contained in the cigarettes sold by British American Tobacco Italia (BAT) was so high that the nicotine was capable of causing consumer addiction. Accordingly, the plaintiffs sought compensation for the costs of the cigarettes purchased under what they asserted was a dependency and for the health damages caused by the nicotine.[28]

However, the alleged facts occurred before Article 140-bis came into force and therefore before the new action had become available for consumers. In addition, the defendant noted that the rights at issue were not homogeneous as required under the law. The Tribunal of Rome partially agreed with BAT

---

[25] Court of Naples, no. 2195/2013, of 18 February 2013 upheld the first *azione di classe* on the merits.

[26] According to art. 96 of the Italian Code of Civil Procedure, the judge can condemn the plaintiff, who began a '*lite temeraria*', to pay the defendant a penalty of an amount determined by the judge.

[27] Court of Appeal of Rome, 27 January 2012, *Codacons v British American Tobacco*, Foro it. (2012) 1908, as observed by Palmieri.

[28] C Roberto, 'Tobacco-Smoke Litigation in Italy: Could the Marketing of Tobacco be a 'Dangerous Activity'?' 4 *Journal of Multidisciplinary Research* (2012) 45. An alternative route to overcome the burden of proving the defective nature of the product is the possibility of starting legal action based on the provisions of art 2050 of the ICC proving strict liability for damages caused by dangerous activities. This also happened with respect to the case of tobacco litigation notwithstanding the fact that art 2050 addresses activities that were, per se, dangerous and not a specific conduct, such as the failure to warn. In that case, manufacturers were held liable for not having taken the necessary measures to avoid damage after circulating the dangerous products, notwithstanding full compliance with applicable laws.

and held that the lawsuit was valid only for those misconducts that had occurred after Article 140-bis became enforceable. It then examined the grounds of the case in order to discover whether there was sufficient legal basis to assume that the plaintiff's right existed. In particular, the Court believed that the action was groundless because every smoker was fully aware of the risks connected to the consumption of cigarettes, and the damages were consequences of their free will and not due to the addictive nature of the nicotine. Moreover, the judges explained that Codacons did not have the power to file the action on its own initiative under Article 140-bis.

Finally, the Court declared that a collective protection could be granted whenever the judge's evaluation focused on the solution of the same questions of law and facts, thus on homogenous rights. Nonetheless, since every consumer had his own smoking 'history' and the nicotine had affected him differently, the Tribunal of Rome held that the class was not homogenous. Accordingly, the Court declared the *azione di classe* as inadmissible. Codacons challenged the ordinance in the Court of Appeal of Rome. The appellate court accepted the reasoning of the trial court and affirmed the decision.

B. The Lack of Driving Forces

Four years after it was launched, it appears that the *azione di classe* still suffers from serious shortcomings. In particular, it should be pointed out that the transplant of collective redress mechanisms for mass torts occurred without contextualizing it. Such actions work effectively in contexts including entrepreneurial lawyers, damages recovery, contingency fees and other judicial case-management mechanisms that are absent from the Italian legal system. Without these driving forces, the *azione di classe*, and indeed, other collective redress mechanisms for damages in Civil law countries may not reach their potential.

1. Consumer associations

Why is the outcome of the *azione di classe* so unsatisfactory? The main point here is the lack of one or more driving forces. Article 140-bis assigns a central role to consumer associations, while it leaves open the possibility for injured consumers to establish a committee to act before the courts. Law firms play a central role in the second option. The reference to associations is a compromise with the class action where every member of the class has standing to sue on behalf of the entire group. It also relies on the previous rules and, more precisely, the above-mentioned Article 139 of the Consumer Code, which gives standing to 'certified' associations to go to court for injunctions to protect the collective interests of the consumers.

In the first few years since the inception of the *azione di classe*, associations have been proactively seeking opportunities to rely on the collective redress mechanism. They seem to be adopting different strategies with respect to class actions. Some, like Codacons, have been filing a comparatively high number of class actions and announcing claims for billions of Euros. Others, like *Unione Nazionale Consumatori*, have filed fewer and financially less ambitious class actions, being more realistic in their aims.

There is evidence that associations, rather than individuals or committees, have been the de facto plaintiffs in this period. However, can consumer associations take the place occupied in the US by plaintiffs' law firms (and institutionally lead plaintiffs)? Like US plaintiff law firms, they may seize the opportunity to articulate legal arguments that will win decisions that may further their interests in future unrelated litigation. Nevertheless, there are many fundamental differences between consumer associations and law firms, as consumer associations have less financial resources to litigate and different economic incentives from those of law firms. The State or the local authorities provide very limited funding to the associations that usually do not have the economic resources or the adequate expertise to deal with product liability mass torts. Because they are typically non-profit and do not stand to gain directly from a settlement, their economic interest is not necessarily the maximization of settlements or recoverable damages. Although their final objective is to promote consumer welfare, they may see consumer welfare as broader than the simple recovery of damages. Consumer associations may aim to send a warning to the entire industry and push for changes in current business practices. They are less likely to be enticed to settle by monetary offer alone because increasing their own visibility and reputation results in increased power and the widening of their association base. Concurrently, consumer associations also have (maybe only implicitly) the goal of increasing the influence of the association. Thus, they may aim to increase their own visibility.

2. *The legal profession*

Surprisingly, associations and their lawyers have been more active in filing *azione di classe* than law firms. However, the legal profession has limited incentives to act due to the rules governing the liquidation of damages, the costs of the legal proceedings and the remuneration of lawyers.

Between 1988 and 2004, Italian courts refused to award non-economic damages in product liability cases. This means that, for a long time, the judges have provided a narrow interpretation of the concept of damages. The traditional position only changed in 2004, when the Italian Supreme Court changed its rule for the first time concerning the possibility of awarding non-economic damages in cases of strict liability, such as product liability cases.[29]

---

[29] *Corte di cassazione*, 27 October 2004, No. 20814/2004, *P c U spa*, (2005) *Resp. civ.* 172.

Also relevant is the fact that the Italian Supreme Court has historically found that punitive damage awards in civil matters are contrary to the Italian system of civil liability that seeks compensation rather than punishment. In its leading case of 2007, the Supreme Court confirmed the Italian lower court's position that punitive damage awards are against public policy.[30] In judgment 1781/2012 of February 8, 2012, the Italian Supreme Court further reinforced this position by finding that foreign judgments which award punitive damages are contrary to domestic public policy and are therefore unenforceable in Italy.[31]

Both judgments involved injured plaintiffs seeking compensation for their damages. In assessing compensation, the Italian courts reviewed the damages incurred and recognized contributions from other tortfeasors. The Courts determined that the awards of 1 million USD and 8 million USD were excessive and meant to punish the defendants rather than fairly compensate the injured plaintiffs.[32]

In addition, European countries usually adopt the 'English rule,' ie, the rule under which a prevailing party recovers his attorney's fees from the loser. Thus, the plaintiff may finance the action by relying on the rule that the losers pay. Nevertheless, Italian courts quite often shift away from a rigid application of the rule and do not require the losing defendant to pay the actual amount of a plaintiff's litigation costs.

In addition, it was unlawful for any law firm to work on contingency or conditional fees before January 2007. Conditional fees are a legal novelty: what Italian attorneys can do is reach an agreement with their clients by which attorneys, instead of receiving a percentage of the damages awarded to their client, are only entitled to receive a success fee on top of their regular fees. If they win, this is calculated according to a mandatory rate approved by the Government. Even today, contingency fee arrangements are still encountering resistance from some law firms that are lobbying to make them unlawful again. The latest developments are probably not sufficient to make *azione di classe* a profitable business for Italian law firms.[33]

---

[30] *Corte di cassazione*, 19 January 2007, No. 1183/2007, *Parrott v Società Fimez*, (2007) 4 *Resp. civ.* 373.

[31] *Corte di cassazione*, 8 February 2012, No.1781/2012, *Società Ruffinatti v Oyola-Rosado*, (2013) *I Giur. It*. 126.

[32] It is unclear whether the Italian courts would have reached similar results if the underlying US decisions had distinguished between compensatory and punitive damages.

[33] Third party funding is possible, since it is not openly forbidden by any legal rules. In spite of the admissibility, the lack of statutory regulations and, even more, of any case law on the matter, puts third party funding of litigation in a sort of twilight zone nobody seems willing to explore.

3. The courts

In Italian civil procedure, there are no pre-trial proceedings, no pre-trial discovery, and no trial by jury. Italian procedural rules allow broad discovery in a very limited and defined set of marginal cases. In other words, the problem is that the party does not know exactly what documents his opponent has, and the court cannot grant a disclosure order unless the party has indicated a specific document. The same is true for German and French laws. Hence, discovery is virtually absent. Given the lack of efficient discovery rules, action against mass wrongdoings are very problematic in Italy, as in the rest of Europe, unless public authorities gather information.

The involvement of the court at the initial stage of *azione di classe* has already been described; the action can proceed only if the court declares it admissible, having found that the requirements laid down by Article 140-bis of the Consumer Code have been met. Among the elements the court is supposed to evaluate, one in particular enables the court to filter prospective actions according to a prognostic evaluation of their merits. The *azione di classe* is not admissible when it is manifestly unfounded, when the representative does not appear able to adequately represent the interests of the group, when there is a conflict of interests and finally, when individual rights to be protected are not homogeneous (Article 140-bis, paragraph 6). In fact, the majority of the actions filed in the initial period of enforcement of the said article (ie 2010–2014) failed to pass the admissibility test. The Court has shown a strict interpretation in evaluating the criteria of admissibility. In 2014, the Court of Appeal of Milan, overturning the first instance, declared the admissibility of the *azione di classe* proposed by Altroconsumo, an association that protects consumers. The action was against Trenord, a railway operator and was due to the poor quality of the transport services.[34] The judgment focused on the requirement of homogeneity of the rights that must exist to declare an action permissible pursuant to Article 140-bis of the Consumer Code. According to the Court of Appeal, the judge should interpret this requirement consistently with the ratio of the *azione di classe* (ie, to facilitate mass litigation) and having ascertained the homogeneity in terms of existence of the same infringement of the law (ie, the event of the offence, or the breach of contract). The diversification in terms of the individual damages and their liquidation do not represent obstacles to admitting the action because the Court may deal with these issues at a later stage of the process.

---

[34] *Corte di Appello di Milano*, 3 March 2014, *Trenord Case*, (2014) *Giur. it.* 1910.

IV. WILL COLLECTIVE REDRESS CHANGE THE PICTURE OF EUROPEAN PRODUCT LIABILITY MASS LITIGATION?

A. A Patchwork of Old and New Procedural Tools

EU Member States have implemented the Product Liability Directive into domestic law, seeking to harmonize a strict liability regime for defective products across the EU. In some countries, the implementing legislation has been in force for more than 10 years.

Until recently, a limited number of cases have been decided in Europe, considering in detail the often critical provisions of Articles 6 (definition of defectiveness) and 7(e) (the development risks defense) of the Product Liability Directive. The limited number of judicial cases may be explained by the lack of collective redress mechanisms for mass torts in many Member States and in particular, Civil Law countries. The latter aspect, however, is now changing.

Before the recent introduction of collective redress mechanisms, Member States were managing mass torts for product liability in various ways. The most common tools are the joinder of parties, the participation of civil parties in criminal proceedings (common in Civil Law countries) and/or out-of-court settlement.[35]

Thus, the picture is becoming increasingly complicated and fragmented with the introduction of new mechanisms for collective redress also covering product liability cases. They include test case procedure, group litigation (England), and representative litigation, class actions (Sweden), mass torts settlements procedures (The Netherlands), and the recent *action de groupe* (France).[36]

With respect to other European countries, the impact of these laws is still unknown because collective redress mechanisms are so new and national courts have not clearly interpreted and applied the new rules. Germany, for example, has not introduced a general collective redress mechanism to protect consumers, and still relies on the joinder of parties and test cases limited to protect investors.[37] Other countries, like Italy, are still relying on procedural devices that existed before the introduction of *azione di classe*, such as the joining of parties before the Criminal Court, or out-of-court settlements for mass torts (eg, joint conciliation).

---

[35] D Fairgrieve, *State Liability in Tort: A Comparative Law Study* (Oxford University Press, 2003), Chapter 8.

[36] In general, see A Stadler, 'The Commission's Recommendation on common principles of collective redress and private international law issues' (2013) *NiPR* 485. Loi Hamon of 17 March 2014 (a new piece of legislation on consumer law) has introduced the new *action de groupe* into French Law.

[37] A Stadler, 'Developments in Collective Redress: What's New in the 'New German KapMug' *European Business Law Review* (2013) 733.

As a result, European jurisdictions deal with product liability cases by applying the various substantive laws resulting from the implementation of the Product Liability Directive into domestic law. In addition, they have very different judicial and non-judicial devices available in European jurisdictions for product liability litigation.

B. Blood Transfusion Case: Litigating in England, Germany, and Italy

Our point asserted above may be better explained by examining a case to see how the legal systems of England, Germany, and Italy were equipped to deal with the blood transfusion mass litigation. It is also interesting to note the developments and their possible impact over the litigation.

1. England

On 26 March 2001, a UK Court decided the case of *A & Others v The National Blood Authority* by applying the strict liability provisions contained in 1987 Consumer Protection Act (CPA) that has implemented the Product Liability Directive in the UK.[38] The claimants successfully argued that the blood and blood products that had infected the claimants were defective under the CPA, and that the development risks defence was not available to the National Blood Authority. The Court considered both issues in detail and in doing so, focused on the wording of the Product Liability Directive.[39]

There are other aspects of UK litigation procedures relevant to the case in issue that are making England a comparatively more favorable legal environment for consumers who suffer injury from defective products compared to other EU jurisdictions, such as, for example, Germany and Italy. England was one of the first EU countries to introduce specific procedural provisions for group actions (Group Litigation Order – GLO) seeking recovery of damages in product liability cases. The group action model under Part 19.11 of the Civil Procedure Rules (CPR) is based upon the desire to achieve the efficient administration and economic disposal of cases where there are common issues of fact and law.[40] The GLO is still at an early stage in England, and it is less used in comparison to the US. In the first period of application, quite a relevant number of multiple-claimant product liability cases have been brought in the United Kingdom, including the Opren (Benoxaprofen) arthritis drug case, tranquillizer claims (Benzodiazepine), whooping cough cases (Pertussis), and the African asbestos group action. Some more recent HIV

---

[38] *A and others v National Blood Authority and another* [2001] 3 All ER 289.
[39] *Ibid.*
[40] The Civil Procedure Rules 1998 (SI 1998/3132) of 10 December 1998 came into force on 26 April 1999.

and contaminated blood transfusion claims have been subject to a GLO procedure. Nevertheless, it is not easy to comment on these cases given that the parties have settled many of the product liability cases before trial, or that consumer groups have been withdrawn due to removal of state funding to pursue the GLO.[41]

The introduction of the GLO, however, may contribute to enhancing the picture of product liability mass litigation in the country. The same civil procedure rules applied in the UK are among the most favorable in Europe to mass litigation and thus to product liability. For example, detailed disclosure rules are available pursuant to which personal injury claimants (among others) are entitled to inspect and copy all non-privileged documents in the possession or control of the manufacturer. Moreover, victims of personal injury can claim both general damages and special damages, both in proceedings under the strict liability regime of the CPA and in negligence at common law. General damages compensate for pain, suffering, and loss of amenity (PSLA), which is non-pecuniary loss.[42] Special damages represent pecuniary loss, which includes the costs incurred in treating the condition, and losses resulting from unemployment, nursing and other medical expenses. The Courts may also award additional sums by way of special damages depending on claimants' individual circumstances.

2. Germany

German law has two principal bases of product liability: strict liability, as circumscribed by the Product Liability Law and sector specific statutes, such as the Drug Law (the separate strict liability regime for licensed medicinal products), and negligence as set out in the *Bürgerliches Gesetzbuch*.[43]

Procedural and cost rules always have a bearing on the viability of bringing or defending product liability claims and it is fair to say that in certain respects, litigation procedures in Germany may seem more restrictive for personal injury claimants than those in England.

---

[41] Although, in general, personal injury claimants are not able to receive state funding for their claims on the basis that such claims are more appropriately funded using conditional fee agreements, state funding may be granted for those personal injury claims, which have a 'wider public interest.' For example, the UK body which makes funding decisions concluded that the appeal to the House of Lords in the asbestos-related disease claims brought in *Lubbe v Cape Plc* [2000] 4 All ER 268 on behalf of South African miners merited a high to exceptional wider public interest rating.

[42] Indicative damages awards for PSLA for particular injuries and conditions are set out in the Judicial Studies Board's Guidelines for the Assessment of General Damages in Personal Injury Cases (5th Edition, 2000) (the 'JSB Guidelines') based on pre-existing case law.

[43] R Best, 'A Comparison of Civil Liability for Defective Products in the United Kingdom and Germany' 3 *German Law Journal* (2002) 4.

Unlike in England, there is no formal group litigation procedure, and, apart from instruments for injunctive relief and for skimming-off illegally gained profits from those violating antitrust laws and rules on fair competition, there exists only the Capital Market Models Case Act which protects investors.[44] In product liability cases, including the blood transfusion case example, the injured consumers may principally rely on the traditional procedural mechanism of the 'joinder of parties,' or out-of-court settlements.

Commenting briefly on the general procedural rules, there are limited disclosure obligations. The courts are more interventionist and more willing to suggest settlement proposals than their English counterparts (this, of course, can be positive or negative, depending on your point of view). The law prohibits both contingency and conditional fee arrangements with lawyers, and the judge decides which witnesses to hear and which experts to call. Furthermore, costs recovery is limited to low statutory fees.

3. Italy

The *Corte di cassazione* has expressly admitted in its case law that there is a presumption of responsibility of the Ministry of Health for infection occurring in the years between 1979 and 1989. The scientific discovery of the predictability of infection was identified in 1978, with the consequent obligation of control and supervision in the field collection and distribution of human blood.[45]

Thousands of victims have sued the Ministry of Health before the courts, claiming damages and compensation. This generated widespread litigation with hundreds of proceedings. In order to define the pending litigation, the Italian government initiated a public process in 2007 aimed at settling the many civil cases pending against damage by transfusion of infected blood and or blood products. The victims were infected in Italian hospitals owned by the State (Ministry of Health) and accordingly, the cases were brought against the Ministry of Health.

The Government introduced a statutory compensation scheme in the year 2007 (Law 29 of November 2007 No. 222; Law 244/2007 paragraphs 361 and 362 and Regulation 132/2009-DM, 4 May 2012). This process has, however, persisted for years, leading to an unacceptable impasse, challenged both by means of specific actions taken before the Italian Supreme Court.[46] It is very interesting to note that, according to the Italian Supreme Court, the

---

[44] Stadler (above n 37).
[45] *Corte di cassazione, sezione* III, 14 March 2014, No. 5954/2014, CED *Cassazione* (2014), *Maccarone e altri c Min. Salute e altri.*
[46] *Corte di cassazione, sezione lavoro*, 27 April 2012, No. 6562/2012 (2013) 3 *Danno e Resp.*, 261.

settlement procedure illustrated earlier concerning the *Blood Transfusion* Case denotes a substantial legislative trend in favouring out-of-court settlements for mass torts.[47]

The trend for out-of-court strategies is not surprising: the *azione di classe* certainly improves the litigation environment in Italy, but the latter is more restrictive in mass tort cases, including product liability mass litigation, than those in England and Germany. This is because of the peculiar problem in the country where the *azione di classe* is part of a system of civil procedure that is not in itself efficient.[48] As a result, in 2013, an association of victims of infected blood products filed an application against the Italian government before the European Court of Human Rights. The association claim concerns the delay in the process of compensating the damages awarded to infected blood victims and established by law.[49]

VI. AN AMERICAN IN ROME

Comparative legal scholarship draws attention to the 'local tuning' affecting legal transplantation – given the influence in the process of transplantation of each country's legal, cultural, accounting, technological, political and economic circumstances. The process of transplantation results in a different effect than in the country of origin once the instrument has been incorporated by a country's legal system.[50] Collective redress mechanisms adopted in European Civil Law countries to protect consumers (Italy and France), or not adopted at all (Germany),[51] are very good examples of the relevance of local tuning to legal transplantation of a collective redress mechanism.

Indeed, the prestigious class actions have influenced the majority of Member States – with few exceptions.[52] However, in the end, they adopted

---

[47] *Corte di cassazione, sezione* VI, 21 October 2014, No. 22298/2014, CED *Cassazione* (2014).

[48] E Silvestri, 'The Never-Ending Reforms of Italian Civil Justice' (2 August 2011).

[49] ECHR, *AA et Autres v Italy*, Case no. 16178/2013.

[50] E Örücü, 'Mixed and Mixing Systems: A Conceptual Search', in E Örücü, E Attwooll and S Coyle (eds), *Legal Systems: Mixed and Mixing* (Kluwer Law International, 1996) 335–351; M Graziadei, 'Comparative Law as the Study of Transplants and Receptions', in M Reimann and R Zimmermann (eds), *The Oxford Handbook of Comparative Law* (Oxford University Press 2006) 441.

[51] Published in the French Official Journal of 18 March 2014, No. 0065, at 54 following a decision by the French Constitutional Council on 13 March 2014 on the constitutionality of arts 1 and 2 of the new law (decision No. 2014-690-DC).

[52] F Valguarnera, 'Legal Tradition as an Obstacle: Europe's Difficult Journey to Class Action', 10 *Global Jurist* (2010). Scandinavian countries, Portugal and the Netherlands have elaborated solutions, which resemble the American class action.

very different collective redress mechanisms from the US class actions for three main reasons.

First, while any member of the class can initiate the class action (as long as certain requirements are met), most European Civil law countries on the contrary reserve the standing to sue to associations (or they favour the role that associations may play, as in Italy). Often, standing is granted to consumer associations that, in some cases, the government has previously approved, according to the criteria indicated in the law.

Second, while the American class action is either mandatory or opt-out, the European models follow what we can loosely call the opt-in system, meaning that the judgment only binds those who have adopted an active stance. A 'silent' and passive group member does not benefit from a victory and retains his or her right to sue autonomously.

Third, while the American class action can be used to litigate all kinds of subject matter, most European models only allow group litigation for certain specific areas of the law. These procedures have a potentially wide application and could cover areas as diverse as consumer claims, competition law, securities law, personal injury, intellectual property, and tax law as well as social welfare law. They often include product liability.

Two other differences between Europe and the United States are of great importance for the functioning of product liability mass litigation: (1) the regulation of the legal profession; and (2) the limited role of the courts in case-management. In the search for a new European model, one author concluded that either collective redress mechanisms do not work effectively or they work too well. However, if those features were to be changed, the system would quickly attract many claims that do not fall under traditional procedures.[53]

In doing so, the majority of the Member States in the EU, like Italy, are trying to strike a difficult balance as they want (at least some of) the advantages of collective redress without the cultural revolution consisting of the Americanization of civil procedure and the legal profession in EU nations. The class action has been de-Americanized in the European context by adopting different legal terminology (ie, 'collective redress' instead of 'class action').

If we accept mass litigation in product liability, we are bound to accept what comes with it: a certain degree of adversarial legalism, meaning the use of litigation as a regulatory tool, and not solely as the formal structure established by

---

[53] C Hodges, 'Collective Redress in Europe: The New Model' 7 *Civil Justice Quarterly* (2010) 370; C Hodges, 'From Class Actions to Collective Redress: A Revolution in Approach to Compensation' 28 *Civil Justice Quarterly* (2009) at 41; In general, C Hodges, *The Reform of Class and Representative Actions in European Legal Systems: A New Framework for Collective Redress in Europe* (Hart Publishing, 2008).

the system to resolve disputes.[54] As one author noted: "procedure is always 'portable,' we just have to remember that it never travels alone."[55] Strong driving forces, consumers and their associations, entrepreneurial lawyers and judicial case-management fail to make collective redress represent a cultural revolution for European consumers. However, this means accepting some aspects of the legal profession in the US, such as entrepreneurial lawyers and conditional fees.

In order to be effective, the transplant of a mechanism for judicial collective redress, as the Italian case confirms, should take place within a well-designed legal framework related to both substantive law and procedural law. Otherwise, there is a clear risk that the mechanism will not give the desired results and, thus, the outcome of the transplant is remains unsatisfactory.

We argue that the legal transplant without contextualization has caused a change in the nature of the original class action. European collective redress mechanisms do not truly empower the 'common man' against powerful corporations, but only provide a certain rationalization of litigation and cost-efficiency improvement in a few well-selected legal fields. Collective redress mechanisms produce positive effects without an important change in the client-attorney relationship and without jeopardizing individual procedural rights.

The result is not, so far, particularly encouraging, as the solutions developed in most European countries are, with some exceptions, extremely fragmented, too conservative and too limited in scope to offer substantial improvements for citizen rights. It is obviously questionable whether this approach has been too conservative because of the fear of opening Pandora's box.

To conclude, forced by public opinion, but reluctant on the basis of their legal cultures, the majority of European Member States have adopted very different collective redress devices from their American counterpart, and this has resulted in the transformative power of class actions not fully having been realised. Collective redress represents a useful procedural tool for mass torts in the EU, a more sophisticated form of joinder of parties based on the representation by an ideological plaintiff of a group.

Collective redress would be more successful in countries characterized by a friendly litigation landscape, like England, and the blood transfusion case briefly examined in this paper confirm this observation.

For all the reasons above, the *azione di classe* has had a very limited impact in product liability in Italy. To quote an old movie, this judicial collective

---

[54] R Kagan, *Adversarial Legalism: The American Way of Law* (Harvard University Press, 2003).
[55] E Silvestri, 'The Difficult Art of Legal Transplants: The Case of Class Actions' 35 *Revista de Processo* (2010) 99.

redress mechanism represents "an American in Rome."[56] Only one case of product liability litigation occurred between 2010 and 2014, while injured consumers are still relying on mechanisms that are different from the *azione di classe*, such as the civil action in the criminal proceedings and various forms of out-of-court settlement schemes (ie, statutory compensation schemes and joint conciliation).

The outcome of the legal transplant of a collective redress judicial mechanism into the Italian legal civil process is not satisfactory. This instrument is scarcely used, and it has not reached the results that were anticipated in terms of enhancement of the level of consumer protection in the country. The reason behind this failure in Italy, as well as in other Civil Law Countries, is that the transplant has occurred without an effective re-contextualization of the collective redress mechanism into the legal system. The problem here is that such a conservative approach may be inadequate to make collective redress a powerful tool to compensate consumers in the EU, even in cases where a defective product has seriously damaged their health.

VII. THE THREAT OF COLLECTIVE REDRESS IN PRODUCT LIABILITY CASES

A. The Boundaries to the Application of the Class Action in Product Liability Cases

The progressive growth of consumer protection in European legal provisions has not had a proportionate impact on litigation. A clear example is given by the small number of product liability cases brought before national courts (with the exception of Austria) since the implementation of European Directive 374/1985. Therefore, the European lawmaker is now stressing access to justice issues, questioning Member States about foreseeable tools more apt to enforce consumer rights of action. Under this concern, in 2008, the European Commission published a Green Paper on collective redress, followed by the other documents mentioned above.

Italy is among one of the first Member States to have incorporated a class action into its legal system. However, the class action introduced in Italy in 2008 has had minimal impact so far. For several reasons, this result is not surprising and hence cannot be considered deceptive at this stage.

At first, there is a sort of comprehensible caution towards a new instrument, which is correctly perceived as foreign in the Italian legal system. This caution is clearly demonstrated by the decision of the courts not to apply the

---

[56] The reference is to one of Alberto Sordi's greatest roles, as the star of *Un Americano a Roma* (1954). In that film Sordi plays Nando Moriconi, a young Italian man obsessed with American music and popular culture. He walks in a bow-legged swagger that seems a parody of John Wayne, sports a baseball cap, and dreams of being the next Gene Kelly.

new instrument for facts occurred before its introduction.[57] The criticised decision on non-retroactive character of the instrument is likely explained by the fear of an excessive number of claims for restitution of undue payments in particular against the banks. Without wishing to enter the debate, the point is that a legal action, which gives rise to refunds of sums unduly paid restricted to the last couple of years (at most), is clearly not very attractive.[58] However, as time goes on, the non-retroactive limitation will be less of an issue and as courts and practitioners become more acquainted with the new instrument, the reluctant attitude will progressively soften.

Furthermore, there is the lack of economic incentive for the promoter of a class action, as well as for those who are asked to opt in. This aspect has been already analysed in detail in the previous part of this chapter. The comparative analysis shows that the lack of economic incentive is mainly because punitive damages are not conceivable in Europe since they are in contrast with the principle of full compensation of the damage, which governs tort law.[59] This means that tort law in Europe aims to ensure a compensatory function as well as a deterrence function, while the punitive function is attributed exclusively to the public authority. The underlying idea is that the activities detrimental to the community are punished by criminal law, which is charged with taking care of public interests. The other activities are allowed providing they internalize all the costs they cause to third parties, and this is the task of private law.[60] In other words, there is a clear divide in Europe among private law and public law which explains the main differences of the European legal system in comparison to the American legal system, where in the latter country, this divide is less prominent. Clearly this divide in Europe is challenged by an instrument such as the class action which takes care of individual interests by combining them into a 'community.'

As regards product liability in particular, the new collective redress provision has been used in only one case.[61] This is also explained by the fact that the new provision is not applicable for every kind of product liability case. At first, cases concerning single manufacturing defects are excluded (and the product liability database provided by the British Institute of International and Comparative Law shows that the majority of cases brought before a

---

[57] S Chiarloni, 'Il nuovo art. 140bis del codice del consumo: azione di classe o azione collettiva?', 1 *Analisi giuridica dell'economia* (2008) 107; P Fiorio, 'L'azione di classe nel nuovo art. 140bis e gli obiettivi di deterrenza e di accesso alla giustizia dei consumatori', available at http://www.ilcaso.it/articoli/172.pdf.

[58] In Italy the time limit for recovery of undue payments is 10 years.

[59] F Quarta, *La funzione deterrente della responsabilità civile* (Napoli, 2010) 100.

[60] U Mattei, *Tutela risarcitoria e tutela inibitoria* (Milano, 1987) 255.

[61] The class action filed against British American Tobacco and decided by *App. Roma Ordinanza*, 27.01.2012.

European national court indeed concern damage allegedly caused by single manufacturing defects).[62]

The class action could come into play either for a manufacturing defect, which affects an entire series of the same product, or for a design defect.

The mass torts caused by a manufacturing defect of an entire series of a product are usually prevented through the regulatory system and most notably through the recall system, which seems to be very effective. Hence, it is unlikely that these kinds of cases come in front of a judge with a collective action.

On the other hand, the design defect cases do not present a chance of success if, given the state of scientific and technical knowledge, the risk of damage was not foreseeable by the manufacturer at the time the product was put into circulation. Otherwise, the development risk defence will frustrate the claim.

In conclusion, collective redress seems to be useful in product liability cases only for design defect issues where the defect was foreseeable in advance by the manufacturer.[63]

However, the cases concerning design defects are more controversial and can give rise to inconsistent judgments depending on the legal doctrine followed by the courts in each Member State in order to detect this kind of defect.

The more controversial issues are the requirement of homogeneous rights for the admission of the collective action (from a procedural point of view), and the application of the risk/utility test (from a substantial point of view).

B. The Admissibility Requirement of Homogeneous Individual Rights

The only collective action on product liability brought before Italian courts has been declared not admissible for lack of homogeneity among the individual rights of the class members.[64]

According to the interpretation given by courts, the requirement of homogenous individual rights can be a serious obstacle for the admission of a collective redress action. Aware of this obstacle, the lawmaker intervened and substituted the word 'identity' with the word 'homogeneity' in order to soften the legal provision. At the same time, courts are shifting to looser interpretations of the legal requirement.

In the case against the Trenord, the Court of Appeal of Milan (cf p 309) has affirmed that homogeneity should be required in regard to the evidence

---

[62] http://www.biicl.org/plf/database.
[63] These cases could also wear the form of a warning defect case, assuming that the manufacturer did not adequately inform the consumer about the design defect that he was aware of.
[64] *App. Roma Ordinanza*, 27.01.2012, *Codacons v Soc. Bat Italia*.

founding the claim, not necessarily in regard to individual damages (which could be separately calculated as explicitly provided by Article 140 bis c 12 Consumer Code).[65] This way the collective action can be effective from an economic perspective. In product liability cases, for example, the collective redress mechanism presents a clear advantage when it is necessary to ascertain causation through complex and expensive expertise. The cost of expertise is in fact easily exorbitant for a single individual, with devastating consequences for access to justice. Under this concern, the law implementing the European directive in Italy on product liability provides that courts may order that expert costs are anticipated by the manufacturer, whenever it is likely that the damage was caused by a defect of the product (Article 120 c 3 Consumer Code). However, this legal provision has not yet been applied. Through collective action, the expert costs are automatically divided among the class members. For this reason, collective redress becomes highly competitive with the alternative instrument of the *costituzione di parte civile* in a criminal procedure mentioned above. This is also because civil courts have weakened the claimant's burden of proof presuming the responsibility of the most probable cause (compared to the others), while under criminal law causation has to be proven "beyond any reasonable doubt."[66]

Furthermore, the ascertainment of causation in one unique collective procedure avoids inconsistent judgments on the same matter (as happens, for example in France, with regard to the vaccine cases individually brought in front of different courts).[67]

However, if causation is perceived as multifactor, then the class action is not admitted by the judge for lack of the homogeneity requirement. This happens when the damage is the consequence of the interaction among the inherently dangerous product with the victim's specific condition, or her specific habits or ways of living. For this reason indeed the class action filed against the British American Tobacco has been declared inadmissible. The court of first instance, and then the Court of Appeal of Milan (vid supra), stated that every smoker has his own history that needs to be examined individually.

C. *The Incoherent Use of the Risk/Utility Test in Design Defect Cases*

The cases on design defects are those which raise different interpretations of

---

[65] *App. Milano Sez.* II, Ord., 3.3.2014.

[66] *Cassazione civile*, 4.3.2004, n. 4400; Cass SU 11 January 2008 n. 581. The *Corte di cassazione* has pointed out that the proof of causation required in a civil court is very different from the one required in a criminal court. The tort law, in fact, is focused on the interests of the victim to get compensation, while the criminal procedure is focused on those of the defendant who might be unjustly punished.

[67] On this concern see JS Borghetti, 'Qu'est-ce qu'un vaccin défectueux?', *Recueil Dalloz* (2012) 2853.

the uniform legal provision among European courts according to the application or non-application of the risk/utility test.

As is well known, the risk /utility test was established by US courts as an instrument to detect a design defect. However, it is not mentioned by the European Product Liability Directive.

A manufacturing defect is easily detected by comparing the product that has caused the damage with the performance of the other products of the same series. If the other products do not present the same risk of damage, then the product in question is certainly defective and the manufacturer is liable. It does not matter if he cannot avoid a certain percentage of his products coming out with a manufacturing defect.[68] It is assumed that the manufacturer, having statistically calculated the risk of damage caused by the manufacturing defect, has consciously accepted this risk because the expected profit of his activity outweighs its costs, including the costs of damages to third parties.[69] Put differently, the strict liability rule for manufacturing defects represents an application of the 'enterprise liability' doctrine that was elaborated by scholars in the '60s and has never been made explicit by lawmakers.[70] The underlying idea is that the market will automatically eliminate those activities that cause more harmful externalities than profits (and the class action has been also set for the purpose of ensuring the internalisation of all damages).

---

[68] For example in a typical case of an exploding bottle of fizzy drink, the German Supreme Court held the manufacturer liable even though he had proven that he had taken all possible precautions in order to detect the defective bottles. In fact, the bottle passed through an initial manual check; they were then passed through an electronic system appropriate to identify cracks through a special lighting technique; subsequently, bottles underwent a pressure test 1.7 times in excess of the pressure of ordinary fizzy water; finally, they were filled with water and once again checked one by one by employees (BGH 9 May 1995, 2162).

[69] The leading case applying a strict liability rule on the producer for manufacturing defect is *Escola v Coca Cola bottling Co.* (24 Cal.2d 453, 150 P.2d 436 (1944)). In his concurrent opinion, J Traynor writes: "Even if there is no negligence [...] public policy demands that responsibility be fixed wherever it will most effectively reduce the hazards to life and health inherent in defective products that reach the market. It is evident that the manufacturer can anticipate some hazards and guard against the recurrence of others, as the public cannot. Those who suffer injury from defective products are unprepared to meet its consequences. The cost of an injury and the loss of time or health may be an overwhelming misfortune to the person injured and a needless one for the risk of injury can be insured by the manufacturer and distributed among the public as a cost of doing business".

[70] GL Priest, 'The Invention of Enterprise Liability: A Critical History of the Intellectual Foundations of Modern Tort Law', 14 *J Legal Stud* (1985) 61, see also WL Prosser, 'The Fall of the Citadel (Strict Liability to the Consumer)', 50 *Minn L Rev* (1966) 791, 793–94. From a viewpoint of economic efficiency of the system the doctrine finds its source in Italy in P Trimarchi, *Rischio e responsabilità oggettiva (*Milano, 1961); from the viewpoint of social solidarity see S Rodotà, *Il problema della responsabilità civile* (Milano, 1964).

Even though the European directive does not mention any distinction among different kinds of defects, within every member state, a strict liability rule for manufacturing defects is made explicit either by courts or by lawmakers.[71]

On the other hand, when the design of an entire type of product is questioned, the detection of a product's defectiveness becomes much more complex since a completely safe product cannot exist. Following the American Third Restatement on torts, in order to prove a design defect, the claimant has to demonstrate that an alternative design of the product would have been possible and would have been cheaper than the overall costs of damages foreseeable at the time when the product has been put into circulation.[72] Because the risk utility test takes into consideration the global costs related to all the products, rather than the marginal costs related to the single case, it becomes an assessment of the benefit of a type of product for the community.[73] This is more evident in cases where an alternative design does not exist, such as for vaccine cases. Therefore, in the US, the public interest is included within the balancing of the individual interests of the parties, while in Europe it is usually treated as an exception that might eventually paralyze the rule generally applied to solve the conflict among individuals.[74] It has already been remarked that this benefit/cost analysis in a general perspective gives the US court the role of a national risk regulator.[75] This is not surprising in a system where courts are also lawmakers as they create precedent; where courts of private law are provided with the power to punish, a power which in other legal systems is normally reserved for criminal courts; where courts may decide class actions through an opt-out mech-

---

[71] For example art 117 of the Italian consumer code states: "a product is defective if it does not provide the safety normally provided by other products in the same series."

[72] D G Owen, 'Risk-Utility Balancing in Design Defect Cases', 30 *U Mich JL Reform* (1996–1997) 239; AD Twerski, 'From Risk-Utility to Consumer Expectation: Enhancing the Role of Judicial Screening in Product Liability Litigation', 11 *Hofstra Law Review* (1983) 861.

[73] J Stapleton, 'Restatement (Third) of Torts: Product Liability, an Anglo-Australian Perspective', 39 *Washburn Law J* (2000) 363.

[74] The cases in which there is a conflict between the general interest and the individual interest are governed in the Directive by those provisions setting out an exception with respect to the general rule of resolution of the conflict between the parties (consider, for example, the exemption of liability of the manufacturer when a defect is due to compliance with a mandatory regulation). The heterogeneity in the concept of general or collective interest with respect to individual interest is analyzed in P Femia, *Interessi e conflitti culturali nell'autonomia privata e nella responsabilità civile* (Napoli, 1996) 124.

[75] The remark is in W Kip Viscusi, *Reforming product Liability* (Harvard University Press, 1991) 83. "(I)f regulatory requirements exist and lead to an efficient level of safety for a product, then a risk/utility test in the courts is extraneous. In effect, the analyses supporting the regulations would have already provided the answers to the risk/utility test in that they have shown that the resulting guidelines are efficient".

anism that automatically applies to an entire class of individuals. In short, the US has a system where the divide between private and public law appears to be somewhat fading in the eyes of a lawyer from continental Europe, and it is therefore not surprising that the general interest may come into play in proceedings among individuals.

However, the point is that in certain cases, the benefit/cost analysis leads to decisions that clash with the general sensibility and coherence of the system. This may happen in particular when a product causes consistent damage in very few cases that are not avoidable by the user, even though the user is well-informed about the risks. A classic example is provided by the well-known *Ford Pinto* case.[76] In May 1972, a Ford Pinto was struck by another car traveling at approximately thirty miles per hour. The impact ignited a fire in the Pinto, which killed the driver and left her thirteen-year-old son with devastating injuries. The plaintiff claimed that Ford had improperly placed the gas tank where the gas could explode if the car was hit from the rear. Ford defended itself, showing that a cost/benefit analysis of different gas tank placements had been done correctly, as the cost of putting the tank in a safer place was too high in relation to the number of lives that would be saved by doing so.[77] The straightforward application of the risk/utility test would lead to arguing that the product is not defective with the consequence that the few unlucky victims shall bear the entire cost of damages on their own. Nevertheless, the jury held Ford liable and awarded the claimant 2.5 million USD in compensatory damages, as well as 125 million USD in punitive damages (subsequently reduced to USD 3.5 million). This example shows that the risk/utility test is not acceptable when the damage is avoidable with an extra cost compared to the damage caused to an individual.[78]

---

[76] *Grimshaw v Ford Motor Co*, 1 19 Cal. App. 3d 757, 174 Cal. Rptr. 348 (1981).

[77] Ford estimated the cost to make this production adjustment to the Pinto would have been $11 per vehicle. Ford contended that its reason for making the cost/benefit analysis was that the National Highway Traffic Safety Administration required them to do so. Moreover, Ford said that the NHTSA supplied them with the $200,000 as the figure for the value of a lost life. Therefore the result of the Ford cost/benefit analysis was:
Benefits:
Savings: 180 burn deaths, 180 serious burn injuries, 2100 burned vehicles
Unit Cost: $200,000 per death, $67,000 per injury, $700 per vehicle
Total Benefit: 180 x ($200,000) + 180 x ($67,000) + 2100 x ($700) = $49.5 Million
Costs:
Sales: 11 million cars, 1.5 million light trucks
Unit Cost: $11 per car, $11 per truck
Total Cost: 11,000,000 x ($11) + 1,500,000 x ($1 1) = $137 Million
From Ford Motor Company internal memorandum: 'Fatalities Associated with Crash-Induced Fuel Leakage and Fires.' Source: D Birsch and JH Fielder, *The Ford Pinto Aase: A Study in Applied Ethics, Business, and Technology* (Albany, 1994) 28.

[78] On one hand, the cost would have been 11 USD for a different placement of the gas tank in one car and, on the other hand, the life and safety of Lily Gray and her son.

When the risk of damage is unavoidable, both by the manufacturer and the user, the risk/utility test is justified by arguing that the user has consciously accepted that risk on the condition that the manufacturer has adequately informed the user. This explains why the cases on cigarettes or vaccines are usually brought before a court claiming a warning defect rather than a design defect. However, this reasoning might be acceptable with regard to hedonistic products, such as cigarettes or alcoholic drinks. In the case of a vaccine or a drug necessary to treat or to prevent a serious disease, it seems more difficult to argue that the user has the free choice not to use the product in order to avoid the inherent risk of damage, since this decision comes at a very high cost.

The point is that the cases on design defects present the very same factors which justify the application of a strict liability rule in manufacturing defects, following the doctrine of enterprise liability.[79] These factors are, on the one hand, that the risk of damage has been foreseen by the manufacturer who has consciously accepted it since it does not exceed the expected benefits of his activity. On the other hand, the user, aware of the risk of damage, does not have any way to avoid it; he can just decide not to use the product, but according to the type of product, this decision can represent an excessive cost (for example, when the product is a drug necessary to treat or to prevent a disease). The application of the enterprise liability doctrine to these cases would condemn the manufacturer to compensating victims for damages that he had already taken into account in his benefit/cost analysis, as they are foreseeable costs. Therefore, these costs are manageable by the manufacturer either through a proportional increase of the price of the product or through insurance. Furthermore, the strict liability rule works as an incentive for the manufacturer to finance research in order to find a way to avoid a design defect of a product which may cause side effects.

Put differently, following this analysis, the distinction among manufacturing, design and warning defect is not really effective from an operational point of view. What really matters for the decision of the courts is if the damage was foreseeable and avoidable.[80] In this case liability will be on the party which was in the best position to avoid the damage. If the damage was foreseeable in theory but unavoidable by both parties, then a strict liability

---

[79] The co-reporters of the Third Restatement recognized the existence of "a special subset of design defects involving products that malfunction, thereby failing to perform their manifestly intended function in a self-defeating manner. In those special design cases the defects are functionally equivalent to manufacturing defects, so strict liability works as well for them" (A Twerski and J Henderson, 'The Products Liability Restatement: Was It a Success? Manufacturers' Liability for Defective Product Designs: The Triumph of Risk/Utility', 74 *Brooklyn L Rev* (2009) 1062).

[80] For a more detailed analysis on this point see: E Rajneri, 'La notion de défectuosité du produit dans les jurisprudences des pays européens', in *Revue Internationale de droit comparé*, forthcoming.

rule should apply for manufacturing, as well as for design defects. Lastly, if the risk of damage was not foreseeable given the state of scientific and technical knowledge, then the manufacturer will not be held liable due to the development risk defence.

Despite its incoherence, the risk/utility test is also present in Europe. It was first applied in Germany through the Drug Act of 1976 (*Arzneimittelgesetz*).[81] The Act states that the manufacturer or distributor is liable if the drug, being used correctly, has harmful effects which, in consideration of the state of medical knowledge, exceed a tolerable level (§ 5 Drug Act). That is, the manufacturer or the distributor of the drug is liable if the risks of the drug outweigh its benefits. Alternatively, he is liable "if the injury is caused by an instruction which does not adequately represent the state of medical knowledge" (§ 84 (1) no. 2 Drug Act). The German Drug Act is a special regime which still exists alongside the Product Liability Directive. Even though the European Directive does not mention the risk/utility test in its definition of defectiveness, German courts also tend to refer to the test in cases of defective products other than drugs.[82]

Interestingly, the French *Cour de cassation* has also recently made reference to a benefit/cost balance in cases concerning vaccines that are allegedly defective.[83] The *Cour de cassation* seems to suggest in its hermetic language that the general benefits and costs assessment could be avoided, by arguing the presence of a manufacturing defect in the specific doses of vaccine injected in the claimant rather than a design defect. Besides the difficulty of proving a manufacturing defect in a single dose of vaccine, which has already been injected, what is interesting is that the French court implicitly accepts the application of the general benefit cost assessment in design defect cases.

On the contrary there are systems, such as the Italian system, where the risk/utility test is not applied at all. Therefore, having proven that the product has caused unavoidable damage in that specific case, the manufacturer is certainly held liable even though the product is beneficial for the community.

In conclusion, the success of a design defect case in an EU Member State's jurisdiction depends on whether or not the risk/utility test is applied. The answer is crucial in order to decide if and where to file a collective action for a product design defect.

D. Conclusion

Product liability law has been enacted to implement a level of consumer protection adequate for an advanced industrial system. As made clear in the

---

[81] AMG 1976.
[82] See for example BGH 16 June 2009, VI ZR 107/08.
[83] Cass., 1ère civ., 26 September 2012.

consideranda of the European Product Liability Directive, consumer protection is intended not as a goal in itself, but as an instrument to make the internal market more efficient. In fact, the asserted strict liability rule is counterbalanced by a series of defences (such as the development risk defence) that are provided in order to protect manufacturers from unpredictable compensation costs and excessive litigation. Other legal tools are provided by the system in order to minimize the number and severity of accidents caused by a defective product, and at the same time, prevent or avoid excessive litigation costs.

First, there is the regulatory system which aims at preventing damages.[84] In order to accomplish its function, the regulatory authority balances and compares the benefits and the risks presented by the product. If the product is beneficial for the community, the regulator authorizes its distribution (even though the product may have side effects in some cases).

On the other hand, there is the instrument of the public or private compensation fund, set up for reasons of solidarity and equity. Its purpose is to award an indemnity (which is less than compensation) to certain victims of the unavoidable side effects of a product (for example, a vaccine). The underlying idea is that whenever an individual has to suffer a sacrifice for the benefit of the community, he deserves compensation from the community.[85]

Furthermore, there is the product liability law, which has both a compensatory and deterrence function.

In this system, the class action has little residual space that is made narrower in Italy by the lack of economic incentive in comparison to those provided in the US legal system. All things considered, it is not surprising that the new instrument has had such a low impact so far in Italy. However, it cannot be concluded that it is useless or disappointing. Even silent and unapplied, the class action is a threat which is effective as a deterrent in cases of mass tort caused by defective products when the defect was foreseeable by the manufacturer. However, its efficacy as a deterrent will vanish automatically if European national courts decide to apply the risk/utility test in order to assess every alleged design defect of a product, despite the fact that the test is not mentioned in the directive on product liability.

---

[84] Concerning the ex ante regulation, the decision of the *Tribunal Adminstratif de Paris* that upheld the State responsible in the case of the Mediator, deeming it 'responsible for misconduct' by the drug agency who had withdrawn the drug too late from the market after its collateral effects were already known (*Trib. admnistratif de Paris* 3 July 2014).

[85] R Caranta, 'Danni da vaccinazione e responsabilità dello Stato', *Resp civ e prev* (1998) 1352.

*Collective Redress in Environmental
Liability Cases: The Spanish Approach*

Albert Ruda González*

I. INTRODUCTION

As is well known, the law of torts allows a victim to recover a loss from the person at fault. It is a branch of the legal system which applies to human victims, since it deals with adverse effects only suffered by individuals. However, some forms of harm affect the general public more than a single individual. A clear example is what is known as pure ecological damage or pure environmental harm. Pure environmental harm is a destruction of the environment which –as in the case of the destruction of the ozone layer, the alteration of the global climate, or the extinction of a species– does not affect the individual interests, goods, or attributes of any specific individual. Instead, one may say that the victim is the environment itself. In this case, no one has a proprietary interest on which to base a claim for damages against the tortfeasor, since the damage affects goods which either belong to no one (*res nullius*) or belong to the public in general (*res communes omnium*).

Therefore, the question to be raised is whether the person who causes pure ecological damage can be held liable for a tort. In this regard, and assuming that liability existed, the subject also raises the question as to whether any form of collective redress would be suitable to sue the polluter. This question has become especially significant after the European Commission has recommended that Member States introduce collective redress mechanisms into their legal systems to ensure access to justice, including *inter alia* the area of environmental protection.[1]

---

* Senior Lecturer in Private Law, Institute of European and Comparative Private Law, University of Girona. Paper written within the framework of the Spanish Ministry of Science and Technology R&D grant (Ref Der2013-40613-R) with the title 'Modernization and harmonization of the law of tort: boundaries of responsibility, compensable damages and assessment', funded by the Ministry of Science and Innovation of Spain for the period 2014–2016). Project directors: Prof. Dr. Miquel Martin-Casals and Dr. Josep Solé Feliu.

[1] See Commission Recommendation of 11 June 2013 on common principles for injunctive and compensatory collective redress mechanisms in the Member States concerning violations of rights granted under Union Law (2013/396/EU, OJ L 201, 26.7.2013). See also the

However, it is also well known that it is very difficult to fit the concept of pure ecological damage into the traditional law of torts for several reasons. An opposing tension exists between the individual and the anthropocentric approach of the law of torts on one hand,[2] and the collective, ecological or as it is sometimes called ecocentric approach on the other. The Spanish legal system clearly does not grant legal standing to any specific individual to claim compensation on behalf of the public.[3]

Instead, public law usually plays a leading role in the attempt to address environmental damage. Indeed, environmental law in Spain remains predominantly in the public law domain. Nevertheless, the public administration generally lacks the resources to enforce regulations and proceed against every person who harms the environment. Moreover, the public administration has no up-to-date information on every environmental risk. The system is heavily influenced by lobbyists, and what is worse is that the public administration itself causes significant damage to the environment. Recent events in Spain show that the acts or omissions of the public administration may in fact cause, increase, or not diminish environmental damage already caused. This phenomenon has been extensively discussed in the *Prestige* oil-spill case.[4] Moreover, in case of misconduct by the public authorities, the negative consequences which may ensue for the environment do not affect the public administration as such, but affect the general public, in the form of externalities.[5] The result will probably hold no one liable for pure ecological damage, and more particularly, the public is going to bear the loss. Therefore, the polluter will not be charged with paying.

Attention must also be given to another scenario, namely, the one where the polluter causes harm to several, perhaps even a large number of victims. As individuals, they may suffer very little harm. However, collectively, the damage may be enormous. Each victim may lack the necessary incentives to sue. Nevertheless, if damage could be aggregated in some way, ie, by providing specifically tailored procedural rules, the lack of incentive for the victims to sue could perhaps be resolved. Again, collective redress is a possibility to be considered.

Communication from the Commission to the European Parliament, the Council, the European Economic and Social Committee and the Committee of the Regions "Towards a European Horizontal Framework for Collective Redress", 11 June 2013, COM(2013) 401 final.

[2] See C de Miguel Perales, *Derecho español del medio ambiente* (3rd edn, Thomson Reuters Civitas, 2009) 517.

[3] See A Ruda, *El daño ecológico puro* (Thomson Aranzadi, 2008) 35 ff.

[4] Decision of the Court of Appeal no 1 of A Coruña 13.11.2013. On which see A Ruda, 'Spain', in E Karner and BC Steininger (eds.) *European Tort Law 2013* (De Gruyter, 2014) 651 with further references.

[5] See DH Cole, *Pollution & Property* (Cambridge University Press, 2002) 39 and 88.

II. THE CASE FOR AND AGAINST COLLECTIVE REDRESS UNDER SPANISH ENVIRONMENTAL LIABILITY LAW

As has already been noted, the claim for compensation for environmental damage may result in many complications from a procedural perspective. To start with, there is the complexity of evidence as regards the causal link, or the apportionment of damage among a plurality of polluters. Complex causal issues usually require the intervention of a number of experts, which delays the procedure and increases litigation costs. Moreover, the number of plaintiffs (victims) and defendants (polluters) may be very high. Generally speaking, Spanish civil procedure is not well-suited for claims with hundreds, if not thousands, of victims. Evidently, it may also be questioned whether private law is the most appropriate tool to solve multi-party litigation with a high number of participants on either side of the case. The traditional law suit consists of a single plaintiff acting against a single defendant. Hence, the procedure may be unsuitable whenever impairment of the environment affects thousands, perhaps even millions, of people.

Apart from these problems, little economic incentive exists for a plaintiff to bring a claim for damage or loss that hardly seems serious or which requires the claimant to bear a lot of expense in order to support his claim. The cost of litigation may be disproportionate to the extent of damage caused to each individual. The damage may be spread among a multitude of victims, who would not be incentivized to bring a claim as an individual (the 'scattered cost' or 'dispersed cost' problem). An example of a lack of incentive is a pollution that causes a mild cough only once a year for victims.[6] Because of this dispersion of the damage suffered, the cost of compensating victims of environmental pollution may exceed the cost of the damage itself.[7] Also, taking into account that in many countries the victims can turn immediately to a social security system, the perverse effect is an incentive to spread the damage among as many people as possible, which is sometimes known as 'tall stacks policy' (*Politik der hohen Schornsteine*). Paradoxically, the more one pollutes, the less he will be accountable for. In these circumstances, even proportional liability – understood as a type of liability where each defendant is held liable according to the probability that he caused damage to the victim – would not increase incentives to litigate. On the contrary, where victims

---

[6] The example is taken from HB Schäfer and C Ott, *Lehrbuch der ökonomischen Analyse des Zivilrechts* (3rd edn, Springer, 2000) 337.

[7] See BL Benson, 'Rent Seeking on the Legal Frontier' in RL Stroup and RE Meiners (eds.), *Cutting Green Tape: Toxic Pollutants, Environmental Regulation and the Law* (The Independent Institute, 2000) 129, 131 and RE Jenkins and JW Kastner, 'Running Aground in a Sea of Complex Litigation: A Case Comment on the Exxon Valdez Litigation' 18 *UCLA J Envtl L & Pol'y* (1999/2000) 151, 159.

may only get a proportional share of compensation from the defendants, incentives to sue will be even lower.[8] Even worse, a civil claim with hundreds, maybe thousands of people affected is less suitable due to the procedural costs. Furthermore, if the kind of damage for which the claim was filed was pure ecological damage, one would have to add the costs related with the financial assessment of damage.[9]

Moreover, lawsuits on environmental issues tend to be terribly long and complex. Therefore, highly specialized courts are needed which are well-prepared to deal with environmental disputes. The complex and lengthy nature of the lawsuit fills victims with dread and discourages them from lodging a civil lawsuit in defence of the environment.

To facilitate a victim's access to justice, the legislator may use several procedural devices, such as attributing a more active role in the procedure to the judge or altering the rules on the burden of proof. Above all, the legislator may give the claimant the possibility of demanding that the defendant brings to court any information related with the causal process of damage, according to the model drafted by the Lugano Convention,[10] as well as the German Act on environmental liability,[11] which provide the victim with the right to disclosure from the facility operator. This is an aspect which is not dealt with by Spanish legislation with a sufficient degree of detail.

Apart from these issues, the true crux of environmental litigation in many cases has to do with legal standing, both active and passive. Standing may be defined on the grounds that the victim has suffered individual damage, which affects the victim in a personal way. In contrast to this, pure ecological damage has a collective nature. Under Spanish law there is no *actio popularis* which would allow anyone to claim damages for harm to the environment, neither in private law nor criminal law. In fact, the absence of a close link between individuals and natural resources affected by pure ecological damage explains the state of affairs.

It has been noted that this situation could be modified in two ways. First, pure ecological damage could be linked with a personality right (as under

---

[8] See Schäfer and Ott (above n 6) 339 and C Katzenmeier, 'Beweismaßreduzierung und probabilistische Proportionalhaftung' *ZZP* (2004) 187, 210. Also, on that paradox, from a sociological perspective, U Beck, *Politik in der Risikogesellschaft* (Suhrkamp, 1991) 123.

[9] See A Endres, *Ökonomische Grundlagen des Haftungsrechts* (Physica-Verlag, 1991) 54.

[10] Art 15, Convention on Civil Liability for Damage Resulting from Activities Dangerous to the Environment, Lugano, 21 June 1993, http://conventions.coe.int/Treaty/en/Treaties/Html/150.htm.

[11] § 8, *Umwelthaftungsgesetz vom 10. Dezember 1990, Bundesgesetzblatt I*, 2634. A translation into English can be found at http://www.utexas.edu/law/academics/centers/transnational/work_new/german/case.php?id=1396.

Greek law),[12] but this could be a problematic solution. Second, the infringement of a collective interest in the environment could be deemed sufficient to grant legal standing to bring a public claim (as under Portuguese law),[13] or the individual could bring such a claim on behalf of the public administration through subrogation, contingent on the administration remaining passive (which is possible under Italian law).[14]

To avoid the risk of abuse, the compensation could always be awarded to the public administration as a representative of the public. At present, the public administration is the sole entity entitled to bring a claim for damage to the environment under Spanish law, and this complies with the European Directive on environmental liability.[15]

The goal of environmental restoration cannot be achieved only through the use of so-called class actions. As is well-known, collective or class actions allow a group of people to claim compensation for damages that are substantially identical. Class actions therefore make it unnecessary for each victim to bring a claim separately insofar as they have a common interest that all claims are tried at trial in a single procedure through one or more representatives of the whole class. If successful, the compensation would be distributed among all members of the class, whether they had been represented at trial or not. The question is whether this mechanism is useful for claims of pure ecological damage.

Certainly, class actions exist in the US and more recently in some European jurisdictions. Regarding environmental cases, they can already be found in the Swedish law.[16] However, they are not possible under Spanish law. The closest Spanish mechanism that resembles a class action are collective claims to protect the interests of consumers.[17]

In Spanish law, class actions do not exist strictly speaking with an all-encompassing scope. Rather, a compensatory collective action is

---

[12] See K Tsekouras, *Zivilrechtliche Abfallhaftung im deutschen, griechischen und europäischen Recht* (Peter Lang, 2001) 91, with further references.

[13] See JS Monteiro, 'Protecção dos interesses económicos na responsabilidade civil por dano ambiental' 81 *Boletim da Faculdade de Direito, Universidade de Coimbra, Studia Iuridica* (2004) 133, 141.

[14] See GC Rosi, 'Civile e penale nella repressione del danno all'ambiente' 1 *Diritto dell'economia* (1989) 161, 162.

[15] Directive 2004/35/CE of the European Parliament and of the Council of 21 April 2004 on environmental liability with regard to the prevention and remedying of environmental damage.

[16] Chapter 32, para 13 of the Environmental Code, *Miljöbalk* (MB)(1998:808), http://www.notisum.se/rnp/sls/lag/19980808.HTM.

[17] As laid down by art 6.1.7 of the Civil Procedure Act (*Ley 1/2000, de Enjuiciamiento Civil* (LEC)) *Boletín Oficial del Estado* [BOE] No. 7, 8 January 2000.

available,[18] that has a limited scope in the protection of consumers and users.[19] This places Spanish law along with others legal systems that provide a similar mechanism, but the system lags behind other jurisdictions in which class actions have general application, most notably class actions in the US. Furthermore, Spanish law does not provide a specific collective action for environmental damage. In this respect, it differs from Swedish law where the legislator has introduced such a class action mechanism through the reform of the Environmental Code by way of the so-called Act on collective procedure (*Grupprättegångslagen*).[20] The latter provides a group claim (*grupptalan*), which will result in a court ruling that may involve individuals who have suffered harm, but did not take part in the procedure.[21]

It seems that the class action could perhaps mitigate rational apathy of the victims who, as mentioned above, prefer not to litigate due to the risk of losing the case, of not collecting any compensation, and of having to pay legal costs. If this is so, class actions may remedy the problem of the dispersed cost. In addition to that, class actions may remedy the fact that the extent of damage may be very small in relation to each victim, but catastrophic as a whole. Both arguments make class action quite attractive in relation to environmental damage.[22]

However, it is risky to import isolated elements of different legal systems, regardless of the context, and have them function properly. The application of doctrines or institutions from other systems could lead to unjust or absurd results. Furthermore, such importation may be unnecessary. In the US, class actions are used, among other reasons, as a specific mechanism to make the

---

[18] See JJ Marín López, 'Las acciones de clase en el derecho español' (2001) *InDret* www.indret.com 1, 3; but see M Cárcaba Fernández, 'Defensa civil del medio ambiente', 171 *Revista de Derecho Urbanístico y Medio Ambiente* (1999) 141, 152; J Conde Antequera, *El deber jurídico de restauración ambiental* (Comares, 2004) 142 and R de Ángel Yagüez, *Tratado de responsabilidad civil* (Civitas and Universidad de Deusto, 1993) 611.

[19] Arts. 6.1.7°, 6.1.8°, 7.7, 11, 13.1, 15, 52.1, 76.2.1., 78.4, 221, 222.3, 249, 250, 256.1.6°, 519 and finally, 711.2 and 728.3 LEC.

[20] *Lag om grupprättegång*, SFS 2002:599. On which see S Rubenson, *Miljöbalken. Den nya miljörätten* (3rd ed., Norstedts Juridik, 2002) 151. Concerning the proposal to create a class action in Canada to claim for environmental damage, see Public Review Panel on Tanker Safety and Marine Spills Response Capability, *Protecting our waters*, Final report (Minister of Supply and Services Canada 1990) 101.

[21] Chapter 32, para 13 of the Environmental Code (above n 16).

[22] Among others see M Alonso Pérez, 'La tutela del derecho civil frente a inmisiones molestas y nocivas', in JL Iglesias Prada (ed.), *Estudios jurídicos en homenaje al profesor Aurelio Menéndez* (Civitas, 1996) vol IV, 4783, 4806; A Crespo Hernández, *La responsabilidad civil derivada de la contaminación transfronteriza ante la jurisdicción estatal* (Eurolex, 1999) 58; cf. J Egea Fernández, *Acción negatoria, inmisiones y defensa de la propiedad* (Marcial Pons, 1994) 88; S Patti, *La tutela civile dell'ambiente* (Cedam, 1979) 119.

defeated litigant pay the fees for the defence and technical representation of the winner. These costs must be met by compensation.[23] It seems unlikely that the class action could become established in systems such as the Spanish that does not recognize the right to recover attorney's fees for winning the lawsuit.[24] However, the legal regime for class actions in the US may still be too controversial even on key issues.[25]

It must also be kept in mind that if environmental damage is widespread, diffuse and does not result in substantial harm to each individual, victims have no incentive to bring a claim. The issue of attorney compensation could be resolved through an agreement that would put it below the actual damage.[26] Furthermore, class actions may work when damages are identical or very similar and occur at the same time, which is not necessarily the case for damage caused by environmental pollution.[27] Moreover, they presuppose individual claims of the class members. Instead, what is required is to litigate for pure ecological damage, ie, for damages which anyone can claim; this is the primary reason why class actions in defence of diffuse interests often fail.[28] Finally, the class action is a very expensive instrument, requiring identification of the class and so-called 'certification,' not to mention the division of compensation.[29] In the case of pure ecological damage, in which the whole community is harmed, the cost would in theory be even greater.[30]

---

[23] See LS Mullenix, *Mass Tort Litigation. Cases and Materials* (West, 1996) 728 n. 28 and P Loser-Krogh, 'Kritische Überlegungen zur Reform des privaten Haftpflichtrecht' 2 *ZSR* (2003) 127, 192.

[24] Article 394 LEC (above n 17). See similarly, although with regard to German law, H Stoll, *Haftungsfolgen im bürgerlichen Recht. Eine Darstellung auf rechtsvergleichender Grundlage* (Müller, 1993) 128.

[25] See RH Klonoff and EKM Bilich, *Class Actions and Other Multy-Party Litigation* (West, 2000) 3; S Ueki, 'Umweltschutz- und Produzentenhaftung in Japan' in G Baumgärtel (ed), *Grundprobleme des Privatrechts. Japanische Veröffentlichungen in deutscher Sprache* (Heymann, 1985) 147, 159 and, in Spanish legal scholarship, R de Ángel Yagüez, *Algunas previsiones sobre el futuro de la responsabilidad civil (con especial atención a la reparación del daño)* (Civitas, 1995) 95.

[26] See Schäfer and Ott (above n 6) 338.

[27] In a similar vein, see D Lungershausen, *Unbekannte Klägerfälle im amerikanischen Umwelthaftungsrecht* (Peter Lang, 1993) 42.

[28] See B Pozzo, *Danno ambientale ed imputazione della responsabilità. Esperienze giuridiche a confronto* (Giuffrè, 1996) 130 and W van Gerven, J Lever and P Larouche, *Tort Law. Common Law of Europe Casebooks* (Hart, 2000) 276.

[29] See RB Stewart, 'Environmental Law', in AB Morrison (ed), *Fundamentals of American Law* (Oxford University Press, 1997) 481, 482.

[30] See L Kaplow and S Shavell, 'Economic Analysis of Law' (1999) NBER Working Paper no. 6960 www.nber.org/papers/w6960.pdf 24.

It has been sometimes noted that the general trend in Europe is to be against class actions.[31] The reason is that other mechanisms already exist that allow a claim to be filed and reach a similar result (eg via legal standing to sue the public administration, or compensation funds, see eg the *Contergan* case, via taxation, or through actions brought by associations).[32]

Class actions would indeed be inadequate in this regard for several reasons. Decisive aspects relating to the functioning of these actions still remain unknown. In addition, they allow the victim to bring a claim in defence of individual interests and could be unsuitable for the protection of collective interests. Finally, in the case of pure ecological damage, the class of victims is the whole community as a collective group.

The fact that pure ecological damage affects interests belonging to the community suggests that the best person to be attributed legal standing to claim compensation would be the State. It has enough resources to bring a claim, and it represents the whole community. Furthermore, the State is charged with a duty to take care of the environment (as laid down by Article 45 of the Spanish Constitution), and it has sovereignty on all natural resources that are not owned by. Under Spanish law, the public administration has legal standing to claim compensation for damage caused to natural resources belonging to the so-called public domain (*dominio público*). This can ordinarily be done by using the possibilities known as public self-defence (*autotutela administrativa*). However, this in theory leaves private law remedies untouched. Nowadays, the Spanish legal system can be classified as a double track system. Nevertheless, it seems that the power or authority conferred on the public administration is insufficient for substantiating a private law claim in tort for damage to natural resources which do not belong to anyone. It is submitted that the legislature could widen the legal standing of the public administration according to the model of other countries (such as Italy or the US). The law could support this solution on the assumption that the State is a custodian of the environment with a legal right of action whenever natural resources are damaged. This is certainly the path followed by the European Directive, but it is believed that it still falls short, because it only covers some, and not all, natural resources to be found within the territory of the EU. In spite of the EU Directive, legal standing

---

[31] See M Taruffo, 'Some Remarks on Group Litigation in Comparative Perspective', 11 *Duke J Comp & Int'l L* (2001) 405, 412; L Dommering-van Rongen, *Schade Vergoeden door Fondsvorming* (Kluwer, 1996) 21–22, and van Gerven, Lever and Larouche, *Tort Law* (above n 28) 268 and 452.

[32] See G Walter, 'Mass Tort Litigation in Germany and Switzerland' 11 *Duke J Comp & Int'l L* (2001) 369, 373; WM Landes and RA Posner, *The Economic Structure of Tort Law* (Harvard University Press, 1987) 52 and H Bocken, *Preventie, toerekening en herstel van schade door milieuverontreiniging. Preadvies Nederlandse Vereniging voor Rechtsvergelijking* (Kluwer, 1983) 27.

conferred to the State could be dysfunctional in the case where the author of pure ecological damage is the State itself. For instance, this would be the case of impairment or damage caused to the environment for military activities. For this reason, it would be convenient for the public custodian of the environment to have a certain degree of autonomy, by way of an Ombudsman of the environment.

Granting the State standing to sue is only a minimal and insufficient solution to resolving the problem of pure ecological damage. This is more evident in Italy, where the legislator was required to pass a new act widening the definition of legal standing by granting environmental organizations a legal right of action to claim damages so that the State would not alone be entitled to bring a claim.[33] Statutory reform was propelled by the fact that public authorities with legal standing to sue the authors of pure ecological damage remained passive in spite of the damage to the environment. The situation raised awareness that the efficacy of legislation on environmental protection was being seriously undermined in Italy.

As for Spain, non-governmental organizations cannot base their claims in tort actions on an analogical interpretation of the rule, as it does not confer to them legal standing to sue in the interest of consumers. The reason is that an identity of reason (*eadem ratio*) is lacking between both situations. As a matter of fact, it is has been noted that there is no need to broaden the scope of norms on consumer protection in that way. Some ecological non-governmental organizations (namely, *EAPAS* and the *Group for the Protection of the Ter River*)[34] have been awarded compensation for pure ecological damage in criminal procedures. This distorts the system of tort law and amounts to an unjustifiable inequality of treatment in the way the legal system deals with compensation of damage depending on which jurisdiction, private or criminal, is chosen. For this reason, the legislator should make it clear which solution should be applied in cases like these and whether environmental NGOs have the right to a compensation award in a private lawsuit, which has in fact been possible in the Netherlands, as the *Borcea* case shows.[35] It is suggested that the legislator could confer legal standing to NGOs under certain conditions, namely, public control and compliance with the legislation on legal persons.

---

[33] See S Patti, 'La valutazione del danno ambientale', *Riv Dir Civ* (1992) 447, 450 n. 7.

[34] See A Cabanillas Sánchez, *La reparación de los daños al medio ambiente* (Aranzadi, 1996) 193.

[35] Rb. Rotterdam 15.3.1991, *NJ* 1992, 91 (*Nederlandse Vereniging tot Bescherming van Vogels/ Intreprindera de Explotoara a Floti Maritimi Navrom*). On which see E Bauw, 'Nieuwe verdragen. De internationalisering van het milieuaansprakelijkheidsrecht', in RJJ van Acht and GC Sicking (eds.), *Privaatrecht en milieu* (WEJ Tjeenk Willink, 1994) 27, 35 n. 37.

Nobody should fear that a flood of claims will occur after legal standing is defined this way. The cost of litigation and the complexity of the procedure may in fact be enough to discourage frivolous claims. At any rate, it seems clear that granting standing to the public administration only is not enough, as the blatant lack of application of the present Environmental Liability Act shows.[36]

All issues considered, private law faces many serious difficulties when it is confronted with the problem of pure ecological damage. It is a form of damage which is difficult to define since it affects the equilibrium of ecosystems more than concrete natural resources. Damage does not affect any goods belonging to private parties nor the public administration, but affects nature belonging to everyone (*res communes omnium*) or to no one (*res nullii*). Pure ecological damage is difficult to prove and to attribute to a specific author, since it may be derived from the sum or interaction of several causal contributions. It is often irreparable in kind, and compensation by an approximately equivalent amount is riddled with difficulties, because money only captures the value of natural resources in a very imperfect way. The potential magnitude of pure ecological damage may be so far-reaching that liability becomes hardly insurable. Existing compensation funds only provide limited compensation for pure ecological damage. The present situation, where full liability for pure ecological damage is lacking, is unsatisfactory. In this regard, it seems necessary for the legislator to redefine legal standing in such a way that tort claims can effectively be brought to obtain compensation for this damage. Both the State as a guardian of the environment, as well as environmental organizations (under conditions to be defined by the law) should have standing to bring a claim for pure ecological damage.

---

[36] See B Lozano Cutanda, 'La responsabilidad medioambiental dos años después: ¿por qué se retrasa su aplicación? Problemas y dudas sin resolver', *Diario La Ley* (2009) 7270.

Collective Redress and Competition Law Claims: Some Specific Issues

Mihail Danov*

I. INTRODUCTION

It is well established that numerous businesses and consumers across Europe may suffer harm caused by competition law infringements.[1] However, the high costs associated with individual antitrust damage actions might be a significant deterrent for claimants[2] in competition law cases.[3] If multiple injured parties were able to combine their claims with the intent to pursue them collectively,[4] then their litigiousness could be boosted. With this in

---

* Associate Professor in Law, University of Leeds.

[1] eg *The Consumer Association v JJB Sports PLC,* [2009] CAT 2, 30 January 2009; *Emerald Supplies v British Airways* [2009] EWHC 741 (Ch) a'ffd *Emerald Supplies v British Airways* [2010] EWCA Civ 1284; *In re: International Air Transportation Surcharge Antitrust Litigation* MDL No 1793 (United States District Court for the Northern District of California, San Francisco Division). See also: R Mulheron, 'The Recognition, and *Res Judicata* Effect, of a United States Class Actions Judgment in England: A Rebuttal of Vivendi' *Modern Law Review* (2012) 180; M Danov, D Fairgrieve and G Howells, 'Collective Redress Proceedings: How to Close the Enforcement Gap and Provide Redress for Consumers' in M Danov, F Becker and P Beaumont (eds), *Cross-Border EU Competition Law Actions* (Hart Publishing, 2013) 253–282.

[2] Commission Recommendation on common principles for injunctive and compensatory collective redress in the Member States concerning violation of rights granted under Union Law [2013] OJ L201/60 (hereafter 'the Commission Recommendation'), Recital (9).

[3] M Danov and S Dnes, 'Cross-Border Competition Litigation: New Evidence from England and Wales' in Danov, Becker and Beaumont (above n 1) 45–47. See also: *2 Travel Group PLC (In Liquidation) v Cardiff City Transport Services Limited* [2011] CAT 30, 14 October 2011 [17]; *Yeheshkel Arkin v Borchard Lines and Others* [2005] EWCA Civ 655. See further J A Ordover, 'Costly litigation in the model of single activity accidents' 7 *Journal of Legal Studies* (1978) 243; S Shavel, 'The social versus the private incentives to bring suit in a costly legal system', 11 *Journal of Legal Studies* (1982) 333; HSE Graville, 'The Efficiency Implications of Cost Shifting Rules', 13 *International Review of Law and Economics* (1993) 3; CF Beckner III and A Katz, 'The Incentive Effects of Litigation Fee Shifting When Legal Standards Are Uncertain,' 15 *International Review of Law and Economics* (1995) 205; C Hodges, M Tulibacka and S Vogenauer (eds), *The Costs and Funding of Civil Litigation* (Hart Publishing, 2010).

[4] The EU legislator defines 'injured party' as "a person that has suffered harm caused by an

mind, the European Commission (EC) has decided that there is a case for the EU policy makers and national legislators to implement common principles for collective redress in order to facilitate the access to justice across Europe. To this end, the EU adopted a Recommendation on common principles for injunctive and compensatory collective redress in the Member States concerning violations of rights granted under EU Law.[5] The EU rule makers have clearly outlined their intentions by stating that:

> The aim of this Recommendation is to facilitate access to justice in relation to violations of rights under Union law and to that end to recommend that all Member States should have collective redress systems at national level that follow the same basic principles throughout the Union, taking into account the legal traditions of the Member States and safeguarding against abuse.[6]

Since Articles 101 and 102 TFEU, which are the main EU competition law provisions, are derived from the Treaty on the Functioning of the European Union, there is no doubt that the Recommendation will certainly be of great relevance in competition law claims.[7] Following the publication of the Commission Recommendation, the UK legislator has tabled legislative proposals which aim to "make it easier for consumers and businesses to gain access to redress where there has been an infringement of antitrust provisions."[8] Although the former proposal is broader than the latter (insofar as it is not limited to antitrust disputes), the purpose of this paper is to examine aspects of the Commission Recommendation and the Consumer Rights Bill in the light of some specific issues which characterise competition law claims.

The author will make a case that there is a need for an empirical study which aims to identify how the competition law enforcement process functions in the EU. The gathered data should allow researchers to assess the effectiveness of the current legislative framework, and evaluate whether there are effective remedies for injured parties across Europe.[9] To this end, the chapter will open with a brief review of the features of the competition law

---

infringement of competition law". See Article 2(6) of the Directive on antitrust damages actions which was adopted by the Council on 10th November 2014 http://ec.europa.eu/competition/antitrust/actionsdamages/proposed_directive_en.html.

[5] [2013] OJ L201/60.
[6] Commission Recommendation (Recital 10).
[7] Commission Recommendation (Recital 7).
[8] *Explanatory Notes – Consumer Rights Bill,* HL Bill 029-EN 2014-15, [407].
[9] The author contributes to the research project JUST/2013/JCIV/AG/4635 on "Cross-Border Litigation in Europe: Private International Law Legislative Framework, National Courts and the Court of Justice of the European Union." As part of this study, the research teams collect empirical evidence which explains the cross-border litigation pattern and assesses the effectiveness of the private international law instruments adopted at Union level.

infringements which might affect the level of litigiousness of private parties who have suffered harm as a result of these infringements. Then, the collective redress regime (as proposed by the Commission Recommendation and the Consumer Rights Bill) will be examined with a view to assessing whether it adequately addresses the specific aspects of competition law claims brought on behalf of multiple claimants. Finally, a case for an empirical study will be made.

II. INJURED PARTIES' LITIGIOUSNESS: ISSUES POSING SPECIFIC CHALLENGES

The purpose of this section is to demonstrate that there are certain features of competition law infringements and competition law enforcement proceedings which may affect injured parties' litigiousness. These specific issues may pose specific challenges,[10] which should be factored in, by national rule makers across Europe with a view to "ensur[ing] that any natural or legal person who has suffered harm caused by an infringement of competition law is able to claim and to obtain full compensation for that harm."[11]

A. Litigiousness of Numerous Injured Parties in Competition Law Cases

It has been submitted that "the legal costs and complexity [remain] an insuperable barrier for the vast majority of SMEs and consumers"[12] in competition cases. In other words, the level of complexity may inflate litigation costs, which may adversely affect an injured party's litigiousness. What are the issues which must be carefully considered in this context?

Some of the complex issues relate to the fact that most competition law infringements will cause mass harm to numerous businesses and consumers.[13] As a result, injured parties may be further up (or further down) the chain of distribution.[14] Since, according to the current legal framework,[15]

---

[10] See Danov, Fairgrieve and Howells (above n 1) 262–269.
[11] See Article 3 of the Directive on antitrust damages actions.
[12] Executive Summary – *Private Actions in Competition Law: A consultation on options for reform – government response*, https://www.gov.uk/government/consultations/private-actions-in-competition-law-a-consultation-on-options-for-reform, at 5.
[13] See the definition of 'mass harm situation.' Commission Recommendation, Section 3(b).
[14] *Emerald Supplies v British Airways* [2009] EWHC 741 (Ch) [36]; *Devenish Nutrition v Sanofi-Aventis* [2008] EWCA Civ 1086 [147] Longmore LJ and [151] Tuckey LJ. Danov, Fairgrieve and Howells (above n 1) 267–268.
[15] Directive on antitrust damages actions, Articles 3 and 12(1). Joined Cases C-295/04–C-298/04 *Manfredi v Lloyd Adriatico* [2006] 5 CMLR 17.

direct and indirect purchasers may both bring claims for competition law damages, there may be a level of uncertainty and complexity as to whether the injured party has "passed on the whole or part of the overcharge resulting from the infringement of competition law."[16] The issues were demonstrated in *Emerald*.[17] In this case, the claimants imported cut flowers using the air freight services provided by the defendant, British Airways. The defendants were members of a cartel which coordinated their pricing behaviour.[18] The claimants, who were direct and/or indirect purchasers, sought damages for breach of Article 101 TFEU. The ability of an injured party to sue had to be determined under CPR Rule 19.6 which requires the parties to have the "same interests in a claim." One of the questions before the English court was whether this requirement was satisfied. The Court held that:

> even if the criteria for inclusion in the class are sufficiently described the relief sought in the action is not equally beneficial for all members of the class. It is not disputed that damage is a necessary element in the cause of action of individual members of the class. Whether or not an individual member of the class can establish that necessary ingredient will depend on where in the chain of distribution he came and who if anyone in that chain had absorbed or passed on the alleged inflated price. Given the nature of the cause of action and the market in which the relevant transactions took place there is an inevitable conflict between the claims of different members of the class.[19]

In spite of the fact that, on many occasions, the end consumer will absorb the illegal overcharge, the individual damage caused to him may be insignificant[20] in comparison to the litigation costs,[21] and as a result, the end consumers may not be willing to sue.

Indeed, a recent comparative study,[22] which was funded by the European Parliament, demonstrated that the number of collective redress actions related

---

[16] Directive on antitrust damages actions, Article 13. *Devenish Nutrition v Sanofi-Aventis* (above n 14) [151] (Tuckey LJ).

[17] *Emerald Supplies v British Airways* (above n 1).

[18] Case COMP/39258 – Airfreight – Commission Decision of 9/11/2010 http://ec.europa.eu/competition/elojade/isef/case_details.cfm?proc_code=1_39258.

[19] *Emerald Supplies v British Airways* (above n 1) [36].

[20] M Handler, 'The Shift from Substantive to Procedural Innovations in Antitrust Suits – The Twenty-Third Annual Antitrust Review' (1971) 71 *Columbia Law Review* 1, 9. Danov, Fairgrieve and Howells (above n 1) 267.

[21] Danov and Dnes (above n 3) 45–47.

[22] P Buccirossi, M Carpagnano, L Ciari and others, *Collective Redress in Antitrust*, http://www.europarl.europa.eu/document/activities/cont/201206/20120613ATT46782/20120613ATT46782EN.pdf.

to antitrust infringements is still very limited in Europe.[23] The 2012 Report on Collective Redress in Antitrust went on to state that "[t]o date collective actions resulting in damages awarded to the victims have been observed only in Austria and in the UK."[24] Nonetheless, there is a strong case that, even in the UK, there are very few claims by SMEs and consumers,[25] so there is hardly any redress for consumers at present.[26] In January 2013, the UK government has stated that, "[c]hallenging anti-competitive behaviour is costly and complex, well beyond the resources of many businesses, particularly SMEs, and the financial costs of going to court makes it impractical for consumers to achieve redress."[27] It may be far from easy and cheap to ascertain the damage suffered by the individual injured parties (and for indirect purchasers in particular), in order to distribute it to them.[28] The EU legislator has recently noted that "it may be particularly difficult for consumers or undertakings that did not themselves make any purchase from the infringer to prove the extent of that harm."[29] This may explain why primarily large companies appear to be suing for EU competition law damages at present.[30]

B. *Competition Law Enforcement Pattern: Public Proceedings and Follow-on Private Proceedings*

The current enforcement pattern suggests that a significant majority of the private claims for damages caused by competition law infringements are preceded by public enforcement actions initiated by competition

---

[23] *Ibid*, 11 and 37.

[24] *Ibid*, 39.

[25] *Private Actions in Competition Law: A consultation on options for reform – government response*, (above n 12), at 5.

[26] Foreword from the Secretary of State, Rt. Hon. Dr. Vince Cable MP, *Private Actions in Competition Law* (above n 12), at 2.

[27] *Ibid*, at 2.

[28] Danov, Fairgrieve and Howells (above n 1) 266-268. LA Sullivan and WS Grimes, *The Law of Antitrust: An Integrated Handbook*, 2nd edn (Thomson West, 2006) 997.

[29] Directive on antitrust damages actions, Recital (41).

[30] Eg *Roche Products Limited, Roche Vitamine Europe AG (Switzerland), F. Hoffmann–La Roche AG (Switzerland) v Provimi Limited* [2003] EWHC 961 (Comm); *SanDisk Corporation v Koninklijke Philips Electronics and others* [2007] EWHC 332 (Ch), [2007] Bus LR 705; *Cooper Tire & Rubber Company v Shell Chemicals UK Limited* [2009] EWHC 2609 (Comm); *Cooper Tire & Rubber Company Europe Limited & Others* [2010] EWCA Civ 864; *Toshiba Carrier UK Ltd and Other v KME Yorkshire Limited & Others* [2011] EWHC 2665 (Ch); *Toshiba Carrier UK Ltd and Other v KME Yorkshire Limited & Others* [2012] EWCA Civ 169; *National Grid Electricity Transmission PLC v ABB Ltd & Others* [2012] EWHC 869 (Ch); *Deutsche Bahn v Morgan Crucible Company* [2012] EWCA Civ 1055; *Nokia Corporation v AU Optronics Corporation* [2012] EWHC 731 (Ch); *Ryanair Limited v Esso Italiana Srl* [2013] EWCA Civ 1450. See also Danov and Dnes (above n 3) 38.

authorities.[31] As noted elsewhere,[32] an inefficient institutional architecture may raise the level of uncertainty, which may in turn fuel the costs of enforcement. This would affect an injured party's litigiousness. If an injured party had to wait for a public authority to adopt a decision finding a competition law infringement, then there would be a significant level of delay, as there would be two sets of proceedings: public proceedings establishing the infringement; and private proceedings awarding damages. This may be an issue insofar as it is well established that "[d]elays can render the judicial protection of the rights ineffectual, reduce the value of the rights, adversely affect economic activity and lead to economic distortions."[33]

A specific challenge, which was put forward by the English Court of Appeal in *Enron*,[34] was how to address "the 'split' jurisdiction of regulator for infringement, tribunal for causation and assessment of damages,"[35] with a view to devising an effective redress mechanism in competition cases. The proposal for a Directive on actions for damages stated that "the existing legal framework does not properly regulate the interaction between the two strands of EU competition law enforcement."[36] The recently adopted Directive *inter alia* addressed the effect of competition authorities' decisions on court proceedings for damages.[37] The Directive went on to state that an injured party, who sues for damages, will not be given access to the leniency statements and/or settlement submissions held by the competition authority.[38] But, would this solve all the problems?

---

[31] Danov and Dnes (above n 3) 54 and the case cited above; Case COMP/E-1/37.512 – *Vitamins*, Commission Decision of 21 November 2001 relating to a proceeding pursuant to Article 81 of the EC Treaty and Article 53 of the EEA Agreement [2003] OJ L6/1; Case COMP/38.899 – *Gas Insulated Switchgear*, Commission Decision of 24 January 2007 relating to a proceeding under Article 81 of the Treaty establishing the European Community and Article 53 of the EEA Agreement, C(2006) 6762 final; COMP/39.309 – *LCD – Liquid Crystal Displays*, Commission Decision of 8 December 2010 relating to a proceeding under Article 101 Treaty on the Functioning of the European Union and Article 53 of the Agreement on the European Economic Area, C(2010) 8761 final.

[32] Danov and Dnes (above n 3) 54. See also Danov, Becker and Beaumont (above n 1).

[33] AAS Zuckerman, 'Justice in crisis: Comparative dimensions of civil procedure' in AAS Zuckerman (ed), *Civil Justice in Crisis: Comparative perspectives of Civil Procedure* (OUP, 1999) 3, 12.

[34] *Enron Coal Services Ltd v English Welsh & Scottish Railway Ltd* [2011] EWCA Civ 2.

[35] *Ibid* [149].

[36] Paragraph 1.2 of the Proposal for a Directive on certain rules governing actions for damages under national law for infringements of the competition law provisions of the Member States and of the European Union – COM(2013) 404 final.

[37] Directive on antitrust damages actions, art 9.

[38] Directive on antitrust damages actions, art 6(6). Case C-360/09 *Pfleiderer AG v Bundeskartellamt* [2011] 5 CMLR 219.

C. Cross-border Aspects of Large-scale Competition Law Infringements

The EU competition law provisions produce direct effects in relations between individuals and create rights for individuals concerned in 28 Member States.[39] It is well established that many "large-scale infringements of competition law often have a cross-border element."[40] As a result, mass harm may be suffered in different jurisdictions. However, some jurisdictions may be less effective than others in dealing with private competition law claims. This may be seen as yet another challenge to be addressed by policy-makers across Europe.

It is well established that the conditions for bringing damages claims in case of infringement of EU competition rules may be different in different Member States.[41] Recent research has shown that there are advantages for an injured party to bring an EU competition law damage action in one Member State rather than another.[42] This is acknowledged by the EU legislator in the Explanatory Memorandum accompanying the recently adopted Directive for Antitrust Damage Actions, in which the drafters have stated that "[b]ecause of th[e] marked diversity of national legislations, the rules applicable in some Member States are considered by claimants to be much more suitable for bringing an antitrust damages action in those Member States rather than in others."[43] As a result, there is a "concentration of antitrust damages actions in three EU jurisdictions: the UK, Germany and the Netherlands,"[44] which suggests that some jurisdictions may provide a less effective remedy (or no effective remedy at all) for breach of competition law.

Approximation might "reduce the differences between the Member States as to the national rules governing actions for damages."[45] However, a level of variation is likely to remain. For example, the lack of experience in the majority of jurisdictions (which may be reasonably expected if actions had been predominately initiated in three jurisdictions out of 28), and the level of delay which may be experienced in some jurisdictions may need to be considered

---

[39] Case 127/73 *BRT v SABAM* [1974] ECR 51 [16]; Case C-282/95 P *Guerin Automobiles v Commission* [1997] ECR I-1503 [39]; Case C-453/99 *Courage Ltd v Crehan* [2001] ECR I-6297 [23].

[40] Directive on antitrust damages actions, Recital (9).

[41] D Waelbroeck, D Slater and G Even-Shoshan, *Study on the Conditions of Claims for Damages in Case of Infringement of EC Competition Rules (Ashurst Report)*, http://ec.europa.eu/competition/antitrust/actionsdamages/comparative_report_clean_en.pdf.

[42] See Danov and Dnes (above n 3); J Kammin and F Becker, 'Cross-Border EU Competition Litigation: Qualitative Interviews from Germany' in Danov, Becker and Beaumont (above n 1) 61–80.

[43] Proposal for a Directive on antitrust damages actions, COM(2013) 404 final, 9.

[44] Commission Staff Working Document – SWD(2013) 204 final [7] – emphasis in the original.

[45] Directive on antitrust damages actions, Recital (9).

carefully by policy makers. In particular, the potential delay of Italian courts was raised as a cause of concern in a claim (which was related to an earlier claim initiated in Italy, and arising out of the same competition law infringement) brought before the English court.[46] Lord Justice Longmore, sitting in the Court of Appeal, held that, in some jurisdictions, the delay may be important. In particular, the judge stated:

> The fact that it may take different periods of time for similar proceedings to come to a conclusion in different jurisdictions, for whatever reasons, [...] is merely a fact of life to which a judge cannot be expected to close his eyes.[47]

The issue is indeed important because the predominant enforcement pattern strongly suggests that an injured party will have to wait for the outcome of the public proceedings in the first place,[48] and then he will have to experience even further delay in some jurisdictions in order to obtain redress. Could this be a significant issue? Will a full compensation which is given too late not "amount to a denial of justice?"[49]

III. COLLECTIVE REDRESS: THE EU COMMISSION RECOMMENDATION AND THE UK CONSUMER RIGHTS BILL

In view of the foregoing, there is a strong case that the end consumers, who will be absorbing the damage caused by competition law infringements, may be the biggest loser under the current regime. Not only will the cartel induced overcharge be eventually passed onto them, but also the infringing undertakings could pass on the cost (or some of the cost) incurred when paying the enormous fines imposed on them by the regulator.[50] How should policy-makers address these issues, and provide redress for consumers? Are the proposed legislative measures adequately addressing the specific challenges, arising in competition law cases, with the intent to provide an effective remedy for consumers who have suffered harm arising out of competition law infringements?

---

[46] *Cooper Tire & Rubber Company v Shell Chemicals UK Limited* (above n 30) [117–118].
[47] *Ibid* [54-55].
[48] See Section II.B above.
[49] Cf Zuckerman (above n 33) 10.
[50] HH Lidgard, 'Due Process in European Competition Procedure: A Fundamental Concept or a Mere Formality?' in P Cardonnel, A Rosas and N Wahl (eds), *Constitutionalising the EU Judicial System: Essays in Honour of Pernilla Lindh* (Hart Publishing, 2012) 403, 421.

Although the authors of the Report on Collective Redress in Antitrust did make a case for a more direct harmonisation (even in the form of Regulation) in the area,[51] the EU legislator has decided to exclude the collective redress proceedings from the scope of the Directive on antitrust damages actions.[52] Instead, only a Recommendation with a view of ensuring that a common set of principles are being used across Europe has been adopted. The adoption of a soft-law (ie non-binding) instrument may be justified by the fact that national procedural laws are fundamental for the success of any collective redress mechanism.[53] The UK legislator has very recently decided that there is a case for more direct legislative intervention at a national level.

The advantages of a soft-law instrument is that it may even promote regulatory competition, by creating incentives for Member States to legislate with the purpose of attracting more cross-border competition law cases.[54] Weatherill has argued that "in a geographically and functionally expanded European Union the establishment of common rules is not only increasingly difficult to achieve, it is also increasingly undesirable as a suppression of competitive and cultural diversity."[55] It is now well established that "in the European Union, there is a diversity of legal cultures, of legal traditions, of languages [...]."[56] A recent commentator has noted:

> While it could be argued that this legal plurality is merely another complicated factor in an already indeterminate integration process, [Hendry] submit[s] that it makes more sense to view it in light of a more nuanced normative ideal of (legal) 'unity in diversity'.[57]

The diverse nature of the EU might suggest that the current Member States may even share different interests when it comes to regulating the conditions

---

[51] *Collective Redress in Antitrust* (above n 22) 88.

[52] Directive on antitrust damages actions, Recital (13). Cf White Paper on Damages actions for breach of the EC antitrust rules COM(2008) 165 final; Green Paper on Consumer Collective Redress COM(2008) 794 final.

[53] Danov, Becker and Beaumont (above n 1).

[54] M Danov and F Becker, 'Governance Aspects of Cross-Border EU Competition Actions: Theoretical Issues and Practical Challenges' *Journal of Private International Law* (2014), 359–401.

[55] S Weatherill, 'Why harmonise?' in T Tridimas and P Nebbia, *European Union Law for the Twenty-First Century: Rethinking the New Legal Order* (Vol. 2, Hart Publishing, 2004) 11. See also M Danov and F Becker, 'Concluding Remarks on Promoting Regulatory Competition' in Danov, Becker and Beaumont (above n 1) 81–93.

[56] R Sefton-Green, 'Cultural Diversity and the Idea of a European Civil Code' in MW Hesselink (ed), *The Politics of a European Civil Code* (Kluwer Law International, 2006) 71, 72. H Collins, *The European Code: The Way Forward* (CUP, 2008) 124–145.

[57] J Hendry, 'The double fragmentation of law: Legal System-Internal Differentiation and the process of Europeanization' in D Augenstein (ed), *'Integration through Law' Revisited: The Making of the European Polity* (Ashgate, 2012) 157, 165.

for bringing damages actions. For example, it might be that some of the export-orientated countries may prefer a relatively weak enforcement regime, whilst some of the import-oriented countries may have incentives to have a more efficient enforcement regime.[58] This poses the question: should the claimant party in competition cases be formed on the basis of the 'opt-in' or 'opt-out' principle?

A. Opt-in Regime or Opt-out Regime: UK Consumer Rights Bill and EU Commission Recommendation

A common principle promoted by the Commission Recommendation on collective redress mechanisms is that "the claimant party should be formed on the basis of express consent of the natural or legal persons claiming to have been harmed ('opt-in' principle)."[59] Making a positive decision to litigate is required for collective redress proceedings in England at present.[60] However, the UK Consumer Rights Bill has recently proposed an 'opt-out' model for collective redress antitrust proceedings. 'Opt-out collective proceedings'[61] may be brought on behalf of each class member (except the one/s who opts out by notifying the representative). Since competition law infringements cause mass harm to numerous claimants, there is a strong case that a reform in England is needed with a view to providing redress for multiple injured parties in competition cases,[62] where "each [injured party] has a loss that is too small to justify an individual action."[63] The OFT (which was succeeded by the Competition and Market Authority) has suggested that, in competition cases, the 'opt-in' and 'opt-out' regimes should co-exist.[64] The White Paper on damages actions also favoured co-existence of a form of representa-

---

[58] AT Guzman, 'International Antitrust and the WTO: The Lesson from Intellectual property' 43 *Virginia Journal of International Law* (2003) 933, 946.

[59] Commission Recommendation, Section 21.

[60] CPR 19.6 and CPR 19.11. Section 47B of the Competition Act 1998. N Andrews, 'Multi-party proceedings in England: representative and group actions' 11 *Duke Journal of Comparative & International Law* (2001) 249, 260. See also R Mulheron, 'Justice enhanced: Framing an opt-out class action for England' *Modern Law Review* (2007) 550. Civil Justice Council, "Improving access to justice through collective actions – developing a more effective and efficient procedure for collective actions", *Final Report*.

[61] Section 47B(11) of the proposed amendments to the Competition Act 1998.

[62] Schedule 8 of the UK Consumer Rights Bill. *Private Actions in Competition Law: A consultation on options for reform – government response* (above n 12).

[63] KW Dam, 'Class actions: efficiency, compensation, deterrence, and conflict of interest' 4 *Journal of Legal Studies* (1975) 47, 49.

[64] See Office of Fair Trading, *Private actions in competition law: effective redress for consumers and business – Recommendations from the Office of Fair Trading*, OFT916 resp [7.28].

tive actions brought on behalf of identifiable victims (ie 'opt-out' system) and 'opt-in' collective actions.[65]

That said, strong arguments against an 'opt-out' regime have been very recently expressed at EU level. The EC has noted that:

> The 'opt-out' system gives rise to more fundamental questions as to the freedom of potential claimants to decide whether they want to litigate. The right to an effective remedy cannot be interpreted in a way that prevents people from making (informed) decisions on whether they wish to claim damages or not. In addition, an 'opt-out' system may not be consistent with the central aim of collective redress, which is to obtain compensation for harm suffered, since such persons are not identified, and so the award will not be distributed to them.[66]

Hence, the Commission Recommendation states that "any exception to [the 'opt-in'] principle, by law or by court order, should be duly justified by reasons of sound administration of justice."[67] However, it should be noted that the principles set in the Recommendation are to be applied not only in EU competition law actions, but also in the areas of "consumer protection, […] environment protection, protection of personal data, financial services legislation and investor protection."[68] This poses the question: do competition law claims justify the national legislator's actions to make an exception to the 'opt-in' principle? Arguments in support of an 'opt-out' regime in competition law have been very recently put forward by the UK legislator:

> [in competition cases, an exception to 'opt-in' principle] is justified by the legitimate aim of establishing effective access to justice for consumers and businesses who would not otherwise have any, or any effective, access to justice. This is because in the absence of opt-out collective actions, it may not be economically worthwhile for potential claimants to bring a claim on the basis that the sums sought are likely to be small (eg the sum due for an over-priced washing machine or an excessively high coach ticket price) when compared to the cost of bringing the case.[69]

---

[65] White Paper (above n 52) [2.1].
[66] Communication from the Commission to the European Parliament, the Council, the European Economic and Social Committee and the Committee of the Regions, 'Towards a European Horizontal Framework for Collective Redress' COM(2013) 401 final,12.
[67] Commission Recommendation, Section 21.
[68] Commission Recommendation, Recital (7).
[69] Consumer Rights Bill, *Explanatory Notes – Bill 003-EN 2014-15* [453]. R Mulheron, 'The case for an opt-out class actions for European Member States: A legal and empirical analysis' 15 *Columbia Journal of European Law* (2008–2009) 409.

The UK rule-maker went on to provide safeguards against abusive competition law claims.[70] 'Opt-out collective proceedings' may continue only if a collective proceedings order has been issued by the Competition Appeal Tribunal.[71] The Tribunal can issue an order to that effect only if the person who brought the proceedings may be authorised to act as the representative,[72] and if the claims are eligible for inclusion in collective proceedings. The latter requirement will be satisfied, if the claims "raise the same, similar or related issues of fact or law",[73] which is intended *inter alia* to addresses some of the issues which were identified in *Emerald*,[74] insofar as the claimants are not required to have the same interest in a claim. The proposed 'opt-out' model is certainly a welcome development, as it may contribute to a more effective competition law enforcement regime in the UK. The proposal has the potential to adequately address some of the issues related to the low level of litigiousness of consumers because, for example, consumer organisations may wish to initiate follow-on collective redress proceedings on the basis of an 'opt-out' model in the UK with a view to raising pressure on defendants and forcing a settlement which provides full compensation to multiple injured parties.

However, a drawback of the UK legislative proposal is that the 'opt-in' principle will continue to apply for claimants who are not domiciled in the UK.[75] One may justify the proposed approach by noting that there is a view that "[an 'opt-out' model] may be unconstitutional in some Member States."[76] That said, having an 'opt-out' regime for the UK-domiciled claimants, and using an 'opt-in' model for the non-UK-domiciled claimants in the same EU competition law case, would fly in the face of the Commission Recommendation to have "a single collective action in a single forum."[77] This will be a significant issue, as many businesses do engage in pan-European (or even global) business activities.

Indeed, given the cross-border nature of many competition law infringements, it is a relatively safe prediction that an 'opt-in' model (applicable for

---

[70] COM(2013) 401 final (above n 66) at 11.
[71] Proposed amendments to the Competition Act 1998, Section 47B(4).
[72] Proposed amendments to the Competition Act 1998, Section 47B(8).
[73] Proposed amendments to the Competition Act 1998, Section 47B(6).
[74] *Emerald Supplies v British Airways* (above n 1).
[75] R Mulheron, 'In Defence of the Requirement For Foreign Class Members to opt in to an English Class Action' in D Fairgrieve and E Lein (eds), *Extraterritoriality and Collective Redress* (OUP, 2012) 245, 247; M Danov, 'The Brussels I Regulation: Cross-border collective redress proceedings and judgments' 6 *Journal of Private International Law* (2010) 359. Cf Danov, Fairgrieve and Howells (above n 1) 277.
[76] COM(2013) 401 final (above n 66) at 11.
[77] Commission Recommendation, Section 17.

non-local domiciled claimants) will (assuming that all Member States have equally effective regimes) inevitably lead to parallel collective redress proceedings,[78] in respect to the same infringement raising similar issues of fact and law. Moreover, the low mobility of consumers and SMEs strongly suggests that the proposal will have only a local effect as one may assume that the damage for the majority of the members of the claimant party (formed on 'opt-out' basis) will have occurred in the UK.[79] Could collective settlements address part of the problem?

B. Collective Settlements

It is well established that a substantial number of claims which are brought in England eventually settle.[80] The high costs and the level of uncertainty which characterise the competition law actions strongly suggest that parties would have strong incentives to settle, [81] because a "settlement avoids the costs and uncertainty associated with further litigation."[82]

The Commission Recommendation states that "[t]he Member States should ensure that the parties to a dispute in a mass harm situation are encouraged to settle the dispute about compensation consensually or out-of-court."[83] In this context, the EU legislator has *inter alia* made a reference to Directive 2008/52/EC on certain aspects of mediation.[84] Therefore, one should distinguish between the use of settlement as a tactical device when parties have started to litigate,[85] and an amicable settlement of disputes in ADR proceedings.[86] In line with this, the UK legislator has made a clear distinction between collective settlements in cases where a collective proceedings order

---

[78] The specific issues with regard to jurisdiction in cross-border case are discussed in M Danov, 'Jurisdiction in Cross-Border EU Competition Law Cases: Some Specific Issues Requiring Specific Solutions' in Danov, Becker and Beaumont (above n 1) 167–196.

[79] Danov and Dnes (above n 3); Kammin and Becker (above n 42).

[80] B Rodger, 'Private Enforcement of Competition Law, The Hidden Story: Competition Litigation Settlements in the United Kingdom, 2000–2005', 29 *European Competition Law Review* (2008) 96. B Rodger, 'Competition Law Litigation in the UK Courts: A Study of all Cases 2005–2008: Part I', 2 *GCLR* (2009) 93; B Rodger, 'Competition Law Litigation in the UK Courts: A Study of all Cases 2005–2008: Part II', 3 *GCLR* (2009) 136. See also SC Salop and LJ White, 'Private Antitrust Litigation: An Introduction and Framework' in LJ White (ed), *Private Antitrust Litigation: New Evidence, New Learning* (MIT Press, 1988) 3, 23.

[81] Danov and Dnes (above n 3).

[82] Salop and White (above n 81) 23.

[83] Commission Recommendation, Section 25.

[84] [2005] OJ L136/3.

[85] Danov and Dnes (above n 3) 49–50.

[86] *Ibid*, 58–59.

has been made (ie court proceedings have been initiated),[87] on the one hand, and on the other hand, collective settlements which are not preceded by such an order.[88] Although a very positive feature of the UK proposal is that the collective settlements may be made on an opt-out basis,[89] its main drawback remains that the opt-out model will apply for the UK-domiciled claimants.

How would these aspects of the proposal affect the dynamics of (collective) settlement? As already noted,[90] given the cross-border nature of many EU competition law infringements and the low mobility of consumers, the cross-border nature of the 'opt-in' collective proceedings for non-UK domiciled claimants strongly suggests that UK proceedings will be for the local harm only. First, the pressure on defendants to settle will be less as the claims will largely be for the local harm. Secondly, the defendant will have no significant incentives to settle, because if they do, they might face similar claims in other jurisdictions, thus incurring even higher litigation expenses. In those circumstances, they might prefer to delay the proceedings, and raise preliminary issues in order to increase pressure on the claimants and get them to settle with terms they would not have accepted otherwise.[91] Danov and Dnes made the following observation: [92]

> Widespread settlements do, however, pose an important question: there are many settlements, but one cannot say in isolation whether they are satisfactory.[93] A well-functioning settlement regime would provide cheap and speedy redress with an appropriate level of compensation. As things stand, there are very few indicators of whether the current state of settlements represents an efficient level of compensation, which might be an interesting area for future research.[94]

Thus, there are some issues which need to be carefully considered because effective settlements do presuppose the availability of an effective and efficient court system which entitles the court to address all the issues arising in a cross-border context.

---

[87] Proposed amendments to the Competition Act 1998, Section 49A.
[88] Proposed amendments to the Competition Act 1998, Section 49B.
[89] Proposed amendments to the Competition Act 1998, Sections 49A(8) and 49B(10).
[90] See Section II.C above.
[91] Danov and Dnes (above n 3); J Lawrence and A Morfey, 'Tactical Manoeuvres in UK Cartel Damages Litigation' in Danov, Becker and Beaumont (above n 1) 149–158.
[92] Danov and Dnes (above n 3).
[93] For a summary of the law and economics literature, see R Cooter and D Rubinfeld, 'Economic Analysis of Legal Disputes and Their Resolution,' 27 *Journal of Economic Literature* (1989) 1067.
[94] Danov and Dnes (above n 3) 50.

If all Member States adopt 'opt-in' models for non-locally domiciled injured parties, then it is highly likely that an enforcement gap (in respect to large-scale EU competition law infringements) will continue to exist across Europe. Some of the jurisdictions may remain less efficient than others in providing full compensation. Since the level of compensation sought by individual consumers is likely to be small, one may safely argue that SMEs and consumers domiciled in other Member State would be reluctant to take cross-border litigation risks and opt-in for the UK proceedings instead. In the circumstances, the injured parties domiciled in other Member States may bring local proceedings (or they may not even bring any proceedings at all) in respect of the same large-scale EU competition law infringement. Could the proposed voluntary redress scheme be a solution?

C. *Voluntary Redress Schemes: The Role of NCAs*

Should the national competition authorities be empowered to approve voluntary redress schemes at the same time as rendering a decision finding an infringement? As noted above, a two-step adjudication model appears to characterise the current enforcement pattern.[95] As a part of the current model, the regulator is considered best placed to detect and establish a competition law infringement, and then a Member State court will be the appropriate place to sue for antitrust damages. Such a two-step adjudication model generates a level of delay and legal uncertainty because, for example, it is far from clear whether the evidence collected by the regulator will be directly relevant to a follow-on claim for damages.[96] In spite of strong arguments for reform with the purpose of adopting a single set of proceedings before a national court,[97] no institutional reform appears to be on the agenda. Indeed, the EC Recommendation clearly states:

> The Member States should ensure that in fields of law where a public authority is empowered to adopt a decision finding that there has been a violation of Union law, collective redress actions should, as a general rule, only start after any proceedings of the public authority, which were launched before commencement of the private action, have been concluded definitively. If the proceedings of the public authority are

---

[95] See above, and also Danov and Becker (above n 54). Danov, Becker and Beaumont (above n 1).

[96] Eg *Enron Coal Services Ltd v English Welsh & Scottish Railway Ltd* (above n 34). KPE Lasok, 'Some Procedural Aspects and How They Could/Should be Reformed' in Danov, Becker and Beaumont (above n 1) 207, 209; J Webber, 'Observations on the Implications of *Pfleiderer* for Leniency Programmes' in Danov, Becker and Beaumont (above n 1) 215, 221.

[97] Danov and Becker (above n 54); Danov, Becker and Beaumont (above n 1).

launched after the commencement of the collective redress action, the court should avoid giving a decision which would conflict with a decision contemplated by the public authority. To that end, the court may stay the collective redress action until the proceedings of the public authority have been concluded.[98]

This would certainly be of great relevance to competition law proceedings, where the inefficient enforcement architecture suggests that the consumers and SMEs would normally have to wait for a public authority to adopt a decision finding a competition law infringement.[99] This is not an entirely satisfactory solution insofar as there might be some important institutional limitations which characterise the proceedings before the national competition authorities.[100] First, it is well established that "public enforcers cannot investigate all complaints, but must set priorities in their treatment of cases."[101] Second, injured parties would not have much control over public-administrative proceedings, and as a result injured parties could not force a settlement. Third, there could be "political problems in terms of finding a sympathetic ear at the NCA."[102] Fourth, a level of delay could be an issue in some cases. Fifth, the regulator would not have jurisdiction to award damages, so that injured parties would still need to bring a claim before courts, which means even more delay.[103]

The UK legislator has tried to address some of the problems by providing a voluntary redress scheme which may be approved by the Competition and Market Authority after the infringement decision has been rendered (which supposedly may be after a decision of the EC, for example), or (in case of a decision of the CMA) at the same time the decision is made.[104] A positive aspect of the proposal is that compensation may be provided at the time when the infringement is being established. Likewise, the proposal provides a voluntary redress scheme which takes into account that most competition law cases would settle. However, a significant problem with the voluntary redress scheme is that it is being proposed at a time when the UK government has concluded that there is no redress for consumers and SMEs under

---

[98] Commission Recommendation, Section 33.
[99] Commission Recommendation, Section 33.
[100] Danov and Dnes (above n 3) 52–53.
[101] Commission Notice on the handling of complaints by the Commission under Articles 81 and 82 of the EC Treaty, OJ C 101, 27.4.2004, 65–77 [8]. See also: WJ Wils, 'Discretion and Prioritisation in Public Enforcement, in Particular EU Antitrust Enforcement' 34 *World Competition* (2011) 353. E Burrows and T Gilbert, 'OFT Competition Act Enforcement: Key Developments over the First Decade' *Competition Law Journal* (2010) 178, 179–82.
[102] Danov and Dnes (above n 3) 52.
[103] Kammin and Becker (above n 42) 63. Danov and Dnes (above n 3).
[104] Proposed amendments to the Competition Act 1998, Section 49C.

the current civil justice system.[105] This poses the question: may the compensating party offer the injured parties a discounted compensation?[106] Could such a discount be significant if there is no adequately functioning EU civil justice system to "create the credible threat of litigation?"[107]

Another problem relates to the issue of jurisdiction of the CMA. The proposed amendment to the Competition Act 1998 states that "[i]n deciding whether to approve a redress scheme, the CMA may take into account the amount or value of compensation offered under the scheme."[108] However, the White Paper on modernisation strongly suggests that an NCA decision is enforceable only within the territory on which the authority in question operates.[109] The limited territorial scope of an NCA decision has recently been reaffirmed by the Directive on antitrust damages actions.[110] The following questions remain: how effective would such a scheme be? If voluntary redress may be offered after a Commission decision, does the UK CMA have the authority to approve a redress scheme for injured parties who are not domiciled in the UK?[111]

IV. ASSESSING THE EFFECTIVENESS OF THE COMPETITION LAW ENFORCEMENT REGIME – A NEED FOR AN EMPIRICAL STUDY

It seems clear that there will be a level of delay under the current enforcement regime, insofar as the inefficient enforcement architecture does suggest that the consumers would normally have to wait for a public authority to adopt a decision finding a competition law infringement.[112] Moreover, it is difficult to see how under the current legislative framework (based on an 'opt-in' model for non-UK domiciled claimants) it is possible to have one set of collective redress proceedings before a single forum in respect to a harm caused to numerous injured parties across Europe.

---

[105] See the UK government response – above.
[106] Cf H Genn, *Judging Civil Justice* (CUP, 2010) 113.
[107] *Ibid*, 21.
[108] Proposed amendments to the Competition Act 1998, Section 49C(3).
[109] White Paper on Modernisation of the Rules implementing Articles 85 and 86 of the EC Treaty, Commission Programme No 99/027, para 60. See A Komninos, *EC Private Antitrust Enforcement: Decentralised Application of EC Competition Law by National Courts* (Hart Publishing 2008) 77; S Brammer, *Co-operation Between National Competition Agencies in the Enforcement of EC Competition Law* (Hart Publishing, 2009) 426–436.
[110] Directive on antitrust damages actions, art 9.
[111] Cf Proposed amendments to the Competition Act 1998, Sections 49A(8) and 49B(10).
[112] Commission Recommendation, Section 33.

There is a strong case that the cross-border implications of many EU competition law actions would make any national legislation, in implementation of common principles for collective redress proceedings,[113] less than effective in a cross-border context.[114] If all Member States adopt 'opt-in' models for non-locally domiciled injured parties, then the access to justice issues would be considerable insofar as the cross-border litigation costs could by far exceed the damage caused to individual consumers. Indeed, the high cross-border litigation costs may be a disincentive for SMEs and consumers who, due to their low level of mobility, would not sue at all (or sue at their home state at best).[115] If only a few jurisdictions continue to attract EU competition law actions in Europe, then there would be no remedies for a significant number of injured parties across Europe. This would be an important issue in a case where there is a large scale competition law infringement. Hence, providing for an effective remedy for consumers and SMEs may be important in cross-border competition law cases.[116]

In view of the foregoing, the following question must be addressed head-on: is the current EU antitrust enforcement system in crisis?[117] How effective is the current enforcement regime in Europe? Is there an effective remedy for consumers in cross-border cases? The responses to these questions are important in light of the fact that the Strasbourg Programme does specify that: [118]

> The EU should pursue its efforts to ensure the respect of the right to an effective remedy before a tribunal in case of violation of EU law (Article 47 of the Charter), including in cases where national procedures make it excessively difficult for citizens to claim the rights granted to them by EU law in cross-border cases.[119]

---

[113] See the recently proposed UK Consumer Rights Bill. Cf the Commission Recommendation.

[114] M Danov, 'Cross-Border Competition Law Cases: Level Playing Field for Undertakings and Redress for Consumers' 35 *European Competition Law Review* (2014) 487. H Muir Watt, 'Integration and diversity: The conflict of laws as a regulatory tool' in F Cafaggi (ed) *The Institutional Framework of European Private Law* (OUP, 2006); H Muir Watt, 'European integration, legal diversity and the conflict of laws' 9 *Edinburgh Law Review* (2005) 6. See also Danov, Becker and Beaumont (above n 1).

[115] Danov and Becker (above n 54).

[116] The Strasbourg Programme – *The EU Justice Agenda for 2020 – Strengthening Trust, Mobility and Growth within the Union*, COM(2014) 144 final.

[117] Cf Zuckerman (above n 33).

[118] The Strasbourg Programme (above n 116).

[119] *Ibid*, para 4.1(ii).

The Charter of Fundamental Rights states that "[e]veryone whose rights and freedoms guaranteed by the law of the Union are violated has the right to an effective remedy before a tribunal in compliance with the conditions laid down in [Article 47]." However, Rawls' theory[120] indicates that an important question would be whether the current institutional framework is capable of safeguarding them with to the purpose of creating "a Europe of law and justice".[121]

There is a need for an empirical study to be conducted in several Member States, sharing different legal traditions/heritages, in order to assess the effectiveness of the current competition law enforcement regime. The following questions must be addressed: do national competition authorities adequately enforce competition laws across Europe? Are there effective remedies for private parties? Data about the enforcement rates (eg "variables relating to number and types of cases filed, adjudicated settled, or otherwise terminated,"[122] leniency applications, follow-on proceedings) must be gathered from across Europe. Furthermore, it will be necessary to examine the views of legal practitioners discussing key questions concerning competition law enforcement. On the basis of such an empirical study, one should consider how to improve the effectiveness of the current framework, which is applied in a diverse and multi-level system of governance.

Chalmers and Chaves have recently submitted that "[m]ost recent accounts accept that no single narrative fully explains European Union (EU) judicial politics [...]. Research will accordingly need to consider the conditions under which one narrative holds rather than another. Comparison of patterns of litigation or adjudication across sectors or from different territories will go some way towards answering this." [123] The need for such an empirical study may be further strengthened by stating that the "Commission should assess the implementation of the Recommendation on the basis of practical experience by 26 July 2017 at the latest."[124]

---

[120] J Rawls, *Theory of Justice – Revised Edition* (OUP, 1999) 208.
[121] The Stockholm Programme – *An open and secure Europe serving and protecting the citizens* [2010] OJ C115/1, 4.
[122] SR Anleu and K Mack, 'Trial courts and adjudication' in P Cane and H Kritzer (eds), *The Oxford Handbook of Empirical Legal Research* (OUP, 2012) 545, 549.
[123] D Chalmers and M Chaves, 'The reference points of EU judicial politics' in SK Schmidt and D Kelemen (eds), *The Power of the European Court of Justice* (Routledge, 2013) 25.
[124] Commission Recommendation, Section 41.

Where to Next? The European Law Institute's Statement on Collective Redress and Competition Damages Claims

Mark Clough QC[*]

I. INTRODUCTION

This chapter is as much about the European Law Institute and its Statement on Collective Redress and Competition Damages Claims[1] (the Statement) as it is about the substantive issues raised by these two documents.

First, what is the European Law Institute (ELI)? Second, what and who is the Project Team that produced the ELI Statement? Third, what does the ELI Statement say about the substantive issues in its two separate sections – one dealing with the European Commission's Recommendation of 11 June 2013[2] and the other addressing Directive 2014/104/EU[3]? Fourth, some thoughts on specific issues and what comes next. As discussed in the extracts from the ELI Statement in the third section, the practical problems relating to disclosure, passing on and limitation periods, as well as cross-border cases and collective alternative dispute resolution will need to be addressed in the European Commission's review of its Recommendation in 2017.

A. *The European Law Institute*

The ELI is an independent non-profit organisation established to initiate,

---

[*] Senior Counsel at Dentons Brussels.
[1] European Law Institute Statement on Collective Redress and Competition Damages Claims (12 December 2014), http://www.europeanlawinstitute.eu/fileadmin/user_upload/p_eli/Projects/S-5-2014_Statement_on_Collective_Redress_and_Competition_Damages_Claims.pdf.
[2] Commission Recommendation of 11 June 2013 on common principles for injunctive and compensatory collective redress mechanisms in the Member States concerning violations of rights granted under Union Law (2013/396/EU, OJEU, L 201/60, 26.7.2013).
[3] Directive 2014/104/EU of the European Parliament and of the Council of 26 November 2014 on certain rules governing actions for damages under national law for infringements of the competition law provisions of the Member States and of the European Union (OJEU L349/1, 5.12.2014).

conduct and facilitate research, make recommendations and provide practical guidance in the field of European legal development. Building on the wealth of diverse legal traditions, its mission is the quest for better law-making in Europe and the enhancement of European legal integration. By its endeavours, the ELI seeks to contribute to the formation of a more vigorous European legal community, integrating the achievements of the various legal cultures, endorsing the value of comparative knowledge and taking a genuinely pan-European perspective. As such, its work covers all branches of the law: substantive and procedural; private and public.

The ELI is committed to the principles of comprehensiveness and collaborative working, thus striving to bridge the oft-perceived gap between the different legal cultures, between public and private law, as well as between scholarship and practice. To further its commitment, it seeks to involve a diverse range of personalities, reflecting the richness of the legal traditions, legal disciplines and vocational frameworks found throughout Europe. The ELI is also open to the use of different methodological approaches and to canvassing insights and perspectives from as wide an audience as possible of those who share its vision.

B. Project Team

Following publication of the Recommendation and the Commission's proposal for the directive in June 2013, an ELI project team, assisted by an Advisory Committee, was established to prepare the Statement which involved meetings and drafting sessions in parallel with the Directive's legislative procedure. The ELI Statement was adopted by a decision of the ELI Council on 12 December 2014 following an electronic vote. Both the Project Team and the Advisory Committee consisted of members of the judiciary, legal practitioners and academics from a broad range of legal traditions.[4]

The outcome of the ELI Project on Collective Redress and Competition Damages Claims is the present Statement, structured in two sections. Section I is an assessment of the Recommendation which identifies its implications for Member States and suggests practical measures that will contribute to its coherent implementation. Section II contains an assessment of the EC's Proposal for a Directive in the light of its practical implications for damages claims in national courts and for the effectiveness of competition damages claims.

---

[4] See page 3, ELI Statement (above n 1) for the list of names including Diana Wallis, President of ELI since September 2013, Koen Lenaerts, judge, and Nils Wahl, Advocate General at the Court of Justice of the European Union.

The Statement which forms the basis of this chapter does not however necessarily reflect the position of all members of the Team.

C. What does the ELI Statement say?

This chapter reproduces the key observations in the form of direct extracts (including footnotes) from the ELI statement, which make a useful contribution to the debate on the main issues raised by the Collective Redress Recommendation and the Competition Damages Directive. In many ways, the Directive is less controversial than the Recommendation so more time is devoted to the latter. Some conclusions are drawn in Section IV by way of further commentary on the ELI Statement.

II. EXTRACTS FROM THE ELI ASSESSMENT OF THE EUROPEAN COMMISSION RECOMMENDATION ON COLLECTIVE REDRESS

A. Introduction

In June 2013, the European Commission finally published its long-awaited policy on collective redress. The documents included separate proposals and recommendations for EU competition law and for the violation of rights granted under European Union law generally. Regarding the latter, the main item was a Recommendation "on common principles for injunctive and compensatory collective redress mechanisms in the Member States concerning violations of rights granted under Union Law" (the 'Recommendation'),[5] which was accompanied by a Communication to the European Parliament and the Council ("Towards a European Horizontal Framework for Collective Redress.")[6] Regarding competition law, the Commission proposed a directive "on certain rules governing actions for damages under national law for infringements of the competition law provisions of the Member States and of the European Union ('Directive')."[7] This Directive, finally adopted in November 2014, was accompanied by an impact assessment[8] and a Communication on what qualifies as harm in competition cases.[9]

---

[5] Commission Recommendation of 11 June 2013 on common principles for injunctive and compensatory collective redress mechanisms in the Member States concerning violations of rights granted under Union Law, (2013/396/EU), OJEU, L 201/60, 26.7.2013).
[6] COM (2013) 401/2.
[7] COM (2013) 404 final.
[8] SWD (2013) 203 final.
[9] COM (2013) 3440.

The documents were the final result of a long and very controversial debate on the reform of the European system of enforcement of consumer rights and the rights of tort victims in mass harm situations. Although the result is disappointing for those who had hoped for a binding European framework of collective redress instruments,[10] it had been clear for some time that the current political situation would not allow a directive or regulation which would impose any obligation on the Member States to implement new instruments for the collective enforcement of damages claims. Therefore it did not come as a surprise that the Commission's documents were rather cautious. Neither the Directive nor the Recommendation will oblige the Member States to reform their existing systems fundamentally.[11]

A brief review of the debate at the European level reveals the extent of the controversy relating to collective redress both in the Member States and within the Commission. With respect to competition law, DG Competition from the outset clearly favoured stronger instruments of private enforcement following the example of US class actions, relying to a large extent on the 'Ashurst Study' of 2004.[12] This stance resulted in a Green Paper in 2005,[13] a White Paper in 2008,[14] and an internal proposal for a regulation (which never appeared in public), which prompted a wave of strong resistance from the business sector all over Europe, particularly in Germany and France. DG Competition's initiative supported rather uncritically the idea that private enforcement would be a more efficient instrument in antitrust cases than public enforcement, notwithstanding the lack of empirical data on and sufficient research into the respective merits of public and private enforcement in Europe. Therefore, there is considerable weight in the argument that class actions—which were developed in a completely different legal system, namely the United States—should not simply be copied in Europe.[15]

---

[10] See especially Opinion of the European Economic and Social Committee on the Communication from the Commission to the European Parliament, the Council, the European Economic and Social Committee and the Committee of the Regions Towards a European Horizontal Framework for Collective Redress, COM(2013) 401 final, INT 708, 10.12.2013.

[11] For more detailed reviews of the Commissions documents see C Hodges, Collective Redress: A Breakthrough or a Damp Squib? *Journal of Consumer Policy*, vol. 67, (2014) 67; A Stadler, 'Die Vorschläge der Europäischen Kommission zum kollektiven Rechtsschutz in Europa – Der Abschied von einem kohärenten europäischen Lösungsansatz?', 67 *Journal of Consumer Policy* (2014) *Zeitschrift für Gemeinschaftsprivatrecht*, (2013) 281.

[12] D Waelbroeck, D Slater and G Even-Shoshan, *Study on the condition of claims for damages in case of infringement of EC competition rules* (Ashurst 2004).

[13] COM (2005) 672.

[14] White Paper on damages actions for breach of the EC antitrust rules, COM (2008) 165.

[15] Particularly in Germany the opposition was and still is quite strong: cf. A Bruns, 'Einheitlicher kollektiver Rechtsschutz in Europa', 125 *Zeitschrift für Zivilprozess* (2012) 399 with further references; H Willems, in C Brömmelmeyer (ed.), *Die EU-Sammelklage,- Status und Perspektiven* (Frankfurter Institut für das Recht der Europäischen Union, 2013) 17.

Unfortunately the Commission passed up the opportunity to develop a new European form of group action which would better harmonise with European traditions and would be able to avoid the negative implications of class actions, such as the encouragement of a claims culture and the blackmailing of defendant companies by unmeritorious but expensive mass claims.

DG Sanco for various reasons was more cautious when it published its Green Paper on collective redress for consumers in 2008,[16] but that was not enough to quieten the strong opposition to collective redress, particularly in the form of opt-out group actions. Consequently, in advance of the re-election of José Manuel Barroso as President of the European Commission in 2009, some Member States took the opportunity to wrest from him the concession not to implement opt-out group or class actions in Europe.[17] As a result, the Barroso II Commission launched a public consultation towards "a more coherent approach to collective redress" in February 2011,[18] with the intention of establishing a common basis for further action. The response to the public consultation was overwhelming in terms of the number of statements filed, but the positions taken by respondents again varied considerably.[19] Finally, as a reaction to the consultation, the European Parliament published a Resolution in 2012,[20] in which it called upon the Commission to take into consideration the potential for misuse of collective redress instruments and to provide sufficient safeguards against such misuse. The Resolution also stressed the need for effective instruments of alternative dispute resolution (ADR), but pointed out that ADR mechanisms cannot provide sufficient protection for consumer rights unless there is some pressure on the business sector to adopt such mechanisms and to make them available to consumers. In reality, it takes both the availability of ADR instruments to consumers, and – as a last resort – procedural mechanisms allowing the enforcement of mass claims, to deal with the problem of defendants who refuse to cooperate in the settlement of claims.[21] Nevertheless, it is also clear that the development of European instruments of collective redress faces a dilemma: how to provide efficient mechanisms allowing the enforcement of

---

[16] Green Paper on Consumer Collective Redress, COM (2008) 794.

[17] *Frankfurter Allgemeine Zeitung*, 20.10.2009 ('Barroso verheddert sich im Sammelklage-Dickicht'); *Frankfurter Allgemeine Zeitung* 26.10.2009 ('Kroes scheitert mit Kollektivklage'); *Financial Times*, 3 October 2009.

[18] COM SEC (2011) 173.

[19] Cf. the study by B Hess and T Pfeiffer, *Evaluation of contributions to the public consultation and hearing: 'Towards a Coherent European Approach to Collective Redress'* (JUST/2010/JCIV/CT/0027/A4), Universität Heidelberg.

[20] Resolution of the European Parliament (2 February 2012) 2011/2089(INI). For detailed discussion of the position of the European Parliament.

[21] See Recommendation, points 25-28: Collective alternative dispute resolution and settlements.

even small and minor damages claims while at the same time avoiding the misuse of the mechanisms developed. The Commission's Recommendation is an attempt to balance these diverging interests. It is a compromise based on the realistic estimation that for political reasons nothing else would have been possible within the remaining time in office of the Barroso II Commission.[22]

B. Overview

The key issues identified by the ELI are:

a) the structure of collective redress actions – whether opt-in or opt-out;
b) the criteria for recognition or admissibility/certification of a representative body to bring an action on behalf of a class or collective group;
c) the permitted methods of funding collective redress actions;
d) the cost rules to be applied to collective redress actions;
e) collective alternative dispute resolution (ADR) for class and representative actions;
f) cross-border collective redress.

The views of the ELI on these issues may be summarised as follows:

1. Opt-in or opt-out?

From the ELI's perspective, the main objective should be to work towards a solution that will make collective redress in Europe effective in mass harm cases. The ELI recognises that, at the moment, it would be very difficult to achieve a consensus at EU level in favour of either opt-in or opt-out. If a principle is to be adopted at EU level, the only viable option seems to be that national courts in the Member States should be given full discretion to select the appropriate structure for collective redress claims on a case by case basis.

The ELI considers that the principled preference for opt-in collective redress expressed in the Recommendation is problematic for reasons explained in the text below. The ELI calls upon the European Commission to study the varying developments of national law and practice currently taking place in order to produce a report based on the empirical evidence available in 2017, when the Recommendation is due to be reviewed.

---

[22] This introductory section is substantially based on A Stadler, 'The Commission's Recommendation on common principles of collective redress and private international law issues', 4 *Nederlands Internationaal Privaatrecht* (2013) 483.

2. Criteria for recognition of representative bodies

The ELI considers that similar requirements as apply under point 4 of the Recommendation to the advance designation of representative entities by Member States should apply to the certification of representative entities by national authorities or courts on an ad hoc basis (for the purposes of a particular representative claim).

The Recommendation recognises that courts should play a key role in the ad hoc certification of entities (Recital 21). This requires Member States and the EU to set up training programs for judges who will be dealing with mass claims and collective actions, bearing in mind that the case management of mass disputes differs from the case management of ordinary claims. Ideally, the EU should facilitate uniform judicial case management training programs at EU level to handle collective redress actions via the European Judicial Network.

National rules should clearly distinguish between the formal certification of an action filed as a necessary requirement for collective redress proceedings and summary judgment on the merits of the case in the early stages of the litigation. If Member States allow an early dismissal of the action on the merits, they should do so only on the basis of clearly defined and strictly limited criteria and should not generally accord such decisions *res judicata* effect.

3. Funding

As a safeguard for claimants, national rules should provide that, if the claimant party is required to declare the origin of its funding, it should do so to the court only. The information provided should not be made available to the defendant.

Member States should in any case ensure that private third party funders do not misuse their position and do not improperly influence procedural decisions made by the claimant party, especially if the claimants are consumers. Judges should be requested to take into account the possible influence of private third party funders when considering whether or not to give approval to collective settlements.

As the impact of different funding regimes for collective redress actions remains to be subjected to detailed empirical study, Member States and the EU should conduct a careful analysis of existing funding options in the light of practical experience. The use of innovative new techniques such as crowd-funding should also be further explored.

4. Cost rules

As contingency fees provide one possible mechanism for the funding of collective redress claims, it would be wrong to limit or exclude their use before careful study of their impact in European legal systems has been undertaken. Therefore, the Commission should review and commission empirical research aiming at assessing the impact of contingency fees on the resolution of claims, and in particular the bringing of frivolous claims, in Members States in which such fee arrangements are currently allowed.

5. Collective ADR

Though the provisions of the Recommendation dealing with collective ADR and collective settlements strictly speaking apply only to collective damages claims, Member States should extend their application to injunctive collective redress as well.

When deciding whether or not to give approval to a collective settlement, the court should consider not only its legality, but also the fairness and adequacy of its terms, including the remuneration agreed to be paid to professional advisers, with respect to all group members.

6. Cross-border collective redress

As the Recommendation is a non-binding instrument it could not provide the regulation necessary for the efficient handling of cross-border mass cases. Currently, neither the new Brussels I Regulation (coming into force in January 2015) nor the Rome I and II Regulations deals with the particular problems of collective redress proceedings. Although there is a need for clear rules on international jurisdiction for mass disputes, courts will have to make do with the Brussels I Regulation for the time being.

The ELI considers that the Recommendation should encourage Member States to accord legal standing to foreign representative entities which have been founded on an ad hoc basis for a particular mass harm situation in another Member State. Member States should be aware of that possibility when implementing new rules on legal standing.

C. Recommendation

In this section, we will review a series of key issues in respect of the Recommendation.

1. Funding

Relevant provisions of the Recommendation:

14. The claimant party should be required to declare to the court at the outset of the proceedings the origin of the funds that it is going to use to support the legal action.

15. The court should be allowed to stay the proceedings if in the case of use of financial resources provided by a third party:
(a) there is a conflict of interest between the third party and the claimant party and its members;
(b) the third party has insufficient resources in order to meet its financial commitments to the claimant party initiating the collective redress procedure;
(c) the claimant party has insufficient resources to meet any adverse costs should the collective redress procedure fail.
16. The Member States should ensure, that in cases where an action for collective redress is funded by a private third party, it is prohibited for the private third party:
(a) to seek to influence procedural decisions of the claimaarty, including on settlements;
(b) to provide financing for a collective action against a defendant who is a competitor of the fund provider or against a defendant on whom the fund provider is dependant;
(c) to charge excessive interest on the funds provided.

a) Comments

The provisions of the Recommendation dealing with funding prompt a number of specific reflections, as well as a number of wider observations (which follow, below).

As regards the specific matters addressed in points 14 to 16:

(1) The requirement in point 14 that the claimant party should declare to the court at the outset of the proceedings the origin of the funds to be used to support the legal action should not be interpreted as requiring the claimant party to disclose details of the funding arrangements in place as that could give the defendant party tactical and strategic advantages in the litigation. A simple declaration by the claimant party about the (private or third party) origin of the funds should suffice.

(2) Point 15 provides that national courts should be able, under certain conditions, to stay the proceedings in the case of use of financial resources provided by a third party, but the Recommendation contains no definition of "third party" and the meaning of this term is likely to give rise to satellite litigation. Arguably, all funds available to representative entities are "financial resources provided by a third party." Further, claims financed out of public funds (legal aid), individual member contributions and legal expenses insurance may also fall within the scope of point 15. The Commission should attempt to resolve these potential ambiguities in its review of the Recommendation's implementation in 2017.

(3) The Recommendation does not make a distinction between consumer representative actions and representative actions on behalf of businesses. In the first case, regulating funding of every kind makes sense from the point of

view of consumer protection, which is a core aim of EU action in the field of collective redress. It is unclear, however, what justification can be advanced for State regulation of litigation funding arrangements between businesses. At the very least, evidence of need for such restrictive measures should be presented.
(4) Point 16(a) recommends that the Member States should ensure that third party funders do not seek to influence procedural decisions of the claimant party, including decisions on settlements. It is, however, unrealistic to expect third party funders to shoulder the procedural risk of the litigation and to leave it completely to the claimant to conduct and ultimately to settle the case. Third party funders have – at least to some extent – a legitimate interest in being involved in important decisions that have to be made by the claimant party. It is, however, necessary to prevent abuse and to make sure that the third party funder's interests do not prevail over the legitimate interests of the claimant group members. Consequently, when scrutinising the proposed settlement courts should examine the influence exerted by third party funders and evaluate its propriety.

b) The wider funding context

The ELI believes that the issue of funding is crucial to the effectiveness of collective redress and regrets that the Commission did not consider funding questions of a general nature, as opposed to the specific issue of restrictions on third-party funding. The ELI therefore calls upon the Commission to address the general issue of funding of collective redress in its four-year review of the Recommendation's implementation, paying special regard to the specific points mentioned below.

Generally speaking, at least six different funding mechanisms can be identified for funding a representative action: i) individual member contributions or donations; ii) legal aid; iii) legal expenses insurance taken out before the event triggering the insurance entitlement occurs; iv) special multi-party and representative action funds; v) third party funding after the event, provided by commercial entities (private equity) working on the basis of a percentage of damages obtained; and vi) lawyers' contingency fees.[23] Each funding source raises different issues. For example, "free-rider problems"[24] and other

---

[23] See RP Mulheron, 'Cost Shifting, Security for Costs, and Class Actions: Lessons from Elsewhere', in D Dwyer (ed.), *The Tenth Anniversary of the Civil Procedure Rules*, (Oxford University Press, 2010), 183–228, at 191–196; RP Mulheron, 'Costs and Funding of Collective Actions: Realities and Possibilities', Feb 2011, http://www.law.qmul.ac.uk/docs/staff/department/71112.pdf; IN Tzankova, 'Funding of Mass Disputes: Lessons from the Netherlands', 8 *JL Econ & Pol'y* 549 (2012) at 571–591.

[24] The free rider problem arises where a group member is able to profit from a representative action without financially contributing to it.

logistical challenges related to the acquisition of funds mean that individual group member contributions will often turn out to be an inadequate source of funding.[25] Likewise, legal aid is unlikely to prove adequate in most jurisdictions because of its generally restrictive eligibility criteria. Even if Member States were to ensure that representative entities are eligible for legal aid, which is currently often not the case, this cannot be viewed as a complete solution. Quite apart from its own budget constraints, legal aid does not offer any assistance in cross-border claims or when claimants are SMEs.

Before-the-event legal expenses insurance *does offer* a potentially useful mechanism for funding collective redress. However, as a result of the ruling of the CJEU in the Austrian *UNIQA* case,[26] legal expenses insurers might choose to exclude mass disputes and group or representative actions from their coverage, as happened in Germany in the aftermath of the *Deutsche Telecom* case.[27] Where insurers have not excluded coverage of mass disputes from their policies, their business models may still prevent them from funding a representative action unless the number of insurers who report a loss is significant. That will rarely be the case for a single insurer. In addition, the business model of before-the-event legal expenses insurers generally favours the quick settlement and resolution of claims,[28] which may not always be in the best interests of the claimant group. Before-the-event legal expenses insurance thus cannot be viewed as a complete solution to the problem of funding collective redress.

Other funding options also merit consideration, for example the creation of special funds to finance claims in mass consumer disputes[29] or representative actions more generally.[30] Mechanisms involving the distribution of damages for substitute purposes ('*cy-près* distribution')[31] also deserve further

---

[25] IN Tzankova, 'Funding of Mass Disputes: Lessons from the Netherlands' (above n 23) 571–591.

[26] Case C-199/08, *Eschig v UNIQA*, 2009, ECR I-8295.

[27] See A Halfmeier, 'Litigation without end? The German approach to private enforcement of securities law', in DR Hensler, C Hodges and IN Tzankova (eds.), *Class Actions in Context* (Edward Elgar, 2014).

[28] WH van Boom, 'Financing Civil Litigation by the European Insurance Industry', in M Tuil and L Visscher (eds.), *New Trends in Financing Civil Litigation in Europe: A Legal, Empirical, and Economic Analysis*, 94–99 where the author provides a general analysis of the business model of before-the-event legal expenses insurers and related agency problems. For a discussion of the differences between the Dutch and German markets for legal expense insurances see IN Tzankova, 'Funding of Mass Disputes: Lessons from the Netherlands' (above n 23) at 578–579.

[29] A-L Sibony, 'Les actions collectives en droit européen: cent fois remettre sur le métier', 3–4 *European Journal of Consumer Law* (2010) 577–602, at 598.

[30] See RP Mulheron, 'Cost Shifting, Security for Costs, and Class Actions', in D Dwyer (ed), *The Tenth Anniversary of the Civil Procedure Rules* (Oxford University Press 2010) at 192–193.

[31] See RP Mulheron, 'Cy-Près Damages Distributions in England: A New Era for Consumer Redress', 20 *European Business L Rev* (2009) 307–342 where she discusses *cy-près* in the UK

analysis, even though they are not currently widely available, and would need an explicit statutory basis in most Member States. 'Crowdfunding' based on the solicitation of multiple voluntary contributions of small amounts provides another relatively novel but promising mechanism for the funding of collective redress; its participatory aspects may be considered an especial advantage. However, European Union law should ensure that it is possible for representative entities to resort to crowdfunding methods and, in particular, should remove the current obstacles to cross-border crowdfunding.[32]

A further option that appealed to members of the ELI Project Team was the creation of a special fund, preferably at EU level, which would receive donations from successful litigants.[33] The idea would be to 'nudge' consumers (or other successful claimants) to donate part of the money they have been awarded in the trial or settlement. After receiving the money, successful consumers would be presented with the choice between taking their share of the damages (often a very small sum), or donating some or all of the money they obtained to a fund which would finance future collective actions.

Consideration could also be given to the creation of a European (or national) fund out of monies obtained from the enforcement of injunctive orders in collective redress proceedings (see below, comments to points 19 and 20), the enforcement of civil fines in cartel cases or the disgorgement of unlawful profits.[34]

However, it should be noted that the Recommendation (at points 15, 16 and 32) restricts the use of contingency fees and third party funding to such an extent that they cannot be considered a realistic option in most representative actions. Therefore, the conclusion could very well be that, at this point, there are no completely viable funding options in the EU in place for the funding of representative actions.

As this wider funding context is not addressed in the current Recommendation, but is vital to the effective implementation of collective

---

context. At 324–342, she discusses a framework and defines a check list about how and when to apply *cy-près*. See also RP Mulheron, *The Modern Cy-Près Doctrine: Applications and Implications* (Cavendish, 2006), chs 7 and 8.

[32] Cf. Communication from the Commission to the European Parliament, The Council, The European Economic and Social Committee and the Committee of the Regions, Unleashing the potential of Crowdfunding in the European Union. Brussels, 27.3.2014, COM(2014) 172 final.

[33] See A-L Sibony (above n 29).

[34] For such a proposal made with respect to German law see HW Micklitz and A Stadler, *Das Verbandsklagerecht in der Informations- und Dienstleistungsgesellschaft*, German Federal Ministry for Consumer Protection, Nutrition and Agriculture (Münster, 2005) at 1270 et seq., http://www.jura.uni-konstanz.de/stadler/forschung/publikationen/hinweisverbands klagerecht/; K-H Fezer, *Zweckgebundene Verwendung von Unrechtserlösen und Kartellbußen zur Finanzierung von Verbraucherarbeit* (2012), http://www.umwelt.nrw.de/verbraucherschutz/ wirtschaft/wettbewerbsrecht/index.php.

redress in Europe, the ELI proposes that the Commission should address funding issues explicitly in its four-year review of the Recommendation's implementation, and in the meantime should review and commission research into the funding mechanisms currently available in collective redress proceedings in Member States and elsewhere. The ELI notes that, in preparation for the current Recommendation, the Commission conducted several studies within the Member States aimed at assessing and demonstrating the need for collective redress and representative actions. It would be consistent with that approach to assess and explore the funding of mass disputes in the various Member States before coming up with any recommendation on the funding issue, having regard in particular to the funding arrangements that are currently available in the Member States to finance multi-party and representative actions, how these operate in practice and what kind of issues the various funding sources raise.

c) Implementation in Member States:
Lastly, to ensure that funding sources do not have different effects in the various Member States,[35] Member States and the EU should conduct a careful analysis of existing funding options in the context of mass disputes and representative actions. Only after such an analysis can it be decided what the most appropriate action with respect to funding should be at EU level and how the use of third party funding and contingency fees should be regulated.

2. Cross-border cases

Relevant provisions of the Recommendation:

17. The Member States should ensure that where a dispute concerns natural or legal persons from several Member States, a single collective action in a single forum is not prevented by national rules on admissibility or standing of the foreign groups of claimants or the representative entities originating from other national legal systems.
18. Any representative entity that has been officially designated in advance by a Member State to have standing to bring representative actions should be permitted to seize the court in the Member State having jurisdiction to consider the mass harm situation.

a) Comments
Cross-border cases should always be kept in mind when dealing with matters

---

[35] For a discussion of the differences between the Dutch and German market of legal expense insurances see IN Tzankova, 'Funding of Mass Disputes: Lessons from the Netherlands (above n23) at 572–573, 583.

of European law.[36] As the Recommendation is a non-binding instrument, it could not provide the regulation which is necessary for the efficient handling of cross-border mass claims. Currently, neither the new Brussels I Regulation (coming into force in January 2015) nor the Rome I and II Regulations deal with the particular problems of proceedings for collective redress. Although there is a need for clear rules on international jurisdiction in respect of mass disputes, courts will have to make do with the Brussels I Regulation for the time being. It is likely that competition among Member States for 'big' cases will increase, which may lead to intensive forum shopping and parallel litigation which cannot be handled by existing legal provisions; these consequently need improvement. The rather individualistic approach taken by the Rome II Regulation which protects the individual expectations of tort victims in product liability and competition cases will often have as its consequence that courts in cross-border mass disputes cannot apply a single set of tort rules to the numerous claims that are brought. These issues are very likely to create obstacles for the efficient enforcement of mass claims in practice. The ELI therefore recommends that the European legislature initiates a broad discussion on private international law issues relating to collective redress in order to come up with a solution when the Commission revisits the situation in its four-year review of the Recommendation's implementation.[37]

The provisions of the Recommendation dealing with cross-border cases (points 17 and 18) only address the issue of the legal standing of representative entities. They should be considered to seek a similar goal to the rule established in Article 4(1) of the Injunctions Directive, which is to allow entities complying with the relevant requirements in one Member State to also be granted legal capacity and legal standing to apply to courts or administrative authorities in another Member State namely the State in which the infringement of European Union law occurred–if this infringement of European Union law affects the interests of stakeholders in the Member State in which the entity is established.

However, the Recommendation and the Injunctions Directive apparently establish different principles in seeking to achieve this objective.

Point 18 of the Recommendation has a broader effect than Articles 3 and 4 of the Injunctions Directive if in a cross-border case the infringement has

---

[36] A Nuyts and NE Hatzimihail (eds.), *Cross-Border Class Actions*. The European Way (Sellier, 2014).

[37] A Stadler (above n 11); for more detailed discussion see A Stadler, 'Conflicts of Laws in Multinational Collective Actions – a Judicial Nightmare?', in D Fairgrieve and E Lein (eds.), *Extraterritoriality and Collective Redress* (Oxford University Press 2012) at 191; D Fairgrieve, 'The Impact of the Brussels I Enforcement and Recognition Rules on Collective Actions', *ibid* at 171.

its origin in one Member State (normally the place where the infringer is domiciled) but causes harm or injury to consumers in various other Member States. Point 18 asks all Member States having jurisdiction over the case to accept the legal standing of particular representative entities from other Member States. This includes the Member States where the injury or harm occurred in the sense of Article 5(3) of the Brussels I Regulation (Article 7 (2) of the Brussels I Regulation Recast), even though the tortious act may have been committed elsewhere. Under the Injunctions Directive the 'country-of-origin' principle applies only to actions filed in the Member States where the 'infringement originated' (which is the place where the tortious act was committed). Thus, the Recommendation invites the Member States to accept the legal standing of foreign representative entities in circumstances going beyond what is provided for in the Injunctions Directive. Given that proceedings for injunctive relief may be more effective in one Member State than in another, point 18 thus allows the necessary forum shopping by representative entities.

With respect to the entities qualified to bring cross-border actions, the scope of application of point 18 of the Recommendation seems to be stricter than under the Injunctions Directive. Points 4 and 6 of the Recommendation distinguish between 'entities which have been officially designated in advance' and 'entities which have been certified on an ad hoc basis by a Member State's national authorities or courts for a particular representative action.' For cross-border situations, point 18 of the Recommendation exclusively refers to the first type of representative entity, not to the latter. This seems to indicate that entities certified on an ad hoc basis for a particular representative action in one Member State are not supposed to act as a representative entity in other Member States. However, according to Articles 3 and 4 of the Injunctions Directive any 'qualified entity" established in one Member State and representing the interests protected has legal standing in the Member States where the infringement originated. The definition of 'qualified entity' in Article 3 refers to organisations which 'being properly constituted according to the law of a Member State' have a legitimate interest in ensuring that certain provisions protecting consumers are complied with. This raises the question whether the definition given in Article 3 includes representative entities certified according to the Recommendation on an ad hoc basis for a particular representative action (with the peculiarity that they would have been created for the purpose of litigating abroad). It is, however, more likely that point 6 of the Recommendation (read together with point 18) establishes that national authorities or courts can certify representative entities on an ad hoc basis only for the particular proceedings taking place before those authorities or courts. Nevertheless, the Recommendation leaves it to them to certify even foreign representative entities which have been founded (on an ad hoc basis for a particular mass harm situation) in another Member State. Member States should be aware of that possibility when implementing new rules on legal standing.

From the cross-border perspective, it should also be noted that Articles 27 and 28 of the Brussels I Regulation (Articles 29 and 30 of the Brussels I Regulation Recast) address the problem of parallel proceedings and irreconcilable judgments by giving preference to the court where proceedings were first initiated. As the *lis pendens* rule requires not only 'the same cause of action' in all proceedings, but also the participation of 'the same parties,' it will not apply to parallel proceedings initiated by (different) representative entities. Article 28 (1) (now 30(1)), however, confers broad discretion on the courts to stay proceedings or even to decline jurisdiction with regard to the possibility of consolidating the proceedings in the court first seized (Article 28(2), now 30(2)). Consolidation depends, however, on the procedural law applicable in the Member State where the first action has been filed. In order to avoid irreconcilable judgments Member States should consider the implementation of national rules generously permitting the consolidation of 'related actions' within the meaning of Article 28(2) of the Brussels I Regulation.

b) Implementation in Member States:
The ELI considers that the Recommendation should encourage Member States to accord legal standing to foreign representative entities which have been founded on an ad hoc basis for a particular mass harm situation in another Member State. Member States should be aware of that possibility when implementing new rules on legal standing.

Member States should also consider the implementation of national rules which generously allow the consolidation of 'related actions' in cross-border mass harm situations thus giving Article 28(2) (now 30 (2)) of the Brussels I Regulations broader application in practice.

3. Constitution of the claimant party by 'opt-in' principle

Relevant provisions of the Recommendation:

21. The claimant party should be formed on the basis of express consent of the natural or legal persons claiming to have been harmed ('opt-in' principle). Any exception to this principle, by law or by court order, should be duly justified by reasons of sound administration of justice.

22. A member of the claimant party should be free to leave the claimant party at any time before the final judgement is given or the case is otherwise validly settled, subject to the same conditions that apply to withdrawal in individual actions, without being deprived of the possibility to pursue its claims in another form, if this does not undermine the sound administration of justice.

23. *Natural or legal persons claiming to have been harmed in the same mass harm situation should be able to join the claimant party at any time before the judgement is given or the case is otherwise validly settled, if this does not undermine the sound administration of justice.*
24. *The defendant should be informed about the composition of the claimant party and about any changes therein.*

a) Comments

In the Recommendation, opt-in is the general principle and opt-out the exception. This calls for several remarks relating to the Commission's forthcoming review of the Recommendation's implementation in 2017 (as provided for by point 41 of the Recommendation).

First of all, the principle/exception relationship between opt-in and opt-out should itself be within the scope of the review planned for 2017. The ELI believes that the arguments in favour of opt-out, at least as a component of the collective redress system, are stronger than the Commission currently recognises.

Secondly, the Commission's review should pay particular attention to the ongoing collective redress reforms which have been introduced or are in the process of being introduced in several Member States, some of which have adopted the opt-out principle (for example, in Portugal, Denmark, the Netherlands and the UK)[38] or a mix of opt-in and opt-out (Belgium).[39] The ELI believes that the impact of the opt-in principle should be reviewed on the basis of the evidence available in 2017, and that the Recommendation should not be read as putting a stop to national experiments with opt-out.[40]

Thirdly, in considering the circumstances in which exceptions from the opt-in principle are justified (point 21, 2nd sentence), the notion of 'the sound administration of justice' should be interpreted broadly. In line with the princi-

---

[38] The British Institute of International and Comparative Law website on Collective Redress (funded by the EU) includes overviews of the relevant national systems, with regular updates on reforms: www.collectiveredress.org.

[39] E Falla, *Powers of the judge in collective redress proceedings*, Université Libre de Bruxelles, February 2012, http://www.beuc.org/publications/2012-00227-01-e.pdf; European Parliament, Overview of existing collective redress schemes in EU Member States, Directorate General for internal policies, Policy department A, July 2011, http://www.europarl.europa.eu/document/activities/cont/201107/20110715ATT24242/20110715ATT24242EN.pdf; BEUC, Country survey of collective redress mechanisms (updated in December 2011), http://www.beuc.eu/publications/2011-10006-01-e.pd; Les actions de groupe. Les documents de travail du Sénat Belge, Mai 2010; Strooischade: Een verkennend (rechtsvergelijkend) onderzoek naar de mogelijkheden tot optreden tegen strooischade, Juli 2009.

[40] The European Consumer Consultative Group, in its Opinion on private damages actions (2010), noted Europe's recent experience that the rate of participation in opt-in procedure for consumer claims was less than one percent, whereas under opt-out regimes, rates are typically very high (97% in the Netherlands and almost 100% in Portugal).

ple of procedural autonomy, a wide margin of appreciation should be left to Member States when determining what the demands of 'the sound administration of justice' are. In particular, Member States should be free to consider that the right to an effective remedy is a component of 'the sound administration of justice.' In this context, the experience of various Member States that the compensation of large-scale loss made up of significant but low-value claims is only viable with some form of opt-out mechanism must be deemed relevant when assessing justifications put forward by national legislators and courts.

As the Recommendation has a strong focus on the compensation of consumers and tort victims, it does not mention the instrument of disgorgement or skimming-off of illegally gained profits from wrongdoers, which has primarily deterrent effects. However, Member States that are reluctant to accept the opt-out mechanism for whatever reasons should instead consider the implementation of such instruments (whether in private or public law) for cases that involve only very small individual damage.[41]

Fourthly, with regards to opt-in/opt-out, the insights of behavioural science are very clear: where there is a default option, people tend not to actively choose a different option even when they could ('inertia bias'). This is why default options constitute such a powerful 'nudge.'[42]

Fifthly, regarding effectiveness, unless the impact of 'nudges' is harnessed by means of an opt-out solution, experience shows that significant but low-value claims will not give rise to viable court proceedings, as illustrated in the United Kingdom by the claim against JJB Sports for price fixing in respect of football shirts.[43] In other words, the effectiveness principle, recalled in Article 3 of the proposed Directive on actions for damages,[44] supports the adoption of opt-out mechanisms by Member States. If the effectiveness principle is taken seriously, it seems paradoxical to insist that opt-in should be the

---

[41] A Stadler, 'Group Actions as a Remedy to Enforce Consumer Interests', in F Cafaggi and HW Micklitz (eds.), *New Frontiers of Consumer Protection – Interplay between Private and Public Enforcement* (Intersentia, 2009) 305, at 325–27. The German rules on the disgorgement of illegal profits in Sec. 10 Unfair Competition Act and Sec. 34a, 33 Antitrust Act are, however, good illustrations of how such regulations should *not* be designed. Private organisations that have legal standing to bring such actions must be given some financial incentives to litigate, given especially the large costs risk if the loser pays rule applies.

[42] C Sunstein and R Thaler, *Nudge*, (Yale University Press, 2008), esp. at 1 and 105 et seq. In the field of consumer policy, the EU legislator draws on such insights, for instance in Directive 2011/83/EU of the European Parliament and of the Council of 25 October 2011 on consumer rights, OJ 2011 L 304/64 (esp. art 22).

[43] UK Competition Appeal Tribunal, Case 1022/1/1/03, *JJB Sports PLC v Office of Fair Trading*.

[44] Proposal for a Directive of the European Parliament and of the Council on certain rules governing actions for damages under national law for infringements of the competition law provisions of the Member States and of the European Union, COM(2013) 404 final. The finally adopted text of the Directive (approved in November 2014) refers to this principle in Article 4.

default solution and that Member States need to adduce special justifications when they adopt (more effective) opt-out mechanisms.

Sixthly, on the need for empirical evidence, differing views regarding the comparative merits of opt-in and opt-out collective redress structures are expressed in the literature. By and large, they are supported by legal and political arguments. What is so far missing is empirical research into the competing models, which is an essential precondition of further progress in this longstanding debate.[45] Without further monitoring and reporting by the Commission of the way collective redress develops over the period to 2017, it would be premature to determine the best approach to collective redress to recommend to the Member States. Empirical evidence – beyond the famous UK *JJB Sports* case – will be necessary with respect to the behaviour of individual claimants when liability has been established in collective redress proceedings or when a collective settlement has been achieved. Every opt-out mechanism applied to claims for damages ultimately involves an opt-in procedure at the distribution stage of proceedings. If the individual loss is small, those theoretically entitled to claim compensation may choose not to do so or may have difficulty in proving their entitlement in practice. Therefore, a decision on the best approach on opt-in/opt-out must also include a debate on the role of deterrence,[46] the proper relationship between private and public enforcement, and the pros and cons of *cy-près* solutions.[47]

Finally, regarding the policy background, the dilemma remains how to choose between opt-out and opt-in systems of collective redress. Opt-out is more likely to produce results, but allows lawyers and third party funders, and others unharmed by the unlawful conduct in question, to make windfall profits from their involvement. Conversely, with opt-in collective redress, inertia is likely to limit the number of claims by those actually harmed, and there is little incentive for relevant third parties to become involved, because the size of the cake is reduced.

b) Implementation in Member States:
While the Commission's Recommendation clearly favours the opt-in system as the default option, it also recognises that too rigid an approach to the structuring of collective redress may not be in the interests of justice. One

---

[45] Mulheron has done some research in this respect: R Mulheron, 'The Case for an Opt-out Class Action for European Member States: A Legal and Empirical Analysis', 15 *Columbia J of European L* (2009) 409–453.

[46] S Issacharoff and GP Miller, 'Will Aggregate Litigation Come to Europe?' (2009) 62 *Vand L Rev* 179,187.

[47] C Hodges, *The Reform of Class and Representative Actions in European Legal Systems* (Hart Publishing 2008) 118–123; R Mulheron, *The Class Action in Common Law Legal Systems, A Comparative Perspective* (Hart Publishing 2004); R Mulheron, *The Modern Cy-près Doctrine*, (Hart Publishing 2006).

possible way for Member States to implement the Recommendation would be to permit their courts to adopt the form of collective redress procedure best suited to the particular circumstances of the case at hand, as under the new Belgian legislation.[48] This is a 'third way' model, which is especially interesting at the present time, at which more data is needed on the operation of both opt-in and opt-out in Europe. While it would be for Member States to decide how to implement such a model, it is suggested that the choice between opt-in and opt-out should be made by national courts taking into account the specific features of each case, including such matters as:

- the characteristics of the claimants (big business, SMEs, trade associations, NGOs such as Consumer Associations, large numbers of individual consumers, or public bodies);
- the nature of the claim (for example, whether the claim is for high value damages suffered by a small number of large business concerns, low value damages suffered by a large number of end consumers, damages to mixed large and small business customers belonging to a trade association, or damages to identifiable residents in a street with a claim against local or central government); and
- the overall context of the proceedings (including, for example, any payment into court by way of an offer of compensation or the initiation of 'Italian torpedo' actions in other jurisdictions as a delaying tactic).[49]

Where a Member State follows the approach set out in the Recommendation which gives preference to the opt-in model but permits opt-out when justified in the interests of the sound administration of justice, the court's case management powers should permit it to decide on the best structure in the light of the particular circumstances of the case in question.

Where a Member State gives preference to the opt-out model,[50] it should equally make it clear that other structures may be selected where justice requires,[51] including an opt-in structure.

It follows that the Member States could implement the Commission's Recommendation by introducing a new mechanism, or streamlining an exist-

---

[48] Loi du 28 mars 2014 – Loi portant insertion d'un titre 2 'De l'action en réparation collective' au livre XVII 'Procédures juridictionnelles particulières' du Code de droit économique et portant insertion des définitions propres au livre XVII dans le livre 1er du Code de droit économique, Moniteur Belge, 29 April 2014, n°2014011217, 35201.

[49] As to 'Italian torpedo' actions, see P Véron, ECJ Restores Torpedo Power, *IIC* 2004, 638; A Wittwer, *Eur. L. Rptr.* 2004, 49; T Hartley, in JAR Nafziger and S Symeonides (eds.), *Essays in Honor of AT von Mehren*, 2002, 73.

[50] As under a current proposal in the UK, favouring an opt-in mechanism with respect to group members domiciled outside the UK: Draft Consumer Rights Bill (Cm 8657).

[51] As under the Draft Consumer Rights Bill in the UK.

ing mechanism, to ensure that effective and efficient class (or group) actions are readily available before their courts without unduly prejudicing the rights of any interested parties. A way to ensure that class (or group) actions are effective and efficient is to give the national courts full case management powers to enable them to determine the most appropriate form of collective redress procedure in the individual case.

4. Collective alternative dispute resolution and settlements

Relevant provisions of the Recommendation:

25. The Member States should ensure that the parties to a dispute in a mass harm situation are encouraged to settle the dispute about compensation consensually or out-of- court, both at the pre-trial stage and during civil trial, taking also into account the requirements of Directive 2008/52/EC of the European Parliament and of the Council of 21 May 2008 on certain aspects of mediation in civil and commercial matters.

26. The Member States should ensure that judicial collective redress mechanisms are accompanied by appropriate means of collective alternative dispute resolution available to the parties before and throughout the litigation. Use of such means should depend on the consent of the parties involved in the case.

27. Any limitation period applicable to the claims should be suspended during the period from the moment the parties agree to attempt to resolve the dispute by means of an alternative dispute resolution procedure until at least the moment at which one or both parties expressly withdraw from that alternative dispute resolution procedure.

28. The legality of the binding outcome of a collective settlement should be verified by the courts taking into consideration the appropriate protection of interests and rights of all parties involved.

a) Comments

As noted in the Comments to Chapter IV above, the ELI recommends that these provisions on collective settlements and ADR should also apply to injunctive collective redress, even though this chapter of the Recommendation is entitled "Specific principles relating to compensatory collective redress."

As regards point 28, the ELI notes that settlements are the most common way in which mass disputes are resolved. A court review of the settlement, which is simply a form of contract, is not necessary in traditional two-party litigation, in which claimant and defendant are expected to negotiate in their own respective interests. Collective settlements negotiated by a representative of the claimant class require judicial oversight, however, as there is the potential for principal-agent conflicts and the group of absent claimants is unable to monitor effectively the representative's performance. Therefore, it is consistent with international standards of mass litigation that collective settlements should be approved by the court in order to have binding effect on group members.[52] However, the ELI submits that the text of point 28 is not clear with respect to its scope of application and the criteria to be applied by courts.

First, a distinction should be drawn between the outcomes of ADR and settlements negotiated during formal court proceedings. The requirement for court approval applies only to the latter and not the former. ADR is a mechanism outside the court system and it would be detrimental to its operation for its outcomes to be subject to court approval regarding the appropriateness of the protection given to the interests and rights of all parties involved. In any case, court approval is not necessary as the outcomes of ADR will normally have no binding effect on the absent group members. Although the context of point 28 (under the heading "Collective alternative dispute resolution and settlements") may be interpreted as indicating that it refers to collective settlements achieved as the outcome of ADR, that interpretation is undesirable and was probably not the intention of the Commission. The ELI accepts, however, that court approval of all collective settlements negotiated in the course of judicial proceedings should be required as a general rule. It is an absolutely necessary safeguard of the interests of absent claimants.[53]

Secondly, the Recommendation requires a verification of the 'legality' of the binding outcome of the collective settlement and thus seems to restrict the scope of examination to mere formalities or to the question of whether the mass settlement violates existing rules. It is not clear why the expression 'legality' has been chosen as the benchmark for the court's review and it is not acceptable for either settlements achieved during ADR proceedings or settlements in the course of contentious litigation. Strictly speaking, it is not even necessary to verify the 'legality' of a settlement because illegal settlements will normally be null and void anyway.

The main risk involved in collective settlements is certainly not the violation of procedural or substantive law. Class action and collective redress regulations all over the world require a review of the settlement by the court because of the potential principal-agent conflicts arising in the nego-

---

[52] Rule 23 (e) US Federal Rules of Civil Procedure; Art. 907 Dutch Civil Code (for settlements under the Dutch Collective Settlement Act); Sec. 26 Swedish Group Litigation Act; Art. 19 Polish Group Litigation Act; Sec. 18 German Capital Market Model Case Act (2012); Sec. 18–19 Israel Class Action Law (2006); Ch. 6 Sec. 29 Ontario Class Proceedings Act 1992, Sec. 35 Class Action Proceedings Act British Columbia, 1996; Class Action Proceedings Act SNS Sec. 38 (Nova Scotia); Sec. 33V Federal Court of Australia Act; Sec. 33A Victoria Supreme Court Act (Australia); Sec. 173 New South Wales Civil Procedure Act (part 10); Art. XVII 44 Belgian Draft for Collective Redress Proceedings (2014).

[53] See the contributions by R Marcus, M Legg, J Kalajdzic, I Tzankova and D Hensler in Hodges and Stadler (eds.) (above n 27).

tiation process and because of the risk that the settlement might not take into consideration the different or even conflicting interests of the group members.[54] Depending on the mechanism by which the mass litigation is funded, the remuneration granted in the settlement to the lawyers may be another issue in respect of which judicial scrutiny and approval is justified. Consequently, courts should first of all assess the reasonableness and fairness of the terms of the settlement, not its legality (which can probably be denied only under extraordinary circumstances).

'Legality' can also hardly be interpreted as allowing the court to withhold its approval if the rights granted under the settlement do not correspond with the factual circumstances and legal entitlements of the group members. Compromise is the essence of settlement and therefore group members will often not receive full compensation under the agreed terms. Nevertheless, the settlement might constitute a fair and reasonable resolution of the collective dispute, having regard to the stage of the proceedings at which it is reached and the risks involved in seeking to establish liability before the court.

b) Implementation in Member States

Though, strictly speaking, points 25 to 28 apply only to collective damages claims, Member States should extend their application to injunctive collective redress as well.

Member States should clearly distinguish between the outcomes of ADR and settlements, negotiated during formal court proceedings. A requirement for court approval would be contrary to the operation of ADR and is not necessary as the outcomes of ADR will normally have no binding effect on absent group members. All settlements negotiated in the course of judicial proceedings should require court approval so as to protect the rights and interests of absent group members. Scrutinising the proposed settlement courts should not only consider its legality, but also the fairness and adequacy of the settlement, including the remuneration to be paid under its terms to professional advisers, with respect to all group members.

III. ASSESSMENT OF THE COMPETITION DAMAGES CLAIMS DIRECTIVE

A. Introduction

The Directive on certain rules governing actions for damages under national law for infringements of the competition law provisions of the Member

---

[54] J Coffee, 'Class Wars: The Dilemma of the Mass Tort Class Action', 95 *Col J Rev* (1995), 1344; M Faure, 'CADR and settlement of claims – a few economic observations', in Hodges and Stadler (eds.), *Resolving mass disputes: ADR and settlement of mass claims* (Edward Elgar 2013) 38 et seq., at 54–59.

States and of the European Union, approved by the European Parliament on 17 April 2014 and by the Council on 10 November 2014, is the result of a long process. This process started back in 2005, when the European Commission published its Green Paper on Damages actions for breach of the EC antitrust rules. The publication highlighted what were considered the main obstacles to a more effective system of antitrust damages actions. Quantification of harm, the absence of clear rules on the passing-on defence or the questionable probative value of NCA's decisions were some of the challenges this Green Paper identified as problems to be solved by future European legislation. Some concrete policy proposals were suggested in that regard by the European Commission, the European Parliament and the European Economic and Social Committee.

But it was only in 2011 when more concrete steps were taken, especially with the public consultation "[t]owards a coherent European approach to collective redress" held by the European Commission with the goal of identifying common legal principles on collective redress and exploring the way those common principles could fit into the EU legal system and into the national legal orders of the Member States. The consultation aimed to improve the enforcement of EU legislation and the protection of the rights to victims. Another milestone in this process was the Resolution of the Meeting of the Heads of the European Competition Authorities of 23 May 2012, which emphasised the importance of the protection of leniency material in the context of civil damages actions. The support to the idea that public enforcement is essential in the competition field also came from the European Parliament whose response to the mentioned public consultation encouraged the Commission to take action in that direction.

With this background, on 11 June 2013 the Commission issued the Proposal for a Directive of the European Parliament and of the Council on certain rules governing actions for damages under national law for infringements of the competition law provisions of the Member States and of the European Union (COM(2013) 404 final). This Proposal for a Directive introduced various significant measures such as a rebuttable presumption that any cartel infringement has caused harm, a power for national courts to order the defendant or third parties to disclose evidence, and the recognition of infringement decisions by national competition authorities before every national court in the EU. The Proposal was accompanied by a Communication and a Practical Guide on how to quantify harm in antitrust cases. In October 2013, the European Economic and Social Committee published its first opinion on the proposed Directive, which was followed by a report from the EP's Committee on Economic and Monetary Affairs, where some amendments were suggested. The Council gave its approval to the proposed Directive but agreed on a modified text on 3 December 2013 as its common position, suggesting amendments regarding the value of NCA's decisions and other issues. The original text proposed by the European Commission was then subject to opinions from the European Parliament's Committee on the Internal Market and Consumer Protection and from the Committee on Legal Affairs. Before the final text was put to a vote at the European Parliament, the European Economic and Social Committee published a second opinion on the proposed Directive. The text of the Directive was finally adopted in the Plenary Session of the European Parliament of 17 April 2014 and by the Council on 10 November 2014.

B. Overview

The proposed Directive of the European Parliament and of the Council on certain rules governing actions for damages under national law for infringements of the competition law provisions of the Member States and of the European Union (COM(2013) 404 final), approved with modifications on 10 November 2014, introduces various significant measures such as a more open system of disclosure of evidence, the facilitation of indirect purchasers actions, the balancing between protecting leniency programs and encouraging private actions. It includes a rebuttable presumption that any cartel infringement has caused harm, a power for national courts to order the defendant or third parties to disclose evidence, and the requirement for national courts to allow follow-on actions based on infringement decisions of their own National Competition Authorities (NCAs). The proposed Directive was accompanied by a Communication and a Practical Guide on how to quantify harm in antitrust cases.

At the same time, the non-binding Recommendation issued by the European Commission (discussed in detail in Section I of this Statement) prescribes that all Member States should have collective redress mechanisms in place for all areas of Union law conferring rights and obligations on individuals and legal entities (as many currently do not) and outlines several principles to which such mechanisms should adhere. This subject is of particular importance in the field of competition law, as anti-competitive practices can often result in relatively small amounts of damage to large groups of consumers. The Directive deals with actions for damages in antitrust cases but does not cover collective redress which is left to the Recommendation.

1. The ELI's work on the Directive

This section of the Statement includes the concrete suggestions that the ELI communicated to European institutions during the legislative process, aiming to improve the effectiveness of competition damages claims in national courts in the light of the Directive and to maximise its practical utility, while endorsing the Communication on quantifying harm in actions for damages based on breaches of Article 101 or 102 of the TFEU.

The Statement contains comments on the text of the Directive originally proposed by the European Commission (COM(2013) 404 final). Only those articles of the proposed Directive for which an alternative wording was suggested or whose scope and interpretation was found to be potentially controversial have been commented upon. Those articles are revised showing the original wording proposed by the European Commission in one column and the alternative wording suggested by the ELI adjacently. Proposals for alternative wording are followed by a summary of the reasons justifying them. The final text of the Directive, adopted by the European Parliament (on 17 April 2014) and the Council (on 10 November 2014) is attached as Annex II to this volume.

2. *Comments on the Proposal COM(2013) 404 final*

In general terms, the ELI agrees with the approach of the European Commission and welcomes this Directive, since it will contribute to a more coherent and stronger legal framework for damages. An example of this contribution is the minimum limitation period for damages claims, positively considered by the ELI as a guarantee that will significantly improve access to justice for victims of competition law infringements.

The main suggestions made by the ELI refer to disclosure of evidence, effect of national decisions, and passing-on of overcharges.

On disclosure of evidence, the ELI considers that private enforcement should not compromise the effectiveness of public enforcement of competition law.

Regarding the effect of national decisions, the ELI supports the proposal of the Commission to give binding effect to the finding of infringement in NCAs' decisions without this giving binding effect to any findings of fact which relate to the issues of damage or causation. This issue should be addressed again as confidence in the European Competition Network grows.

For passing-on of overcharges, the need to establish transnational rules in order to allow consolidated actions (direct and indirect purchasers) is highlighted.

Finally, as a general comment on the Directive, the ELI welcomes the existing funding programmes for training in EU Competition Law for judges. In any case, it invites the European Commission to consider the establishment of new funding programmes in EU Competition Law, focused on this new Directive.

IV. COMMENTARY: WHAT NEXT AND KEY ISSUES?

The following are a few conclusions on collective redress and the new

Competition Damages Directive prompted by the ELI Statement presented above:

1. The EU institutions have been wise to be cautious to avoid the US class action system (which is often perceived to be protectionist in the light of the nationality of those business people sent to prison for antitrust law violations).
2. The challenge for the EU and its 28 Member States is to develop a system for collective redress which will work in Europe where the culture is not instinctively litigious. In fact, there are precedents in the US for a regulatory administered compensation system, such as the models provide by the Securities and Exchange Commission Fair Funds and the September 11th Victim Compensation Fund which have proved that they can provide a more effective and efficient restitution to victims than traditional litigation.[55]
3. The UK Consumer Rights Bill is surprisingly close to what could be a workable collective redress system for individual consumers (although one wonders whether they will ever be bothered if not pushed by lawyers with ulterior motives). In reality it will not prevent the court from deciding on a case by case basis not to follow the chosen opt-out class-action approach if it determines that exceptional circumstances militate in favour of an opt-in or other approach. It is also clear that the Consumer Rights Bill, if it ever passes into law, is intended to provide a litigation backbone threat to encourage ADR and settlements.
4. In the context of ADR, it is notable that both the Competition Damages Directive and the UK Consumer Rights Bill encourage ADR and settlement and in particular encourage the NCAs to promote them. It will be interesting to see how the procedures under discussion in the UK may achieve this objective.
5. The new Competition Damages Directive gives each Member State the opportunity to become jurisdictions of choice for competition law damages cases by requiring them all to provide for proportionate disclosure on request (which arguably goes beyond the current rights of claimants in most Member States other than those with a common law system). However, forum shopping disputes, such as the Italian Torpedo, are still left to the Brussels I Recast Regulation, in force from January 2015. Cross-border damages claims, including collective redress cases, require further study and eventual guidance following the Commission's review of collective redress in 2017.

---

[55] See, EE Litwin and MJ Feder, 'European Collective Redress: Lessons from the US Experience', in J Langenfeld (ed.) *The Law and Economics of Class Actions* (Emerald Books 2014) at 209 to 248.

6. One of the main issues with the new evidence disclosure obligations (which are well drafted to protect public enforcement) is the appropriate approach to disclosure of business secrets and confidential information. This has been an issue with regard to disclosure or publication in the OJEU of the confidential version of Commission competition law (cartel) decision since the *Pergan* case. It is currently occupying the time of over 40 parties and 'non-parties' to the Air Freight Cartel damages case in the English High Court, which ordered disclosure of the full text of the confidential version of the Commission's decision to a confidentiality ring on the condition that the Claimants gave an undertaking not to use any of the information disclosed (for example, to claim damages in a foreign jurisdiction) without the permission of the English Court. This decision of the High Court is subject to an appeal to the Court of Appeal, so the position remains unclear and is not clarified by Recital 18 of the new Directive which appears to permit the English Court to decide as it has to disclose the entire confidential version of the Decision to a confidentiality ring.
7. The rules on limitation periods in the new Directive may require amendment to the English Limitation Act provision on tort, if not in Scotland where the limitation period does not exceed the Directive's five year period. However, the approach of the Directive is similar to that of the English courts in practice.
8. Finally, it is to be noted that presumptions, albeit rebuttable, are not favoured by English courts. The presumptions of harm and of passing-on (interfering with the ordinary law of causation) are unlikely to find favour with English judges, if respectable arguments for challenging the presumptions are put before them.

Collective Redress and Health Care Law: The Specific Characteristics of Group Compensation under Portuguese Law

*Rafael Vale e Reis**

I. THE IMPORTANCE OF COLLECTIVE REDRESS IN HEALTH AND MEDICAL RELATED CLAIMS

Several examples can be identified where a collective redress mechanism would be useful to obtain group compensation in international health law and in particular health care liability cases.[1] Collective Redress in this respect refers to civil procedure mechanisms allowing victims to seek either compensatory or injunctive relief via a bundling of claims in a single procedure.[2]

---

* Invited assistant Professor at the Faculty of Law of the University of Coimbra, Portugal.

[1] The Recommendation of the European Commission of 11 June 2013 makes a clear distinction between injunctive collective redress mechanisms (a legal mechanism that allows two or more natural or legal persons or an entity entitled to bring a representative action to claim cessation of an illegal behaviour) and compensatory collective redress mechanisms (a legal mechanism that allows two or more natural or legal persons claiming to have been harmed in a mass harm situation or an entity entitled to bring a representative action to claim compensation).

[2] For a comprehensive analysis on collective litigation in a comparative perspective: JB Weinstein 'Compensating Large Numbers of People for Inflicted Harms', 11 *Duke Journal of Comparative & International Law,* (2001) 165–178; DR Hensler, 'Revisiting the Monster: New Myths and Realities of Class Action and Other Large Scale Litigation', 11 *Duke Journal of Comparative & International Law,* (2001) 179–214; EH Cooper, 'Class Action Advice in the Form of Questions', 11 *Duke Journal of Comparative & International Law,* (2001) 215–248; N Andrews, 'Multi-Party Proceedings in England: Representative and Group Actions', 11 *Duke Journal of Comparative & International Law,* (2001) 249–268; GD Watson, 'Class Actions: The Canadian Experience', 11 *Duke Journal of Comparative & International Law,* (2001) 269–288; SS Clark and C Harris, 'Multi-Plaintiff Litigation in Australia: A Comparative Perspective', 11 *Duke Journal of Comparative & International Law,* (2001) 289–320; C Hodges 'Multi-Party Actions: A European Approach', 11 *Duke Journal of Comparative & International Law,* (2001) 321–354; H Koch, 'Non-Class Group Litigation Under EU and German Law', 11 *Duke Journal of Comparative & International Law,* (2001) 355–368; G Walter, 'Mass Tort Litigation in Germany and Switzerland', 11 *Duke Journal of Comparative & International Law,* (2001) 369–380; R Nordh, 'Group Actions in Sweden: Reflections on the Purpose of Civil Litigation, the Need for Reforms, and a Forthcoming Proposal', 11 *Duke Journal of Comparative & International Law,* (2001) 381–404; M Taruffo, 'Some Remarks on Group Litigation in

Outside of Europe, in Canada, the first known medical malpractice class action was certified in 2001 and involved a neurologist and his technologist who allegedly failed to follow proper sterilisation procedures and, as a result, triggered an outbreak of hepatitis B.[3]

Another case concerned hip implants in the US. Stryker Orthopaedics developed a revolutionary two-piece hip implant that allowed physicians to perform more personalised treatment. However, once implanted in patients and subjected to normal stress, two pieces of the implant began to wear against one another, leaving metallic debris in a patient's surrounding tissues. Instead of having an implanted artificial hip lasting for 10–15 years, some patients faced replacement within the first 18 months. Many patients were forced to undergo revision surgery, and were at risk that their corrective surgery could become more complicated than the original hip replacement surgery.[4]

Within the European Union (EU) frontiers, other examples have occurred recently in Spain, with the soya oil breast implants and thalidomide cases. In the first case, Trilucent breast implants were designed to make mammographic exams more reliable, as soya bean oil is translucent.[5] Those implants, first licensed in 1995 in Germany, have since become widely used throughout Europe. However, in March 1999, the suppliers of Trilucent voluntarily withdrew the implants from circulation. The decision to withdraw them was taken after many adverse events occurred, including swelling and leakage of the implants.[6]

In the second situation in 2013, a first instance court ruled for the first time in Spain, on tort liability for damages caused by thalidomide between 1960 and 1965.[7] These cases are well-known to the public, sometimes referred to as the 'thalidomide babies' cases. In the 60s, several babies were born with deformities (limbs failing to develop properly, and in some cases also eyes, ears and internal organs) due to side-effects of the drug thalidomide that was taken by mothers during pregnancy to ease their morning sickness. While the first instance court in Madrid granted compensation to the victims represented by an association, the Court of Appeal overturned the decision.[8]

Comparative Perspective', 11 *Duke Journal of Comparative & International Law*, (2001) 405–422; R Mulheron, *The Class Action in Common Law Legal Systems: A Comparative Perspective* (Hart, 2004).

[3] Referring to the case, see: http://www.ncbi.nlm.nih.gov/pmc/articles/PMC81425/.

[4] On these cases, see http://www.drugwatch.com/stryker/recall-hip-stems/.

[5] On these cases, see CG Membrado, *La responsabilidad civil por implante mamario – mala práxis, consentimento informado y prótesis defectuosas* (Editorial Comares, 2014) 124 ct seq.

[6] On the problems detected, see http://www.dhsspsni.gov.uk/niaic_an(ni)1999_01.pdf.

[7] Commenting the decision, see P Salvador Coderch, C Gómez Ligüerre, A Rubí Puig, S Ramos González, and A Terra Ibáñez, *Daños tardíos Avite c. Grünenthal. Comentario a la SJPI no 90 Madrid, 19.11.2013, sobre los daños causados por la talidomida*, 1/2014 indret, *passim*, available at http://www.indret.com/pdf/1036_revisado.pdf.

[8] See S Ramos González, *Nota a La Sentencia de la Audiencia Provincial (Sección 14ª), Madrid,*

When looking at the situation in Portugal, there are cases which demand group compensation in relation to health, but not necessarily to health care liability. Many years ago, in the 1980s, more than 100 Portuguese haemophiliacs were infected with the AIDS virus after receiving transfusions of contaminated plasma that had been imported and distributed by the public health service.[9] Furthermore, recently in 2014, there was a Legionella outbreak in Vila Franca de Xira, a suburban area of Lisbon, which infected more three hundred people and caused eleven deaths. The source of this outbreak is alleged to have been the cooling tower of a plant nearby.[10]

Taking into account the features of the abovementioned cases, prominent academics have pointed out that in these cases, the main goal is to provide compensation for the injuries suffered by each individual, although they belong to a group that was affected by the same unlawful actions.[11] Nevertheless, harmful conduct affecting a large number of victims challenges the traditional two-party litigation on which most of the continental procedural rules are still based.[12] Taking this into account, the question arising is how Portuguese legislation on collective redress deals with the demand for a group of identified injured people to initiate one single judicial procedure in order to get compensation. Undoubtedly, one should not forget that these types of cases could be considered to be subject to 'traditional forms of litigation' such as plural standing (coalition or *litisconsortium*) under the general rules of the Civil Procedure Code (Articles 32 *et seq*).[13] However, this customary approach to collective litigation does not give the victims any special regime for representation and is very unfavourable in terms of costs, as each victim is required to pay for his/her part.[14]

In fact, the reason for having a collective redress mechanisms lies in the many advantages such mechanism has for the claimants: litigation by

---

13.10.2014 (Mp: Sagrario Arroyo García), *Sobre los Daños Asociados a la Talidomida*, http://www.revista.uclm.es/index.php/cesco/article/view/630).

[9] The former Portuguese Health Minister (amongst others) was criminally charged of 'spreading contagious disease' but the case was dropped. The Constitutional Court ruled that limitation period for the procedure was exceeded.

[10] On the outbreak see: http://www.ecdc.europa.eu/en/publications/Publications/legionnaires-disease-portugal-RRA-14-nov-2014.pdf.

[11] See M Taruffo, 'Some Remarks on Group Litigation in Comparative Perspective', 11 *Duke Journal of Comparative & International Law*, (2001) 407, in which the author says that the second purpose is to achieve changes in the practice of some subjects.

[12] M Teixeira de Sousa, *A Legitimidade Popular na Tutela dos Interesses Difusos* (Lex, 2003) 9.

[13] Coalition is more likely to be applicable to these cases than *litisconsortium* due to their respective legal requirements. For a coalition of claimants, one of the following conditions has to be met (art 36 of the Civil Procedure Code): same grounds for claims; one or some claims have to be decided first or depend on the decision on other(s); claims are based on the same facts; or on the application of similar legal or contractual rules.

[14] Unless requirements for legal aid are fulfilled, according to Law 34/2004, of 29 July 2004.

representation; a much more favourable regime of costs even when the claim is not successful; group decision to resort to the judicial system; a strengthening of the claimant's bargaining power against powerful entities; and better technical support (especially in cases where injuries have to be evaluated).[15]

These advantages may largely compensate for the drawbacks of collective trials, which are: (1) less control over proceedings (especially for unnamed plaintiffs); (2) lesser focus on individual solutions; and (3) difficulties with the collection of evidence or with getting compensation that effectively covers the suffered harm.

II. THE PORTUGUESE 'POPULAR ACTION' AS A WAY TO PROTECT INDIVIDUAL RIGHTS IN THE SECTOR OF HEALTH CARE LIABILITY

A. The Portuguese Collective Redress Mechanism – A General Description

The Portuguese legislator has opted for the creation of a general collective redress mechanism.[16] In 1995, the Portuguese parliament passed the Law 83/95, of 31 August 1995 (hereafter Law 83/95), which regulates the so-called *acção popular* ('popular action') and the right of citizens to participate in administrative procedures in order to influence decisions of the public administration.[17] Additionally, there are some sectoral laws dealing with specific forms of collective redress.[18]

---

[15] Regarding the reimbursement of legal costs of the winning party, the European Commission Recommendation of 11 June 2013 on common principles for injunctive and compensatory collective redress mechanisms in the Member States concerning violations of rights granted under Union Law states that "the Member States should ensure that the party that loses a collective redress action reimburses necessary legal costs borne by the winning party ('loser pays principle'), subject to the conditions provided for in the relevant national law" (cfr. Para 13 of the Recommendation, http://eur-lex.europa.eu/legal-content/EN/TXT/?Uri=OJ: JOL_2013_201_R_NS0013).

[16] For more details on the Portuguese collective redress system, see http://www.collective redress.org/collective-redress/reports/portugal/overview.

[17] In addition to the popular action, mass processes are regulated by art 48 of the Code of Administrative Court Procedure, approved by Law 15/2002, of 22 February 2002. This mechanism only applies in administrative court proceedings, where more than 20 cases are initiated which relate, for instance, to the same factual or legal relationship. Only one or some processes (depending on a judicial decision) are referred to for judgement and the final decision may, under certain conditions, be applicable to other cases that were suspended.

[18] In the area of consumer law, art 13/b and c of Law 24/96, of 31 July 1996 grants standing to consumers and consumer associations and, under the terms of Law 83/95, to the Public Prosecutor (*Ministério Público*) and to the Consumer Institute. In financial market law, Decree-Law 486/99, of 13 November 1999, approved the Securities Code; arts 31 and 32 enable the use of the popular action for the protection of homogeneous individual interests or collective interests of investors in securities. Also, in the area of environmental law (Art 45 of Law 11/87, of April 7th changed by Law 13/2002 of 19 February 2002), the protection of environmental values may be achieved using the popular action.

With Law 83/95, the Portuguese legislator enacted Article 52 (3) of the Constitution of the Portuguese Republic of 1976, as amended in 1989. In fact, until the constitutional revision of 1989, the 'popular action' was only possible to enable jurisdictional control of certain administrative acts and to deal with the omissions of local public entities in the defence of property and rights of the administration.[19]

Today, the 'popular action' is a considerably broader mechanism, applicable namely when interests such as public health, environment, quality of life, protection of consumers, cultural heritage and the public domain are involved. These types of interests are specifically listed in the Portuguese Constitution, but not in an exhaustive way.[20] Despite its broad scope of application, however, the Portuguese collective redress mechanism has been rarely used in practice, and even then, mainly with the aim of consumer protection.[21]

Rules on legal standing are also broad. Generally, standing is granted to any citizen, as well as to associations and foundations defending the interests referenced above, regardless of whether they have a direct interest in an action.[22]

Regarding the proceedings, the civil popular action may take '(...) any of the forms provided for in the Civil Procedure Code (Article 12, no. 3 of Law 83/95).' The action is, therefore, declaratory, condemnatory or constitutive

---

[19] H Sousa Antunes, 'Portuguese Report, Class Actions, Group Litigation & Other Forms of Collective Litigation', http://globalclassactions.stanford.edu/sites/default/files/documents/Portugal_National_Report.pdf, 6.

[20] Art 52 (3). Both civil courts and administrative courts are competent to hear popular actions, depending on the nature of the conflict. If administrative rules are at stake, administrative courts are competent. If the conflict concerns private law matters (in a very broad sense), civil courts have jurisdiction.

[21] A few cases were referred to in the Portuguese media. For example, the 'Dulce Pontes Bizet's Carmen' case, where in 1998, several newspapers publicized the show 'Bizet's Carmen', with singer Dulce Pontes in the main role, acting on a rotating stage at Campo Pequeno in Lisbon; the show ended up being performed by the London Philharmonic Orchestra, who played some excerpts from opera, on a stage that was not rotating. Hundreds of spectators found themselves defrauded; after the refusal of the show organiser to return the money from the ticket sales, the court decided in favour of the claimant (DECO – Portuguese Association for Consumer Protection). DECO is also known for the 'Opening School' case: in 2002, DECO received numerous complaints from consumers who faced the closure of Opening School (School of English), which offered teaching in various parts of the country. The closure left 1,200 students without the possibility of continuing their studies; when registering, Opening School offered the students two payment options: immediate or by entering into a consumer credit contract (provided by BBVA Finanziamento) which continued to be performed despite the closure of this school; in 2010, the Supreme Court of Justice (STJ) ruled against Opening School and BBVA Finanziamento and ordered these institutions to reimburse consumers.

[22] Art 2, no. 1 of Law 83/95.

depending on the interests involved.[23] This means that, once initiated, the action is conducted as a normal procedure, although with several particularities as provided for by Law 83/95.[24]

One of the main features of the Portuguese popular action is that it operates basically as an opt-out system.[25] The claimant represents, without the need for a mandate or express authorisation, all the other holders of the rights or interests in question.

After the procedure is initiated by an entity with standing, interested parties are notified within a term fixed by the judge: (a) to intervene in the main proceedings; (b) to declare whether they agree to be represented by the claimant; or (c) to exclude themselves from the representation. In the latter case, the final decision will not be applicable to them. In the event that the interested parties do not take any of the actions described above, the law considers the omission as an acceptance of the representation. Nevertheless, the representation by the claimant can be expressly refused by interested entities until the end of the collection of evidence.

To protect the interest of individuals that are represented by the claimant, the Public Prosecutor (*Ministério Público*) is charged with the responsibility of protecting legality, and may replace the claimant in case of withdrawal from the procedure, or any conduct which may be harmful to the interests at stake.[26]

Pursuant to Article 19 of Law 83/95, judicial decisions have overall effectiveness. However, the *res judicata* effect does not cover parties that have specifically opted-out. There are some exceptions to the *erga omnes* effect, notably where the case is dismissed due to insufficient evidence or where the judge decides otherwise based on reasons specific to the case in question.

Law 83/95 also provides that the judgment, once having *res judicata* effect, is to be published in two newspapers and thereby made accessible to those interested in the case.[27] The defendant has to pay for the costs of publication.

---

[23] Art 4, no. 2 of the Civil Procedure Code.

[24] Those particularities include: preliminary rejection of the claim if the judge finds it manifestly unfounded; special regime for representation, with the 'opt-out' solution; possibility for the Public Prosecutor (*Ministério Público*) to replace the claimant in case of withdrawal from the procedure or conduct which may be harmful to the interests at stake; special regime regarding the effects of an appeal; special *res judicata* regime; more favourable cost regime.

[25] See arts 14 and 15 of Law 83/95. Portugal, Denmark, the Netherlands and the UK have already implemented 'opt-out' systems and Belgium has implemented a mix between 'opt-in' and 'opt-out' (cf. Statement on Collective Redress and Competition Damages Claims, http://www.europeanlawinstitute.eu/fileadmin/user_upload/p_eli/Projects/S-5-2014_Statement_on_Collective_Redress_and_Competition_Damages_Claims.pdf, 42).

[26] See Art 16, no. 3 of Law 83/95.

[27] It is up to the court to decide whether the entire ruling or only the most relevant parts are published (art 19 no. 2 of Law 83/95).

Regarding legal costs, Article 21 of the Law 83/95 specifies that the court decides on these, depending on the complexity of the case and its value. It should be noted that no preliminary costs are charged to the claimant. After the judgment has been rendered, the claimant is exempt from any payment in cases of a favourable or even only partially favourable judgment. In case the judgment is not favourable, costs are determined by the court, which will take into account the economic situation of the claimant and the reasons for the judgment being unfavourable.[28]

B. *The Protection of Homogeneous Individual Rights in the Field of Health and Medical Liability – Some Difficulties with the Portuguese Popular Action*

Michele Taruffo has stated that mechanisms for group litigation are not normally allowed for the compensation of damages suffered by individuals.[29] However, various countries, including civil law systems such as Portugal, have effectively adopted mechanisms similar to the US class action model.[30]

In general, in accordance with the Civil Procedure Code (Article 30) to appear in a Portuguese court as a claimant, one has to (allegedly) be the subject of the disputed right or, at least, the legally protected interests at stake.

However, as stated above, the specific mechanism of the 'popular action' does not require the claimant to have a 'direct' interest. This raises the question whether a 'popular action' is at all suitable for cases where the claimant asks for group compensation in order for the compensation to be divided by people affected as occurs in health and medical liability cases. In other words, it is questionable whether the 'popular action' can be used to protect individual rights in a collective perspective, or whether it is restricted to the protection of collective rights and diffuse interests.

Portuguese doctrine establishes a clear distinction between collective interests and diffuse interests.[31] Diffuse interests refer to legal assets that are not open to individual appropriation and do not belong to any specific entity, public or private. Collective interests belong to a group, and not individually to any of its members.[32]

---

[28] In addition, Law 34/2004, of 29 July 2004, grants legal aid for the resolution of any type of legal dispute or litigation where a party does not have sufficient financial means to pay the fees of the legal representatives and to pay, in full or in part, the costs of legal proceedings.

[29] Taruffo (above n 2) 406.

[30] *Idem*.

[31] M Teixeira de Sousa, 'Legitimidade Processual e Acção Popular no Direito do Ambiente', in *Direito do Ambiente* (INA, 1994); LFC Antunes, 'Para uma Tutela Jurisdicional dos Interesses Difusos', *Boletim da Faculdade de Direito, Sep.Vol. LX, Universidade de Coimbra*, (1986).

[32] This theoretical division between collective and diffuse interests is also taken into account by the Spanish Code of Civil Procedure in its art 11. According to this provision, interests are

In group compensation cases like those referred above, it cannot be said that the main purpose of the action is to protect a diffuse interest or a collective interest.

The key to solve this problem rather seems to allow the use of a popular action in these types of cases, based on the concept of homogeneous individual interests.[33] These homogeneous individual interests are the refraction of diffuse or collective interests in the sphere of each of their subjects.[34]

In those cases where we can identify homogeneous individual interests, the use of the 'popular action' for collective redress or group compensation should be permitted under the collective redress rules.[35]

A problem, however, lies in the reference made in Article 22 to the types of interests in Article 1 no. 2. This reference seems to suggest that a 'popular action' is only permissible when the homogeneous individual interests at stake have a specific diffuse interest identified in Article 1 no. 2 and Article 52 of the Portuguese Constitution (public health, environment, quality of life, protection of consumers, cultural heritage and public domain). Furthermore, considering that the list of interests referred in Article 1 and Article 52 of the Portuguese Constitution is not exhaustive, the question arises whether homogeneous individual interests can be protected via a 'popular action' in cases of non-listed but similar diffuse interests.

Although the Portuguese legislator made no effort to make this clear, the 'popular action' should be allowed in all cases where protection of homogeneous individual interests is claimed provided that these have a relation to a diffuse interest, even where the latter is not listed in Article 1 no. 2 or Article 52 of the Portuguese Constitution. This solution more accurately reflects the spirit of the 'popular action' as well as the special regime contained in the Securities Code.[36]

Evidently, when we deal with compensation for medical malpractice injuries, there is always a connection to at least two of the interests listed, being public health and quality of life.

---

collective if the injured parties are known or easy to identify; however, if the aggrieved parties are an indeterminate number of persons or a number which is difficult to ascertain, the interests are defined as diffuse. For further details, see the chapter by García Rubio and Otero Crespo in this volume.

[33] Law 24/96, of 31 July 1996, expressly references this concept (arts 3/f and 13/c). This Law establishes the legal regime applicable to the protection of consumers.

[34] M Teixeira de Sousa, *A Legitimidade Popular na Tutela dos Interesses Difusos* (Lex, 2003) 53.

[35] Contained in arts 22 et seq. of Law 83/95.

[36] Arts 31 and 32 of Securities Code, expressly allow the use of the 'popular action' for the protection of homogeneous individual interests or collective interests of investors in securities, giving standing to non-institutional investors, investor protection associations and foundations protecting investors in the securities industry, approved by Decree-Law 486/99, of 13 November 1999.

This leads to the conclusion that in Portugal, it is possible to use the 'popular action' when group compensation is sought in cases of medical malpractice or health liability.

Nevertheless, further problems arise. In this regard, it was stated that Article 22, which concerns subjective liability, distinguishes between compensation for injury done to identified holders of interests, calculated under the general rules of civil liability and the global fixing of compensation for violations of interests of unidentified holders.[37] Some doctrines restrict global compensation to the violation of collective or diffuse interests or, at least, to situations where the amount due to each of the injured parties is small, not justifying the costs incurred by the calculation of individual harm.[38]

Regarding medical malpractice or health liability the 'popular action' is useful in those cases where identified holders of interests appear together in court, claiming compensation together and individually, thus avoiding the problem of fixing global compensation for unidentified holders. In case of participation of unidentified holders of interests, the aforementioned difficulties will arise.

III. PORTUGUESE LEGISLATION ON COLLECTIVE REDRESS IN PERSPECTIVE: POSSIBLE IMPLICATIONS OF THE EC RECOMMENDATION

Another interesting question is whether Portuguese legislation is in compliance with the Commission Recommendation of 11 June 2013.[39] Considering the scope of this chapter, the Recommendation will only be assessed in light of malpractice compensation. To that extent, the chapter focuses on two topics that are of interest in this field: firstly, the 'opt-in'/'opt-out' solutions, and secondly, the danger of mass litigation when contingency fees and punitive damages are allowed.

---

[37] Sousa Antunes (above n 19) 26.

[38] The fact that the Portuguese legislator did not establish any system for sharing compensation between injured parties has also given rise to criticism. António Payan Martins states that: "... It seems to us that de *iure condendo* (in law as it should be) the payment should be made by resorting exclusively to arbitration, setting up a highly specialized court or arbitration committee alongside the court in question which processes the payment of all the indemnities. This process would thus be relatively simple, non-litigious, informal, and with low costs and would increase the number of injured parties that would come to court to receive compensation" (A Payan Martins, *Class Actions em Portugal* (Lisboa, 1999) 122.

[39] European Commission Recommendation from of 11 June 2013 on common principles for injunctive and compensatory collective redress mechanisms in the Member States concerning violations of rights granted under Union Law, http://eur-lex.europa.eu/legal-content/EN/TXT/?Uri=OJ:JOL_2013_201_R_NS0013.

A. Is there a Need to Change the Portuguese 'Opt-out' System?

On the 'opt-in' versus 'opt-out' debate, the Recommendation states that the claimant party should be formed on the basis of express consent of the natural or legal persons claiming to have been harmed ('opt-in' principle).[40] Exceptions are allowed, by law or by court order, but they should be "duly justified by reasons of sound administration of justice."

It is evident that the EC prefers the 'opt-in' system for collective redress mechanisms. This could lead to future changes regarding the 'popular action', in particular a reconsideration of the 'opt-out' system.[41]

In fact, it was an obscure choice in 1996 when the 'opt-out' solution was implemented in the Portuguese civil law system, since an 'opt-out' system is more characteristic of common law systems, or at least typical of the US class action system.

The adoption of an 'opt-in' system and the consequent abolition of the 'opt-out' system would not constitute a dramatic change for the Portuguese legal system. [42]

However, litigation habits in southern European countries are not very compatible with class actions in the sense of group litigation. The use of collective redress in Portugal is rare,[43] probably, as stated by Cooper, due to individualism or the tradition that each person is entitled to his day in court.[44] But under the 'opt-out' system, once actions are initiated, the case magically lifts judicial inertia by creating proceedings with many stakeholders (those who are not self-excluded from the action).[45] By changing the opt-out rules, the insignificance of collective actions will remain or will even be fostered.

---

[40] *Ibid*, para 21.

[41] The European Law Institute, in its Statement on Collective Redress and Competition Damages Claims (http://www.europeanlawinstitute.eu/fileadmin/user_upload/p_eli/ Projects/S-5-2014_Statement_on_Collective_Redress_and_Competition_Damages_ Claims.pdf), considers that the arguments in favour of 'opt-out' are stronger than the Commission currently recognises and that the Recommendation should not be read as putting a stop to national experiments with 'opt-out' (at 42).

[42] Note that the EC Recommendation allows for exceptions to the opt-in mechanism (see above n 39).

[43] Sousa Antunes (above n 19) 20.

[44] Cooper (above n 2) 224.

[45] As mentioned above, the 'Recommendation' admits exceptions, by law or by court order, if they are duly justified by reasons of 'sound administration of justice.' Following the reasoning of the European Law Institute, the notion of 'sound administration of justice' should be interpreted broadly giving a wide margin of appreciation to Member States so that they can consider that the right to an effective remedy is a component of 'the sound administration of justice' (cfr. Statement on Collective Redress and Competition Damages Claims (http://www.europeanlaw-institute.eu/fileadmin/user_upload/p_eli/Projects/S-5-2014_Statement_on_Collective_ Redress_and_Competition_Damages_Claims.pdf, 43).

B. Risks of Contingency Fees and Punitive Damages

Two topics that appear important in cases concerning health care law, especially considering the examples from US class actions, are contingency fees and punitive damages. The Recommendation strongly rejects both.

Regarding contingency fees, the Recommendation states in Paragraph 29 that the Member States should ensure that the lawyers' remuneration and the method by which it is calculated do not create any incentive to litigation that is unnecessary from the point of view of the interest of any of the parties. Paragraph 30 continues, stating that the Member States should not permit contingency fees, which risk creating such an incentive.

For most European countries, the 'no-win, no-fee' agreement is unacceptable, as is the possibility for lawyers to collect a percentage of the damages awarded to their client, because this provides an incentive to go to court.[46]

This topic is particularly important in health related compensation cases. Most cases that reach the court are certainly important. However, in medical malpractice, personal rights of individuals are always at stake. This being the case, the social dimension of the attorneys' profession should be stressed here, because they should primarily focus on protecting the interests of the client, and only then on receiving the fees to which they are rightfully entitled. Contingency fees regimes may have, of course, many merits, but undoubtedly, they contribute to an aggressive litigation system that harms victims and, ultimately, the health system.

It should be noted that in Portugal, *quota litis* it is not allowed and no evidence suggests that the legislator intends to change this rule.[47]

Concerning punitive damages, it needs to be recalled that this is probably one of the most problematic concepts in US collective redress from a European perspective.[48] The possibility of awarding huge punitive damages in US class actions (which is completely alien to European lawyers) has enhanced the reluctance in Europe to introduce similar mechanisms, although this might be a distorted perspective since 'punitive damages may also be awarded in individual actions, and class actions do not necessarily result in high punitive damage awards.'[49]

Paragraph 31 of the Recommendation states that the compensation awarded to natural or legal persons harmed in a mass harm situation should not exceed the compensation that would have been awarded if the claim had been pursued by means of individual actions. It also states that punitive damages should be prohibited.

---

[46] Sousa Antunes (above n 19) 1.
[47] Article 101 of the Bar Association Statute, approved by Law 15/2005, of 26 January 2005.
[48] On the importance of punitive damages in Europe, see L Meurkens and E Nordin (eds), *The power of punitive damages. Is Europe missing out?* (Intersentia, 2012).
[49] Taruffo (above n 2) 414 and 415.

In accordance with the majority of civil law countries, punitive damages are not permissible as a remedy in Portugal. Furthermore, compensation may never exceed the injuries. However, the fact that compensation cannot exceed the injuries does not signify that Portuguese tort law does not, to some extent, follow an auxiliary punitive goal (without accepting the concept of punitive damage). This seems to be confirmed in doctrine. Gomes for instance acknowledges the importance of the preventive and punitive purpose of civil liability. Even though playing a secondary role, this purpose of Portuguese law is accepted today.[50]

From our perspective, for both contingency fees and punitive damages, the EC's position is to be welcomed. In civil liability cases involving health professionals, particularly in countries with strong national health services treating the majority of the population, it is too dangerous for physicians to be subject to an aggressive and repressive liability system.

A compensatory system based on fault with a purpose of obtaining large sums of compensation can have very harmful effects, leading to the installation of defensive medicine and to a rise in the costs of the system.[51] The prohibition of *quota litis* and punitive damages will help the system to concentrate on what truly matters, the 'pure' compensation for damage caused to the victim.

IV. FINAL REMARKS

Collective Redress is a useful tool in health care liability cases. In Portugal the 'popular action' can be used for such cases.

The EC's initiative, which is to be followed by initiatives of national legislators, it is commendable and, in general, the recommendations made in the area of collective redress are to be approved. Its cautious approach will help reduce the risk of serious disturbances to the European legal space which could potentially be caused by mass access to justice based on imported practices which are not compliant with the judicial traditions of the old continent. The Recommendation might in the long term have an impact on the existing rather liberal collective redress structure in Portugal.

---

[50] J Gomes, 'Uma função punitiva para a responsabilidade civil e uma função reparatória para a responsabilidade penal?' *Revista de Direito e Economia Coimbra* (1989), 15, 106. In the same way V Varela *João de Matos, Das Obrigações em Geral* (Almedina, 2000) 930 and L Menezes and LM Teles, *Direito das Obrigações* (Almedina, 2000) 283 et seq.

[51] Defensive medicine is an expression used in Medical Law to explain how the fear of law suits and liability can lead doctors to be unreasonably proactive, for instance, prescribing expensive exams that are not necessary, in order to make sure that the diagnosis is correct, or at least, to use it as a defence later.

3

Alternative Dispute Resolution and Collective Redress

Collective Consumer ADR in the European Union

*Magdalena Tulibacka**

I. INTRODUCTION

At present, there is a gap in consumer law enforcement across the European Union. This has become more and more significant as, with the growth in cross-border trade which the EU encourages, the number of cross-border consumer disputes is also increasing.[1] The gap is particularly prevalent in cases involving large numbers of small consumer claims.[2] The majority of consumers who experience a problem with a product or service complain directly to the provider.[3] However, in 2009, only about 50% of the complaints were satisfied with the trader's response to the complaint.[4] Almost half of those who were dissatisfied did not pursue the problem any further.[5] The 2010 Consumer Empowerment Survey determined that only 16% of consumers who experienced problems in dealing with traders contact consumer organizations or public regulators dealing with consumer law enforcement for help.[6] Courts are used very rarely. Almost half of consumers declare they would not use the courts for claims valued at less than EUR 200,

---

* Dr Magdalena Tulibacka is BIICL Consultant in Collective Redress, Associate Researcher at the European and Comparative Civil Justice Programme of the University of Oxford's Centre for Socio-Legal Studies, and Scholar in Residence at Emory Law School in Atlanta.

[1] SI Strong, 'Cross-Border Collective Redress in the European Union: Constitutional Rights in the Face of the Brussels I Regulation', 45 *ArizStLJ* 233 (2013) 237 discusses the increasing number of cross-border disputes.

[2] 'An analysis and evaluation of alternative means of consumer redress other than redress through ordinary judicial proceedings. Final Report.' A Study for the European Commission prepared by the Study Centre for Consumer Law (Prof J Stuyck), 2007 (Stuyck ADR Study) 13.

[3] One in ten EU consumers made such complaints to sellers or providers in 2009. Flash Eurobarometer No. 282, 'Attitudes towards cross-border sales and consumer protection. Analytical Report', 2010, 5 and 18.

[4] *Ibid*, 19.

[5] 'Consultation Paper on the use of Alternative Dispute Resolution as a means to resolve disputes related to commercial transactions and practices in the European Union', DG SANCO, 2011, 3.

[6] Flash Eurobarometer No. 282 (above n 3).

and in 8% of the claims, the claimants would never use the court system for resolving their dispute with a trader.[7] What is striking in the context of this chapter is that only 3% of European consumers who were dissatisfied with the trader's response to their complaint took their case to an ADR body in 2009.[8] The EU is set on filling this gap with effective redress and dispute resolution mechanisms available to consumers. In search of such mechanisms, EU institutions are looking to, among others, the ADR and to collective redress.

Various EU Member States have already adopted judicial collective redress procedures or are considering introducing such a procedure. The EU itself, with the aim of harmonising the national models of judicial collective redress, embarked on an ambitious work programme that climaxed in 2013 with the adoption of non-binding recommendations.[9] Yet judicial collective redress may not always present an attractive redress path for consumers, because of its complexity and the time and resource demands it places on the group members, lawyers and the judiciary.[10] Certainly, ADR has the potential to provide an effective mechanism through which consumers would be able to seek redress via mass claims, especially those of small value. Collective ADR mechanisms are already in place in some Member States.[11] The question is whether there is a need and a scope for adopting such a mechanism at the EU level. One finds very little discussion about this issue – both within EU policy and legal instruments, as well as in academic papers and research documents conducted by European scholars.[12] This is perhaps not as surprising as both ADR and collective redress surfaced on the research and policy agenda relatively recently.

---

[7] Consultation Paper on the use of Alternative Dispute Resolution, DG SANCO, 2011, 5.

[8] *Ibid*, 7.

[9] See below.

[10] Some scholars take this for granted and focus on seeking valuable alternatives to litigation in solving mass disputes: see C Hodges and A Stadler (eds.), *Resolving Mass Disputes: ADR and Settlement of Mass Claims* (Edward Elgar, 2013) where the authors take it as a starting point that new methods of resolving mass consumer disputes must be sought, as litigation should be avoided in such cases. This sentiment can be found not only in a growing body of academic writings on the design and operation of European civil justice systems, but also in policy papers deriving from the EU. See below for a further brief analysis of the current tendencies.

[11] These are not examined here in detail: the reader should refer to the chapter by Strong (above n 1). Instead, this chapter analyses specific types of collective ADR mechanisms and procedures.

[12] The DG SANCO Study on the use of Alternative Dispute Resolution in the European Union, Berlin, Civic Consulting, 2009 (2009 SANCO Study) contains an analysis of the existing national ADR mechanisms offering collective resolution (or investigation) of disputes. Other EU research and policy documents rather focus on ADR or on collective redress as separate mechanisms. The recent EU Directive on Consumer ADR (see below for reference and analysis) refers to collective ADR in the Preamble only – Recital 27. Scholars follow the same tendency, with the most prominent exception being. Strong (see above n 1 and *Class, Mass and Collective Arbitration in National and International Law* (OUP, 2013)).

This chapter offers some thoughts concerning the utility and possible disadvantages of ADR for resolution of collective claims, and also preliminary suggestions on whether introducing an EU-wide collective ADR mechanism is feasible and desirable. While the recent EU activity with regard to collective redress as well as ADR is impressive, it shows limitations and caveats which may make the introduction of an EU-wide collective ADR scheme problematic. National approaches to ADR and collective redress continue to differ across the EU. Some of the reservations to establishing an EU-wide judicial collective redress procedure are also present when a collective ADR mechanism is considered. Further, there is no agreement as to the ultimate utility of ADR versus traditional civil litigation, most notably in mass litigation cases and when the outcome of the ADR proceedings is a non-binding decision or recommendation. It is believed that because no consensus exists on the desired framework of the collective redress system for consumers (including judicial collective redress), a legislative measure on collective ADR is not desirable. Moreover, some of the existing EU laws already cover collective ADR procedures.

The chapter proceeds as follows. It starts with establishing the context and the nature of ADR and collective redress. Following these introductory remarks, it provides a picture of the European ADR, albeit a somewhat simplified one – a fragmented, diverse mixture of mechanisms and approaches, with some functioning collective procedures. Subsequently, the EU position is presented. So far, it has mainly focused on ADR in individual cases, but the most recent policy documents and legislative measures also cover collective ADR. The position with regard to judicial collective redress is also briefly described to further illustrate two points. First of all, the EU has no ultimate vision of a collective redress system for consumers. Second, putting forward any approach with regard to collective ADR would be premature – what is needed is thorough research into the appropriate responses to specific types of consumer problems: judicial procedures, ADR, and possibly other mechanisms which are not examined here.

II. ESTABLISHING THE CONTEXT – THE ROLE AND PLACE OF ADR AND COLLECTIVE REDRESS WITHIN CIVIL JUSTICE SYSTEMS

Across Europe, discussions concerning efficiency, effectiveness and fairness of civil justice systems resulted in reforms of court-based individual litigation,[13] and also revealed the need to search for procedural mechanisms beyond this

---

[13] For analyses of reforms in England and Wales, see D Dwyer (ed.) *The Civil Procedure Rules Ten Years On,* (OUP, 2009), and in Poland (in the same volume) M Tulibacka, 'The Ethos of the Woolf Reforms in the Transformations of Post-socialist Civil Procedures: Case Study of Poland', 395.

traditional civil justice framework. Policy-makers and law-makers seek such mechanisms in regulatory enforcement and various other alternatives to the judicial system (such as mediation, arbitration, conciliation, ombudsmen and others), in small claims procedures, and in collective litigation procedures. In most States, a combination of different forms of each is now in operation. These developments are often informed and inspired by the growing body of academic writings from which what could be called a multi-level approach to civil justice arose.[14] Professor Stuyck and his colleagues presented in their 2007 ADR Study all the European 'intermediate methods' of dealing with claims,[15] which included ADR in the narrow sense, as well as judicial collective redress, which they determined was crucial in ensuring access to justice for European consumers. More recently, Hodges has been a particularly strong proponent of the 'integrated approach,' with litigation as the mechanism rather to be avoided in favour of regulatory redress and ADR.[16]

The EU's focus on civil justice was prompted by the deepening process of integration and legal harmonization, and the ensuing need for enhancing *effet utile* of EU law and for individual legal protection.[17] Within the constraints of its legislative mandate, as part of the policy of judicial cooperation in civil and commercial matters, the EU started coordinating national civil justice mechanisms through private international law measures as well as introducing its own procedural mechanisms.[18] The latest phenomenon in the growing emphasis on civil justice is the appearance of procedural provisions and even distinct procedural legislation in substantive areas (sectors) of EU law: especially consumer law, competition law and intellectual protection law.[19] The multi-level approach to civil justice reaching beyond individual court-based procedures seems to have first surfaced within these sectoral policies and legislative measures, especially in the area of consumer law. Collective redress and ADR feature strongly in this approach. They present

---

[14] This approach was already advocated by Mauro Cappelletti in 1975 (M Cappelletti, 'La protection d'interets collectifs et le groupe dans le process civil – Metamorphoses de la procedure civile', *Rev Int Dr Comp* (1975) 571), and currently its greatest proponent is Christopher Hodges (C Hodges, *The Reform of Class and Representative Actions in European Legal Systems: A New Framework for Collective Redress in Europe* (Hart Publishing, 2008). Hodges refers to it as the 'integrated approach'.

[15] The Stuyck ADR Study.

[16] See Hodges (above n 14) and C Hodges, 'Collective Redress in Europe: The New Model', 29 *CJQ* 3 (2010) 370–395.

[17] See M Tulibacka, 'Europeanization of Civil Procedures: in Search of a Coherent Approach', 46 *Common Market Law Review* (2009) 1527–1565 and M Tulibacka, 'Proceduralisation of EU Consumer Law', *European Review of Administrative Law*, forthcoming 2015.

[18] See H Micklitz 'The ECJ between the Individual Citizen and the Member States: A Plea for a Judge-Made European Law on Remedies' (December 1, 2011), EUI Working Papers LAW 2011/15, and Tulibacka (above n 17).

[19] See Tulibacka (above n 17).

an opportunity to bring to the fore cases and complaints which would not have otherwise been brought (because of their small individual value).

There is no uniform understanding of ADR. Studies such as the Commission's 2002 Green Paper on alternative dispute resolution in civil and commercial law,[20] the study conducted under the direction of Professor Stuyck for the European Commission,[21] the 2009 DG SANCO Study on ADR in the EU, and the current research by the European and Comparative Civil Justice Systems Programme at Oxford's Centre for Socio-Legal Studies, uncovered the breadth and depth of ADR techniques, procedures and mechanisms across Europe.[22] For the purposes of this chapter, ADR covers a range of possible techniques and mechanisms used to resolve disputes and provide redress outside the realm of the civil procedure before courts. It does not include direct negotiations or small claims procedures. It also excludes in-litigation settlement procedures, as well as the Dutch collective settlement mechanism which requires judicial approval.[23]

Collective redress is a wide concept which encompasses 'any mechanism that may accomplish the cessation or prevention of unlawful business practices which affect a multitude of claimants or the compensation for the harm done by such practices.'[24] In the context of judicial collective enforcement it was defined as 'collective procedures for redress of multiple individual damages and collective damages, suffered by an entity.'[25] Judicial collective

---

[20] COM/2002/0196 final.
[21] The 'Stuyck ADR Study': its authors adopt the ultimate user's perspective to obtaining redress and see ADR as a continuum between taking no action at all on the one end and using ordinary court procedures on the other. This approach places collective redress within the scope of ADR, together with direct negotiations, traditional ADR measures such as mediation and arbitration, and small claims procedures. The study defines ADR as 'means of consumer redress other than redress through ordinary judicial proceedings' (2).
[22] See C Hodges, I Benohr and N Creutzfeldt-Banda, *Consumer ADR in Europe. Civil Justice Systems* (Hart, CHBeck, Nomos, 2012). The Oxford Civil Justice research project in fact coined the new term: CADR (Consumer ADR). Its authors argue that, in contrast to the traditional understanding of ADR as a *technique* existing particularly but not exclusively with relation to or even within the court system, CADR is a unique system with its own rationale and architecture (at 389). They suggest that the way to examine it is through a range of possible techniques of dispute resolution, and especially: mediation, conciliation, arbitration, adjudication, and ombudsman schemes (xxix).
[23] See XE Kramer, 'Enforcing Mass Settlements in the European Judicial Area: EU policy and the strange case of Dutch Collective Settlements (WCAM)', in Hodges and Stadler (above n 10), at 63; and I Tzankova and D Hensler, 'Collective settlements in the Netherlands: some empirical observations', in Hodges and Stadler (above n 10), 91.
[24] 'Overview of existing collective redress schemes in EU Member States', European Parliament's Directorate General for Internal Policies, IP/A/IMCO/NT/2011/16, 2011, at 6. The same definition was used by the European Commission's Consultation Paper 'Towards a Coherent European approach to Collective Redress', SEC (2011) 173 final, 3.
[25] F Cafaggi and H-W Micklitz, '*Administrative and Judicial Collective Enforcement of Consumer Law in the US and the European Community*', EUI Working Papers, LAW 2007/22, 25.

actions can take a variety of forms, and in particular: (1) a representative action; (2) a group action (also referred to as multi-party action or collective action); and (3) a model or test case proceedings.

As mentioned above, within the EU policy agenda, as well as at the national level of the Member States, collective redress has mostly been discussed in relation to judicial procedures. Only recently have policy papers and legislation started referring to collective ADR.

III. INDIVIDUAL AND COLLECTIVE ADR IN EU MEMBER STATES:

A. Introduction

The numbers, scope and diversity of ADR schemes across Europe are impressive. European States each constructed a 'cocktail' of various ADR processes and techniques.[26] In fact, the 2009 SANCO Study revealed that 750 mechanisms exist within the EU, and the number has certainly grown since then. It is somewhat surprising that only one in five of the national mechanisms identified in 2009 offered some type of collective procedure. The majority do not deal with collective claims, although some indicate that they could potentially do so.

The exact trajectory of development of an ADR system in a particular State and its features depend upon the shape of the judicial system, the legal culture and civil procedure, and the socio-economic conditions of the State.[27] Thus, while ADR as a concept and a viable alternative to court-based justice that has been universally recognized, its place within the justice system, its features and popularity are very different in various EU Member States. These issues are briefly examined here. It appears from the analysis below that the framework and position of ADR – whether ADR is prominent and popular or rather merely an addition to the more frequently used civil litigation – do not always have a significant impact on whether collective ADR is offered. Leaving aside collective ADR in the Scandinavian countries (Sweden and Finland)[28] where ADR is a crucial civil justice mechanism and where a specific type of opt-out collective ADR operates, it can be said that the presence of collective ADR procedures is rather the result of the organizational and functional features of each ADR body.

B. The Main Trends of Development of ADR Systems

If litigation is a complex, long and expensive process and small claims proce-

---

[26] Stuyck ADR Study, 7.
[27] Stuyck ADR Study, 77.
[28] For further details, L Ervo and A Persson (in this volume).

dures are unavailable or unpopular, it is likely that alternatives to litigation will be sought. This has certainly been the case in England and Wales, where ADR, especially in consumer cases, is highly developed.[29] The position is different if, as in Germany, the costs of litigation are low and often covered by the wide-spread Litigation Expenses Insurance or third-party funders, the length of litigation is not disproportionate, and lawyers have monopoly for legal advice and assistance.[30] As a result, ADR mechanisms tend not to develop rapidly, and even if present they are not widely used.[31] The German system of consumer law enforcement, largely privatized – relying on private actions in courts by individual consumers and assisted by powerful consumer organizations – has only recently included ADR mechanisms such as mediation and ombudsmen.[32]

Specific features of civil procedures, such as discovery or cross-examination, may be very problematic and costly, and may also trigger interest in alternative mechanisms.[33] The position of judges in litigation (for instance, how managerial they can be in referring parties to mediation) and their flexibility in applying the rules of civil procedure also can affect the emergence and the popularity of certain ADR methods.[34]

Further factors which affect the evolution of ADR mechanisms are the organization, level of regulatory coverage, presence or absence of self-regulation, and the general economic shape of industry in a particular state. It is said, for instance, that the prominence of German guilds contributed to the appearance of sector-specific ADR schemes.[35] Further, strong regulatory bodies combined with the 'national policy and [the] culture of self-regulation' in the United

---

[29] N Creutzfeldt-Banda, C Hodges and I Benohr, 'The United Kingdom', in Hodges, Benohr and Creutzfeldt-Banda (above n 22), 253.

[30] The monopoly of German lawyers ended only in 2007 (Legal Service Act allowed non-lawyers such as charities, consumer organizations and other associations to provide legal advice within their areas of expertise).

[31] See N Creutzfeldt-Banda, C Hodges and I Benohr 'Germany', in Hodges, Benohr and Creutzfeldt-Banda (above n 22) 73, 73–75. The authors suggest that the number of ADR bodies identified in Germany by the 2009 Civic Study and those registered with the European Commission is misleading: the number of ADR bodies providing a completely out-of-court pathway is much lower (74).

[32] Mediation taking place in courts is very common indeed (Creutzfeldt-Banda, Hodges and Benohr, 'Germany' (above n 31) 79), but here, the remark concerns mediation mechanisms independent of the judicial proceedings and the judicial system.

[33] This is said to have motivated the development of ADR mechanisms in common law states (Stuyck ADR Study, 77). For a review of UK's ADR mechanisms see M Tulibacka, *'Civil Justice in England and Wales – Beyond Courts. Mapping Out Non-Judicial Civil Justice Mechanisms'*, (Centre for Socio-Legal Studies, 2009), www.csls.ox.ac.uk/CivilJusticeSystems.php.

[34] This approach resulted in the popularity of court-based mediation in common law states (Stuyck ADR Study, 77), but also in popularity and use of mediation outside of the scope of litigation.

[35] Stuyck ADR Study, 77.

Kingdom entailed the emergence of a large number of private sector ombudsmen overseen by public authorities.[36] On the other hand, the still-forming markets and their new regulatory infrastructure in the countries of Central and Eastern Europe only recently saw the emergence of ADR schemes.[37]

Lastly, important factors affecting the development of ADR are the social attitudes to courts and dispute resolution, as well as civic awareness and activity. The culture of amicable settlement in the Netherlands has long been explored,[38] and it certainly was one of the material factors in developing the extensive ADR framework.[39] A somewhat new phenomenon is the emergence of new Member States of the EU (Central and Eastern Europe), where the regained democracy and respect for human rights entail reliance on access to courts as a realization of one's human and civic rights. ADR might not be as attractive an option there.[40]

The Nordic States (Sweden, Denmark, Finland and Norway) merit a separate note here, as they were the pioneers in establishing ADR schemes, in particular for consumer disputes. Their ADR systems, the key elements of which are consumer dispute boards (for instance: the Swedish National Board for Consumer Complaints, and the Danish Consumer Complaint Board) as well as numerous other private or self-regulatory ombudsmen and boards, cover most types of claims.[41]

C. Types of Existing Collective ADR Mechanisms and Procedures

Only about one in five of all the national ADR schemes (18%) offered collective dispute settlement or redress in 2009. Some more would be capable of applying collective dispute settlement techniques (16% specified that they could possibly use such techniques).[42] Only one mechanism was established specifically to deal with collective claims (the Spanish consumer arbitration), while others merely apply collective approaches when required. The SANCO 2009 Study identified three different types of approaches: collective investigation, representative collective ADR procedures, and the collective ADR procedures of the Scandinavian type.

---

[36] Creutzfeldt-Banda, Hodges and Benohr, 'The United Kingdom' (above n 22) 253.

[37] See Tulibacka, 'Poland', in Hodges, Benohr and Creutzfeldt-Banda (above n 22).

[38] See for instance E Blankenburg, 'Civil Litigation Rates as Indicators for Legal Cultures', in D Nelken (ed.) *Comparing Legal Cultures* (Aldershot, Dartmouth, 1997), and G Hofstede, *Culture's Consequences: comparing values, behaviours, institutions, and organisations across nations* (2nd edition, Thousand Oaks, CA, Sage Publications, 2011).

[39] F Weber and C Hodges, 'The Netherlands', in Hodges, Benohr and Creutzfeldt-Banda (above n 22) 130.

[40] M Tulibacka, 'Poland', in Hodges, Benohr and Creutzfeldt-Banda (above n 22).

[41] Hodges, Benohr and Creutzfeldt-Banda (above n 22) 390.

[42] 2009 SANCO Study, 49–51.

1. Collective investigation

Some ADR bodies are able to join a number of similar complaints in a single investigation. The most common example is ADR bodies that deal with complaints pertaining to advertising. Complaints concerning the same advertisement and its potential non-compliance with the applicable codes of conduct can be investigated together. These ADR mechanisms have purely injunctive powers. They normally use one or a small number of selected representative cases to consider the general position, and their overall conclusion applies to all the remaining complaints. For instance, the Dutch *Stichting Reclame Code* (Advertising Code Committee) selects one complaint which appears most representative of the rest and investigates it. After the decision is taken concerning this complaint, all complainants are informed of its contents.[43]

In fact, the collective investigation model is the only one which attracts larger numbers of cases, with the other two analysed below being used rarely or never. The German Advertising Standards Council reported 260 cases handled in this manner between 2002 and 2008.[44] This could be the result of the types of complaints for which it is used, entailing quite uniform claims and not requiring much attention to be devoted to each individual consumer. However, there is potential for such bundling of cases to be used wider, in many other types of cases. Indeed, certain other ADR bodies indicated that they use this approach; for instance the Polish Centre for Mediation (*Polskie Centrum Mediacji*), in operation since 2000, offering mediation in civil law, family law, labour, commercial and criminal law areas.[45] Other bodies using the collective investigation approach are the GDF SUEZ mediation in France, the Consumer Complaint Committee in Estonia and the Teleoff in Slovenia.

In many respects, it is quite difficult in practice to distinguish the collective investigatory approach from the representative collective procedures examined below. The claims are looked at collectively to select the highest number of claimants which are investigated, and the final decision applies to all.

2. Representative collective ADR procedures

These mechanisms allow a representative (normally a consumer organization or a consumer) to bring a complaint before an ADR body on behalf of a larger number of consumers. The consumers covered by the complaint

---

[43] 2009 SANCO Study, 525.
[44] 2009 SANCO Study, 49.
[45] *Ibid*.

should be named, and the decision on the substance of the complaint applies only to those who opted in. The most prominent example is the Spanish consumer arbitration scheme, examined in this volume by SI Strong.[46] The arbitration is conducted in the local *Juntas Arbitrales de Consumo*,[47] or in the National Arbitration Board in cases of multi-jurisdictional disputes.[48] The mechanism offers an opt-in procedure for consumer claims. These claims must be related to conduct of traders, which is capable of injuring collective interests of consumers or users and of affecting a 'determined or determinable number of such persons.'[49] Respondent traders have an option of not consenting to the collective procedure, in which case consumers must pursue their claims individually. Further, there is one crucial exception to the opt-in rule. This issue has not been finally settled yet, but the system appears to include a rather restrictive lock-in procedure for those consumers who already initiated individual arbitration proceedings in the same matter before a local board. These individual cases are automatically suspended and the matter taken over by the collective procedure, with no apparent right for the consumer involved to opt-out. If the arbitral tribunal was already appointed, the proceedings may continue on an individual basis provided the respondent trader does not object.[50] While such safeguards on procedural rights of respondents are justified in binding arbitration, leaving the decision on whether collective arbitration is to take place entirely to them is a controversial approach.[51] Nevertheless, the Spanish consumer arbitration is a promising mechanism. It is specifically designed for collective cases, and thus may effectively gain required expertise to deal with such cases. It may also be dynamic and flexible enough to respond proactively to issues that may arise. It is therefore disappointing that it is not used in practice:[52] both the consumers and the traders seem suspicious of it and rather opt for individual ADR or judicial proceedings (also collective proceedings).

Other mechanisms providing a representative collective procedure are for instance: the Lisbon Arbitration Centre, the *Service de médiation auprès du Grupe SNCB* (Belgian Rail Ombudsman Service), and the Belgian *Service de*

---

[46] See also by SI Strong, 'Collective Consumer Arbitration in Spain: A Civil Law Response to US-Style Class Arbitration', 30 *Journal of International Arbitration* 5 (2013) 495–510.

[47] These *Juntas arbitrales de consumo* may be found at different administrative levels (local, provincial, regional, etc). For further details, visit http://consumo-inc.gob.es/arbitraje/juntas.htm

[48] Each local board has jurisdiction only with regard to consumers resident in its area of jurisdiction. Strong (above n 46) 500.

[49] *Real Decreto-Ley* 231/2008, of 15 February 2008, *Boletín oficial del Estado*, 25.02.2008, Núm. 48, pág. 11072, art 56, quoted by Strong, (above n 46) 499.

[50] Strong (above n 46) 502.

[51] *Ibid.*, at 503.

[52] *Idem*.

médiation pour le secteur postal.[53] The Lisbon Arbitration Centre offers a procedure that can lead to an award of damages, either to each consumer involved or to the group representative who subsequently distributes them.[54] The number of such cases brought before the Centre is very low: between 2002 and 2008 the highest number was 7 per year.[55] The Belgian Rail Ombudsman Service considers complaints brought by consumers representing a larger group of identified rail users. The Ombudsman's decisions are not binding on the rail companies, and it has been submitted that they are not often followed. However, in practice most complaints result in settlement and compensation offers before the Ombudsman makes a decision (88% overall as of 2009).[56] Again, numbers of cases considered by means of this representative collective procedure are low, with the highest number being 11 for 2002 and 2008.[57]

3. Collective procedure of the Scandinavian type

These procedures, as the name suggests, function in the Scandinavian countries, namely in Sweden and Finland. The Swedish Consumer Ombudsman (alternatively, a consumer or a trade union) and the Finnish Consumer Ombudsman have the power to bring proceedings before the National Board for Consumer Complaints (Sweden) and Consumer Disputes Board (Finland) on behalf of a number of consumers who have claims stemming from the same circumstances.[58] These are opt-out proceedings, and not all affected consumers must be identified. As with the representative proceedings above, the numbers of such collective proceedings are low, with 17 in Sweden and none in Finland as of 2009.[59]

D. *Common Tendencies and Problems in Collective ADR across EU Member States*

The number of ADR bodies using collective procedures is relatively low. This is indeed surprising if one takes into account the ever-increasing numbers of consumer complaints, including cross-border complaints, and the potential time and money-saving benefits of the collective approach. The relatively small percentage of ADR bodies using collective techniques and procedures

---

[53] 2009 SANCO Study, 50.
[54] *Ibid*, 503.
[55] *Ibid*, 505.
[56] *Ibid*, 419.
[57] *Ibid*, 424.
[58] *Ibid*, 50.
[59] See Ervo and Persson in this volume.

to resolve consumer disputes is accompanied by a noticeably low count of actual cases. The only types of cases where numbers are higher concern advertising complaints processed with the use of collective investigation techniques.

Significant problems with coupling ADR with collective procedures can be identified:[60]

1. Collective redress entails the level of complexity of proceedings which ADR bodies may not be ready for and indeed capable of handling. ADR proceedings are meant to be faster, cheaper and less complex than litigation. The demands of a collective case involve gathering evidence, finding all affected consumers, and keeping in touch with them during the proceedings, which requires both time and resources.
2. Many ADR bodies do not have the power to issue binding decisions. Considering the potentially high costs and other resources required to conduct collective proceedings, this may not be an efficient mechanism for seeking redress if the traders do not follow the final decision. Further, consumer trust in these collective mechanisms may suffer if no finality is guaranteed.
3. Mediation may be particularly ill-suited for collective procedures because it is based on the idea of communication and negotiations between the two parties, and instead of a final decision taken by a third party, the persons concerned are encouraged to reach an amicable settlement.[61] The position may be different if, as in the case of the French Mediation Service of the energy company GDF SUEZ, the decisions of the mediator are binding on the trader (and not on the consumer). There, mediation may well be conducted collectively.[62]
4. Attitudes to ADR are also crucial. For many consumers, as well as traders, the courts are simply more appropriate venues to deal with collective cases.[63] This is particularly significant because judicial decisions can create precedents to be used in other similar cases.

It may well be that collective ADR is not suitable for cases where consumer claims differ from one another. On the other hand, the collective investigation model may offer an answer. Some common elements may be investi-

---

[60] Some of these problems were indicated by the ADR bodies interviewed by Civic Consulting (2009 SANCO Study, 109).

[61] This point was made by the *Service Médiateur Du Net* (a French Online Mediation Service of the Internet Rights Forum), 2009 SANCO Study, 440.

[62] According to the 2009 SANCO Study, the Mediation Service of GDF SUEZ had no problems with the idea of collective mediation, and in fact conducted one such mediation in 2008 (453).

[63] 2009 SANCO Study, 109.

gated together and subsequently transferred to a more individualized procedure which would conclude each consumer's complaint. With regard to the very significant problem of complexity of proceedings, there could be possibilities of consumer organizations participating in evidence-gathering and group management in conjunction with the ADR body, or the proceedings being brought following investigations by the public regulator. As far as lack of a binding effect of decisions and the problems with compliance are concerned, and in addition to potential changes in rules or regulations governing these decisions, an appropriate response could be a robust judicial collective redress system. Its mere presence may entice parties to strive for settlement and finality. Attitudes towards collective ADR, which are shaped by all the problems identified here, can be detrimental to its practical use and popularity. While it is difficult to challenge the belief in superiority of judicial decisions, a more proactive response to the problems with collective ADR and an active campaign encouraging the use of the schemes may increase the numbers of cases.

IV. EU FOCUS ON CONSUMER ADR

A. Genesis

The EU looked into ADR mechanisms as part of its consumer protection policy as early as the 1980s, when it commenced work on consumer access to justice.[64] The importance of access to justice was confirmed in the European Parliament's Resolution of 11 March 1992 and the Council Resolution of 13 July 1992 on future priorities for the development of consumer protection policy.[65] In its Green Paper on access of consumers to justice and the settlement of consumer disputes in the Single Market, the Commission made proposals aimed at resolving individual and collective cross-border disputes, including simplified settlement of claims.[66] The 1995 Commission Study 'The Cost of Legal Barriers to Consumers in the Internal Market' revealed that in cross-border situations, consumers were unlikely to pursue claims valued at less than 2,000 ECU. The Study resulted in the 1996 Commission's Action Plan on consumer access to justice and the settlement of consumer disputes in the internal market,[67] where ADR was highlighted.

---

[64] The first Commission Communication on consumer redress was drafted as a memorandum: COM (84) 692 final. The European Parliament adopted a Resolution on 13 March 1987 (OJ No C 99, 13.4.1987), and the Council adopted its own Resolution on consumer redress on 25 June 1987 (87/C 176/02, OJ No C 176, 4/7.1987, 2).
[65] OJ No C 94, 13.4.1992, 217; OJ No C 186, 23.7.1992, 1.
[66] COM (1993) 576.
[67] COM (1996) 0013.

B. Early Policies and Law

ADR is becoming an important part of the EU consumer law enforcement system. Its regulatory coverage at the EU level is also gradually developing. The process started with non-binding recommendations. In 1998, the Commission adopted a Recommendation on the principles applicable to bodies responsible for out-of-court consumer dispute settlements.[68] The principles which the Recommendation suggests as the necessary requisites of an effective ADR mechanism for consumers are: (1) transparency of procedures and operation; (2) independence and expertise; (3) fair and adversarial nature of proceedings; (4) legality and (5) efficiency (fast and cheap proceedings). The Recommendation also included a complaint form which was meant to improve communication between consumers and traders. In 2001, the Recommendation on the principles for out-of-court bodies involved in the consensual resolution of consumer disputes was adopted.[69] This instrument is aimed at mechanisms where a third party encourages the solution to be reached by consent. It does not cover internal complaints procedures established by businesses, or consumer arbitration.[70] The list of suggested criteria includes: impartiality, transparency, effectiveness, and fairness.[71] The Recommendations do not distinguish between individual ADR and collective ADR, and thus it can be concluded that they apply to both. While they lack legally binding force, the Recommendations were quite influential in popularizing consumer ADR. The suggested principles/criteria were often adopted by consumer ADR bodies on the Member State level.[72] In fact, the Commission composed a database of over five hundred ADR mechanisms operating across the EU that, according to Member States, meet the criteria set out in the Recommendations.[73]

In 2002, the Commission issued the Green Paper on alternative means of dispute resolution. The consultation process which followed the Green Paper led to two important instruments. The first one was the Code of Conduct for Mediators (2004) drafted by the European Commission with the participation of a considerable number of practitioners and mediators.[74] It is a volun-

---

[68] Recommendation 98/257/EC of the Commission of 30 March 1998 regarding the principles applicable to bodies responsible for out-of-court consumer dispute settlements, OJ L 115, 18 April 1998, 31.

[69] Commission Recommendation (EC) 2001/310 on the principles for out-of-court bodies involved in the consensual resolution of consumer disputes, OJ L 109/56.

[70] Recommendation 2001/310, Part I (1).

[71] Recommendation 2001/310, part II (A-D).

[72] I Benohr, 'Alternative Dispute Resolution for Consumers in the European Union', in Hodges, Benohr and Creutzfeldt-Banda, (above n 22) 8.

[73] *Ibid*, at 8. The database can be accessed at: http://ec.europa.eu/consumers/redress_cons/schemes_en.htm.

[74] *Idem*.

tary Code, and the mediators who decide to adhere to its recommendations can notify the Commission and be inserted into a European Code of Conduct for Mediators list, which is available online.[75] The second instrument, the Directive on certain aspects of mediation in civil and commercial matters, was adopted in 2008.[76] The Directive is quite limited in scope: it applies to cross-border mediation only.[77] It does not create an EU-wide mediation procedure, but it does provide a somewhat harmonized approach to mediation. It defines mediation (including voluntary mediation, and mediation to which parties are referred to by court or by law),[78] as well as mediators.[79] It also sets out common standards as regards mediator training, quality of mediation, confidentiality of mediation and prescription or limitation periods.[80]

C. Recent Tendencies: Multi-dimensional Approach to Civil Justice

More recent policy documents and action plans deriving from the Commission and other EU institutions focus on improving enforcement of consumer law through a multi-dimensional approach combining ADR mechanisms, self-regulatory measures, small claims, enforcement by public regulatory bodies, judicial redress and other mechanisms providing dispute resolution and redress. The Consumer Policy Strategy 2002–2006,[81] and the Council's Resolution on the Strategy,[82] emphasized the need for greater coordination in national enforcement of EU consumer laws, both through public regulatory bodies, and through judicial and extra-judicial measures. The Consumer Policy Strategy for 2007–2013 emphasized consumer empowerment.[83] One of the priorities was continuing the work on consumer redress, and the areas of focus the Commission mentioned were ADR, as well as collective redress for breaches of consumer law and antitrust law.[84] The 2011

---

[75] http://ec.europa.eu/civiljustice/adr/adr_ec_code_conduct_en.htm.
[76] Directive 2008/52/EC of the European Parliament and of the Council of 21 May 2008 on certain aspects of mediation in civil and commercial matters, OJ L 136, 24 May 2008 ('Mediation Directive').
[77] This is the result of the limited legislative powers of the EU in the area of judicial cooperation in civil matters. See Tulibacka (above n 17) for an analysis of this issue.
[78] Mediation Directive, art 2.
[79] Art 3(b).
[80] Arts 4, 7, 8.
[81] Doc. 8907/02.
[82] Council Resolution of 2 December 2002 on Community consumer policy strategy 2002–2006, [2003] OJ C 11/1.
[83] Communication from the Commission to the Council, the European Parliament and the European Economic and Social Committee 'EU Consumer Policy Strategy 2007–2013. Empowering consumers, enhancing their welfare, effectively protecting them', 13 March 2007, COM (2007) 99 final.
[84] Consumer Policy Strategy 2007–2013, 11.

Consultation Paper on the use of ADR to resolve disputes concerning commercial transactions and practices in the EU concludes that encouraging the availability of collective ADR procedures should improve the handling of mass claims.[85] The 2012 European Consumer Agenda deals with a very wide range of issues including providing redress in an efficient manner.[86] ADR and collective redress are again highlighted.[87] Although no significant emphasis was placed upon the issue, the Commission is aware of the fact that only a small percentage of ADR bodies offer collective proceedings.

These policy instruments were informed by comprehensive research projects. In particular, the 2009 SANCO study conducted by Civic Consulting confirmed that the main problems with ADR across Europe were the fragmentation of coverage, the lack of consumer awareness, the tendency of businesses to refuse to engage in ADR or to follow non-binding decisions of ADR schemes, as well as the deficiencies in expertise and consumer trust.[88] As a response, DG SANCO published a Consultation Document, mentioned above in 2011.[89] The Directive 2013/11/EU on Consumer ADR,[90] and Regulation 524/2013 on Consumer ODR soon followed.[91]

D. Consumer ADR and ODR Measures

The ODR Regulation is a complementary mechanism to the Directive on Consumer ADR. It sets up an online platform which consumers and traders can use as a single point of entry for dispute resolution. The platform is to be linked to the ADR bodies operating according to the principles established by the Directive.

The Directive on Consumer ADR is an example of the new type of sectoral procedural measure in the EU. The emergence of the phenomenon of proceduralisation of various substantive areas (sectors) of EU law is significant because it offers a much wider power to legislate, without the cross-

---

[85] DG SANCO 'Consultation Paper on the use of Alternative Dispute Resolution as a means to resolve disputes related to commercial transactions and practices in the European Union', Brussels, DG SANCO, 2011, 10 ('Consultation on ADR').

[86] Communication from the Commission to the European Parliament, the Council, the Economic and Social Committee and the Committee of the Regions 'A European Consumer Agenda – Boosting confidence and growth', Brussels, 22 May 2012, COM (2012) 225 final (the 2012 European Consumer Agenda).

[87] *Ibid*, 10–12.

[88] 2009 SANCO Study.

[89] Consultation on ADR.

[90] Directive 2013/11/EU of the European Parliament and of the Council of 21 May 2013 on consumer ADR, OJ L 165/63.

[91] Regulation (EU) No 524/2013 of 21 May 2013 on Consumer ODR, OJ L 165/1.

border limitation.[92] A large number of consumer Directives contain provisions requiring adequate enforcement, including alternative mechanisms of resolving claims. Further, purely procedural measures were also adopted within the realm of consumer policy, including the Consumer ADR Directive.[93]

The Directive applies to 'procedures for the out-of-court resolution of domestic and cross-border disputes concerning contractual obligations' stemming from sales and services contracts between traders and consumers (established or resident in the EU) 'through the intervention of an ADR entity which proposes or imposes a solution or brings the parties together with the aim of facilitating an amicable solution.'[94] Thus, a wide variety of ADR mechanisms are included, such as mediation bodies (but not mediation conducted by a judge during civil proceedings), consumer arbitration (including binding arbitration), conciliation, ombudsmen and others. Recital 6 explains that ADR mechanisms ought to be available for all domestic and cross-border disputes covered by the Directive. The aim of the Directive is to ensure that, in the disputes stipulated in it, consumers have access to an ADR mechanism meeting the specified criteria (the mechanism could be located in another Member State). Member States are not required to establish new ADR mechanisms and may rely on mechanisms that are already in place (even if they entail complaints handled by a public body). However, a 'residual' ADR body must be in existence for all those types of disputes not covered by any other ADR mechanism available.[95] The Directive introduces quality requirements for all ADR bodies so that consumers can rely on having access to high-quality, transparent, fair and effective mechanisms.[96]

The Directive does not make an express provision for collective ADR schemes. However, Recital 27 reads:

> This Directive should be without prejudice to Member States maintaining or introducing ADR procedures dealing jointly with identical or similar disputes between a trader and several consumers. Comprehensive impact assessments should be carried out on collective out-of-court settlements before such settlements are proposed at Union level. The existence of an effective system for collective claims and easy recourse to ADR should be complementary and they should not be mutually exclusive procedures.

---

[92] This chapter does not examine the constitutional dimension of EU lawmaking in the area of civil justice. See Tulibacka (above n 17) for an analysis of the EU's legislative powers in this matter (art 81 TFEU). Sectoral rules are based on art 114 TFEU which does not contain a cross-border limitation.
[93] Tulibacka (above n 17).
[94] Art 2.1.
[95] Recital 24 and art 5.3.
[96] Art 2.3.

E. Conclusions

It is clear that EU legislators are not yet ready to regulate collective ADR, but they surely recognize its importance. The Directive on Consumer ADR applies to schemes offering collective ADR if they fulfil the criteria established by it. The Preamble to the Directive explains that more research is required before any collective ADR scheme is proposed by the EU. This is the sentiment that the chapter draws upon. It is supported by the unsettled EU position with regard to judicial collective redress, introduced below.

V. JUDICIAL COLLECTIVE REDRESS – NATIONAL MODELS AND THE EU RESPONSE

Many national models for collective redress, as well as the EU policies and legislation on the matter, are examined elsewhere in this volume. Below is a brief note focusing on the differences in national approaches and the resulting lack of consensus on what the EU response ought to be.

Collective redress for consumers has been on the agenda of DG SANCO for some time. In 2007 and 2008, the cause of enhancing collective redress mechanisms gained momentum. They are seen as an important element of the consumer law enforcement system, essential for consumer empowerment. The interest in this specific form of action at the EU level coincided with a much greater interest within Member States. The latter was triggered by the potential benefits of bundling together consumer claims and thus saving judicial time and resources which are under increasing pressure across Europe. The focus was on judicial mechanisms. During 1980s, but especially 1990s and beyond, almost all Member States (including the accession States of Central and Eastern Europe) at least looked into establishing a judicial collective redress procedure.[97] Many in fact succeeded, although the differences in national models are very significant, from the settlement approval model in the Netherlands,[98] through representative-style actions in Spain,[99]

---

[97] See the Stanford Law School's Global Class Actions Exchange website for updates on national developments across Europe and the Globe, http://globalclassactions.stanford.edu/about. See also D Hensler, C Hodges and M Tulibacka (eds.) 'The Globalization of Class Actions' 622 *The Annals of the American Academy of Political and Social Science* (2009).

[98] See I Tzankova and DL Scheurleer, 'The Netherlands', in Hensler, Hodges and Tulibacka (above n 97) 149–160.

[99] P Gutierrez de Cabiedes, 'Spain' in Hensler, Hodges and Tulibacka (above n 97) 170-178. The recent Act 3/2014 of March 27 amends the 2007 Consumer Protection Act. It adds the power of the public prosecutor to bring compensatory actions in the name of consumers (the power to bring injunctive actions already existed before).

to class actions in Sweden or Poland.[100] The latest national model is the one adopted in France.[101] It is an opt-in system limited to consumer law violations.[102]

The national initiatives illustrated a number of pressing issues, notably the perceived gap in access to justice that the collective mechanisms aimed to fill, the difficulties with balancing the need for access to justice with the potential risks of abuses of collective procedures, and the challenges of fitting this new procedural model in the continental civil law systems to which, in many respects, is considered foreign. So far, the judicial collective redress mechanisms have not been very popular. Indeed, in most States they are used very rarely. There are a number of factors which make them unattractive from the perspective of a mass consumer claim:

1. The significant costs of mass litigation, combined with the risks of having to cover the defendant's costs (loser pays rule) and problems with obtaining funding;
2. The complexity of such litigation, including problems with gathering evidence and the complex task of managing the group, resulting in the increased demands on time, resources and the required expertise of group representatives (for instance consumer associations) and law firms;
3. The potential length of proceedings – some European systems have problems with overly lengthy litigation even in individual cases, and a collective case brings an even greater challenge;
4. Restrictive rules concerning standing and certification, as well as some peculiar limitations to the scope of application of the collective redress procedures.[103]

The European Commission recognized the significance of these challenges, as well as the differences in national approaches, and started seeking ways in which the national models can be coordinated and made useful on a cross-border basis. On 27 November 2008 the Commission adopted the Green

---

[100] See for analysis of the Swedish class actions http://globalclassactions.stanford.edu/content/national-report-group-litigation-sweden and http://www.collectiveredress.org/collective-redress/reports/sweden/overview; and for Poland: http://globalclassactions.stanford.edu/content/whats-going-poland-update-class-actions-and-litigation-funding and http://www.collective redress.org/collective-redress/reports/poland/overview.

[101] *Loi 2014-344 du 17 mars 2014 relative à la consommation*, http://www.legifrance.gouv.fr/affichTexte.do?cidTexte=JORFTEXT000028738036&categorieLien=id.

[102] Only designated consumer organizations can bring actions in the name of consumers.

[103] For instance in Poland the claims concerning personal interests (including personal injury) cannot be pursued in a class action. Further, the Polish Class Actions law requires that monetary claims be standardized (made equal). For further details, M Tulibacka, Country report 'Poland', http://www.collectiveredress.org/collective-redress/reports/poland/overview.

Paper on Consumer Collective Redress.[104] The Green Paper set out 4 options, including no immediate action, and co-operation between Member States extending national collective redress systems to consumers from other Member States that do not have a collective redress mechanism. The third option is very interesting in the context of this chapter – it was a mix of policy instruments aimed at strengthening consumer redress (including collective consumer ADR mechanisms, powers for national enforcement authorities to request traders to compensate consumers and extending small claims to deal with mass situations). Clearly, collective ADR was seen as a viable alternative to judicial collective redress. Even though the last option was a binding or non-binding measure for a judicial collective redress procedure, there was never much potential for a binding instrument due to lack of consensus on what exactly the new EU procedure should look like.[105] Further, the opposition to an EU-level collective redress mechanism was very significant: coming from the industry, political circles and even academia.[106]

More recent consultation papers,[107] and discussions in the European Parliament,[108] revealed the extent of political, legal, social and economic problems with any contemplated EU-level collective redress model. Further, extensive academic input in this field, as well as voices from stakeholders, demonstrated that collective redress should be seen as an element of a wider law enforcement model and only one element of a well-functioning justice system. The example of the United States system was quoted on numerous occasions to illustrate a number of important points. Certain features of justice systems – such as contingency fees for lawyers or punitive damages – may encourage weak or unmeritorious mass claims, and putting too much emphasis on private enforcement risks overemphasizing judicial redress (also class actions) over other mechanisms which may well be more economically

---

[104] Commission of the European Communities, 'Green Paper on Consumer Collective Redress', 27 November 2008, COM (2008) 794 final.

[105] DG SANCO's efforts in this regard were taking place at the same time as the DG COMP's work on collective redress in the antitrust area. See Commission of the European Communities, 'White Paper on damages actions for breaches of EU antitrust rules', 2 April 2008, COM (2008) 165 final.

[106] See the responses to the DG SANCO Green Paper on consumer collective redress: http://ec.europa.eu/consumers/archive/redress_cons/response_GP_collective_redress_en.htm.

[107] Consultation Paper for Discussion on the Follow-up to the Green Paper on Consumer Collective Redress (2009), http://ec.europa.eu/consumers/archive/redress_cons/docs/consultation_paper2009.pdf. It proposed five options: including no action, self-regulation, non-binding or binding setting up of collective ADR and collective judicial schemes, with increased powers under the Consumer Protection Cooperation Regulation, and an EU-wide judicial collective redress mechanism including an ADR element.

[108] European Parliament Resolution 'Towards a Coherent European Approach to Collective Redress', 2 February 2012 (2011/2089), was preceded by the European Commission's Consultation on a coherent approach to collective redress (COM (2010) 135 final).

efficient and effective, such as public regulatory pressure, ADR or self-regulation. Another point which appeared in academic and policy writings concerned the need for respecting the legal systems, cultures and traditions of the Member States.

Following these discussions, in 2013, the Commission adopted a set of non-binding recommendations for collective redress mechanisms.[109] They establish a set of principles which apply to judicial and out-of-court collective redress.[110] The recommendations concern both injunctive and compensatory types of actions, and they also go beyond consumer law to include any rights conferred by EU law (consumer protection, competition, environment protection, protection of personal data, financial services regulation, investor protection and any other area where collective actions may be relevant).[111] They emphasize that judicial collective redress is a supplementary form of enforcement of EU rights, alongside public enforcement, judicial private enforcement (for instance using the small claims procedures), and ADR. The Commission recommends that all Member States have collective redress mechanisms at national level for:

> Both injunctive and compensatory relief, which respect the basic principles set out in this Recommendation. These principles should be common across the Union, while respecting the different legal traditions of the Member States. These are the principles as to which there is relatively wide consensus across the EU: for instance the loser pays principle or no opt-out proceedings in compensatory actions. Member States should ensure that the collective redress procedures are fair, equitable, timely and not prohibitively expensive.[112]

There are also provisions encouraging settlement between the parties, and requiring Member States to make sure that 'judicial collective redress mechanisms are accompanied by appropriate means of collective alternative dispute resolution available to the parties before and throughout the litigation.'[113] While these rather apply to the forms of settlement mechanisms related to litigation, the Recommendations may trigger a much wider interest in collective ADR and its further development, at least on the national level.

---

[109] Commission Recommendation of 11 June 2013, on common principles for injunctive and compensatory collective redress mechanisms in the Member States concerning violations of rights granted under Union Law, OJ L 201/60.
[110] Recital 13.
[111] Recital 7.
[112] Recommendation I.2.
[113] Recommendation 26.

Two main conclusions transpire from the European experience with judicial collective redress so far. First of all, even though there is probably no risk of European systems repeating US-style abuses to class actions,[114] there are significant problems with the existing European models of judicial collective redress. Furthermore, while these problems are generally acknowledged, the EU has so far not reached consensus with regards to how to respond to them. In other words, the EU is not yet close to establishing its own collective redress mechanism.

VI. CONCLUSIONS: IS THERE SCOPE AND APPETITE FOR AN EU MEASURE ON COLLECTIVE ADR?

The purpose of the chapter is not to argue that collective ADR is better, more effective or efficient than judicial collective redress. Clearly, within the EU policy documents and academic writings, the two are presented as complementary and not mutually exclusive. Collective ADR works for some consumer cases. On the other hand, its functioning is not without challenges, and it may not be suitable for all potential types of cases. ADR does not always work in mass cases, especially complex cases where individual claims are different or of high value. The existing collective ADR mechanisms across Europe are not very popular among consumers and traders, and this seems to be the most crucial issue the policymakers must tackle if they wish for collective ADR to provide a meaningful redress mechanism for consumers.

While ADR tends to offer a cheaper, quicker and less formalized resolution of disputes, collective mechanisms often involve expensive, long and extremely complex proceedings. In attempting to structure an EU-wide collective ADR mechanism, the following questions must be considered: can these contrasting tendencies be reconciled? Can ADR replace the court-based collective redress and provide a mechanism which combines the benefits of a collective approach and a less formal and cheaper procedure? What are the types of cases/problems that are more efficiently dealt with by the use of ADR, and which cases should be channelled towards courts? If one or both mechanisms (judicial collective redress and collective ADR) are introduced without much thought given to their respective roles, and their interaction with other civil justice mechanisms such as regulatory enforcement, small claims procedures and others, it can potentially lead to an unbalanced, ineffective justice system.

---

[114] The US class actions operate within the specific context of no loser pays rule, contingency fees, jury verdicts, punitive damages, lack of a universal public health system, and the more general approach to private litigation as a regulatory mechanism.

The EU recognizes the importance of collective ADR, but also its complementarity with other forms of redress, including judicial collective redress. It is in the process of building its own civil justice system, and its own ideas of an efficient justice system have not yet resulted in a harmonized approach. The EU justice system is a decentralized network of systems, bound by the growing number of generally binding principles. Europe does not yet have a clear picture of what an effective collective ADR system for consumer claims should be. The existing EU measures on ADR, including the Consumer ADR Directive examined in this paper, create quite a comprehensive legislative footing for almost all consumer ADR bodies, including those offering collective procedures. They seem to be sufficient for the moment. The EU is not ready to adopt a binding measure on collective consumer ADR.

Non-Judicial Means of Collective Redress

S.I. Strong*

I. INTRODUCTION

Most discussions relating to European forms of collective redress focus primarily, if not exclusively, on actions arising in the judicial context. However, courts are not always the best or only place to resolve large-scale legal disputes.[1] Indeed, both the European Commission (EC) and the European Parliament (EP) have repeatedly mentioned the need to develop alternative forms of dispute resolution (ADR) in cases involving collective redress.[2]

As it turns out, several European nations have already established non-judicial means of resolving large-scale legal disputes. Additional options are waiting in the wings, should the proper circumstances arise. However, many of these procedures have not been fully discussed in the scholarly literature,

---

* DPhil, University of Oxford; PhD (law), University of Cambridge; JD, Duke University; MPW, University of Southern California; BA, University of California, Davis. The author, who is admitted to practice as a solicitor in England and Wales and as an attorney in New York, Illinois and Missouri, is Professor of Law at the University of Missouri and Senior Fellow at the Center for the Study of Dispute Resolution.

[1] Questions relating to the relative benefits of judicial and non-judicial types of collective redress are beyond the scope of the current discussion. However, further reading on this issue is available. See SI Strong, *Class, Mass, and Collective Arbitration in National and International Law* (OUP, 2013) 284–304 (discussing benefits of large-scale arbitration); SI Strong, 'Beyond International Commercial Arbitration? The Promise of International Commercial Mediation' 45 *Washington U J of Law and Policy* 11 (2014) 16–17, 26 (discussing benefits of large-scale mediation and conciliation) ('ICM').

[2] See Commission Recommendation of 11 June 2013 on common principles for injunctive and compensatory collective redress mechanisms in the Member States concerning violations of rights granted under Union Law [2013] OJ L201/60, recital 16, paras 25–28 ('Commission Recommendation'); Communication from the Commission to the European Parliament, the Council, the European Economic and Social Committee and the Committee of the Regions, 'Towards a European Horizontal Framework for Collective Redress', paras 1.1, 3.8, COM(2013) 401 final ('Commission Communication'); European Parliament resolution of 2 February 2012 on 'Towards a Coherent European Approach to Collective Redress' (2011/2089(INI)), recitals 10, 25 ('Parliament Resolution'); European Commission, Public Consultation: Towards a Coherent European Approach to Collective Redress, SEC (2011) 173 (4 February 2011).

and are therefore largely unknown to both parties and policymakers. This chapter intends to cure this gap by analysing both existing and future forms of non-judicial collective redress in Europe. The discussion will cover consensual procedures, such as mediation and conciliation (Section II),[3] as well as adjudicative procedures such as arbitration (Section III).

II. EUROPEAN FORMS OF LARGE SCALE MEDIATION AND CONCILIATION

When the EC and EP promote the development of ADR in the collective context, they are clearly contemplating consensual mechanisms such as mediation and conciliation.[4] In many ways, this emphasis on mediation and conciliation may be attributed to the fact that consensual forms of collective redress are already known in the European Union as a result of the Dutch Act on Collective Settlements (WCAM), which provides judicial confirmation to large-scale settlement agreements.[5] The WCAM is available on an opt-out basis for parties to both domestic and cross-border disputes, and has been largely praised by commentators working in the field.

Unfortunately, critical support for the WCAM has not ensured wide usage. Although the Act has been in place since 2005, parties have only sought to confirm a settlement agreement under the Act seven times, thereby giving rise to questions as to why the procedure is not relied upon more often.[6]

---

[3] There has been a great deal of debate over the years about the difference between mediation and conciliation. See JM Nolan-Haley, 'Is Europe Headed Down the Primrose Path With Mandatory Mediation?' 37 *North Carolina J International L and Commercial Regulation* 981 (2012) 1009–1010; NA Welsh and A Kupfer Schneider, 'The Thoughtful Integration of Mediation Into Bilateral Investment Treaty Arbitration' 18 *Harvard Negotiation L Rev* 71 (2013) 84–85. Although some experts identify certain differences in the procedural processes used by the third party neutral, with conciliation being more evaluative than 'pure' mediation, most people have now concluded that the two terms are basically synonymous. See Guide to Enactment and Use of the UNCITRAL Model Law, 2002, 11, available at <http://www.uncitral.org/pdf/english/texts/arbitration/ml-conc/03-90953_Ebook.pdf>; T Gaultier, 'Cross-Border Mediation: A New Solution for International Commercial Settlement?' 26 *International L Practicum* 38 (2013) 42, n 25. That is the approach that will be adopted herein.

[4] See Commission Recommendation (above n 2) recital 16, paras 25-28; Commission Communication (above n 2) paras 1.1, 3.8; Parliament Resolution (above n 2) recitals 10, 25.

[5] See *Wet collectieve afwikkeling van massaschades* (WCAM), Law of 23 June 2005, Stb 340; I Tzankova and D Lunsingh Scheurleer, 'The Netherlands' in D Hensler *et al* (eds), *The Annals of the American Academy of Political and Social Science*, vol 622 (Sage Publications, 2009) 153–55. Notably, the WCAM does not require the assistance of a third party neutral. Instead, the parties may simply negotiate a settlement on their own.

[6] See B Krans, 'The Dutch Act on Collective Settlement of Mass Damages' 27 *Global Business and Development L J* (2014) 281, 282.

Research suggests that decisions relating to the choice of a particular dispute resolution process are affected by a wide variety of factors. For example, scholars in law and economics describe how default rules can affect parties' decision-making processes,[7] while experts in public international law discuss how disparities in different legal regimes can drive parties toward a certain type of procedure.[8] However, much of this jurisprudence is overlooked in discussions about the development of collective redress in Europe because of the prevailing view that European parties are largely disinclined toward consensual forms of dispute resolution.[9] The thought is that if parties do not want mediation or conciliation, then it makes little sense to spend time and political capital developing such mechanisms.

Certainly it is true that mediation and conciliation have failed to flourish in many European nations despite numerous top-down efforts to encourage consensual dispute resolution in the region.[10] Some observers find this phenomenon unproblematic and consistent with the principle of subsidiarity. However, recent empirical studies into the use and perception of international commercial mediation and conciliation suggest that one of the major reasons why parties do not use consensual means of dispute resolution is because parties and counsel have not been presented with compelling empirical evidence regarding potential benefits and success rates.[11]

This data goes a long way towards explaining why mediation and conciliation have not been more widely adopted in two-party disputes in Europe.[12] However, the results also help explain why the WCAM has not been more popular. Not only is there is very little research currently available concerning

---

[7] See M Barendrecht and BR de Vries, 'Fitting the Forum to the Fuss With Sticky Defaults: Failure in the Market for Dispute Resolution Services?' 7 *Cardozo J Conflict Resolution* (2005) 83, 83–84; SI Strong, 'Use and Perception of International Commercial Mediation and Conciliation: A Preliminary Report on Issues Relating to the Proposed UNCITRAL Convention on International Commercial Mediation and Conciliation' 39 ('Preliminary Report'), available at <http://papers.ssrn.com/sol3/papers.cfm?abstract_id=2526302> (discussing how law and economics can aid in this analysis).

[8] Strong, ICM (above n 1) 27–28; Strong, Preliminary Report (above n 7) 45–46.

[9] See R Tromans, 'Challenging the Conflict Culture: Mediation's Struggle for Acceptance in Europe' 58 *European Lawyer* (2007) 19, 19–22.

[10] See Directive 2013/11/EU of the European Parliament and of the Council of 21 May 2013 on alternative dispute resolution for consumer disputes and amending Regulation (EC) No 2006/2004 and Directive 2009/22/EC (Directive on consumer ADR); Directive 2008/52/EC, of the European Parliament and of the Council of 21 May 2008 on Certain Aspects of Mediation in Civil and Commercial Matters (2008) OJ L136/ 3; Tromans (above n 9) 19.

[11] See Strong, Preliminary Report (above n 7) 13, 28–29.

[12] Although there are a number of empirical studies on costs and success rates of mediation and conciliation in the United States, there are very few such studies in Europe. The preliminary report cited herein is the first empirical study of any type on international commercial mediation and conciliation. See *ibid* 5.

multiparty mediation and conciliation,[13] but parties' concerns about costs and success rates are even more heightened in multiparty matters than in two-party disputes, since the risks and costs associated with large-scale procedures are proportionally greater than those associated with bilateral proceedings.

This analysis suggests that European reluctance to use consensual means of large-scale dispute resolution could accurately be framed as a rational choice resulting from insufficient data on the one hand, and decisional inertia on the other.[14] If and when evidence is presented demonstrating that mediation and conciliation are superior to the other alternatives, then parties will likely shift their preferences, assuming that there is nothing in the legal environment to skew the decision-making process.[15]

Parties and policymakers need to keep a close eye on this latter element, since some types of legal disincentives can be very difficult to recognize.[16] For example, some commentators have suggested that legal systems can unconsciously drive parties toward adjudicative means of dispute resolution by making the enforcement regime surrounding litigation and arbitration easier than the enforcement regime surrounding mediation and conciliation.[17]

When considering how to remedy these inequities, policymakers must be sure to look at the whole picture, since partial measures can be as ineffective as inaction. Thus, for example, empirical studies have suggested that legal systems wishing to support mediation and conciliation may need to provide assistance in enforcing agreements at both the front end of the procedure (ie,

---

[13] Most of the existing research is theoretical rather than empirical. See Strong, ICM (above n 1) 22–24 (citing sources).

[14] Parties have a tendency to prefer the legal status quo, even if doing so is not necessarily to their benefit. See R Korobkin, 'Inertia and Preference in Contract Negotiation: The Psychological Power of Default Rules and Form Terms' 51 *Vanderbilt L Rev* (1998) 1538, 1626–27. Since mediation and conciliation must be affirmatively chosen by the parties in lieu of litigation, the benefits of mediation and conciliation must be clearly in excess of litigation for parties to overcome the attractiveness of the default. See C Sunstein, 'Choosing Not to Choose' 64 *Duke L J* 1 (2014) 38, 44. The preference for traditional forms of dispute resolution may be exacerbated by the fact that lawyers are often involved in parties' decisions whether to mediate or conciliate and most lawyers are by nature risk-adverse and therefore loathe to adopt new procedures and innovations. See JR Macey, 'Lawyers in Agencies: Economics, Social Psychology, and Process' 61 *L and Contemporary Problems* (1998) 109, 110–11; Strong, Preliminary Report (above n 7) 52 (discussing survey data indicating that counsel can sometimes be an obstacle to mediation and conciliation).

[15] See Korobkin (above n 14) 1626–27; Strong, ICM (above n 1) 27–38; Sunstein (above n 14) 44.

[16] For example, the attraction of the status quo is often difficult to overcome. See Korobkin (above n 14) 1626–27; Sunstein (above n 14) 44.

[17] See Strong, ICM (above n 1) 27–28.

agreements to mediate or conciliate a dispute) as well as the back end of the procedure (ie, settlement agreements arising out of a mediation or conciliation).[18] The WCAM only focuses on the latter of these two processes, which may explain why the WCAM has not been more widely used by parties. By only supporting part of the mediation and conciliation process, the WCAM may not provide sufficient incentive for parties to adopt consensual means of dispute resolution.

Empirical research has identified a number of additional reasons why Europeans have avoided mediation and conciliation. For example, studies suggest that a lack of familiarity with mediation and conciliation procedures can lead a party to avoid using such mechanisms.[19] Fear of the unknown may be particularly prevalent in cases involving collective redress, since there are very few public examples of successful multiparty mediations for parties to use as models and no procedural rules aimed specifically at multiparty scenarios.[20]

In fact, parties' concerns about consensual forms of collective redress may in some ways be justified. Although research is only now beginning in this field, multiparty mediation appears to give rise to a number of structural issues that are qualitatively different than those found in bilateral disputes.[21] For example, the concept of Pareto-efficiency, which is central to the identification of a reasonable resolution of a bilateral dispute, is inapplicable in the multiparty context.[22] Conversely, large-scale disputes generate concerns about group decision-making dynamics that do not exist in two-party conflicts.[23]

Commentators have suggested that parties to multiparty disputes face three challenges that are absent in two-party proceedings:

> First, as the number of parties increase, the likelihood that coalitions will emerge also increases. Coalitional behavior can make it difficult to reach agreement in complex problem-solving situations as subgroups seek to

---

[18] See *ibid* 32; Strong, Preliminary Report (above n 7) 46.

[19] See Strong, Preliminary Report (above n 7) 29.

[20] Although commentators have suggested that there is nothing about large-scale disputes that prohibits the use of consensual forms of resolution (indeed, some scholars go so far as to suggest that mediation and conciliation may be the best way to address such matters), the truth is that there are very few known examples of large-scale mediation and conciliation. See Strong, ICM (above n 1) 22–24.

[21] See *ibid* (citing sources).

[22] See RM Mnookin, 'Strategic Barriers to Dispute Resolution: A Comparison of Bilateral and Multilateral Negotiations' 159 *J Institutional and Theoretical Economics* (2003) 199.

[23] See L Susskind *et al*, 'What We Have Learned About Teaching Multiparty Negotiation' 21 *Negotiation J* (2005) 395; CR Sunstein, 'Deliberative Trouble? Why Groups Go to Extremes' 110 *Yale L J* (2000) 71.

form either 'winning' or 'blocking' coalitions. Second, as the number of parties at the table increases, the task of managing the conversation becomes more complicated. Coordinating a problem-solving dialogue (ie, who gets to speak, what information is shared, how written summaries of what has been agreed to are prepared, and how those not at the table are kept informed) requires not just process management skill, but legitimacy in the eyes of all the stakeholders. Finally, as the number of parties increases, the analytical challenges facing the stakeholders – especially as they try to examine and evaluate offers and counteroffers – increase exponentially. Representatives involved in multiparty negotiation must focus not just on what they want or do not want, but also on the changing nature of 'their next best option' given what others at the table might conclude without them.[24]

There are ways that a good mediator can avoid or minimize these problems, but the process requires an experienced and well-informed neutral.[25] Until such mediators can be easily and consistently identified, consensual forms of collective redress may be slow to develop in Europe. However, the fact that the evolutionary process may take some time does not make the goal any less worthy. If there are benefits to be gained from mediation and conciliation of multiparty disputes, then policymakers should strive to make such processes a realistic option for European parties.

III. EUROPEAN FORMS OF LARGE SCALE ARBITRATION

Mediation and conciliation are not the only ways to resolve collective claims outside of court. Parties can also turn to arbitration.

Many Europeans shy away from the notion of arbitration in the collective context because the most well-known form of large-scale arbitration – class arbitration (also known as class action arbitration) – is extremely similar to US-style class actions.[26] The largely negative view among European policymakers of US class actions makes it highly unlikely that class arbitration will ever develop in the EU or in individual Member States.[27]

---

[24] LE Susskind and L Crump, 'Multiparty Negotiation: An Emerging Field of Study and New Specialization' in LE Susskind and L Crump (eds), *1 Multiparty Negotiation: Complex Litigation and Legal Transactions* (Sage Publications, 2008) xxv, xxv; see also Strong, ICM (above n 1) 22–24.

[25] See Strong, ICM (above n 1) 22–23.

[26] See Strong, *Class, Mass, and Collective Arbitration* (above n 1) 93–94, 96, 312–13.

[27] See *ibid*. For additional views on this issue, see P Billiet *et al* (eds), *Class Actions and Arbitration in the European Union* (Maklu Publishers, 2012).

However, class arbitration is not the only way to provide large-scale legal relief in arbitration.[28] Instead, there are a variety of types of so-called 'collective' arbitration already in existence.[29] Many of these mechanisms have been developed by European parties and European nations seeking to find a way of pursuing collective relief in arbitration.

There is no limit to the types of procedural innovations that can arise with respect to large-scale arbitration.[30] Indeed, three very different models have already been developed for use by European parties: a Spanish form of collective consumer arbitration, a German procedure for corporate arbitration, and international investment proceedings involving large numbers of Italian bondholders. The following discussion considers each of these procedures in turn and then tackles the question of whether and to what extent large-scale arbitration could arise under the arbitration rules of several international arbitration organizations based in Europe.

A. Collective Consumer Arbitration in Spain

One of the most innovative and well-structured forms of large-scale arbitration in the world is found in Spain. In 2008, the Spanish legislature enacted a statute known as Ley (Law) 231/2008 which created a novel type of collective consumer arbitration.[31] Although Ley 231/2008 does not appear to have yet been used in practice (possibly as a result of Spanish antipathy to arbitration as a general concern), recent developments arising out of the financial crisis in Spain may herald an increase in interest in this mechanism.[32]

---

[28] See Strong, *Class, Mass, and Collective Arbitration* (above n 1) 6–19 (distinguishing between class, mass and collective proceedings). Although class arbitrations, like class actions, can include extremely large numbers of claimants, the size of the group does not determine whether a proceeding is a class arbitration. See *ibid* 6, 118. Instead, class arbitration is typically defined by the use of a single 'lead' claimant acting for numerous others in a representative capacity. See *ibid* 6. Class arbitrations also typically operate on an opt-out, rather than opt-in, basis. See *ibid* 7. Opt-in proceedings are usually characterized as collective in nature, since such procedures involve individualized consent from all claimants. See *ibid*; see also n 29.

[29] One hallmark of collective arbitration is the existence of individualized consent to the arbitration. See Strong, *Class, Mass, and Collective Arbitration* (above n 1) 18–19.

[30] See *ibid* 304–05; SI Strong, 'Class and Collective Relief in the Cross-Border Context: A Possible Role for the Permanent Court of Arbitration' 23 *The Hague Yearbook of International Law 2010* (2011) 133-38 ('PCA'); SI Strong, 'From Class to Collective: The De-Americanization of Class Arbitration' 26 *Arbitration International* (2010) 493 ('De-Americanization').

[31] See Real Decreto-ley 231/2008 de 15 de febrero, por el que se regula el Sistema Arbitral de Consumo, Boletín Oficial del Estado, 25.2.2008, n 48, 11072, arts 56–62 ('Ley 231/2008'), translation available in Strong, *Class, Mass, and Collective Arbitration* (above n 1) Appendix.

[32] See SI Strong, 'Collective Consumer Arbitration in Spain: A Civil Law Response to U.S.-Style Class Arbitration' 30 *J International Arbitration* (2013) 495, 497–98 ('Spanish Statute').

It is impossible to conduct a detailed analysis of Ley 231/2008 in the space available.[33] Therefore, this section will instead focus on a few salient issues so as to suggest how Ley 231/2008 might be adapted for use in other countries and in other contexts.

In many ways, Ley 231/2008 is a relatively narrow device, since it applies only to consumer disputes arising out of a common factual scenario.[34] Initially, all arbitrations are filed by consumers on a bilateral basis without any centralized coordination. However, if enough cases are filed, the president of one of the regional Consumer Arbitration Boards may seek to establish a collective proceeding, either on his or her own initiative or in response to a request from a local consumer association.[35]

Notice of a potential collective proceeding is sent to the respondent, who may decide to accept or decline the opportunity to proceed collectively. If the respondent decides not to proceed on a collective basis, the Consumer Arbitration Board archives the file and proceedings continue on a bilateral basis.[36] If, however, the respondent agrees to collective treatment, all pending arbitrations are transferred to the Consumer Arbitration Board with jurisdiction over the dispute.[37] The Consumer Arbitration Board also provides notice to other potential claimants through publication in the Official Journal of Spain, a process which will likely increase, perhaps significantly, the size of the collective.[38] Once the notice period (typically two months from the time of publication in the Official Journal) has run, the president of the Consumer Arbitration Board appoints the arbitral tribunal.[39]

The Spanish approach to collective arbitration is very effective in overcoming a number of potential problems with large-scale arbitration. First, Ley 231/2008 avoids any issues concerning the European Union directive on unfair terms in consumer contracts which has been interpreted in some Member States, including Spain, as prohibiting the use of pre-dispute arbitration clause in cases involving consumers.[40] The Spanish approach is a true innovation, since many people believed that it would not be possible to devise a mechanism for large-scale arbitration on a post-dispute basis.

---

[33] For a detailed discussion of Ley 231/2008 in English, including a full translation of the text of the statute itself, see ibid. Additional information can be found in BM Cremades and R Cortés, 'Class Actions and Arbitration Procedures – Spain' in *Class Actions and Arbitration in the European Union* (above n 27) 153, 155–56.

[34] See Ley 231/2008 (above n 31) art 56.

[35] See *ibid* art 58. The statute also offers the means of creating a nationwide collective action.

[36] See *ibid*.

[37] See *ibid* art 60. The one exception is in cases where an arbitral tribunal has already been appointed in an individual dispute. Those matters continue on a bilateral basis.

[38] See *ibid* art 59(1). Other forms of notice may be used if necessary or useful.

[39] See *ibid* art 59(3).

[40] See Council Directive 93/13/EEC of 5 April 1993 on unfair terms in consumer contracts [1993] OJ L95/29; J Hill, *Cross-Border Consumer Contracts* (OUP, 2008) 215.

Second, by giving respondents the ultimate authority to decide whether the dispute should be heard collectively, Ley 231/2008 avoids the problem often seen in other contexts of ensuring that the respondent agrees with the idea of proceeding on a group basis.[41] Respondents often resist large-scale arbitration as a tactical matter, based on the belief that forcing parties to proceed individually will reduce or eliminate the number of claims that are brought. By allowing the respondent to decide whether to proceed collectively, Ley 231/2008 avoids any expense or delays that might arise as a result of a procedural dispute about whether a group proceeding is permissible.

However, Ley 231/2008 is not perfect. Some difficulties still remain from the respondent's perspective. For example, even though a respondent proceeding under Ley 231/2008 understands that the arbitration will be collective in nature, there is no way to know in advance how large the final group will be. As a result, respondents might view Ley 231/2008 as somewhat risky, since the notice process could inspire claimants who might not otherwise be inclined to file a claim to do so.[42] This inability to anticipate the size of a collective dispute might explain why no Spanish respondent has yet relied on the procedure, despite the advantages of 'global peace.'

Claimants may have slightly different problems with Ley 231/2008. For example, nowhere in the statute are existing claimants given the opportunity to opt out of the collective proceeding and pursue their claims individually. Furthermore, claimants who file during the notice period are not allowed to proceed on a bilateral basis.[43] These features could result in a challenge to Ley 231/2008 based on the claimant's constitutional right to choose whether, when, where and in particular how to assert a legal claim.[44]

Even if it is possible for parties to withdraw a claim that has been transferred to the collective action so that they can bring those claims individually at a later date, there is no language in Ley 231/2008 describing whether and to what extent the collective award would have any sort of *res judicata* effect on any claimants who refiled after the collective proceeding was completed. This issue also affects claimants who chose not to file during the notice period, either because they did not receive notice or because they did not want to proceed on a collective basis. This gap in the law is extremely

---

[41] See Strong, *Class, Mass, and Collective Arbitration* (above n 1) 340–44.
[42] Some claimants might not know that they had a compensable right prior to receipt of the notice, while others might have found the burdens of proceeding on a bilateral basis too onerous.
[43] See *ibid* arts 58–61 (providing respondent with various options regarding the conduct of the case, but not claimants).
[44] See SI Strong, 'Cross-Border Collective Redress and Individual Participatory Rights: Quo Vadis?' 32 *CJQ* (2013) 508, 511 ('Quo Vadis') (discussing whether parties have a right to decide how a claim will be resolved); Strong, Spanish Statute (above n 31) 505–06.

troubling, since it is often unclear how principles of preclusion operate in both arbitration and collective actions.[45]

Although this analysis suggests that a number of issues remain to be worked out, Ley 231/2008 nevertheless provides a very good, practical model of how collective arbitration can arise without the existence of a pre-dispute arbitration agreement. Furthermore, this mechanism could be extended from the consumer context to include other situations where a pre-dispute arbitration agreement is impossible to obtain, including mass torts, human rights actions or environmental suits.[46] The procedure could also be easily adapted for use in international disputes, with either a public or private organization acting as the central clearinghouse for claims.[47] Such an option may be particularly attractive given the rising number of cross-border collective injuries in Europe and around the world.[48]

B. Corporate Arbitration in Germany

Ley 231/2008 provides European parties and policymakers with an intriguing statutory model of collective arbitration. However, Spain is not the only European jurisdiction to have adopted large-scale arbitral proceedings. Germany has also developed a form of collective arbitration, although German innovation has not come through legislative action. Instead, Germany has adopted group arbitration through a combination of judicial and private efforts.

The issue first arose in 1996, when the German Federal Court of Justice (*Bundesgerichtshof* or BGH) heard a case concerning the arbitrability of corporate law concerns.[49] Although the BGH's decision was not entirely negative, the court did express some reservations about the arbitrability of shareholder disputes and indicated that such questions might be better handled through legislative action. However, the legislature did not take up the court's invitation, and in 2009, when the issue arose again, the BGH stated affirmatively that corporate law disputes were arbitrable so long as certain minimum conditions were met.[50]

---

[45] See Strong, Quo Vadis (above n 44) 512–14, 532.

[46] See Strong, *Class, Mass, and Collective Arbitration* (above n 1) 24, 330.

[47] For example, the Permanent Court of Arbitration at the Hague may be amenable to acting in this capacity. See Strong, PCA (above n 30) 133–39.

[48] Strong, Quo Vadis (above n 44) 533; see also Parliament Resolution (above n 2) paras D, H.

[49] See C Borris, 'Arbitrability of Corporate Law Disputes in Germany' in CJM Klaassen *et al* (eds), *Onderneming en ADR* (Kluwer, 2011) 55, 59.

[50] See *S v M*, Case No II ZR 255/08 (BGH, 6 April 2009), Kriendler Digest for ITA Board of Reporters, available at www.kluwerarbitration.com; Borris (above n 49) 61.

Later that year, the German Institution of Arbitration (*Deutsche Institution für Schiedsgerichtsbarkeit* or DIS) incorporated the principles outlined in the BGH's decision into a new set of specialized arbitral rules known as the DIS Supplementary Rules for Corporate Law Disputes (DIS Supplementary Rules).[51] The DIS Supplementary Rules provide a means of collectively resolving corporate law disputes involving partnerships (*Personengesellschaften*) and limited liability companies under German law (*GmbH*).[52]

At this point, most of the disputes that have been heard under the DIS Supplementary Rules have been relatively modest in size, since large, publicly traded companies are excluded from the scope of the Rules.[53] Nevertheless, the DIS Supplementary Rules provide useful insights on how to organize large-scale proceedings.

It is impossible to analyse the DIS Supplementary Rules in their entirety in the space available.[54] Instead, the emphasis here is on a number of key features that distinguish the DIS Supplementary Rules from Ley 231/2008 and other types of large-scale arbitration.

One of the most innovative aspects of the DIS Supplementary Rules involves the form and timing of the arbitration agreement. According to the BGH, an arbitration provision found in a corporation's articles of incorporation can bind current, future, and former shareholders even though that document is not a contract in the technical sense.[55] The DIS Supplementary Rules are founded on this principle and not only provide countries, commentators, and competing arbitral institutions with a procedural framework that can be followed in other contexts, but also offer a model arbitration clause that can be used as the basis for such proceedings.[56]

The second remarkable aspect of the DIS Supplementary Rules is the notion that shareholders do not need to participate actively in the proceedings to be bound by the decision rendered by the arbitral tribunal. Although

---

[51] *See* DIS Supplementary Rules for Corporate Law Disputes, effective 15 September 2009 ('DIS Supplementary Rules'), available at <http://www.dis-arb.de/ download/DIS_SRCoLD_%202009_Download.pdf>; Strong, *Class, Mass, and Collective Arbitration* (above n 1) 86–101.

[52] See DIS Supplementary Rules (above n 51).

[53] The DIS heard seven proceedings under the DIS Supplementary Rules between September 2009 and December 2012. See DIS, Statistics, <http://www.dis-arb.de/en/39/content/statistics-id54>. Though this number may appear low, it will likely take some time for arbitration provisions to be inserted into the relevant corporate documents and disputes involving those entities to arise.

[54] A full discussion of the rules is available elsewhere. See Borris (above n 49); Strong, *Class, Mass, and Collective Arbitration* (above n 1) 86–101.

[55] Many jurisdictions require an arbitration agreement to be or be found in a contract, although this principle is weakening in some countries. See SI Strong, 'Arbitration of Trust Disputes: Two Bodies of Law Collide' 45 *Vanderbilt J Transnational L* (2012) 1157, 1209.

[56] See DIS Supplementary Rules (above n 51), Model Clause; see also *ibid* s 11.

all shareholders must be given the opportunity to participate and the corporation itself must be named as a party, any shareholder who does not want to be actively involved in the arbitration does not have to be.[57] Shareholders who wish to participate in the proceedings may do so as full parties or compulsory intervenors, although the two categories of participants have slightly different rights and responsibilities.[58]

The DIS Supplementary Rules also indicate that shareholders do not need to have been named as parties at the time the arbitration was filed for them to be bound by the decision. Instead, shareholders merely need to have been provided notice as a 'Concerned Other' at an appropriate point during the proceedings so as to enjoy both the benefit and the burden of any award that ensues.[59]

The process of providing notice to Concerned Others is relatively complicated, with parties on both sides of the dispute being allowed to name Concerned Others, as well as Concerned Others being able to name additional Concerned Others. Though time-consuming, this approach is necessary because all shareholders must be provided notice of the proceeding if the award is to be enforceable.[60]

The DIS Supplementary Rules are also unusual, in that they allow Concerned Others to decide for themselves how they will be aligned within the proceedings.[61] Other arbitral rules typically allow either the arbitral institution or the initial parties to the dispute to indicate who is a claimant and who is a respondent. While the traditional approach may be relatively unproblematic in standard multiparty proceedings, it can create difficulties in disputes relating to corporate policy since it may not be apparent how new parties want to affiliate themselves. Therefore, the DIS approach is preferable in the type of cases that arise under the DIS Supplementary Rules.

Some observers may find the concept of passive and initially unnamed parties to be uncomfortably similar to certain procedures seen in US class actions and class arbitrations.[62] However, the DIS Supplementary Rules cannot be framed as a type of representational action similar to a US class proceeding. Not only are all shareholders explicitly given the opportunity to be involved before the action proceeds, but they are allowed to participate in

---

[57] See *ibid* ss 2, 4.
[58] See *ibid* s 4.
[59] See *ibid* ss 4, 11. The term 'Concerned Others' is defined in a comment to section 2 of the DIS Supplementary Rules and includes all shareholders.
[60] See *ibid* s 2–5. The corporation must also be named as a party to the dispute.
[61] See *ibid* s 3.
[62] See Federal Rule of Civil Procedure 23 (providing rules of procedure on a trans-substantive basis); *ibid* rule 23.1 (providing rules of procedure for derivative actions).

the conduct of the proceedings in a much more realistic and involved manner than unnamed plaintiffs in a US class action or class arbitration are.[63]

One of the most intriguing aspects of the DIS Supplementary Rules relates to the nature of the proceeding. Close analysis suggests that arbitrations under the DIS Supplementary Rules operate on something of an *in rem* basis.[64] Characterizing the DIS proceedings in this way is helpful because it distinguishes matters heard under the DIS Supplementary Rules from standard types of compensatory or declaratory proceedings, and therefore helps identify other types of multiparty disputes that might be amenable to DIS-style procedures. Thus, the DIS Supplementary Rules could be adapted for use in other types of large-scale corporate disputes, such as those involving publicly traded companies, as well as disputes involving trusts, *stiftung* or foundations involving large numbers of parties.[65]

Anyone seeking to adopt DIS-style proceedings in other contexts would need to be able to identify a document similar to a corporate charter that is common to all parties and that generates the relative rights and responsibilities between the parties. If such a document exists, then it might be possible to adopt procedures similar to those outlined in the DIS Supplementary Rules. Of course, any procedure that is eventually adopted would have to comply with fundamental principles of procedural fairness.[66]

C. Investor-State Arbitration Involving Italian Bondholders

The preceding two subsections discussed large-scale arbitration from the perspective of private domestic law. However, group arbitration is also possible as a matter of public international law. Although most people who think of large-scale arbitration in the public international realm focus on mass claims, commissions, and inter-state tribunals, those types of proceedings are essentially bilateral in nature.[67] Instead, the emphasis in this section is on

---

[63] See DIS Supplementary Rules (above n 51) s 4.

[64] See Strong, *Class, Mass, and Collective Arbitration* (above n 1) 25, 86, 89, 93; see also DIS Supplementary Rules (above n 51) comment to s 2.

[65] See SI Strong, 'Mandatory Arbitration of Internal Trust Disputes: Improving Arbitrability and Enforceability Through Proper Procedural Choices' 28 *Arbitration International* (2012) 591, 601-04 (discussing the size and prevalence of trusts worldwide, including commercial or business trusts, and the size of potential claimant groups); see also SI Strong (ed), *Arbitration of Trust Disputes Under National and International Law* (OUP, forthcoming 2016). It might also be possible to use DIS-style proceedings in disputes arising out of a will or other testamentary document, although those matters would not be as large as other types of actions, such as those involving commercial trusts.

[66] The BGF decision on shareholder arbitration might be useful in helping identify the necessary standards. See Borris (above n 49) 61.

[67] See Strong, *Class, Mass, and Collective Arbitration* (above n 1) 331–32.

large-scale forms of treaty-based arbitration which resolve multiple claims at a single time in a single forum.

The proceedings in question arise in the context of investor-state arbitration, which is in some ways distinguishable from private forms of arbitration, particularly with respect to issues of respondent consent.[68] Nevertheless, parties and policymakers in Europe can learn some valuable lessons from these cases. Indeed, these procedures have already won the support of a large number of Italian claimants.

At this point, the international legal community has witnessed three large-scale investment arbitrations. The first of these matters, *Abaclat v. Argentine Republic*,[69] saw 60,000 Italian bondholders bringing a single action against Argentina for injuries suffered as a result of Argentina's default on approximately 100 billion US dollars' of sovereign debt in 2001. This procedure was framed as a 'mass' arbitration rather than a class arbitration, due to the 'hybrid' nature of the claims.[70]

The other two proceedings involved the same substantive dispute, but were much more modest in size. Thus, *Ambiente Ufficio v. Argentine Republic* involved only 90 claimants,[71] while *Alemanni v. Argentine Republic* involved only 74 claimants.[72] Because investment arbitration does not follow a formal system of precedent, the tribunals in *Ambiente Ufficio* and *Alemanni* were not bound to follow the reasoning reflected in *Abaclat*.[73] However, investment tribunals can and often do consider previous investment decisions to be a form of persuasive authority. In this case, the latter two tribunals cited *Abaclat* favourably on a number of substantive and procedural points, even

---

[68] Investor-state arbitration is not based on a contract between the parties, but is instead based on a standing 'offer to arbitrate' made by the state which individual investors can subsequently accept. See C McLachlan *et al*, *International Investment Arbitration: Substantive Principles* (OUP, 2008) 52–54. The 'offer to arbitrate' is often found in a bilateral or multilateral treaty, although certain national laws and contracts between the investor and the state can also include an offer to arbitrate. See *ibid*.

[69] See *Abaclat and others v Argentine Republic*, ICSID Case No ARB/07/5, Decision on Jurisdiction and Admissibility (4 August 2011) (Pierre Tercier, President; Georges Abi-Saab; Albert Jan van den Berg) ('*Abaclat*'). On 28 October 2011, Professor Abi-Saab issued a dissenting opinion.

[70] See *ibid* paras 483, 488.

[71] See *Ambiente Ufficio S.p.A. and others v Argentine Republic*, ICSID Case No ARB/08/9, Decision on Jurisdiction and Admissibility (8 February 2013) (Brunno Simma, President; Karl-Heinz Böckstiegel; Santiago Torres Bernárdez) ('*Ambiente Ufficio*'). On 2 May 2013, Dr Torres (appointed by Argentina) issued a dissenting opinion.

[72] See *Alemanni and others v Argentine Republic*, ICSID Case No ARB/07/8, Decision on Jurisdiction and Admissibility (17 November 2014) (Sir Franklin Berman, President; Karl-Heinz Böckstiegel; J Christopher Thomas) ('*Alemanni*'). On 17 November 2014, Mr Thomas (appointed by Argentina) issued a concurring opinion.

[73] See G Kaufmann-Kohler, 'Arbitral Precedent: Dream, Necessity or Excuse?' 23 *Arbitration International* (2007) 357, 361–378.

though the arbitrators in the latter two actions declined to frame their proceedings as constituting 'mass' arbitrations.[74]

At the time of writing, none of these disputes had yet reached conclusion on the merits. However, all three tribunals had issued preliminary decisions on jurisdiction and admissibility which contain important insights into how large-scale arbitrations might arise in practice.[75] Parties and policymakers who are contemplating the possibility of collective arbitration in Europe might find these decisions helpful with respect to various matters concerning large-scale proceedings. Although it is impossible to discuss each of these matters in detail in the space available, the following discussion will raise a few issues of particular interest.[76]

One of the most useful lessons arising out of this trio of cases involves the manner in which claimant's consent can be obtained in a large-scale proceeding. This chapter previously discussed how Spain uses a centralized filing system to identify claims that are suitable for aggregation on a post-dispute basis. *Abaclat*, *Ambiente Ufficio* and *Alemanni* also involve post-dispute aggregation, but on an entirely ad hoc basis. Rather than relying on a formal or state-sponsored filing process, all of the claimants – which in *Abaclat* numbered in the tens of thousands – found each other privately before the arbitration was filed.[77]

Abaclat is particularly instructive with respect to how consent to collective arbitration can be obtained from a large number of individual claimants, since a number of relevant documents are publicly available and can be used as models. Thus, parties and policymakers can look to *Abaclat* for excellent examples of: (1) a letter of instruction explaining the purposes and procedures of the arbitral proceedings; (2) a declaration of consent, delegation of authority, and power of attorney for the law firm in question to act on behalf the bondholder; (3) a grant of mandate to the entity acting as claimant's

---

[74] The arbitral tribunal in *Ambiente Ufficio* considered the matter to be a multiparty proceeding while the arbitrators in *Alemanni* declined to characterize the proceedings in any particular manner.

[75] Arbitral awards and procedural orders are often made publicly available in treaty-based proceedings.

[76] More detailed discussions are available elsewhere. See Strong, *Class, Mass, and Collective Arbitration* (above n 1) 75–83; SI Strong, 'Heir of *Abaclat*? Mass and Multiparty Proceedings: *Ambiente Ufficio S.p.A. v. Argentine Republic*' 29 ICSID Review-Foreign Investment L J (2014) 149. Because investment arbitration uses a somewhat unique approach to respondent's consent to arbitration (ie, a standing offer to arbitrate), the analysis here will focus on matters unrelated to respondent's consent. See McLachlan *et al* (above n 68) 52–54; Strong, *Class, Mass, and Collective Arbitration* (above n 1) 340–44 (discussing respondent's objections to matters of consent in *Abaclat*).

[77] The process was coordinated by counsel and by certain organizations that eventually acted as the claimants' agent, but was still remarkable in its scope. See *Abaclat* (above n 69) paras 65, 550–54; *Ambiente Ufficio* (above n 71) paras 85, 186, 202–03.

agent, allowing that entity to coordinate the arbitration; (4) a questionnaire asking for documents and information relating to the underlying claim and (5) additional instructions regarding the gathering of documents.[78]

Another intriguing issue arises out of the fact that all three proceedings saw an organization acting as an agent for purposes of coordinating the members of the claimant group, although the bondholders all asserted their claims in their individual capacities. In *Abaclat*, the organization in question was an *associazione non riconosciuta* known as *Task Force Argentina* (TFA) and created under Italian law to represent the interests of the claimants.[79] In *Ambiente Ufficio* and *Alemanni*, the agent was the *North Atlantic Société d'Administration* (NASAM), an entity created under the law of Monaco.[80]

The presence of TFA and NASAM in these proceedings raises the question of whether it would be possible for an organization to proceed independently on behalf of a large group of individuals who were not themselves parties to the dispute. This is a model that has a number of benefits and is judicially available in several European nations.[81]

At this point, there are no known cases of large-scale arbitrations involving representative claims brought exclusively by an agent or other representative organization. Actions of this type would be potentially problematic in investment arbitration due to jurisdictional requirements relating to the nationality and status of the claimant as an 'investor' under the relevant treaty or law.[82] However, this type of approach could very well be possible in private (contract-based) arbitration.[83]

A third issue that is worth mentioning involves the concept of third party funding. Investment arbitration is a very expensive undertaking, and there is no way that the individual claimants in any of these three cases would be willing or able to pay the necessary fees and costs, particularly given that each party suffered relatively small individual damages.[84] However, all three cases saw the claimants' agent (TFA or NASAM) agreeing to fund the proceedings.

---

[78] See *Abaclat* (above n 69) para 85; Strong, *Class, Mass, and Collective Arbitration* (above n 1) 334–40. Although similar documents were compiled in *Ambiente Ufficio* and *Alemanni*, the procedure was slightly problematic, at least in the case of *Alemanni*, and does not provide as good a model for future claimants to follow. See *Alemanni* (above n 72) para 279 (noting some potential difficulties with respect to the powers of attorney).

[79] See *Abaclat* (above n 69) paras 65–66.

[80] See *Alemanni* (above n 72) para 45; *Ambiente Ufficio* (above n 71) para 274.

[81] See Strong, *Class, Mass, Collective Arbitration* (above n 1) 311.

[82] The injury in question would also have to arise from an 'investment' that is covered under the relevant treaty or law. The author is grateful to Mark Kantor and Mick Smith for insights into these issues.

[83] See *ibid*.

[84] See *ibid* 82.

Argentina objected to the payment structure in all three cases on a variety of grounds but was overruled in each instance. In the words of the tribunal in *Alemanni*,

> many of the aspects criticized are merely characteristic of the incidents of third-party funding in international investment arbitration. Individual views may differ as to whether third-party funding is or is not desirable or beneficial, either at the national or at the international level, but the practice is by now so well established both within many national jurisdictions and within international investment arbitration that it offers no grounds in itself for objection to the admissibility of a request to arbitrate.[85]

Although that statement was made within the context of investment arbitration, there is no reason to believe that the same principle would not hold true in private forms of arbitration. This development could be crucial to the development of large-scale arbitration in Europe, since there is often a heightened need for third party funding in matters involving collective redress.[86]

One question that remains unanswered involves the procedures to be used in resolving these three disputes on the merits. Because the arbitrations are still underway, little is known about the tribunals' case management methods.[87] However, answers on these and other issues will undoubtedly come with time. Until then, all three proceedings stand as excellent examples of how large numbers of parties can band together to file their claims without the use of a representative mechanism similar to that used in US class actions and class arbitrations.

D. Large-Scale International Commercial Arbitrations Involving European Arbitral Institutions

One of the reasons why the tribunals in *Abaclat*, *Ambiente Ufficio*, and *Alemanni* were able to allow large-scale procedures to go forward was that the governing treaties and arbitration rules left a sufficient gap for the tribunal to exercise its procedural discretion.[88] Similar situations could arise in private (contract-based) arbitration, giving rise to the question of whether

---

[85] *Alemanni* (above n 72) para 278. The tribunal in *Ambiente Ufficio* made a similar statement. See *Ambiente Ufficio* (above n 71) para 202–03. The funding arrangement was slightly different in *Abaclat* but was still considered appropriate. See *Abaclat* (above n 69) para 458.

[86] See Strong, *Class, Mass, and Collective Arbitration* (above n 1) 323.

[87] Some interim procedural orders have been made public, but those provide only a piecemeal account of the procedures adopted to date.

[88] *Abaclat* framed this as a 'qualified silence', although that characterization was disputed by later tribunals. See *Alemanni* (above n 72) paras 264, 265, 267.

an arbitral tribunal in a commercial or related setting would ever have the authority to allow large numbers of claimants to bring a joint claim absent express authority in the arbitration agreement.[89]

To decide this issue, arbitral tribunals must determine whether implicit consent can support this type of procedure, and if so, whether the arbitration agreement reflects that type of consent.[90] In so doing, tribunals will doubtless consult any arbitration rules that the parties have chosen to govern the proceedings to see whether those procedures allow a large-scale dispute to be brought.[91] Interestingly, two arbitral institutions based in the EU have adopted procedural rules that could conceivably support some form of large-scale arbitration.

The first set of rules to consider are promulgated by the London Court of International Arbitration (LCIA Arbitration Rules).[92] Although any tribunal considering the propriety of large-scale proceedings would have to consider the rules in their entirety, arbitrators would doubtless focus much of their attention on Article 14, which indicates that:

> 14.4 Under the Arbitration Agreement, the Arbitral Tribunal's general duties at all times during the arbitration shall include:
>
> (i) a duty to act fairly and impartially as between all parties, giving each a reasonable opportunity of putting its case and dealing with that of its opponent(s); and
> (ii) a duty to adopt procedures suitable to the circumstances of the arbitration, avoiding unnecessary delay and expense, so as to provide a fair, efficient and expeditious means for the final resolution of the parties' dispute.
>
> 14.5 The Arbitral Tribunal shall have the widest discretion to discharge these general duties, subject to such mandatory law(s) or rules of law as the Arbitral Tribunal may decide to be applicable; and at all times the parties shall do everything necessary in good faith for the fair, efficient and expeditious conduct of the arbitration, including the Arbitral Tribunal's discharge of its general duties.

The second set of rules to consider are promulgated by the Paris-based

---

[89] This issue is hotly debated in a number of contexts. See Strong, *Class, Mass, and Collective Arbitration* (above n 1) 340–44.

[90] See *ibid* 185–205.

[91] The analysis in each individual instance will be guided by standard contract principles contained within the law governing the construction of the arbitration agreement. See *ibid*.

[92] See LCIA Arbitration Rules, effective 1 October 2014, http://www.lcia.org/Dispute_Resolution_Services/lcia-arbitration-rules-2014.aspx.

International Chamber of Commerce (ICC Arbitration Rules).[93] The ICC Arbitration Rules also give arbitral tribunals a great deal of discretion in crafting procedures in situations where a gap arises, which could be quite useful to proponents of large-scale arbitration.[94] Furthermore, Article 22 of the ICC Arbitration Rules explicitly states that:

> 1 The arbitral tribunal and the parties shall make every effort to conduct the arbitration in an expeditious and cost-effective manner, having regard to the complexity and value of the dispute.
> 2 In order to ensure effective case management, the arbitral tribunal, after consulting the parties, may adopt such procedural measures as it considers appropriate, provided that they are not contrary to any agreement of the parties.[95]

The breadth of the language in both of these rule sets would appear to provide a sufficient basis for arbitrators to adopt large-scale proceedings in appropriate cases. However, arbitrators would also have to consider various provisions relating to multiparty arbitration. Though helpful in some ways,[96] these provisions could create a number of problems in large-scale disputes. For example, questions might arise as to whether collective claims should be considered under language dealing with joinder or consolidation.[97] Although some tribunals in the investment context have concluded that joinder and consolidation provisions are inapplicable in matters that are initially filed as multiparty proceedings,[98] resolution of that particular issue could be costly and time-consuming.

Neither the LCIA nor the ICC are known to have administered any large-scale proceedings in recent years,[99] although the ICC administered a case involving over 140 parties in the late 1990s under an older set of procedural

---

[93] See ICC Arbitration Rules, effective 1 January 2012, http://www.iccwbo.org/Products-and-Services/Arbitration-and-ADR/Arbitration/Rules-of-arbitration/Download-ICC-Rules-of-Arbitration/ICC-Rules-of-Arbitration-in-several-languages.

[94] See *ibid* art 19.

[95] *Ibid* art 22.

[96] For example, the ICC recently amended its rules so as to make multiparty arbitration easier, particularly in cases involving multiple contracts. See *ibid* arts 7–10. Large-scale arbitration can arise under a single contract or under multiple joined contracts, which could reflect either a 'string' or 'hub and spoke' pattern. See Strong, *Class, Mass, and Collective Arbitration* (above n 1) 123–24.

[97] See ICC Arbitration Rules (above n 93) arts 7–10; LCIA Arbitration Rules (above n 92) art 22.1 (vii–x).

[98] See *Alemanni* (above n 72) paras 261–67 (discussing *Abaclat* and *Ambiente Ufficio*).

[99] Unlike investment arbitration, which has a relatively high degree of transparency due to the public nature of the claims, commercial arbitration tends to proceed on a private and confidential basis. However, an award may become public during judicial enforcement or annulment proceedings.

rules.[100] As a result, it is impossible to predict the form of any large-scale arbitration proceeding under the LCIA Arbitration Rules or ICC Arbitration Rules. However, there is no reason to assume that an arbitral tribunal faced with a possible large-scale action will adopt procedures akin to US class arbitrations. To the contrary, it would seem far more likely that a tribunal overseeing a dispute involving European parties would consider how collective redress is structured in the national courts of the parties involved.[101] Arbitrators would also seem likely to consider the types of procedures that are used in non-class forms of large-scale arbitration that are already in existence, such as those discussed herein.

Both the LCIA and the ICC specialize in international commercial disputes, which means that these rules will likely only be invoked in matters arising in the cross-border business context. However, there are a number of commercial disputes that could give rise to large-scale claims. For example, the coming years might see collective redress sought in the context of international insurance and reinsurance disputes or with respect to international construction projects. The LCIA Arbitration Rules and ICC Arbitration Rules would both appear capable of providing collective redress in either of those two scenarios.

IV. CONCLUSION

As the above discussion has shown, European parties seeking non-judicial means of collective redress currently have recourse to an impressive number of options. While more work needs to be done to make these alternatives more widely known and more widely available, Europe could very well become the leader in large-scale arbitration, mediation and conciliation in the coming years.[102]

---

[100] See The Decision, Judgment of the Swiss Federal Court, (1999) 10 *American Rev International Arbitration* 559, 564–68; Y Derains and EA Schwartz, *Guide to the ICC Rules of Arbitration* (Kluwer Law International, 2005) 101–02; BR Ostrager et al, 'Andersen v Andersen: The Claimants' Perspective' 10 *American Rev International Arbitration* (1999) 443, 443.

[101] See Strong, De-Americanization (above n 30) 493; see also Strong, *Class, Mass, and Collective Arbitration* (above n 1) 305–07.

[102] The United States Supreme Court has recently issued several decisions that have effectively restricted the use of class arbitration in a number of situations. See Strong, *Class, Mass, and Collective Arbitration* (above n 1) 12, 129, 206. However, the United States could be in the process of developing various forms of non-class collective arbitration as an alternative to class arbitration. See *ibid* 13 n 74, 84–85, 215–17, 341 n 382.

The Effect of EU Public Enforcement Proceedings on Collective ADR

*Vincent Smith**

I. INTRODUCTION

Collective alternative dispute resolution is becoming increasingly common as a means of addressing a wide range of compensation actions by groups of plaintiffs who have suffered harm as a result of breach of EU law by one or more economic operators. In Europe, many of the collective redress mechanisms developed in recent years have an ADR component, the most prominent regime being the Dutch mass tort settlement action.[1] The groups are usually through appointing a representative (either a public body or private law institution) to negotiate on behalf of the plaintiffs who have suffered harm.

This consensual approach to the compensation of mass harm contrasts with the approach taken in the US, where collective ADR has developed by adapting the pre-existing class mechanism, used in court based civil procedure to arbitrations.[2] In the US, class arbitration is based on the class litigation rule contained in the Federal Rules of Civil Procedure.[3]

How then does collective ADR fit into the EU law enforcement landscape? First, many of the activities causing harm to groups in Europe are sanctioned by public enforcement authorities under EU law, whether the sanctions are administered directly by EU institutions (as in the case of competition law) or indirectly by a Member State's administrative authorities applying powers given to them by EU Regulations and Directives. The outcomes of those enforcement activities are usually binding both on Member States and on the private parties to whom they are addressed.[4]

---

* Vincent Smith is Consultant in Collective Redress and Visiting Fellow of the British Institute of International and Comparative Law. He is also Visiting Professor at ESCP Europe.
[1] *Wet collectieve afwikkeling massaschade*, 16 July 2005, inserted as arts 907–910 of the Dutch Civil Code.
[2] *Bazzle v Green Tree Corp* (2003) 539 USC 444.
[3] United States Federal Rules of Civil Procedure, rule 23.
[4] See Treaty on the Functioning of the European Union (TFEU), art 288, which specifies that decisions of the EU institutions shall be binding on those to whom they are addressed.

Further, EU law requires that effective civil law redress is available in the legal systems of each Member State to allow national courts to remedy breaches of directly effective EU law rights, which may include rights given under Directives which are sufficiently precise and unconditional to be justiciable without Member State legislative intervention.[5] The question of whether the right to an effective remedy includes the procedural possibility of grouping together claims, so as to ensure that a compensation action can effectively be brought, has not yet been directly addressed by the CJEU. In contrast, the European Commission has in its recent Recommendation on collective redress recommended that all Member States should introduce general collective redress mechanisms to ensure the effective application of the EU law requirement of full compensation for harm caused by breach of a directly effective EU rule.[6]

EU institutions have also encouraged alternative dispute resolution as a means of ensuring compliance with, and the availability of, redress for breaches of EU law. In particular, Directive 2008/52/EC requires Member States to ensure an adequate opportunity for mediation in commercial and consumer law matters in order to provide an effective means for consumers to obtain compensation (or other remedy) for breaches of EU-sourced consumer protection legislation.[7] Similarly, the Directive[8] on compensation for victims of EU competition law infringements contains requirements for Member States to ensure that their national rules governing civil recovery also permit ADR.[9]

How then, do these three elements: the public enforcement of EU law in a number of areas; the EU Recommendation on collective redress (and other EU legislation to facilitate effective access to redress under EU law); and the encouragement of ADR at an EU level all fit together in theory and in practice?

---

[5] A principle (called 'vertical direct effect') first set out by the CJEU in Case 41/74 *Van Duyn v Home Office* [1974] ECR 1337.

[6] Commission Recommendation on common principles for injunctive and compensatory collective redress mechanisms in the Member States concerning violations of rights granted under Union law, 11 June 2013, 2013/396/EU, OJ (2013) L 201/60, Recital 10.

[7] Directive 2008/52/EC of the European Parliament and of the Council of 21 May 2008 on certain aspects of mediation in civil and commercial matters, OJ (2008) L136/3.

[8] Directive 2014/104/EU of the European Parliament and of the Council of 26 November 2014 on certain rules governing actions for damages under national law for infringements of the competition law provisions of the Member States and of the European Union, OJ (2014) L 349, 1–19 ('Damages Directive').

[9] Damages Directive, arts 18–19.

II. WHEN CAN COLLECTIVE ADR AND PUBLIC ENFORCEMENT OF
EU LAW INTERACT?

Both the procedural and substantive aspects of the interface between collective ADR and public administrative enforcement of EU law may give rise to difficulties. Procedural concerns may arise at the effect of collective redress actions (including collective ADR) during an ongoing public enforcement investigation. There is also a need to ensure that, later in the process, the decision of the public authorities is not undermined by inconsistency with any collective redress ADR action.

Both of these procedural aspects of the public investigation/private action interface have most prominently been dealt with in competition law claims – mainly at the interface between national court proceedings and public enforcement – in the Commission Recommendation, and in the Damages Directive and related case law, both of which will be examined below.[10]

Substantive overlap is likely to occur in those policy areas where EU law is directly enforced by the EU or national institutions. The private enforcement of competition law is the most prominent of these areas. However, collective ADR will also be (or become) very relevant in compensating victims of mass breaches of EU consumer law, environmental law, and also – in all probability – many aspects of the burgeoning EU intervention in financial services regulation, especially those which impact 'retail' markets.[11]

III. DEVELOPMENT OF EU LAW ON ADR AND REDRESS BY THE CJEU

Until the very recent legislative interventions by the EU institutions, EU law dealing both with the interface between ADR and EU law enforcement, and with the rights of private parties to redress for breaches of directly effective EU law, was exclusively developed by the CJEU, mainly in the course of its dialogue with national courts under Article 267 TFEU. There is limited case law on ADR in EU law and a rather larger body of jurisprudence on the right of private parties to redress. To date, however, the two strands have yet to properly knit together.

The Court has confirmed that arbitrators (and therefore necessarily mediators) are not "national courts" within the definition of Art 267 TFEU, as they do not derive their powers from the exercise of State authority, but rather from the agreement of the parties.[12] It follows from this that arbitral

---

[10] *Ibid*, eg Recitals 11–13, 21, 25–26, 32, 34, 38, arts 6, 7, 9, 11(4).
[11] The Recommendation gives an indicative list of areas where collective ADR is likely to be most useful in Recital 7.
[12] Case 102/81, *Nordsee Deutsche Hochseefischerei v Rederei Mond* [1982] ECR 1095.

tribunals are not required, nor even permitted, to make a preliminary ruling request to the CJEU. If a novel question of EU law arises during arbitration proceedings, the arbitral tribunal must therefore seek to resolve it on its own motion.

However, it does not follow that the CJEU has no locus to intervene in arbitration proceedings – in the wider sense of proceedings leading to the final resolution of a dispute. Where a party seeks to enforce an arbitral award in the courts of an EU Member State, the enforcing court(s) are required – if necessary of their own motion[13] – to consider whether the award complies with directly effective EU law norms. The CJEU has confirmed that compliance EU competition law (at least) is a matter of public policy for the courts in each EU Member State and overrides any contrary provisions of national laws on the enforcement of arbitration awards.[14] Consequently, in case of doubt, an enforcing court will be able, or even required,[15] to make a reference to the CJEU in Luxembourg. Given the reputational damage to the arbitral process, and the likely additional delay and expense caused by such a reference, most arbitrators will do their utmost to ensure compliance with EU law when presented with a relevant question of a disputed EU law.

The jurisprudence of the CJEU on the right to redress is considerably more developed, and perhaps leads to a more satisfactory outcome in practice. The competition context has again provided the basis for the CJEU to develop the basic principles in this area and the recent legislation and guidance from the EU institutions are based on them. Perhaps surprisingly it was not until 2001, in the *Courage v Crehan* decision,[16] that the CJEU confirmed that the general principle of effectiveness in EU law required Member States to interpret existing law, or create additional provisions to ensure that anyone suffering harm as a result of a breach of EU competition law must be entitled to money compensation for the harm caused to them. This was the case even where – as in the *Crehan* case – the claimant was party to the agreement, which contained the unlawful restriction of competition. The previous English law rule, which prevented any recovery by a party to an unlawful agreement in all circumstances, could not be applied; the national court had to have the power to award compensation (with a discretion to reduce it if

---

[13] The consent of the parties to the reference is not a requirement of EU law – eg *R v Secretary of State for the Home Department* [1994] 4 All ER 352.

[14] Case C-126/97 *Eco Swiss China Time v Benetton International* [1999] ECR I-3055.

[15] Art 267 requires national courts whose decision are not amenable to appeal to refer a question of interpretation of EU law unless the answer is irrelevant to the issue before them, the question has already been decided by the CJEU or the answer is so obvious as to admit of only one answer, Case 283/81 *CILFIT v Ministero della Sanita* [1982] ECR 3415.

[16] Case C-453/99 *Courage Ltd v Bernard Crehan* [2001] ECR 6297.

appropriate to reflect any culpability by the claimant for the infringement in question).[17] The CJEU has also set out the heads of loss which must be compensated by the national court in a competition claim[18] – in addition to the 'raw' harm caused (*damnum emergens*), the national court must also be able to compensate successful claimants for loss of profit (*lucrum cessans*) and the time value of money (interest) between the infringement and judgment.[19]

In addition to the general EU law principle of effectiveness, the CJEU has also developed the EU "right to redress," using its sister principle of equivalence – procedural rights available to enforce national laws must also be available to claimants wishing to rely on their directly effective EU law rights. In particular, all means of discovery or compelled disclosure of documents available under national laws – even as against public authorities (such as national competition authorities) – must also be allowed for the enforcement of EU law rights.[20] Using the example of Germany, since documents would be accessible to claimants if an investigation had been carried out under domestic German competition law, the *Bundeskartellamt* could be required to allow a claimant in a German court access to its file when it carries out an investigation into breaches of Article 101 TFEU (as it is entitled to do under Regulation 1/2003),[21] even though the same documents held by the European Commission following an Article 101 investigation would not be accessible to the claimant.

So, the CJEU has created a right to money compensation for harm caused by breach of directly effective EU law, a framework for calculating its amount, and the means for claimants to gain access to at least some of the evidence needed to mount a successful claim.

IV. HOW HAS THE POSITION CHANGED WITH THE 'NEW' LEGISLATIVE PACKAGE?

The Recommendation and Directive on damages in competition cases build on the case law of the CJEU. However, in some respects – particularly on access to evidence – [22] the new legislation appears to be a backward step for claimants' rights. Similarly, although both the Recommendation and the

---

[17] *Ibid*, para 36.
[18] Case C-295/04, *Vincenzo Manfredi v Lloyd Adriatico Assicurazione SpA* [2006] ECR I-6619.
[19] *Ibid*, para 100.
[20] Case C-360/09 *Pfleiderer AG v Bundeskartellamt* [2011] ECR I-5161.
[21] Council Regulation (EC) 1/2003 of 16 December 2002 on the implementation of the rules on competition laid down in arts 81 and 82 [now 101 and 102] of the Treaty, OJ (2003) L 1, 1–25. art 5.
[22] Damages Directive, art 7.

Directive have provisions relating to ADR, they both take only fairly tentative steps towards creating a coherent EU framework, which properly takes account of ADR as a means of promoting collective redress.

Although the Recommendation covers the full spectrum of directly effective EU law, as it is a Recommendation it has no binding force under the Treaties. In contrast, the Directive has binding force on Member States (as of the date when it is due to be transposed into national law), but it only deals with claims for breach of Article 101 and 102 TFEU, not specifically collective claims, nor those in other areas of EU law. However, despite these limitations, the principles set out in both of these instruments will, it is suggested, be a good guide for national courts, as well as arbitrators and mediators, on how to approach the issues raised by the EU public enforcement/arbitration interface.

As the more general of the two instruments, the Recommendation appears – perhaps paradoxically – to be the more important. It recommends that:

> The Member States should ensure that judicial collective redress mechanisms are accompanied by appropriate means of collective alternative dispute resolution available to the parties before and throughout the litigation. Use of such means should depend on the consent of the parties involved in the case.[23]

This is an important development on the current situation, as EU law did not address the need for collective ADR mechanisms, and not all Member States have such a procedure.[24] It is also noteworthy to mention that collective ADR, cited in the Recommendation, should be available to accompany court based collective redress; it is unlikely to be sufficient for Member States to rely on existing ADR opportunities designed solely for bilateral and/or out-of-court situations.

Also worthy of note in the Recommendation is that collective ADR should be possible not only before any collective court proceedings, but also during those proceedings. This implies that the types of ADR covered include not only those which give rise to negotiated contractual settlement (eg mediation), but also those which lead to outcomes equivalent to a court judgment (ie arbitration), and can therefore take the place of a judgment within the scope of the parties' arbitration agreement.

The Recommendation also indicates that Member States should provide for a suspension of any applicable time limits in civil court proceedings for

---

[23] Recommendation, para 26.
[24] See the Study *Collective redress in Antitrust*, Lear and University of Trent, commissioned by the European Parliament Committee on Economic and Monetary Affairs, June 2012, IP/A/ECON/ST/2011-19, PE 475.120, http://www.europarl.europa.eu/studies, 18–19.

the duration of a party's involvement in an ADR process – that is, until one or both of them (expressly) withdraw from the process.[25] This may go a significant way towards addressing the procedural issues in the public enforcement/private ADR interface noted above. Where public enforcement proceedings are underway, the Damages Directive now provides for extended time limits where time would run out so that the claimant will have at least one year after the public enforcement decision is made to bring a compensation claim.[26] It follows that any ADR process will further extend this fallback limitation period.

The case law of the CJEU,[27] the procedural law on public enforcement – notably Article 16 of Regulation 1/2003 – as well as the 'soft law' which surrounds it,[28] appear only to apply to the relationship between public enforcement and the proceedings before national courts. Arbitral tribunals are therefore not formally part of the system of co-operation set up under the public enforcement regime.[29] However, since the law which governs their proceedings (assuming they sit in an EU Member State) incorporates EU law, they will need to ensure that the conduct of their arbitral proceedings is consistent with directly effective EU law rules.[30]

Article 16 has two relevant branches. Firstly, national courts may not give a judgment which runs counter to a decision already made by the European Commission. Secondly, they should avoid taking decisions which would conflict with any Commission decision in an investigation which has already been started. Exactly how far do these two principles apply to arbitrators?

It appears uncontroversial that an arbitral award should comply with the first branch and not run counter to any existing EC decision. This is particularly true where parties to the arbitration agreement are also addressees of the EC decision – although, given the breadth of findings in some Commission cases, care is also likely to be needed where there is simply a possible substantive overlap between the decision findings and the subject matter of the arbitration. Indeed the Recommendation itself provides that:

---

[25] Recommendation, para 27.
[26] Damages Directive, art 10(4).
[27] Case C-344/98 *Masterfoods v HB Ice Cream* [2000] ECR I-11369, para 60, which refers only to national courts. Article 16 of Regulation 1/2003 (n 21 above), which codifies this jurisprudence, similarly only applies to national courts.
[28] In particular Commission Notice on the co-operation between the Commission and the EU Member States in the application of Articles [101] and [102], 27 April 2004, OJ (2004) C 101/54, para 1.
[29] See eg *Nordsee* (n 12 above); case C-516/99 *Schmid* [2002] ECR I-4573.
[30] See the discussion in R Nazzini, *Concurrent Proceedings in Competition Law* (OUP, 2004) at Chapter 11, esp. at 351–353.

> The legality of the binding outcome of a collective settlement should be verified by the courts taking into consideration the appropriate protection of interests and rights of all parties involved.[31]

A national court endorsement of a collective settlement (by way of mediation or arbitration) which ignores that court's duties under Article 16, would not be a proper 'verification of the legality' of the settlement embodied in the mediated agreement or the arbitral award. Consequently the enforcement order would likely be set aside on appeal.

The position appears less clear-cut in relation to the second point (ongoing Commission investigations). Firstly, national courts have taken the view that this second point does not prevent them from taking steps in civil proceedings before them short of giving judgment, if they consider it appropriate,[32] a position which appears consistent with the wording of Article 16 and which should also be respected by arbitrators. But can an arbitrator lawfully make a final award in relation to a claim where a Commission investigation is ongoing? This should depend on the gravity of the perceived risk of conflict concerning the possible outcome of the investigation.

The most common example will be collective ADR proceedings by a group including one or more undertakings being investigated by the Commission for having participated in cartel activities contrary to Article 101 TFEU. The fact that those undertakings are willing to engage in (consensual) ADR with a collective claimant should give the mediator or arbitrator at least some comfort that there is a *prima facie* liability for breach of Article 101, in which case it is unlikely that the Commission would make a finding that there is no infringement at all. Furthermore, it is the near invariable practice of the Commission in making infringement decisions against cartels to do so on the basis of finding the cartel has infringed Article 101 by object. In contrast, the outcome of the ADR will necessarily have to address the issue of harm to the claimant group, and would therefore address the effect of the practice on competition. It is difficult to conceive how any outcome making a finding relating to effect could conflict with a Commission object finding – which would not address the question of effect at all – in the same case.

However, in the less likely situation where the impending outcome of a collective ADR process against a cartel might *not* award any compensation to the group at all, it would be prudent to suspend the ADR to allow consideration of the detail of the Commission's final decision when given. A finding of "no effect" from the practices examined by the arbitrator might well conflict

---

[31] Recommendation, para 28.
[32] An example is in England, *National Grid Electricity Transmission v ABB Ltd and Others* [2009] EWHC 1326 (Ch) where disclosure of documents was ordered even during the stay of pending appeals against the Commission's decision.

with the Commission's possible finding that there is a cartel infringement by object. There is a strong presumption that cartels will have an effect on competition and therefore cause harm.[33] The implication of a finding of no effect at all is the equivalent of ruling that a cartel does not exist and hence conflicting with a possible outcome of the European public enforcement proceedings.

Further, where the collective ADR process relates to practices which would need to include a finding of effect on competition to cement the infringement (for example alleged abuse under Article 102 TFEU), the interface becomes considerably more complex. It is unlikely that a collective ADR process could sensibly be concluded before the Commission's decision is available.

The question of what a mediator or arbitrator should do if faced with the possibility that a consensual collective settlement may conflict with the outcome of EU public enforcement proceedings will not, of course, be limited to the competition sphere. As the discussion above shows, it will be difficult to set out hard and fast rules as to how the ADR process should proceed, if at all. Much will depend on the gravity and imminence of the potential conflict, which is necessarily fact specific.

The Commission itself may also wish to take account of ongoing collective ADR proceedings when reaching its own decision. The competition Damages Directive now expressly allows competition authorities in the EU[34] (including the Commission) to take account of compensation paid as a result of a consensual settlement, which therefore includes collective ADR. [35] This implies first that the Commission should be made aware of the collective ADR proceedings by the parties if they wish to consider whether to take up this possibility, and second, that the Directive envisages that ADR can indeed conclude before the Commission has reached a decision in the related public enforcement action. There would not appear to be anything in principle to prevent the Commission or national authorities from adopting a similar approach in other policy areas where public enforcement of EU law is carried out.

V. WHAT FORMS OF ADR CAN BE 'SETTLEMENTS'?

The emphasis put on the benefits of 'consensual settlement'[36] by the EU and the advantages to parties who engage with ADR – as regards their exposure

---

[33] See Damages Directive, art 17(2) and Commission Communication on quantifying harm in actions for damages based on breaches of Article 101 or 102 of the TFEU (2013/C 167/07), OJ (2013) C 167/19, 140–145.

[34] Damages Directive, art 18(3).

[35] See the discussion of the meaning of 'settlement' in this context below and also more generally on the interface between arbitration and public enforcement, Nazzini (above n 30) 369–375.

[36] Recommendation, para 25; Damages Directive, Recital 51.

to damages to other claimants and co-defendants,[37] and also as possible mitigation of any public enforcement penalty – indicate that the importance placed on deciding what ADR processes are within the scope of the term 'settlement' has significantly increased.

The answer to this is not assisted by the Recommendation and the Damages Directive in adopting a somewhat different terminology in this area. The Recommendation provisions talk of 'collective alternative dispute resolution' and 'settlements',[38] whereas the Damages Directive uses the terms 'consensual dispute resolution' and 'consensual settlement.'[39]

If we focus on the two main 'assisted' ADR processes, mediation and arbitration, it is apparent that an agreement between the parties reached with the assistance of a mediator falls within all of the descriptions above. However, there may be more doubt in the case of an arbitration award. Although clearly within the ambit of alternative dispute resolution, it is not immediately obvious that an arbitral award – which may have been made after a lengthy and hard fought process – is a 'settlement,' nor that it is of a 'consensual' nature.

However, arbitration can only come about with the consent of the parties. In many cases, where public enforcement of EU law is accompanied by arbitration proceedings, there will be no pre-existing contractual nexus between the parties to the arbitration. For example, victims seeking compensation from a cartel may well be unaware that the cartel existed before the public enforcement proceedings, and may not have purchased directly from members of the cartel. Any arbitration agreement will therefore have been made 'after the event' with a view to reaching a 'settlement,' but accompanied by the undoubted benefits of an arbitral award, especially international enforceability under the New York Convention.[40]

The Damages Directive has defined the relevant terms as follows:[41]

(21) 'consensual dispute resolution' means any mechanism enabling the parties to reach the out-of-court resolution of a dispute concerning a claim for damages;

---

[37] The Damages Directive sets out fairly detailed rules (in art 19) which require an enforcing court to reduce the claimants' continuing claim by the share of damages represented by the settling defendant and to release the settling defendant from further liability (including from co-infringers). There are some exceptions to this rule.

[38] Recommendation, para 25 and in particular its heading – "*Collective alternative dispute resolution and settlements*".

[39] Damages Directive, art 2(21) and art 2(22).

[40] United Nations Conference on International Commercial Arbitration, Convention on the recognition and enforcement of foreign arbitral awards, New York, 1958, 330 UNTS 38 ('New York Convention').

[41] See n 39.

(22) 'consensual settlement' means an agreement reached through consensual dispute resolution;

Arbitration proceedings are clearly within the scope of the definition of 'consensual dispute resolution.' What is less clear is whether arbitration can be a 'consensual settlement.' It appears from the wording of the Directive that the 'consensual dispute resolution' mechanism, which has enabled the parties to reach an out-of-court settlement of their dispute, must have operated before the agreement constituting the settlement is formed. But an arbitral award (after the agreement to arbitrate) will not necessarily be agreed to by all of the parties to the arbitration. If it were agreed to, the award would probably not have been made, as the matter would have been resolved earlier by negotiation.

However, this interpretation may be unduly strained. The arbitral award is clearly achieved as a result of an agreement between the parties to arbitrate, and it is at least implied (although, perhaps better in this context, made expressly in the submission agreement) that they agree to abide by the arbitrator's findings even if they are adverse to their own interests. The 'settlement' is delegated by agreement to a third party, the arbitrator, and all parties agree to abide by the award after it is given. This view is reinforced by the New York Convention (to which all EU Member States are signatories) which defines its scope as covering:

> ... all or any differences which have arisen [...] between [the parties] in respect of a defined legal relationship, whether contractual or not, concerning a subject matter capable of *settlement by arbitration* (emphasis added).[42]

In any event, an important general principle of EU law is that all EU legislation should be interpreted so as to give useful effect to EU law in accordance with the legislation's general purpose, and therefore to avoid complex 'black letter' interpretations.[43] The useful effect of the Damages Directive's provision on ADR would likely be undermined if an important and well respected method of resolving disputes out-of-court were excluded due to an overly close interpretation of the Directive's text.

The same considerations apply to the use of the term 'settlement' in the Recommendation. On any sensible purposive reading, the 'settlements' described should include arbitral awards following express consent to submit to arbitration to resolve a dispute.

---

[42] New York Convention, art II.1.
[43] See eg *Garland v British Rail Engineering* [1983] 2AC 751 (House of Lords) per Lord Diplock at 771 A-B; Case 14/83, *von Colson v Nordrhein-Westfalen* [1984] ECR 1891 and subsequent case law.

VI. CONCLUSIONS

From an unpromising start in the *Nordsee* case,[44] the role of ADR in the overall scheme of EU law enforcement has become increasingly recognised. As the profile of ADR as a useful part of the enforcement landscape increases, the importance of issues concerning the way in which ADR – and collective ADR in particular, given its place in supporting redress for groups of individual (eg consumer) victims of EU law breaches – will also increase.

The new legislative initiatives launched by the Commission and by EU legislation have taken steps towards addressing the most obvious areas of potential friction. However, more remains to be done and it is likely that the CJEU will continue to play a prominent role in the development of the law in this area. However, unlike the dialogue between the CJEU and the national courts, a dialogue between arbitrators and the CJEU (and other EU institutions) is lacking and probably unlikely.

This relatively low degree of information and dialogue is probably due to the confidential nature of many ADR proceedings, but it is to be hoped that the new impetus given by the European institutions to ADR,[45] in parallel with the public enforcement effort, will encourage arbitration institutes and other representative bodies to cooperate with the Commission in order to improve the workings of an EU ADR system which is currently still being crafted.

---

[44] Case 102/81, see (n 12 above).
[45] Through possible mitigation of administrative fines for infringers who use ADR to give compensation to victims – see Damages Directive art 17(2) and n 34 above.

Finnish and Swedish Legislation in Light of the ADR Directive – Boards and Ombudsmen

*Laura Ervo and Annina H. Persson**

I. EU REGULATION

A. Introduction

On 21 May 2013, two new EU legal instruments regarding alternative dispute resolutions for consumers were approved, namely the Directive 2013/11/EU on alternative dispute resolution for consumers disputes (ADR Directive)[1] and the Regulation on online dispute resolution for consumer disputes (ODR Regulation).[2] The new legislation will allow consumers and traders to resolve their disputes through an out-of-court procedure in a simple, quick, and inexpensive manner. According to Article 1, the purpose of the ADR Directive is to contribute to the proper functioning of the internal market – through the achievement of a high level of consumer protection – by ensuring that consumers can, on a voluntary basis, submit complaints against traders to entities offering independent, impartial, transparent, effective, fast, and fair alternative dispute resolution procedures. Enacted as a complement to the directive, the purpose of the ODR Regulation is to give consumers access to an online platform available across the EU, which will help consumers contact an ADR entity when disputes arises from online cross-border transactions. Given that the Directive must be implemented by 9 July 2015 at the latest, and that the ODR platform will be operational on 9 January 2016, the purpose of this article is, first, to give a brief overview on how Finland and Sweden are going to implement the new legislation.

---

* Professor of Procedural Law, Örebro University; Professor of Private Law, Örebro University.
[1] Directive 2013/11/EU of the European Parliament and of the Council of 21 May 2013 on alternative dispute resolution for consumer disputes and amending Regulation (EC) No 2006/2004 and Directive 2009/22/EC.
[2] Regulation (EU) No 524/2013 of the European Parliament and of the Council of 21 May 2013 on online dispute resolution for consumer disputes and amending Regulation (EC) No 2006/2004 and Directive 2009/22/EC.

Secondly, a brief comment will be made on how the two countries will handle the Recommendation of the European Commission on collective redress.[3] Thirdly, we will present the role of different Scandinavian boards in dispute resolutions, notably the role of the ombudsmen in this regard. Finally, we will comment on how the ADR system currently functions in practice and how it will be designed in the future.

B. *The ADR Directive and the ODR Regulation*

As a result of the new EU legislation, the Swedish government initiated an inquiry on 28 February 2013[4] examining appropriate measures to ensure that consumers have access to convenient and cost-effective out-of-court dispute settlement mechanisms. A proposal was delivered in June 2014.[5] It presented a new Law (2014: XX) on alternative dispute resolution for consumer relationships, which is set to come into force on 1 July 2015. Furthermore, several amendments will be made to the Ordinance for the Swedish National Board for Consumer Disputes,[6] to the Ordinance for the Consumer Agency,[7] and to the Law regarding the Market Court.[8]

In Finland, a committee has been created to research and decide how to implement both the Directive and the Regulation. Their deadline was intended to be the end of 2014, however there are still no substantive instructions on how to properly implement the ADR Directive, nor the ODR Regulation.

Both Finland and Sweden already have a good system for handling out-of-court consumer disputes, primarily through their respective National Boards for Consumer Disputes.[9] However, the Directive contains rules that address the quality of the procedure itself and the activities of the dispute resolution body to which it applies (Article 5-11 ADR Directive). These provisions not only concern the National Board for Consumer Disputes in both countries, but also self-regulatory bodies of the industry that may be approved as ADR entities under the Directive in the future. In both Finland and Sweden, there already exist many alternative boards to resolve disputes in consumer matters like the Consumer Disputes Board, as well as the Insurance, Banking, and Securities Complaints Boards. The Finnish committee which is currently

---

[3] Commission Recommendation of 11 June 2013 on common principles for injunctive and compensatory collective redress mechanisms in the Member States concerning violations of rights granted under Union law (2013/396/EU), OJ L 201, 26.7.2013, 60–65.

[4] Directive 2013:23. *Hantering av konsumenttvister utanför domstol.*

[5] SOU 2014: 47. *Förbättrad tvistlösning på konsumentområdet – ny EU-lagstiftning och en översyn av det svenska systemet.*

[6] See Ordinance 2007:1041, amended 2009:608, and 2011:617, 916.

[7] See Ordinance 2009:607, amended 2011:1218.

[8] See SFS 1970:417.

[9] In Finland *Konsumenttvistenämnden* and in Sweden *Allmänna reklamationsnämnden*.

working on how to implement the Directive and the Regulation, wants especially to ensure that alternative dispute resolution is organized in an effective and reasonable way in terms of insurance.[10] This seems to imply that the duties and procedures of the Insurance Complaint Board will be reformed thanks to the new EU Regulation.[11]

The Directive also contains other provisions which require States to implement new provisions. These provisions concern the obligation for traders to inform consumers about ADR (Article 13 ADR Directive) and about the impact of ADR on limitation and prescription periods (Article 12 ADR Directive). The procedure for approval and supervision of ADR entities must also be regulated (Article 19 ADR Directive). In order to make it transparent and clear, all provisions concerning the ADR Directive and ODR Regulation will be compiled into a new law in Sweden.[12] Thus, the Directive will be implemented in Sweden, mainly through the new proposed law, but also through amendments made to the Ordinance regarding the National Board for Consumer Disputes.[13] In doing so, its activities will also generally be adapted to comply with the Directive.

The ADR Directive requires that consumers have access to alternative dispute resolution for all kinds of consumer disputes. According to Article 2 of the Directive, it applies to domestic and cross-border disputes concerning contractual obligations stemming from sales contracts or service contracts between a trader established in the EU and a consumer resident in the EU. However, certain disputes do not fall within the scope of the Directive, ie those regarding health services provided by health professionals to patients to assess, maintain, or restore their state of health and those concerning public providers of further or higher education. In order to comply with the Directive, the Swedish National Board for Consumer Disputes must extend the scope of competence to certain types of disputes that, in the current situation, are exempted from the Board's competence. The scope of competence must apply to disputes regarding categories such as art and antiques, telephone and electricity supplies, games, lotteries, plants, food, certain disputes over leasing of immovable property, and disputes concerning heat pumps. Some of these disputes are currently handled by self-regulatory bodies created by the industry. However, as these disputes fall within the scope of the Directive, the self-regulatory bodies must meet the demands of EU legislation and become authorized if they are to continue their activities and therefore serve as a

---

[10] http://oikeusministerio.fi/fi/index/valmisteilla/lakihankkeet/velvoiteoikeusjakuluttajansuoja/vaihtoehtoinenkuluttajariitojenratkaisu.html.
[11] *Ibid.*
[12] See SOU 2014:47, 300.
[13] See SOU 2014:47, 299.

complement to the Board. If not, these disputes will have to fall under the scope of competence of the Board.[14] In Finland, the situation is simpler since the decisions of the Finnish Consumer Disputes Board already cover all consumer products, as well as certain disputes in both the areas of banking and housing.[15]

Furthermore, the ADR Directive requires ADR entities to establish pre-specified monetary thresholds in order to limit access to ADR procedures. However, the thresholds cannot be set to a level which impairs consumer access to complaint services provided by ADR entities.

The Swedish National Board for Consumer Disputes currently only examines disputes exceeding a certain value. Currently, the threshold is 500 SEK if the dispute concerns shoes, textiles, etc. If the dispute concerns electronics, motor vehicles, travel etc, the threshold is set at 1000 SEK. If the matter concerned falls under banking, housing, insurance, etc., the threshold is 2000 SEK. Given the increasing supply of low-priced products, the inquiry believed that there is a strong interest among consumers in bringing small-value complaints against traders. In this context, the abovementioned proposal suggested that the Directive require the limits to be lowered from current levels. The proposed thresholds are now 300 SEK instead of 500 SEK, 600 SEK instead of 1000 SEK, and 1000 SEK instead of 2000 SEK.[16] In Finland, no such limits exist.[17]

The ADR Directive also requires the introduction of provisions into Swedish law regarding an obligation for traders to provide consumers with information about ADR. All traders who have a dispute with a consumer shall be required, when the trader opposes the claim, to provide the consumer with information on the ADR entity, which the consumer can use to bring his claim. Furthermore, a new obligation is introduced for an entrepreneur who has committed himself to use ADR to resolve disputes with consumers to provide general information before a dispute arises outlining which method of ADR he would use.[18]

The ODR Regulation also implies further specific provisions on the obligation for traders who engage in online trading to inform consumers of the presence of the European online platform. Such information shall be provided on the business's website, in the written terms of the contract between the trader and the consumer and also be offered by e-mail. A trader who does not give information under the new disclosure requirements will be subject to legal sanctions under the 2008 Swedish Marketing Act.

---

[14] Cf art 20 and art 5–12 ADR Directive.
[15] The Act on the Consumer Disputes Board, Chapter 1, Section 2.
[16] See SOU 2014:47, 213–219.
[17] See the Act on the Consumer Disputes Board.
[18] See SOU 2014:47, 264–280.

The Swedish National Board of Consumer Disputes estimates that the number of cases will increase due to the new EU legislation. Therefore, a number of measures are proposed to streamline and improve the management practices at the Board. For example, changes will be introduced regarding general grounds for inadmissibility.[19] Another change is that the Board must be able to try a case within 90 days.[20] The result will be an increase in demand for resources, as the time to settle a dispute is presently around 180 days.[21] A third change is that the Board must inform the parties when the case is ready to be decided.[22] A fourth category of modifications to be made are the technical and practical improvements in order for the Board to adhere to the new EU legislation.[23] The Board must improve its handling routines and enhance its internal organization.[24]

The Swedish National Board of Consumer Disputes will also begin providing settlement mechanisms to the parties,[25] if it is not inappropriate as a result of the character of the case.[26] Consumers who choose to apply to the Board will therefore generally be able to get help to achieve an amicable solution.

C. The EU Recommendation on Common Principles for Injunctive and Compensatory Collective Redress

On 11 June 2013, the European Commission published its Recommendation on common principles for injunctive and compensatory collective redress mechanisms in the Member States concerning violations of rights granted under Union law (2013/396/EU). The key issues in the Recommendation are questions regarding: (1) the constitution of the claimant party by opt-in or opt-out systems; (2) the criteria for recognition or admissibility of a representative body to bring an action on behalf of a class or collective group; (3) permitted methods for funding; (4) the rules on costs and contingency fees; (5) mechanisms for both injunctive and compensatory

---

[19] Cf art 5.4 ADR Directive; SOU 2014:47, 204–226.
[20] Cf art 8.e ADR Directive.
[21] See SOU 2014:47, 241–245, compare 75.
[22] See SOU 2014:47, 243 and cf art 8.d. ADR Directive.
[23] See art 15 ADR Directive.
[24] See SOU 2014:47, 313–355.
[25] Compare mediation mechanisms in civil cases in court. According to Chapter 42, Section 1 of the Code of Judicial Procedure 7, if the matter at issue is amenable to an out-of-court settlement, the court shall, to the extent appropriate considering the nature of the case and other circumstances, work for the parties to reach a settlement. If, considering the nature of the case, it is more appropriate that special mediation occur, the court can direct the parties to appear at a mediation session before a mediator appointed by the court.
[26] See SOU 2014:47, 332–337.

relief and questions regarding punitive damages; and (6) cross-border collective redress. The Member States are obliged to implement the principles set out in the Recommendation in their respective national collective redress systems by 26 July 2015 at the latest. They should also collect reliable annual statistics on the number of out-of-court and judicial collective redress procedures, information about the parties, the subject matter and the outcome of the cases. The Member States must then communicate the information collected to the Commission on an annual basis starting on 26 July 2016. The Commission will then assess whether Member States have implemented the provisions of the Recommendation by 26 July 2017 at the latest.

According to the Swedish Justice department, the Commission Recommendation on collective redress for consumers has not yet resulted in any new inquiry to propose changes to the existing Group Proceedings Act.[27] This is not surprising, as most of the points raised in the Recommendation are already fulfilled by the present legislation, as will be seen below. Thus, the Swedish government will probably not legislate further on the matter, with the exception of creating a national registry of collective redress actions.[28]

The Finnish Ministry of Justice has not yet modified the Finnish collective redress mechanism to correspond with the Commission Recommendation, even though Finland needs to make the collective redress system more efficient in practice. However, group actions have been set as one of the medium-term objectives in 2013–25, where it will be determined whether there are possibilities to expand the scope of group actions to also include non-consumer cases. Findings of the study will be assessed in light of the Commission Recommendation. This review will, however, not be launched before the new government enacts it in spring 2015.[29]

The need to develop the group action mechanism is urgent due to the fact that there has not been one group action case in Finland. The reason appears to be that only public group action is allowed, and the only authority which has the competence to sue is the Consumer Ombudsman. Furthermore, group action is limited to consumer cases. Therefore, the scope of group actions, as well as the possibilities to sue and represent the group should be broadened.[30] In Finland there is no registry on group actions, even though there seems to be no need for a registry due to the lack of group action cases. There has been debate in the media on the situation and the Consumer

---

[27] According to Kanslirådet Rebecca Heinemann, 29 September 2014.
[28] See points 35–37 of the Commission Recommendation.
[29] *Oikeudenhoidon uudistamisohjelma vuosille* 2013–2025. OMML 16/2013, 37.
[30] See for instance L Ervo and E Martínez García 'Class action – a solution to access to justice problems in consumer cases?: Some thoughts between the North, South and Europe', in 17 *ZZPInt* (2012) 207–229, at 201.

Ombudsman has been criticised for not bringing group actions, even though there have been situations where a group action would have been a proper instrument for consumers to obtain compensation for damages suffered. However, the requirements to bring a group action suit seem to be rather difficult to satisfy.

The other more severe lack in the group action mechanism is the scope of group actions. In modern society, it is not enough to restrict group actions to only consumer cases, especially due to environmental issues, problems in medical care, or other issues concerning social welfare as well as claims against the State and State authorities.[31] Victims should be allowed to bring group action suits on issues present in modern society.[32] The reason for the narrow scope in Finland has been the active resistance by industry and other businesses. For instance, the Chamber of Commerce has campaigned and continues to campaign strongly against group actions.[33] This type of societal consensus and the resistance of the business sector are the reasons why the scope of the group action only covers consumer cases and not environmental cases, even though it was planned to include the latter, as stated in the working group's report.[34]

D. Welfare State in Crisis?

ADR can be seen as an alternative to court for consumers and can also be seen as a form of privatization, as it is a way for the State to save money and court resources. At least in Finland, this trend seems to be rather transparent and evident on the home page of the Ministry of Justice's website, where the new plans to increase court fees are cited.[35] However, the same conclusion can be made with regard to Sweden.

Improved opportunities for consumers to get their complaints tried through ADR will eventually lead to many positive effects for society and the economy. It can cause a shift towards production of more sustainable products and more reputable services. This is particularly true in sectors with a wide selection of low-priced products such as shoes, clothing, and electronics. If

---

[31] For instance, it was reported on the media that the consumer ombudsman had refused to start a group action in the situation where a huge amount of patients had got a defective hip replacement because s/he has no jurisdiction in such cases, http://www.hs.fi/kotimaa/a1305581561697.

[32] Ervo and Martínez García (above n 30) 210.

[33] http://kauppakamari.fi/2013/06/12/eulta-siedettava-ryhmakannesuositus/.

[34] See more about the legislative history on the Finnish group actions in L Ervo, 'Class actions in consumer cases – a Finnish start' in R Stürner and M Kawano (eds) *Comparative Studies on Business Tort Litigation* (Mohr Siebeck, 2011) 203–212.

[35] http://oikeusministerio.fi/fi/index/valmisteilla/lakihankkeet/oikeudenkayntijaoikeuslaitos/tuomioistuinmaksujakoskevansaantelynuudistaminen.html.

consumers have access to ADR in more areas than before, this option will become favoured over litigation through court. Another positive aspect of ADR is that it is also much cheaper. Under Swedish law, the application fee for court proceedings has increased significantly in the past few years. It is currently at 900 SEK for simplified civil disputes and 2800 SEK for ordinary civil disputes. This can be compared with the previous application fee of 450 SEK. Consumers may now have access to a cost-effective, quick alternative to court proceedings through ADR by the National Board of Consumer disputes, so that courts may allocate resources to be used for cases where there is a real need for litigation.[36]

As mentioned above, there are similar plans in Finland to increase court fees in many ways. First of all, the scope of the payment system will be expanded, and the main rule will require that the plaintiff be charged for court services. However, there will be exceptions to this main rule, due to the requirement to guarantee sufficient legal protection. The objective is also to raise the level of payments towards the cost correlation which should in theory be better than it is at present. The goal is to get 20 percent of the court costs covered directly from court fees paid by litigants. The Ministry of Justice is of the opinion that this could be possible without hindering legal protection. It has even been suggested that court fees be based on the interest of the case. The Ministry of Justice also plans to collect court fees in advance. Still, it remains to be seen what would happen to the case if the fee has not been paid beforehand. At the same time, it has been stressed that payments must not be an obstacle for access to justice, even in the future. Furthermore, the payment system must be simple, clear, consistent and fair.[37]

To reach the goal of 20 percent of total costs of court fees, the payments should be significantly raised. In 2012, the fees were set at 33.7 million euros which covered 13 percent of the expenses.[38] In Sweden, the court fees are very low in comparison to other European nations, and in spite of the rise in costs for court resources for the government over the years, court fees have remained the same. The revenue from application fees represents only 0.8 percent of the total annual budget for Swedish courts.[39]

With changes to the payment system, the economic position of courts will be strengthened. The other aim is to intensify the control effect and use

---

[36] SOU 2014:47, 90 and 412.
[37] http://oikeusministerio.fi/fi/index/valmisteilla/lakihankkeet/oikeudenkayntijaoikeuslaitos/tuomioistuinmaksujakoskevansaantelynuudistaminen.html.
[38] *Tuomioistuinten maksujärjestelmien kehittäminen*, OMML 75/2012.
[39] See Dv rapport 2012:1 (Domstolsverket, *Ansöknings- och kungörandeavgifter vid allmän domstol*) 34, Regeringens proposition 2013/14:1 *Budgetproposition för 2014. Utgiftsområde 4, Rättsväsendet*, 57.

court fees as a sanction mechanism. The control effect will be most intense if the court fee is collected beforehand.[40] With this, the Finnish legislator means to prevent unnecessary suits being brought to court. The intention here is to limit access to court in minor or otherwise 'unnecessary' cases.

Officially, it is said that the objective of the reform is to improve access to courts and legal protection by improving the economic position of courts. This is probably ineffective in terms of improving access to courts, however what is more transparent is the objective to intensify the control effect through higher fees. So, even if the official aim is for plaintiffs to choose alternative forms to resolve their disputes, it appears as if it is privatization in disguise. The more pressing issue is that when the control effect achieved through higher fees is working effectively, the courts are able to focus their resources on cases where the need for legal assistance is greatest. However, it can also be said that court fees can help parties decide whether they should take the case to the court, whether they should apply for appeal, or whether they choose an alternative way of resolving the conflict.[41] Therefore, it seems to be clear that the aim is to reduce the amount of claims presented at court, as well as frequency of access to courts, and to increase the use of alternative methods to resolve disputes. The other issue is whether it will provide access to justice or if it will hinder a plaintiff's access to justice.

II. ARE BOARDS AND OMBUDSMEN AN ALTERNATIVE?

A. Scandinavia – A Wonderland of Boards and Ombudsmen

Traditionally, boards have played a great role in Scandinavia in providing access to justice in rapid and economically efficient ways without resorting to trial. This kind of system is cheap and otherwise simple and less problematic for the plaintiff. The problem, however, is that it does not strengthen the plaintiff's right to access to court and the result is not a judgment, but rather a recommendation, even though the board works more or less like a court. Therefore, the procedure can be seen as a type of conciliation.[42] If the opposite party does not voluntarily follow the recommendation, the winning party must evidently go to court in order to get an enforceable judgment. Therefore, the power of the resolutions made by boards is only 'political,' and such pressure on companies when a consumer has won may

---

[40] OMML 16/2013.
[41] http://oikeusministerio.fi/fi/index/valmisteilla/lakihankkeet/oikeudenkayntijaoikeuslaitos/tuomioistuinmaksujakoskevansaantelynuudistaminen.html.
[42] L Ervo and L Sippel, 'Scandinavian Countries' in C Esplugues, JL Iglesias and G Palao (eds) *Civil and Commercial Mediation in Europe* (Intersentia, 2013) 373.

not be truly effective. In spite of the aforementioned weaknesses, the boards have been useful and the opposing parties normally follow the resolutions.[43]

In Denmark, the Consumer Complaint Board exists, as well as 17 other approved private complaint boards. In addition, there are a number of non-approved private complaint boards. These boards deal with complaints from consumers concerning goods and services provided by business.[44]

Norway is famous for its practice of conciliation. The Conciliation Board was founded in 1795.[45] In the new Code of Civil Proceedings,[46] Chapter 10 contains provisions on processing a case before the Conciliation Boards. Its scope is similar to that of Chapter 21 of the Dispute Act of 1915. However, measures have been taken to make rules simpler, as the rules need to be understood and practiced by non-lawyers.[47] The Conciliation Board aids the parties to achieve a simple, swift, and inexpensive resolution of a case through conciliation or judgment and it is a mandatory step to be taken before ordinary court proceedings with exceptions in certain situations.[48] The purpose of the board is to provide a simple and inexpensive way to resolve disputes.[49]

In Finland, the group action mechanism was first introduced by a consumer complaint board in 2007, and its late introduction in Scandinavian law is due to Scandinavian significance and tradition of using boards in consumer cases. However, only a public group complaint is allowed. Before the reform in March 2007, only single complaints were possible. If a recommendation issued by the Consumer Complaint Board is not respected, the Consumer Ombudsman can take the matter to court as a group action.[50]

---

[43] K Viitanen, *Lautakuntamenettely kuluttajariitojen ratkaisukeinona* (Suomalainen Lakimiesyhdistys, 2003) 438.

[44] More information can be found at www.ukecc-services.net/dkadr.cfm.

[45] J Hov, *Rettergang III. Sivilprosess* (Papinian, 2000) 46.

[46] The parliament accepted the new legislation for civil proceedings on 17 June, 2005. The new Code of Civil Proceedings and Mediation came into force on 1 January, 2008.

[47] *Rett på sak. Lov om tvisteløsning (tvisteloven)*, NOU 2001:32. More information on the old procedure before the Conciliation Board in JEA Skoghøy *Tvistemål* (2nd ed. Universitetsforlaget, 2001), 469–486.

[48] According to the Code of Civil Proceedings, Chapter 10, Section 2, Paragraph 2 the Municipal Court is not allowed to try a case before the Conciliation Board has tried it. The exceptions to this rule are mentioned in the same paragraph. These exceptions include, for instance, situations where the amount of the monetary claim is at least 125 000 NOK and both parties have used advocates or if the non-judiciary mediation according to Chapter 7 of the Code has already been done. For more on the conciliation system, see, for instance Hov (above n 45) 46–59 and Skoghøy (above n 47) 56–62.

[49] Ot.prp.nr 51 (2004–2005), 383.

[50] S Laukkanen 'Last trends in the Finnish civil procedure and judicial administration' in Simaitis R, *The Recent Tendencies of Development in Civil Procedure Law – Between East and West*. International Conference to Celebrate the 100th Anniversary of the Birth of Professor Jonas Žėruolis (Vilnius, 2007) 72–82, at 81.

Together with the reform in March 2007, the competence of the Consumer Complaints Board (CCB) was broadened to include certain housing matters as well.[51] The procedural rules of the CCB do not completely mirror those of court proceedings. Thus, the definitions of the demand are not exactly the same. However, the CCB decides if multiple complaints can be resolved in one decision.[52]

In Sweden, there is the National Board of Consumer Disputes, as well as several private self-regulatory bodies for ADR. The Consumer Ombudsman can act as a representative of an individual consumer before an ordinary court in proceedings between a consumer and a business operative. According to a proposal for a new law, the Consumer Ombudsman will be able to take over a consumer claim for damages against a trader and thus intervene as a party to the dispute. This opportunity may be utilized when a Consumer Ombudsman believes that a decision to grant the consumer counsel is not enough to pursue the dispute so that precedent is created, with the purpose of avoiding a settlement between the consumer and the trader.

In Scandinavia, there have traditionally existed alternatives to court proceedings, including softer as well as simpler procedures. Various boards are available, and mediation is strong in Finland and Denmark, and most notably in Norway where it is deeply rooted in Norwegian society.[53] Due to this common practice in Scandinavian countries, we have not been in dire need of group action mechanisms, especially for straightforward individual claims. Therefore, it is also worth considering whether the existing practice of using boards and mediation could be used for collective redress in the form of, for instance, mass mediation. Although the group complaint already exists in a form, it could easily be applied towards more comprehensive group complaints, including not only public and organizational suits, but even individual suits in collective situations. Together with the EU Regulation, it is possible to take the next step towards mass mediation and friendly settlements by collective means. In this regard, ombudsmen could also play their own role and be one instrument available as an alternative dispute resolution mechanism.[54]

---

[51] Act 8/2007 on the Consumer Complaints Board.
[52] Laukkanen (above n 50) 81.
[53] For more on mediation in Scandinavian countries, see Ervo and Sippel (above n 42) 402.
[54] The exception is the Spanish doctoral thesis of Ana Isabel Blanco García, *Conflictos bancarios: su tutela extrajurisdiccional*, University of Valencia, Spain 2014 (unpublished), where she researched, especially from a comparative point of view, how mediation and ombudsmen could be used as a solution to solve conflicts between consumers and banks.

B. *The Obligations of the Ombudsman and Statistical Data*[55]

The institution of ombudsmen originated in Sweden when the Swedish Parliament created the position of a Parliamentary Ombudsman in 1809. The next country was Finland which got a Parliamentary Ombudsman in 1920. After that, ombudsmen were created in other Nordic countries in the mid-20th century. In 1955, Denmark created the post of *Folketingets ombudsmand,* and in Norway the *Stortingets ombudsman* assumed his post in 1962. In Norway and Denmark, the powers of the Ombudsman are more limited than in Sweden and Finland. However, this more limited Danish model was later replicated in many other parts of the world.[56]

The Ombudsman is a supreme overseer of legality and is elected by the Parliament. They exercise oversight to ensure that fundamental human rights are guaranteed, and that the law is respected in public tasks and activities they perform. The scope of the Ombudsman's oversight encompasses courts, authorities, and public servants as well as other individuals and bodies who perform public tasks. The Ombudsman does not survey private instances and individuals not entrusted with public tasks.[57] However, it is possible to have extraordinary Ombudsmen for such tasks, like the Consumer Ombudsman, who is charged with the duty of observing and guaranteeing the rights of consumers.

Concerning the Parliamentary Ombudsman, anyone may file a complaint with the Ombudsman, and there is no fee charged for investigating a complaint. A complaint in a matter within the ombudsman's competence may be filed by anyone who thinks an entity or individual in public service has acted unlawfully or neglected a duty in the performance of their task. It is therefore possible to bring a claim on one's behalf, but a claim can also be brought on behalf of another or collectively together with others. Therefore, the instrument is simple and effective for control, as well as a good guarantee for access to justice in many cases.

The complaint shall be filed in writing. It shall contain the name and contacts of the plaintiff, as well as the necessary information on the matter to which the claim relates. The Ombudsman then investigates a complaint if it gives ground for suspicion that an authority or official has acted unlawfully

---

[55] On Scandinavian ombudsmen see also L Ervo, 'Liability and Social Control of Scandinavian Judge' in M Gizyzska and A Piszcz (eds) *In Liability of Public Officers – selected issues* (Pock, 2013) 117–132, at 124–127.

[56] Parliamentary Ombudsman of Finland, *Summary of the Annual Report 2011*, 23, http://www.oikeusasiamies.fi/dman/Document.phx?documentId=in29012125858656&cmd=download.

[57] *Ibid*, 23 and Parliamentary Ombudsman Act, Chapter 1, Section 1.

or violated their duty.[58] The Ombudsmen are well respected in practice and their control is effective due to the fact that authorities and civil servants take the system seriously. Therefore, their decisions are well followed. The scope of their power is a mix of both legal and social (in this case professional) control, which seems to work well in practice. Therefore, the scope of jurisdiction of Ombudsmen could be widened, as has already occurred for the Consumer Ombudsman. Their duties and powers could be developed in the future towards the Parliamentary Ombudsman to make the system even more effective.

Investigating complaints is the Parliamentary Ombudsman's central task and activity. The Ombudsman investigates those complaints with respect to which there is a reason to suspect unlawful action or neglect of duty, or where investigation is warranted for any other reason. Arising from a complaint, the Ombudsmen take measures that they deem justified from the perspective of observance of the law, legal protection, or implementation of fundamental and human rights. Ombudsmen can also act on their own initiative to investigate shortcomings that manifest themselves and they are required by law to conduct inspections of official agencies and institutions.[59]

If an Ombudsman concluded that a subject has acted unlawfully or neglected his/her duty, but considers that a criminal charge or disciplinary proceedings are nonetheless unwarranted, the Ombudsman may issue a reprimand to the subject for future guidance. If necessary, the Ombudsman may express to the subject his/her opinion concerning what constitutes proper observance of the law, or draw the attention of the subject to the requirements of good administration or to considerations of fundamental and human rights.[60]

In a matter within the Ombudsman's remit, they may issue a recommendation to the competent authority that an error be redressed or a shortcoming rectified. In the performance of his or her duties, the Ombudsman may draw the attention of the Government or another body responsible for legislative drafting to the defects in legislation or official regulations, as well as make recommendations concerning the development and elimination of the defects.[61]

According to most recent statistics, the amount of initiated cases was 5506 in 2013 in Finland, whereas the amount of inhabitants of Finland is

---

[58] Parliamentary Ombudsman Act, Chapter 1, Section 2 and http://www.oikeusasiamies.fi/Resource.phx/eoa/english/complaints/index.htx.
[59] Parliamentary Ombudsman Act, Chapter 1, Sections 4 and 5 and Parliamentary Ombudsman of Finland (above n 56), 25, http://www.oikeusasiamies.fi/dman/Document.phx?documentId=in29012125858656&cmd=download.
[60] Parliamentary Ombudsman Act, Chapter 1, Section 10.
[61] Parliamentary Ombudsman Act, Chapter 1, Section 11.

approximately 5 million at present. There were 4975 complaints made to the Ombudsman, and 68 complaints were transferred from the Chancellor of Justice. 67 cases were taken up on the Ombudsman's own initiative. In addition, there were 80 submissions and attendances at hearings, and 316 other kinds of written communications. The total amount of resolved cases were 5762, 275 of which were cases regarding courts. 232 of the cases concerned civil and criminal courts, 42 cases concerned administrative courts, and one case concerned special courts.[62]

In Finland, the Ombudsman took 787 decisions leading to measures in 2013. There were no prosecution cases. However, there were 31 reprimands and 590 opinions of which 304 were rebukes, 286 for future guidance, 38 recommendations, 4 of which resulted in a recommendation from the Ombudsman to redress the error. In 16 cases, the Ombudsman made an initiative to develop legislation or regulations, 18 cases concerned the provision of compensation for a violation, there were 45 matters redressed in the course of investigation, and in 83 cases, the Ombudsman resorted to other measures, of which 22 cases involved mediation.[63]

C. Consumer Ombudsman's Duties

The most essential responsibility of the Consumer Ombudsman is to supervise the application and respect of the Consumer Protection Act and other laws protecting consumers. Particular attention is paid to ensure that marketing activities and contractual terms conform to the laws. The goal of the supervisory activities is to require the company to alter its marketing activities or unreasonable contractual terms so that they conform to current legislation. The Consumer Ombudsman does not primarily resolve individual disputes where the consumer is seeking reimbursement for an error concerning a product or service. These cases are handled by consumer rights advisors and the Consumer Disputes Board. The Consumer Ombudsman may, however, aid the consumer if necessary to resolve an individual dispute if its resolution carries a significant impact on the interpretation of the law or the general well-being of consumers, or in instances where a business is not compliant with the decision of the Consumer Disputes Board. The Consumer Ombudsman may also refer group complaints to the Consumer Disputes Board for resolution or to initiate group actions.[64]

---

[62] Parliamentary Ombudsman of Finland, *Annual Report 2013*, 348–350, http://www.oikeusasiamies.fi/Resource.phx/eoa/english/publications/annual.htx.

[63] Parliamentary Ombudsman of Finland (above n 62), 350.

[64] http://www.kkv.fi/en/about-us/the-consumer-ombudsman/.

The Consumer Ombudsman annually receives thousands of claims and communications from consumers, companies, and other officials and associations. They are all processed and recorded in the Competition and Consumer Authority's information system. The Consumer Ombudsman uses the collected information in selecting which issues to supervise. The Consumer Ombudsman may also intervene on issues he/she has identified on his/her own. Identified problems are often handled just like larger entities, where several problems are addressed at once. According to law, the Consumer Ombudsman must be particularly active in areas that are of substantial importance to consumers or where problems can be presumed common to consumers. The focus of the supervisory activities varies between different industries. The current Consumer policy program also affects areas on which the Consumer Ombudsman focuses for a specific time period. The primary goal of the Consumer Ombudsman activities is to influence a business that is non-compliant with the law in order to cease such activities or alter them voluntarily. If the company cannot be persuaded to cease the unlawful activities, the Consumer Ombudsman must take the necessary enforcement actions or refer the issue to the court for resolution. In practice, these situations are subject to imposing a prohibition reinforced with a penalty.[65]

D. The Situation in Practice

The Swedish National Board for Consumer Complaints had 11531 cases in 2012, which is a 23 percent increase compared to 2011. The possible explanation for this is that it was made possible to file a complaint on the web. On the other hand, the number of cases in 2013 was 11301, a decrease of 2 percent.[66] The enforcement of decisions has increased from 71 percent in 2011 to 76 percent in 2012. The Swedish Consumer Ombudsman has filed several (19 to be exact) group proceedings with the Swedish National Board for Consumer Complaints ('Board'). At least 7 have been successful; however, the figure is probably even higher if it includes group proceedings in the form of friendly settlements. During 2010, the Board received a group complaint concerning district heat delivery. The complaint was filed by the Ombudsman against a district heating company, Hammarö Energi AB. The Ombudsman alleged that the company was not entitled to charge certain district heating customers for administrative overheads as no provision to this effect was made in the contract between the parties. The case was successful, and the company was ordered to return the extra payments. The Consumer Ombudsman recently started a group action against the company Gotland

---

[65] Ibid.
[66] See SOU 2014:47, 74.

Boat AB at the National Board for Consumer Disputes. The Consumer Ombudsman received requests in a group action that the Board should oblige the company Gotland Boat AB to pay compensation to all consumers who purchased a ticket from the company for the ferry trip between Västervik and Visby in the summer of 2014. Consumers should receive compensation for the damages they suffered since Gotland Boat AB cancelled the ferry service.[67] The case is still pending.

The first and only public group action against an electricity company was successful for the Consumer Ombudsman, who initiated an action on 15 December 2004 against an energy supplier in northern Sweden.[68] The company failed to supply electricity to 7,000 consumers at the price agreed to in the contract. The case concerned damages of EUR 100 to 1,000 per subscriber for additional expenses following the respondent's failure to deliver electric power in accordance with a fixed price agreement. The Consumer Ombudsman filed a performance action in the first instance, requesting an interlocutory judgement in the matter of liability in damages. The Consumer Ombudsman had conducted a group action before The National Board for Consumer Disputes. The respondent, who had lost a number of individual cases concerning the same matter, but who had also won one or two cases, refused to comply with the Board's recommendation concerning payment of damages. The proceedings were delayed by the respondent who asserted, among other things, that the special procedural conditions under the Group Proceedings Act were not followed. The district court overruled the respondent's objections on 20 June 2005. The respondent then took the matter to appeal, which was, however, dismissed on 16 December 2006, whereupon the respondent appealed to the Supreme Court. In a ruling on 25 September 2007, the Supreme Court found no cause for granting a review dispensation. The proceedings were then resumed by the district court, which in January 2010 ordered the respondent to pay damages in an intermediate judgment to the consumers concerned.[69] This judgment was affirmed by the Court of Appeal for Upper Norrland. The Supreme Court refused to review the judgment. The case was still pending – as the question on how much each consumer was entitled to receive was not settled – when the Consumer Ombudsman announced on 7 October 2014 that an agreement had been reached with the company, granting all plaintiffs compensation. Although the Consumer Ombudsman only got half of the amount claimed, the present Consumer Ombudsman, Mr Gunnar Larsson, expressed in a press release that the agreement was a success for the consumers. He highlighted that the case

---

[67] See 'Allmänna Reklamationsnämndens hemsida', www.arn.se.
[68] The Court of Appeal in *Övre Norrland*, Case T 154-10, 4 November 2011.
[69] *Umeå tingsrätt*, Case T 5416-04.

in question was very complex, and that it could have taken several years more before a final judgment would have been reached.[70]

In Finland, there have been no group action cases until now, which has led to some debate in the media as mentioned above.[71] Ombudsmen have been criticized, as the threshold required to commence a group action appears to be very high. The other actors in the field were of the opinion that the group action could have served more often as a useful tool to get access to justice and access to court, especially in consumer cases.[72] However, the Ombudsmen indicated that there has been no need for group actions because the mechanism has been efficient as a threat and situations could be resolved by other means. Furthermore, the Ombudsman stated that it has been sufficient to have the option of group actions and to use them as a threat to promote the rights of consumers. The Consumer Agency stresses another reason, namely that its collective actions affect the fear of difficult and lengthy legal proceedings: if the group actions were dismissed, the State would not only pay the defendant's costs, but all attorneys' fees as well. Therefore, the Consumer Ombudsman can refuse to start a group action on the basis that a procedure would be too complicated because of the complexity of the case.[73]

There has been one group complaint in Finland, which was, however, dismissed. The Consumer Disputes Board rejected the Consumer Ombudsman's group complaint against the construction company Peab Oy. The group complaint concerned the marketing of new houses and the information given on the maintenance charge. Namely, housing costs for residents were higher than they had originally estimated. The Consumer Complaints Board noted in its decision that the financing plan is just an estimate, and therefore it should not be regarded as fully binding.[74]

E. Lessons to be Learned

In Finland, only the public group action and the public group complaint are possible and the Consumer Ombudsman is the only actor in the field that has the right to bring a group action or a group complaint to court and to the Consumer Disputes Board.[75] Therefore, the system is ineffective in reality.

---

[70] http://www.konsumentverket.se/Nyheter/Pressmeddelanden/Pressmeddelanden-2014/Ersattning-till-tusentals-konsumenter-efter-tio-ars-rattsprocess/.
[71] See, for instance, http://www.hs.fi/kotimaa/AL+Ryhm%C3%A4kanteet+eiv%C3%A4t+etene+kuluttaja-asiamiehelt%C3%A4+oikeuteen/a1305581561697.
[72] http://kuningaskuluttaja.yle.fi/node/2234.
[73] *Ibid.*
[74] Decision 1070/81/11, 15 May 2012, http://www.kuluttajariita.fi/lautakunnan-ratkaisuja/?action=read&id=828.
[75] Act on Class Actions, Section 4 and Act on the Consumer Complaints Board, Section 4.

In Sweden, there are more options for consumers. Even private and organisational group actions are allowed. A group complaint formed by a group of private persons is also allowed where an Ombudsman has made the decision not to start a group complaint. Therefore, the system has been more effective in practice, and there are a few successful examples of group complaints and group actions filed by the Consumer Ombudsman. However, the threshold to start the group action is still too high, even in Sweden, and this can evidently cause problems for a consumer's access to justice.[76]

As mentioned above, Swedish and Finnish legislators have yet to take steps in promulgating the conditions of the Commission Recommendation in their legal systems. It is not a surprising statement, as most of the principles of the Recommendation are already fulfilled in the present legislation. The reason for that decision is the following:

First, the opt-in principle, included as general principle in point 21 of the Recommendation, is already applied in Sweden. This means that it will not be a problem for the Swedish legislator to meet the demands of the Recommendation for the time being. The same applies for Finland, where the system is based on opt-in only.[77]

Secondly, according to points 4–7 of the Recommendation, the Member States should designate representative entities to bring representative actions on the basis of clearly defined conditions of eligibility. An eligible entity should have a non-profit making character and have sufficient capacity in terms of financial resources, human resources, and legal expertise. The entity should also have a main objective of ensuring the protection of the rights granted under Union law which allegedly have been violated. The entity must be officially designated in advance and it can be a public authority. Sweden's system permitting Consumer Ombudsmen to initiate group actions both before a court or the National Board of Consumer Disputes, fits well with the Recommendation. The same applies to Finland, despite the fact that the Finnish system of basing group actions on public suits by the Consumer Ombudsman can be strongly criticized.

Thirdly, as stated in points 14–16 and 32 of the Recommendation, the Member States should provide national rules to ensure that the claimant only has to declare the origin of the funding for the court proceedings to the court. Furthermore, there should be national rules that prevent third party funders from abusing their position. As there have been very few cases on

---

[76] See for instance L Ervo, 'Group proceedings in Sweden – a moderate start' in V Harsági and CH van Rhee (eds) *Multi-Party Redress Mechanisms in Europe: Squeaking Mice?* (Intersentia, 2014) 243–259.

[77] However, the opt-in system can be criticized as ineffective. See Ervo *ibid*, 257 and PH Lindblom, '*Utvärdering av lagen om grupprättegång*' 10 *Svensk Juristtidning* (2008) 833, 843.

group proceedings in Sweden, it is difficult to say whether any problems with permitted methods of funding have occurred. In at least four cases regarding private group actions, private entities who have not been parties or group members have contributed to the financing and sponsoring of such trials as they considered them worthy of support. The third party funders have also provided expertise to the plaintiff or the group members. The funding in these cases has come from individuals, but also trusts, companies, or special associations formed for this specific purpose.[78] The special procedural rules in Section 8 of the GRL have probably been sufficient in preventing third-parties funding the proceedings from abusing their position, but a new and practical analysis of the funding methods is necessary in order to be certain. In Finland, where only public group actions are allowed, such funding problems are no issue. However, the real problem with funding is that the Consumer Ombudsman does not seem to have enough resources to bring group actions, which can be seen as a serious limit to plaintiffs' access to justice given the Ombundsman's monopoly to bring group action suits.

Fourthly, points 29–31 of the Recommendation state that the Member States must make sure that the lawyer's remuneration and the method by which it is calculated do not create any incentive for litigation. As Swedish lawyers can, in principle, only demand fees that are in harmony with Chapter 18, Section 8 RB,[79] and as contingency fees and punitive damages are not allowed under Swedish or Finnish law, it will not be difficult for Sweden or Finland to meet this requirement of the Recommendation. In Finland, remuneration is even less problematic due to fact that only public group actions are possible.

Fifthly, Member States should provide mechanisms for both injunctive and compensatory relief. Point 20 of the Recommendation states that the Member States should establish appropriate sanctions against the losing defendant with a view to ensuring effective compliance with the injunctive order, including payments for a fixed amount for each day of delay or any other amount provided for in national legislation.[80] Under Swedish and

---

[78] See PH Lindblom, *Grupptalan i Sverige* (Norstedts Juridik, 2008) 163, 242–243.

[79] Compensation for litigation costs shall fully cover the costs of preparation for trial and presentation of the action including fees for representation and counsel, to the extent that the costs were reasonably incurred to safeguard the party's interest. Compensation shall also be paid for the time and effort expended by the party by reason of the litigation. Negotiations aimed at settling an issue in dispute that bear directly on the outcome of a party's action are deemed to be measures for the preparation of the trial. Compensation for litigation costs shall also include interest under the Interest Act (1975: 635), Section 6, running from the date of the court's determination until the date of payment (SFS 1987: 328).

[80] Commission Recommendation, Point 20 "Efficient enforcement of injunctive orders". The Member States should establish appropriate sanctions against the losing defendant with a view to ensuring the effective compliance with the injunctive order, including the payments of a fixed amount for each day's delay or any other amount provided for in national legislation.

Finnish law, the provisions on group actions do not set any limitations on the civil law remedies to be obtained. Therefore, the Recommendation can be respected through legislation. Furthermore, in Sweden, the Consumer Ombudsman can also ask for a prohibition order or an information disclosure order according to Section 28 of the Market Practises Act (2008:486). The order can be sanctioned with a fine. In Finland, the law on group actions is very short and covers only the main parts of group actions, while the normal civil procedure rules remain applicable in group actions. This sort of 'frame law' undoubtedly causes many problems when applied in practice, but also leaves all doors open when needed. Mechanisms for both injunctive and compensatory relief are therefore already in place with the present legislation in both Sweden and Norway.

Sixthly, Member States should ensure efficient handling of cross-border collective redress. Point 17 of the Recommendation requires the Member States to ensure that where a dispute concerns natural or legal persons from several Member States, a single collective action in a single forum is not prevented by national rules on admissibility, on standing of the foreign groups of claimants or on representative entities from other national legal systems. As the Swedish Group Proceedings Act does not establish any limitation in terms of the nationality of the group members and there are no restrictions as to the participation of foreign plaintiffs, it will not be a problem to meet the Recommendation in this point. In Finland, no rules exist concerning cross-border cases, and therefore a similar interpretation is possible. However, the Finnish law on Group Proceedings only includes 19 Sections, and should be more comprehensive. There is therefore a strong need to develop both the system and the legislation on it in the near future. Therefore, the Finnish legislator should take the Recommendation into account and consider whether this is the right moment to take the next step in developing collective redress as promised in the *travaux preparatoires*.[81]

The Consumer Ombudsman institutions were created for their preventive effects. They are mostly tools for mediation or social pressure. Therefore, one can wonder if these tools are too soft. The Ombudsmen have different roles, such as the Parliamentary Ombudsman, whose role is a controller, and their power is also derived from Parliament, which consequently intensifies the pressure to obey their decisions even in cases where they are "just" recommendations. In comparison, the Consumer Ombudsman is a simple instrument, and the next steps which should be taken in their development are either to broaden their jurisdiction to include mass mediation or to allocate

---

[81] *Lakivaliokunnan mietintö* 30/2006 vp. *Hallituksen esitys ryhmäkannelaiksi ja laiksi Kuluttajavirastosta annetun lain muuttamisesta* 30/2006, 4.

more resources to start public group actions. It is possible that more jurisdictional power could be delegated to them in the form of legally binding decisions. The trend of delegating adjudicative power away from the courts is not a new one in Scandinavia, where prosecutors often make decisions which are included in traditional adjudication.

As Blanco García mentioned, the Ombudsman system is an ADR category of its own. An Ombudsman is a sensible, cost effective, and quick alternative dispute resolution compared to civil procedure.[82] Ombudsmen could easily have more power in decision making or mediation than they do today. However, this also means that the whole system should be updated.[83]

The other available option are public group actions which are based on an opt-out method and which work effectively. This is greatly desired by consumers but time and money are needed to realise that dream. Furthermore, the Consumer Ombudsman should not hold a monopoly in the field, as is the case in Finland. In Sweden, private and organisational group actions are also possible.[84]

F. Easier Solutions or Strict Enforcement?

Until now, the Ombudsmen have not been successful in taking group actions to judgment in Finland or Sweden. As we have stated above, no group actions have existed so far in Finland, and in Sweden, the first public group action ended with a friendly settlement where the consumers got only half of the amount to which they could have been entitled. Ombudsmen appear to be more like peacemakers rather than institutions that impose harsh sanctions on violators of consumer law.

As long as Ombudsmen lack resources to take *ex officio* care of consumer protection including in a group action case, and as long as the current group actions are still rather complicated and time consuming, it is impossible to examine consumer access to court, or their access to justice.

Current group actions have often been seen as preventive tools, which are often deemed effective.[85] However, is it enough? Are procedural tools needed if they are only threats and do not work in practice? Procedural tools

---

[82] Blanco García (above n 54) 577.
[83] Blanco García (*ibid* 577–578, 581 and 584) stresses for instance that the non-binding legal nature of the final decisions and the absence of fixed deadlines lead to legal uncertainty for both parties. She recommends that the decisions made by Ombudsmen should be binding in a way which does, however, not limit access to courts or any other administrative protection.
[84] Ervo and Martínez García (above n 30) 207–229.
[85] For instance, this is typically brought forward as a defense when the Finnish public group action system is criticized.

are a means for a plaintiff to access justice but they are not coercive measures. The current procedural instruments, which are successful only during negotiations, have not fulfilled their task. The procedural system should be alive and working in practice, not only in books.[86]

According to Viitanen, a group action can, by its mere existence among other legal procedures, facilitate the opportunity of reaching an agreement without the need to take the case to court. He asserts that this preventive effect of group actions should not be underestimated. He refers to Sweden, where there have been several cases in which the threat of group actions has been successfully used to persuade the party causing damage to voluntarily pay compensation. Viitanen believes that persuasion is the most effective way to use a group action mechanism because it saves a lot of time and both parties' money. However an essential precondition for this preventive effect is that there are practical possibilities for bringing a group claim to court if the persuasion fails.[87] In order to work, the preventive effect therefore needs to be real and it will not be effective if it is illusory. Still, the essential existence of a procedural tool is not to be a 'coercive measure,' but rather an instrument for access to court and by that means, access to justice.

There shouldn't be any need for procedural threats because this presupposes that the existing juridical tools are not functioning well, and that the system of providing access to justice is failing. A normal, well-functioning procedural system is not based on the use of threat as a means to achieving a remedy, but on effective access to justice, in which procedural tools are used. Group actions should be one of those functioning and effective tools which belong to the daily repertoire available to resolve a dispute whenever needed.[88]

Group actions in their current form are still too complicated, time consuming, and difficult for consumers. Both Swedish and especially Finnish legislation leave many questions open and there is not enough case law or doctrine. Plaintiffs therefore bear certain risks when starting a suit because there are too many gaps. So far, group actions are not common for courts or lawyers, so how could they be standard for individual consumers? We would like to argue that the group action system will not be effective and useful until it provides a simple and rapid process for everyone. As soon as this has been realized, we can move on to consumer service.[89]

One option to develop consumer access to justice could be to expand the role of boards and Ombudsmen. Boards are traditional and typical dispute resolution forums in the Nordic countries. They fit well into our legal

---

[86] Ervo and Martínez García (above n 30) 220–221.
[87] Viitanen (above n 43) 613.
[88] Ervo and Martínez García (above n 30) 221.
[89] *Ibid* 207–229.

culture. Their procedure could be cheap, simple, rapid, and sufficiently consumer-friendly. Requesting the board's aid for legal issues is not intimidating, but is rather stress-free. Even these types of experimental elements of fairness and procedural justice are important in modern society and they are highly appreciated according to empirical studies among the general audience.[90] With the EU legislation, Scandinavia can finally put this resource of boards fully into servicing group actions.[91] The group complaint has traditionally been seen as an easy tool to gain access to justice when group actions seem time-consuming and requiring a large amount of resources.[92] Scandinavia should use the opportunity through the Commission Recommendation to develop the role of boards in consumer dispute resolution by giving them an even bigger role in the future as a decision-maker.

The other possibility is to develop the mediation systems. The new tool could be mass mediation (not conciliation which is prevalent today) done by boards or ombudsmen.[93] Furthermore, mediation is a simple, quick, and friendly tool in consumer cases, which is needed especially in smaller claims where the interest in the case is not very high. In those situations, there is no need to cause extra harm to consumers through highly complicated, long-lasting, and risky procedures which are often considered to be the characteristics of group actions. A regular individual, even in a group, needs effective and simple tools.[94] From this point of view, the consumer can be compared to a victim who often suffers when they are pushed to go through the trial. Based on research, it has been found that a trial is added stress for the victim who claims to have already suffered from a tort. Therefore, alternatives or tools otherwise to reduce the suffering must be found.[95] The same applies to consumers. They feel often like 'victims,' with their claims against banks or other types of rich and powerful entrepreneurs. The same applies to situations where individuals, for instance patients, try to bring claims against State or communal authorities where each party begins on unequal grounds.

---

[90] See for instance L Ervo, 'Changing Civil Proceedings – Court Service or State Economy' in *Recent Trends in Economy and Efficiency of Civil Procedure* (Vilnius University, 2013) 51–71, 52 and other sources mentioned there.

[91] See also Ervo and Martínez García (above n 30) 207–229.

[92] J Bärlund, 'Reklamation som förutsättning för påföljder vid gruppklagomål och grupptalan' 5 *JFT* 6 (2007) 481, 492.

[93] See also Blanco García (above n 54) 575–585 where she recommends that the solutions made by ombudsmen should be binding like in the UK and Australia to make the system more effective and 'proper'. The other tool she recommends for the future to intensify the mediation and ombudsmen systems are the publicity of information with the help of webpages and free consumer helplines.

[94] See also Ervo and Martínez García (above n 30) 222.

[95] See for instance L Ervo, *Oikeudenmukainen oikeudenkäynti* (WSOY, 2005) 439–452 and sources mentioned in that discussion.

Protecting consumers does not only mean to help them defend their rights, but also to facilitate their access to justice in the most comfortable way.

In consumer protection, the individual claimants with their problems and feelings should be central. That is why Scandinavia needs mechanisms for reoccurring cases. Therefore, group actions should be developed towards simpler and more effective procedures in the future. Still, effective group actions should also assist in the fight against injustice, especially in situations where the parties have very unequal positions (eg individual consumers, trying to reach equity against State authorities where a group action is perhaps the only effective way to achieve an equitable solution).[96] Due to the economic crisis and privatization of the welfare state, these situations may become even more frequent in the future and functioning mechanisms to access justice will be needed even more.[97]

As explained above, State courts are likely to focus only on hard cases, whereas common cases should be presented to boards and mediation. In this context, the boards and ombudsmen could be useful instruments in realizing mass mediation. However, consumers should not compromise all the time. Also, solutions are needed for complex cases, and an effective group action system is a vital tool for consumers' access to justice. It is especially important when the defendant is the State itself. The public group action brought by the Ombudsman could also be a difficult solution but in that case, their independence and sufficient resources to operate should be granted.

---

[96] However, the Swedish group actions against the state have not been successful so far but the district courts have dismissed them at the early level due to formal reasons. The cases are called 'Stulen barndom' and 'Lexbase'.

[97] See also Ervo and Martínez García (above n 30) 222–223.

4
Lessons from Public International Law

Mass Claims Processes under Public International Law

*Sandrine Giroud and Sam Moss**

I. INTRODUCTION

The processes developed under public international law to deal with international mass claims arising from various types of crises and incidents (Mass Claims Processes) have a long history and have played an important role in shaping public international law. Indeed, the arbitrations under the Jay Treaty of 1794, which involved hundreds of claims, marked the beginning of the practical application of public international law, which had previously been largely an academic discipline.[1]

Although there is no fixed definition of Mass Claims Processes under international law, the term is generally understood to encompass *ad hoc* tribunals, quasi-judicial commissions or administrative programmes established to resolve claims "when a large number of parties have suffered damages arising from the same diplomatic, historic or other event."[2] These programmes "sometimes [borrow] concepts and procedures from each other, but often [invent] unique solutions in light of particular legal and practical perspectives."[3] Mass Claims Processes under international law therefore come in various forms, although they share a common purpose. The common purpose is to adjudicate large numbers of claims, whether for restitution or compensation for death, personal injury or damage to or confiscation of property resulting from extraordinary events such as armed conflicts, breaches of international humanitarian law or environmental disasters.

In recent times, mass claims arising from financial and economic crises have also been advanced in the framework of international investment treaty

---

* Sandrine Giroud is an attorney-at-law with LALIVE in Geneva. Sam Moss is an attorney-at-law with LALIVE in Geneva.

[1] V Heiskanen, 'Arbitrating Mass Investor Claims: Lessons of International Claims Commissions' in Permanent Court of Arbitration (ed), *Multiple Party Actions in International Arbitration* (OUP 2009) 297, 299.

[2] HM Holtzmann, 'Mass Claims' in *Max Planck Encyclopedia of Public International Law* http://www.mpepil.com, para 1.

[3] *Ibid*.

arbitration, in particular in proceedings before the International Centre for Settlement of Investment Disputes (ICSID). Unlike past international Mass Claims Processes, the investment treaty arbitration framework was not specifically designed to handle mass claims. As a result, the use of the framework for mass claims has triggered much debate, in particular as to whether international investment tribunals have the authority to hear mass claims in the absence of the specific consent of the respondent State, and whether such tribunals can borrow from the techniques used in other Mass Claims Processes.

This paper aims to provide an overview of the evolution of Mass Claims Processes in international law and their status in today's dispute resolution landscape. It will first discuss the history of Mass Claims Processes in international law, which dates back more than two centuries, before setting out a few examples of modern processes. It will then turn to identifying the main characteristics of such processes, before discussing the emergence of mass claims in investment treaty arbitration and the future of Mass Claims Processes in international law.

II. HISTORY OF MASS CLAIMS PROCESSES

The history of Mass Claims Processes can be divided into three successive periods.[4] Starting at the end of the eighteenth century, Mass Claims Processes took the form of claims commissions and flourished until World War II. However, the inefficiencies of such commissions, in particular those set up to address claims arising from World War I, became notorious and after World War II, they were largely replaced by agreements between governments for the payment of lump sum amounts, which were then distributed through domestic claims processes. The period approaching the end of the Cold War saw a resurgence of international Mass Claims Processes. This so-called 'third-generation' of Mass Claims Processes, of which many examples still exist today, proved to be far more effective than their predecessors due to the adaptation of methods and techniques developed in domestic mass claims procedures and the development of information technology.

---

[4] V Heiskanen, 'Virtue Out of Necessity: International Mass Claims and New Uses of Information Technology' in Permanent Court of Arbitration (ed), *Redressing Injustices Through Mass Claims Processes: Innovative Responses to Unique Challenges* (OUP 2006) 25–37 (which distinguishes three main periods in the history of Mass Claims Processes). M Henzelin, V Heiskanen and A Romanetti, 'Reparations for Historical Wrongs: From ad hoc Mass Claims Programs to an International Framework Programs?' 2 *Uluslararası Suçlar ve Tarih* (2006) 91, 92–101.

A. The Era of Mixed Commissions

The expression 'mixed commissions' was commonly used between the end of the eighteenth century and the beginning of the twentieth century to designate mainly, but not exclusively, bilateral inter-State *ad hoc* dispute settlement institutions, encompassing both arbitral commissions and mixed claims commissions.[5] These commissions were established with the purpose of settling claims between nationals of different States, between nationals of one State and the other State, or between the States themselves in formal and final proceedings.[6]

The Treaty of Amity, Commerce and Navigation between Great Britain and the United States (US),[7] the so-called 1794 Jay Treaty, which dealt with a number of outstanding issues after the end of the American revolutionary war, created the first mixed commission procedure which could be designated a Mass Claims Process.[8] In addition to establishing an arbitral tribunal to determine the boundary between the US and Canada (the 'St. Croix River Commission'), the Jay Treaty created two mixed claims commissions. The first of these rendered more than 500 awards dealing with disputes in relation to the unlawful seizure of merchant ships by British privateers, and by French privateers outfitted in US ports. The second commission was set up to hear claims by British creditors against US debtors in respect of colonial-era debts. However, its mission was unsuccessful due essentially to insurmountable disagreement between the British and American commissioners on fundamental procedural and substantial issues.[9]

Scores of claims commissions were subsequently established in the late nineteenth century and the early part of the twentieth century to address claims resulting from war, civil unrest and efforts to suppress the African slave trade.[10] The peace treaties following World War I later established mixed

---

[5] L Boisson de Chazournes and D Campanelli, 'Mixed Commissions' in *Max Planck Encyclopedia of Public International Law* http://www.mpepil.com, para 1. See also M Indlekofer, *International Arbitration and the Permanent Court of Arbitration* (Kluwer Law International 2013) 200.

[6] R Dolzer, 'Mixed Claims Commissions' in *Max Planck Encyclopedia of Public International Law* http://www.mpepil.com, para 1.

[7] Treaty of Amity, Commerce and Navigation (the Jay Treaty) (signed 19 November 1794).

[8] DJ Bederman, 'The Glorious Past and Uncertain Future of International Claims Tribunals' in MW Janis (ed), *International Courts for the Twenty-First Century* (Martinus Nijhoff Publishers 1992) 161 at 161.

[9] Holtzmann (above n 2) para 5; JR Crook, 'International Claims Litigation I: Is Rough Justice Too Rough? Thoughts on Mass Claims Processes' 99 *Am Soc'y Int'l L Proc* (2005) 80, 80. See generally RB Lillich, 'The Jay Treaty Commissions' 37 *St. John's Law Review* (1963) 260.

[10] For instance, several mixed commissions addressed the seizure of vessels suspected of trading in African slaves after the trade had been declared illegal (L Bethel, 'The Mixed Commissions for the Suppression of the Transatlantic Slave Trade in the Nineteenth Century', *Journal of*

claims commissions and arbitral tribunals to address claims arising out of the Great War.[11] At the same time, several mixed claims commissions were set up to settle disputes between Mexico and the nationals of a number of other States, including the US, France, and Germany, arising out of repeated revolutionary disturbances within the country.[12]

However, the mixed claims commissions of the early twentieth century, in particular those created after World War I, generally dealt exclusively with property and other economic rights, and not personal injury suffered by individuals,[13] and were plagued by cumbersome administrative processes, inefficiency, and significant delays in processing claims, causing them to fall into disuse after World War II.[14]

B. Lump Sum Agreements

International claims commissions all but disappeared in the aftermath of World War II due to their reputation for inefficiency, as well as to the unprecedented number of international claims arising from large-scale breaches of international law during World War II.[15] Instead, claims by nationals of one State against another were more commonly resolved by the two States entering into a lump sum settlement agreement. The recipient State would then establish its own domestic claims authority or national commission to decide claims and distribute the lump sum amount.[16] As a result, functions previously exercised by international claims commissions became nationalized.[17]

The advantages of this type of Mass Claims Process were to ensure prompt payment and reduce procedural and administrative costs. For the paying

---

African History (1996) 79). See also Henzelin, Heiskanen and Romanetti (above n 4) 92–93; Bederman (above n 8) 161 (listing over 65 such bodies until 1991); I Bottigliero, *Redress for Victims of Crimes Under International Law* (Springer 2004) 80.

[11] For instance, the Polish-German mixed commission adjudicated over 10,000 claims, while the United States-German mixed commission rendered over 7,000 awards.

[12] Holtzmann (above n 2) paras 5–6.

[13] Henzelin, Heiskanen and Romanetti (above n 4) 92–93.

[14] Heiskanen (above n 4) 28.

[15] RB Lillich and BH Weston, *International Claims: Their Settlement by Lump Sum Agreements* (Procedural Aspects of International Law Series, vol 1, University Press of Virginia 1975) (originally Transnational Publishers, Inc 1999, now Martinus Nijhoff Publishers) xi (pointing to the nationalization of foreign investments in many countries, which also gave rise to numerous claims, coupled with the reluctance of the communist countries and many developing countries to have such claims submitted to third-party adjudication); see also Bottigliero (above n 10).

[16] Holtzmann (above n 2) para 7; R Bank and F Foltz, 'Lump Sum Agreements' in *Max Planck Encyclopedia of Public International Law* http://www.mpepil.com, para 8; SD Murphy, W Kidane and TR Snider, *Litigating War: Mass Civil Injury and the Eritrea-Ethiopia Claims Commission* (OUP 2013) 32–35.

[17] Henzelin, Heiskanen and Romanetti (above n 4) 95.

State, it also had the benefit of determining in advance the extent of its liability, allowing for the compensation of victims without an admission of responsibility, and providing for a more favourable standard of compensation – generally 'adequate' rather than 'full compensation.'[18]

Between the end of World War II and 1995, more than 200 lump sum settlement agreements were concluded, settling claims relating to property and personal injuries, including injuries arising from persecution and detention. A recent example of such a lump sum agreement is that concluded in 1990 between the US and Iran with respect to a group of claims of less than USD 250,000 which had originally fallen under the jurisdiction of the Iran-US Claims Tribunal (Iran-US CT), but which the Tribunal had not taken any significant steps to address.[19] A notable illustration of a national commission set up to oversee the domestic distribution of a lump sum is the US Foreign Claims Settlement Commission (FCSC), which administered 45 international and war-related claims programmes involving claims against eighteen countries, including Yugoslavia, Panama, the former Soviet Union, Cuba, China, Vietnam, Iran and the Federal Republic of Germany.[20]

The prevalence of lump sum agreements has, however, declined. Since the 1980s, claims arising out of some of the most prominent conflicts have been addressed by international commissions. One reason for this development is that lump sum settlement agreements inadequately addressed victims' compensation, which narrowed their scope of application. Considering the growing support in international literature and by domestic courts for an individual right for compensation in cases involving breaches of international human rights or humanitarian law, lump sum settlement agreements have been considered by some to be ill-adapted to handle the type of claims that the current state of international law affords to individuals.[21] Moreover, the remedies granted by lump sum settlement institutions could consist of financial compensation only, and generally not full compensation for damage to property or other economic interests.[22] By contrast, modern Mass Claims

---

[18] *Ibid*, 96.

[19] JR Crook, 'Mass Claims Processes: Lessons Learned Over Twenty-Five Years' in Permanent Court of Arbitration (ed) *Redressing Injustices Through Mass Claims Processes: Innovative Responses to Unique Challenges* (OUP 2006) 41, 46. See generally MN Leich, 'Contemporary Practice of the United States Relating to International Law' *AJIL* (1990) 885, 890.

[20] See generally Foreign Claims Settlement Commission of the US http://www.justice.gov/fcsc.

[21] R Bank and F Foltz, 'Lump Sum Agreements' in *Max Planck Encyclopedia of Public International Law* http://www.mpepil.com, para 27.

[22] The acceptance of less than the full amount of compensation in a lump sum agreement gives rise to numerous legal problems, particularly in light of the ILC Articles on State Responsibility, which provide for full compensation: International Law Commission Articles on Responsibility of States for Internationally Wrongful Acts, GA Res 56/83 of 12 December 2001, Annex, art 34, UN Doc A/RES/56/83; Bank and Foltz (above n 21) para 26.

Processes have allowed for a wider array of remedies, such as restitution of property.[23]

C. Modern Mass Claims Processes

The last thirty years have marked a return to international claims commissions and a multiplication of international claims programmes.[24] The establishment of these modern Mass Claims Processes has been facilitated by the increased cooperation between States following the end of the Cold War, as well as significant developments in information technology and the adaptation of methods and techniques developed in domestic mass claims procedures, which have allowed for greater efficiency in processing mass claims.[25] Key examples of modern Mass Claims Processes included Iran-US CT, the United Nations Compensation Commission (UNCC), and the Eritrea-Ethiopia Claims Commission (EECC).

1. Iran-United States Claims Tribunal

The first of the modern Mass Claims Processes was the Iran-US CT. The Tribunal was set up as part of the Algiers Accords of 1981, which were concluded in order to put an end to the hostage crisis at the US Embassy in Tehran.[26] It had the mission of adjudicating thousands of claims of individuals and entities relating to debts and contracts affected by the Iranian revolution, as well as expropriations and other measures affecting property rights.[27] The Algiers Accords did not address either side's liability for claims falling within the Iran-US CT's jurisdiction, and therefore left the issue of liability to be determined by the Tribunal on a case-by-case basis. The Iran-US CT also ruled that it had no jurisdiction over claims concerning personal injuries, such as physical and psychological harm suffered by victims.[28]

---

[23] Henzelin, Heiskanen and Romanetti (above n 4) 96.
[24] HM Holtzmann and E Kristjánsdóttir, *International Mass Claims Processes: Legal and Practical Perspectives* (OUP 2007) 17–37; Crook (above n 19) 45. See also Indlekofer (above n 5) 202–205.
[25] Henzelin, Heiskanen and Romanetti (above n 4) 98.
[26] Settlement of the Hostage Crisis, US-Iran, 19 January 1981, 20 ILM 223 (Algiers Accords).
[27] *Ibid*, art II.
[28] *Grimm v Islamic Republic of Iran* 2 Iran-US Cl Trib Rep 78 (1983) (holding that a claim for both loss of support and punitive damages due to the mental anguish resulting from the assassination of the plaintiff's husband, based on an alleged failure by Iran to provide him security and protection, did not fall within the Tribunal's jurisdiction on the basis of "other measures affecting property rights").

The Iran-US CT, which was faced with over 850 large commercial and bank claims, approximately 2,800 small claims of less than USD 250,000, and numerous large claims between the two States, "demonstrated that case-by-case arbitration of disputes in an international, multi-cultural setting was possible, but also showed that it could be expensive, slow and time-consuming."[29] Indeed, the Tribunal is still operating more than thirty years after it was formed. Although the bulk of the 850 large commercial and bank claims was resolved within the first decade of its inception, a number of cases have lingered, and the Tribunal is still hearing the last claims between the two States. In addition, the Tribunal "never developed an effective strategy for dealing with the approximately 2,800 small claims on its docket."[30] As mentioned above, the claims were ultimately settled by the two States by way of a lump sum agreement, after the Tribunal had decided a small number of test cases.[31]

2. United Nations Compensation Commission

A myriad of international claims commissions and claims resolution bodies followed in the footsteps of the Iran-US CT, starting with the UNCC.[32]

The UNCC was set up in 1991 as a subsidiary organ of the United Nations (UN) Security Council to resolve millions of claims relating to Iraq's invasion and subsequent occupation of Kuwait in 1990.[33] Compensation for losses resulting from Iraq's actions was paid from a special fund (the 'Compensation Fund') that received a percentage of the proceeds from Iraqi oil sales. The UNCC concluded its claims-processing exercise in 2005 and made its last payments to claimants in 2007. Having resolved 2.6 million claims, it has been the largest Mass Claims Process to date.

The UNCC was the first attempt by the international community to set up a claims resolution process through a multinational facility within the UN system. Security Council Resolution 687, which was adopted under Chapter VII of the UN Charter, established Iraq's liability under international law for any direct loss, damage – including environmental damage and depletion of natural resources – and injury to foreign governments, nationals and corporations caused by its invasion and occupation of Kuwait.[34] The UNCC was

---

[29] Crook (above n 19) 44.
[30] *Ibid*, 45.
[31] *Ibid*.
[32] See generally V Heiskanen, *The United Nations Compensation Commission* (Hague Academy of International Law ed, Collected Courses of the Hague Academy of International Law (Martinus Nijhoff 2002).
[33] SC Res 687 UN Doc S/RES687 (3 April 1991).
[34] N Wühler, 'The United Nations Compensation Commission' in Permanent Court of Arbitration (ed), *Institutional and Procedural Aspects of Mass Claims Settlement Systems* (Kluwer Law International 2000) 17.

not therefore set up as an arbitral tribunal, as the Iran-US CT had been, but as a claims commission which mainly had a fact-finding role, "namely to establish for each claim whether or not the damage was directly linked to Iraq's unlawful invasion and occupation of Kuwait."[35]

The UNCC consisted of three organs. The first, the Governing Council, was the policy-making organ. The second organ was composed of three Panels of Commissioners, which verified and evaluated claims, assessed the value of losses suffered by claimants and recommended compensation awards for approval by the Governing Council. Finally, the Secretariat provided administrative, technical and legal support to the Governing Council and the panels of Commissioners, in addition to administering the Compensation Fund. The Secretariat played an important role in streamlining the adjudication of claims by the UNCC. Indeed, the UNCC's procedural rules provided for a delegation of claims review functions to the Secretariat for claims under USD 100,000,[36] as well as for the grouping of larger claims with common legal and factual issues.[37] Another procedure used by the UNCC to handle the numerous claims before it included the verification of claims under USD 100,000 by matching them against the information contained in a computerised database. In respect to the claims that could not be verified through the matching of database information, the UNCC was entitled to limit its review to a statistical sample, rather than having to review every claim individually, with further verification required only if the circumstances warranted it.[38]

After twelve years of processing claims, the UNCC completed its work in June 2005. During its existence, the UNCC granted approximately 1.55 million claims, and awarded a total of approximately USD 52.4 billion in compensation, representing roughly 15 percent of the USD 352.5 billion claimed.[39] The resolution of such a significant number of claims with such a large asserted value over such a short time is unprecedented in the history of international claims resolution.

3. *The Eritrea-Ethiopia Claims Commission*

The EECC was established to address claims arising from the 1998-2000 war between Ethiopia and Eritrea. Unlike the UNCC, the EECC was an arbitral body established bilaterally by Eritrea and Ethiopia, as part of the 2000

---

[35] UNCC, 'UNCC at a Glance' (UNCC Website) http://www.uncc.ch/uncc-glance.
[36] UNCC's Provisional Rules for Claims Procedure, S/AC.26/1992/10, 26 June 1992, art 37(c).
[37] *Ibid*, art 38(a).
[38] *Ibid*, art 37(a) and (b).
[39] UNCC at a Glance (above n 35).

Algiers Agreement.[40] The EECC was given the mandate to "decide through binding arbitration all claims for loss, damage or injury by one government against the other, and by nationals (including both natural and juridical persons) of one party against the Government of the other party or entities owned or controlled by the other party" arising from the war, and from "violations of international humanitarian law, including the 1949 Geneva Conventions or other violations of international law."[41] The Commission did not have jurisdiction over claims arising from the cost or preparation of military operations, or the use of force, except to the extent that they related to violations of international humanitarian law.[42] Claims could be brought by the two States on their own behalf or on behalf of their nationals.

The EECC's Rules of Procedure contemplated procedures for mass claims brought by individuals including prisoners of war, for unlawful expulsion, displacement, or detention, or for any other loss, damage or injury.[43] The Rules provided in particular for the grouping of the mass claims into sub-categories according to the alleged violation of international law, after which the Commission was to determine in respect of each sub-category whether the violation was proved. If the violation was proved, the Commission was to use "random sampling of [the] evidence to ascertain the percentage of ... claims for which the evidence is inadequate to establish the claim," and reduce the compensation awarded for that sub-category by that percentage.[44] However, the special procedural rules for mass claims were never implemented.[45]

Indeed, Ethiopia and Eritrea instead filed government-to-government claims, and the vast majority of these were:

---

[40] Agreement between the Government of the Federal Democratic Republic of Ethiopia and the Government of the State of Eritrea, 12 December 2000, 40 ILM 260 (2001), http://www.pca-cpa.org/showpage.asp?pag_id=1151. See generally W Kidane, 'Civil Liability for Violations of International Humanitarian Law: The Jurisprudence of the Eritrea-Ethiopia Claims Commission in The Hague' 25 *Wis Int'l L J* (2007) 23; N Klein, 'State Responsibility for International Humanitarian Law Violations and the Work of the Eritrea Ethiopia Claims Commission So Far' 47 *Germ YB Int'l L* (2005) 214.

[41] Agreement between the Government of the Federal Democratic Republic of Ethiopia and the Government of the State of Eritrea, 12 December 2000, 40 ILM 260 (2001), http://www.pca-cpa.org/showpage.asp?pag_id=1151, art 5.

[42] *Ibid*.

[43] EECC Rules of Procedure, October 2011, http://www.pca-cpa.org/showpage.asp?pag_id=1151, arts 30–32.

[44] Arts 30–32, EECC Rules of Procedure, October 2011, http://www.pca-cpa.org/showpage.asp?pag_id=1151.

[45] Holtzmann and Kristjánsdóttir (above n 24) 168. See generally SD Murphy, W Kidane and TR Snider, *Litigating War: Mass Civil Injury and the Eritrea-Ethiopia Claims Commission* (OUP 2013).

filed as claims of the governments themselves, [and] not as claims of persons that were transmitted to the [C]ommission by the governments … . Thus, rather than Ethiopia filing, for example, 3,000 or so claims by named individuals injured along the Central Front for harm to person or property, Ethiopia filed a signed claim on behalf of the government itself alleging harm to its unnamed nationals and property along the Central Front.[46]

In this sense, the "Commission's practice marks an unusual retreat to the diplomatic protection philosophy of 19th century inter-state arbitration."[47]

Nevertheless, the Commission addressed a wide range of claims relating to the conduct of military operations, the treatment of prisoners of war and civilians as well as their property, diplomatic immunity and the economic impact of certain government actions during the conflict.[48] Ultimately, it awarded approximately USD 161.5 million to Eritrea and USD 174 million to Ethiopia,[49] although it left open the question of how these amounts would be used to provide redress to the victims of the conflict, noting that it "would probably be impossible, and certainly inordinately expensive, to attempt to identify the specific individuals who suffered injuries as a result of the various illegal acts committed against them."[50] Instead, it contemplated that the funds would be used for "relief programs for categories of victims,"[51] although no such programmes have been implemented, as it appears that neither party has paid the awarded amounts to date.[52] Despite this failure, commentators have pointed to successes of the EECC of another nature, namely "helping to end the war and securing the full repatriation of prisoners of war … and broader successes in providing the two countries a forum to air their differences, giving a voice to the victims of wrongful conduct, and establishing an impartial historical record of key events that unfolded during the war."[53]

4. Other Modern Mass Claims Processes

Since the 1990s, Mass Claims Processes have been used in various other contexts such as the Commission for Real Property Claims of Displaced

---

[46] Murphy, Kidane and Snider (above n 16) 61.
[47] Heiskanen (above n 4) 311.
[48] See generally Eritrea-Ethiopia Claims Commission http://www.pca-cpa.org/showpage.asp?pag_id=1151.
[49] Murphy, Kidane and Snider (above n 16) 407.
[50] EECC, Decision No. 8, Relief to War Victims, 27 July 2007, para 2.
[51] *Ibid*, para 5.
[52] Murphy, Kidane and Snider (above n 16) 408.
[53] *Ibid*, 407.

Persons and Refugees (CRPC),[54] which dealt with the aftermath of the dissolution of the Socialist Federal Republic of Yugoslavia, in addition to claims relating to the 1992-1995 war in Bosnia and Herzegovina, and the Housing and Property Claims Commission (HPCC),[55] which dealt with claims relating to the 1999 conflict in Kosovo. More recently, Mass Claims Processes have been envisaged for other situations of armed conflicts and massive displacement of persons such as in Iraq,[56] Cyprus,[57] and Darfur.[58]

A number of Mass Claims Processes were also instituted to deal with the extensive losses of assets resulting from the Holocaust, although unlike the processes mentioned above, these were not created under public international law, but rather as private arbitral tribunals or as part of domestic court proceedings.

The first of these was the Claims Resolution Tribunal for Dormant Accounts in Switzerland (CRT-I), which was established in 1997 as an independent international arbitral tribunal under Swiss law to resolve claims relating to approximately 6,000 accounts in Swiss banks which had been dormant or inactive since the end of World War II and whose holders or their heirs were unable to recover. The CRT-I was established pursuant to the Memorandum of Understanding between the Swiss Bankers Association, the World Jewish Restitution Organization and the World Jewish Congress.[59]

The CRT-I was followed by another Mass Claim Process set up in 2000, which related to additional accounts held by Swiss banks. The Second Claims Resolution Tribunal for Dormant Accounts in Switzerland (CRT-II) was the result of a settlement agreement reached in the context of US class action lawsuits in 1996 and 1997 which were based on the alleged failure of banks to identify and return assets deposited by victims of Nazi

---

[54] General Framework Agreement for Peace in Bosnia and Herzegovina, ILM (Dayton Peace Agreement) (14 December 1995). Holtzmann and Kristjánsdóttir (above n 24) 23.

[55] UNMIK Regulation No. 1999/23 on the Establishment of the Housing and Property Directorate and the Housing and Property Claims Commission (15 November 1993) UN Doc UNMIK/REG/1999/23 http://www.unmikonline.org/regulations/1999/re99_23.pdf. See generally See generally Holtzmann and Kristjánsdóttir (above n 24) 27.

[56] International Organization for Migration, *Property Restitution and Compensation: Practices and Experiences of Claims Programmes* (2008) 20–21, 54–57, 91, 127–130, 169–175.

[57] *Ibid*, 39, 232–233.

[58] International Commission of Inquiry on Darfur 'Report of the International Commission of Inquiry on Darfur to the United Nations Secretary-General' (25 January 2005), 149–153.

[59] Independent Committee of Eminent Persons, *Memorandum of Understanding Between The World Jewish Restitution Organization and The World Jewish Congress, representing also the Jewish Agency and Allied Organizations, and The Swiss Bankers Association* (Final Report on Dormant Accounts of Victims of Nazi Persecution in Swiss Banks, 2 May 1996) http://www.crt-ii.org/icep_report.phtm.

persecution.[60] Plaintiffs also contended that the banks had accepted and laundered assets looted by the Nazis and profits generated by Nazi use of slave labour. The lawsuits were settled in January 1999, when the banks agreed to create a USD 1.25 billion settlement fund. Pursuant to a Plan of Allocation and Distribution approved in November 2000,[61] the CRT-II was responsible for processing claims relating to assets deposited in accounts which were open or opened between 1933 and 1945.[62]

Two other Mass Claims Processes, the German Forced Labour Compensation Programme (GFLCP) and the Holocaust Victim Asset Programme (HVAP), were established in 2000 to compensate victims of certain injustices committed by the Nazi regime during World War II. These mechanisms were established pursuant to settlements and private or governmental agreements following numerous Holocaust-related lawsuits brought in the US against the German and Swiss Governments, banks and corporations. Both are administered by the International Organization for Migration (IOM).[63] Additional Mass Claims Processes set up to deal with post-Holocaust claims include the Austrian General Settlement Fund (AGSF),[64] the French Commission for the Compensation of Victims of Spoliation (CCVS),[65] and the International Commission on Holocaust Era Insurance Claims (ICHEIC).

III. CHARACTERISTICS OF MASS CLAIMS PROCESSES

The nature of Mass Claims Processes can be difficult to define, however it is possible to identify a number of largely common and interrelated characteristics.

A. *The Number and Commonality of Claims*

The first characteristic of Mass Claims Processes is that they involve large

---

[60] See *In re Holocaust Victim Assets Litigation* F Supp 2d (EDNY, 2000). The text of the Settlement Agreement can be found at http://www.crt-ii.org/court_docs/Settleme.pdf.

[61] See Special Master's Proposed Plan of Allocation and Distribution of Settlement Proceeds, approved by Judge Korman on 22 November 2000, see *In re Holocaust Victim Assets Litigation* and http://www.swissbankclaims.com.

[62] Holtzmann and Kristjánsdóttir (above n 24) 17–37; Holtzmann (above n 2) para 12.

[63] Holtzmann and Kristjánsdóttir (above n 24) 29.

[64] H Lessing, R Rebernik and N Spitzy, 'The Austrian General Settlement Fund: An Overview' in Permanent Court of Arbitration (ed), *Redressing Injustices Through Mass Claims Processes: Innovative Responses to Unique Challenges* (OUP 2006) 95.

[65] Decree No. 99-778 of 10 September 1999 (p 13633, Fr, 11 September 1999). See generally E Freedman, 'The French Commission for the Compensation of Victims of Spoliation: A Critique' in Permanent Court of Arbitration (ed), *Redressing Injustices Through Mass Claims Processes: Innovative Responses to Unique Challenges* (OUP 2006) 139–149.

numbers of claims. Although it is unclear how large that number has to be for a process to be characterised as a Mass Claims Process,[66] it can vary greatly, meaning that the nature of and challenges faced by different processes can be very different. For example, the Iran-US CT dealt with several thousand claims, while the number of claims addressed by the UNCC, which reached a total of 2.6 million, was on an entirely different scale. A second characteristic of Mass Claims Processes is that they involve claims which arise from common circumstances and involve common factual and legal issues, making it possible and more efficient to resolve them within a single process rather than in separate proceedings.[67] However, as with the number of claims, the level of commonality between claims varies between Mass Claims Processes, which can have an impact on the nature and complexity of the proceedings.

B. Reparative Function

Despite the different backgrounds and institutional frameworks of Mass Claims Processes,[68] their reparative function is one of their main characteristics. They share the common goal of providing effective remedies and a 'measure of justice'[69] for the damage or injury caused to a large number of individuals or entities due to an armed conflict or similar events with widespread effects.[70] As such, they often serve to allay the societal discontent that unresolved wrongs perpetuate, and can thereby contribute to stability within a society.

Mass Claims Processes have evolved beyond the boundaries of traditional diplomatic protection to better provide relief to those who have been injured, notably by widening the scope of remedies available to affected individuals and entities.[71] Indeed, the remedies are among a number of features of Mass Claims Processes that "can be tailored ... in whatever ways are required to address the ... human, political and economic dimension" of the problem being addressed.[72] Besides providing an opportunity for compensation for injuries and losses sustained by victims of extraordinary events,[73] Mass

---

[66] It has been suggested by at least one commentator that it would have to be at least in the low thousands: Heiskanen (above n 4) 28.

[67] H Das, 'The Concept of Mass Claims and the Specificity of Mass Claims Processes' in Permanent Court of Arbitration (ed), *Redressing Injustices Through Mass Claims Processes: Innovative Responses to Unique Challenges* (Oxford 2006) 7.

[68] See generally PA Karrer, 'Mass Claims Proceedings in Practice: A Few Lessons Learned' 23 *Berkeley J Int'l L* (2005) 463.

[69] Crook (above n 19) 55.

[70] Das (above n 67) 5.

[71] Crook (above n 19) 55.

[72] *Ibid*, 55–56.

[73] Eg the CRT-I, the CRT-II, the GFLCP and the HVAP.

Claims Processes can provide for the restitution of property,[74] as well as serve the political and psychological function of recognising and legitimising the claims of injured groups.

C. Hybrid Nature of Mass Claims Processes

The structure and framework of modern Mass Claims Processes vary. Some Mass Claims Processes are designed essentially as arbitrations, as was the case for the Iran-US CT, the CRT-1 and the EECC, even though the procedures used may differ from those in 'full-fledged arbitration' due to the commonality of the factual and legal issues to which the claims give rise.[75] For instance, "hearings at the [Iran-US CT] were, with few exceptions, generally much shorter than in cases of a similar level of complexity in international commercial arbitration."[76] Other Mass Claims Processes are structured as 'quasi-judicial' administrative procedures,[77] and others still are a hybrid of the two forms.[78] An example of such a hybrid form is the UNCC, which was an administrative body that performed essentially a fact-finding function of examining claims, verifying their validity, evaluating losses and paying out compensation.[79] Yet, for certain large cases, it operated more like an arbitral body, with adversarial proceedings which included submissions by parties.[80]

The suitability of one structure or another for a Mass Claims Process is case-specific and depends on a number of factors, including the number of claims to be addressed. An arbitral method of dispute resolution may be more costly and time-consuming due to, among other things, minimum requirements of due process,[81] and may not even be practicable in certain cases involving particularly high numbers of claims. Administrative procedures are less constrained by considerations of due process, and therefore afford greater flexibility in adopting an appropriate mechanism to resolve claims quickly and efficiently.

Another important factor is whether the question of liability has been settled beforehand. Most modern Mass Claims Processes were constituted on the basis of settlement agreements or other instruments which already determined that individuals or entities falling within a class or group are entitled

---

[74] Eg the CRPC and the HPCC.
[75] Heiskanen (above n 2) 304.
[76] *Ibid*, note 23.
[77] Eg the CRT-II, the CRPC and the HVAP.
[78] Eg the UNCC. See generally Holtzmann and Kristjánsdóttir (above n 24) 97–103; N Wühler, 'The Different Contexts in Which International Arbitration Is Being Used: International Claims Tribunals and Commissions' (2003) 4 *J World Investment* 379.
[79] Wühler (above n 34) 17.
[80] Holtzmann and Kristjánsdóttir (above n 24) 98 & n 5.
[81] Karrer (above n 68) 463–466.

to certain types of relief.[82] Therefore, the liability of one of the parties was either recognised,[83] or simply left out of the process.[84] This was for example the case for the UNCC, which operated on the basis of a UN Security Council resolution which established Iraq's liability for damage caused by its invasion and occupation of Kuwait. In these kinds of circumstances, administrative, rather than arbitral procedures, are often deemed more appropriate for Mass Claims Processes:

> In the absence of a live dispute regarding the basis of liability, which has been settled by the settlement agreement, there is necessarily no need for the decision-making body to employ fully-fledged adversar[ial] proceedings to process and verify the claims. Since the liability issue has been settled, there is effectively no respondent on the level of legal principle; the sole task for the claims commission is to receive the claims, assess whether they meet the applicable eligibility requirements, verify the evidence and, if necessary, quantify the claim.[85]

In the rare cases in which the issue of liability remains disputed, it is likely that an arbitral procedure will be more appropriate.[86] For instance, the Iran-US CT, which had to address the issue of liability on a case-by-case basis, was structured as an arbitral tribunal.

D. A Process of 'Practical' Justice

The pressure of processing and deciding very large numbers of claims, together with the desire to expedite payments of compensation and the difficulties encountered by victims in locating documentary evidence, most notably in cases involving armed conflict, have required procedural innovations and a standard of justice which often differs from that provided for in traditional international dispute resolution proceedings.

1. Guarantee of Due Process

Inherent to all Mass Claims Processes is "the tension ... between the search

---

[82] Crook (above n 9) 80.
[83] Eg the UNCC (compensating damages arising out of the Iraqi invasion of Kuwait based on the UN's Security Council's establishment of Iraq's liability under international law). *Contra*, eg the EECC.
[84] Eg the CRPC (arising out of the Dayton Peace Agreement which, while establishing the right of return of refugees, did not confirm the legal liability of any of the parties to the conflict for damage caused during the conflict).
[85] Heiskanen (above n 2) 303.
[86] *Ibid.*, 305.

for individual justice and fairness and the requirement of an expedient process that resolves all the claims within a reasonable time period,"[87] leading some to describe the outcome of Mass Claims Processes as 'rough justice.'[88] Nevertheless, it has been suggested that such Processes do comply with the requirements of due process, although not necessarily in the same form as in court or arbitral proceedings.[89] Due process is guaranteed for the system and less for each individual case, as a traditional conception of due process would be too onerous and could lead to a denial of justice for the victims of the often tragic and extraordinary events which give rise to Mass Claims Processes. The guiding principle is therefore one of "practical justice," in other words "justice that would be swift and efficient, yet not rough."[90]

2. Flexible Rules of Procedure

Whether Mass Claims Processes are of an arbitral or administrative nature, they are governed by procedural rules that typically are referred to in their constituting instruments.[91] Some of these refer to an existing set of procedural rules, either incorporating them by reference or citing them as a basis for drafting new rules.[92] Others provide, without incorporating a set of rules by reference, that procedures may be 'guided by' a set of existing rules.[93] Regardless of the method used, the success of Mass Claims Processes rests in the flexibility of their rules and the possibility to adjust them to the particularities of their context.

---

[87] Wühler (above n 34) 20.

[88] Crook (above n 9) 80; PA Karrer, 'Mass Claims to Provide Rough Justice: The Work of he Property Claims Commission of the German Foundation "Remembrance, Responsibility and the Future"' in B Bachmann et al (eds), *Grenzüberschreitungen: Beiträge zum internationalen Verfahrensrecht und zur Schiedsgerichtsbarkeit: Festschrift für Peter Schlosser zum 70. Geburtstag* (2005) 339; Wühler (above n 34) 22.

[89] Wühler (above n 78) 380. See generally H Houtte and I Yi, 'Due Process in International Mass Claims' 1 *Erasmus L Rev* (2008) 63 (analysing Mass Claims Processes in light of art 6 of the European Convention on Human Rights, and concluding that standards of due process applicable to individual justice cannot apply directly to mass claims proceedings, but that such proceedings must still meet the test of due process, albeit in a slightly different form).

[90] DD Caron and B Morris, 'The United Nations Compensation Commission: Practical Justice, Not Retribution' 13 *Eur J Int'l L* (2002) 183, 188.

[91] See generally Holtzmann and Kristjánsdóttir (above n 24) 205–210.

[92] Eg Iran-US CT which used the UNCITRAL Arbitration Rules (UN Doc A/RES/31/98, 15 December 1976) http://www.uncitral.org/pdf/english/texts/arbitration/arb-rules/arb-rules.pdf (UNCITRAL Rules), or the EECC, which referred to the PCA Rules.

[93] Eg the UNCC which took inspiration from the UNCITRAL Rules.

3. Adapted Standards of Proof and Evidentiary Rules

The sheer number of claims and the difficulty encountered in many cases in obtaining evidence in respect to events which occurred years or decades earlier, and for which the records may have been destroyed in part or in full, means that the evidence supporting claims in Mass Claims Processes often cannot be assessed in the same manner judges and arbitrators assess cases in traditional judicial or arbitral proceedings. Modern Mass Claims Processes therefore have often been designed to require only the level of documentary or other evidence that can reasonably be expected in the circumstances.[94] As a result, Mass Claims Processes have generally used a relaxed standard of proof; instead of applying traditional legal standards such as requiring facts to be established by a preponderance of the evidence, Mass Claims Processes often resort to a test of 'plausibility.'[95]

In conjunction with, or instead of, relaxed standards of proof, Mass Claims Processes have also resorted to techniques, such as the discovery of evidence on their own motion and evidentiary presumptions. Administering institutions or secretariats can play an active role in seeking out evidence to support claims,[96] especially in cases in which it is difficult for claimants to access such evidence. Such a role raises issues of procedural fairness, as it impacts the allocation of the burden of proof. However, in certain cases, "the accuracy of outcome [is, for policy reasons,] considered more important than procedural neutrality."[97] Evidentiary presumptions, which also impact the allocation of the burden of proof, are sometimes used for large-scale claims programmes in which individual research to substantiate individual claims would be too time-consuming and expensive, or in which the claimants have difficulties accessing the evidence. Such presumptions can, for example, be developed on the basis of research as to frequently occurring claim scenarios.[98]

4. Mass Processing Techniques

A number of other techniques which have been developed in modern Mass Claims Processes, many of which originated in US class action lawsuits,[99]

---

[94] See generally JJ Haersolte-van Hof, 'Innovations in Mass Claims Dispute Resolution: Using New Standards of Proof' 58 *Disp Resol J* (2003) 70.

[95] Holtzmann (above n 2) 16. The plausibility standard was first explicitly enunciated by the RT-I. See Rules of Procedure for the Claims Resolution Process (15 October 1997) http://www.crt-ii.org/crt-i/rules_procedure.html, art 22.

[96] Crook (above n 19) 56.

[97] Heiskanen (above n 2) 318.

[98] International Organization for Migration, 'Property Restitution and Compensation: Practical and Experiences of Claims Programmes' (2008) 246.

[99] V Heiskanen, 'Innovations in Mass Claims Dispute Resolution: Speeding the Resolution of Mass Claims Using Information Technology' 58 *Disp Resol J* (2003) 79, 80.

have contributed greatly to their efficiency. Among these are the extensive use of large-scale computerization,[100] which can facilitate the verification and evaluation of thousands of individual claims through computerised matching and advanced techniques, such as sampling and statistical modelling. The UNCC, for instance, used a large database to store all relevant data pertaining to the claims before it and to perform a number of statistical operations.[101] These processing techniques are not new and have generally been borrowed from US class action lawsuits. Besides speeding up the management of the process, computer technology also facilitates the grouping of claims, which permits Mass Claims Processes to identify and resolve common issues in a single decision applicable to an entire group of claims, without having to resort to case-by-case adjudication.[102]

In addition to computerization and other related techniques, such as the use of statistical methods, modern Mass Claims Processes have in many cases delegated review functions either to an administrative institution, such as a secretariat, or to an expert. For example, as mentioned above, the UNCC's procedural rules provided for the delegation to its Secretariat of claims review functions in respect of claims under USD 100,000. In addition, delegation of review functions can be used to assist in the grouping of claims, allowing common issues to be determined together, rather than on a case-by-case basis.[103]

IV. MASS CLAIMS AND INTERNATIONAL INVESTMENT DISPUTES

An important development in recent years has been the submission of mass claims arising from economic and financial crises to international investment treaty arbitration.[104] Only one such arbitration has been initiated so far, namely the still ongoing *Abaclat v. Argentina* case, which involves the claims of 60,000 (initially 180,000) Italian nationals who are alleged holders of bonds on which Argentina defaulted. Other cases have also involved large numbers of claimants, such as the similar *Ambiente v. Argentina* and *Alemanni v. Argentina* cases, which were initiated by 90 (initially 119) and 183 Argentinian bondholders respectively; however, it is generally considered that these do not constitute mass claims.[105] Nevertheless, the emergence of mass claims in investment treaty arbitration has given rise to much debate.

---

[100] See generally *ibid*, 80.
[101] Wühler (above n 34) 20.
[102] Heiskanen (above n 99) 81. See eg the UNCC which resorted to this technique by grouping similar claims together and by submitting them to the same panel of Commissioners.
[103] Heiskanen (above n 2) 314.
[104] *Ibid*, 297–298, 302.
[105] The tribunal in the *Ambiente v. Argentina* case noted that the term 'mass claims' was not a

Unlike past Mass Claims Processes, the investment treaty arbitration framework was not specifically designed to handle mass claims. Indeed, the procedural rules applicable to investment treaty arbitrations, such as those set out in the ICSID Convention and in the ICSID Arbitration Rules, are silent on the specific issue of mass claims, and in particular, on the issue of arbitral tribunals' jurisdiction over such claims and their power to adopt the procedures or techniques which, from a practical point of view, would be necessary to deal with such claims. This has raised the question as to whether international investment tribunals can hear mass claims in the absence of a specific consent of the respondent State, as well as what procedures or techniques tribunals may resort to when hearing mass claims.

With respect to the first question, the respondent in *Abaclat v. Argentina* argued, ia, that it had not consented, in the applicable bilateral investment treaty (BIT) or in the ICSID Convention, to an "unprecedented mass action" which would "change the nature of ICSID claims."[106] While one of the arbitrators dissented, noting in particular that all past Mass Claims Processes in international law were based on the consent of the States involved (or on the powers of the UN Security Council),[107] the tribunal ruled that no specific consent for mass claims was required. It explained in particular that if it could have jurisdiction over several individual claimants, there was no reason why it would lose that jurisdiction "where the number of [c]laimants outgrows a certain threshold."[108] It also noted that the investments at issue in the case, namely bonds, which were protected by the applicable BIT, were:

> susceptible of involving ... a high number of investors, and where such investments require a collective relief in order to provide effective protection

---

technical term with a precise meaning, and, after comparing the number of claimants in the proceedings before it with that in the *Abaclat v. Argentina* case, concluded that it would 'stick to qualifying [the case] as a "multi-party action".' (*Ambiente v. Argentina*, Decision on Jurisdiction and Admissibility, 8 February 2013, ICSID Case No. ARB/08/9, paras 119–122; see S Blanchard, 'Ambiente Ufficio S.p.A. and Others v. Argentine Republic' 15 *Journal of World Investment and Trade* (2014) 314–323). The *Alemanni v. Argentina* tribunal reached a similar conclusion, noting that the number of claimants in the arbitration 'does not in ordinary usage fit the descriptor "mass".' (*Alemanni v. Argentina*, Decision on Jurisdiction and Admissibility, 17 November 2014, ICSID Case No. ARB/07/8, para 276.) See also B Demirkol, 'Does an Investment Treaty Tribunal Need Consent for Mass Claims?' 2 *Cambridge Journal of International and Comparative Law* 3 (2013) 616–617.

[106] *Abaclat v. Argentina*, Decision on Jurisdiction and Admissibility, 4 August 2011, ICSID Case No. ARB/08/9, para 471.

[107] *Abaclat v. Argentina*, Decision on Jurisdiction and Admissibility, Dissenting Opinion of Professor Georges Abi-Saab, 28 October 2011, ICSID Case No. ARB/08/9, para 185.

[108] *Abaclat v. Argentina*, Decision on Jurisdiction and Admissibility (above n 106), para 490.

to such investment, it would be contrary to the purpose of the BIT and to the spirit of ICSID, to require in addition to the consent to ICSID arbitration in general, a supplementary express consent to the form of such arbitration.[109]

The tribunal's decision to hear the mass claims proved to be controversial.[110] However, it has certainly opened the door to mass claims being brought in investment treaty arbitrations.

With respect to the procedures or techniques for hearing mass claims, the *Abaclat v. Argentina* tribunal ruled that it had the power under Article 44 of the ICSID Convention and Rule 19 of the ICSID Arbitration Rules to "fill the gaps" left by the ICSID framework in respect of mass claims, and therefore to adopt the necessary procedural mechanisms.[111] However, the tribunal recognized that its authority in this respect was limited by the provisions of the ICSID Convention and the ICSID Arbitration Rules, which it could not modify,[112] and that any procedural mechanism it adopted could not affect its duty to examine the elements necessary to establish its jurisdiction and the merits of the claims.[113] In addition, certain procedures or techniques which are commonly provided for in the constituting instruments of Mass Claims Processes could raise issues concerning due process rights in the context of investment treaty arbitration.

The tribunal in *Abaclat v. Argentina* provided little indication in its Decision on Jurisdiction and Admissibility as to what procedural mechanisms it would adopt, although it did address the issue to a certain extent. In particular, the tribunal indicated that it would resort to "group treatment" or common issue determination, which is "one of the most commonly employed mass claims processing techniques,"[114] by dividing the merits phase into two parts: the first will be "a general phase aimed at determining the core issues regarding the merits of the case, and in particular establishing what conditions must be fulfilled for further resolving claimants' claims and determining the best method to examine these issues and conditions."[115] In the second phase, the tribunal will "rule on how to examine the relevant issues and conditions" and

---

[109] *Ibid*.
[110] SI Strong, 'Mass Procedures as a Form of "Regulatory Arbitration" – *Abaclat v. Argentine Republic* and the International Investment Regime' 38 *The Journal of Corporation Law* 2 (2012/2013) 259–260.
[111] *Abaclat v. Argentina*, Decision on Jurisdiction and Admissibility (above n 119) paras 518–528.
[112] *Ibid*, para 520. See D Donovan, 'Case Comment: Abaclat and others v Argentine Republic As a Collective Claims Proceeding' 27 *ICSID Review* 2 (2012) 261–267.
[113] *Abaclat v. Argentina*, Decision on Jurisdiction and Admissibility (above n 119) para 529.
[114] Heiskanen (above n 2) 315.
[115] *Abaclat v. Argentina*, Decision on Jurisdiction and Admissibility (above n 119) para 671.

"put in place an appropriate mechanism of examination and will proceed with such examination."[116] In assessing whether or not group treatment was appropriate, the tribunal explored "whether claimants have homogeneous rights of compensation for a homogeneous damage caused to them by potential homogeneous breaches by Argentina of homogeneous obligations provided for in the BIT," which it found to be the case.[117] According to commentators, the application of such common issue determination in investment treaty arbitration would not raise due process concerns provided that the parties are given the opportunity to be heard on the issue and as to the applicability of a decision on an issue to a particular group of claims.[118] Similarly, pilot cases or bellwether proceedings, which were also considered by the *Abaclat v. Argentina* tribunal,[119] and which can assist parties to settle the remaining cases, should also not impact procedural fairness as they do not affect the parties' rights to be heard on individual claims.[120]

As mentioned above, another procedural mechanism used in Mass Claims Processes is the delegation of claims review to a secretariat or an expert. This was the approach adopted by the tribunal in *Abaclat v. Argentina* in order to verify whether the 60,000 claimants in the case met the specific jurisdictional requirements set out in its Decision on Jurisdiction and Admissibility.[121] The tribunal in that case appointed an expert to review the information contained in the database of individual claims, which the claimants had set up, to verify whether each claimant met the specific jurisdictional requirements, which included the requirement that natural persons had held Italian nationality between certain specific dates.[122] The expert then submitted a report of his findings to the tribunal and the parties. Some commentators have taken the position that such delegation by an arbitral tribunal may be permissible provided that the tribunal does not delegate its decision-making function, and that the expert's review is conducted under the guidance and supervision of the tribunal.[123] However, the approach adopted in *Abaclat v. Argentina*

---

[116] *Ibid*.
[117] *Ibid*, paras 541 and 543.
[118] Donovan (above n 112) 265; Heiskanen (above n 2) 316.
[119] *Abaclat v. Argentina*, Decision on Jurisdiction and Admissibility (above n 119) para 666.
[120] Donovan (above n 112) 264.
[121] *Abaclat v. Argentina*, Procedural Order No. 12, 7 July 2012, ICSID Case No. ARB/08/9, para 4.
[122] See *Abaclat v. Argentina*, Decision on Jurisdiction and Admissibility (above n 106) para 501(iii).
[123] Heiskanen (above n 2) 314–315. See also Donovan (above n 112) 265, who states that the delegation of any decision-making function, "if permissible at all, would need to be provisional – that is, any initial determination would need, upon objection, to be subject to plenary review and determination by the tribunal."

may raise due process concerns. Indeed, the respondent in the case objected that the expert's review, which would be limited to a mere six minutes per claim, would fail "to provide for an analysis of the circumstances of each claim," including the validity of the documentary evidence submitted, and therefore would "fail to provide [it] with the opportunity to respond to each claim."[124]

The use of statistical sampling in investment treaty arbitration, in the absence of the agreement of the parties, raises even greater due process concerns. Indeed, the tribunal granting claims without having reviewed all of them "may be considered an excess of powers or 'a serious departure from a fundamental rule of procedure,' thus creating a risk of annulment of the award under Article 52 of the ICSID Convention."[125] The tribunal in *Abaclat v. Argentina* appears to have recognized this concern, as it declined to accept a proposal by the expert it appointed to only review whether jurisdictional requirements were met in respect to a sample of claims when it was faced with an objection from the respondent that such sampling would deprive it of "the right to defend itself against each claim and claimant individually."[126] Resorting to certain other procedural mechanisms used in Mass Claims Processes, such as the discovery of evidence *ex officio* by the tribunal or secretariat, or the use of evidentiary presumptions and relaxed standards of proof will also likely be considered inappropriate in investment treaty arbitration.

V. CONCLUSION

It is unclear how international Mass Claims Processes, which historically have contributed greatly to the development of public international law, will develop in the future. As public international law evolves to grant individuals and entities greater rights and protection, Mass Claims Processes may play an even more important role than in the past in the wake of various crises and incidents, such as armed conflicts, environmental disasters or large-scale economic crises. However, there has been a tendency towards the nationalization of Mass Claims Processes. Indeed, a number of Mass Claims Processes which might have been "created under an international umbrella" are now being established under domestic law, due in part to the "increasing reluctance on the part of the international community to carry the burden of financing international claims programs and the practical difficulties associ-

---

[124] *Abaclat v. Argentina*, Procedural Order No. 17, 8 February 2013, ICSID Case No. ARB/08/9, para 14(iii).
[125] Heiskanen (above n 2) 322.
[126] *Abaclat v. Argentina*, Procedural Order No. 17 (above n 124), para 8(iv).

ated with ensuring the funding of compensation awards."[127] This development underlines the importance of strong political support for the success of international Mass Claims Processes, in particular with respect to funding.

An exception to the trend of nationalization has been the emergence of mass claims in international investment treaty arbitration, the legal framework of which was not specifically designed to address mass claims. It remains to be seen whether the *Abaclat v. Argentina* case will open the door to a significant influx of mass claims in investment treaty arbitration. Nevertheless, the case has stirred an important debate as to the suitability of the investment treaty arbitration framework for hearing mass claims, and in particular as to the policy implications of its use with respect to issues such as sovereign debt restructuring, which the tribunal in *Abaclat v. Argentina* declined to take into consideration.[128]

Time will tell whether mass claims will become more prevalent in international investment arbitration, as well as what role other types of Mass Claims Processes will play and what form they will take in the future. In any event, traditional mechanisms of dispute resolution will, in many cases, be unable to provide adequate redress to high numbers of individuals and entities affected by extraordinary events with widespread impact. Mass Claims Processes, in their various forms, will therefore undoubtedly remain relevant as extraordinary mechanisms to address extraordinary disputes.

---

[127] Heiskanen (above n 2) 302.
[128] *Abaclat v. Argentina*, Decision on Jurisdiction and Admissibility (above n 106) para 660: "Respondent's policy arguments regarding the appropriateness of ICSID proceedings in the context of sovereign debt restructuring are irrelevant for the determination of the admissibility of the claims."

Annex 1

COMMISSION RECOMMENDATION
of 11 June 2013
on common principles for injunctive and compensatory collective redress mechanisms in the Member States concerning violations of rights granted under Union Law
(2013/396/EU)

THE EUROPEAN COMMISSION,
Having regard to the Treaty on the Functioning of the European Union, and in particular Article 292 thereof,

Whereas:
(1) The Union has set itself the objective of maintaining and developing an area of freedom, security and justice, inter alia, by facilitating access to justice, as well as the objective of ensuring a high level of consumer protection.
(2) The modern economy sometimes creates situations in which a large number of persons can be harmed by the same illegal practices relating to the violation of rights granted under Union law by one or more traders or other persons ('mass harm situation'). They may therefore have cause to seek the cessation of such practices or to claim damages.
(3) The Commission adopted a Green Paper on antitrust damages actions in 2005[1] and a White Paper in 2008, which included policy suggestions on antitrust-specific collective redress[2]. In 2008 the Commission published a Green Paper on consumer collective redress[3]. In 2011 the Commission carried out a public consultation 'Towards a more coherent European approach to collective redress'[4].

---

[1] COM(2005) 672, 19.12.2005.
[2] COM(2008) 165, 2.4.2008.
[3] COM(2008) 794, 27.11.2008.
[4] COM(2010) 135 final, 31.3.2010.

(4) On 2 February 2012 the European Parliament adopted the resolution 'Towards a Coherent European Approach to Collective Redress', in which it called for any proposal in the field of collective redress to take the form of a horizontal framework including a common set of principles providing uniform access to justice via collective redress within the Union and specifically but not exclusively dealing with the infringement of consumer rights. The Parliament also stressed the need to take due account of the legal traditions and legal orders of the individual Member States and enhance the coordination of good practices between Member States[5].

(5) On 11 June 2013 the Commission issued a Communication 'Towards a European Horizontal Framework for Collective Redress'[6], which took stock of the actions to date and the opinions of stakeholders and of the European Parliament, and presented the Commission's position on some central issues regarding collective redress.

(6) It is a core task of public enforcement to prevent and punish the violations of rights granted under Union law. The possibility for private persons to pursue claims based on violations of such rights supplements public enforcement. Where this Recommendation refers to the violation of rights granted under Union Law, it covers all the situations where the breach of rules established at Union level has caused or is likely to cause prejudice to natural and legal persons.

(7) Amongst those areas where the supplementary private enforcement of rights granted under Union law in the form of collective redress is of value, are consumer protection, competition, environment protection, protection of personal data, financial services legislation and investor protection. The principles set out in this Recommendation should be applied horizontally and equally in those areas but also in any other areas where collective claims for injunctions or damages in respect of violations of the rights granted under Union law would be relevant.

(8) Individual actions, such as the small claims procedure for consumer cases, are the usual tools to address disputes to prevent harm and also to claim for compensation.

(9) In addition to individual redress, different types of collective redress mechanisms have been introduced by all Member States. These measures are intended to prevent and stop unlawful practices as well as to ensure that compensation can be obtained for the detriment caused in mass harm situations. The possibility of joining claims and pursuing them collectively may constitute a better means of access to justice, in

---

[5] 2011/2089(INI).
[6] COM(2013) 401 final.

particular when the cost of individual actions would deter the harmed individuals from going to court.

(10) The aim of this Recommendation is to facilitate access to justice in relation to violations of rights under Union law and to that end to recommend that all Member States should have collective redress systems at national level that follow the same basic principles throughout the Union, taking into account the legal traditions of the Member States and safeguarding against abuse.

(11) In the area of injunctive relief, the European Parliament and the Council have already adopted Directive 2009/22/EC on injunctions for the protection of consumers' interests[7]. The injunction procedure introduced by the Directive does not, however, enable those who claim to have suffered detriment as a result of an illicit practice to obtain compensation.

(12) Procedures to bring collective claims for compensatory relief have been introduced in some Member States, and to differing extents. However, the existing procedures for bringing claims for collective redress vary widely between the Member States.

(13) This Recommendation puts forward a set of principles relating both to judicial and out-of-court collective redress that should be common across the Union, while respecting the different legal traditions of the Member States. These principles should ensure that fundamental procedural rights of the parties are preserved and should prevent abuse through appropriate safeguards.

(14) This Recommendation addresses both compensatory and – as far as appropriate and pertinent to the particular principles – injunctive collective redress. It is without prejudice to the existing sectorial mechanisms of injunctive relief provided for by Union law.

(15) Collective redress mechanisms should preserve procedural safeguards and guarantees of parties to civil actions. In order to avoid the development of an abusive litigation culture in mass harm situations, the national collective redress mechanisms should contain the fundamental safeguards identified in this Recommendation. Elements such as punitive damages, intrusive pre-trial discovery procedures and jury awards, most of which are foreign to the legal traditions of most Member States, should be avoided as a general rule.

(16) Alternative dispute resolution procedures can be an efficient way of obtaining redress in mass harm situations. They should always be available alongside, or as a voluntary element of, judicial collective redress.

---

[7] OJ L 110, 1.5.2009, p. 30.

(17) Legal standing to bring a collective action in the Member States depends on the type of collective redress mechanism. In certain types of collective actions, such as group actions where the action can be brought jointly by those who claim to have suffered harm, the issue of standing is more straightforward than in the context of representative actions, where accordingly the issue of legal standing should be clarified.

(18) In the case of a representative action, the legal standing to bring the representative action should be limited to ad hoc certified entities, designated representative entities that fulfil certain criteria set by law or to public authorities. The representative entity should be required to prove the administrative and financial capacity to be able to represent the interest of claimants in an appropriate manner.

(19) The availability of funding for collective redress litigation should be arranged in such a way that it cannot lead to an abuse of the system or a conflict of interest.

(20) In order to avoid an abuse of the system and in the interest of the sound administration of justice, no judicial collective redress action should be permitted to proceed unless admissibility conditions set out by law are met.

(21) A key role should be given to courts in protecting the rights and interests of all the parties involved in collective redress actions as well as in managing the collective redress actions effectively.

(22) In fields of law where a public authority is empowered to adopt a decision finding that there has been a violation of Union law, it is important to ensure consistency between the final decision concerning that violation and the outcome of the collective redress action. Moreover, in the case of collective actions following a decision by a public authority (follow-on actions), the public interest and the need to avoid abuse can be presumed to have been taken into account already by the public authority as regards the finding of a violation of Union law.

(23) With regard to environmental law, this Recommendation takes account of the provisions of Article 9(3), (4) and (5) of the UN/ECE Convention on Access to Information, Public Participation in Decision-Making and Access to Justice in Environmental Matters ('the Aarhus Convention') which, respectively, encourage wide access to justice in environmental matters, set out criteria that procedures should respect, including criteria that they be timely and not prohibitively expensive, and address information to the public and the consideration of assistance mechanisms.

(24) The Member States should take the necessary measures to implement the principles set out in this Recommendation at the latest two years after its publication.

(25) The Member States should report to the Commission on the implementation of this Recommendation. Based on this reporting, the Commission should monitor and assess the measures taken by Member States.

(26) Within four years after publication of this Recommendation, the Commission should assess if any further action, including legislative measures, is needed, in order to ensure that the objectives of this Recommendation are fully met. The Commission should in particular assess the implementation of this Recommendation and its impact on access to justice, on the right to obtain compensation, on the need prevent abusive litigation and on the functioning of the single market, the economy of the European Union and consumer trust,

HAS ADOPTED THIS RECOMMENDATION:

I. PURPOSE AND SUBJECT MATTER

1. The purpose of this Recommendation is to facilitate access to justice, stop illegal practices and enable injured parties to obtain compensation in mass harm situations caused by violations of rights granted under Union law, while ensuring appropriate procedural safeguards to avoid abusive litigation.

2. All Member States should have collective redress mechanisms at national level for both injunctive and compensatory relief, which respect the basic principles set out in this Recommendation. These principles should be common across the Union, while respecting the different legal traditions of the Member States. Member States should ensure that the collective redress procedures are fair, equitable, timely and not prohibitively expensive.

II. DEFINITIONS AND SCOPE

3. For the purposes of this Recommendation:

   (a) collective redress' means: (i) a legal mechanism that ensures a possibility to claim cessation of illegal behaviour collectively by two or more natural or legal persons or by an entity entitled to bring a representative action (injunctive collective redress); (ii) a legal mechanism that ensures a possibility to claim compensation collectively by two or more natural or legal persons claiming to have been harmed in a mass harm situation or by an entity entitled to bring a representative action (compensatory collective redress);

(b) 'mass harm situation' means a situation where two or more natural or legal persons claim to have suffered harm causing damage resulting from the same illegal activity of one or more natural or legal persons;

(c) for damages' means an action by which a claim for damages is brought before a national court;

(d) 'representative action' means an action which is brought by a representative entity, an ad hoc certified entity or a public authority on behalf and in the name of two or more natural or legal persons who claim to be exposed to the risk of suffering harm or to have been harmed in a mass harm situation whereas those persons are not parties to the proceedings;

(e) 'collective follow-on action' means a collective redress action that is brought after a public authority has adopted a final decision finding that there has been a violation of Union law.

This Recommendation identifies common principles which should apply in all instances of collective redress, and also those specific either to injunctive or to compensatory collective redress.

III. PRINCIPLES COMMON TO INJUNCTIVE AND COMPENSATORY COLLECTIVE REDRESS

Standing to bring a representative action

4. The Member States should designate representative entities to bring representative actions on the basis of clearly defined conditions of eligibility. These conditions should include at least the following requirements:
   (a) the entity should have a non-profit making character;
   (b) there should be a direct relationship between the main objectives of the entity and the rights granted under Union law that are claimed to have been violated in respect of which the action is brought; and
   (c) the entity should have sufficient capacity in terms of financial resources, human resources, and legal expertise, to represent multiple claimants acting in their best interest.

5. The Member States should ensure that the designated entity will lose its status if one or more of the conditions are no longer met.

6. The Member States should ensure that representative actions can only be brought by entities which have been officially designated in advance as recommended in point 4 or by entities which have been certified on an ad hoc basis by a Member State's national authorities or courts for a particular representative action.

7. In addition, or as an alternative, the Member States should empower public authorities to bring representative actions.

Admissibility

8. The Member States should provide for verification at the earliest possible stage of litigation that cases in which conditions for collective actions are not met, and manifestly unfounded cases, are not continued.
9. To this end, the courts should carry out the necessary examination of their own motion.

Information on a collective redress action

10. The Member States should ensure that it is possible for the representative entity or for the group of claimants to disseminate information about a claimed violation of rights granted under Union law and their intention to seek an injunction to stop it as well as about a mass harm situation and their intention to pursue an action for damages in the form of collective redress. The same possibilities for the representative entity, ad hoc certified entity, a public authority or for the group of claimants should be ensured as regards the information on the ongoing compensatory actions.
11. The dissemination methods should take into account the particular circumstances of the mass harm situation concerned, the freedom of expression, the right to information, and the right to protection of the reputation or the company value of a defendant before its responsibility for the alleged violation or harm is established by the final judgement of the court.
12. The dissemination methods are without prejudice to the Union rules on insider dealing and market manipulation.

Reimbursement of legal costs of the winning party

13. The Member States should ensure that the party that loses a collective redress action reimburses necessary legal costs borne by the winning party ('loser pays principle'), subject to the conditions provided for in the relevant national law.

Funding

14. The claimant party should be required to declare to the court at the outset of the proceedings the origin of the funds that it is going to use to support the legal action.
15. The court should be allowed to stay the proceedings if in the case of use of financial resources provided by a third party:
    (a) there is a conflict of interest between the third party and the claimant party and its members;
    (b) the third party has insufficient resources in order to meet its financial commitments to the claimant party initiating the collective redress procedure;

(c) the claimant party has insufficient resources to meet any adverse costs should the collective redress procedure fail.
16. The Member States should ensure, that in cases where an action for collective redress is funded by a private third party, it is prohibited for the private third party:
   (a) to seek to influence procedural decisions of the claimant party, including on settlements;
   (b) to provide financing for a collective action against a defendant who is a competitor of the fund provider or against a defendant on whom the fund provider is dependant;
   (c) to charge excessive interest on the funds provided.

Cross-border cases
17. The Member States should ensure that where a dispute concerns natural or legal persons from several Member States, a single collective action in a single forum is not prevented by national rules on admissibility or standing of the foreign groups of claimants or the representative entities originating from other national legal systems.
18. Any representative entity that has been officially designated in advance by a Member State to have standing to bring representative actions should be permitted to seize the court in the Member State having jurisdiction to consider the mass harm situation.

IV. SPECIFIC PRINCIPLES RELATING TO INJUNCTIVE COLLECTIVE REDRESS

Expedient procedures for claims for injunctive orders
19. The courts and the competent public authorities should treat claims for injunctive orders requiring cessation of or prohibiting a violation of rights granted under Union law with all due expediency, where appropriate by way of summary proceedings, in order to prevent any or further harm causing damage because of such violation.

Efficient enforcement of injunctive orders
20. The Member States should establish appropriate sanctions against the losing defendant with a view to ensuring the effective compliance with the injunctive order, including the payments of a fixed amount for each day's delay or any other amount provided for in national legislation.

V. SPECIFIC PRINCIPLES RELATING TO COMPENSATORY COLLECTIVE REDRESS

Constitution of the claimant party by 'opt-in' principle

21. The claimant party should be formed on the basis of express consent of the natural or legal persons claiming to have been harmed ('opt-in' principle). Any exception to this principle, by law or by court order, should be duly justified by reasons of sound administration of justice.
22. A member of the claimant party should be free to leave the claimant party at any time before the final judgement is given or the case is otherwise validly settled, subject to the same conditions that apply to withdrawal in individual actions, without being deprived of the possibility to pursue its claims in another form, if this does not undermine the sound administration of justice.
23. Natural or legal persons claiming to have been harmed in the same mass harm situation should be able to join the claimant party at any time before the judgement is given or the case is otherwise validly settled, if this does not undermine the sound administration of justice.
24. The defendant should be informed about the composition of the claimant party and about any changes therein.

Collective alternative dispute resolution and settlements

25. The Member States should ensure that the parties to a dispute in a mass harm situation are encouraged to settle the dispute about compensation consensually or out-of-court, both at the pre-trial stage and during civil trial, taking also into account the requirements of Directive 2008/52/EC of the European Parliament and of the Council of 21 May 2008 on certain aspects of mediation in civil and commercial matters.[8].

26. The Member States should ensure that judicial collective redress mechanisms are accompanied by appropriate means of collective alternative dispute resolution available to the parties before and throughout the litigation. Use of such means should depend on the consent of the parties involved in the case.
27. Any limitation period applicable to the claims should be suspended during the period from the moment the parties agree to attempt to resolve the dispute by means of an alternative dispute resolution procedure until at least the moment at which one or both parties expressly withdraw from that alternative dispute resolution procedure.

---

[8] OJ L 136, 24.5.2008, p. 3.

28. The legality of the binding outcome of a collective settlement should be verified by the courts taking into consideration the appropriate protection of interests and rights of all parties involved.

Legal representation and lawyers' fees
29. The Member States should ensure that the lawyers' remuneration and the method by which it is calculated do not create any incentive to litigation that is unnecessary from the point of view of the interest of any of the parties.
30. The Member States should not permit contingency fees which risk creating such an incentive. The Member States that exceptionally allow for contingency fees should provide for appropriate national regulation of those fees in collective redress cases, taking into account in particular the right to full compensation of the members of the claimant party.

Prohibition of punitive damages
31. The compensation awarded to natural or legal persons harmed in a mass harm situation should not exceed the compensation that would have been awarded, if the claim had been pursued by means of individual actions. In particular, punitive damages, leading to overcompensation in favour of the claimant party of the damage suffered, should be prohibited.

Funding of compensatory collective redress
32. The Member States should ensure, that, in addition to the general principles of funding, for cases of private third party funding of compensatory collective redress, it is prohibited to base remuneration given to or interest charged by the fund provider on the amount of the settlement reached or the compensation awarded unless that funding arrangement is regulated by a public authority to ensure the interests of the parties.

Collective follow-on actions
33. The Member States should ensure that in fields of law where a public authority is empowered to adopt a decision finding that there has been a violation of Union law, collective redress actions should, as a general rule, only start after any proceedings of the public authority, which were launched before commencement of the private action, have been concluded definitively. If the proceedings of the public authority are launched after the commencement of the collective redress action, the court should avoid giving a decision which would conflict with a decision contemplated by the public authority. To that end, the court may stay the collective redress action until the proceedings of the public authority have been concluded.

34. The Member States should ensure that in the case of follow-on actions, the persons who claim to have been harmed are not prevented from seeking compensation due to the expiry of limitation or prescription periods before the definitive conclusion of the proceedings by the public authority.

VI. GENERAL INFORMATION

Registry of collective redress actions
35. The Member States should establish a national registry of collective redress actions.
36. The national registry should be available free of charge to any interested person through electronic means and otherwise. Websites publishing the registries should provide access to comprehensive and objective information on the available methods of obtaining compensation, including out of court methods.
37. The Member States, assisted by the Commission should endeavour to ensure coherence of the information gathered in the registries and their interoperability.

VII. SUPERVISION AND REPORTING

38. The Member States should implement the principles set out in this Recommendation in national collective redress systems by 26 July 2015 at the latest.
39. The Member States should collect reliable annual statistics on the number of out-of-court and judicial collective redress procedures and information about the parties, the subject matter and outcome of the cases.
40. The Member States should communicate the information collected in accordance with point 39 to the Commission on an annual basis and for the first time by 26 July 2016 at the latest.
41. The Commission should assess the implementation of the Recommendation on the basis of practical experience by 26 July 2017 at the latest. In this context, the Commission should in particular evaluate its impact on access to justice, on the right to obtain compensation, on the need to prevent abusive litigation and on the functioning of the single market, on SMEs, the competitiveness of the economy of the European Union and consumer trust. The Commission should assess also whether further measures to consolidate and strengthen the horizontal approach reflected in the Recommendation should be proposed.

Final provisions

42. The Recommendation should be published in the *Official Journal of the European Union*.

Done at Brussels, 11 June 2013.

For the Commission
The President
José Manuel BARROSO

Annex 2

DIRECTIVE 2014/104/EU OF THE EUROPEAN PARLIAMENT AND OF THE COUNCIL
of 26 November 2014
on certain rules governing actions for damages under national law for infringements of the competition law provisions of the Member States and of the European Union
(Text with EEA relevance)

THE EUROPEAN PARLIAMENT AND THE COUNCIL OF THE EUROPEAN UNION,

Having regard to the Treaty on the Functioning of the European Union, and in particular Articles 103 and 114 thereof,

Having regard to the proposal from the European Commission,

After transmission of the draft legislative act to the national parliaments,

Having regard to the opinion of the European Economic and Social Committee,[1]

Acting in accordance with the ordinary legislative procedure,[2]

Whereas:

(1) Articles 101 and 102 of the Treaty on the Functioning of the European Union (TFEU) are a matter of public policy and should be applied effectively throughout the Union in order to ensure that competition in the internal market is not distorted.

(2) The public enforcement of Articles 101 and 102 TFEU is carried out by the Commission using the powers provided by Council Regulation (EC) No 1/2003.[3] Upon the entry into force of the Treaty of Lisbon

---

[1] OJ C 67, 6.3.2014, p. 83.
[2] Position of the European Parliament of 17 April 2014 (not yet published in the Official Journal) and decision of the Council of 10 November 2014.
[3] Council Regulation (EC) No 1/2003 of 16 December 2002 on the implementation of the rules of competition laid down in Articles 81 and 82 of the Treaty (OJ L 1, 4.1.2003, p. 1).

on 1 December 2009, Articles 81 and 82 of the Treaty establishing the European Community became Articles 101 and 102 TFEU, and they remain identical in substance. Public enforcement is also carried out by national competition authorities, which may take the decisions listed in Article 5 of Regulation (EC) No 1/2003. In accordance with that Regulation, Member States should be able to designate administrative as well as judicial authorities to apply Articles 101 and 102 TFEU as public enforcers and to carry out the various functions conferred upon competition authorities by that Regulation.

(3) Articles 101 and 102 TFEU produce direct effects in relations between individuals and create, for the individuals concerned, rights and obligations which national courts must enforce. National courts thus have an equally essential part to play in applying the competition rules (private enforcement). When ruling on disputes between private individuals, they protect subjective rights under Union law, for example by awarding damages to the victims of infringements. The full effectiveness of Articles 101 and 102 TFEU, and in particular the practical effect of the prohibitions laid down therein, requires that anyone – be they an individual, including consumers and undertakings, or a public authority – can claim compensation before national courts for the harm caused to them by an infringement of those provisions. The right to compensation in Union law applies equally to infringements of Articles 101 and 102 TFEU by public undertakings and by undertakings entrusted with special or exclusive rights by Member States within the meaning of Article 106 TFEU.

(4) The right in Union law to compensation for harm resulting from infringements of Union and national competition law requires each Member State to have procedural rules ensuring the effective exercise of that right. The need for effective procedural remedies also follows from the right to effective judicial protection as laid down in the second subparagraph of Article 19(1) of the Treaty on European Union (TEU) and in the first paragraph of Article 47 of the Charter of Fundamental Rights of the European Union. Member States should ensure effective legal protection in the fields covered by Union law.

(5) Actions for damages are only one element of an effective system of private enforcement of infringements of competition law and are complemented by alternative avenues of redress, such as consensual dispute resolution and public enforcement decisions that give parties an incentive to provide compensation.

(6) To ensure effective private enforcement actions under civil law and effective public enforcement by competition authorities, both tools are required to interact to ensure maximum effectiveness of the competition rules. It is necessary to regulate the coordination of those two

forms of enforcement in a coherent manner, for instance in relation to the arrangements for access to documents held by competition authorities. Such coordination at Union level will also avoid the divergence of applicable rules, which could jeopardise the proper functioning of the internal market.

(7) In accordance with Article 26(2) TFEU, the internal market comprises an area without internal frontiers in which the free movement of goods, persons, services and capital is ensured. There are marked differences between the rules in the Member States governing actions for damages for infringements of Union or national competition law. Those differences lead to uncertainty concerning the conditions under which injured parties can exercise the right to compensation they derive from the TFEU and affect the substantive effectiveness of such right. As injured parties often choose their Member State of establishment as the forum in which to claim damages, the discrepancies between the national rules lead to an uneven playing field as regards actions for damages and may thus affect competition on the markets on which those injured parties, as well as the infringing undertakings, operate.

(8) Undertakings established and operating in various Member States are subject to differing procedural rules that significantly affect the extent to which they can be held liable for infringements of competition law. This uneven enforcement of the right to compensation in Union law may result not only in a competitive advantage for some undertakings which have infringed Article 101 or 102 TFEU but also in a disincentive to the exercise of the rights of establishment and provision of goods or services in those Member States where the right to compensation is enforced more effectively. As the differences in the liability regimes applicable in the Member States may negatively affect both competition and the proper functioning of the internal market, it is appropriate to base this Directive on the dual legal bases of Articles 103 and 114 TFEU.

(9) It is necessary, bearing in mind that large-scale infringements of competition law often have a cross-border element, to ensure a more level playing field for undertakings operating in the internal market and to improve the conditions for consumers to exercise the rights that they derive from the internal market. It is appropriate to increase legal certainty and to reduce the differences between the Member States as to the national rules governing actions for damages for infringements of both Union competition law and national competition law where that is applied in parallel with Union competition law. An approximation of those rules will help to prevent the increase of differences between the Member States' rules governing actions for damages in competition cases.

(10) Article 3(1) of Regulation (EC) No 1/2003 provides that '[w]here the competition authorities of the Member States or national courts apply national competition law to agreements, decisions by associations of undertakings or concerted practices within the meaning of Article [101(1) TFEU] which may affect trade between Member States within the meaning of that provision, they shall also apply Article [101 TFEU] to such agreements, decisions or concerted practices. Where the competition authorities of the Member States or national courts apply national competition law to any abuse prohibited by Article [102 TFEU], they shall also apply Article [102 TFEU].' In the interests of the proper functioning of the internal market and with a view to greater legal certainty and a more level playing field for undertakings and consumers, it is appropriate that the scope of this Directive extend to actions for damages based on the infringement of national competition law where it is applied pursuant to Article 3(1) of Regulation (EC) No 1/2003. Applying differing rules on civil liability in respect of infringements of Article 101 or 102 TFEU and in respect of infringements of rules of national competition law which must be applied in the same cases in parallel to Union competition law would otherwise adversely affect the position of claimants in the same case and the scope of their claims, and would constitute an obstacle to the proper functioning of the internal market. This Directive should not affect actions for damages in respect of infringements of national competition law which do not affect trade between Member States within the meaning of Article 101 or 102 TFEU.

(11) In the absence of Union law, actions for damages are governed by the national rules and procedures of the Member States. According to the case-law of the Court of Justice of the European Union (Court of Justice), any person can claim compensation for harm suffered where there is a causal relationship between that harm and an infringement of competition law. All national rules governing the exercise of the right to compensation for harm resulting from an infringement of Article 101 or 102 TFEU, including those concerning aspects not dealt with in this Directive such as the notion of causal relationship between the infringement and the harm, must observe the principles of effectiveness and equivalence. This means that they should not be formulated or applied in a way that makes it excessively difficult or practically impossible to exercise the right to compensation guaranteed by the TFEU or less favourably than those applicable to similar domestic actions. Where Member States provide other conditions for compensation under national law, such as imputability, adequacy or culpability, they should be able to maintain such conditions in so far as they comply with the case-law of the Court of Justice, the principles of effectiveness and equivalence, and this Directive.

(12) This Directive reaffirms the acquis communautaire on the right to compensation for harm caused by infringements of Union competition law, particularly regarding standing and the definition of damage, as stated in the case-law of the Court of Justice, and does not pre-empt any further development thereof. Anyone who has suffered harm caused by such an infringement can claim compensation for actual loss (damnum emergens), for gain of which that person has been deprived (loss of profit or lucrum cessans), plus interest, irrespective of whether those categories are established separately or in combination in national law. The payment of interest is an essential component of compensation to make good the damage sustained by taking into account the effluxion of time and should be due from the time when the harm occurred until the time when compensation is paid, without prejudice to the qualification of such interest as compensatory or default interest under national law and to whether effluxion of time is taken into account as a separate category (interest) or as a constituent part of actual loss or loss of profit. It is incumbent on the Member States to lay down the rules to be applied for that purpose.

(13) The right to compensation is recognised for any natural or legal person – consumers, undertakings and public authorities alike – irrespective of the existence of a direct contractual relationship with the infringing undertaking, and regardless of whether or not there has been a prior finding of an infringement by a competition authority. This Directive should not require Member States to introduce collective redress mechanisms for the enforcement of Articles 101 and 102 TFEU. Without prejudice to compensation for loss of opportunity, full compensation under this Directive should not lead to overcompensation, whether by means of punitive, multiple or other damages.

(14) Actions for damages for infringements of Union or national competition law typically require a complex factual and economic analysis. The evidence necessary to prove a claim for damages is often held exclusively by the opposing party or by third parties, and is not sufficiently known by, or accessible to, the claimant. In such circumstances, strict legal requirements for claimants to assert in detail all the facts of their case at the beginning of an action and to proffer precisely specified items of supporting evidence can unduly impede the effective exercise of the right to compensation guaranteed by the TFEU.

(15) Evidence is an important element for bringing actions for damages for infringement of Union or national competition law. However, as competition law litigation is characterised by an information asymmetry, it is appropriate to ensure that claimants are afforded the right to obtain the disclosure of evidence relevant to their claim, without it being necessary for them to specify individual items of evidence. In

order to ensure equality of arms, those means should also be available to defendants in actions for damages, so that they can request the disclosure of evidence by those claimants. National courts should also be able to order that evidence be disclosed by third parties, including public authorities. Where a national court wishes to order disclosure of evidence by the Commission, the principle in Article 4(3) TEU of sincere cooperation between the Union and the Member States and Article 15(1) of Regulation (EC) No 1/2003 as regards requests for information apply. Where national courts order public authorities to disclose evidence, the principles of legal and administrative cooperation under Union or national law apply.

(16) National courts should be able, under their strict control, especially as regards the necessity and proportionality of disclosure measures, to order the disclosure of specified items of evidence or categories of evidence upon request of a party. It follows from the requirement of proportionality that disclosure can be ordered only where a claimant has made a plausible assertion, on the basis of facts which are reasonably available to that claimant, that the claimant has suffered harm that was caused by the defendant. Where a request for disclosure aims to obtain a category of evidence, that category should be identified by reference to common features of its constitutive elements such as the nature, object or content of the documents the disclosure of which is requested, the time during which they were drawn up, or other criteria, provided that the evidence falling within the category is relevant within the meaning of this Directive. Such categories should be defined as precisely and narrowly as possible on the basis of reasonably available facts.

(17) Where a court in one Member State requests a competent court in another Member State to take evidence or requests that evidence be taken directly in another Member State, the provisions of Council Regulation (EC) No 1206/2001[4] apply.

(18) While relevant evidence containing business secrets or otherwise confidential information should, in principle, be available in actions for damages, such confidential information needs to be protected appropriately. National courts should therefore have at their disposal a range of measures to protect such confidential information from being disclosed during the proceedings. Those measures could include the possibility of redacting sensitive passages in documents, conducting hearings in camera, restricting the persons allowed to see the evidence,

---

[4] Council Regulation (EC) No 1206/2001 of 28 May 2001 on cooperation between the courts of the Member States in the taking of evidence in civil or commercial matters (OJ L 174, 27.6.2001, p. 1).

and instructing experts to produce summaries of the information in an aggregated or otherwise non-confidential form. Measures protecting business secrets and other confidential information should, nevertheless, not impede the exercise of the right to compensation.

(19) This Directive affects neither the possibility under the laws of the Member States to appeal disclosure orders, nor the conditions for bringing such appeals.

(20) Regulation (EC) No 1049/2001 of the European Parliament and of the Council[5] governs public access to European Parliament, Council and Commission documents, and is designed to confer on the public as wide a right of access as possible to documents of those institutions. That right is nonetheless subject to certain limits based on reasons of public or private interest. It follows that the system of exceptions laid down in Article 4 of that Regulation is based on a balancing of the opposing interests in a given situation, namely, the interests which would be favoured by the disclosure of the documents in question and those which would be jeopardised by such disclosure. This Directive should be without prejudice to such rules and practices under Regulation (EC) No 1049/2001.

(21) The effectiveness and consistency of the application of Articles 101 and 102 TFEU by the Commission and the national competition authorities require a common approach across the Union on the disclosure of evidence that is included in the file of a competition authority. Disclosure of evidence should not unduly detract from the effectiveness of the enforcement of competition law by a competition authority. This Directive does not cover the disclosure of internal documents of, or correspondence between, competition authorities.

(22) In order to ensure the effective protection of the right to compensation, it is not necessary that every document relating to proceedings under Article 101 or 102 TFEU be disclosed to a claimant merely on the grounds of the claimant's intended action for damages since it is highly unlikely that the action for damages will need to be based on all the evidence in the file relating to those proceedings.

(23) The requirement of proportionality should be carefully assessed when disclosure risks unravelling the investigation strategy of a competition authority by revealing which documents are part of the file or risks having a negative effect on the way in which undertakings cooperate with the competition authorities. Particular attention should be paid to preventing 'fishing expeditions', i.e. non-specific or overly broad

---

[5] Regulation (EC) No 1049/2001 of the European Parliament and of the Council of 30 May 2001 regarding public access to European Parliament, Council and Commission documents (OJ L 145, 31.5.2001, p. 43).

searches for information that is unlikely to be of relevance for the parties to the proceedings. Disclosure requests should therefore not bedeemed to be proportionate where they refer to the generic disclosure of documents in the file of a competition authority relating to a certain case, or the generic disclosure of documents submitted by a party in the context of a particular case. Such wide disclosure requests would not be compatible with the requesting party's duty to specify the items of evidence or the categories of evidence as precisely and narrowly as possible.

(24) This Directive does not affect the right of courts to consider, under Union or national law, the interests of the effective public enforcement of competition law when ordering the disclosure of any type of evidence with the exception of leniency statements and settlement submissions.

(25) An exemption should apply in respect of any disclosure that, if granted, would unduly interfere with an ongoing investigation by a competition authority concerning an infringement of Union or national competition law. Information that was prepared by a competition authority in the course of its proceedings for the enforcement of Union or national competition law and sent to the parties to those proceedings (such as a 'Statement of Objections') or prepared by a party thereto (such as replies to requests for information of the competition authority or witness statements) should therefore be disclosable in actions for damages only after the competition authority has closed its proceedings, for instance by adopting a decision under Article 5 or under Chapter III of Regulation (EC) No 1/2003, with the exception of decisions on interim measures.

(26) Leniency programmes and settlement procedures are important tools for the public enforcement of Union competition law as they contribute to the detection and efficient prosecution of, and the imposition of penalties for, the most serious infringements of competition law. Furthermore, as many decisions of competition authorities in cartel cases are based on a leniency application, and damages actions in cartel cases generally follow on from those decisions, leniency programmes are also important for the effectiveness of actions for damages in cartel cases. Undertakings might be deterred from cooperating with competition authorities under leniency programmes and settlement procedures if self-incriminating statements such as leniency statements and settlement submissions, which are produced for the sole purpose of cooperating with the competition authorities, were to be disclosed. Such disclosure would pose a risk of exposing cooperating undertakings or their managing staff to civil or criminal liability under conditions worse than those of co-infringers not cooperating with the competition

authorities. To ensure undertakings' continued willingness to approach competition authorities voluntarily with leniency statements or settlement submissions, such documents should be exempted from the disclosure of evidence. That exemption should also apply to verbatim quotations from leniency statements or settlement submissions included in other documents. Those limitations on the disclosure of evidence should not prevent competition authorities from publishing their decisions in accordance with the applicable Union or national law. In order to ensure that that exemption does not unduly interfere with injured parties' rights to compensation, it should be limited to those voluntary and self-incriminating leniency statements and settlement submissions.

(27) The rules in this Directive on the disclosure of documents other than leniency statements and settlement submissions ensure that injured parties retain sufficient alternative means by which to obtain access to the relevant evidence that they need in order to prepare their actions for damages. National courts should themselves be able, upon request by a claimant, to access documents in respect of which the exemption is invoked in order to verify whether the contents thereof fall outside the definitions of leniency statements and settlement submissions laid down in this Directive. Any content falling outside those definitions should be disclosable under the relevant conditions.

(28) National courts should be able, at any time, to order, in the context of an action for damages, the disclosure of evidence that exists independently of the proceedings of a competition authority ('pre-existing information').

(29) The disclosure of evidence should be ordered from a competition authority only when that evidence cannot reasonably be obtained from another party or from a third party.

(30) Pursuant to Article 15(3) of Regulation (EC) No 1/2003, competition authorities, acting upon their own initiative, can submit written observations to national courts on issues relating to the application of Article 101 or 102 TFEU. In order to preserve the contribution made by public enforcement to the application of those Articles, competition authorities should likewise be able, acting upon their own initiative, to submit their observations to a national court for the purpose of assessing the proportionality of a disclosure of evidence included in the authorities' files, in light of the impact that such disclosure would have on the effectiveness of the public enforcement of competition law. Member States should be able to set up a system whereby a competition authority is informed of requests for disclosure of information when the person requesting disclosure or the person from whom disclosure is sought is involved in that competition authority's investi-

gation into the alleged infringement, without prejudice to national law providing for ex parte proceedings.

(31) Any natural or legal person that obtains evidence through access to the file of a competition authority should be able to use that evidence for the purposes of an action for damages to which it is a party. Such use should also be allowed on the part of any natural or legal person that succeeded in its rights and obligations, including through the acquisition of its claim. Where the evidence was obtained by a legal person forming part of a corporate group constituting one undertaking for the application of Articles 101 and 102 TFEU, other legal persons belonging to the same undertaking should also be able to use that evidence.

(32) However, the use of evidence obtained through access to the file of a competition authority should not unduly detract from the effective enforcement of competition law by a competition authority. In order to ensure that the limitations on disclosure laid down in this Directive are not undermined, the use of evidence of the types referred to in recitals 24 and 25 which is obtained solely through access to the file of a competition authority should be limited under the same circumstances. The limitation should take the form of inadmissibility in actions for damages or the form of any other protection under applicable national rules capable of ensuring the full effect of the limits on the disclosure of those types of evidence. Moreover, evidence obtained from a competition authority should not become an object of trade. The possibility of using evidence that was obtained solely through access to the file of a competition authority should therefore be limited to the natural or legal person that was originally granted access and to its legal successors. That limitation to avoid trading of evidence does not, however, prevent a national court from ordering the disclosure of that evidence under the conditions provided for in this Directive.

(33) The fact that a claim for damages is initiated, or that an investigation by a competition authority is started, entails a risk that persons concerned may destroy or hide evidence that would be useful in substantiating an injured party's claim for damages. To prevent the destruction of relevant evidence and to ensure that court orders as to disclosure are complied with, national courts should be able to impose sufficiently deterrent penalties. In so far as parties to the proceedings are concerned, the risk of adverse inferences being drawn in the proceedings for damages can be a particularly effective penalty, and can help avoid delays. Penalties should also be available for non-compliance with obligations to protect confidential information and for the abusive use of information obtained through disclosure. Similarly, penalties should be available if information obtained through access to the file of a competition authority is used abusively in actions for damages.

(34) Ensuring the effective and consistent application of Articles 101 and 102 TFEU by the Commission and the national competition authorities necessitates a common approach across the Union on the effect of national competition authorities' final infringement decisions on subsequent actions for damages. Such decisions are adopted only after the Commission has been informed of the decision envisaged or, in the absence thereof, of any other document indicating the proposed course of action pursuant to Article 11(4) of Regulation (EC) No 1/2003, and if the Commission has not relieved the national competition authority of its competence by initiating proceedings pursuant to Article 11(6) of that Regulation. The Commission should ensure the consistent application of Union competition law by providing, bilaterally and within the framework of the European Competition Network, guidance to the national competition authorities. To enhance legal certainty, to avoid inconsistency in the application of Articles 101 and 102 TFEU, to increase the effectiveness and procedural efficiency of actions for damages and to foster the functioning of the internal market for undertakings and consumers, the finding of an infringement of Article 101 or 102 TFEU in a final decision by a national competition authority or a review court should not be relitigated in subsequent actions for damages. Therefore, such a finding should be deemed to be irrefutably established in actions for damages brought in the Member State of the national competition authority or review court relating to that infringement. The effect of the finding should, however, cover only the nature of the infringement and its material, personal, temporal and territorial scope as determined by the competition authority or review court in the exercise of its jurisdiction. Where a decision has found that provisions of national competition law are infringed in cases where Union and national competition law are applied in the same case and in parallel, that infringement should also be deemed to be irrefutably established.

(35) Where an action for damages is brought in a Member State other than the Member State of a national competition authority or a review court that found the infringement of Article 101 or 102 TFEU to which the action relates, it should be possible to present that finding in a final decision by the national competition authority or the review court to a national court as at least prima facie evidence of the fact that an infringement of competition law has occurred. The finding can be assessed as appropriate, along with any other evidence adduced by the parties. The effects of decisions by national competition authorities and review courts finding an infringement of the competition rules are without prejudice to the rights and obligations of national courts under Article 267 TFEU.

(36) National rules on the beginning, duration, suspension or interruption of limitation periods should not unduly hamper the bringing of actions for damages. This is particularly important in respect of actions that build upon a finding by a competition authority or a review court of an infringement. To that end, it should be possible to bring an action for damages after proceedings by a competition authority, with a view to enforcing national and Union competition law. The limitation period should not begin to run before the infringement ceases and before a claimant knows, or can reasonably be expected to know, the behaviour constituting the infringement, the fact that the infringement caused the claimant harm and the identity of the infringer. Member States should be able to maintain or introduce absolute limitation periods that are of general application, provided that the duration of such absolute limitation periods does not render practically impossible or excessively difficult the exercise of the right to full compensation.

(37) Where several undertakings infringe the competition rules jointly, as in the case of a cartel, it is appropriate to make provision for those co-infringers to be held jointly and severally liable for the entire harm caused by the infringement. A co-infringer should have the right to obtain a contribution from other co-infringers if it has paid more compensation than its share. The determination of that share as the relative responsibility of a given infringer, and the relevant criteria such as turnover, market share, or role in the cartel, is a matter for the applicable national law, while respecting the principles of effectiveness and equivalence.

(38) Undertakings which cooperate with competition authorities under a leniency programme play a key role in exposing secret cartel infringements and in bringing them to an end, thereby often mitigating the harm which could have been caused had the infringement continued. It is therefore appropriate to make provision for undertakings which have received immunity from fines from a competition authority under a leniency programme to be protected from undue exposure to damages claims, bearing in mind that the decision of the competition authority finding the infringement may become final for the immunity recipient before it becomes final for other undertakings which have not received immunity, thus potentially making the immunity recipient the preferential target of litigation. It is therefore appropriate that the immunity recipient be relieved in principle from joint and several liability for the entire harm and that any contribution it must make vis-à-vis co-infringers not exceed the amount of harm caused to its own direct or indirect purchasers or, in the case of a buying cartel, its direct or indirect providers. To the extent that a cartel has caused harm to those other than the customers or providers of the infringers, the contribution of

the immunity recipient should not exceed its relative responsibility for the harm caused by the cartel. That share should be determined in accordance with the same rules used to determine the contributions between infringers. The immunity recipient should remain fully liable to the injured parties other than its direct or indirect purchasers or providers only where they are unable to obtain full compensation from the other infringers.

(39) Harm in the form of actual loss can result from the price difference between what was actually paid and what would otherwise have been paid in the absence of the infringement. When an injured party has reduced its actual loss by passing it on, entirely or in part, to its own purchasers, the loss which has been passed on no longer constitutes harm for which the party that passed it on needs to be compensated. It is therefore in principle appropriate to allow an infringer to invoke the passing-on of actual loss as a defence against a claim for damages. It is appropriate to provide that the infringer, in so far as it invokes the passing-on defence, must prove the existence and extent of pass-on of the overcharge. This burden of proof should not affect the possibility for the infringer to use evidence other than that in its possession, such as evidence already acquired in the proceedings or evidence held by other parties or third parties.

(40) In situations where the passing-on resulted in reduced sales and thus harm in the form of a loss of profit, the right to claim compensation for such loss of profit should remain unaffected.

(41) Depending on the conditions under which undertakings are operating, it may be commercial practice to pass on price increases down the supply chain. Consumers or undertakings to whom actual loss has thus been passed on have suffered harm caused by an infringement of Union or national competition law. While such harm should be compensated for by the infringer, it may be particularly difficult for consumers or undertakings that did not themselves make any purchase from the infringer to prove the extent of that harm. It is therefore appropriate to provide that, where the existence of a claim for damages or the amount of damages to be awarded depends on whether or to what degree an overcharge paid by a direct purchaser from the infringer has been passed on to an indirect purchaser, the latter is regarded as having proven that an overcharge paid by that direct purchaser has been passed on to its level where it is able to show prima facie that such passing-on has occurred. This rebuttable presumption applies unless the infringer can credibly demonstrate to the satisfaction of the court that the actual loss has not or not entirely been passed on to the indirect purchaser. It is furthermore appropriate to define under what conditions the indirect purchaser is to be regarded as having established such prima facie proof.

As regards the quantification of passing-on, national courts should have the power to estimate which share of the overcharge has been passed on to the level of indirect purchasers in disputes pending before them.

(42) The Commission should issue clear, simple and comprehensive guidelines for national courts on how to estimate the share of the overcharge passed on to indirect purchasers.

(43) Infringements of competition law often concern the conditions and the price under which goods or services are sold, and lead to an overcharge and other harm for the customers of the infringers. The infringement may also concern supplies to the infringer (for example in the case of a buyers' cartel). In such cases, the actual loss could result from a lower price paid by infringers to their suppliers. This Directive and in particular the rules on passing-on should apply accordingly to those cases.

(44) Actions for damages can be brought both by those who purchased goods or services from the infringer and by purchasers further down the supply chain. In the interest of consistency between judgments resulting from related proceedings and hence to avoid the harm caused by the infringement of Union or national competition law not being fully compensated or the infringer being required to pay damages to compensate for harm that has not been suffered, national courts should have the power to estimate the proportion of any overcharge which was suffered by the direct or indirect purchasers in disputes pending before them. In this context, national courts should be able to take due account, by procedural or substantive means available under Union and national law, of any related action and of the resulting judgment, particularly where it finds that passing-on has been proven. National courts should have at their disposal appropriate procedural means, such as joinder of claims, to ensure that compensation for actual loss paid at any level of the supply chain does not exceed the overcharge harm caused at that level. Such means should also be available in cross-border cases. This possibility to take due account of judgments should be without prejudice to the fundamental rights of the defence and the rights to an effective remedy and a fair trial of those who were not parties to the judicial proceedings, and without prejudice to the rules on the evidentiary value of judgments rendered in that context. It is possible for actions pending before the courts of different Member States to be considered as related within the meaning of Article 30 of Regulation (EU) No 1215/2012 of the European Parliament and of the Council.[6] Under that Article, national courts

---

[6] Regulation (EU) No 1215/2012 of the European Parliament and of the Council of 12 December 2012 on jurisdiction and the recognition and enforcement of judgments in civil and commercial matters (OJ L 351, 20.12.2012, p. 1).

other than that first seized may stay proceedings or, under certain circumstances, may decline jurisdiction. This Directive is without prejudice to the rights and obligations of national courts under that Regulation.

(45) An injured party who has proven having suffered harm as a result of a competition law infringement still needs to prove the extent of the harm in order to obtain damages. Quantifying harm in competition law cases is a very fact-intensive process and may require the application of complex economic models. This is often very costly, and claimants have difficulties in obtaining the data necessary to substantiate their claims. The quantification of harm in competition law cases can thus constitute a substantial barrier preventing effective claims for compensation.

(46) In the absence of Union rules on the quantification of harm caused by a competition law infringement, it is for the domestic legal system of each Member State to determine its own rules on quantifying harm, and for the Member States and for the national courts to determine what requirements the claimant has to meet when proving the amount of the harm suffered, the methods that can be used in quantifying the amount, and the consequences of not being able to fully meet those requirements. However, the requirements of national law regarding the quantification of harm in competition law cases should not be less favourable than those governing similar domestic actions (principle of equivalence), nor should they render the exercise of the Union right to damages practically impossible or excessively difficult (principle of effectiveness). Regard should be had to any information asymmetries between the parties and to the fact that quantifying the harm means assessing how the market in question would have evolved had there been no infringement. This assessment implies a comparison with a situation which is by definition hypothetical and can thus never be made with complete accuracy. It is therefore appropriate to ensure that national courts have the power to estimate the amount of the harm caused by the competition law infringement. Member States should ensure that, where requested, national competition authorities may provide guidance on quantum. In order to ensure coherence and predictability, the Commission should provide general guidance at Union level.

(47) To remedy the information asymmetry and some of the difficulties associated with quantifying harm in competition law cases, and to ensure the effectiveness of claims for damages, it is appropriate to presume that cartel infringements result in harm, in particular via an effect on prices. Depending on the facts of the case, cartels result in a rise in prices, or prevent a lowering of prices which would otherwise have occurred but for the cartel. This presumption should not cover the concrete amount

of harm. Infringers should be allowed to rebut the presumption. It is appropriate to limit this rebuttable presumption to cartels, given their secret nature, which increases the information asymmetry and makes it more difficult for claimants to obtain the evidence necessary to prove the harm.

(48) Achieving a 'once-and-for-all' settlement for defendants is desirable in order to reduce uncertainty for infringers and injured parties. Therefore, infringers and injured parties should be encouraged to agree on compensating for the harm caused by a competition law infringement through consensual dispute resolution mechanisms, such as out-of-court settlements (including those where a judge can declare a settlement binding), arbitration, mediation or conciliation. Such consensual dispute resolution should cover as many injured parties and infringers as legally possible. The provisions in this Directive on consensual dispute resolution are therefore meant to facilitate the use of such mechanisms and increase their effectiveness.

(49) Limitation periods for bringing an action for damages could be such that they prevent injured parties and infringers from having sufficient time to come to an agreement on the compensation to be paid. In order to provide both sides with a genuine opportunity to engage in consensual dispute resolution before bringing proceedings before national courts, limitation periods need to be suspended for the duration of the consensual dispute resolution process.

(50) Furthermore, when parties decide to engage in consensual dispute resolution after an action for damages for the same claim has been brought before a national court, that court should be able to suspend the proceedings before it for the duration of the consensual dispute resolution process. When considering whether to suspend the proceedings, the national court should take into account the advantages of an expeditious procedure.

(51) To encourage consensual settlements, an infringer that pays damages through consensual dispute resolution should not be placed in a worse position vis-à-vis its co-infringers than it would otherwise be without the consensual settlement. That might happen if a settling infringer, even after a consensual settlement, continued to be fully jointly and severally liable for the harm caused by the infringement. A settling infringer should in principle therefore not contribute to its non-settling co-infringers when the latter have paid damages to an injured party with whom the first infringer had previously settled. The corollary to this non-contribution rule is that the claim of the injured party should be reduced by the settling infringer's share of the harm caused to it, regardless of whether the amount of the settlement equals or is different from the relative share of the harm that the settling co-infringer

inflicted upon the settling injured party. That relative share should be determined in accordance with the rules otherwise used to determine the contributions among infringers. Without such a reduction, non-settling infringers would be unduly affected by settlements to which they were not a party. However, in order to ensure the right to full compensation, settling co-infringers should still have to pay damages where that is the only possibility for the settling injured party to obtain compensation for the remaining claim. The remaining claim refers to the claim of the settling injured party reduced by the settling co-infringer's share of the harm that the infringement inflicted upon the settling injured party. The latter possibility to claim damages from the settling co-infringer exists unless it is expressly excluded under the terms of the consensual settlement.

(52) Situations should be avoided in which settling co-infringers, by paying contribution to non-settling co-infringers for damages they paid to non-settling injured parties, pay a total amount of compensation exceeding their relative responsibility for the harm caused by the infringement. Therefore, when settling co-infringers are asked to contribute to damages subsequently paid by non-settling co-infringers to non-settling injured parties, national courts should take account of the damages already paid under the consensual settlement, bearing in mind that not all co-infringers are necessarily equally involved in the full substantive, temporal and geographical scope of the infringement.

(53) This Directive respects the fundamental rights and observes the principles recognised in the Charter of Fundamental Rights of the European Union.

(54) Since the objectives of this Directive, namely to establish rules concerning actions for damages for infringements of Union competition law in order to ensure the full effect of Articles 101 and 102 TFEU, and the proper functioning of the internal market for undertakings and consumers, cannot be sufficiently achieved by the Member States, but can rather, by reason of the requisite effectiveness and consistency in the application of Articles 101 and 102 TFEU, be better achieved at Union level, the Union may adopt measures, in accordance with the principle of subsidiarity as set out in Article 5 TEU. In accordance with the principle of proportionality, as set out in that Article, this Directive does not go beyond what is necessary in order to achieve those objectives.

(55) In accordance with the Joint Political Declaration of 28 September 2011 of Member States and the Commission on explanatory documents,[7]

---

[7] OJ C 369, 17.12.2011, p. 14.

Member States have undertaken to accompany, in justified cases, the notification of their transposition measures with one or more documents explaining the relationship between the components of a directive and the corresponding parts of national transposition instruments. With regard to this Directive, the legislator considers the transmission of such documents to be justified.

(56) It is appropriate to provide rules for the temporal application of this Directive,

HAVE ADOPTED THIS DIRECTIVE:

CHAPTER I

SUBJECT MATTER, SCOPE AND DEFINITIONS

Article 1

Subject matter and scope

1. This Directive sets out certain rules necessary to ensure that anyone who has suffered harm caused by an infringement of competition law by an undertaking or by an association of undertakings can effectively exercise the right to claim full compensation for that harm from that undertaking or association. It sets out rules fostering undistorted competition in the internal market and removing obstacles to its proper functioning, by ensuring equivalent protection throughout the Union for anyone who has suffered such harm.
2. This Directive sets out rules coordinating the enforcement of the competition rules by competition authorities and the enforcement of those rules in damages actions before national courts.

Article 2

Definitions

For the purposes of this Directive, the following definitions apply:
(1) 'infringement of competition law' means an infringement of Article 101 or 102 TFEU, or of national competition law;
(2) 'infringer' means an undertaking or association of undertakings which has committed an infringement of competition law;
(3) 'national competition law' means provisions of national law that predominantly pursue the same objective as Articles 101 and 102 TFEU and that are applied to the same case and in parallel to Union

competition law pursuant to Article 3(1) of Regulation (EC) No 1/2003, excluding provisions of national law which impose criminal penalties on natural persons, except to the extent that such criminal penalties are the means whereby competition rules applying to undertakings are enforced;

(4) 'action for damages' means an action under national law by which a claim for damages is brought before a national court by an alleged injured party, or by someone acting on behalf of one or more alleged injured parties where Union or national law provides for that possibility, or by a natural or legal person that succeeded in the right of the alleged injured party, including the person that acquired the claim;

(5) 'claim for damages' means a claim for compensation for harm caused by an infringement of competition law;

(6) 'injured party' means a person that has suffered harm caused by an infringement of competition law;

(7) 'national competition authority' means an authority designated by a Member State pursuant to Article 35 of Regulation (EC) No 1/2003, as being responsible for the application of Articles 101 and 102 TFEU;

(8) 'competition authority' means the Commission or a national competition authority or both, as the context may require;

(9) 'national court' means a court or tribunal of a Member State within the meaning of Article 267 TFEU;

(10) 'review court' means a national court that is empowered by ordinary means of appeal to review decisions of a national competition authority or to review judgments pronouncing on those decisions, irrespective of whether that court itself has the power to find an infringement of competition law;

(11) 'infringement decision' means a decision of a competition authority or review court that finds an infringement of competition law;

(12) 'final infringement decision' means an infringement decision that cannot be, or that can no longer be, appealed by ordinary means;

(13) 'evidence' means all types of means of proof admissible before the national court seized, in particular documents and all other objects containing information, irrespective of the medium on which the information is stored;

(14) 'cartel' means an agreement or concerted practice between two or more competitors aimed at coordinating their competitive behaviour on the market or influencing the relevant parameters of competition through practices such as, but not limited to, the fixing or coordination of purchase or selling prices or other trading conditions, including in relation to intellectual property rights, the allocation of production or sales quotas, the sharing of markets and customers, including bid-rigging, restrictions of imports or exports or anti-competitive actions against other competitors;

(15) 'leniency programme' means a programme concerning the application of Article 101 TFEU or a corresponding provision under national law on the basis of which a participant in a secret cartel, independently of the other undertakings involved in the cartel, cooperates with an investigation of the competition authority, by voluntarily providing presentations regarding that participant's knowledge of, and role in, the cartel in return for which that participant receives, by decision or by a discontinuation of proceedings, immunity from, or a reduction in, fines for its involvement in the cartel;

(16) 'leniency statement' means an oral or written presentation voluntarily provided by, or on behalf of, an undertaking or a natural person to a competition authority or a record thereof, describing the knowledge of that undertaking or natural person of a cartel and describing its role therein, which presentation was drawn up specifically for submission to the competition authority with a view to obtaining immunity or a reduction of fines under a leniency programme, not including pre-existing information;

(17) 'pre-existing information' means evidence that exists irrespective of the proceedings of a competition authority, whether or not such information is in the file of a competition authority;

(18) 'settlement submission' means a voluntary presentation by, or on behalf of, an undertaking to a competition authority describing the undertaking's acknowledgement of, or its renunciation to dispute, its participation in an infringement of competition law and its responsibility for that infringement of competition law, which was drawn up specifically to enable the competition authority to apply a simplified or expedited procedure;

(19) 'immunity recipient' means an undertaking which, or a natural person who, has been granted immunity from fines by a competition authority under a leniency programme;

(20) 'overcharge' means the difference between the price actually paid and the price that would otherwise have prevailed in the absence of an infringement of competition law;

(21) 'consensual dispute resolution' means any mechanism enabling parties to reach the out-of-court resolution of a dispute concerning a claim for damages;

(22) 'consensual settlement' means an agreement reached through consensual dispute resolution.

(23) 'direct purchaser' means a natural or legal person who acquired, directly from an infringer, products or services that were the object of an infringement of competition law;

(24) 'indirect purchaser' means a natural or legal person who acquired, not directly from an infringer, but from a direct purchaser or a subsequent

purchaser, products or services that were the object of an infringement of competition law, or products or services containing them or derived therefrom.

Article 3

Right to full compensation

1. Member States shall ensure that any natural or legal person who has suffered harm caused by an infringement of competition law is able to claim and to obtain full compensation for that harm.
2. Full compensation shall place a person who has suffered harm in the position in which that person would have been had the infringement of competition law not been committed. It shall therefore cover the right to compensation for actual loss and for loss of profit, plus the payment of interest.
3. Full compensation under this Directive shall not lead to overcompensation, whether by means of punitive, multiple or other types of damages.

Article 4

Principles of effectiveness and equivalence

In accordance with the principle of effectiveness, Member States shall ensure that all national rules and procedures relating to the exercise of claims for damages are designed and applied in such a way that they do not render practically impossible or excessively difficult the exercise of the Union right to full compensation for harm caused by an infringement of competition law. In accordance with the principle of equivalence, national rules and procedures relating to actions for damages resulting from infringements of Article 101 or 102 TFEU shall not be less favourable to the alleged injured parties than those governing similar actions for damages resulting from infringements of national law.

CHAPTER II

DISCLOSURE OF EVIDENCE

Article 5

Disclosure of evidence

1. Member States shall ensure that in proceedings relating to an action for damages in the Union, upon request of a claimant who has presented a reasoned justification containing reasonably available facts and evidence sufficient to support the plausibility of its claim for damages, national courts are able to order the defendant or a third party to disclose relevant evidence which lies in their control, subject to the conditions set out in this Chapter. Member States shall ensure that national courts are able, upon request of the defendant, to order the claimant or a third party to disclose relevant evidence.

    This paragraph is without prejudice to the rights and obligations of national courts under Regulation (EC) No 1206/2001.

2. Member States shall ensure that national courts are able to order the disclosure of specified items of evidence or relevant categories of evidence circumscribed as precisely and as narrowly as possible on the basis of reasonably available facts in the reasoned justification.
3. Member States shall ensure that national courts limit the disclosure of evidence to that which is proportionate. In determining whether any disclosure requested by a party is proportionate, national courts shall consider the legitimate interests of all parties and third parties concerned. They shall, in particular, consider:

    (a) the extent to which the claim or defence is supported by available facts and evidence justifying the request to disclose evidence;
    (b) the scope and cost of disclosure, especially for any third parties concerned, including preventing non-specific searches for information which is unlikely to be of relevance for the parties in the procedure;
    (c) whether the evidence the disclosure of which is sought contains confidential information, especially concerning any third parties, and what arrangements are in place for protecting such confidential information.

4. Member States shall ensure that national courts have the power to order the disclosure of evidence containing confidential information where they consider it relevant to the action for damages. Member States shall

ensure that, when ordering the disclosure of such information, national courts have at their disposal effective measures to protect such information.
5. The interest of undertakings to avoid actions for damages following an infringement of competition law shall not constitute an interest that warrants protection.
6. Member States shall ensure that national courts give full effect to applicable legal professional privilege under Union or national law when ordering the disclosure of evidence.
7. Member States shall ensure that those from whom disclosure is sought are provided with an opportunity to be heard before a national court orders disclosure under this Article.
8. Without prejudice to paragraphs 4 and 7 and to Article 6, this Article shall not prevent Member States from maintaining or introducing rules which would lead to wider disclosure of evidence.

Article 6

Disclosure of evidence included in the file of a competition authority

1. Member States shall ensure that, for the purpose of actions for damages, where national courts order the disclosure of evidence included in the file of a competition authority, this Article applies in addition to Article 5.
2. This Article is without prejudice to the rules and practices on public access to documents under Regulation (EC) No 1049/2001.
3. This Article is without prejudice to the rules and practices under Union or national law on the protection of internal documents of competition authorities and of correspondence between competition authorities.
4. When assessing, in accordance with Article 5(3), the proportionality of an order to disclose information, national courts shall, in addition, consider the following:

   (a) whether the request has been formulated specifically with regard to the nature, subject matter or contents of documents submitted to a competition authority or held in the file thereof, rather than by a non-specific application concerning documents submitted to a competition authority;
   (b) whether the party requesting disclosure is doing so in relation to an action for damages before a national court; and
   (c) in relation to paragraphs 5 and 10, or upon request of a competition authority pursuant to paragraph 11, the need to safeguard the effectiveness of the public enforcement of competition law.

5. National courts may order the disclosure of the following categories of evidence only after a competition authority, by adopting a decision or otherwise, has closed its proceedings:
   (a) information that was prepared by a natural or legal person specifically for the proceedings of a competition authority;
   (b) information that the competition authority has drawn up and sent to the parties in the course of its proceedings; and
   (c) settlement submissions that have been withdrawn.

6. Member States shall ensure that, for the purpose of actions for damages, national courts cannot at any time order a party or a third party to disclose any of the following categories of evidence:

   (a) leniency statements; and
   (b) settlement submissions.

7. A claimant may present a reasoned request that a national court access the evidence referred to in point (a) or (b) of paragraph 6 for the sole purpose of ensuring that their contents correspond to the definitions in points (16) and (18) of Article 2. In that assessment, national courts may request assistance only from the competent competition authority. The authors of the evidence in question may also have the possibility to be heard. In no case shall the national court permit other parties or third parties access to that evidence.

8. If only parts of the evidence requested are covered by paragraph 6, the remaining parts thereof shall, depending on the category under which they fall, be released in accordance with the relevant paragraphs of this Article.

9. The disclosure of evidence in the file of a competition authority that does not fall into any of the categories listed in this Article may be ordered in actions for damages at any time, without prejudice to this Article.

10. Member States shall ensure that national courts request the disclosure from a competition authority of evidence included in its file only where no party or third party is reasonably able to provide that evidence.

11. To the extent that a competition authority is willing to state its views on the proportionality of disclosure requests, it may, acting on its own initiative, submit observations to the national court before which a disclosure order is sought.

Article 7

Limits on the use of evidence obtained solely through access to the file of a competition authority

1. Member States shall ensure that evidence in the categories listed in Article 6(6) which is obtained by a natural or legal person solely through access to the file of a competition authority is either deemed to be inadmissible in actions for damages or is otherwise protected under the applicable national rules to ensure the full effect of the limits on the disclosure of evidence set out in Article 6.
2. Member States shall ensure that, until a competition authority has closed its proceedings by adopting a decision or otherwise, evidence in the categories listed in Article 6(5) which is obtained by a natural or legal person solely through access to the file of that competition authority is either deemed to be inadmissible in actions for damages or is otherwise protected under the applicable national rules to ensure the full effect of the limits on the disclosure of evidence set out in Article 6.
3. Member States shall ensure that evidence which is obtained by a natural or legal person solely through access to the file of a competition authority and which does not fall under paragraph 1 or 2, can be used in an action for damages only by that person or by a natural or legal person that succeeded to that person's rights, including a person that acquired that person's claim.

Article 8

Penalties

1. Member States shall ensure that national courts are able effectively to impose penalties on parties, third parties and their legal representatives in the event of any of the following:

    (a) their failure or refusal to comply with the disclosure order of any national court;
    (b) their destruction of relevant evidence;
    (c) their failure or refusal to comply with the obligations imposed by a national court order protecting confidential information;
    (d) their breach of the limits on the use of evidence provided for in this Chapter.

2. Member States shall ensure that the penalties that can be imposed by national courts are effective, proportionate and dissuasive. The penalties available to national courts shall include, with regard to the behaviour of

a party to proceedings for an action for damages, the possibility to draw adverse inferences, such as presuming the relevant issue to be proven or dismissing claims and defences in whole or in part, and the possibility to order the payment of costs.

CHAPTER III

EFFECT OF NATIONAL DECISIONS, LIMITATION PERIODS, JOINT AND SEVERAL LIABILITY

Article 9

Effect of national decisions

1. Member States shall ensure that an infringement of competition law found by a final decision of a national competition authority or by a review court is deemed to be irrefutably established for the purposes of an action for damages brought before their national courts under Article 101 or 102 TFEU or under national competition law.
2. Member States shall ensure that where a final decision referred to in paragraph 1 is taken in another Member State, that final decision may, in accordance with national law, be presented before their national courts as at least prima facie evidence that an infringement of competition law has occurred and, as appropriate, may be assessed along with any other evidence adduced by the parties.
3. This Article is without prejudice to the rights and obligations of national courts under Article 267 TFEU.

Article 10

Limitation periods

1. Member States shall, in accordance with this Article, lay down rules applicable to limitation periods for bringing actions for damages. Those rules shall determine when the limitation period begins to run, the duration thereof and the circumstances under which it is interrupted or suspended.
2. Limitation periods shall not begin to run before the infringement of competition law has ceased and the claimant knows, or can reasonably be expected to know:

    (a) of the behaviour and the fact that it constitutes an infringement of competition law;

(b) of the fact that the infringement of competition law caused harm to it; and
(c) the identity of the infringer.

3. Member States shall ensure that the limitation periods for bringing actions for damages are at least five years.
4. Member States shall ensure that a limitation period is suspended or, depending on national law, interrupted, if a competition authority takes action for the purpose of the investigation or its proceedings in respect of an infringement of competition law to which the action for damages relates. The suspension shall end at the earliest one year after the infringement decision has become final or after the proceedings are otherwise terminated.

Article 11

Joint and several liability

1. Member States shall ensure that undertakings which have infringed competition law through joint behaviour are jointly and severally liable for the harm caused by the infringement of competition law; with the effect that each of those undertakings is bound to compensate for the harm in full, and the injured party has the right to require full compensation from any of them until he has been fully compensated.
2. By way of derogation from paragraph 1, Member States shall ensure that, without prejudice to the right of full compensation as laid down in Article 3, where the infringer is a small or medium-sized enterprise (SME) as defined in Commission Recommendation 2003/361/EC,[8] the infringer is liable only to its own direct and indirect purchasers where:

    (a) its market share in the relevant market was below 5 % at any time during the infringement of competition law; and
    (b) the application of the normal rules of joint and several liability would irretrievably jeopardise its economic viability and cause its assets to lose all their value.

3. The derogation laid down in paragraph 2 shall not apply where:

    (a) the SME has led the infringement of competition law or has coerced other undertakings to participate therein; or

---

[8] Commission Recommendation 2003/361/EC of 6 May 2003 concerning the definition of micro, small and medium-sized enterprises (OJ L 124, 20.5.2003, p. 36).

(b) the SME has previously been found to have infringed competition law.

4. By way of derogation from paragraph 1, Member States shall ensure that an immunity recipient is jointly and severally liable as follows:

(a) to its direct or indirect purchasers or providers; and
(b) to other injured parties only where full compensation cannot be obtained from the other undertakings that were involved in the same infringement of competition law.

Member States shall ensure that any limitation period applicable to cases under this paragraph is reasonable and sufficient to allow injured parties to bring such actions.

5. Member States shall ensure that an infringer may recover a contribution from any other infringer, the amount of which shall be determined in the light of their relative responsibility for the harm caused by the infringement of competition law. The amount of contribution of an infringer which has been granted immunity from fines under a leniency programme shall not exceed the amount of the harm it caused to its own direct or indirect purchasers or providers.

6. Member States shall ensure that, to the extent the infringement of competition law caused harm to injured parties other than the direct or indirect purchasers or providers of the infringers, the amount of any contribution from an immunity recipient to other infringers shall be determined in the light of its relative responsibility for that harm.

CHAPTER IV

THE PASSING-ON OF OVERCHARGES

Article 12

Passing-on of overcharges and the right to full compensation

1. To ensure the full effectiveness of the right to full compensation as laid down in Article 3, Member States shall ensure that, in accordance with the rules laid down in this Chapter, compensation of harm can be claimed by anyone who suffered it, irrespective of whether they are direct or indirect purchasers from an infringer, and that compensation of harm exceeding that caused by the infringement of competition law to the claimant, as well as the absence of liability of the infringer, are avoided.

2. In order to avoid overcompensation, Member States shall lay down procedural rules appropriate to ensure that compensation for actual loss

at any level of the supply chain does not exceed the overcharge harm suffered at that level.
3. This Chapter shall be without prejudice to the right of an injured party to claim and obtain compensation for loss of profits due to a full or partial passing-on of the overcharge.
4. Member States shall ensure that the rules laid down in this Chapter apply accordingly where the infringement of competition law relates to a supply to the infringer.
5. Member States shall ensure that the national courts have the power to estimate, in accordance with national procedures, the share of any overcharge that was passed on.

Article 13

Passing-on defence

Member States shall ensure that the defendant in an action for damages can invoke as a defence against a claim for damages the fact that the claimant passed on the whole or part of the overcharge resulting from the infringement of competition law. The burden of proving that the overcharge was passed on shall be on the defendant, who may reasonably require disclosure from the claimant or from third parties.

Article 14

Indirect purchasers

1. Member States shall ensure that, where in an action for damages the existence of a claim for damages or the amount of compensation to be awarded depends on whether, or to what degree, an overcharge was passed on to the claimant, taking into account the commercial practice that price increases are passed on down the supply chain, the burden of proving the existence and scope of such a passing-on shall rest with the claimant, who may reasonably require disclosure from the defendant or from third parties.
2. In the situation referred to in paragraph 1, the indirect purchaser shall be deemed to have proven that a passing-on to that indirect purchaser occurred where that indirect purchaser has shown that:
    (a) the defendant has committed an infringement of competition law;
    (b) the infringement of competition law has resulted in an overcharge for the direct purchaser of the defendant; and

(c) the indirect purchaser has purchased the goods or services that were the object of the infringement of competition law, or has purchased goods or services derived from or containing them.

This paragraph shall not apply where the defendant can demonstrate credibly to the satisfaction of the court that the overcharge was not, or was not entirely, passed on to the indirect purchaser.

Article 15

Actions for damages by claimants from different levels in the supply chain

1. To avoid that actions for damages by claimants from different levels in the supply chain lead to a multiple liability or to an absence of liability of the infringer, Member States shall ensure that in assessing whether the burden of proof resulting from the application of Articles 13 and 14 is satisfied, national courts seized of an action for damages are able, by means available under Union or national law, to take due account of any of the following:

   (a) actions for damages that are related to the same infringement of competition law, but that are brought by claimants from other levels in the supply chain;
   (b) judgments resulting from actions for damages as referred to in point (a);
   (c) relevant information in the public domain resulting from the public enforcement of competition law.

2. This Article shall be without prejudice to the rights and obligations of national courts under Article 30 of Regulation (EU) No 1215/2012.

Article 16

Guidelines for national courts

The Commission shall issue guidelines for national courts on how to estimate the share of the overcharge which was passed on to the indirect purchaser.

CHAPTER V

QUANTIFICATION OF HARM

Article 17

Quantification of harm

1. Member States shall ensure that neither the burden nor the standard of proof required for the quantification of harm renders the exercise of the right to damages practically impossible or excessively difficult. Member States shall ensure that the national courts are empowered, in accordance with national procedures, to estimate the amount of harm if it is established that a claimant suffered harm but it is practically impossible or excessively difficult precisely to quantify the harm suffered on the basis of the evidence available.
2. It shall be presumed that cartel infringements cause harm. The infringer shall have the right to rebut that presumption.
3. Member States shall ensure that, in proceedings relating to an action for damages, a national competition authority may, upon request of a national court, assist that national court with respect to the determination of the quantum of damages where that national competition authority considers such assistance to be appropriate.

CHAPTER VI

CONSENSUAL DISPUTE RESOLUTION

Article 18

Suspensive and other effects of consensual dispute resolution

1. Member States shall ensure that the limitation period for bringing an action for damages is suspended for the duration of any consensual dispute resolution process. The suspension of the limitation period shall apply only with regard to those parties that are or that were involved or represented in the consensual dispute resolution.
2. Without prejudice to provisions of national law in matters of arbitration, Member States shall ensure that national courts seized of an action for damages may suspend their proceedings for up to two years where the parties thereto are involved in consensual dispute resolution concerning the claim covered by that action for damages.

3. A competition authority may consider compensation paid as a result of a consensual settlement and prior to its decision imposing a fine to be a mitigating factor.

Article 19

Effect of consensual settlements on subsequent actions for damages

1. Member States shall ensure that, following a consensual settlement, the claim of the settling injured party is reduced by the settling co-infringer's share of the harm that the infringement of competition law inflicted upon the injured party.
2. Any remaining claim of the settling injured party shall be exercised only against non-settling co-infringers. Non-settling co-infringers shall not be permitted to recover contribution for the remaining claim from the settling co-infringer.
3. By way of derogation from paragraph 2, Member States shall ensure that where the non-settling co-infringers cannot pay the damages that correspond to the remaining claim of the settling injured party, the settling injured party may exercise the remaining claim against the settling co-infringer.

    The derogation referred to in the first subparagraph may be expressly excluded under the terms of the consensual settlement.
4. When determining the amount of contribution that a co-infringer may recover from any other co-infringer in accordance with their relative responsibility for the harm caused by the infringement of competition law, national courts shall take due account of any damages paid pursuant to a prior consensual settlement involving the relevant co-infringer.

CHAPTER VII

FINAL PROVISIONS

Article 20

Review

1. The Commission shall review this Directive and shall submit a report thereon to the European Parliament and the Council by 27 December 2020.
2. The report referred to in paragraph 1 shall, inter alia, include information on all of the following:

(a) the possible impact of financial constraints flowing from the payment of fines imposed by a competition authority for an infringement of competition law on the possibility for injured parties to obtain full compensation for the harm caused by that infringement of competition law;
(b) the extent to which claimants for damages caused by an infringement of competition law established in an infringement decision adopted by a competition authority of a Member State are able to prove before the national court of another Member State that such an infringement of competition law has occurred;
(c) the extent to which compensation for actual loss exceeds the overcharge harm caused by the infringement of competition law or suffered at any level of the supply chain.
3. If appropriate, the report referred to in paragraph 1 shall be accompanied by a legislative proposal.

Article 21

Transposition

1. Member States shall bring into force the laws, regulations and administrative provisions necessary to comply with this Directive by 27 December 2016. They shall forthwith communicate to the Commission the text thereof.
When Member States adopt those measures, they shall contain a reference to this Directive or be accompanied by such a reference on the occasion of their official publication. Member States shall determine how such reference is to be made.
2. Member States shall communicate to the Commission the text of the main provisions of national law which they adopt in the field covered by this Directive.

Article 22

Temporal application

1. Member States shall ensure that the national measures adopted pursuant to Article 21 in order to comply with substantive provisions of this Directive do not apply retroactively.
2. Member States shall ensure that any national measures adopted pursuant to Article 21, other than those referred to in paragraph 1, do not apply to actions for damages of which a national court was seized prior to 26 December 2014.

Article 23

Entry into force

This Directive shall enter into force on the twentieth day following that of its publication in the Official Journal of the European Union.

Article 24

Addressees

This Directive is addressed to the Member States.

Done at Strasbourg, 26 November 2014.

For the European Parliament *The President* M. SCHULZ	*For the Council* *The President* S. GOZI